Ius Gentium: Comparative Perspectives on Law and Justice

Volume 138

Ius Gentium is a book series which discusses the central questions of law and justice from a comparative perspective. The books in this series collect the contrasting and overlapping perspectives of lawyers, judges, philosophers and scholars of law from the world's many different jurisdictions for the purposes of comparison, harmonisation, and the progressive development of law and legal institutions. Each volume makes a new comparative study of an important area of law. This book series continues the work of the well-known journal of the same name and provides the basis for a better understanding of all areas of legal science.

The *Ius Gentium* series provides a valuable resource for lawyers, judges, legislators, scholars, and both graduate students and researchers in globalisation, comparative law, legal theory and legal practice. The series has a special focus on the development of international legal standards and transnational legal cooperation.

Ama F. Hammond · Prosper Batariwah
Editors

The Law on Marital Property in Africa

Comparative Perspectives

Springer

Editors
Ama F. Hammond
School of Law
University of Ghana
Accra, Ghana

Prosper Batariwah
Harvard Law School
Cambridge, MA, USA

ISSN 1534-6781 ISSN 2214-9902 (electronic)
Ius Gentium: Comparative Perspectives on Law and Justice
ISBN 978-3-032-19357-5 ISBN 978-3-032-19358-2 (eBook)
https://doi.org/10.1007/978-3-032-19358-2

This Springer imprint is published by the registered company Springer Nature Switzerland AG
The registered company address is: Gewerbestrasse 11, 6330 Cham, Switzerland

Foreword

> That a woman should leave a marriage empty-handed and homeless, meets with much sympathy, some disapproval, but little surprise.[1]

CEDAW General Recommendation 29, paragraph 5 states that regardless of the vast range of economic arrangements within the family, in developing and developed countries, women generally share the experience of being worse off economically than men in family relationships, and following the dissolution of these relationships.

Numerous and complex strands govern the distribution of marital property in Africa before, during, and after marriage. They are influenced by the forms of marriage contracted, which include civil, religious, and customary marriages (registered and unregistered), as well as permutations of these forms of marriage, and civil unions or prolonged cohabitation. Correspondingly, due to the plural legal systems evolved through a history of British, French and Dutch colonial rule and law, the governance structure—customary, state law, federal and state and religious law, common law, civil law, and religious law systems—also govern the determination of property rights, bringing with them conflict of laws issues. Each system of law espouses either a separate or joint marital property regime, which influences the legal principles governing the ownership, distribution, and determination of property rights. Varying degrees of judicial discretion compound predictable adjudication.

Several tensions emerge within these crosshairs that engage academics, researchers, practitioners, judges, as well as law and policymakers in navigating property rights regimes. History, patriarchy, the incidents of colonialism and the legal system's endorsement of the nature of marriage as an institution of status or contract, often constitute starting points for the various linear and layered legal systems.

The Law on Marital Property in Africa: Comparative Perspectives is a valuable resource within the context of human rights. The contributors from Cameroon, Côte d'Ivoire, Ethiopia, Eswatini, Ghana, Kenya, Malawi, Mauritius, Morocco, Nigeria, Seychelles, South Africa, Tanzania, Zambia, Uganda, and Zimbabwe explore the

---

[1] Musembi (2023), p. 160.

definition and contestations of marital property, and provide an analysis of the legal framework and tensions around marital property rights during marriage and on divorce. They also assess the impact of international and domestic human rights law on their national laws. All papers in this volume emanate from countries that have ratified the United Nations Convention on the Elimination of All Forms of Discrimination against Women (CEDAW), and almost all are States Parties to the Protocol to the African Charter on the Rights of Women in Africa (the Maputo Protocol). The framework for the contributions provides material for comparative research across jurisdictions, legal systems, and themes, for which the Nigeria and Uganda *Comparative Appraisal* provides a microcosm.

The scope of the publication covers property rights before, during, and after marriage. However, there is usually scant focus on marital property rights during the pendency of marriage. The Zambia chapter observes that the question of ownership of such property between the parties is not often discussed while the marriage subsists. This is rationalised in the Tanzania chapter as, 'while the question of property rights between spouses may not be a big issue during the subsistence of marriage, it becomes more complex when the marriage ends, whether due to death, divorce, separation, or annulment and after'. It may imply that spouses do not usually seek ownership declarations during marriage, for example, to collateralise marital property for entrepreneurial ventures, in line with the rights provided to women in CEDAW Article 16 (h) on equal spousal rights to the administration of property, thereby preventing contestations. There is a taboo element alluded to in the Zambia chapter about marriage creating a unit of existence which inherently prevents spouses from making individual claims to property ownership while the marriage subsists.

Several interesting themes run through the publication. Apart from the historical, patriarchal, and colonial antecedents, almost all papers trace how national constitutions, legislation, and judicial pronouncements provide the conduit for incorporating international and regional human rights treaties and standards into local law, while harmonising matrimonial law across marriage systems. The human rights texts provide guarantees of rights to equality during the subsistence of marriage and upon dissolution.

The terminology of equality and equity is evident in the publication's chapters. It juxtaposes the tendency of formal equality to produce inequality with substantive equality, which advances justice and enshrines fairness by awarding spouses that which they duly deserve when their marriage ends. CEDAW, in General Recommendation 28, insists that States parties not use the concept of gender 'equity', but exclusively use 'equality'. CEDAW has pointed out that a state party's (Gambia) legislation providing for women's 'equitable' access to property was non-compliant with CEDAW's standard of equality. Therefore, whereas CEDAW and the Human Rights Council use the identical terminology of equality—'the *same* rights'—regarding the ownership, acquisition, management, administration, enjoyment and disposition of spousal property, the Maputo Protocol uses 'the right to *equitable* sharing of the joint property'. It subsequently clarified in its General Comment 6 that the equitable sharing represents at least half the property acquired during marriage.

A clear understanding of 'marital property' is important for consistency, predictability, and establishing precedents, a concern raised in the Seychelles and Ghana chapters. The Maputo Protocol's General Comment 6 defines marital property to include 'all property acquired during the marriage, regardless of who holds the title to it'. Within a community property regime, Halperin-Kaddari and Freeman provide some specific components of a comprehensive definition that would include 'real estate; household goods; savings and investments; business enterprises; interest in pensions, retirement accounts, or other entitlements that are acquired during the relationship but paid out later in life', thus flagging 'new property'.[2]

A recurring and significant theme that emerges from the papers is the recognition and valuation of non-financial contributions within marriage. In line with this, the UN CEDAW General Recommendation 29, paragraph 47, recommends valuing non-financial contributions to marital property subject to division, including household and family care, lost economic opportunities, and tangible or intangible contributions to either spouse's career development and other economic activities that assist in the development of their human capital.

Another theme is the trend towards community of property as the default marital property regime as pertains in Ethiopia. In Côte d'Ivoire, incremental reforms led to a shift from community to separate property within which spouses may execute marriage contracts. Some other countries operate a hybrid. In its concluding observations, CEDAW has requested that a state party (Togo) replace its default separate property regime with a community property one, as gender-based economic disparities tend to disadvantage women under the separate property regime.[3] (Halperin-Kaddari and Freeman, 612).

In addition, Paragraph 45 of General Recommendation 29 provides the guiding principle that the economic advantages and disadvantages related to the relationship and its dissolution should be borne equally by both parties, without resulting in detrimental economic consequences for either party. Parties, therefore, should be made aware of the consequences of an evolution towards a separate property regime, provisions should be made for an opt-out clause, and safeguards should be provided against the use of unequal bargaining power.

Pre-nuptial agreements are an emerging trend which the Morocco chapter discusses as advantageous to women who earn a decent income, but disadvantage those without economic wherewithal due to power asymmetry. The Ethiopia chapter acknowledges, in line with CEDAW, the rights of spouses to enter into marriage contracts, with the caveat of arms-length dealings, mindfulness of formalities, and the state's responsibility to ensure that women are informed and fully aware of the consequences of the agreements.

The courts have played a significant role in transforming matrimonial property rights, as evidenced by the South Africa chapter, which references numerous judicial decisions. In Tanzania as well, the changing economic, social, and cultural dynamics of the community have complicated the law, prompting the courts to continually

---

[2] Halperin-Kaddari and Freeman (2022), pp. 613, 610.

[3] Halperin-Kaddari and Freeman (2022), p. 612.

interpret, challenge, and reshape it to promote equality and fairness between spouses. There are outstanding issues of polygamy, which pose a difficult fit within marital property distribution. While stating a preference for monogamy, the Maputo Protocol cautions that the rights of women in polygamous unions should be protected.

However, contributors have noted the deficit in academic writing and literature on the impact of legal changes on women's property rights. This volume fills that gap as it represents an intellectually rigorous intervention in the field of family law and gender justice in Africa. Through its comprehensive exploration of the historical, cultural, and legal complexities surrounding spousal property ownership and distribution in sixteen African countries, the book offers a unique blend of comparative depth and analytical clarity. Its examination of legal pluralism and the interplay between national and international legal norms not only enriches academic discourse but also holds profound policy relevance. For scholars, policymakers, legal practitioners, and reform advocates, this work provides an indispensable foundation for crafting coherent, context-sensitive reforms that promote substantive gender equality and align domestic legal systems with evolving modern human rights standards.

Accra, Ghana

Hilary Gbedemah
Former Member, Chair, UN Committee
on the Elimination of All Forms
of Discrimination against Women

References

Halperin-Kaddari Ruth, Freeman MA (2022) Article 16. In: Schulz P et al (eds) The UN Convention on the Elimination of All Forms of Discrimination Against Women and its Optional Protocol: A Commentary, 2nd edn. Oxford University Press, Oxford, New York, pp. 577–626.

Musembi CN (2023) Article 7: Separation, divorce and annulment of marriage. In: Rudman A, Musembi CN, Makunya TM (eds) The Protocol to the African Charter on Human and Peoples' Rights on the Rights of Women in Africa: A Commentary pp. 160–178.

Acknowledgements

The editors are sincerely grateful to the authors for their thoughtful contributions, rigorous scholarship, and commitment to this project. Their diverse perspectives and expertise have enriched the content and scope of this volume. We also extend our deep appreciation to the reviewers, whose critical insights, constructive feedback, and careful evaluation of the chapters played a vital role in shaping the final quality of this work.

We further thank our research and editorial assistants, Richard Adjei Kyeremateng, Kofi Appiadjei Asante-Krobea, Stephen Menya-Amoako, and Solomon Omani-Mensah, for working efficiently and tirelessly throughout the preparation of this volume. A special note of gratitude goes to Ms Katherine Aglobitse for the accurate and careful translation of the chapters from Côte d'Ivoire and Mauritius from French to English.

We are also sincerely thankful to the University of Ghana School of Law for its financial support in producing this volume. Editing this book has been a rewarding experience, and we hope that readers will find it both intellectually stimulating and action-inspiring.

Contents

Introduction: Legal Pluralism and Spousal Property Rights in Africa

Ama F. Hammond and Prosper Batariwah

Abstract This chapter examines the historical context and legal implications of the plurality of legal systems for spousal property ownership and distribution in Cameroon, Côte d'Ivoire, Ethiopia, Eswatini, Ghana, Kenya, Malawi, Mauritius, Morocco, Nigeria, Seychelles, South Africa, Tanzania, Uganda, Zambia, and Zimbabwe. Marital property regulation in Africa is shaped by legal pluralism, producing a diversity of spousal property regimes that often disadvantage women by restricting property rights during and beyond marriage. In recent decades, international human rights law has influenced constitutional, legislative, and judicial reforms aimed at promoting gender equality and eliminating discriminatory marital property rules. Progress, however, remains uneven and is frequently constrained by entrenched patriarchal norms, inconsistent judicial interpretation, and limited political will. Adopting a comparative approach and situating contemporary marital property regimes within their broader historical and legal contexts, the chapter identifies shared trends and tensions across jurisdictions, particularly concerning the definition and classification of spousal property and recognition of non-financial contributions. It also examines property claims arising from irregular unions and the growing impact of international human rights norms on domestic approaches to spousal equality. The chapter concludes that achieving equity requires context-sensitive legal reform, strengthened judicial capacity, and expanded public legal education.

A. F. Hammond (✉)
School of Law, University of Ghana, Legon, Ghana
e-mail: afhammond@ug.edu.gh

P. Batariwah
Harvard Law School, Cambridge, MA, USA
e-mail: pbatariwah@sjd.law.harvard.edu

A. F. Hammond and P. Batariwah (eds.), *The Law on Marital Property in Africa*, Ius Gentium: Comparative Perspectives on Law and Justice 138,
https://doi.org/10.1007/978-3-032-19358-2_1

1 Introduction

This introductory chapter explores the historical context and legal implications of the plurality of systems for spousal property ownership and distribution in Cameroon, Côte d'Ivoire, Ethiopia, Eswatini, Ghana, Kenya, Malawi, Mauritius, Morocco, Nigeria, Seychelles, South Africa, Tanzania, Zambia, Uganda, and Zimbabwe. The ownership and distribution of marital property upon the dissolution of marriages has long been a contentious issue in African family law. In each African country, the laws on the subject are drawn from different systems of law, whether customary, state law, or religious law, creating a complex and intriguing scheme of legal pluralism and resulting in legal diversity in spousal property arrangements. The laws formulated by these diverse internal systems of law have not always been fair to women.

Women have often found themselves at a disadvantage, facing routine discrimination and possessing limited property rights both within and outside of matrimony. However, in recent decades, international human rights law has prompted many African countries to reassess their legal frameworks governing the ownership and distribution of marital property, aligning them with the countries' international obligations to promote gender equality. This has led to increased constitutional protections, statutory reforms, and judicial interventions aimed at ensuring equitable treatment of spouses and dismantling discriminatory customary practices that historically disadvantaged women in the division of marital assets.

However, progress has often been undermined by deeply rooted patriarchy, judicial reluctance, or inconsistency in applying gender-sensitive interpretations and limited political will. These challenges continue to constrain the transformative potential of the legal reforms.

Despite the individual efforts of scholars researching African family law, there is currently no African text that provides a comparative analysis of how property rights are regulated within the context of marriages and divorces in Africa. A comparative study of marital property sharing across African countries is crucial for understanding how legal systems address the complexities of marriage, property ownership, and gender relations. While African nations share historical experiences, such as colonial rule and post-independence legal reforms, they differ significantly in legal frameworks. This diversity allows for comparison, highlighting convergences and divergences in the structuring and enforcement of marital property rights. Such analysis also enables reflection on how effectively different systems promote fairness, protect vulnerable spouses, particularly women, and respond to social change. By examining these systems side by side, the volume aims to show best practices, expose enduring challenges, and contribute to ongoing debates on legal harmonisation, reform, and the role of international human rights norms in shaping family law across Africa.

This introduction begins with a brief account of legal pluralism in Africa. This is followed by an overview of the significance of property rights. It then situates marital property regimes within their broader historical and legal contexts, examining the enduring influence of colonial legacies, the evolution of post-independence legal reform, and the classification of key types of property regimes. The discussion then turns to the central themes and comparative insights explored throughout the volume, including patterns of legal pluralism, the recognition of non-financial contributions, the role of contracts in property division, the growing influence of international human rights norms, and the property rights implications of irregular unions. It concludes with a set of recommendations to advance legal reform in marital property rights in Africa.

2 Navigating Marital Property Rights in Plural Legal Systems

Most African states experienced colonial rule, during which foreign legal systems were imposed on societies that already had systems of customary laws.[1] This foreign imposition gave rise to a plurality of legal systems that continue to coexist today, albeit with contestations over superiority in some spheres of life. Religious laws, especially Islamic law, have also been very prominent in the lives of many Africans, a people described as 'notoriously'[2] and 'incurably[3] religious. While both customary law and religious norms have long been embedded in African societies, the introduction of European legal systems has left a lasting imprint on the legal, political, and institutional structures of African states, deeply influencing the evolution of their contemporary legal frameworks. The plurality of legal systems in African states, also known as legal pluralism, generally describes 'a situation in which two or more legal systems coexist in the same social field'.[4] At its core, legal pluralism rejects the ideology of legal centralism, which, though described as "a myth, an ideal, a claim, an illusion," asserts the supremacy of State law.[5]

The predominant approach to legal pluralism, recognised by countries to varying degrees, is state legal pluralism. It denotes the coexistence of multiple normative systems officially recognised by the state, which remains the ultimate source of legal authority.[6] This form of pluralism involves the formal recognition and incorporation of customary law within state-regulated domains.[7] However, such recognition of customary law as a fact does not equate to an acknowledgement of its legal nature.[8] In this approach to pluralism, the state may adopt customary rules in whole or in part, thereby granting them legal effect within the state's legal framework.[9] Nonetheless,

[1] Sarbah (1904).

[2] Mbiti (1969, p. 1).

[3] Parrinder (1970, p. 9).

[4] Merry (1988, p. 870).

[5] Griffiths (1986, p. 4); See also Tamanaha (2021, pp. 4–5).

[6] Corrin (2017, p. 306).

[7] Woodman (1996, p. 158).

[8] Morse and Woodman (1988, p. 10).

[9] Morse and Woodman (1988, p. 11–12).

state law maintains supremacy by defining and regulating non-state legal systems on its own terms, thereby reinforcing legal centralism.

In the contributions, legal pluralism is evident in the coexistence of statutory law, practised and judicial customary law, and religious law. This layered legal heritage accounts for the multiple forms of marriage, each granted differing levels of official recognition, in countries like Cameroon, Ghana, Kenya, Ethiopia and eSwatini, among others. As seen in the ensuing chapters, each system of marriage may have its own prescriptions on the same issue, some more favourable than others when viewed through a modern human rights lens.

It must be noted that these variations are not merely theoretical; they have direct implications for individuals who must determine which norms govern their personal relationships, including marriage. People may encounter the challenge of navigating multiple legal systems, often finding themselves positioned between state law and non-state law.[10] A limited awareness of the legal options available to them further exacerbates this difficulty, underscoring the need for education and capacity-building initiatives to enhance legal literacy and informed decision-making. Navigating these options is not as straightforward as simply opting for state law.

For many Africans, customary or personal law remains deeply intertwined with their cultural identity and social belonging, and the fact remains that in communal societies, the need for acceptance and legitimacy within one's community cannot be disregarded. Realistically, in most postcolonial African countries:

> It would be difficult to find any individual, in the past or today, who has abandoned the entirety of their indigenous culture and replaced it by taking the imported culture as the sole guide to their social relations. Those who, often skilfully and with conviction, adopted the imported culture for some parts of their lives, continued to live other parts according to one or another of the indigenous cultures.[11]

This legal hybridity explains why, in some jurisdictions, like Ghana and Zambia, civil marriages are often preceded by customary marriages, thereby honouring both systems of law, while securing the protections provided by the former.

Customary law is frequently criticised for offering weaker protections to women and children, and for enabling practices that conflict with modern human rights standards. However, it has been argued that this accusation is more with respect to official customary law than practised or living customary law,[12] which, according to Chuma Himonga, a legal scholar, embodies an 'enduring attribute' in that 'it adapts

---

[10] For the purposes of this chapter's discussion of legal pluralism, "state law" is used in a narrow sense to refer to legislation enacted by Parliament. In contrast, "non-state law" refers to other normative or regulatory systems whose authority does not derive from legislative enactment. The latter includes customary law.

[11] Woodman (2010, p. 259).

[12] We use the terms official or judicial customary law to refer to the customary laws developed and formalised by the courts through adjudication, in contrast to the lived or practised customary law of communities. Living or practised customary law refers to the body of norms, rules, and procedures actually observed by a community, reflecting their lived customs and social practices, as distinct from the version of customary law formalised or interpreted by courts. Kludze (1972, p. 92); See also Himonga (2011, pp. 33–35).

and develops according to changing socio-economic, political, and other conditions in society.'[13] It is important to challenge the assumption that customary or non-state systems are merely "poor substitutes for Western-style formal systems."[14] Arguably, 'they represent alternative conceptions of justice, grounded in socio-cultural realities with their own definition of what constitutes an offense and what is an effective remedy'.[15] With its focus on "reconciliation and compromise," among other qualities, '[c]ustomary law thinking was very prominent in the transitional justice programs that addressed the genocide in Rwanda and other gross violations of human rights that occurred in parts of Africa, such as Sierra Leone, Uganda, and Kenya, within the last few decades'.[16]

The view that customary law does not take human rights seriously is, however, not unjustified. While the contributors to this volume do not employ a clean distinction between living and official customary law, they each note how customary law limits the property a woman can acquire in marriage and what she may be entitled to in the event of divorce. In jurisdictions like Nigeria, where state law does not apply uniform marital property rules, women receive substantially less property upon the dissolution of customary marriages. In other countries like Zimbabwe, courts have characterised some customary marriages as 'universal partnerships', to obviate injustices that would occur if customary law were applied to marital property disputes.

In light of these observations, it is essential to find a middle ground that integrates elements from state and non-state legal systems in a way that aligns with modern human rights norms and reflects people's lived experiences. Melton argues that for the law to achieve its intended purposes, it must be grounded in the lived realities of the people, noting that this 'requires attention to the everyday experience of the citizenry.'[17]

Building on Melton's emphasis on grounding law in lived realities, Fitzpatrick shows how these experiences, expressed through diverse social and normative orders, actively reshape law itself. He argues that state and non-state systems mutually influence one another, making law an evolving product of these interactions. As Fitzpatrick puts it, 'Law is the unsettled resultant of relations with a plurality of social forms.'[18] This insight provides a useful framework for harmonising property rights in marriages and related relationships across internal legal systems.

However, traversing multiple legal systems raises practical concerns. We are cautioned that, 'pluralism, just as deconstruction, ultimately ends in immobilization, since if everything is complex and variable, just as if everything is a matter of interpretation, how can one say anything?'[19] This concern points to a broader

[13] Himonga (2011, p. 35).

[14] See footnote 12; Isser (2011, p. 328).

[15] Isser (2011, p. 328).

[16] Oba (2011, p. 59).

[17] Melton (1992, p. 385).

[18] Fitzpatrick (1984, p. 138).

[19] Merry (1988, p. 885).

tension within pluralist theory: how to meaningfully engage diverse legal systems without becoming paralysed by relativism. Instead of viewing pluralism as inherently paralysing, it could be seen as a space for dialogue, while bearing in mind that legal interventions can be anchored in broadly recognised normative principles of dignity, reciprocity, and respect for individuals, all of which are central to customary law.[20]

3 The Importance of Property Rights

Property rights are the bedrock of economic prosperity. They regulate how property is used and have the potential to guarantee financial security and stability. In other words, ensuring the security of property rights is not just about safeguarding individual liberty; it's about fostering economic growth. This freedom is a cornerstone of a free society, enabling individuals to choose how best to utilise their resources.

Ordinarily, the acquisition of property confers a presumptive entitlement to ownership, which, barring exceptional conditions, is seldom contested. However, in cases where the property is obtained jointly with others, particularly in the context of marriage, it is crucial to establish the precise extent of each partner's stake in the property, especially in the absence of a clearly defined agreement or legal prescriptions about ownership. This is due to the inherent nature of the marital relationship and the legal presumptions that come with it.

Admittedly, marriage is fertile ground for the exhibition of opportunistic behaviours, and clearly defined property rights reduce the risks of such behaviours. While Dnes, a law and economics scholar observes that marriage 'gives a means of protecting long-term investment in marital property',[21] he is quick to caution that 'the gains from marriage are surpluses that arise after sunk investments have been made, which can tempt the less-tied spouse into opportunistic behavior, specifically into attempts to appropriate the product of the sunk investments'.[22]

Legally precise and clearly articulated property rights within marriage are essential, as they ensure fairness and protect the interests of both partners, prevent exploitation, and secure financial stability, thereby promoting a just and equitable society.

4 Property Ownership: Historical and Legal Context

Understanding the historical and legal foundations of property ownership at common law, as well as in the civil law and Islamic legal systems, is essential to any analysis of marital property regimes in African countries shaped by colonial and religious legal

---

[20] Cobbah (1987).

[21] Dnes (2019, p. 1344).

[22] Dnes (2019, p. 1344).

traditions. This section examines how common law principles, such as coverture, influenced early conceptions of spousal property rights, while also exploring the parallel development of property rights in civil law and Islamic legal systems. It highlights the lasting impact of these systems on contemporary approaches to the division of marital property in Africa.

4.1 Common Law

Coverture had real consequences for the rights of married women; it created difficult challenges for them, particularly regarding their autonomy and independence.[23] It flourished as a legal fiction predicated on the 'unity of personhood', a concept inspired by the Bible.[24] Coverture was a legal union in which a married woman's legal identity was merged into her husband's, placing her under his protection and control.[25] The merger 'was not mere metaphysics, but imposed real disabilities on the married woman'.[26] Women were not permitted to own personal property; it became their husbands' upon marriage.[27] They could own immovable property, though its management and any rent income derived from it belonged to their husbands.[28] Two rights characterised the property ownership regime: the woman's dower rights and the man's curtesy rights.[29] Dower rights meant that the woman had a life interest in a third of her husband's property on the husband's death.[30] On the other hand, courtesy rights entitled the husband to all the woman's estate on her death only if there was a child of the marriage.[31] Under coverture, married women in England and its colonies suffered severe legal and social disadvantages.[32] They lacked legal autonomy, unable to enter into contracts or sue without their husbands.[33]

In the nineteenth century, however, the rigidity of coverture began to soften as reformers in England and America, driven by social and economic change, pushed for wives' protection and greater economic efficiency. Equity, through the law of

---

23 Dnes (20201919, p. 1344).

24 Dnes (2019, p. 1344).

25 Blackstone (1765, p. 468). See also, Stretton and Kesselring (2013, p. 1).

26 Ronner (1996, p. 132). It must be noted that Husbands were free to will their wives' personal property, save her personal clothing and jewellery. Combs (2005, p. 1031).

27 Combs (2005, p. 1031).

28 Combs (2005, p. 1032).

29 Kha (2021, pp. 13–14).

30 Haskins (1948, p. 43).

31 Seabourne (2019, p. 44).

32 When in debt, men relied on their wives' property and were unwilling to give it up, even resulting in violence. See Stretton and Kesselring (2013, p. 15); By the eighteenth century, English law so firmly upheld husbands' entitlement to their wives' property that courts treated assets brought into marriage as outright gifts to the husband, free of any duty towards the wife's family or children, Bailey (2002, p. 352).

33 Antognini (2019, p. 2142).

trusts, contributed to the development of a more liberal approach to the doctrine of coverture than existed under common law.[34] Also, the 19th-century Industrial Revolution, particularly in England and America, brought more women into the workforce, increasing their property ownership and challenging the traditional legal restrictions.[35] Feminist advocacy and economic necessity spurred reforms, leading to the enactment of Married Women's Property Acts in several American states in the 1830s[36] and in Britain in 1870.[37] While these statutes expanded married women's property rights, they did not entirely abolish the doctrine of coverture. Among other setbacks, property still passed through the husband, and women lacked the right to their own earnings or property acquired with those earnings.[38] The Married Women's Property Act of England was revised in 1882 to correct the deficiencies of the earlier Act by allowing women to acquire, hold, and dispose of property as their own without a trustee.[39]

The Married Women's Property Acts of 1870 and 1882 were transplanted into the colonies of the British Empire, and the development of a separate property system in the colonies was brought into parity with that of Britain. In this volume, Ghana, Nigeria, and Kenya are examples of countries whose colonial legal systems adopted Married Women's Property Acts, Ghana being the first to adopt one in 1890.

Formal equality did not guarantee women substantial property upon divorce, as the common law property rules prioritised formal ownership, and unpaid domestic work was undervalued.[40] Support for wives was often predicated on maintenance orders, which, it seems, were hardly complied with.[41] Reforms, such as statutes granting claims to housekeeping funds, offered limited relief.[42] Real reform came in the 1960s and 1970s in England. By that time, many common law African colonies had become independent states and were no longer bound by English law or subsequent legal developments in England. However, these laws continued to exert some influence on their legal systems. The equitable trust, for example, has been used in Ghana and Nigeria in line with English case law to reorder the property rights of spouses.[43]

---

[34] *Duncombe v. Greenacre* (1860). Combs (2013, p. 220). Wives started using trusts to manage their separate estates, and this practice rapidly became widespread. Tait (2014, pp. 165–216).

[35] Basch (1979, p. 348).

[36] Holton (2015, p. 314–315).

[37] The US states of Arkansas and Mississippi were the first to pass Married Women's Property Acts in 1835 and 1839 respectively, see McCammon et al. (2014, p. 225).

[38] Married Women's Property Act 1870, s. 1. See also s. 7 on inheritance rights.

[39] Married Women's Property Act 1882, s 1; for a background of the debates leading up to the enactment of this law, see Griffin (2003).

[40] Thompson (2018, pp. 1–2).

[41] Thompson (2018, pp. 1–2).

[42] The Married Women's Property Act 1964 had just two sections. Section 1 states: 'If any question arises as to the right of a husband or wife to money derived from any allowance made by the husband for the expenses of the matrimonial home or for similar purposes, or to any property acquired out of such money, the money or property shall, in the absence of any agreement between them to the contrary, be treated as belonging to the husband and the wife in equal shares'.

[43] *Pettitt v Pettitt* [1968] 1 WLR 443.

In common law Africa, the formal equality provisions of English law, which remained or were absorbed into postcolonial legal systems, left homemakers and low-income-earning women disadvantaged. The contributions from Nigeria, Ghana, Malawi, Kenya, Tanzania and Zambia highlight how common law created inequality, prompting each to reform it differently. Malawi and Ghana have drawn on human rights and constitutional law to establish a consistent, uniform legal framework for all internal legal orders. Nigeria and Zambia, have modified the common law as it applies to statutory and civil marriages. Kenya appears to occupy a middle position because it gives Muslims the choice to opt for the application of Islamic law instead of the provisions of the Matrimonial Property Act.

4.2 *Civil Law*

Some of our contributions are from civil law countries or mixed-legal systems that blend elements of civil law with English common law. The civil law itself, traceable to the Roman Emperor Justinian I's *Corpus Juris Civilis*, and popularised in continental Europe, has different iterations introduced to Africa.[44] The two most popular iterations of civil law in some African countries are those heavily influenced by France's Napoleonic Code or the Roman-Dutch Law.[45] Côte d'Ivoire and Morocco are the only contributions in this volume where civil law of the Napoleonic sort prevails to a greater extent. Others from Southern Africa, such as South Africa, Zimbabwe and eSwatini, are largely mixed legal systems where Roman-Dutch Law is widely received. In general, the introduction of civil law in these countries was largely the result of colonisation, especially by the French and the Dutch.[46] Where subsequent European powers, especially the English, displaced the French or the Dutch, they introduced variants of their own legal systems while retaining aspects of the civil law.[47] Thus, in many countries of Southern Africa, Roman-Dutch law coexists with received English law, and in Mauritius and Seychelles, French civil law coexists with English law. Not all countries were compelled to adopt civil law, however. Ethiopia, as Gebreyesus notes, voluntarily introduced the civil law as part of a modernising mission.[48]

Returning to the Napoleonic Code, it is important to note that women did not fare any better under this system than they did under the English doctrine of coverture, reflecting a general European legal tradition that arguably tended to limit women's rights. Brenda notes that the Code 'reflected Napoleon's view that women were inferior to men and consequently placed married women under the tutelage of their

[44] Pérez-Perdomo and Merryman (2018, p. 33).

[45] See Blanc-Jouvan (2004, p. 5), Fagan (1996) and Pain (1978).

[46] Blanc-Jouvan (2004, p. 5) and Fagan (1996).

[47] Girvin (1996).

[48] See in this volume Ethiopia Chapter: Gebreyesus, 'Marital Property Division under the Ethiopian Family Law'.

husbands despite the promise of equality embodied in both the French Revolution and certain provisions of the Code itself'.[49] She describes some of the provisions which bluntly impacted women's property rights as follows:

> Once married, women were legal minors subject to their husbands who were designated the head of the family and endowed with 'paternal power' (Title IX). Under Article 213, "[t]he husband owes protection to his wife, the wife obedience to her husband". Additionally, husbands chose the familial residence (Article 214); wives required their husbands' authorisation to contract (Articles 215 and 217)...[50]

Therefore, while it was generally agreed that husbands and wives owned property under a community of property regime with an equal division of the community property upon the dissolution of the marriage, it was quite difficult for women to administer or manage the community property, as they were considered perpetual minors. As Heuer, a historian, notes:

> Once individuals were married, they were constrained to act according to the roles determined by their position within the household. They became spouses with different rights and duties, a rule that they could not change even if they wanted to do so.[51]

A similar position prevailed in Roman-Dutch Africa, where men possessed similar powers over community property. Only recently, as our South African and eSwatini contributions show, have steps been taken to equalise the powers of management and administration of community property.[52]

Reforms made in France did not extend to France's colonies. To this day, countries that adopted the Napoleonic Code continue to debate family law reforms that better reflect their socio-economic realities and the rigorous equality demands of human rights law.[53]

4.3 Islamic Law

What is remarkable about this volume is the ubiquity of Islamic law. Islam has been introduced to many parts of Africa in various ways, including the Arab conquest of North Africa, trade, and the Islamicisation of centralised states in Africa.[54] As a law applicable only to Muslims, almost all the countries in this volume recognise Islamic law to varying degrees. Islamic law is not just ubiquitous; it is also pliable, sometimes existing as a separate legal order on its own, and at other times overlaying

---

[49] Kombo (2021, pp. 711–712).

[50] Kombo (2021, p. 712).

[51] Heuer (2018, p. 131).

[52] See in this volume Eswatini Chapter: Dlamini, 'Proprietary Consequences of Marriage in Eswatini'; see also South Africa Chapter: Mokoena and Mopai, 'A Critical Analysis and Overview of the South African Legal Framework on Matrimonial Property Rights and Divorce'.

[53] Kombo (2021, p. 705).

[54] Salvaing (2020).

a civil law or common law order. For instance, Morocco, a civil law country, operates a separate property system which codifies the Islamic separate property order.

However, in each of these countries, the place of Islamic law is highly circumscribed because of what Christelow calls 'judicial centralisation'. That is:

> the introduc[tion] [of] clearly defined hierarchies of appeal, and often codified law, in order to assure the uniform operation-and thus the predictability of law… [with[] Judges becom[ing] part of nationwide bureaucratic systems, at least partially insulated from local political haggling, but, in the bargain, all the more subject to central control.[55]

Through this centralism, we see the 'relegation of Islamic law to a limited domain, particularly family law, while European codes are applied in criminal matters and the modern commercial sector, and the modern court system is grafted onto local custom when it comes to real property'.[56] Interestingly, property rights under Islamic law bear a striking resemblance to the common law concept of separate property. There is no concept of community of property under Islamic law, and property jointly acquired is shared in proportion to the contributions made by each party.

Together, these legal traditions continue to shape the complex and pluralistic landscape of marital property regimes across Africa, underscoring the importance of contextualised legal reform that acknowledges historical legacies while advancing equitable and culturally sensitive frameworks for property ownership and spousal rights.

5 The Changing Phase of Family Law in Africa

The triumph of marital property rights in African family law is a direct consequence of deliberate national economic modernisation projects pursued in many postcolonial African states, as it reflects the success of market liberalism on the continent. In an intriguing and seminal essay, Kang'ara, an African private law theorist, observes that the various evolutions of African family law have developed in lockstep with Anglo-American legal thought.[57] In the infant and constituent stages of the colonial state, African marriages, despite the recognition of African law as part of the sources of law, were often invalidated because they hardly conformed to the metropole's view of marriage as one of 'individualism, free will, and exclusivity'.[58] As the African family, often described as a union of families, was also the site for the distribution and use of economic resources, such as land, the derecognition of African marriages effectively applied market logic to the African family and its resources.[59]

---

[55] Christelow (2000, p. 374).

[56] Christelow (2000, p. 375).

[57] Kang'ara (2012, p. 1).

[58] Kang'ara (2012, p. 7).

[59] Kang'ara (2012, pp. 10–13).

It would be later that the Savignian pattern of treating marriage as a question of status rather than a contract would emerge,[60] and with it the transformation of marriage, converting it from a customary practice to a statutory institution, with an apparent change in personal law. The change in personal law in this way was significant, as it subjected the colonised to a new legal order, one that dictated characteristically different property, succession, and inheritance rights than those previously available under customary law. In Nigeria, for instance, the Married Women's Property Act only applied to marriages under the Ordinance.[61] Post independence, Wangui remarks that the construction of African family law from the ground up, that is, from codification of the lived experiences of customary societies, together with a broad judicial discretion in reforming and finetuning the law to reflect individual autonomy and supported by international human rights law, has become the dominant reform method of African family law.[62]

The reform project is not just a matter for the courts. Across the continent, as the contributions in this volume show, countries are imposing uniform statutes on the field of spousal property arrangements untethered to specific marriage forms.[63] Marital property rights, therefore, emerge from broader reform context, where the communitarianism of African marriages has generally given way to the discrete relationship of husband and wife, accompanied by a panoply of legal regulations governing the acquisition, ownership, and division of property acquired. It is this material relationship between husband and wife that we explore in this volume.

6 Spousal Property Arrangements

This section provides a brief overview of the various forms of matrimonial property regimes presented in this volume.

The first is the community property regime. In jurisdictions that adhere to community property laws, any assets acquired during a marriage are regarded as jointly owned by both spouses, regardless of who earned or acquired them. Assets are collected into a 'community' that both parties co-own. Additionally, both spouses are regarded as having contributed to the ownership of such property, whether as a

[60] '...as the European colonizer repeatedly imposed its own commercial law (and criminal, procedural, and other bodies of law adjunct to an ever-less mercantilist and ever-more capitalist colonial enterprise) and left the law of marriage, divorce, and parentage to persist under what then became local or "customary" law. Whether the resulting body of law was called Personal Status Law (a mark of French legal influence), or Family Law (a German legal idea), it was transformed—modernized—by being thus segregated and integrated as a new, distinct legal domain'. See Halley and Rittich (2010, p. 771).

[61] See in this volume Nigeria Chapter: Kekere, Kolade-Faseyi and Ajidasile, 'Settlement of Matrimonial Property upon Divorce in Nigeria: The Rights of Spouses, Challenges and Urgent Need for Reforms'.

[62] Kang'ara (2012, pp. 18-34).

[63] Kang'ara (2012, p. 2).

breadwinner, a homemaker, or both. Assets may include income, property, and debts. Community property laws are a common feature in civil and mixed legal systems. In this volume, Côte d'Ivoire, Mauritius, Seychelles, and South Africa substantially privilege the common community property system. Interestingly, none of these jurisdictions can be described as a 'pure' community property system, as each provides options for spouses to opt out of the community property system. The most comprehensive form of the community property regime is the universal community property regime. Under this regime, all property belonging to either spouse, acquired before and during the marriage, is held jointly by the parties. Only South Africa and eSwatini provide for this regime.

Contradistinguishing the position in civil and mixed legal systems from common law systems, the default regime in common law countries is the separate property regime. In separate property regimes, any assets obtained before the marriage or received as gifts or inheritances during the marriage are regarded as the exclusive property of the individual spouse. This may encompass assets acquired before the marriage, as well as those received as gifts and inheritances during the marriage.[64] In short, separate property belongs to one spouse individually and is not subject to division in a divorce. This arrangement's effect is that neither spouse is considered to have an inherent interest in the property acquired by the other. Thus, in divorce proceedings, where this spousal arrangement is practised, the courts can typically only order a transfer of part of the property to the other spouse.[65] Consequently, spouses who choose to become homemakers and subordinate their careers may find that their efforts are undervalued by the courts in such proceedings, as they would have contributed little to nothing in monetary terms to the acquisition of property. They would not have been considered to have contributed to the purchase of property through their particular efforts.[66] Separate property regimes are a feature not only of common law but also of Islamic law, as shown in the chapters from Morocco and Kenya, and of customary law, as demonstrated in the chapters from Ghana and Nigeria.

Both the community property and separate property regimes have undergone substantial reforms to reflect an ethos of equality. Community property systems have taken steps to abolish or reduce the husband's power and control over marital assets.[67] In this volume, South Africa, eSwatini, Mauritius, and Côte d'Ivoire have abolished what was known as the marital power, thereby putting the husband and wife on an equal footing. On the other hand, the separate property systems are evolving towards a greater recognition of joint property and the associated sharing of such property.[68]

---

[64] Davie (1993, p. 855).

[65] Leong Kai Wun has stated that under the separation of property regime as practiced in England for example, the 'power to adjust' merely allows the divorce court to order a transfer of part of the property to the other spouse. Leong (1993, p. 353).

[66] Leong (1993, p. 353).

[67] Rheinstein and Glendon (1980).

[68] Rheinstein and Glendon (1980).

The distinctions among the various matrimonial property regimes are far more complex than the brief overview provided above suggests. Admittedly, most of the countries in this volume endorse a default position that would apply in the absence of the other relevant factors, such as the parties' intention. Yet, none of the countries in this volume exclusively encodes one matrimonial regime into their family laws. In the civil and mixed-legal systems in this volume, the non-exclusivity is much more explicit through the introduction of an optional separate property regime. Common law countries in this volume adopt a less explicit stance on the incorporation of the community property system, but their family laws reflect certain attributes; for instance, Zambia, Malawi and Tanzania presumed all property acquired during the marriage to be marital property.[69] Ghana, until recently, followed this approach. Other countries stress equal division in the absence of other countervailing factors. In community property regimes generally, sharing of property upon divorce is done on an equal basis, though some community property regimes are evolving towards equitable division, a nod to the common law property regime. The cross-jurisdictional pollination of family law rules raises some interesting questions. Why do civil and mixed-legal systems provide the separate property regime option? And why are common law countries increasingly enshrining equality as the criterion for property division? If the aim is equality between spouses, why has a uniform system not emerged across jurisdictions? The contrast raises important considerations about the values shaping family law.

7 Key Themes and Comparative Insights

The contributions in this volume reveal common themes that emerge across jurisdictions despite differing legal systems, cultures, and histories. Central among these are the definition and classification of spousal property as well as the complex patterns of legal pluralism that shape the operation of matrimonial property regimes in practice. The role of marriage contracts as tools for navigating rights and obligations also features prominently. Another emerging theme concerns the treatment of property rights in irregular unions, highlighting how courts seek to achieve equitable outcomes beyond the bounds of formal marriage. Several contributions also engage with the influence of international human rights norms and standards on spousal equality. Together, these themes offer a comparative lens through which to assess the existing legal frameworks in their promotion of fairness and justice in the sharing of property.

[69] See in this volume Zambia Chapter: Chewe, 'Ownership of Marital Property in Zambia'; see also Malawi Chapter: Mwenelupembe, 'The Protection of Women's Property Rights on Dissolution of Marriage in Malawi'; and Tanzania Chapter: Buchumi, 'Marital Property Rights During and After the Dissolution of Marriage in Tanzania'.

7.1 Definition of Marital Property

Some jurisdictions have adopted clear definitions of marital property, promoting greater consistency and predictability in the division of marital assets. In light of ongoing contestations over what constitutes marital property, it is essential that the law clearly articulates its meaning and scope. Such clarity is vital to ensuring fairness and equity in the distribution of assets upon divorce. Malawi's Marriage, Divorce, and Family Relations Act of 2015 (MDFRA) defines marital property to include the matrimonial homes, household possessions within those homes, and any other property acquired during the marriage that the spouses, by agreement or conduct, regard as shared assets. Similarly, Section 6 of Kenya's Matrimonial Property Act (MPA) defines marital property to include the matrimonial home(s), household goods, and any movable or immovable property jointly owned and acquired during the marriage. Ethiopia's Revised Family Code (RFC), under Article 62, also defines marital property, adopting a default community property regime in which all property acquired after marriage is presumed to be jointly owned by the spouses. Likewise, eSwatini, currently in the process of enacting new matrimonial property legislation, defines such property in its bill to include the matrimonial home(s), household goods and effects, and any jointly acquired movable or immovable property during the marriage.

These definitions reveal a clear and deliberate legal trend towards recognising marriage as a partnership, where both spouses are presumed to have equal stakes in property acquired during the marriage. A clear definition, however, must extend beyond mere clarity to include detailed guidelines that permit limited judicial discretion, promote gender equality and ensure consistent standards.

In other jurisdictions, the meaning of marital property is left to judicial interpretation and other legal actors, such as those in customary legal systems, resulting in varied and often inconsistent approaches to sharing marital property. Such countries include Tanzania, Uganda, Ghana, Eswatini, and Seychelles, where statutory law on the meaning of marital property is either silent or underdeveloped. Indeed, the chapters in this volume demonstrate that, particularly in jurisdictions where marital property is undefined, the scope of such property is uncertain, and the general legal framework on this subject appears arbitrary. The Tanzanian case of *Bi Hawa Mohamed v. Ally Sefu* set a precedent by defining matrimonial assets as those acquired with the intention of providing for the family and used for the benefit of all members during the marriage. Similarly, in Cameroon, there appears to be a general recognition of the definition of marital property in *Wachtel v Wachtel*,[70] as 'those things, which one, other or both parties acquire, with the intention that there should be a continuing provision for them and their children during their joint lives, and used for the benefit of the family as a whole.'[71] In Seychelles, Tuyau clarifies that matrimonial property

[70] *Wachtel v Wachtel* [1973] EWCA 10.

[71] See in this volume Cameroon Chapter: Valery, 'The Resolution of Disputes Over Ownership of Marital Property Under the Common Law System in Cameroon'.

refers to any assets jointly owned by spouses or acquired during the marriage through their combined efforts.[72]

Admittedly, these case-based definitions create space for courts to consider a broad range of contributions as well as the contextual dynamics of marriage. However, they lack the specificity and consistency needed to provide legal certainty. Extensive reliance on judicial discretion could lead to unpredictable outcomes, thereby undermining the protection of property rights. In Ghana, for instance, the reliance on courts to define marital property has led to conflicting judicial decisions, with limited clarity on the criteria guiding these outcomes. In *Arthur v. Arthur*, Ghana's Supreme Court advanced marital property law by presuming that all property acquired during marriage is jointly owned, recognising both financial and non-financial contributions. However, in a subsequent decision, *Adjei v. Adjei,* the High Court reintroduced the need to prove contribution, limiting joint ownership to cases where shared effort could be demonstrated.[73]

To avoid such situations and ensure fairness and predictability in the resolution of property disputes, there is a pressing need for legal reforms that establish clear, objective criteria to guide equitable distribution.

7.2 Patterns of Legal Pluralism

As earlier noted, in most African jurisdictions, the regulation of matrimonial property reflects a complex intersection of legal traditions. This pluralism gives rise to multiple systems governing spousal property, each offering different rights and entitlements. Although there is a shared recognition of the importance of marital property in divorce proceedings, the criteria for defining, classifying, and distributing such property vary considerably, both in theory and in practice.

According to Dlamini, a marriage contracted under Eswatini customary law is governed by the principles and norms of Eswatini customary law. However, the proprietary consequences arising during the subsistence of such a marriage, as well as upon its dissolution by divorce, remain largely indeterminate due to the absence of judicial precedent clearly articulating these rules, though what is known undermines women's rights. In contrast, under Roman-Dutch law, also applicable in Eswatini, a more defined and structured framework governs matrimonial property, comprising two principal regimes: marriage in community of property and of profit and loss, and marriage out of community of property, with or without the exclusion of community of profit and loss,[74] offering spouses in these unions a stronger foundation for legal redress. This contrast underscores the need to harmonise and reform customary law to ensure equal protection, particularly for women.

[72] See in this volume Seychelles Chapter: Tuyau, 'Marital Property in Seychelles'.

[73] See in this volume Ghana Chapter: Hammond and Batariwah, 'Spousal Property Rights in Ghana'.

[74] See in this volume Dlamini, 'Proprietary Consequences of Marriage in Eswatini'.

Similarly, in Zimbabwe, Chikaonda explains that Shona customary law reflects a distinctly gendered approach to property division upon divorce. Under this customary framework, a woman's entitlement is typically limited to property she has acquired through personal effort beyond her ordinary domestic responsibilities and a symbolic cow received as part of the bridewealth. In contrast, the husband retains rights to all other property accumulated during the marriage.[75] This reflects a 'legal' imbalance that entrenches male control over marital assets and exposes women to economic vulnerability despite their contributions. Conversely, under the civil law regime in Zimbabwe, matrimonial property is governed by principles that distinguish between property acquired before the marriage, which remains the exclusive property of the acquiring spouse, and property acquired during the marriage, which remains separately owned by each spouse unless an antenuptial contract is executed to alter this default out-of-community property system.[76]

Like Eswatini and Zimbabwe, those married under customary law in Nigeria also appear to be at a disadvantage, embedded in a legal framework that consistently discriminates against women, especially in matters related to property. For instance, Kekere, Kolade-Faseyi, and Ajidasile reveal that in *Igbo* customary law, a woman is generally not permitted to own property independently of her husband, thereby limiting her autonomy over property. In contrast, other ethnic groups, such as the *Idoma,* recognise the capacity of a woman married under customary law to acquire and hold both personal and real property,[77] showing that customary law is not monolithic; there are different 'legal' orders within the customary legal system with differing norms, values, and degrees of gender equity. It also highlights that legal reforms need not reject customary law outright, but can build on the more progressive practices already present in some traditions.

However, in many places, customary laws significantly undermine property rights, often favouring men. Zambia and Ghana exhibit a strong influence of customary law, which frequently limits women's property rights despite statutory or constitutional protections. Ghana's legal landscape is further complicated by the divergence between judicial customary law, and the living customary law, resulting in different legal rules on the same subject. Within the legal landscape in Ghana is also Islamic law, which, like living customary law, often operates beyond the effective reach of the state, particularly in the regulation of marital property and in areas where rights may differ from constitutional standards. This underscores the challenges of legal pluralism, where multiple legal systems with conflicting prescriptions coexist, creating unequal property rights.

Significant legal strides have been made in Zambia, where courts have resolved property rights disputes arising from customary law unions based on the principles

[75] See in this volume Zimbabwe Chapter: Chikaonda, 'A Double-Edged Sword: Zimbabwe's New Marriage Act and The Implications for The Matrimonial Rights of Women in Unregistered Customary Marriages'.

[76] See in this volume Chikaonda, 'A Double-Edged Sword: Zimbabwe's New Marriage Act and The Implications for The Matrimonial Rights of Women in Unregistered Customary Marriages'.

[77] See in this volume Kekere, Kolade-Faseyi and Ajidasile, 'Settlement of Matrimonial Property upon Divorce in Nigeria: The Rights of Spouses, Challenges and Urgent Need for Reforms'.

of law and equity, rather than strictly adhering to traditional customary law rules, which often favour men. Chebe explains that in the landmark case of *Rosemary Chibwe v. Austin Chibwe*, the Supreme Court provided important guidance on the application of legal and equitable principles in divorce proceedings arising from customary law marriages. She adds that in a 2024 case of *Julius Sibanda v Flat Mooyo*, the High Court refused to give effect to an *Ndebele* custom that would have deprived a woman of a share in property acquired during her marriage.[78] This case illustrates a progressive shift in the judicial approach to customary law, where courts are increasingly willing to reject discriminatory practices and affirm gender equity and fairness in property division.

Nevertheless, property rights are applied consistently in Malawi, regardless of the type of marriage. Section 24(1)(b)(i) of the Constitution guarantees women's property rights upon the dissolution of marriage, stating that women are entitled to full and equal legal protection and must not be discriminated against based on gender or marital status, including the right to a fair division of jointly held property.[79] Accordingly, women in civil, customary, or religious marriages have a constitutional guarantee of non-discrimination and equal property rights upon marital breakdown.

In theory, Malawi's approach resembles Ghana's, where Christian and civil marriages may be dissolved under the Matrimonial Causes Act (Act 367) based, arguably, on principles of justice, fairness, and good conscience. Customary and Islamic marriages, though potentially polygamous, can also be terminated under the same Act, allowing spouses in polygamous unions to obtain similar property rights as those in monogamous marriages.

The Kenyan situation, as described by Jadeed, shows that in addition to establishing the mainstream legal framework, the Matrimonial Property Act (MPA) incorporates provisions for Islamic marital property law. Section 3 explicitly states that a person who professes the Islamic faith may be governed by Islamic law in all matters relating to matrimonial property. This provision grants Muslims the option to apply Islamic law in place of the substantive provisions set out in the MPA. But how would the substantive provisions under the MPA be applied to Islamic marriages if 'the concept of marital property law is foreign to Islam?'[80] Will the state accept Islamic law on its terms, or will it undercut Islamic law with standards such as equity, good conscience, and modern human rights considerations, as happens in most states that recognise the norms of other legal systems?[81]

Unsurprisingly, Kenya's MPA also permits the conditional application of customary marital property laws. Under Section 11, customary law applies only to the extent that it aligns with constitutional values; where it conflicts, the provisions

---

[78] See in this volume Chewe, 'Ownership of Marital Property in Zambia'.

[79] See in this volume Mwenelupembe, 'The Protection of Women's Property Rights on Dissolution of Marriage in Malawi'.

[80] See in this volume Kenya Chapter: Jadeed, 'Contemporary Matrimonial Property Law in Kenya: An Exposition of Substantive Equality'.

[81] Woodman (1996, pp. 158).

of the MPA take precedence. Jadeed explains that this has been criticised as undermining the autonomy of the customary legal system, and privileging statutory frameworks.[82] While it is imperative to align customary law with constitutional values of non-discrimination, it remains a valid concern that the insistence on the supremacy of the state's legal system may marginalise customary law, thereby undermining cultural rights.

South Africa, on the other hand, distinguishes polygamous customary marriages from monogamous marriages and makes provision for spouses in such unions. Historically, customary marriage in South Africa was patriarchal, denying wives property rights after the husband's death despite their contributions. This began to change with the 1996 Constitution, lauded by Mokoena and Mopai as 'one of the world's most progressive', which required customs to align with constitutional values.[83] The Recognition of Customary Marriages Act 120 of 1998 (RCMA), effective from 2000, legally recognised customary marriages and spelt out attendant property rights. Under section 7(1), pre-Act polygamous marriages share joint control of property between husbands and wives, while section 7(6) requires court-approved matrimonial contracts, with safeguards for first wives previously married in community of property. Mokoena and Mopai argue that this system ensures equitable property sharing in customary marriages.[84]

It must be noted that in South Africa, marriage in community of property is the default matrimonial property system for all monogamous civil marriages. If a couple wishes to be married out of community of property, either with or without the accrual system, they must enter into a valid antenuptial contract before the marriage, otherwise, the marriage will automatically be regarded as in community of property. This means that spouses will share equally in all assets and liabilities, reflecting the legal view of marriage as a shared partnership.

It is essential to stress that religious law, particularly Islamic law as applied in Morocco and among Muslim communities in Kenya, adopts a distinct approach. Property ownership is treated similarly inside and outside marriage, with each spouse retaining separate rights unless they voluntarily enter into a joint arrangement. Even where communal ownership exists, each party's interest remains individually defined. In contrast to Mauritius's emphasis on community property, this illustrates the deeply ingrained value of financial independence in Islamic marriages.

In Mauritius, the default community property regime, as noted by Gunputh, can lead to unjust outcomes. By treating salaries and earnings as common property, it renders both spouses generally liable for debts incurred during the marriage, unless

82 See in this volume Jadeed, 'Contemporary Matrimonial Property Law in Kenya: An Exposition of Substantive Equality'.

83 See in this volume Mokoena and Mopai, 'A Critical Analysis and Overview of the South African Legal Framework on Matrimonial Property Rights and Divorce'.

84 See in this volume Mokoena and Mopai, 'A Critical Analysis and Overview of the South African Legal Framework on Matrimonial Property Rights and Divorce'.

one can prove the debts were manifestly excessive and unrelated to family maintenance. He maintains that this structure may inadvertently promote irresponsible spending, as financial liability is shared regardless of individual conduct.[85]

In sum, the regulation of matrimonial property in Africa underscores the challenges of legal pluralism. This highlights the ongoing need for dialogue and reform to ensure greater consistency and fairness in spousal property regimes.

7.3 The Treatment of Contributions to Marital Property

Many jurisdictions adopt a broader and more inclusive understanding of matrimonial property, often rooted in common law or judicial development. In Nigeria, Section 72 of the Matrimonial Causes Act governs the settlement of property upon divorce, granting the courts discretionary authority to distribute assets acquired during the marriage. Although the Act does not explicitly define marital property, it endorses the principle of equitable distribution, taking into account both the spouses' financial and non-financial contributions. In Zambia, parties must prove their contribution to the acquisition of property. Chewe notes regarding Zambia, that 'In all the decisions on property settlement, the reasoning of the courts is that for a party to claim a share of the matrimonial property, that party must show their contribution, whether in kind or in cash'.[86] Unsurprisingly, she laments the widespread failure to recognise women's non-financial contributions, highlighting a longstanding and nearly universal issue.[87]

In determining the ownership of marital property in Malawi, courts assess each party's contributions to the acquisition and distribute the property proportionately. If contributions cannot be established, the property is divided equally.[88] This approach reflects a balance between acknowledging each spouse's individual contributions and promoting fairness in situations where exact contributions cannot be determined precisely. Similarly, in Tanzania, the courts consider the contributions of spouses to property acquired during the marriage, with Buchumi explaining that the 'Courts have ruled that the requirement to incline towards equality does not entail a 50/50 distribution but should be based on the contribution of each party in acquiring the properties'.[89] The courts in Tanzania thus strive for an equitable, rather than an equal division. It could be argued that the courts are committed to substantive justice rather than formal equality, recognising that a strict equal division may not always lead to just outcomes. In Uganda, the guiding principle in determining each spouse's share

[85] See in this volume Mauritius Chapter: Gunputh, 'An Overview of Matrimonial Property Rights in Mauritius'.

[86] See in this volume Chewe, 'Ownership of Marital Property in Zambia'.

[87] See in this volume Chewe, 'Ownership of Marital Property in Zambia'.

[88] See in this volume Mwenelupembe, 'The Protection of Women's Property Rights on Dissolution of Marriage in Malawi'.

[89] See in this volume Buchumi, 'Marital Property Rights During and After the Dissolution of Marriage in Tanzania'.

of marital property is their contribution to its acquisition. The courts consider both monetary and non-monetary efforts, thereby placing value on unpaid labour, often performed by women.[90]

Contribution is so central to the ownership of marital property that the Malawian courts in *Tewesa v Tewesa*,[91] were faced with the issue of whether educational qualifications obtained during the subsistence of the marriage formed part of marital property and whether a spouse can claim an interest in those qualifications. The court recognised educational qualifications as a form of property vested in the individual who acquired them and thus not subject to distribution. However, it acknowledged that a beneficial interest may arise during the marriage, allowing for possible compensation upon divorce, particularly in light of the future earning potential of the qualified spouse.[92] Mwenelupembe laments that, despite this decision, the court did not quantify such compensation and failed to adequately address the contributing spouse's role in acquiring the qualifications.[93] Indeed, this case reflects the complex and evolving nature of marital property law as it relates to intangible assets, such as educational qualifications, highlighting the need for legal frameworks to also evolve in ways that meaningfully address non-financial contributions.

Seychellois courts have stressed the importance of considering spouses' non-monetary contributions, though they have rejected the notion of marriage as a business partnership in which each party's contributions are meticulously tracked and accounted for. In Seychelles, when a matrimonial asset is registered in the name of one spouse, the court may initially presume sole ownership; however, this presumption can be rebutted if the other spouse demonstrates a shared intention and contribution toward its acquisition, as pertains also in Kenya and Ethiopia. This demonstrates a judicial willingness to look beyond formal ownership and to recognise interests arising from joint efforts within a marriage. Kenyan law also explicitly recognises both monetary and non-monetary contributions when determining each spouse's share in matrimonial property.

As earlier noted, Ghana appears to have moved away from the progressive approach that treated all assets acquired during marriage as marital property, reverting to an emphasis on individual contribution in determining ownership. On the other hand, Dlamini explains that under the community of property system in eSwatini, both spouses hold equal, undivided shares in the joint estate, regardless of the nature or value of their individual contributions. Upon the dissolution of the marriage, all liabilities are first settled from the joint estate, after which the remaining assets are divided equally between the spouses. Though this appears advantageous, he hastens to add that the parties are not protected from each other's creditors.[94] Does this

---

[90] See in this volume Uganda Chapter: Olomola, 'Marital Property Settlement after the Dissolution of Marriages in Nigeria and Uganda: A Comparative Appraisal'.

[91] *Tewesa v Tewesa* [2020] MWHC 28.

[92] *Tewesa v Tewesa* [2020] MWHC 28.

[93] See in this volume Mwenelupembe, 'The Protection of Women's Property Rights on Dissolution of Marriage in Malawi'.

[94] See in this volume Dlamini, 'Proprietary Consequences of Marriage in Eswatini'.

suggest that true equality in some property regimes requires adequate safeguards against the risks of shared liability?

While it may be argued that a more inclusive understanding of marital property enables a more comprehensive evaluation of each party's role in the accumulation of matrimonial assets, it can also introduce complexities in proving contribution, potentially disadvantaging spouses whose efforts are less tangible or undocumented. This is particularly relevant in cases where one spouse has assumed non-financial roles, such as caregiving, household management, or supporting the other spouse's career. While these contributions are often critical to the family's well-being, they are difficult to quantify in economic and, arguably, legal terms.

Consequently, the focus on contribution, while seemingly equitable, may unintentionally reinforce economic disparities and undermine the principle of partnership that marriage embodies. As such, there is ongoing debate as to whether such a framework adequately reflects the realities of modern marital relationships and the diverse forms of contribution that sustain them.

7.4 Contracts in Property Division

Marital contracts are an important feature of marital property law in Africa. Couples may choose to have a prenuptial agreement outlining how their assets will be divided in the event of a divorce. This can help protect separate property or specify terms for spousal support. Prenuptial agreements, also called ante-nuptial agreements, and post-nuptial agreements, are marital property agreements. Prenuptial agreements are made before the marriage, and post-nuptial agreements are made during the marriage to provide for the distribution of property upon divorce.[95] The effect of these agreements is to control the division of the parties' assets upon divorce.[96] Prenuptial and post-nuptial agreements are thus contractual agreements between spouses made to avoid what some perceive as the unfair legal arrangements in operation for the distribution of property upon divorce.[97] The rights of marriage dependent on the nuptial contract are determined by the lex loci contractus.[98]

---

[95] Newbury (2024).

[96] Law Commission (2014, paras 3.65–3.67), confirming that qualifying nuptial agreements may determine financial division on divorce, provided parties' needs are met; *see also Radmacher (formerly Granatino) v Granatino* [2010] UKSC 42, [75], where the Supreme Court held that such agreements should generally be upheld if fairly entered into with full appreciation of implications.

[97] From the perspective of Baroness Deech, a prenup can prevent the richer spouse from being deprived of all that he or she has worked for, as without an agreement: 'The wife who is least likely ever to have put her hand in cold water during the marriage is the one most likely to walk off with millions, regardless of her contributions or conduct. Hence, we find that … the phrases 'gold digger' or 'alimony drone' have been coined'. See UK Parliamentary Debate, HL Deb 27 June 2014, vol. 754, col. 1491.

[98] *Decocuche Savetier* & al 3 Johnson Chy. 100.

In civil and mixed-legal systems such as Côte d'Ivoire, Ethiopia, Morocco, South Africa, eSwatini, and Seychelles, the marital contract offers an opportunity for spouses to opt out of the default matrimonial system. Except for Morocco, these countries generally adopt a default community of property regime, and the marital contract serves as a means of adopting an alternative property regime. Morocco appears to be the outlier. Drawing from principles of Islamic law, it stipulates a separate property regime as the default matrimonial regime, while giving parties the liberty to adopt some form of joint community of property regime.[99] This contractual flexibility is key in systems that prioritise individual ownership and autonomy, but it also places the burden on spouses to proactively formalise joint arrangements, which may not reflect the social and economic realities of marriage in practice.

In many common law-based jurisdictions, by contrast, property classifications often emerge through conduct, implied agreements, or judicial inference rather than formal contracts. This can leave room for discretion but also create legal uncertainty, particularly when evidence of intent or contribution is contested. However, common law countries are increasingly legislating on marital contracts, for example, Kenya.[100]

The place of contract highlights the tension between status and contract in a marriage. Côte d'Ivoire's reform law of 2019 predicates the recognition of marital contracts on compliance with the dictates of morality, explained by Kouassi to mean the values of 'loyalty, probity, conscience, decency and honesty'.[101] On the other hand, as Hammond and Batariwah note, a Ghanaian Court of Appeal has held that marriage is a contract, for which reason the court can give effect to a prenuptial contract to the exclusion of the equitable framework provided for by the Ghanaian constitution and associated case law.[102] While the Ivorian position suggests a state's willingness to interfere with a marital contract along the lines of fairness, the Ghanaian Court of Appeal gives us the most radical and far-reaching expression of contractual freedom in a marital relationship from a common law jurisdiction. With the rise of the market economy and the canonical place given to private property rights, it goes without saying that in African countries, the move from status to contract is underway, and the role of the contract as a way of redistributing property rights in a marital union is gaining influence.

---

[99] See in this volume Morocco Chapter: Hafid, 'An Economic Interpretation of Morocco's New Family Code of 2004: Divorce and Marital Property'.

[100] Kenya's Matrimonial Property Act, s 6(3) and (4) allow spouse to 'enter into an agreement before their marriage to determine their property rights' if they are the agreement is affected by 'fraud, coercion or is manifestly unjust'.

[101] See in this volume Côte D'Ivoire Chapter: Kouassi, 'Ivorian Matrimonial Property Law Reform: Between Resurgence And Emergence'.

[102] See in this volume Hammond and Batariwah, 'Spousal Property Rights in Ghana'.

7.5 *Marital Property Rights in Irregular Unions and Polygamous Marriages*

7.5.1 Presumption of Marriage

Cohabitation appears widespread and has implications for property acquired in such unions. The contributions in this volume show that legal systems diverge in whether and how such relationships are granted legal effect, especially regarding property rights. The chapters reflect what appears to be a divide between formalist and functional approaches to property rights in cohabiting relationships. Countries such as Seychelles, Côte d'Ivoire, Morocco, Ghana, and Zambia have a formalist approach; only legally recognised marriages confer protections such as property division, maintenance, and inheritance rights on the parties.[103] Cohabitation, however long or socially recognised, neither results in a presumption of marriage nor the property rights associated with marriage. This reflects the ongoing tension not just between legal certainty and justice, but also between the moral integrity of the law and moral fairness in recognising informal relationships and the rights associated with them. Furthermore, it echoes the broader theoretical divide between legal positivism and natural law. Nevertheless, in Mauritius, it appears that a narrow presumption of civil marriage exists when documentary proof is absent following a civil ceremony.[104]

By contrast, functional systems permit courts to infer marriage from conduct and reputation; cohabitation and public acknowledgement can suffice to establish a presumption of marriage in the absence of a legal marriage. In Nigeria, the presumption under the Evidence Act, 2011, allows access to property and succession rights, provided it is not rebutted,[105] while Ethiopia accepts familial and communal recognition as proof of marital status.[106] In Tanzania, the Law of Marriage Act recognises a presumption of marriage, and even when the presumption is rebutted, courts can exercise discretion to order equitable distribution of property.[107] Malawi, on the other hand, recognises marriage by repute or permanent cohabitation, based on factors defined by law, and as such, allows parties to benefit from various reliefs regarding property distribution, child custody and maintenance.[108] Historically, Zimbabwe followed a formalist approach. Their 2022 Marriages Act adopts a functionalist

---

[103] See in this volume Tuyau, 'Marital Property in Seychelles'; Kouassi, 'Ivorian Matrimonial Property Law Reform: Between Resurgence And Emergence'.; Hafid, 'An Economic Interpretation of Morocco's New Family Code of 2004: Divorce and Marital Property'; Hammond and Batariwah, 'Spousal Property Rights in Ghana'; and See in this volume Chewe, 'Ownership of Marital Property in Zambia'.

[104] See in this volume Gunputh, 'An Overview of Matrimonial Property Rights in Mauritius'.

[105] See in this volume Kekere, Kolade-Faseyi and Ajidasile, 'Settlement of Matrimonial Property upon Divorce in Nigeria: The Rights of Spouses, Challenges and Urgent Need for Reforms'.

[106] See in this volume Gebreyesus, 'Marital Property Division under the Ethiopian Family Law'.

[107] See in this volume Buchumi, 'Marital Property Rights During and After the Dissolution of Marriage in Tanzania'.

[108] See in this volume Mwenelupembe, 'The Protection of Women's Property Rights on Dissolution of Marriage in Malawi'.

approach by recognising civil partnerships, where partners may claim property division under the Matrimonial Causes Act upon evidentiary proof of the relationship.[109] Collectively, these legal frameworks reflect a shift towards recognising the realities of informal unions and ensuring the equal protection of property rights. Added to this mix is eSwatini, whose Constitution recognises what it calls 'common law husband and wife', a reference to an intimate relationship solidified by cohabitation.[110]

The South African system demonstrates an evolving effort to balance legal certainty with the recognition of informal unions. While their law does not explicitly recognise presumptions of marriage, when cohabiting partners live in a manner resembling marriage, courts may presume marriage when distributing property under the Matrimonial Property Act.[111] Kenya's Supreme Court, in *Mayaka v Mayaka*, emphasised that presumptions of marriage require strict evidentiary proof. Nevertheless, even where a presumption is not upheld, courts may resolve proprietary disputes equitably.[112]

No country is obligated to presume the existence of marriage for cohabiting couples. However, recognising the existence of such relationships and developing guidelines to protect the parties involved should be considered. Laws should clearly define conditions for recognition, ensure equitable property and succession outcomes, and maintain high evidentiary standards. This approach will protect vulnerable partners while preserving legal certainty, ensuring that statutory law is consistent with social realities, and promoting fairness in intimate relationships.

7.5.2 Invalid Marriages

Judicial approaches to property rights in invalid marriages remain diverse. Unlike legally valid unions, where matrimonial property laws clearly govern asset division, invalid marriages require courts to rely on principles of equity, fairness, and proven contributions. Marriages may be declared void or invalid for various reasons, including the existence of a prior subsisting marriage, prohibited degrees of consanguinity or affinity, failure to meet legal formalities, or lack of capacity to marry. Although such marriages are void ab initio, meaning they are treated as if they never legally existed, the contributions suggest that courts often develop mechanisms to protect the rights of innocent parties and children affected by these unions. A comparative analysis across the countries reveals a layered approach to property sharing in invalid marriages.

---

[109] See in this volume Chikaonda, 'A Double-Edged Sword: Zimbabwe's New Marriage Act and The Implications for The Matrimonial Rights of Women in Unregistered Customary Marriages'.

[110] See in this volume Dlamini, 'Proprietary Consequences of Marriage in Eswatini'.

[111] See in this volume Mokoena and Mopai, 'A Critical Analysis and Overview of the South African Legal Framework on Matrimonial Property Rights and Divorce'.

[112] See in this volume Jadeed, 'Contemporary Matrimonial Property Law in Kenya: An Exposition of Substantive Equality'.

It would appear that in cases where courts emphasise equity, the property is usually divided on the basis of demonstrable contributions rather than the formal status of the union, suggesting that judicial reasoning prioritises fairness over technicalities. This approach is evident in countries such as Cameroon, eSwatini, Ghana, and Zambia, where courts recognise contributions to the joint life or to the acquisition of property as the basis for claims.

Some legal systems, on the other hand, maintain a more formal distinction between valid and invalid unions, which arguably limits the scope of protection for 'spouses' acting in good faith. It would seem that these frameworks restrict claims in void or invalid marriages, highlighting a preference for legal certainty over equitable outcomes. Kenya and Morocco are examples of countries where courts either apply ordinary property rules or preserve rights primarily for formally recognised unions.

A recurring theme across jurisdictions, however, is the nuanced application of good faith and contribution. Even in formalistic systems, courts may grant limited remedies where it can be demonstrated that one party materially contributed to jointly held property. This suggests that judicial intervention seeks to mitigate the problems associated with property rights in invalid marriages by recognising substantive contributions and protecting vulnerable parties. This is commendable.

However, it is contended that, in determining property rights in invalid marriages, courts should place less emphasis on financial contributions to the property and instead focus on the circumstances of each case in making their decision. For instance, a party who enters into a void marriage in good faith, and by agreement between the 'spouses', remains at home to undertake domestic and caregiving responsibilities, should not be prejudiced merely because they cannot establish a direct contribution to the acquisition of property. This position can only be facilitated by clearly defined rules for such circumstances and detailed guidelines to aid judges in making decisions.

7.5.3 Polygamous Marriages

Polygamous marriages are an enduring feature of many legal systems on the continent, particularly within common law and some mixed-legal systems. The choice among customary, Islamic, and civil marriage forms represents one of the clearest manifestations of legal pluralism. The form of polygamy discussed in this book is polygyny, that is, a man's ability to marry more than one woman. The property rights of spouses in polygamous marriages provokes very vexed questions of fairness, justice, and equity. In Nigeria, Zimbabwe, and Zambia, customary law principles place barriers on married women's rights to property, ultimately ensuring that most of the property acquired by the spouses during the marriage belongs to the husband.[113] The legal restrictions on women's property ownership create a lopsided

[113] See in this volume Kekere, Kolade-Faseyi and Ajidasile, 'Settlement of Matrimonial Property upon Divorce in Nigeria: The Rights of Spouses, Challenges and Urgent Need for Reforms'; Chikaonda, 'A Double-Edged Sword: Zimbabwe's New Marriage Act and The Implications for The

separate property regime, reducing the category of property that might property be called joint property and complicating difficult questions about contributions towards acquisition for each wife and her husband, as well as for all the wives collectively and their husband. This invites a broader question: to what extent can legal pluralism deliver fairness and equity if customary law consistently limits women's rights to property?

However, the courts in some jurisdictions have attempted to mitigate inequalities. In eSwatini and Zimbabwe, the courts have applied the concept of a universal partnership to rebalance the parties' respective property rights.[114] While these judicial innovations represent an important step toward equity, they also raise a further question: can the courts alone achieve systemic reform? Moreover, the reliance on judicial discretion means that women's property rights may depend heavily on the progressiveness of individual judges rather than a clear legislative mandate.

Civil law jurisdictions take a markedly different approach. Morocco, for instance, acknowledges polygamy, but under strict conditions, requiring the first wife's consent to marry a second wife and allowing her to seek divorce if the marriage contract so permits.[115] In contrast, Côte d'Ivoire, Ethiopia, Seychelles, and Mauritius do not recognise polygamous marriages at all.[116] This prompts an enquiry into whether legal prohibitions can truly suppress polygamous practices in communities where they are culturally and religiously entrenched, or whether they merely push customary marriages underground, leaving women even more vulnerable and unprotected.

These examples reveal the uneven responses of African legal systems to the issue of polygamy and underscore that women remain economically vulnerable unless their property rights are clearly defined and enforced. The challenge lies in reconciling cultural and religious practices with gender equality in a way that genuinely protects the rights of all spouses.

7.6 International Legal Framework

International human rights law as a liberal normative paradigm is crucial to family law reform in Africa, as noted at the beginning of this chapter. Thus, the picture of marital property rights in Africa will be far from complete without any mention of how human rights law has shaped the trajectory of family law reform. Throughout

---

Matrimonial Rights of Women in Unregistered Customary Marriages'; and Chewe, 'Ownership of Marital Property in Zambia'.

[114] See in this volume Dlamini, 'Proprietary Consequences of Marriage in Eswatini'; and Chikaonda, 'A Double-Edged Sword: Zimbabwe's New Marriage Act and The Implications for The Matrimonial Rights of Women in Unregistered Customary Marriages'.

[115] See in this volume Hafid, 'An Economic Interpretation of Morocco's New Family Code of 2004: Divorce and Marital Property'.

[116] See in this volume Kouassi, 'Ivorian Matrimonial Property Law Reform: Between Resurgence And Emergence'.; Dlamini, 'Proprietary Consequences of Marriage in Eswatini'; Tuyau, 'Marital Property in Seychelles'; and Gunputh, 'An Overview of Matrimonial Property Rights in Mauritius'.

this introduction, we have identified ways in which marital property laws across the continent have disadvantaged women, regardless of the legal order under study. Women are unable to own property under the laws of some customary communities. Formal equality reduces a woman's access to property under common law to a question of her contribution. In civil and mixed legal systems, the marital power negates the assurances of equality expressed in community property and the equal sharing thereof.

The Convention on the Elimination of All Forms of Discrimination Against Women (CEDAW) is inarguably one of the most comprehensive international human rights conventions which directly addresses the issue of marital property. Part of a more comprehensive provision on equality of the sexes in family law, article 16(h) requires state parties to remove discriminatory practices to ensure 'the same rights for both spouses in respect of the ownership, acquisition, management, administration, enjoyment and disposition of property, whether free of charge or for a valuable consideration'.[117] CEDAW projects women as autonomous individuals, as against defining them by the roles they undertake in the family context.[118] CEDAW thus possesses a unique potential as a human rights instrument, with a focus on women, to serve as the foundation from which gender-based inequities in all their forms could be addressed, if appropriately amended and suitably interpreted.

The CEDAW Committee has identified at least four ways in which women's property rights in marriages can be adversely impacted. These are the non-recognition of women's rights to own property like their husbands, the inability of women, especially in community property regimes, to manage community property, the prioritisation of financial contribution against other forms of contributions towards the acquisition of property, and the precarious property rights of women in de facto relationships simply because those relationships are unlike marriage.[119] The CEDAW General Recommendation on Equality in Marriage and Family Relations was adopted in 1994, and we are pleased to report that the contributions in this volume demonstrate the progress made in reforming African marital property laws to conform with the aspirations of the CEDAW and other related human rights treaties. We admit, nonetheless, that more work still needs to be done.

Also of note is the African Charter on Human and Peoples' Rights, via the Maputo Protocol, specifically guarantees women the right to equitable sharing of marital property, including upon divorce, separation, or annulment.[120] General Comment No. 6 on the Maputo Protocol underscores the need to value women's contributions to family life, whether financial or non-financial, and urges member states to ensure that matrimonial regimes reflect gender equity.[121] Similarly, individual complaints brought before international bodies reveal persistent gaps in implementation. In the case of *E.S. and S.C. v United Republic of Tanzania*, the CEDAW Committee found

[117] CEDAW, art. 16(h).

[118] Zwingel (2016, p. 18).

[119] CEDAW General Recommendation No. 21 on Equality in Marriage and Family Relations (1994).

[120] Maputo Protocol (2003).

[121] African Commission (2020).

that denying widows the right to inherit or access property constituted a violation of Article 16 and the broader principles of non-discrimination.[122]

Some countries have taken steps to constitutionally protect women's property rights and promote equality. Malawi provides constitutional guarantees that ensure women's right to a fair disposition of jointly held property upon marriage dissolution, without discrimination based on gender or marital status.[123] Ghana's constitution includes provisions mandating equal access to and equitable distribution of jointly acquired property, inspired by international human rights law such as CEDAW.[124] Despite these progressive measures, implementation gaps remain, as Ghana's Parliament has yet to pass necessary legislation to fully realise these protections, leaving many women vulnerable in property disputes. Constitutionalising equality in property relations typically imposes an overarching constitutional norm on all internal legal orders, serving as a yardstick against which all other legal norms on property relations are validated or rejected.

Where a customary law norm conflicts with a constitutional provision, some courts have, in addition to the adoption of a strong positivist adjudicatory stance of invalidating the customary norms because of a conflict with a superior constitutional norm, resolutely applied the repugnancy test, natural justice, equity and good conscience, to overrule these customs. As our Nigerian authors, Kekere, Kolade-Faseyi, and Ajidasile, demonstrate, the Nigerian courts have done so when called upon to pronounce on the validity of customary laws that conflicted with women's constitutional entitlements.[125] Similarly, while the concept of marital property is generally foreign to Islamic law, some progress has been made under human rights principles. According to Buchumi, when parties in Tanzania seek divorce in court, the Law of Marriage Act (LMA) applies, often superseding customary or Islamic rules deemed discriminatory. Though Islamic law limits a divorced woman to a fixed sum, courts have applied section 114 of the LMA to distribute matrimonial assets. In *Bi. Hawa Mohamed,* the Court of Appeal recognised a wife's right to a share of property based on her contribution.[126]

The abolition of marital power in civil and mixed-legal systems, as discussed in this volume, can be attributed to a commitment to international human rights law. In

---

[122] See *E.S. and S.C. v United Republic of Tanzania* (Committee on the Elimination of Discrimination against Women, 2 March 2015). In *E.S. and S.C. v United Republic of Tanzania* (Committee on the Elimination of Discrimination against Women, 2 March 2015), two widows were denied property rights under customary law, which favored male relatives. The CEDAW Committee held that this discriminatory practice violated Tanzania's international obligations under CEDAW, especially Articles 2, 13, 15, and 16. It emphasised that cultural norms must not undermine gender equality and stressed the need to recognize women's domestic and caregiving roles as valid contributions to marital property.

[123] Constitution of the Republic of Malawi 1994, s. 24(1)(b).

[124] Constitution of the Republic of Ghana 1992, art 22.

[125] See in this volume Kekere, Kolade-Faseyi and Ajidasile, 'Settlement of Matrimonial Property upon Divorce in Nigeria: The Rights of Spouses, Challenges and Urgent Need for Reforms'.

[126] The woman's share was denied due to evidence of mismanagement. See in this volume Buchumi, 'Marital Property Rights During and After the Dissolution of Marriage in Tanzania'.

eSwatini, for example, the courts have incrementally abolished the marital power, first by ruling that women have the legal standing in respect of marital property, and then holding that the marital power is unconstitutional and discriminates against women in the management and control of property.[127] In both cases, the eSwatini courts relied on principles of equality, albeit in different ways.[128] In the former, the courts relied on the International Covenant on Civil and Political Rights and the comments of the Human Rights Committee to tease out the ambit of equality; in the latter, the court was not willing to embark on so broad an excursion, content to rest its decisions on constitutional principles.[129]

This volume highlights the growing recognition of spousal contributions to marital property. Across Africa, legal reforms and judicial decisions increasingly value non-financial contributions, reflecting human rights influences and advancing equality in the division of marital assets.

8 Analytical Focus and Organisation of Chapters

This volume is enriched by the thematic latitude afforded the contributors, enabling a multidimensional exploration of marital property relations. Notably, Hafid analyses Morocco's 2004 New Family Code from an economic perspective, exploring how legal reforms interact with socio-economic changes. His study reveals both the economic impact of legal empowerment and the limits of reform in addressing structural inequalities. Olomola also provides a comparative analysis of the legal frameworks in Uganda and Nigeria, highlighting similarities, differences, and the influence of cultural and statutory norms on the treatment of marital property.

The contributors from Cameroon, Côte d'Ivoire, Ethiopia, Eswatini, Ghana, Kenya, Malawi, Mauritius, Nigeria, Seychelles, South Africa, Tanzania, Zambia, and Zimbabwe focus on their respective countries, highlighting the interactions between the different internal legal systems regarding property rights. However, occasional comparisons with other jurisdictions are included, especially in the recommendations sections, as potential models for reform. Collectively, these approaches are essential for a comprehensive understanding of property rights and their broader legal, socio-cultural and economic effects.

The definition of conceptual categories, the influences on law reform, and the legislative and judicial approaches to marital property rights are uniquely shaped by the legal traditions represented in this volume. To examine the paradox between the uniformity of legal traditions and states' efforts to develop context-specific solutions, the contributions are organised by legal tradition.

---

[127] *Sacolo & Another v Sacolo & Others* [2019] SZHC 166.

[128] *Aphane v Registrar of Deeds & Others* [2010] SZHC 29 and *Sihlongonyane v Sihlongonyane* [2013] SZHC 144.

[129] See in this volume Dlamini, 'Proprietary Consequences of Marriage in Eswatini'.

The volume opens with contributions from the common law tradition, followed by those from the civil law, bijural and mixed legal systems.

Common law contributions from Ghana, Nigeria, Malawi, Tanzania, Uganda and Zambia reflect systems influenced by British common law and diverse customary laws. These jurisdictions have often favoured separate property regimes that undervalue women's contributions, while simultaneously seeking equity through legislative and judicial reform.

Côte d'Ivoire, Ethiopia and Morocco illustrate Africa's civil law mosaic. While Côte d'Ivoire and Morocco inherited the French civil law tradition, Ethiopia adopted it voluntarily to 'modernise' its legal system. Civil law traditions in these jurisdictions emphasise civil marriage and community property regimes. Although alternative regimes exist, spouses must actively choose them. Morocco also highlights the strong influence of Islamic law on marital property division. In these countries, state law largely excludes customary law and offers limited recognition of customary marriages.

Cameroon has a unique bijural system, combining French civil law and British common law, applied in the Francophone and Anglophone regions respectively.

Contributions from Southern Africa, including Eswatini, Mauritius, Seychelles, South Africa and Zimbabwe, reflect mixed or hybrid systems that draw on common law, Roman-Dutch law and, in some cases, civil law. These jurisdictions feature some of Africa's most developed property regimes, particularly advanced community property systems with modifications to accrual. While Mauritian and Seychellois law largely ignore customary marriages, Zimbabwe, South Africa, and Eswatini recognise them. Notably, courts in these countries also use the concept of universal partnership to equitably divide property where constitutional or legislative guidance is lacking.

Grouping chapters by legal tradition highlights how colonial legacies and socio-political contexts continue to shape property ownership across Africa.

9 Recommendations

Despite significant advancements in the sharing of marital property, particularly through the growing influence of international human rights norms, several critical challenges persist. As this chapter reveals, key issues include the incomplete realisation of marital equality, the complex operation of legal pluralism, and the continued inferior treatment of women, especially under certain customary law frameworks. Additionally, inconsistent judicial interpretation of non-financial contributions undermines equitable outcomes. The absence of explicit statutory definitions of marital property in some jurisdictions further complicates the legal landscape, creating uncertainty and limiting the effectiveness of legal protections for vulnerable spouses. To address these shortcomings, we propose the following recommendations to strengthen the legal frameworks governing marital property.

First, states should adopt clear and comprehensive statutory definitions of marital property in both monogamous and polygamous marriages. These definitions should be sufficiently detailed to minimise excessive judicial discretion and should explicitly recognise both financial and non-financial contributions, including domestic work, caregiving, and other forms of unpaid labour typically undertaken by women. In respect of legal definitions, Tie argues that 'the notions of fairness and just adjudication retain their vitality only ... when they remain beyond the reach of legal definition', noting that once ideals are codified into law, they lose their context-sensitivity, which is essential to achieving justice in individual cases.[130] He states specifically of such notions that 'Their instantiation within legal convention inevitably reifies their meaning, producing discursive frameworks that – while enabling for those whose subjectivity mirrors that of the discourse - fail to recognize those whose sense of self is other than that prescribed'.[131] However, predictability and consistency matter in the protection of rights. Moreover, when we fail to define expressions upon which vital rights rest, these expressions remain vague, subjective, and unevenly applied, and this does more harm than good. In addition, legal meanings need not be permanently fixed; through litigation, activism, and reinterpretation, meanings can be reshaped to reflect changing sensibilities.

Alternatively, where states choose to grant judges discretion in the division of marital property to account for varying circumstances, the law should provide a clear set of guiding factors to assist in identifying, classifying, and distributing marital property as has been done in other jurisdictions. This arrangement has the potential to offer a balanced and context-specific solution to property rights. Although anchoring judges' discretion to defined criteria, it allows for the unique dynamics of each marriage to be accounted for. It also provides transparency and consistency across cases, without what may be perceived as the rigidity of legal rules. Such guided discretion will enhance equitable outcomes and likely reflect the realities of diverse marital relationships.

Second, legal harmonisation efforts should seek to reconcile customary, religious, and statutory laws with constitutional and international legal principles of gender equality. As seen in countries like Ghana, where customary law in rural communities differs from customary law decided by judges, it is crucial to educate legal actors in non-state legal systems and strive for legal harmony. Such harmonisation is essential for promoting consistency and fairness in the regulation and enforcement of matrimonial property rights across different legal systems. This is not a rejection of legal pluralism. On the contrary, we affirm that diversity in legal systems should be respected and preserved, but with a firm commitment to gender equality. We acknowledge that historically, men and women had distinct socio-cultural roles,

[130] Tie (1999, p. 21).

[131] Tie (1999, p. 21).

which influenced how rights and responsibilities were allocated upon the dissolution of marriage. For example, men were often expected to care for children post-divorce, which influenced property arrangements.[132] However, societal roles have evolved. Today, women are active economic contributors, often providing equally for their families. There is, therefore, little justification for continuing to disadvantage women in divorce settlements based on outdated assumptions about gender roles and the relative value of those roles.

Third, African countries need to pay attention to the status of couples in irregular unions and take steps to either regularise their status, or design rules which account for these specific unions. The plight of parties who have cohabited for long periods is especially acute. While it is up to each jurisdiction to either recognise these unions as marriages or not, the division of property upon the dissolution of the relationship should not be contingent on proof of only financial contribution. Unions of cohabitation mimic marriages, if they are not already marriages in all but name. If a case can be made for non-financial contributions for married people, little justifies the hesitation to extend these forms of contribution to unions of cohabitation. Furthermore, innocent parties in void marriages, particularly those whose marriages are void because the other party is already married, should be adequately protected. It would appear that in many cases, the women who enter into the subsequent marriages have no knowledge of the existing marriage between their perceived husbands and third parties. Men who take advantage of innocent women should not be allowed to invoke the invalidity of the marriage against those women when they claim a portion of property acquired during the course of the void marriage.

Fourth, sustained judicial training and capacity-building are essential to promoting consistent, gender-sensitive interpretations of matrimonial property law. As demonstrated throughout this volume, the reluctance by judges and other legal actors to challenge patriarchal norms remains a significant barrier to the effective protection of women's property rights. Targeted training for judges and other legal professionals should focus on promoting gender equality, recognising non-financial contributions, and applying constitutional and international human rights standards in family law adjudication.

Fifth, legal reforms should incorporate mechanisms that protect vulnerable spouses, particularly women, by ensuring meaningful access to legal representation. Legal aid services should be expanded and strengthened to prioritise family law matters, especially for individuals in rural or low-income communities where access to legal assistance is limited and often prohibitively expensive. Non-governmental organisations must also be encouraged to continue to play meaningful roles in this regard.

[132] See in this volume Hammond and Batariwah, 'Spousal Property Rights in Ghana'; Kekere, Kolade-Faseyi and Ajidasile, 'Settlement of Matrimonial Property upon Divorce in Nigeria: The Rights of Spouses, Challenges and Urgent Need for Reforms'; and Chikaonda, 'A Double-Edged Sword: Zimbabwe's New Marriage Act and The Implications for The Matrimonial Rights of Women in Unregistered Customary Marriages'.

Sixth, public education and legal awareness campaigns are critical for the protection of rights. Widespread ignorance about legal rights and what constitutes a contribution to marital property, especially the non-financial forms, continues to undermine equitable outcomes. Public education must therefore be seen not as a supplementary measure but as a foundational tool in promoting gender equality in the distribution of marital property. We support the assertion that 'it is not the law which changes attitudes so much as the accompanying education.... There is a great risk of attributing to the law the transforming effect which belongs to the education.'[133] Education not only informs citizens of their rights and responsibilities but also equips them to engage more intentionally with legal systems.

It must be stressed that spouses themselves, especially women, must be educated about their property rights. Such awareness can help prevent exploitation and injustice, especially in contexts where gendered power imbalances exist. In fact, women, especially the uneducated, must be educated about the value of their contributions, both monetary and non-monetary, to marriages. It is only when they understand the significance of their roles, that they can effectively assert their rights and advocate for an equitable share of marital property.

Ultimately, legal reforms must extend beyond the formal recognition of property rights to address the deeply rooted structural and socio-economic barriers that prevent women from acquiring and controlling property. This is because although many postcolonial African legal systems recognise women's right to own property, persistent gender inequality rooted in patriarchal norms and socio-economic disadvantages continues to restrict women's real access to property. Indeed, it has been argued that, 'Empowering legal provisions can all too easily be overshadowed by the enduring social inequalities that lie beneath liberal images of a fundamentally cohesive polity, inequalities that pattern the daily lives of those for whom the provisions are intended'.[134] While progressive in principle, such legal provisions may fail to produce meaningful change when they are introduced into contexts marked by deep-rooted social and structural inequalities.

These provisions may offer formal rights, but for many, especially women and marginalised groups, such rights remain inaccessible due to poverty, illiteracy, entrenched power hierarchies, and socio-cultural norms. As a result, the law's promise of equality is frequently undermined by the lived realities of those it aims to protect. The illusion of a codified rights-based order can obscure these disparities, creating a false sense of progress while systemic injustice persists. Without parallel efforts to transform the social and economic conditions that sustain inequality, legal empowerment provisions risk becoming symbolic and superficial rather than substantive.

Consequently, efforts to promote gender equality must include targeted measures such as economic empowerment initiatives, legal literacy campaigns, and enforcement mechanisms that enable women to exercise their rights meaningfully within marriage and upon its dissolution.

---

[133] Allott (1980, p. 236).

[134] Tie (1999, p. 7).

10 Conclusion

The sharing of marital property remains a deeply complex and often under-regulated issue across Africa. Despite notable progress in some areas of family law, such as the establishment of clear legal frameworks for marriage celebration and dissolution, property division has not kept pace, leaving many parties vulnerable to inequitable outcomes and socio-economic insecurity. This volume demonstrates that closing this regulatory gap is not merely a technical necessity; it is central to ensuring the meaningful realisation of property rights within marriages and other intimate relationships. Legal systems must address this issue through reforms that are both contextually grounded and firmly rooted in the overarching principles of gender equality, fairness, equity, and justice. This requires not only codifying property rights for all marriages, including monogamous and polygamous unions, but also recognising and protecting the property rights of partners in irregular unions, ensuring that such rights are effectively enforceable in practice. Harmonising statutory, customary, and religious laws, strengthening judicial capacity, and expanding access to legal representation and public legal education are all essential to translating legal recognition into meaningful protection. Above all, reforms must tackle the structural and socio-economic barriers that prevent spouses, particularly women, from acquiring and controlling property. By providing comparative insights and practical recommendations, this volume aims to make a meaningful contribution to ongoing legal and policy efforts aimed at achieving equitable property rights. It is hoped that the coming years will see Africa making significant strides in protecting the property rights of spouses and intimate partners in line with contemporary human rights norms, while remaining sensitive to the social and cultural contexts in which unions take place.

References

African Commission on Human and Peoples' Rights (2020) General Comment No. 6 on the protocol to the african charter on human and peoples' rights on the rights of women in Africa (Maputo Protocol): the right to property during separation, divorce or annulment of marriage (Article 7(d)), 4 March 2020. Available at: https://achpr.au.int/en/node/906. Accessed 2 Nov 2025

Allott AN (1980) The limits of the law. Butterworths, London

Antognini A (2019) Nonmarital Coverture. B U L Rev 99(5):2139–2210

Bailey J (2002) Favoured or oppressed? Married women, property and 'coverture' in England, 1660–1800. Contin Chang 17(3):351–372

Basch N (1979) Invisible women: the legal fiction of marital unity in nineteenth-century America. Fem Stud 5(2):346–366

Beattie C, Stevens MF (eds) (2013) Married women and the law in premodern Northwest Europe. Boydell Press, Woodbridge

Blackstone W (1765) Commentaries on the Laws of England. Clarendon Press, Oxford

Blanc-Jouvan X (2004) Worldwide influence of the French Civil Code of 1804, on the occasion of its bicentennial celebration, Cornell Law School Berger International Speaker Papers. Paper 3. http://scholarship.law.cornell.edu/biss_papers/3. Accessed 2 Nov 2025

Christelow A (2000) Islamic law in Africa. In: Levtzion N, Pouwels RL (eds) The history of Islam in Africa. Ohio University Press, Athens, pp 374–393
Cobbah JAM (1987) African values and the human rights debate: An African perspective. Hum Rts Q 9:309–331
Combs MB (2005) "A measure of legal independence": The 1870 Married Women's Property Act and the portfolio allocations of British wives. J Econ Hist 65(4):1028–1057
Committee on the Elimination of Discrimination against Women (CEDAW) (1994) General Recommendation No. 21: Equality in marriage and family relations. UN Doc. A/49/38
Committee on the Elimination of Discrimination against Women (CEDAW) (2015) E.S. and S.C. v United Republic of Tanzania, Communication No. 9/2015, UN Doc. CEDAW/C/60/D/9/2015
Corrin J (2017) Exploring the deep: looking for deep legal pluralism in the South Pacific. Law Rev 48(2):305–322. https://doi.org/10.26686/vuwlr.v48i2.4738
Davie M (1993) Matrimonial property in English and American conflict of laws. Int Comp Law Q 42(4):855–881
Dnes AW (2019) Litigation and marital property rights. In: Marciano A, Ramello GB (eds) Encyclopedia of Law and Economics. Springer, New York, pp 1342–1352
Fagan E (1996) Roman-Dutch Law in its South African historical context. In: Zimmermann VD (ed) Southern cross: Civil Law and Common Law in South Africa. Oxford University Press, Oxford, pp 32–64
Fernandez A (2013) Tapping Reeve, Nathan Dane, and James Kent: three fading federalists on marital unity. In: Stretton T, Kesselring KJ (eds) Married women and the law: coverture in England and the common law world. McGill-Queen's University Press, Montreal, pp 205–225
Fitzpatrick P (1984) Law and Societies. Osgoode Hall L J 22(1):115–138
Girvin SD (1996) The architects of the mixed legal system. In: Zimmermann VD (ed) Southern cross: Civil Law and Common Law in South Africa. Oxford University Press, Oxford, pp 95–139
Griffin B (2003) Class, gender, and liberalism in Parliament 1868–1882: the case of the Married Women's Property Acts. Hist J 46(1):59–87
Griffiths J (1986) What is legal pluralism? Leg Plur Crit Soc Anal 18(24):1–55. https://doi.org/10.1080/07329113.1986.10756387
Halley J, Rittich K (2010) Critical directions in comparative family law: Genealogies and contemporary studies of family law exceptionalism. Am J Comp Law 58(4):753–776
Haskins GL (1948) The development of common law dower. Harv Law Rev 62(1):42–55
Himonga C (2011) The future of living customary law in African legal systems in the twenty-first century and beyond, with special reference to South Africa. In: Fenrich J, Galizzi P, Higgins T (eds) The future of African customary law. Cambridge University Press, Cambridge, pp 31–57
Heuer JN (2018) The family and the nation: Gender and citizenship in revolutionary France, 1789–1830. Cornell University Press, Ithaca
Holton W (2015) Equality as unintended consequence: the Contracts Clause and the Married Women's Property Acts. J South Hist 81(2):313–340
Isser D (2011) Understanding and engaging customary justice systems. In: Isser D (ed) Customary justice and the rule of law in war-torn societies. United States Institute of Peace Press, Washington, DC, pp 325–368
Kang'ara SW (2012) Beyond bed and bread: Making the African state through marriage law reform—Constitutive and transformative influences of Anglo-American legal thought. Comp Law Rev 3:1–35
Kha H (2021) A history of divorce law reform in England from the Victorian to interwar years. Routledge, London
Kludze AKP (1972) Problems of intestate succession in Ghana. UGLJ 9:89–122.
Kombo BK (2021) Napoleonic legacies, postcolonial state legitimation, and the perpetual myth of non-intervention: Family code reform and gender equality in Mali. Soc Leg Stud 30(5):704–723
Law Commission. Matrimonial Property, Needs and Agreements (2014). (Law Com No 343). London: The Stationery Office. Retrieved from https://www.gov.uk/government/publications/matrimonial-property-needs-and-agreements

Leong KW (1993) Division of matrimonial assets: recent cases and thoughts. Sing J Legal Stud 353–364
Maputo Protocol (2003) Protocol to the African Charter on Human and Peoples' Rights of Women in Africa
Mbiti JS (1969) African religions and philosophy, 2nd edn. Heinemann, London
McCammon HJ, Arch SC, Bergner EM (2014) A radical demand effect: early US feminists and the Married Women's Property Acts. Soc Sci Hist 38(2):225–250
Melton GB (1992) The law is a good thing (psychology is, too): human rights in psychological jurisprudence. Law Hum Behav 16(4):381–398
Merry SE (1988) Legal pluralism. Law Soc Rev 22(5):869–896
Morse BW, Woodman GR (1988) Introductory essay: the state's options. In: Morse BW, Woodman GR (eds) Indigenous law and the State. Foris Publications, Dordrecht, pp 5–24
Newbury A (2024) Nuptial Agreements. Law Gazette, 12 January. Retrieved from https://www.lawgazette.co.uk/legal-updates/nuptial-agreements/5118405.article
Oba AA (2011) The future of customary law in Africa. In: Fenrich J, Galizzi P, Higgins T (eds) The future of African customary law. Cambridge University Press, Cambridge, pp 58–82
Pain JH (1978) The reception of English and Roman-Dutch Law in Africa with reference to Botswana. Lesotho and Swaziland Comp Int Law J South Afr 11:137–167
Parrinder EG (1970) African traditional religion, 3rd edn. Greenwood Press, Westport, CT
Pérez-Perdomo R, Merryman JH (2018) The civil law tradition: An introduction to the legal systems of Europe and Latin America, 4th edn. Stanford University Press, Stanford
Rheinstein M Glendon MA (1980) III. Community property systems. In: Zweigert K, Drobnig U (eds), International Encyclopedia of Comparative Law Online. Brill|Nijhoff. https://doi.org/10.1163/2589-4021_IECO_COM_040404
Ronner AD (1996) Husband and wife are one—him: Bennis v. Michigan as the resurrection of coverture. Mich J Gend Law 4(1):132–162
Salvaing B (2020) Islam in Sub-Saharan Africa, 800–1900', In: Fallou N, Mustapha HK, Toyin F (eds) The Palgrave handbook of Islam in Africa, Springer International Publishing AG, Switzerland, ProQuest Ebook Central. https://ebookcentral-proquest-com.ezp-prod1.hul.harvard.edu/lib/harvard-ebooks/detail.action?docID=6357800. pp 45–74
Sarbah JM (1904) Fanti customary laws, 2nd edn. William Clowes & Sons Limited, London
Seabourne G (2019) "It is necessary that the issue be heard to cry or squall within the four [walls]": Qualifying for tenancy by the curtesy of England in the reign of Edward I. J Legal Hist 40(1):44–66
Stretton T (2018) Women, marriage, property, and law: contextualizing the Witch of Edmonton. Early Theatre 21:137–149
Stretton, T, Kesselring KJ (eds) (2013) Married women and the law: Coverture in England and the common law world. McGill-Queen's University Press, Montreal
Tait AA (2014) The Beginning of the end of coverture: a reappraisal of the married woman's separate estate. Yale J L Fem 26(2):165–216
Tamanaha B (2021) Legal pluralism explained: history, theory and consequences. Oxford University Press, Oxford
Thompson S (2018) Married Women's Property Act 1964 In: Rackley E, Auchmuty R (eds). Women's legal landmarks: celebrating the history of women and law in the UK and Ireland, Hart Publishing, Oxford, pp 263–269
Tie W (1999) Legal pluralism: towards a multicultural conception of law. Ashgate Publishing Ltd., Aldershot
Woodman GR (1996) Legal pluralism and the search for justice. J Afr Law 40(2):152–167
Woodman GR (2010) Ghana: how does state law accommodate religious, cultural, linguistic and ethnic diversity? In: Foblets M-C, Gaudreault-Desbiens J-F, Renteln AD (eds) Cultural diversity and the law: state responses from around the world. Bruylant, Brussels / Éditions Yvon Blais, pp 255–276

Zwingel S (2016) Translating international women's rights: the CEDAW Convention in context. Palgrave Macmillan, London

Ama F. Hammond is an Associate Professor at the University of Ghana School of Law, where she teaches Contract Law, Equity, and Succession and coordinates the School's graduate programmes. She serves as Deputy Editor of the University of Ghana Law Journal and has edited a number of books in her areas of expertise. Her research focuses on family law, legal pluralism, the law of succession, and human rights, with particular attention to the interaction between law, society, and policy. Hammond holds a BA from the University of Cape Coast, an LLB from the University of Ghana, an LLM from Harvard Law School, and a Ph.D. from the University of British Columbia.

Prosper Batariwah is an S.J.D. candidate at Harvard Law School. His research interests include family law, legal pluralism, and natural resource governance. His work has appeared in peer-reviewed journals, including the Journal of African Law, Journal of Comparative Law, University of Ghana Law Journal, and African Journal of International and Comparative Law. He holds an LLB (first class honours) from the University of Ghana and a Qualifying Certificate for the Practice of Law from the Ghana School of Law. He is co-editor of Family Law in Africa: Perspectives on Selected Systems of Marriage (Talbot, 2023)

Common Law Systems: Ghana, Kenya, Malawi, Nigeria, Tanzania, Uganda, Zambia

Spousal Property Rights in Ghana

Ama F. Hammond and Prosper Batariwah

Abstract This chapter critically examines Ghana's legal framework governing marital property ownership, focusing on its limitations and proposing reforms. It highlights the importance of well-defined property rights for ensuring equity and empowering spouses in managing and distributing marital property. The chapter investigates the complexities of Ghana's legal system, which is shaped by its colonial history and persistent gender inequality, and how these factors continue to influence spousal property arrangements. It reviews the evolution of property rights under customary law, the common law regime introduced by the Matrimonial Causes Act of 1971, and the constitutional changes of 1992. Despite attempts at reform, the lack of clear definitions and criteria for marital property division has led to inconsistent judicial outcomes. The chapter evaluates the impact of these legal shifts, emphasising the need for clear, equitable guidelines that account for both financial and non-financial contributions. Drawing on international models from the UK and the US, the chapter advocates for comprehensive reform of the Matrimonial Causes Act, recommending specific factors to guide property division and better alignment with Ghana's socio-economic realities. The chapter concludes that a more consistent and inclusive legal framework is necessary to ensure fairness and equality in marital property rights.

1 Introduction

This chapter evaluates the legal framework for marital property ownership in Ghana, focusing on its shortcomings and proposing recommendations for reform. Establishing legal rights to marital property has significant implications for its division

A. F. Hammond (✉)
School of Law, University of Ghana, Accra, Ghana
e-mail: afhammond@ug.edu.gh

P. Batariwah
Harvard Law School, Cambridge, MA, USA
e-mail: pbatariwah@sjd.law.harvard.edu

A. F. Hammond and P. Batariwah (eds.), *The Law on Marital Property in Africa*, Ius Gentium: Comparative Perspectives on Law and Justice 138,
https://doi.org/10.1007/978-3-032-19358-2_2

in the event of divorce, separation, or the death of one spouse. Undoubtedly, well-defined ownership rules ensure equity and empower partners to engage in well-informed deliberations regarding the management and distribution of assets, a critical aspect of financial planning. The rules governing spousal property rights in Ghana are unique, not just because of the country's legal diversity, resulting from its colonial past, but also because gender inequality, fuelled by relentless patriarchy, remains a significant challenge to equity in spousal property arrangements.

This chapter provides an overview of the legally recognised types of marriage in Ghana, highlighting the interdependence of various legal systems in defining spouses' property rights. It discusses customary law principles on joint property ownership, the views of legal scholars, and judicial reforms that have sought to align customary law with modern standards of equality and non-discrimination. The chapter also covers the evolution and reform of Ghana's common law property regime, particularly the Matrimonial Causes Act 1971 (Act 367), which governs divorce and property distribution. It assesses the impact of Act 367, noting its shortcomings in defining marital property and setting criteria for division. The chapter further examines the legal shift introduced by the 1992 Constitution and the ongoing debates about marital property and its distribution. It also critically evaluates the judicial approach to property settlement in divorce, considering the impact of international gender equity obligations, Western legal models, and changing perceptions of fairness. Finally, it makes reform proposals.

2 Types of Marriage in Ghana and the Impact of Legal Pluralism

Like many post-colonial nations, Ghana has a plural legal system.[1] The diverse sources of law in Ghana outlined in Article 11 of the 1992 Constitution include the common law, equity, and customary law.[2] In practice, this legal pluralism is reflected in the co-existence of State law with judicial customary law, the living customary law of various ethnic groups, and Islamic law.[3] As a result, the Marriages Act of Ghana (CAP 127) acknowledges Christian, civil, Islamic, and customary marriages, each governed by distinct legal principles.

Part Three of the Marriages Act regulates Christian and civil marriages, introduced in Ghana, then the Gold Coast, as a monogamous form of marriage in 1884 by the British colonialists. The Marriages Act provides for the solemnisation and registration of marriages by a Registrar of Marriages or a licensed Christian priest or minister referred to as a Marriage Officer in a licensed church building.[4] Under such marriages, a man and woman who are adults and not closely related by blood or

---

[1] Woodman (1996, pp.158–159).

[2] Constitution of the Republic of Ghana 1992, art. 11.

[3] Bond (2008, p. 394).

[4] Marriages Act of Ghana (CAP 127, ss. 42–55).

marriage and are either unmarried or already married to each other under customary law, are permitted to marry.[5] Where the couple is already married under customary law, their marriage is converted from a potentially polygamous marriage to a monogamous marriage,[6] inviting the regulation of the State and customary legal systems.[7] Of this arrangement, Mensa-Bonsu, a legal academic, explains that 'A unique feature of Ghanaian marriages is that the majority of couples, to the eyes of a stranger to the legal system, are married twice'.[8] However, to Ghanaians, this is the norm, highlighting a form of legal hybridisation, where individuals navigate and integrate diverse legal systems, thus maintaining a sense of identity within both systems.[9] Christian and civil marriages may be dissolved under Act 367 if broken down beyond reconciliation.[10]

Islamic marriages are governed by Part Two of the Marriages Act.[11] These marriages are formed under the applicable Islamic rules, but according to the courts, they are regarded as customary marriages unless registered under the Marriages Act.[12] In other words, registering a customary law marriage celebrated according to Islamic rites under Part Two of the Marriages Act effectively transforms it into an Islamic marriage. The judicial recognition of unregistered Islamic marriages as customary marriages reflects a complex interplay between customary law, religious practices, and state law, where the distinction between what Muslims consider 'Islamic' and what the State formally recognises as such is unclear. Such legal ambiguity often denies individuals, particularly those involved, access to certain legal rights.[13] While Islamic marriages may be dissolved in accordance with Islamic rites, such divorces will only be valid if they are registered.[14]

Customary marriages, regulated under Part One of the Marriages Act, account for about 80% of all marriages in Ghana and are *potentially* polygamous, and therefore,

---

[5] Marriages Act (Cap 127, ss. 74 and 76).

[6] This is because the conception of Christian and civil marriages under the common law, as codified into the Marriages Act, can only be monogamous, for as Lord Penzance stated in *Hyde v. Hyde Woodmansee*, (1866) L.R IP & D 130, 133: 'I conceive that marriage as understood in Christendom, may for this purpose be defined as the voluntary union for life of *one man and one woman to the exclusion of all others*' (emphasis ours); any purported subsequent marriage after such conversion will be void and bigamous under the Criminal Offences Act, 1960 (Act 29), ss 264–265.

[7] Woodman (2010, pp. 264–265).

[8] Mensa-Bonsu (2023, p. 109), Mensa-Bonsu adds that this is: 'first under customary law, and then in accordance with Part 3. However, the correct position of the law is that by undergoing a Part 3 marriage process, the couple has converted their customary law marriage into a Part 3 marriage. The import of this is that if the conversion fails due to the failure of the couple to adhere to the rules under Part 3, the Part 3 marriage is held to be null and void. The union reverts to a customary marriage, and issues arising under the marriage are determined by recourse to customary law.'

[9] Hammond (2016, p. 637).

[10] Matrimonial Causes Act 1971 (Act 367, s 41).

[11] Marriages Act (CAP 127), pt 2; see also Dowuona-Hammond et al. (2023, p. 27).

[12] *Kwakye v Tuba and Others* [1961] GLR 720.

[13] Sezgin (2023, p. 1303).

[14] Marriages Act (Cap 127, s 27).

distinguishable from the definition of marriage under English common law.[15] This marriage unifies the families of the man and woman.[16] They have been described not as the 'union of *this man* and *this woman*' but the 'union of the *family of this man* and *this woman*'.[17] The actual rites for celebrating a customary law marriage differ from one ethnic group to another, even though there appear to be common characteristics.[18] While these marriages may be dissolved under the applicable customary law rules on the grounds of adultery,[19] desertion[20] and lack of maintenance,[21] among other grounds, they may also be dissolved by the courts, like all non-monogamous marriages. In this context, courts will consider the distinctive aspects of a customary law marriage when determining suitable relief, financial support, and child custody arrangements. The court may provide reliefs acknowledged under customary law, either in addition to or as a replacement for the matrimonial reliefs outlined in the Matrimonial Causes Act.[22] Additionally, the court will assess the facts recognised by the personal law of the parties as adequate grounds for a divorce.[23] Islamic marriages may also be dissolved under Act 367. However, these considerations must always synchronise with the principles of justice, fairness, and good conscience.[24] Where there is a conflict among the different choice of law rules in a marriage with elements of both statutory and customary marriage law, the ordinance marriage principle of monogamy prevails.[25]

The legal rules regulating these marriages show the interdependence and complementarity among the different systems, not to mention the competition that sometimes characterises their relationship. The State chooses the terms on which to recognise the other legal systems. Indeed, in Africa, state legal pluralism, the more dominant legal arrangement, involves acknowledging and integrating various legal systems, including customary law, within the State's official legal framework.[26] Thus, Woodman, a legal academic, explains that 'state law contains one set of rules on marriage and divorce derived from Islamic law, perhaps several other sets derived from different ethnic customary laws, and a set derived from English law....'[27] More

---

[15] About 15% of currently married women aged 15–49 in Ghana report that their husband has multiple wives. Ghana Statistical Service and ICF (2024, p. 67)

[16] *Yaotey v. Quaye* [1961] 2 GLR 573, 578.

[17] *Yaotey v. Quaye* [1961] 2 GLR 573, GLR 573, Ollennu J (as he then was).

[18] See generally Sarbah (1904, p. 1) and Rattray (1929, p. 1).

[19] See generally Sarbah (1904, p. 1) and Rattray (1929, p. 1).

[20] Rattray (n 19) 31; Sarbah (n 19) 53. According to Rattray, the husband's duty to maintain his wife and children is an essential aspect of customary law, and Sarbah highlights that customary law does not tolerate the neglect of marital responsibilities. As a result, failure to provide maintenance constitutes a valid ground for divorce under customary law.

[21] Matrimonial Causes Act 1971 (Act 367), s. 41(2).

[22] Matrimonial Causes Act 1971 (Act 367), s 41(2).

[23] Matrimonial Causes Act 1971 (Act 367), s 41(3).

[24] Matrimonial Causes Act 1971 (Act 367), s 41(2).

[25] Criminal Offences Act 1960 (Act 29), s.265(2), Woodman (2010, p. 268).

[26] Woodman (1996, p. 158).

[27] Woodman (1996, p. 37).

importantly and relevant to our discussion, the incidents of the various types of marriage have had a profound impact on how the courts have shared property between divorcing spouses.

2.1 *Marital Property and Rights Under Customary Law*

Generally, under customary law, spouses held separately property they acquired individually during the subsistence of the marriage. Such property was not regarded as joint property. Sarbah, a prominent Gold Coast (now Ghana) lawyer, explained that at customary law, 'Married people have no community of goods, but each has his or her particular property'.[28] This meant that a spouse was entitled to acquire and use property separately, and whatever property the spouses acquired before and during the marriage remained their exclusive property during and beyond the period of the marriage.[29] This is primarily because spouses under customary law are unrelated by blood and do not belong to each other's traditional family, which may be matrilineal or patrilineal.[30]

As a result, spouses could not even lay claim to each other's intestate estate. According to scholars writing between the early and late 20th century, customary law treated spouses' property as separate, and marriage did not automatically change their property rights. Daniels, a legal academic, noted that as a general principle of customary law, marriage did not alter property rights of spouses.[31] As with most matrilineal societies, Rattray confirmed that among the Ashanti, a spouse's personal property remained theirs in the event of a divorce.[32] Daniels noted that some gifts exchanged between spouses were recoverable in the event of divorce.[33] This was corroborated by Offei, who, writing about Aburi in Akuapim, noted that on divorce, spouses could choose not to accept the items lent to each other.[34] Danquah highlighted an exception to the general rule of property ownership in marriage among the Akim Abuakwa, noting that spouses could be entitled to half of certain property or trading profits, subject to specific conditions.[35]

Largely, the customary rule on separate property worked to the disadvantage of women, especially on divorce, as societal and legal expectations restricted opportunities for the attainment of financial independence. It has been asserted that:

> Even though this principle appears to be gender neutral, its implementation within the Ghanaian social and marital context and against the background of gender roles and relations

---

[28] Sarbah (1904, p. 6).

[29] Dowuona-Hammond (2005, p. 107).

[30] *Fordjour v Nimo* [1962] 1 GLR 305 and Daniels (1965, p. 20).

[31] Daniels (1965, p. 38).

[32] Rattray (1929, p. 31).

[33] Daniels (1965, p. 49).

[34] Offei (1998, p. 200).

[35] Danquah (1928, p. 154).

> within the matrimonial home, tends to place wives at a great disadvantage vis-à-vis their husbands.[36]

This reflects a broader challenge in aligning legal principles with the realities of gender dynamics, where women may face systemic disadvantages despite laws that seem neutral.

Gradually, the courts began issuing rulings on customary law property ownership that appeared more consistent with principles considered fair and equitable, thereby developing judicial customary law. So, in the case of *Yeboah v Yeboah,* Hayfron-Benjamin J. (as he then was) explained that although customary law did not encourage joint ownership of property between persons who were not connected by blood, there was no positive rule of customary law which prohibited the creation of joint interests in property between persons not connected by blood.[37] While it is generally known that parallel customary and Islamic practices regarding the sharing of marital property operate outside the formal court system, there appears to be minimal current data on these practices.

The only relatively recent report on the distribution of marital property in divorce cases under customary law was based on interviews with traditional leaders in the Volta, Eastern, and Greater Accra regions in 2013.[38] These interviews reflect the practised customary laws of the specific communities discussed, rather than representing the entirety of Ghana. While the rules have changed a bit since the days of Sarbah, Rattray and Daniels, the report concluded that the applicable customary law rules discriminated against women. It explained that:

> There is a great deal of flexibility and subjectivity to the decisions made by the traditional leaders when it comes to the property rights of spouses. There are no set rules or precedents and certainly no reference is made to the rights of the parties under the *Constitution*. Rather, every situation is weighed on its own merits and will, sometimes, take into consideration whether either party has a good or bad relationship with the traditional leader in question and also whether the woman, specifically, is thought to be of good or bad character. Essentially, the idea conveyed was that if the woman brought the divorce on herself by her poor or disrespectful behaviour, there was a far lesser chance she would be awarded any particular share in the marital property. However, if the woman was of good reputation…then there may be cause to compensate her for her contribution to the marriage.[39]

According to the report, a chief from the Volta region explained that if the wife was with the husband when the property was acquired, she could claim a share. In the absence of children, the property was sold, and the proceeds were divided equally between the husband and the wife. However, if there are children, all proceeds from the sale are given to them.[40]

In the Greater Accra Region, a focus group of local chiefs, queen mothers, and stool council members in Amasaman explained that if a wife's financial contribution

---

[36] Dowuona-Hammond (2005, p. 107).

[37] *Yeboah v Yeboah* [1974] 2 GLR 114.

[38] Evelyn (2013, pp. 31–33).

[39] Evelyn (2013, p. 31).

[40] Evelyn (2013, p. 42).

to marital property is clear and publicly acknowledged, she can appeal for a fair division. If she initiates the divorce, however, no property is divided.[41]

Another focus group of the Paramount Chief, local chiefs, and queen mothers from Suhum-Koforidua in the Eastern Region explained that spouses must disclose finances upon divorce. In polygamous marriages, property is divided among the husband and all wives, with the departing wife receiving one share. In a single-wife marriage, the husband retains all property for the children. If the divorce results from the wife's misconduct or her insistence on divorce, she is not entitled to any property, and any allocation is at the husband's discretion.[42]

Among the Muslim community, it was reported that Imams are responsible for handling marriage and divorce matters according to Islamic traditions and principles. As a general rule, marital property is not divided upon divorce except under special circumstances such as the husband's terminal illness or incapacity. Instead, the wife departing the marriage is provided with a negotiated sum of money.[43] Where the property is divided, the husband is entitled to two-thirds, while the wife receives one-third. This division is based on the tradition that, in Muslim communities, children usually stay with their fathers on divorce. The author concludes that 'The cases …indicate that the situation in the Muslim community is generally as problematic for women as in other traditional communities under customary law'.[44]

The discussion underscores how patriarchal norms limit women's property rights by overlooking non-financial contributions and their evolving societal roles. Education can play a role in challenging these norms by fostering awareness, promoting gender equality, and encouraging recognition of women's diverse contributions at home and in the broader economy.

We now turn to case law on marital property in customary law marriages, highlighting the gap between practised and judicial customary law. It must be pointed out that we did not find any cases in which the courts applied Islamic principles in the sharing of marital property. In *Ayishetu Abdul Kadiri v. Abdul Dwamena*,[45] discussed below, although the parties were Muslims, the court treated the case as a matter of property division in a polygynous marriage. Accordingly, information on how courts share property in Islamic marriages is omitted from the subsequent discussion.

The first case on customary law was *Quartey v Martey*, where it was held that property acquired by a man during marriage, even with his wife's assistance, belonged solely to him. Under customary law, a wife's required support in her husband's work grants her no property rights, only a right to maintenance. According to Ollennu J.:

> By customary law, it is the domestic responsibility of a man's wife and children to assist him in the carrying out of the duties of his station in life e.g. farming or business. The proceeds of this joint effort of a man and his wife and/or children and any property which the man acquires with such proceeds are by customary law the individual property of the man. It is

[41] Evelyn (2013, pp. 32–33).

[42] Evelyn (2013, p. 32).

[43] Evelyn (2013, p. 42).

[44] Evelyn (2013, p. 43).

[45] Civil Appeal (J4/36/2024) [2025] GHASC 16.

> not the joint property of the man and his wife and /or children. The right of the wife and the children is a right to maintenance and support from the husband and father.[46]

Thus, the courts upheld the customary law that property acquired with the wife's assistance remains the husband's sole property, not joint property. This position is unsurprising given the prevailing male-centric social norms in 1959, the low literacy rate and the lack of gender-specific dimensions to human rights and gender activism in Ghana at the time.

The 1976 case of *Abebreseh v Kaah*[47] modified the *Quartey v Martey* principle by introducing what has come to be known in Ghanaian law as the substantial contribution doctrine. The wife, a trader of means, contributed substantially to building the parties' matrimonial home. The wife and husband equally contributed to the purchase price of the land, with the wife also providing timber, sand, and iron sheets, as well as carrying water and supervising labourers during construction. She covered household expenses and fed the family when the husband's finances were depleted. Although she did not record her contributions, the court determined that her financial and material support was significant. The court concluded that she made direct contributions to the house's construction, granting her co-ownership of the property. The decisive factor was the substantial contribution that the court decided went beyond the 'mere' contribution of *Quartey v Martey*. The case highlights three types of contributions: direct monetary, indirect monetary, and non-monetary, though the court focused only on the direct monetary contributions of the wife in its decision.

The issue of determining the exact extent of a significant contribution remained a persistent problem for the courts. The court in *Abebreseh* asserted that it could not precisely define the concept of substantial contribution using mathematical accuracy and would instead rely on the specific circumstances of each case as '...ordinary incidents of commerce have no application in the ordinary relations between husband and wife'.[48]

Also, in *Domfe v Adu*,[49] the husband and wife jointly ran a business, with the wife providing the initial capital through loans she secured in her own name, while the husband made no financial contribution. The husband later dissolved their customary marriage and, having transferred the business premises she had rented and paid for into the company's name without her consent, refused to share the business with her. The trial court ruled that the wife had a beneficial interest in the business and was entitled to one-half. Endorsing the trial court's use of equitable principles to resolve the case, the Court of Appeal dismissed the husband's appeal and held, among other things, that where a wife provides the purchase money for the matrimonial home but the property is registered in the husband's name, he holds the property in trust for her; the same principle applies if the roles are reversed.

---

46 [1959] GLR 377, 380 (High Court).

47 [1976] 2 GLR 46 (High Court).

48 [1976] 2 GLR 46, 53.

49 [1984–86] 1 GLR 653.

In *Sykes v Abbey*,[50] a 27-year marriage ended in divorce, resulting in a dispute over the ownership of a house. The Supreme Court held that the inability of the plaintiff-wife to establish her contributions with 'mathematical exactitude' ought not to constitute a bar to her claim to the house. The court emphasised that transactions between spouses living together should not be scrutinised rigorously like commercial transactions, where documentation is expected.[51] The foregoing decisions indicate that as long as the wife could prove a 'substantial contribution' to the property in question, she acquired a beneficial interest in the property. This chapter will demonstrate that this legal position remains largely unchanged.

2.2 *Property Rights Under the Common Law*

Ghana's matrimonial property law is rooted in English common law, introduced in 1876 through the Supreme Court Ordinance. The regime draws heavily from the English Married Women's Property Acts of 1870 and 1882, which curtailed the doctrine of coverture by extending property rights to married women.[52] To incorporate the 1870 Act, the Gold Coast enacted the Married Women's Ordinance in 1890,[53] as the English statute was not one of general application.[54] However, there is little authority on its application to matrimonial property settlements.[55] In one case, where a husband sued his wife over property, the High Court held that the Ordinance protected a wife's earnings and property and barred suits by a husband against his wife in tort, though property suits were permissible.[56] Although the Married Women's Property Acts empowered courts to determine property disputes, they offered no guidance on how such disputes were to be resolved,[57] leaving the development of principles to the English courts.

Ghanaian courts have largely followed English developments conservatively. In England, disputes over the matrimonial home under section 17 of the Married Women's Property Act 1882 saw the activist Lord Denning hold that jointly acquired property with mutual benefit intent gave each spouse an equal beneficial interest,

---

[50] [1995–96] 1 GLR 81.

[51] [1995–96] 1 GLR 81, 87.

[52] For the background to the Married Women's Property Acts, see Griffin (2003, p. 59) and Combs (2005, p. 1028).

[53] The Statute Law Revision (No. 2) Decree, 1973 (N.R.C.D. 228), repealed the Married Women's Property Ordinance because it was considered 'obsolete' or 'unnecessary'. N.R.C.D 228 has only one section; Daniels (1974, p. 143).

[54] Daniels (1974, p. 143).

[55] See generally, Zabel (1969, pp. 65–67).

[56] *Smith v Smith* [1965] GLR 730.

[57] Married Women's Property Act 1882, ss. 9 and 17.

regardless of registration.[58] The House of Lords rejected this, ruling that spousal property rights follow general property law and that any division should be governed by trust law, whether resulting, implied, or constructive. The downside of this approach was that the legal title remained with the spouse named in the property deed, while the other spouse only had an equitable interest.[59]

The trust concept was applied by the Ghana High Court in 1971, barely three months before the coming into force of Act 367. In *Yeboah v Yeboah*,[60] the couple married under the Marriage Ordinance, and before their marriage, the wife applied for a State Housing Corporation house, paying a deposit for the land. This was returned to her after their marriage, when she withdrew her application in favour of her husband to enable him to take advantage of a bank's housing loan scheme. As the couple lived in London when construction of the house began, she flew to Ghana at her own expense to supervise the construction and made structural changes with her husband's consent. After returning to Ghana, the marriage ended, and the husband sought to evict the wife from the marital home. An intriguing aspect of this case was the court's consideration of customary law in relation to an Ordinance marriage. However, the court was quick to state that:

> In this case the parties were married under the Marriage Ordinance and the relations between each other are not governed exclusively by customary law. English legal concepts cannot be completely excluded in the determination of this case.[61]

Applying English law, the court ruled that the wife and husband were joint owners of the house based on their conduct and intention to own the property since 'in so many branches of English law… legal rights and obligations depend on the intentions of the parties to a transaction…'[62] Further basing his decision on the trust model propounded by the House of Lords in *Pettitt*, Hayfron-Benjamin J. noted that:

> any claim to a beneficial interest in land by a person, whether spouse or stranger, in whom the legal estate in the land is not vested must be based on the proposition that the person in whom the legal estate is vested holds it as trustee on trust to give effect to the beneficial interest of the claimant as cestui que trust.[63]

The court considered the wife's financial contributions, including her spending on improvements, airfare, and the 'time and effort' she devoted to the house, although the judge acknowledged these efforts were difficult to quantify in monetary terms. What is clear from this case was the uncertainty in Ghanaian law on the property rights of spouses. The Matrimonial Causes Act of 1971 was later enacted to reform the law on the property rights of spouses upon divorce. Section 20(1) of the Act states:

---

[58] *Rimmer v Rimmer* [1953] 1 QB 63, 73.

[59] *Pettitt v Pettitt* [1968] 1 WLR 443.

[60] *Yeboah v Yeboah* [1974] 2 GLR 114.

[61] *Yeboah v Yeboah* [1974] 2 GLR 114, 121.

[62] *Yeboah v Yeboah* [1974] 2 GLR 114, 124; where the court speaking through Hayfron-Benjamin J. quoted Lord Diplock in *Gissing v Gissing* [1970] 2 All E.R 780, 790–791.

[63] *Yeboah v Yeboah* [1974] 2 GLR 114, 124; where the court speaking through Hayfron-Benjamin J. quoted Lord Diplock in *Gissing v Gissing* [1970] 2 All E.R 780, 790–791.

> the court may order either party to the marriage to pay the other party such sum of money or convey to the other party such movable or immovable property as settlement of property rights or in lieu thereof or as part of financial provision as the court thinks just and equitable.

Act 367 does not only apply to monogamous or Ordinance marriages, even though it replicates many provisions of the matrimonial causes law of England. As previously mentioned, parties in other types of marriages can apply to the court for its provisions to be applied, considering the peculiarities of the marriage.[64]

While attempting to simplify the law on property settlements, section 20(1) of Act 367 left many questions unanswered. What constitutes 'property' in this context? What do property rights even mean? What factors should the courts consider when dividing property jointly acquired? Inevitably, the interpretation and application of Act 367 have depended on the courts. Thus, we turn to the courts to examine and analyse the property settlement rules within the Act.

3 The Matrimonial Causes Act in Motion

There are two components to section 20(1) of the Matrimonial Causes Act. Firstly, it enables the payment of money or the conveyance of property, whether movable or immovable, to either party to the divorce suit as *settlement of property rights*. Secondly, it authorises the court to make *financial provision* for either party. In this regard, the court may order the conveyance of movable or immovable property or/ and the transfer of money to a spouse as the court thinks just and equitable.

Given the lack of explicit legislative provisions governing property division in divorce, the courts have looked to general principles of equity to determine how to divide the marital assets fairly. Case law has established a consistent or discernable pattern regarding how courts have applied equity principles to guarantee 'justice' in dividing marital property rights upon dissolution.

3.1 Judicial Approach to the Making of Financial Provision

Judicial decisions have established that the criterion for claiming financial provision is based on the applicant's needs without requiring evidence of their contribution towards obtaining the specific property. This principle was applied in *Barake v Barake*,[65] where the court stated that in granting financial provision to a spouse under the law, the primary consideration was the needs of the parties rather than proof of ownership or contributions to property acquisition. In this case, since the first respondent (husband) had promised to give the petitioner (wife) a house, a car, and a monthly allowance, the former was ordered to fulfil these promises as part of

64 Matrimonial Causes Act 1971 (Act 367), s. 41.

65 *Barake v Barake* [1993–94] 1 GLR 635.

the financial provision or property settlement. Additionally, he was directed to pay a sum of money over a period.

In *Ribeiro v Ribeiro*,[66] a similar decision was made by the courts. In this case, the parties married in 1953 and divorced in 1981. The wife requested financial provision under the Matrimonial Causes Act, section 20(1). The husband owned 10 houses, and the wife was a full-time housewife for 34 years. Both parties agreed that the divorced wife was entitled to maintenance and accommodation. Therefore, the court did not consider whether or not she had made a substantial financial contribution. The evidence showed that her dedication as a housewife, caring for the home and children, including the husband's children from a previous marriage, helped him accumulate wealth. The court ordered that one of the 10 houses be given to the divorced wife as part of the financial provision under section 20 of Act 367.

The husband appealed to the Supreme Court and even obtained a review.[67] The court upheld the trial court's order to convey a house to the wife. The Supreme Court ruled that a court can order the conveyance of immovable property to provide financial support for a spouse if it is just and equitable. The majority stated that such an order did not require determining whether the wife had an interest in the property due to her contributions to its acquisition. Thus, the court held that the claimant's contribution was irrelevant when making a financial provision order under section 20(1) of the Matrimonial Causes Act, even if it involved conveying immovable property to the petitioner.

However, the judicial approach to the settlement of property rights upon divorce under section 20(1) of the Matrimonial Causes Act, typically necessitates the claimant to provide evidence of significant financial contributions towards acquiring the property or an agreement between the parties acknowledging the claimant's beneficial interest in the property. It would appear that, especially in cases where the claimant's alleged contribution to the property's acquisition is indeterminate or relatively insignificant, applying for financial provision under section 20(1) is better than claiming a beneficial interest in the property as property settlement under the provisions.[68]

---

[66] *Ribeiro v Ribeiro* [1989–90] 2 GLR 109.

[67] The review decision of the Supreme Court is reported as *Ribeiro v Ribeiro (No. 2)* [1989–90] 2 GLR 131.

[68] For instance, in *Yeboah v Yeboah* [1974] 2 GLR 114, headnote 3 Hayfron-Benjamin J said in part: 'The wife was the joint owner of the house with the husband because judging from all the factors attending the acquisition of the house and the conduct of the parties subsequent to the acquisition, it was clear that they intended to own jointly the matrimonial home'. And in *Anang v Tagoe* [1989–1990] 2 GLR 8, Brobbey J. stated: 'where a wife made contributions towards the requirements of a matrimonial home in the belief the contribution was to assist in the joint acquisition of property, the court of equity would take steps to ensure that belief materialised'. It would appear from the requirements set out in these cases that, contribution to the joint acquisition of the property must be demonstrated by the claimant in the absence of which the beneficial interest claimed in the property would not be granted. In such circumstances, it is submitted that it would be better for such parties to claim financial provision under s. 20(1) where no such substantial contribution requirement exists.

3.2 Settlement of the Property Rights of the Claimant

The interpretation of section 20(1) regarding property rights before adopting the 1992 Constitution was still very conservative. No matter how revolutionary it may have appeared, the provision hardly made a dent in judicial behaviour in the settlement of property rights. The trust model developed in England and adopted in cases like *Yeboah* continued to influence Ghanaian jurisprudence. *In Achiampong v. Achiampong*,[69] the court introduced a model based on an agreement between spouses concerning ownership of the matrimonial home. After marriage, the couple moved into a hire-purchase estate house, with the wife using her savings for household expenses while the husband paid the instalments. When the house became too small, the wife borrowed from her employer to add two bedrooms, sold her car to fund their wedding, and later, while the husband served as a diplomat in Peking, worked part-time and helped purchase household goods.

Upon returning to Ghana, the wife sought divorce and a declaration of joint ownership of the house and its contents. The High Court held that both parties had equal beneficial interest, but the husband appealed. The Court of Appeal found evidence of an agreement granting the wife a beneficial interest, creating equity in her favour. Even absent a formal agreement, the court held that equity would prevent either spouse from claiming exclusive ownership, as an implied trust arose from their financial contributions.[70] In dismissing the appeal, the court considered the applicability of section 20(1) and reaffirmed the conservative separate property principle guiding the settlement of matrimonial property rights. Their Lordships made several key observations as follows:

1. Any award of financial provision or property settlement is subject to the judge's discretion.
2. In the absence of guidelines in the provision, courts are to exercise their discretion within the confines of the law, and that means their discretion 'must not be vague, arbitrary or fanciful'.[71]
3. Property should not be transferred from one spouse to another 'on some vague basis' so that 'where the rights of the spouses in respect of any property are established or agreed, the court should uphold those rights'.[72]
4. Where no agreement exists between the parties about the settlement of property, only financial contribution, whether direct or indirect, will suffice to entitle a party to share in the property.[73]

Overall, these principles aim to balance discretion with fairness, ensuring that financial and property settlements reflect the contributions and rights of each spouse while maintaining a legal framework that prevents arbitrariness.

---

[69] *Achiampong v Achiampong* [1982–83] 2 GLR 1017.

[70] This trust model in *Achiampong* was applied in *Domfe v Adu* [1984–86] 653.

[71] *Achiampong v Achiampong* [1982–83] 2 GLR 1017, 1035.

[72] *Achiampong v Achiampong* [1982–83] 2 GLR 1017, 1035.

[73] *Achiampong v Achiampong* [1982–83] 2 GLR 1017, 1036.

4 Problems with the Legal Framework Before the 1992 Constitution

It must be stressed that over the years, there has been a gradual convergence between the customary law rules for the settlement of property rights on the one hand and the common law and statutory rules on the other hand. The evolution is most captured in the development of the principles on substantial contribution. However, from a discussion of the cases above, the rules on substantial contribution were in themselves not capacious because they implicitly excluded certain forms of contribution. Other than *Yeboah v Yeboah*, where the court mentioned time and effort, terms which themselves are vague, the courts often looked for evidence of 'financial contribution' without more. Thus, non-financial contributions were often excluded.

Our observation is corroborated by Ulrike, a legal scholar who, in the 1980s, studied a number of cases and concluded that the courts routinely ignored women's non-financial contribution, specifically the tasks performed by women in the matrimonial home.[74] Daniels, criticising the rule in *Quartey v Martey*, noted much earlier in the 1970s that the rule in *Quartey v Martey* excludes forms of contribution such as 'helping with the clearing of the husband's farmland, the casual carrying of pails of water or pieces of bricks to the site of a building being put up by the husband'.[75] For many homemaker wives, decisions like this were bound to occasion great hardship, if not suffering.

4.1 Human Rights, the 1992 Constitution and Marital Property Rights

The progressive constitutional provisions discussed in the next part can be attributed to the inclusion of women in political spaces and the impact of international human rights law, particularly the United Nations Convention for the Elimination of All Forms of Discrimination Against Women (CEDAW) of 1979. Commenting on the advocacy efforts of women on the Committee of Experts tasked to prepare proposals for the 1992 Constitution, the Report of the Committee noted that,

> With regard to women, the 1978 proposals only paid lip service to the rights of women on the ground that the Commission did not consider it necessary or useful to make elaborate provisions; adding that 'to their credit the women's representatives asked for no more'. Happily and equally to their credit, the women members of the Committee this time around did ask for more, which, in the view of the Committee, is quite legitimate.[76]

---

[74] Wanitzek (1991, pp. 95–99); the cases studied in Ulrike's work include *Gyang v Gyang* (HC, 30 January 1987), *Clerk v Clerk* 55 GLRD 160 and *Ribeiro v Ribeiro* [1989–90] 2 GLR 109.

[75] Daniels (1978, p. 143).

[76] Report of the Committee of Experts Constitution on Proposals for a Draft Constitution of Ghana (1991), para. 166.

The Committee's sympathy was evident in the list of abuses catalogued in the report. It noted in paragraph 167:

> Although strictly according to law, men and women are of equal status in Ghana, there are many social practices and prejudices which undermine this equality. For example, there are in many parts of this country, customary rights of widowhood which, in effect, abase and humiliate the widow.... In order to prevent such violations of the rights of women, the Committee proposes that the laws of the land must carefully spell out the rights of women when their husbands die, and the enforcement of these rights against those who may infringe them.

The Committee, drawing inspiration from CEDAW, proposed that a provision be inserted in the Constitution requiring Parliament to enact legislation to ensure equal access to property jointly acquired during marriage and the equitable distribution of such property upon divorce.[77] The CEDAW's property provisions are derived from two rights in articles 15 and 16 of the Convention: equality of the sexes before the law and the rights of spouses to own and manage property.[78] Expounding on the scope of the latter right, the CEDAW Committee states that, '[t]he guiding principle should be that the economic advantages and disadvantages related to the relationship and its dissolution should be borne equally by both parties. The division of roles and functions during the spouses' life together should not result in detrimental economic consequences for either party'.[79]

The Committee proposal eventually made it into the Constitution as article 22(3) as follows:

> 22(2) Parliament shall, as soon as practicable after the coming into force of this Constitution, enact legislation regulating the property rights of spouses.
>
> 22(3) With a view to achieving the full realisation of the rights referred to in clause (2) of this article-
>
> a) spouses shall have equal access to property jointly acquired during marriage;
>
> b) assets which are jointly acquired during marriage shall be distributed equitably between the spouses upon dissolution of the marriage.

However, for over 30 years, Parliament has failed in its duty to pass a law regulating spouses' property rights. The courts have, therefore, had to rise to the occasion to provide a foundation mainly for equitable property distribution upon dissolution of marriage. We study the judicial decisions of the Ghanaian Courts under two headings: what constitutes marital property, and how is marital property distributed upon divorce?

---

[77] Report of the Committee of Experts Constitution on Proposals for a Draft Constitution of Ghana (1991), para. 169. This was the fourth of eight proposals of the committee with regard to women's rights to be stipulated under the 1992 Constitution.

[78] Convention on the Elimination of All Forms of Discrimination Against Women (adopted 18 December 1979, entered into force 3 September 1981) 1249 UNTS 13 (CEDAW), art. 16(h) states, 'The same rights for both spouses in respect of the ownership, acquisition, management, administration, enjoyment and disposition of property, whether free of charge or for a valuable consideration'; for a detailed treatment of the subject, see Alvarez and Bauder (2024, chapter 2).

[79] CEDAW Committee (2013), para 45.

4.2 What Is Jointly Acquired Marital Property?

The Constitution does not define jointly acquired property, and Parliament has not enacted any legislation to regulate the distribution of jointly acquired property. Consequently, the courts continued to determine what constitutes jointly acquired property, which increasingly recognised in-kind contributions as capable of giving rise to joint property. The case of *Mary Oparebea v S.A. Mensah*,[80] accepted the fact that 'substantial contribution' could be in cash or kind.

Gladys Mensah v Stephen Mensah[81] is regarded as a landmark decision, in that, the Supreme Court, through Dotse, JSC, placed considerable value on household chores, equating its value to a wage-earning activity, and indicating that it would be 'inequitable' and 'unconstitutional' not to do so. The court, relying 'on the constitutional interpretation and applicability of the *equality is equity* principle contained in article 22 (3) [and 33(5)] of the Constitution 1992, in the sharing of marital properties acquired during the subsistence of a marriage and the principle of *jurisprudence of equality*' concluded that 'the time has come for this court to institutionalise this principle of equality in the sharing of marital property by spouses, after divorce, of *all property acquired during the subsistence of a marriage in appropriate cases*'.[82] International human rights law and the judicial decision from Kenya's Court of Appeal influenced the jurisprudence of the equality concept.[83] The concept encourages courts to apply international human rights to cases involving discrimination against women.[84] For this reason, the State's obligations in the CEDAW on eliminating discriminatory cultural practices were deemed relevant in the interpretation of article 22.[85]

The case of *Arthur v Arthur*[86] represents a bold and dynamic attempt by the Supreme Court to develop the law on the ownership and sharing of property. In this case, the Supreme Court, through Date-Bah JSC (as he then was), drawing on the Nova Scotia Matrimonial Property Act,[87] held that marital property was to be understood as 'property acquired during the marriage irrespective of whether the

---

[80] [1993–94] 1 GLR 61.

[81] [2012] 1 SCGLR 391.

[82] Our emphasis; art. 33(5) states, 'The rights, duties, declarations and guarantees relating to the fundamental human rights and freedoms specifically mentioned in this Chapter shall not be regarded as excluding others not specifically mentioned which are considered to be inherent in a democracy and intended to secure the freedom and dignity of man'.

[83] *Tabitha Wangechi Nderitu v Simon Nderitu Kariuki* [1998] eKLR.

[84] Gayoye (2022, p. 74).

[85] The approach adopted was endorsed by the CEDAW Committee (2014), para 41(d) where they recommended 'the wide dissemination of the Supreme Court decision in *Mensah v Mensah*, in particular in the district courts, and ensure that women married under religious or customary law who apply to a court for divorce receive the improved protection arising from the Matrimonial Causes Act 1971 (Act 367) in respect of all aspects of the consequences of divorce'.

[86] [2013–2014] 1 SCGLR 543.

[87] Matrimonial Property Act, R.S.N.S. 1989, c. 275 (Nova Scotia).

other spouse has made a contribution to its acquisition',[88] with possible exceptions, such as an award or settlement of damages in court in favour of one spouse, and gifts. Thus, the court clarified that proof of a spouse's contribution to acquiring marital property was no longer essential. Once the property was acquired during the subsistence of the marriage, it was marital property. However, the court did not specify the considerations that should guide the courts in distributing marital property. It is important to note that the Supreme Court couched the new definition of joint property as a presumption, meaning it is rebuttable by evidence to the contrary. This is important because Article 18(1) preserves every person's right to own property alone or in association with others. In the case of *Fynn v Fynn*, Wood CJ (as she then was) explained that:

> the decided cases envisage situations where within the union parties may still acquire property in their individual capacities as indeed is their guaranteed fundamental right as clearly enshrined under article 18 of the 1992 Constitution, in which case they would also have the legal capacity to validly dispose of same by way of sale.[89]

Within the current framework of Article 22, the most suitable interpretation of joint property is property, the acquisition, maintenance or improvement of which was made possible by both parties, either in cash or in kind. It must be noted that if the Constitution intended joint property to result from the sole effort of only one of the parties, it would have stated so. Nevertheless, the contributions of each party need not be of equal measure. After all, the Supreme Court in the case of *Nartey v Gati*,[90] stated that:

> no two human beings are equal in all respects…if the law were to treat all human beings rigidly equally, it would in fact result in unequal outcomes. Rigid equal treatment would often result in unfair and unequal results…. The law must be able to differentiate between unequals and accord them the differentiated treatment which will result in enabling them, as far as practicable, to attain the objective of equality of outcomes or of fairness.[91]

In applying this principle to spousal rights to property, the determination of joint property should not necessarily defer to the industry of each individual in contributing to the acquisition of the property.

4.3 The Distribution of Marital Property

Change was not immediately perceptible in post-1992. However, incremental changes occurred over time. The judgment of the High Court in *Oparebea v Mensah* in 1984 represents a radical departure from the courts' traditional approach, which

88 [2013–2014] 1 SCGLR 543, 560.

89 *Fynn v Fynn* [2013–2014] 1 SCGLR 727, 741.

90 [2010] SCGLR 745.

91 [2010] SCGLR 745, 755.

has viewed contributions in strictly cash terms.[92] The court, in recognition of this, stated that 'there is hardly any precedent for such a stark departure from set traditions and social norms'.[93] It indicated that 'if we never do anything which has not been done before, we shall never get anywhere. The law will stand still whilst the rest of the world goes on, and that will be bad for both'.[94] The court took the view that times have changed, and the courts should have the courage and conviction to change with the times. The notion that a wife's services in the home need not be remunerated is probably no longer valid in its entirety, and where she works in the business of the husband, helping and keeping the shop as the wife in the present case, then it is 'an affront to common sense and a gross violation of all notions of equity, justice and fair play to deny such a woman a share in the property acquired over 28 years because of custom which is unsteadily rooted in anachronism'. Though the Court of Appeal in 1993 allowed an appeal by the wife on the grounds that the award of one house to her was inadequate considering the husband's wealth, the decision of the High Court was not impugned on the merits but on the husband's dishonesty in failing to disclose all his assets.[95]

4.4 Judicial Approach: Equality Principle

It would seem that, from the substantial contribution principle, the courts moved to the equality principle. In the case of *Mensah v Mensah*,[96] there was a dispute over a marital home and an extension, and the court, relying upon the evidence, found that the parties' intention in acquiring the main house was to use it jointly. Similarly, the parties' intention in proceeding with the extension to the property was to provide more space for their joint benefit and that of their children. The court specifically found that property jointly acquired during marriage becomes joint property of the parties, which should be shared equally on divorce. The court, speaking through Bamford-Addo JSC, thus stated:

> In such circumstances, the principle that property jointly acquired during marriage becomes joint property of the parties applies and such property should be shared equally on divorce, because the ordinary incidents of commerce have no application in marital relations between a husband and wife who jointly acquired property during marriage... On the facts and the law, both parties are joint and equal beneficial owners of the main house and extensions.[97]

However, the court's approach had not undergone substantive normative change. A closer reading of *Mensah v Mensah* reveals that the court inferred an intention by the parties to jointly hold the property, including both the main house and its extensions.

---

[92] [1993–94] 1 GLR 61.

[93] [1993–94] 1 GLR 61.

[94] [1993–94] 1 GLR 61.

[95] [1993–94] GLR 61.

[96] [1998–99] SCGLR 350.

[97] [1998–99] SCGLR 350, 355.

However, the court copiously cited Lord Denning in *Rimmer v Rimmer* and a host of other English authorities to hold that, in the division of property, each spouse is entitled to an equal share in the property. Though section 20 of Act 367 and article 22(3)(b) of the Constitution on the equitable distribution were mentioned, they were to anchor the principles derived from English law and not to serve as a normative basis which deserved to be expounded. In other words, they were the endpoint and not the starting point for the derivation of the principles.

The Supreme Court established that, upon divorce or the husband's death, the wife and husband are each entitled to 50% ownership. This principle was reaffirmed by Date-Bah JSC in *Boafo v. Boafo*,[98] where he declared:

> what is equitable in essence, what is just, reasonable and accords with common sense and fair play is a pure question of fact dependent purely on the particular circumstances of each case.....Where there is a substantial contribution by both spouses, the respective shares of the spouses will not be delineated proportionally like a shareholding in a company for the marriage relationship is not a commercial relationship. Where there is a substantial contribution by both spouses, *equalitywill usually be an equitable solution* to the distribution issue.[99]

It must be noted that the court took human rights considerations into account in arriving at its decision. It noted that:

> article 22 [of the Constitution] firmly places within the domain of social human rights the distribution of the property of spouses, on divorce... It was meant to right the imbalance that women have historically suffered in the distribution of assets jointly acquired during marriage. An equal division will often, though not invariably, be a solution to this imbalance.[100]

The case of *Boafo v Boafo* concluded that sharing jointly owned property equally represents what is just and equitable. In this case, the Supreme Court reaffirmed the equality is equity principle from *Mensah v. Mensah* and further clarified section 20(1) of the Matrimonial Causes Act and article 22(3)(b) of the 1992 Constitution. The Court held that property should be distributed according to the equities of each case, taking into account specific circumstances such as proof of separate ownership or differing ownership proportions.

Gladys Mensah v Stephen Mensah[101] ended the substantial contribution doctrine and rather determined the spouse's right within the framework of human rights and constitutionally guaranteed rights, marking a sharp departure from the past.[102] Thus, the Supreme Court per Dotse JSC relied on article 22 of the 1992 constitution to

---

[98] [2005–2006] SCGLR 705.

[99] *Boafo v Boafo* [2005–2006] SCGLR 705, 714.

[100] *Boafo v Boafo* [2005–2006] SCGLR 705, 713.

[101] *Mensah v Mensah* [2012] 1 SCGLR 391.

[102] Before the decision in *Gladys Mensah v Stephen Mensah*, decisions in cases such as *Quartey v Martey[1959] GLR 377, 380), Abrebeseh v Kaah* [1976] *2 GLR 46.* and *Anang v Tagoe* [1989–1990] 2 GLR 8 had established the doctrine of substantial contribution as the prevailing principle in the distribution of marital property.

rule that the principle of 'substantial contribution' was not only inequitable but also unconstitutional.[103]

The Supreme Court observed that the framers of the 1992 Constitution envisioned equal access to property jointly acquired during marriage and the equitable distribution of such assets upon its dissolution. The Court held that common sense and fundamental human rights require that a spouse who contributes to the household should not be disadvantaged in the division of marital property, since such contributions facilitate the acquisition of those assets. It emphasised that the application of this principle depends on the facts of each case, with the aim of achieving equality in the sharing of marital property. As noted earlier, the Court thereby introduced and advanced the principle of the jurisprudence of equality.

As earlier noted, in *Arthur v Arthur*,[104] the Supreme Court instituted the concept of marital property in Ghana, clarifying that proof of a spouse's contribution to acquiring marital property was no longer essential.

5 Recent Developments

In 2020, Ghana enacted a new Land Act to consolidate existing laws on immovable property and introduce moderate reforms. Where spouses jointly acquire land, both are deemed parties to the transaction unless the document states otherwise.[105] If only one spouse is named, that spouse holds the land in trust for the other.[106] A spouse may not transfer the land to a third party without the other's written consent.[107] Presumably, these provisions aim to address the lack of documentation proving women's contributions towards the acquisition of landed property and to prevent men from using the absence of women's names on land documents as a defence against claims to jointly acquired property.

In the hotly contested case of *Adjei v. Adjei*,[108] the Supreme Court, by a 5–2 majority, appeared to reinstate the requirement of proof of contribution. Notably, all male justices formed the majority, while the female justices dissented. The High Court had settled the matrimonial home on the wife, awarded her a lump sum of GHC 400,000 as financial provision, and granted her custody of the children, with reasonable visitation rights to the husband. It based its decision on the presumption that the matrimonial home, acquired during the marriage, was jointly owned. The Court of Appeal reversed this, holding that the home, one of four flats, was built on land the husband had acquired before the marriage and financed with an outstanding loan in his name. The Supreme Court majority, citing earlier precedents, held that

[103] *Mensah v Mensah* [2012] 1 SCGLR 391, 393.

[104] [2013–2014] 1 SCGLR 543.

[105] Land Act 2020 (Act 1036), s. 38(3).

[106] Land Act 2020 (Act 1036), s. 38(4).

[107] Land Act 2020 (Act 1036), s. 48.

[108] [2021] GHASC 5.

while such cases recognise a presumption of joint acquisition, parties must still provide evidence of contribution to prove their respective entitlements. The majority articulated the rationale as follows:

> …the duties performed by the wife in the home, like cooking for the family, cleaning and nurturing the children of the marriage, etc. which go a long way to create an enabling atmosphere for the other spouse to work in peace towards the acquisition of the properties concerned, was enough contribution that should merit the wife a share in the said properties.[109]

In an interesting turn of events, the Supreme Court upheld the Court of Appeal's decision, holding that a spouse's contribution must be proven at trial before property can be deemed jointly acquired. The spouse alleging joint ownership bears the burden of proving how the property was acquired. Although the Court acknowledged the presumption of joint ownership as rebuttable for evidentiary purposes, it appeared to conflate the issues of what constitutes joint property with how such property should be shared. Consequently, proof of contribution now determines not only the extent of a spouse's entitlement but also whether the property qualifies as joint property at all.

One of the principal reasons why the court adopted the presumption of jointly acquired property was to guarantee that a spouse's non-financial contributions, whether in the home or in the acquisition of the property, will be automatically considered in property settlement. The decision in *Adjei* appears to reverse that. It seems that spouses will now have to prove non-financial contributions. The question remains: What evidence must a spouse present to the court? In *Adjei,* the majority did not answer this question because of its preoccupation with the loan contracted by the husband. The concurring judge who applied the presumption and proceeded to rebut it considered the husband's allegation that his wife was 'torturing him emotionally in the marriage' as material to the rebuttal of the presumption. However, a homemaker's services are not limited to the provision of emotional support; the care of children and responsibilities related to household tasks, among other factors, are equally important, yet the judge did not evaluate these against the presumption. Unsurprisingly, the minority emphasised the domestic services provided by the wife as material in affirming the presumption of jointly acquired property.

It seems the majority were concerned with women taking advantage of men. Pwamang JSC, in his concurring opinion, noted that:

> The highest policy of the law is to be fair to all parties who come before the court. Our thoughts ought not to focus only on protecting female spouses where the ostensible owner is the male spouse, which is more frequent, but the principles we evolve should equally aspire to protect a female spouse when she is the ostensible property owner and a male spouse wants to take advantage of her. That explains why the Constitution uses the gender neutral term, spouse.[110]

This statement implies that the core principle of law in sharing property acquired during the marriage should be fairness to all parties involved, regardless of gender, in

---

[109] [2021] GHASC 5, pp. 11–12.

[110] [2021] GHASC 5, p. 20.

order to safeguard the rights of both men and women. While we recognise the court's intentions, it is impossible to overlook that *Adjei* stands in contrast to earlier rulings considered progressive. In fact, the decision was foreseeable, given the comments made by the courts after the decision in *Gladys Mensah v Stephen Mensah,* which appeared to end the substantial contribution principle, making way for equitable distribution as provided for under article 22(3) of the Constitution 1992. For example, *Quartson v Quartson* quickly warned that

> The decision in *Gladys Mensah v Stephen Mensah*, is not to be taken as a blanket ruling that affords spouses unwarranted access to property when it is clear on the evidence that they are not so entitled. Its application and effect will continue to be shaped and defined to cater for the specifics of each case.[111]

It was only a matter of time before the courts would reinstate the substantial contribution doctrine. In 2023, the Supreme Court decided a similar case involving several properties, some of which had been acquired with loans. The case of *Anyetei v Anyetei*, while reaffirming that article 22 of the Constitution did not mean equal division of property, emphasised proof of contribution along the lines of *Adjei*.[112] However, the case diverges from *Adjei* in ways that make it quite difficult to reconcile the two cases at certain points. For instance, *Adjei* held that until a loan was repaid, the property did not constitute marital property. On the other hand, the Court in *Anyetei* awarded one spouse properties which were the subject of loans and directed the spouse to pay off the loans on those properties! Also quite strange is Pwamang JSC trying to draw an unhelpful distinction between 'marital property' and 'assets which are jointly acquired during marriage'.[113] These terms are used interchangeably in the cases. However, Pwamang JSC suggested that while 'marital property' fell under section 20 of Act 367, 'assets which are jointly acquired during marriage' came under article 22.[114] No further help to distinguish between the two was offered because the Court did 'not [want to] venture into the litigation minefield of the definition of marital property'.[115] When used within the context of marriages, these terms are conceptually the same, and the distinction being introduced in *Anyetei* is quite artificial. These conceptual problems are becoming more palpable in recent Supreme Court decisions.

In *Ayishetu Abdul Kadiri v. Abdul Dwamenah*,[116] the Supreme Court in March 2025 affirmed that property acquired by a spouse or by both spouses during the subsistence of a marriage, whether customary, Mohammedan, or Ordinance, is prima facie matrimonial property. However, the Court acknowledged that acquisition during marriage may be joint or sole, depending on the peculiar facts of each case and the circumstances of the acquisition. In determining whether a property is jointly or

---

[111] [2012] 2 SCGLR 1077, 1090, Ansah JSC delivered the judgment of the court.

[112] [2023] GHASC 54, see generally the judgment of the court per Pwamang JSC.

[113] [2023] GHASC 54.

[114] [2023] GHASC 54, pp. 21–22.

[115] [2023] GHASC 54, pp. 21–22.

[116] Civil Appeal (J4/36/2024) [2025] GHASC 16.

solely acquired, the Court indicated that relevant factors include whether one spouse exclusively financed or acquired the property without contribution, in cash or kind, from the other, and whether it was at all times recognised as belonging only to that spouse.

This framework was, however, refined in *Abena Pokua v. Yaw Kwakye*,[117] where the Supreme Court emphasised that a sweeping presumption converting all property acquired during marriage into matrimonial property violates the constitutional right to acquire and own property independently. According to the Court:

> to state that every property acquired during marriage is presumed to be marital property is to deprive couples of their constitutional right to acquire property either alone or in association with others as guaranteed by article 18(1) of the Constitution, 1992. … Marriage must not be an instrument of deprivation or a burden …. The Court must not trample upon constitutional rights in its quest to ensure equity and justice in the distribution of property acquired during marriage. The definition given by the Court to 'marital property' in Arthur (No.1) vs. Arthur (No.1) has the potential to provoke injustice. The decision does not conform to the doctrine of harmonious interpretation of statutes….[118]

The shifting meaning of "marital property" in Ghana has created legal uncertainty. It will be recalled that in *Gladys Mensah v Stephen Mensah*, the Court introduced a presumption of marital property resembling community property. *Arthur v Arthur* reinforced this presumption, drawing on comparative law from the US, Canada, and the UK, while also addressing property that could be excluded from marital property. The Court quoted at length Nova Scotia's Matrimonial Property Act, defining 'matrimonial assets' as property acquired by either or both spouses before or during the marriage. Clearly, Nova Scotia's marital regime is a universal property system, and it is from this that the confusion in Ghanaian law begins. By extrapolating from these foreign jurisdictions, the Court in effect institutionalised a rebuttable community property regime with a strong preference for equal division. Although subsequent courts have treated *Gladys Mensah v Stephen Mensah* as establishing a full community property regime, the decision itself did not expressly do so, and this interpretative overreach has generated uncertainty regarding the scope and application of the presumption of marital property.

Two more recent cases illustrate this uncertainty. In *Ayishetu,* with Justices Lovelace-Johnson and Asiedu on the panel, the Court declared all property acquired during marriage to be marital property but limited division to only jointly acquired property, creating confusion between the community and separate property systems. Interestingly, a few months later, in *Abena Pokua*, Justices Lovelace-Johnson and Asiedu again sat on the panel, and the unanimous judgment was written by Justice Asiedu, but the Court departed from *Arthur* without citing *Ayishetu.* We are therefore faced with conflicting Supreme Court decisions on the scope of marital property and its distribution between spouses, leaving open the possibility that *Mensah* and *Arthur* may be revived in future cases.

---

[117] (J4/17/2025) [2025] GHASC 45.

[118] (J4/17/2025) [2025] GHASC 45, p. 16.

6 Property Rights in Informal Relationships, Invalid Marriages and Polygynous Marriages

6.1 Informal Relationships

There is no presumption of marriage in Ghana. No matter how long a couple has lived together or presented themselves as husband and wife, the law does not infer the existence of a valid marriage. In *Re Blankson-Hemans,* Koranteng Addow J. explained that 'when the fact of marriage is in dispute ... it has to be proved strictly and affirmatively like any other disputed fact. It does not have to be inferred.'[119] Similarly, in the case of *Badu v Boakye,* the High Court held that "where a man lives with a woman not as a real wife but only as a concubine..., that association cannot be translated into a valid customary marriage because the man and the woman are reputed to live as man and wife.'[120]

Nevertheless, Ghana's legal system recognises the existence of cohabitating unions, commonly referred to as 'concubinage.'[121] These unions do not carry the legal status or the formal protections afforded to married couples, especially with respect to property rights, as was held by the Supreme Court in *Marian Obeng Mintah v Francis Ampenyin.*[122] Specifically, the Court explained that 'the principle of equality is equity...applies in an environment of spousal relationship which creates a status that goes with certain rights and duties which are fixed by law and custom, but the same cannot be said of [a] concubinage relationship.'[123] The Supreme Court further held that, in a concubinage relationship, contributions in kind to property owned by the other party do not confer co-ownership; rather, the contributing party may seek an equitable remedy, including reimbursement or compensation, in accordance with the principles of equity.[124] Thus, in *Abisah Faustina v Bediako Cosmos,* a plaintiff (woman) was awarded compensation for her labour in supervising a house financed by the defendant, with whom she lived in concubinage before the breakdown of the relationship.[125] Considering the specific facts of the case, this award arguably reflects principles of fairness and equitable distribution, consistent with the general rule that contributors to the acquisition of property are entitled to a share proportionate to their contribution. Thus, property acquired during cohabitation in

---

[119] *In re Blankson-Hemans (decd..); Blankson-Hemans v. Monney and Another* [1973] 1 GLR 464, 467. (HC).

[120] [1975] 1 G.L.R 283, 290.

[121] On the rights of women in informal conjugal unions generally, see Morhe and Adomako-Kwakye (2019, p. 88).

[122] [2015–2016] 2 SCGLR 1277; See also *Badu v Boakye* [1975] 1 GLR 283 where the court held that a woman in a concubinage relationship cannot maintain an action against the man with whom she cohabits for maintenance.

[123] [2015–2016] 2 SCGLR 1277, 1283–1284.

[124] [2015–2016] 2 SCGLR 1277, 1282–1284.

[125] [2023] GHADC 1183.

unmarried relationships appears to be treated according to ordinary property law principles.

6.2 *Invalid Marriages*

A related issue arises where a marriage is legally invalid or void in Ghana. For instance, a person already married under customary law cannot validly contract a marriage with a third party under Part Three of the Marriages Act, which governs Christian and civil marriages, and vice versa; either situation constitutes bigamy.[126] In *Owuo v. Owuo*, the Supreme Court held that a party to an invalid marriage claiming a share of property must 'prove with sufficient particularity that …[they] made substantial contribution towards the acquisition of the property.'[127]

In that case, Mr. and Mrs. Owuo married under customary law in 1989 and later formalised their union as monogamous in 1999. Mrs. Owuo subsequently petitioned for divorce and claimed joint ownership of property. The High Court declared the marriage void, finding that Mr. Owuo lacked capacity to remarry due to an existing marriage, and dismissed her property claim for lack of proof of contribution. The Court of Appeal partially upheld her appeal, acknowledging the marriage's invalidity but awarding her half the property's value as 'compensation on grounds of equity and public policy',[128] holding it unjust for Mr. Owuo to benefit from his own wrongdoing.[129] On appeal by Mr Owuo, the Supreme Court upheld the order for the transfer of half the value of the property in question to Mrs Owuo, but based its decision on her contribution to its acquisition. In ordering the transfer, the Supreme Court relied on section 21 of the Matrimonial Causes Act, which provides that:

> When a decree of divorce or nullity is granted, if the court is satisfied that either party to the marriage holds title to movable or immovable property, or part or all of which rightfully belongs to the other, the court shall order transfer or conveyance of the interest to the party entitled to it, on the terms that the court thinks just and equitable.[130]

Without such legislative protections, parties, especially women, who in good faith enter into marriages that are subsequently declared invalid, remain highly vulnerable. Thus, we acknowledge the Court of Appeal's decision ordering compensation on the basis of *equity* and *public policy*, and consider its approach persuasive in promoting fairness. However, clearer laws are needed to regulate property settlement in invalid marriages to ensure fairness, protect individuals who enter into such unions, and

---

[126] See Marriages Act, 1884–1985 (CAP 127), ss. 68(3) and 74(1)(b).

[127] *Mrs Theresa Owuo v Mr Francis Owuo* [2017] DLSC2490, Civil Appeal No. J4/20/2017(SC), p. 6.

[128] *Mrs Theresa Owuo v Mr Francis Owuo* [2017] DLSC2490, Civil Appeal No. J4/20/2017(SC), p. 6.

[129] *Mrs Theresa Owuo v Mr Francis Owuo* [2017] DLSC2490, Civil Appeal No. J4/20/2017(SC), p. 6.

[130] Matrimonial Causes Act 1971 (Act 367), s. 21.

maintain appropriate judicial flexibility. In this regard, we propose that where a party in an invalid marriage entered into the union in good faith and contributed financially to the acquisition of property, they should be recognised as a joint owner of such property, as was done by the Supreme Court. Where a party's contribution in an invalid marriage is primarily non-financial, courts may award compensation rather than ownership. To strengthen the existing legal framework, section 21 of the Matrimonial Causes Act should be amended not only to include an explicit definition or criteria for what constitutes property that 'rightfully belongs' to a party, but also to reflect the suggested proposals.

6.3 Polygynous Marriages

In the context of polygynous marriages, the Court held in *Ayishetu* that the mere existence of a polygynous union does not, in itself, disentitle a wife from obtaining an equal or equitable share of the matrimonial property upon divorce. Where a spouse establishes, by credible evidence, that a particular property was jointly acquired, such property ought to be equitably distributed between the parties, notwithstanding the existence of other wives. The Court further emphasised that the number of wives or children of the husband should not be the determining factor in apportioning property between him and the divorcing wife; rather, the decisive consideration is whether the property in question was jointly acquired during the subsistence of that specific marriage. However, *Abena Pokua* held that in polygynous marriages, where the husband has multiple wives and children, distribution cannot be treated the same as in monogamous marriages. The husband's obligations to other wives and children, and the unique circumstances of the marriage, must guide equitable allocation. According to the court:

> where the Respondent has as many as three wives, it will be most unreasonable and inequitable for the Petitioner/Appellant wife to expect that whatever property that was acquired during her marriage with the Respondent herein should be shared equally between her and the Respondent. What happens to the interest of the remaining wives of the marriage? In such instances, this Court will rather apply the provisions under section 20 of the Matrimonial Causes Act and settle, in a reasonable manner, property on the divorcing wife, the Petitioner herein, taking into consideration all the surrounding circumstances of the case.[131]

Perhaps, the apparent contradiction resolves into a complementary interpretation. While *Ayishetu* allows a wife in a polygynous marriage to obtain an equal or equitable share if joint acquisition is proven, *Abena Pokua* clarifies that distribution must remain fair and context-sensitive.

[131] (J4/17/2025) [2025] GHASC 45, p. 40.

7 Property Rights of Spouses Bill 2024

The Property Rights of Spouses bills have been proposed or introduced in successive Parliaments with little result to show for it, the latest being in 2024. The Property Rights of Spouses Bill 2024 is the culmination of efforts by the bi-partisan women's caucus in Parliament. In many ways, the bill attempts to incorporate the principles enunciated by the courts while allowing for some innovative adjustments where necessary. The bill is intended to apply to all forms of marriage in Ghana, irrespective of the system of law from which they derive their validity.[132]

The presumption of marital property is given prominence in section 3, which even provides a list of property that can be classified as marital property: the matrimonial home and other immovable property; household property, any property (other than separate property) obtained during the marriage; a business established with seed money provided by one spouse; and property that was initially separate but to which a spouse has contributed, except when related to the sale of family land.[133] The list is not exhaustive. The bill also addresses the issue of conversion, specifically the circumstances under which separate property will be converted into marital property. To that end, a spouse will be deemed to have a beneficial interest in the property of the other to the extent of the spouse's contribution.[134] The bill intends to give the Courts additional powers to restrain the sale of marital property by a spouse or even a third party to protect a spouse's interest.[135]

The Act also allows a spouse to acquire and keep separate property during the subsistence of the marriage.[136] This crystallises the principle iterated in the cases that marriage does not prevent individual ownership. The bill, however, imposes procedural requirements to distinguish between separate and marital property. Spouses may maintain property as separate by signing a declaration or providing oral evidence from two independent witnesses specifying which property is separate.[137] Separate property is not subject to equitable division unless otherwise agreed[138] Property considered separate includes assets and profits acquired before marriage, gifts or inheritances, and personal injury damages.[139]

Upon the dissolution of a marriage, the bill contains a provision empowering the court to make orders to 'equitably distribute property jointly acquired during the marriage'.[140] Importantly, the bill intends to exclude fault from the distribution

[132] Property Rights of Spouses Bill 2024, s.2.
[133] Property Rights of Spouses Bill 2024, s. 3(1).
[134] Property Rights of Spouses Bill 2024, s. 3(2).
[135] Property Rights of Spouses Bill 2024, s. 3(3).
[136] Property Rights of Spouses Bill 2024, s. 4(1).
[137] Property Rights of Spouses Bill 2024, s. 4(2).
[138] Property Rights of Spouses Bill 2024, s. 4(3).
[139] Property Rights of Spouses Bill 2024, s. 4(5).
[140] Property Rights of Spouses Bill 2024, s. 6(1).

process and, to that end, indicates that the ground for the dissolution of the marriage is inconsequential.[141]

As we have seen in this chapter, the Ghanaian courts have long grappled with the criteria for the distribution of marital property. Though the courts have equivocated between 'equitable' and 'equal' distribution, very little guidance has been given beyond the courts' insistence that the facts of each case will control what each spouse gets. The bill innovatively intends to fill this gap by providing clear standards to channel and guide judicial discretion. This bill will allow judges to consider the length of the marriage, the spouses' ages and needs, and monetary and non-monetary contributions towards the acquisition, including a spouse's non-monetary contributions towards housekeeping and family maintenance.[142] In line with judicial precedents, the bill affirms that '[t]he non-monetary contribution shall not be proved in monetary terms'.[143]

The bill has special provisions on the matrimonial home. Apart from spouses acting together in transactions relating to the matrimonial home, transactions involving a matrimonial home that is not jointly acquired will involve at least six months' notice being given to the non-owning spouse.[144]

In other proceedings where the court has to settle property, the court will be given the power to alter the property rights of the parties by ordering that some property be settled on a spouse in satisfaction of the spouses' interest in some other property, or direct the spouses to settle or transfer property in the manner determined by the court.[145]

The bill also makes provision for the determination of ownership of property in polygamous marriages. Property acquired by the first and second wives will belong to the first and second wives jointly; otherwise, all the spouses—the husband and his wives—will hold the property jointly proportionate to their respective contributions unless there is some agreement to the contrary.[146]

The bill would also enhance the maintenance provisions in the Matrimonial Causes Act by introducing some factors which the court should consider. These include the spouses' needs and financial abilities, their employment, the impact of the marriage on their earning capacity and careers, among others.[147]

If ever passed, the bill will likely take us closer to a more equitable framework for sharing marital property. A stakeholders' forum was convened in 2024 to deliberate and improve the draft bill before its official introduction in Parliament. Nothing seems to have been done after this process. In light of Parliament's inertia, the principles developed by the courts will continue to dominate the field of marital property.

---

[141] Property Rights of Spouses Bill 2024, s. 6 (1).

[142] Property Rights of Spouses Bill 2024, s. 6(2).

[143] Property Rights of Spouses Bill 2024, s. 6(3).

[144] Property Rights of Spouses Bill 2024, s. 7(1) and (2).

[145] Property Rights of Spouses Bill 2024, s. 8.

[146] Property Rights of Spouses Bill 2024, s. 13(2).

[147] Property Rights of Spouses Bill 2024, s. 16(3).

8 Recommendations

8.1 Inconsistency in Legal Decisions

Despite the reform of the law as far back as 1971 and the constitutionalisation of the property rights of spouses in 1992, we are no closer to answering the question of what constitutes marital property, nor are we certain about how marital property should be distributed upon the dissolution of the marriage. The cases before *Gladys Mensah v Stephen Mensah* in 2012 seemed to value financial contribution in establishing ownership. Thereafter, *Mensah v Mensah* seemed to have turned the questions of ownership into a presumption and emphasised that a non-monetary contribution will suffice to distribute property. *Adjei v Adjei* is moving towards a stronger version of proof, with spouses asked to prove their financial and non-financial contributions to establish ownership and the extent of each spouse's interest in the property. In the court's defence, it is trying to balance the spouses' property interests with the primary human rights goal of equality. Two more recent cases, *Ayishetu* and *Abena Pokua,* have very different views on *Gladys Mensah v Stephen Mensah* and its corollary case, *Arthur*. The inconsistencies in judicial principles are unsurprising, as the language of legislative and constitutional guidelines has been the least helpful, placing the responsibility for fashioning new principles on the courts. And if stare decisis is anything to go by in a common law country, judicial principles are far from uniform.

8.2 Overbreadth in Law and Reforming the Matrimonial Causes Act

The judicial principles being developed are often too broad. For example, the presumption of joint property once threatened to render separate property meaningless until later cases reaffirmed spouses' right to own separate property. Courts also advocate equitable distribution without clear standards, but equity' cannot vary entirely by case; concrete factors should reflect Ghana's socio-economic realities. Generally, courts have emphasised equality and human rights over the incremental development of family law principles. Recognising non-monetary contributions in classifying property carefully balances spousal interests, whereas treating all acquired property as marital prioritises formal equality, an approach international human rights law, particularly in women's rights, is moving away from.[148]

As evidenced in this chapter, the real challenge concerns the definition of contribution in a way that excludes homemaker wives and other working spouses who provide substantial non-monetary contributions. Additionally, there are issues related to evidentiary proof and the complexities of determining what constitutes an equitable property division. These can be resolved with clear standards guiding judges on

[148] See generally, Sheppard (2004, pp. 57–58).

what to include or exclude in classifying and dividing property. A presumption that converts everything acquired and further blurs the lines between marital and separate property goes a tad too far. The guiding light should be substantive equality, which:

> …requires using the actual conditions of women's lives, rather than the wording used in laws, as the true measure of whether equality has been achieved. The State thus must do more than just ensuring that there are no existing laws that directly discriminate against women. It must also take whatever measures are needed to ensure that women actually experience equality in their lives.[149]

8.3 Specific Reforms to the Matrimonial Causes Act

The bigger problem is that, over time, the Matrimonial Causes Act appears to be retreating, and considerable ground has been ceded to the human rights provisions of the 1992 Constitution. In cases post-1992, the Matrimonial Causes Act is only mentioned in passing and not given the actual treatment it deserves. Therefore, the courts have developed the jurisprudence on article 22(3) in a way that creates the impression that the property rights era of 1992 is fundamentally distinct from the pre-1992 property rights regime. Activists have fallen for this, and instead of calling for the amendment of the Matrimonial Causes Act, they have directed their best energies towards an entirely new piece of legislation that has minimal prospects of becoming law. Activists and law reformers must begin to view the Matrimonial Causes Act as the starting point for matrimonial causes, including the property rights of spouses, and advocate for amendments to the Matrimonial Causes Act to conform to the provisions of the 1992 Constitution.

Generally, we recommend a comprehensive reform of section 20 of the Matrimonial Causes Act. Financial provision should be separated from marital property. Specific suggestions for reform are as follows:

8.3.1 Defining Marital Property

The part on marital property should define what constitutes marital property. In this regard, we suggest that marital property should be defined as property acquired through the joint efforts and contributions of the parties. One important area which should be sufficiently considered is non-monetary contributions. We support the courts' approach of not requiring strict proof of contribution and believe they should continue to rely on the probative value of the evidence adduced at trial. Contributions should extend beyond financial input to include a broad spectrum of non-monetary contributions.

---

[149] UN Women Asia and the Pacific (2023, para 2).

8.3.2 Factors to Guide Discretion in Dividing Marital Property

We further recommend including a list of factors to guide judges in classifying and dividing marital property. Some Ghanaian scholars have proposed some policy options. For example, Dowuona-Hammond, a legal academic, has suggested adopting a one-third rule, requiring courts to give wives a one-third interest in all marital property.[150] The problem with this rule is that it contradicts substantive equality by prefixing a fraction, which may not reflect the circumstances of the case. Barnes has also suggested that the courts may want to start from the presumption of equal division and then adjust the parties' share in light of the circumstances of the case to 'remove[s] the likelihood for some courts to be reluctant about recognising the value of such services, or where they do acknowledge there is some value in domestic services, the possibility of them under-valuing same'.[151] As noted earlier, the challenge with Barnes' proposal is the over-inclusiveness of the equality rule, which categorises all property acquisitions as marital property. However, it is important to note that the factors considered significant in each jurisdiction are highly context-dependent. They are influenced by the lived experiences of women, the nature of structural injustices they face, and the legal system's overall commitment to equality. We lay out options from two jurisdictions from which Ghana's legislature may draw inspiration. The first is the United Kingdom, whose matrimonial law is arguably the progenitor of Ghana's Matrimonial Causes Act. The second is the United States.

In the UK's Matrimonial Causes Act of 1973, judges are empowered to consider a range of factors when dividing marital property or awarding financial relief. These include each party's current and foreseeable income, earnings, property, and financial resources, as well as their financial needs, obligations, and responsibilities. The family's standard of living before the breakdown of the marriage, the age of the parties, the duration of the marriage, and any physical or mental disabilities are also relevant. Contributions to the family's welfare, including homemaking and childcare, are taken into account, along with the conduct of the parties if it would be inequitable to disregard it. In divorce or nullity proceedings, courts also consider the value of benefits a party will lose due to the marriage's dissolution.[152] This approach aims to create a fairer and more nuanced distribution of property, taking into account both monetary and non-monetary contributions, while considering each party's future needs and potential.

In the United States, the Uniform Law Commission, a nonprofit body responsible for developing model laws to reduce disparities among state laws, has also developed factors to be considered in settling property rights in the Uniform Marriage and Divorce Act of 1973 (the UMDA). While two alternative models are presented in the UMDA, the common law model is instructive. The UMDA states, among other things, that:

---

150 Dowuona-Hammond (2005, pp. 122–123).

151 Barnes (2020, pp. 405–406).

152 Matrimonial Causes Act, s 25(2).

> [The court]… shall divide community property, without regard to marital misconduct, in just proportions after considering all relevant factors including (1) contribution of each spouse to acquisition of the marital property, including contribution of a spouse as homemaker; (2) value of the property set apart to each spouse; (3) duration of the marriage; and (4) economic circumstances of each spouse when the division of property is to become effective, including the desirability of awarding the family home or the right to live therein for a reasonable period to the spouse having custody of any children.[153]

Both the UK and US models overlap, particularly in recognising homemaking as a contribution, considering the duration of the marriage, and assessing the parties' needs and financial circumstances. The UK model is broader, also accounting for potential future income, resource acquisition, and any disability. These similarities and differences show that relevant factors depend on both jurisdiction and the facts of each case. Any framework drawn from these models should be established democratically with input from all stakeholders. Crucially, courts must consider non-monetary contributions, including homemaking, as their inclusion or omission can advance fairness or perpetuate injustice.

8.3.3 Private Ordering

The status of prenuptial and post-marriage contracts in Ghana is unclear, as there are no specific legal provisions governing such contracts. In one case, the Court of Appeal, *per obiter*, has explained that:

> Since a marriage is a contract, the parties have the right to enter into a prenuptial agreement by which their right to create their individual property would be outlined. Where such a premarital agreement is made on property rights, neither the provisions of article 22 (3) of the Constitution, section 20 of the Matrimonial Causes Act, section 38 (3) and (4) of the Land Act or any of the Supreme Court cases, including Mensah v Mensah and Adjei v Adjei becomes applicable.[154]

This view from the Court of Appeal is quite far-reaching, suggesting that parties can contract outside of the legal framework discussed thus far. This view may render the protections afforded to vulnerable spouses nugatory. It should also not be forgotten that prenuptial contracts or during-marriage contracts are entered into in circumstances where coercive pressures may operate on the minds of either of the spouses. The court's view that marriage is a 'contract' also oversimplifies the nature of marriages in Ghana. Marriages confer both legal and social status. Therefore, the view that marriage is a contract should be counterbalanced by its nature as a social institution. If marriage were entirely contractual, its dissolution would not be tightly regulated by the State. Mensa-Bonsu has intimated that:

> Given the cultural circumstances of Ghana, it is unlikely that this provision (Marital Property Agreement) would inure to the benefit of any but a few Ghanaian women. If anything it would offer an opportunity to many men and their families to get intended spouses to renounce

[153] The Uniform Marriage and Divorce Act, s 307.

[154] *Obeng v Nyamekye* (CA, 20 July 2023).

> any interest in their future property. This provision lacks cultural sensitivity, and clearly illustrates the dangers in borrowing ideas without acculturation, for anyone familiar with how marriages are contracted in Ghana would have difficulty appreciating the practicalities of such an idea.[155]

We, therefore, propose that a provision be inserted into the Matrimonial Causes Act, subjecting all forms of marital contracts preceding dissolution to an equitable standard of equity and fairness. We further propose that a court should have the power to disregard such contracts when it deems them unfair and inequitable. We have excluded divorce settlement contracts because, in practice, they are usually negotiated under a court's instructions during divorce proceedings. Courts, therefore, have greater control over such contracts.

8.4 Customary Law Reforms

The State must influence the principles that guide property division outside the court system. In this regard, we recommend that traditional leaders, family heads, Imams, and other legal actors be educated to shift their perceptions of gender roles, property rights, and women's status in marriage, to ensure more equitable treatment and opportunities for women. Indeed, such education requires a multifaceted approach that combines cultural sensitivity with modern human rights considerations. While we acknowledge and respect the cultural beliefs that influence property distribution in customary and Islamic legal systems, we believe educating traditional leaders about the values enshrined in the 1992 Constitution and the Matrimonial Causes Act, among other laws, is essential. They should be empowered to recognise that these values do not conflict with the principles of dignity, responsibility, reciprocity, and respect for individuals, which are also central to customary law.[156] By combining education, legal awareness, and community engagement, these leaders can be equipped to foster more equitable property sharing in their communities while respecting both modern human rights norms and cultural traditions.

9 Conclusion

Ghana's legal framework for property division in divorce is simply unsatisfactory, and this must change. Admittedly, the complexities surrounding property rights in Ghana stem from its diverse legal landscape, shaped by colonial history and a continuing struggle with gender inequality rooted in patriarchal traditions, which undermine equitable spousal property arrangements. Unquestionably, though, the current legal framework reflects an effort to balance property rights with gender equality, but its

---

[155] Mensa-Bonsu (2011–2012, pp. 139–140).

[156] See Cobbah (1987, pp. 309–331).

vagueness and irreconcilable principles have failed to adequately protect the interests of spouses, particularly women. While evolving, the judicial approach to marital property division remains inconsistent with contradictory legal decisions. The inconsistencies in legal decisions are further compounded by a lack of concrete legislative guidelines, leaving courts to develop principles on a case-by-case basis.

To address these shortcomings, this chapter advocates comprehensive reform of the Matrimonial Causes Act provisions on the sharing of marital property. A more robust framework, drawing on international models such as those in the UK and the US, should include clear definitions of marital property that consider both financial and non-financial contributions, and should provide specific factors to guide judges in equitably dividing property, taking into account the unique socio-economic context of Ghana. Hopefully, these guidelines will foster fairness and consistency and ensure that Ghana's legal system truly upholds the principles of equality and justice for all spouses, regardless of gender. It must be emphasised that establishing just and equitable rules for the division of marital property must aim solely at fairness to prevent marriage from being exploited to acquire property through opportunism.

Lastly, we cannot overemphasise the importance of education, within or outside the formal court system, about the different roles spouses play in acquiring property. All relevant stakeholders, especially judges and the relevant traditional and Islamic leaders, must be sensitised to the varied contributions of spouses. Indeed, if marriages are to be respected in Ghana and not viewed merely as contractual, it behoves Ghanaians to insist on a legal framework that is meaningfully detached from discriminatory norms and entrenched biases, and adapted to the principles of fairness, equity and respect.

References

Alvarez JE, Bauder J (2024) Women's property rights under CEDAW. Oxford University Press, Oxford

Barnes MYA (2020) Equality is equity...or is it? a critical examination of the "equality principle" in the distribution of marital property. In: Dowuona-Hammond C, Hammond AF, Atuguba R (eds) Mobilizing the law for Ghana's future: appraising to revolutionise. School of Law—University of Ghana, Accra

Bond J (2008) Pluralism in Ghana: the perils and promise of parallel law. Or Rev Int Law 10(2):391–418

CEDAW Committee (2014) Concluding observations on the Combined Sixth and Seventh Periodic Reports of Ghana, UN Doc CEDAW/C/GHA/CO/6-7, adopted 14 November 2014

Cobbah JAM (1987) African values and the human rights debate: An African perspective. Hum Rts Q 9:309–331.

Combs MB (2005) A measure of legal independence: the 1870 Married Women's Property Act and the portfolio allocations of British wives. J Econ Hist 65(4):1028–1057

Cooper E (2010) Challenges and opportunities in African societies. Chronic Poverty Research Centre Working Paper 19/2010

Daniels WCE (1965) Towards the integration of the laws relating to husband and wife in Ghana. Univ Ghana Law J 2(2):20–60

Daniels WCE (1974) Married women's property ordinance. Rev Ghana Law 6:143–146

Daniels WCE (1978) The ascertainment of property rights between husband and wife. Rev Ghana Law 10:137–151
Danquah JB (1928) Gold Coast: Akan laws and customs and the Akim Abuakwa constitution. George Routledge & Sons, London
Dowuona-Hammond C (2005) Ensuring equity in the distribution of matrimonial property upon divorce in Ghana: preparing the path for legislation. Univ Botswana Law J 2:101–127
Dowuona-Hammond C, Bamba ABA, Mahamah MA (2023) The regulation of Islamic marriage and divorce in Ghana: legislative and policy roots of discrimination. J Comp Law 18(1):27–62
Evelyn GAS (2013) Property rights of spouses in relation to economic violence against women in Ghana. https://www.researchgate.net/publication/264051209_Property_Rights_of_Spouses_in_Relation_to_Economic_Violence_Against_Women_in_Ghana. Accessed 2 Nov 2025
Gayoye M (2022) Why women judges really matter: the impact of women judges on property law outcomes in Kenya. Soc Leg Stud 31(1):72–98
Ghana Statistical Service (GSS) and ICF. 2024. Ghana Demographic and Health Survey 2022. Accra, Ghana, and Rockville, Maryland, USA: GSS and ICF.
Griffin B (2003) Class, gender, and liberalism in Parliament, 1868–1882: the case of the Married Women's Property Acts. Hist J 46(1):59–87
Hammond AF (2016) Legal reforms in Ghana and the reality of a hybrid legal personality. In: Oppong RF, Agyebeng K (eds) A commitment to law, development and public policy: A festschrift in honour of Nana Dr. SKB Asante. Wildy, Simmonds and Hill, London
Mensa-Bonsu HJ (2011–2012) Ensuring equitable access to marital property when the holy estate becomes an unholy ex-state—will the legislature walk the road paved by the courts? Univ Ghana Law J 25:99–151
Mensa-Bonsu MYA (2023) Customary marriage in Ghana. J Comp Law 18(1):95–120
Morhe RAS, Adomako-Kwakye C (2019) Property rights of Ghanaian women in informal conjugal unions. KNUST Law J 8:88–107
Offei WE (1998) Family law in Ghana, 2th edn. Sebewie Publishers, Kwahu
Rattray RS (1929) Ashanti laws and constitution. Clarendon Press, Oxford
Sarbah JM (1904) Fanti customary laws. London: W. Clowes and Sons
Sezgin Y (2023) Undignified jurispathy: Muslim family law at Ghanaian courts. Law Soc Inq 48(4):1303–1333
Sheppard C (2004) Inclusive equality and new forms of social governance. Supreme Court Law Rev 24:45–76
UN Women Asia and the Pacific (2023) Frequently asked questions about CEDAW. Available at https://asiapacific.unwomen.org/en/focus-areas/cedaw-human-rights/faq. Accessed 2 Nov 2025
Wanitzek U (1991) Integration of personal laws and women's access to property in ghana: the Matrimonial Causes Act of 1971. Third World Leg Stud 10:75–107
Woodman GR (1996) Legal pluralism and the quest for justice. J Afr Law 40(2):152–167.
Woodman GR (1998) Ideological combat and social observation: recent debates about legal pluralism. J Leg Plur Unoff Law 42:21–59
Woodman GR (2010) Ghana: How does state law accommodate religious, cultural, linguistic and ethnic diversity? In: Foblets MC, Gaudreault-Desbiens J-F, Dundes Renteln A (eds) Cultural diversity and the law: State responses from around the World. Bruylant; Éditions Yvon Blais.
Zabel S (1969) The legislative history of the Gold Coast and Nigerian Marriage Ordinances. J Afr Law 13:64–79

Ama F. Hammond is an Associate Professor at the University of Ghana School of Law, where she teaches Contract Law, Equity, and Succession and coordinates the School's graduate programmes. She serves as Deputy Editor of the University of Ghana Law Journal and has edited a number of books in her areas of expertise. Her research focuses on family law, legal pluralism, the law of succession, and human rights, with particular attention to the interaction between law, society, and policy. Hammond holds a BA from the University of Cape Coast, an LLB from the University of Ghana, an LLM from Harvard Law School, and a PhD from the University of British Columbia.

Prosper Batariwah is an S.J.D. candidate at Harvard Law School. His research interests include family law, legal pluralism, and natural resource governance. His work has appeared in peer-reviewed journals, including the Journal of African Law, Journal of Comparative Law, University of Ghana Law Journal, and African Journal of International and Comparative Law. He holds an LLB (first class honours) from the University of Ghana and a Qualifying Certificate for the Practice of Law from the Ghana School of Law. He is co-editor of Family Law in Africa: Perspectives on Selected Systems of Marriage (Talbot, 2023)

Contemporary Matrimonial Property Law in Kenya: An Exposition of Substantive Equality

Moza Ally Jadeed

Abstract This chapter explores Kenya's matrimonial property regime through the lens of substantive equality, as anchored in the Constitution and the Matrimonial Property Act. While these legal instruments both affirm spousal equality before, during, and after marriage, the chapter argues that this is not a matter of formal sameness but of context-sensitive, substantive justice. Drawing on the jurisprudence of the African Commission on Human and Peoples' Rights, the analysis illustrates how a purely formal application of equality may entrench inequities rather than address them. The chapter examines key concepts such as the definition of matrimonial property, the relevance of contributions (monetary and non-monetary), the timing of division, and the role of equitable doctrines like trust. It also considers the treatment of matrimonial property under Islamic and customary law, highlighting how plural legal systems shape marital rights. By situating the doctrine of substantive equality within Kenya's legal and cultural context, the chapter advocates for reforms that operationalise fairness, particularly in protecting women's marital property rights upon dissolution of marriage.

1 Introduction

The principle of equality in Kenya has long been misunderstood. Many lawyers and judges believe it means strictly identical treatment of similarly placed persons. Thus, their interpretation of article 45(3) of the Kenyan Constitution, which guarantees spouses equal rights at the time of marriage, throughout its duration, and upon its dissolution, extends to sharing matrimonial property on a 50:50 basis.[1] Recent courts

[1] Kameri-Mbote and Muriungi (2016, p. 88).

M. A. Jadeed (✉)
Faculty of Law, University of Nairobi, Nairobi, Kenya
e-mail: moza@uonbi.ac.ke

A. F. Hammond and P. Batariwah (eds.), *The Law on Marital Property in Africa*, Ius Gentium: Comparative Perspectives on Law and Justice 138,
https://doi.org/10.1007/978-3-032-19358-2_3

have correctly held that this provision embodies substantive equality.[2] This means that parties to a marriage will receive a share of the marital property commensurate with their contribution towards its acquisition and improvement.[3] As a matter of fact, the institution of marriage in itself does not automatically confer 'common ownership or co-ownership of property'.[4]

The journey to this pinnacle of justice has been fairly long. Until the application of the English Married Women's Property Act (MWPA)[5] in 1971,[6] a substantial number of Kenyans divided their marital property according to their ethnic, customary, or religious laws.[7] Both of these early laws restricted the property to which women were entitled upon the dissolution of the marriage to their personal belongings, such as clothes and jewellery, and other self-acquired property.[8] The MWPA, which generally anchored married women's substantive individual property rights,[9] also offered a procedural panacea for accession to matrimonial property.[10] This law provided an existing or former husband or wife with the means to approach the court to seek a determination and declaration of their proprietary rights in marital property through expedited legal proceedings known as a summary process.[11] This arrangement was intended to make matters easy, especially 'for the spouse who is not in possession of the disputed property'.[12]

Thus, although the Act was silent on the entitlements of each party to this property, the jurisprudence that emerged in the late 1990s and early 2000s appeared to grant the parties identical shares.[13] This happened when a property was jointly registered in unspecified shares.[14] It also occurred when the property was registered in one spouse's name, but the other spouse substantially contributed to its acquisition, whether directly or indirectly.[15] The Court of Appeal, the then highest court of the land, once discounted this coincidence as predicated on 'any general principle of equality of division'. Instead, the court insisted that each decision was based on

---

[2] *JOO v MBO; Federation of Women Lawyers (FIDA Kenya) and another (Amicus Curiae)* (Petition 11 of 2020) 4 KLR (KESC 2023); *PNN v ZWN* [2017] eKLR (per Kiage, JA).

[3] *PNN v ZWN* [2017] eKLR, pp. 17–19.

[4] *JOO v MBO* (Petition 11 of 2020) 4 KLR (KESC 2023) para. 82.

[5] Married Women's Property Act (1882), 45 & 46 Vict. c. 75 (UK Statute).

[6] Though the legislation became operative in 1897 when Kenya received English law, MWPA was first invoked in the case of *I v I* [1971] EA 278. See Nyamu-Musembi (2002, p. 230).

[7] Muslims have largely observed Islamic property laws in distributing marital property.

[8] Human Rights Watch and FIDA-Kenya (2020, p. 4) and *Kivuitu v Kivuitu* [1991] KLR 248, 252.

[9] Norbert (1977, pp. 73–78) and Nyamu-Musembi (2002, p. 229).

[10] *PNN v ZWN* [2017] eKLR.

[11] Married Women's Property Act (1882), s. 17, *Pettitt v Pettitt* [1969] 2 All ER 385, 411 and LSData (n.d.).

[12] *Muthembwa v Muthembwa* [2002] 1 EA 186, 192.

[13] *Kivuitu v Kivuitu* [1991] KLR 248, 252, *Kamore v Kamore* [2000] 1 EA 80, *Tabitha Wangechi Nderitu v Simon Nderitu Kariuki* [1998] eKLR and *Muthembwa v Muthembwa* [2002] 1 EA 186.

[14] *Kivuitu v Kivuitu* [1991] KLR 248, 252 and *Kamore v Kamore* [2000] 1 EA 80.

[15] *Tabitha Wangechi Nderitu v Simon Nderitu Kariuki* [1998] eKLR and *Muthembwa v Muthembwa* [2002] 1 EA 186.

its peculiarity and that each such decision had independently assessed the wife's contribution as the same as the husband's.[16]

However, the nearly uniform 50:50 split in shares changed in 2007 when the Court of Appeal reviewed and clarified its previous decisions. The court held that where property is registered in the joint names of the spouses, the law presumes it is held in identical shares, unless cogent evidence proves otherwise. Where, however, the title is in the name of one spouse, the other spouse must prove their direct or indirect financial contribution to the acquisition of the property to gain beneficial interest. That proof had to be documentary or such other concrete evidence. When this is done, the court grants the non-holding spouse an interest equivalent to their contribution or identical to the holding partner's if it deems that contribution 'substantial but unascertainable'.[17] The court, however, discredited indirect non-monetary contributions, such as childbearing and rearing, as well as domestic chores, in support of a claim to ownership of property registered to one spouse.[18]

Women's rights advocates contested this 2007 decision for its insensitivity to women who contribute to improving a property but keep no receipts for their purchases.[19] The decision also defeated the court's earlier view (albeit in passing) that the typical contribution of 'a Kenya African wife' was management of the matrimonial home.[20] While the court conceded that considering such non-financial contribution was just and, perhaps, in tandem with Kenya's international and regional women's rights obligations, it insisted that such an approach required legislative backing. The court thus implored Parliament to enact a Matrimonial Property law that recognises non-monetary contributions, as Britain did in the 1960s and 1970s, to replace the 1882 MWPA.[21]

Therefore, adopting the Constitution in 2010 provided some relief to these women's rights lawyers.[22] The Constitution instructed Parliament to enact a law to guide the ascertainment and protection of matrimonial property, particularly the matrimonial home, both during and after marriage.[23] Several pieces of legislation responded to this constitutional call in the subsequent three years.[24] These were the Land Act,[25] the Land Registration Act,[26] and the Matrimonial Property Act.[27]

---

[16] *Echaria v Echaria* [2007] eKLR, pp. 9–10.

[17] *Echaria v Echaria* [2007] eKLR, pp. 9–10.

[18] *PNN v ZWN* [2017] eKLR, p. 8 and *Echaria v Echaria* [2007] eKLR, pp. 9–15.

[19] Human Rights Watch and FIDA-Kenya (2020, p. 4).

[20] *Kivuitu v Kivuitu* [1991] KLR 248, 258–259.

[21] *Echaria v Echaria* [2007] eKLR, pp. 11–13.

[22] Kameri-Mbote and Muriungi (2016, p. 75).

[23] Constitution of Kenya (2010), art. 68(c)(iii).

[24] *FIDA v Attorney General* [2018] eKLR, para. 43.

[25] Land Act, Ch. 280, Laws of Kenya (2012, ss. 79, 105).

[26] Land Registration Act, Ch. 300, Laws of Kenya (2012, s. 93).

[27] Matrimonial Property Act (MPA), Ch. 152, Laws of Kenya (2013).

The Matrimonial Property Act (MPA) elaborately explains the constitutional edifice of spousal equality and marital property. While its bill was under discussion before 2010, the resulting Act echoes substantive equality in the proprietary rights of the spouses. The Act also defines matrimonial property and acknowledges non-monetary contributions. This law further enshrines that contribution is pivotal to gaining a beneficial interest in marital property. While it repeals the 1882 MPWA, the MPA retains the former law's provision on resulting trusts, which generally presumed ownership to a non-holding spouse.[28] This 2013 legislation also recognises property rights derived from Islamic law and customary law, although those arising from customary law will only be recognised if they are in tandem with the values and principles of the Constitution. These values and principles include human dignity, equity, social justice, equality, human rights, and non-discrimination.[29]

However, the law has been criticised for limiting the division of marital property to a party's contribution to its acquisition, thereby violating article 45(3) of the Constitution and discriminating against married women upon divorce.[30] Article 45(3) of the Constitution emphatically states that, 'Parties to a marriage are entitled to equal rights at the time of the marriage, during the marriage and at the dissolution of the marriage'. Critics assert that the Act's recognition of the seemingly inherent disproportionate Islamic and customary regimes as discriminating against Muslims and a majority of rural women.[31] Both interpretations represent an incorrect understanding of 'equal' and 'equality'. Equality, if understood in its substantive form, embodies inclusiveness and equity (or fairness). Inclusiveness means respecting different conceptions of rights, even when those constructions differ starkly from the majority view.[32] Fairness, on the other hand, means handling or treating individuals or groups in accordance with their concrete realities or circumstances.[33]

So far, the courts have applied fairness (and consciousness) in individual marital property rights disputes. Indeed, in applying both the Constitution and MPA, courts have now held that while article 45(3) espouses equality, this equality means that each party is entitled to a share in a matrimonial property equivalent to his or her contribution.[34] That provision does not entitle the courts to take one spouse's property and grant half of it to the other spouse who did not contribute to its acquisition just because they are or were married.[35] Instead, article 45(3) still respects the right to individual property ownership, as ensconced in article 40(1) and (2), even in a

---

[28] MPA (2013, ss. 2, 4, 6-9, 14).

[29] MPA (2013, s. 10(2)(b)).

[30] This position is found in section 7. See also *FIDA v Attorney General* [2018] eKLR and Kameri-Mbote and Muriungi (2016, p. 74).

[31] Human Rights Watch and FIDA-Kenya (2020, p. 26), IDLO and UN Women (2024, p. 40) and Chan and Mbogoh (2016, pp. 20–21).

[32] Jadeed (2020, p. 93).

[33] *JOO v MBO* (Petition 11 of 2020) 4 KLR (KESC 2023), para 91.

[34] *JOO v MBO* (Petition 11 of 2020) 4 KLR (KESC 2023), para 82 and *AWM v JGK* [2021] eKLR, p. 8.

[35] *JOO v MBO* (Petition 11 of 2020) 4 KLR (KESC 2023), para 81, *PNN v ZWN* [2017] eKLR, p. 17 and *UMM v IMM* [2014] eKLR, para. 21.

marriage.[36] Article 45(3) does no more than enshrine spousal equality in relation to fundamental rights and freedoms generally.[37]

This chapter now appraises the present matrimonial property law in the country as embodied in the Constitution and the MPA. The chapter asserts that these dual laws do not conflict. They both reflect equality of parties before, during, and after marriage, regardless of the marital regime. However, this equality is not formal equality per se; it is substantive, meaning it is determined by the context in which it is applied. Substantive equality, as explained by the African Commission on Human and Peoples' Rights, advances justice because it enshrines fairness and awards spouses that which they duly deserve when their marriage ends. Formal equality in and of itself may, sometimes, result in inequality of the sexes and disadvantage either the man or the woman.[38] It is therefore important for women's rights advocates to interpret the constitutional equality provisions through this lens.

This chapter is divided into five sections. Following this introduction, Sect. 2 discusses the substantive provisions of the MPA as they relate to state law, Islamic law, and customary law. It addresses the written law or what may loosely be described as state or statutory law, particularly the meaning and impact of contribution, the timing of property division, the protection of marital interests, the equitable principles of trust, and individual property rights. The section then identifies the Islamic and customary law property rights, respectively, to the extent that they are recognised by the MPA. Section 3 presents the concerns raised by critics about the MPA and responds to these criticisms through the lens of substantive equality. Section 4 proposes a better application of marital laws in the country, and Sect. 5 concludes the chapter.

2 An Overview of the MPA

2.1 The State Law

The statutory mainstream law begins by defining matrimonial property and the concept of contribution. Seemingly, the law responds to criticisms that its predecessor, the 1882 MWPA, failed to demarcate the boundaries of matrimonial property.[39] The law also settles the questionable jurisprudence on what amounts to contribution. Furthermore, it establishes the legal autonomy of married women and outlines the rights and liabilities of spouses in relation to property acquired or inherited before marriage. The Act also explains these liabilities when such property becomes matrimonial property. It further explains gifts between spouses and the effects of joint

[36] *JOO v MBO* (Petition 11 of 2020) 4 KLR (KESC 2023), para 82.

[37] *PNN v ZWN* [2017] eKLR, pp. 16–17 and *EGM v BMM* [2020] eKLR, p. 4.

[38] African Commission on Human and Peoples' Rights (2020, para. 42, 43).

[39] Kameri-Mbote and Muriungi (2016, p. 83).

or unilateral registration of matrimonial property. Finally, the Act outlines the legal protections for matrimonial property and indicates the circumstances under which a party may seek the court's intervention for the ascertainment of property rights and order the division of the property.

2.1.1 The Definition of Matrimonial Property

Section 6 of the MPA categorises matrimonial property into three distinct types. These are the matrimonial home, the household goods in that home, or such other property (immovable or movable) '*jointly* owned *and* acquired' during marriage.[40] Section 2 of the Act clarifies what constitutes a matrimonial home. It is any property leased or owned by one or both spouses '*and* occupied or utilized' by them as their family home.[41] Any property attached to this matrimonial home is likewise deemed part of the matrimonial home.[42] In *TMW v FMC*, the High Court found that the property which constituted the subject matter of the suit was matrimonial property because it was acquired during marriage for the 'purposes of building a family home'.[43] Similarly, in *RCL v MKK*, the court found one of the contested properties qualified as marital property because 'the matrimonial home was built there' and the respondent's family lived there.[44] The respondent had contended that he inherited the property from his father, and it was therefore not matrimonial under section 5 of the MPA which excludes property inherited before marriage from being considered matrimonial.[45]

Both section 6 of the Act and relevant case law clearly establish the status of the matrimonial home and household goods. However, questions remain regarding the third category, the omnibus clause, which grants matrimonial property status to any other property, provided it is jointly acquired and owned, and importantly, during the marriage. In many Kenyan communities, women hardly inherit their fathers' land, and most Kenyan women are housewives. Some argue that this description of matrimonial property reinforces men's monopoly over land ownership. This view is discussed more fully in section 3.

[40] MPA (2013, s. 6) (emphasis added).

[41] MPA (2013, s. 2) (emphasis added). Both sections 2 to the Land Act and the Land Registration Act bear a similar definition.

[42] MPA (2013, s. 2).

[43] *TMW v FMC* [2018] eKLR, p. 3.

[44] *RCL v MKK* [2022] KEHC 10719 (KLR), para. 73.

[45] Section 5 provides that any property interest acquired or inherited before marriage is not matrimonial property.

2.1.2 The Meaning and Impact of Contribution

Section 2 of the MPA defines the term contribution as encompassing both 'monetary and non-monetary' and including: 'domestic work and management of the matrimonial home; child care; companionship; management of family business and property; and farm work'. This provision also clarifies that a family business is an enterprise run by either or both spouses that generates income used wholly or partially for the benefit of the family. Undoubtedly, the word 'includes' in section 2 indicates that this list of non-financial contributions is non-exhaustive. So, courts can consider such other activity linked to the home as non-monetary contributions. This is a fulfilment of the wish previously expressed by the Court of Appeal in *Kivuitu.*

In *Kivuitu,* the court held that an urban woman who manages the family home by preparing meals, cleaning, and caring for the children and her husband has contributed to property acquired by her husband through his salary or business, even if the husband provided the funds she used to perform these domestic duties. The court added that it would make a similar finding for a rural woman who manages the household and cultivates both subsistence and cash crops while her husband works in town, sends her monthly maintenance, and acquires property through his salary or business.[46]

What is also clear from section 2 is that the MPA has departed from the 2007 *Echaria* jurisprudence, which discounted non-financial contribution as being capable of conferring beneficial interest in marital property. Kiage JA in *PNN* correctly pointed out the present law, thus: -

> What has changed, from my point of view, is *the narrow conception of contribution* espoused by ECHARIA in that *it went as far only as recognizing indirect contribution which had essentially to be viewed in money or monetary equivalent* leaving out *such unquantifiable as child care and companionship which fall under non-monetary contribution* which is now expressly recognized under the Matrimonial Property Act.[47]

Kiage JA's perspective introduces a new dimension of understanding direct and indirect contributions on the one hand, and financial and non-financial contributions on the other hand. Many legal practitioners and women's rights advocates interchange these two categories,[48] but they do not mean the same thing. While the latter group is easy to understand, the former requires clarification. Omolo JA aptly reminded us of the meanings of direct and indirect contributions in *Kivuitu.* He observed that:

> There is no difficulty as to what a *direct financial contribution* is: either the wife or the husband *has paid so much money towards the purchase of the property.* Again, there is little difficulty in what an indirect financial contribution is. Where *both the husband and the wife are in salaried employment or one of them or the other is in business* and *uses the income to pay household expenses* such as food, clothing, school fees and so on; *such a spouse is making an indirect contribution to the purchase* of the property because the other spouse can then use his or her income to pay for the property.[49]

[46] *Kivuitu v Kivuitu* [1991] KLR 248, 258–59.

[47] *PNN v ZWN* [2017] eKLR, p. 18 and *Echaria v Echaria* [2007] eKLR.

[48] *AWM v JGK* [2021] eKLR, p. 7.

[49] *Kivuitu v Kivuitu* [1991] KLR 248, 258.

In this regard, both direct and indirect contributions may be financial. However, non-financial contributions are exclusively indirect in nature. They are typically service-oriented, non-monetised, and involve the application of one's time, effort, care, and intellect rather than financial resources.

Whether a party's contribution is direct or indirect, monetary or non-monetary, they acquire an interest in the matrimonial property proportionate to the extent of that contribution. This conclusion is supported by section 7 of the MPA, which states that: 'subject to section 6(3), *ownership of matrimonial property* vests in the spouses *according to the contribution of either spouse* towards its *acquisition* ...'.[50] On its part, section 6(3) prescribes that 'parties to an intended marriage may enter into an agreement before their marriage to determine their property rights'.[51] Therefore, section 7 provides that, in the absence of a prenuptial agreement specifying otherwise, a spouse acquires a beneficial interest in matrimonial property proportionate to their contribution. Indeed, in *JOO v MBO*, the Supreme Court confirmed that equity favours a party who contributes, albeit indirectly, to the acquisition of marital property.[52]

2.1.3 The Time for Dividing the Property

Section 7 of the MPA prescribes that the division of the matrimonial property shall take place after the marriage ends or is declared terminated. This provision thus distinguishes between the court's role in determining the parties' respective shares and its role in the actual division of the property. The ascertainment of the spouses' proprietary rights is done under section 17 of the Act, and this can happen even when divorce proceedings are ongoing. Recently, the High Court clarified the meaning of section 7 in *AWK v PNW*.[53] The court held that, since the marriage had not yet been dissolved, the summary application for distribution was premature.[54]

About a decade ago, this court made a similar observation, but more succinctly. The court observed that it lacked jurisdiction to hear the matter because the marriage had not been dissolved nor a divorce granted.[55] In particular, the court noted that:

> The applicant seeks the division of matrimonial property. It is clear that the time for that has not come. She is not seeking *a mere declaration of her rights as contemplated by section 17* of the Act. She seeks *both declaration of her rights and the division of the property*. She has to wait for divorce, or dissolution of the marriage.[56]

---

[50] MPA (2013, s. 7) (emphasis added).

[51] MPA (2013, s. 6[3]).

[52] *JOO v MBO; FIDA Kenya and another (Amicus Curiae)* (Petition 11 of 2020) 4 KLR (KESC 2023, p. 95).

[53] *AWK v PNW* (Family Originating Summons E001 of 2023) [2024] KEHC 3970 (KLR), Judgment of 23 April 2024, para. 17.

[54] *AWK v PNW* [2024] KEHC 3970 (KLR), para. 19.

[55] *RNR v AAR* [2014] KEHC 8395 (KLR), para. 7.

[56] *RNR v AAR* [2014] KEHC 8395 (KLR), para. 5 (emphasis added).

The court was right in both *RNR* and *AWK* on the prematurity of the applications before it. However, it was too quick to abandon these applications. To develop jurisprudence to demonstrate the distinction of the courts' powers in sections 7 (division of property when marriage ends) and 17 (declaration of rights during or after marriage), the court could have invoked its inherent powers and entertained the applications in section 17 only, as Muigai J did in *CNNW v JWM*.[57] Despite the plaintiff filing her summons under section 7, the court found no evidence of the dissolution of the marriage. The court, nonetheless, declared the parties' beneficial interests in the matrimonial property and ordered actual division upon divorce.

The approach adopted by Muigai J is an available mechanism within our legal system, employed in the interest of justice. The Supreme Court in *Outa v Okello & 3 others* demonstrated how the law can be interpreted expansively to serve the ends of justice.[58] While the Supreme Court noted that the review application before it was filed out of time, it heard the application because it raised novel and weighty issues.[59]

Previously, in the 1882 Act, the courts were divided on whether their authority was limited to determining property rights or extended to the actual distribution of the property. In *Kamore v Kamore*, for instance, the Court of Appeal held that section 17 of the MPWA did not confer power on the court to distribute the contested properties. Doing so, the court observed, was to 'effectively change the title of the property from one name to another'—a move it described as a 'drastic innovation'.[60] However, two years later, in *Muthembwa v Muthembwa*, the court changed its views. It held that section 17 grants the courts 'wide and unfettered discretion' to make such orders as justice demands, including ordering the sale of property. To the court, such a definitive decision is required to resolve the dispute between the parties, who were often not on speaking terms and unlikely to reach an agreement on their own.[61]

The Court reaffirmed its position in *Muthembwa* five years later in *Echaria*, stating that it has the authority to allocate shares in the disputed property and, where necessary, to order the transfer of those shares to the identified owners to give effect to the court's decision.[62] The MPA acknowledges the court's powers in this regard but it distinguishes between the circumstances under which courts may declare beneficial interests and those in which they may distribute them. Thus, when the court pronounces that a marriage has ended, it can ascertain the parties' beneficial interests and order the distribution of these interests. However, during divorce proceedings, the court's power is limited to determining those interests.

---

[57] *CNNW v JWM* [2022] KEHC 16321 (KLR), para. 50.

[58] *Outa v Okello & 3 others* (Petition 6 of 2014) [2017] KESC 25 (KLR), para. 83.

[59] Jadeed (2023, p. 241).

[60] *Kamore v Kamore* [2000] 1 EA 80, 88–89.

[61] *Muthembwa v Muthembwa* [2002] 1 EA 186, 192.

[62] *Echaria v Echaria* [2007] eKLR.

2.1.4 Identical Individual Property Rights

While it recognises the spousal interests in marital property, the MPA also maintains the spouses' individual property rights. Section 4 of the Act provides that '…a married woman has the *same* rights as a married man—(a) to acquire, administer, hold, control, use and dispose of property, whether movable or immovable; (b) to enter into a contract; and (c) to sue and be sued in her own name'.[63] This provision reiterates spousal equality enshrined in article 45(3) and section 3(2) of the Marriage Act.[64] Although section 3(4) of theMarriage Act qualifies the spousal equality set out in section 3(2) as it pertains to Muslims,[65] section 4 of the MPA is categorical that these property rights apply identically, even when the spouses are Muslims.

The concept of married women's individual property rights (and men's) is expounded in section 13 through 16. Section 14 is discussed below under the equitable principles of trusts. This part discusses the remaining provisions. Thus, section 13 provides that marriage does not affect previous proprietary rights or the ability of a spouse to acquire, hold, or dispose of any other property during marriage. Only marital property (as defined in section 2) can be adjudged joint property. Similarly, where the parties have entered into a prenuptial agreement specifying that property owned before or during the marriage is to be treated as jointly owned, the law would treat the property as such.

In essence, section 13 echoes article 40(1) and (2) of the Constitution, which protects the right to own property. Article 40(1) reads, thus: 'subject to Article 65, every person has the right, *either individually* or in association with others, to acquire and own property (a) *of any description*; and (b) in any part of Kenya'.[66] Article 65 qualifies the part 'of any description' by limiting foreigners to leasehold titles only and for a maximum period of 99 years. Article 40(2), on its part, bars Parliament from enacting any law that permits the State or any person—

> (a) to *arbitrarily deprive* a person of property of any description or of any interest in, or right over, any property *of any description*; or
>
> (b) to *limit*, or in any way *restrict the enjoyment* of any right under this Article on the basis of any of the grounds specified or contemplated in Article 27(4).[67]

Therefore, the gist of article 40 (1) and (2) is that a person has a right to hold property on their own, whether they are married or not. Marriage does not forestall individual property rights.[68] To do so is to counter article 40(1). Similarly, no legislation can empower the courts to take away someone's proprietary interests and give them to

---

[63] MPA (2013), s. 4 (emphasis added).

[64] Section 3(2) of the Marriage Act (2014) reads that parties to a marriage 'have equal rights at the time of marriage, during the marriage and at the dissolution of the marriage.'

[65] Section 3(4) of the Marriage Act (2014) prescribes that '[S]ubject to section 3(2), the parties to an Islamic marriage shall only have the rights granted under Islamic law.'

[66] Constitution of Kenya (2010), art. 40(1) (emphasis added).

[67] Constitution of Kenya (2010), art. 40(2) (emphasis added).

[68] *Christine Nekesa Wafula v Janerose Sakina Nduguyu* [2021] KEELC 2976 (KLR), para. 47.

another just because the two are married. The term 'State' in article 40(2) includes courts because article 260 of the Constitution defines it to include judicial officers such as judges and magistrates. It also means any institution established by the Constitution, including the courts. Article 40(2) (b) further prohibits a law which would limit or restrict an individual's enjoyment of their property just because of their sex or marital status. This provision underscores the point that a man should not be deprived of or dictated to about how to employ his property just because he is a married male, even though males have a propensity for titled properties.

Meanwhile, section 15 recognises gifts shared between the spouses as an absolute property of the donee, unless the donor produces strong evidence to the contrary. In *FS v EZ*, the applicant pleaded that both the matrimonial home and car which were registered in her name belonged solely to her. The applicant argued that the respondent had bought her the car as a 31st birthday present and had told everyone about it. She also identified the matrimonial home, signed its sale agreement, received the purchase payments from the respondent, and remitted them to the vendor while the respondent was abroad. The respondent denied gifting either of the properties to his wife. He indicated that the house was registered in her name because he was outside Kenya at the time of its purchase. The High Court agreed with the respondent that both properties were meant for the common use of the parties. The Court noted that the applicant failed to produce any written evidence to support her claim. She also presented no witnesses, despite her claim that the respondent told everyone that the car was a gift to her. Also, the parties lived together in the matrimonial home. The Court ultimately found that the matrimonial home and the vehicle, were not gifts as claimed. If the applicant had provided the requisite evidence, she may have succeeded in obtaining a separate indefeasible title to the car under section 15.

Section 16 prescribes that marriage does not make a spouse liable for debts incurred by the other spouse before the union. This provision augments the elaborate section 10, which provides for spousal liability. Section 10(1) reiterates section 16. However, section 10(2) qualifies these dual prescriptions by stating that if that liability was reasonably and justifiably incurred and the property subsequently becomes matrimonial, the spouses shall share the liability equally. Nevertheless, this outcome can be avoided if the parties enter into a prenuptial agreement that suggests otherwise. Section 10(3) also mandates parties to share equally any liability or reasonable and justifiable expenses incurred during marriage for the benefit of the marriage.

2.1.5 Equitable Principles of Trust

As part of protecting individual property rights, the MPA creates presumptions of interests for a non-holding spouse. Section 14(a) establishes a rebuttable presumption that when property is acquired during marriage and registered in one spouse's name, that spouse holds it in trust for the other. A rebuttable presumption means that the law infers the assumption as factual unless the holding spouse tenders strong and weighty evidence to the contrary.[69] They must prove that there was no intention at the time of acquiring the property that it would be owned jointly or that it would become family property.[70] Section 93 of the Land Registration Act (LRA), which deals with land property, also supports the MPA provisions on trusts.[71] It reads that when a spouse acquires an interest in land during marriage that is intended for the 'co-ownership and use by both or more spouses,' the property will be deemed matrimonial property and shall be governed by the MPA.

It is worth noting that both section 14(a) and section 93 reiterate the pre-2014 position.[72] Under the 1882 MWPA regime, the Court of Appeal upheld the common law doctrine of resulting trusts without hesitation, even in the *Echaria* case, except that in that case, the court insisted that contributions had to be financial.[73] It is important to note that if section 14(a) infers ownership of a property to a non-holding spouse, it means that this spouse has a right to move the court to prevent the holding spouse from disposing of the property.[74] Only then would the court determine if the presumption still applies, and if so, whether it prevents the disposal of the entire property or the interest of the non-holding spouse.

This is exactly what happened in *ENM v SNM & another*.[75] The plaintiff sought a declaration that the matrimonial home, which was registered in the first defendant's name, was held in trust for her. Therefore, she subsequently prayed for an injunction to restrain both defendants from disposing of the property. The second defendant had since bought the property from the first defendant and registered it jointly in his name and his wife's. The court found that the property was a matrimonial home because both the plaintiff and the first defendant were named in the sale agreement, jointly built the house, and lived there. The court also found that the plaintiff acquired spousal rights over the property because, though her 'financial contribution could not be quantified, being a wife, she must have contributed to the welfare and upkeep of the family'.[76] The court, however, noted that, since the second defendant was an innocent purchaser for value without notice, his title was indefeasible. Therefore, the court ordered the first defendant to share identically with the plaintiff the income generated from another property he had bought with the proceeds of the matrimonial home. The court also ordered a rectification of the title of this new property to reflect the names of both the plaintiff and the first defendant.

---

69 *Mary Njoki v John Kinyanjui Mutheru* [1985] eKLR, p. 16.

70 Nyamu-Musembi (2002, p. 238).

71 Gaafar (2014, p. 6).

72 *Tabitha Wangechi Nderitu v Simon Nderitu Kariuki* [1998] eKLR, p. 2–3. While the MPA was enacted in 2013, it became operational in January 2014.

73 *Echaria v Echaria* [2007] eKLR, p. 11.

74 MPA (2013, s. 12(2)).

75 *ENM v SNM & another* [2017] eKLR.

76 *ENM v SNM & another* [2017] eKLR, p. 10.

2.1.6 Protection of Marital Property Interests

In addition to prescribing the rights and liabilities of spouses to marital property, the MPA protects the property from alienation by one spouse or a third party, such as a bank. This protection stems from the constitutional call in article 68(c)(iii) for Parliament to enact a law for the '*recognition* and *protection* of matrimonial property *and in particular* the matrimonial home' during the marriage and at its dissolution.[77] Thus, under section 12(1), a party to a monogamous marriage cannot dispose of marital property, whether through a sale, a gift, a lease, or a mortgage, without the consent of the other. In *ENM v SNM & another*, the court found that the matrimonial home was not legally sold to the second defendant because the first defendant did not obtain the consent of his wife, the plaintiff.[78] The first defendant had his subsequent wife provide the consent; however, since he was married to the plaintiff under a monogamous regime, he had no capacity to contract a further marriage.[79]

Section 12(5) of the MPA, as well as sections 79(3) and 105 of the Land Act, offer particular protection to the matrimonial home. Section 12(5) stipulates that the matrimonial home can only be mortgaged or leased if both spouses provide written and informed consent. Section 79(3) concentrates on charges and prescribes that a matrimonial home will only be charged if both spouses execute the application or the charge itself. Meanwhile, section 105 empowers the courts to open a charge, notwithstanding its value, secured on a matrimonial property if the interests of justice dictate so.

Therefore, in consonance with these provisions, where both spouses consent to a mortgage, for example, courts are hesitant to stop the statutory sale of such property by banks on the guise that it is matrimonial. In *Wilstone Mwawugunga v Kenya Women Microfinance Bank*, the High Court observed that 'by charging their matrimonial property willingly, the applicant and his family, in this case the wife, lifted the protection vail (sic) and therefore converted the property into a trading commodity'.[80]

Though the consent provisions have been widely praised, some concerns have also been raised. First, some argue that a plain reading of section 12(1) suggests protection for monogamous relationships only. Yet a sizeable number of women in rural areas are in polygynous marriages, and it is in these latter relationships that 'power dynamics are more complicated'.[81] Second, it is also suggested that both the MPA and the Land Act assume that wives will willingly consent to such transactions without coercion, duping, or pressure from the husband, his family, and/or society. The situation is said to worsen when the wife's education level is lower.[82]

---

[77] Constitution of Kenya (2010), art. 68(c)(iii) (emphasis added).

[78] *ENM v SNM & another* [2017] eKLR, p. 11.

[79] The first defendant had been married under the African Christian Marriage Act which recognises monogamous marriages only.

[80] *Wilstone Mdindi Mwawugunga v Kenya Women MicrofinanceBank* [2022] eKLR, para. 29.

[81] Kameri-Mbote and Muriungi (2016, p. 94).

[82] Kameri-Mbote and Muriungi (2016, pp. 94–95).

These are genuine concerns. In *EKN v AS & 2 others*, the Environment and Land Court held the same view that Parliament did not provide for spousal consent in polygynous marriages.[83] However, the court proceeded by analogy, holding that if consent is required from monogamous spouses, it is likewise required from all spouses in a polygynous marriage, although such consent cannot be unreasonably withheld due to greed or jealousy. The court also opined that in some unique situations, such as serious illness rendering a spouse incapable of giving consent, a party may apply to the court to dispense with this requirement.[84]

This court's rendition is apt, but seemingly, the court jumped to quick conclusions. Yes, section 12(1) addresses monogamous marriages only. But a reading of section 12(2), which recognises identical rights to parties in either a monogamous or polygynous marriage to lodge a caveat, a caution, or such other instrument to forestall alienation of an interest in matrimonial property, supposes the need for consent in polygynous relationships. It just so happens that this consent is restricted to the man and the specific wife who has an interest in that particular matrimonial property. This is exactly what section 8(1)(b) and (2) of the MPA points to.[85]

The instances of coercion, pressure, and taking advantage of a woman's low level of education or understanding in property matters are real. However, Parliament has provided numerous mechanisms to void any transaction that arises from these methods. A wife may act independently of her husband to register a caution, caveat, or restriction on the title. She can move the court to vitiate a charge under section 105 of the Land Act. These moves might bring friction in the family. However, spousal consent is a reasonable first line of protection against the arbitrary alienation of marital property.

The other protection for matrimonial property interests is against eviction. Section 12(3) prohibits a spouse from evicting the other from the matrimonial home except by the court's order. This provision reduces homelessness. A party can leave the matrimonial home voluntarily or after a court process. This provision particularly favours women who, together with their children, are traditional occupiers of the matrimonial home and risk being rendered homeless if the husband were to chase them from the house because of a disagreement, a new relationship, or such other reasons. In many instances, however, courts have been inclined to allow the spouse occupying the matrimonial home to continue residing there whenever marital property is divided.[86] Meanwhile, section 12(4) allows for the eviction of a spouse from matrimonial property by a third party only in three specific instances: first, if the party is a liquidation manager; second, if the party has sold an interest in the home

[83] *EKN v AS & 2 others* [2019] eKLR, para. 28.

[84] *EKN v AS & 2 others* [2019] eKLR, para. 33–36.

[85] Section 8 of the Matrimonial Property Act addresses how matrimonial property is to be distributed upon the dissolution of a polygamous marriage. Property acquired before polygamy is retained equally by the man and the first wife, while property acquired afterward is shared among all parties according to their contribution—unless a separate property arrangement was agreed upon between the husband and any wife.

[86] See *Kivuitu v Kivuitu* [1991] KLR 248 and *FS v EZ* [2016] eKLR.

pursuant to a court order; and third, if the party is a financial institution exercising its statutory power of sale.

2.2 The Islamic Marital Property Law

Apart from laying out the mainstream law, the MPA further introduces Islamic marital property law. This is evident in section 3, which reads that 'a person who professes the Islamic faith *may* be governed by Islamic law in all matters relating to matrimonial property'.[87] This prescription creates a choice for Muslims to employ Islamic law instead of the MPA's substantive provisions. The wording is 'may' and not 'shall'. So contrary to criticisms,[88] section 3 does not oust Muslim women from the MPA. The High Court was, therefore, partly correct and partly incorrect in *AWA v HDD* when it pronounced that section 3 introduces Islamic law but does not confine it to a particular forum.[89] The court correctly indicated that a marital property dispute can be handled by either the Kadhis' courts or the mainstream ones. It was, however, incorrect to direct that either court must employ Islamic law. Instead, the choice of both the forum and the law is the parties'.

Even then, the concept of marital property law is foreign to Islam.[90] Put differently, Islamic law does not treat property ownership inside a marriage dissimilarly from property ownership outside marriage. The tenets remain the same and determine individual property rights. While it is possible to have communal ownership of property in a marriage, the interests therein would, nonetheless, be distinct for every party. Thus, joint ownership of property, whether a matrimonial home or in general, emanates from the spouse's direct financial contributions. A beneficial interest in property acquired during marriage does not arise by operation of law, as it does in the case of equitable trusts. Where a party acquires property, however, and the other improves it, the interest of such other party in the property is limited to their financial investment. This Islamic standpoint is equivalent to the dictates of section 7 of the MPA.

On the other hand, if a spouse makes an indirect financial contribution, such as paying for other household needs, they must clearly express their intention. Are these payments voluntary and charitable, or does the spouse expect reimbursement at some point? Regardless of how substantial the payments are, they will follow the intent of the person making them. However, such payments will not grant the spouse a beneficial interest in the property acquired by the other.

Islamic law further treats non-monetary contributions differently. While some roles can be compensated, others are considered the bona fide duties of a wife and

---

[87] MPA (2013, s. 3) (emphasis added).

[88] See IDLO and UN Women (2024, pp. 39–40) and Human Rights Watch and FIDA-Kenya (2020, pp. 24–25).

[89] *AWA v HDD* [2018] eKLR, p. 2.

[90] Jadeed (2020, p. 109).

mother. Yet still, even those compensated roles would be confined to their equivalent monetary value, unless a spouse chooses to reward the homemaker beyond that amount. The demarcation of compensable and non-compensable non-financial contributions is discernible from both the *Qur'an* and the Prophetic sayings.[91] The *Qur'an* defines marriage as one of the signs of God, whose purpose is to provide tranquillity for the parties.[92] It is also an avenue for procreation.[93] Thus, unlike section 2 of the MPA, courts applying Islamic law shall not regard pregnancy and companionship as forms of indirect contribution to the properties acquired by the husband.

At least two Prophetic sayings are relevant in this discourse on marital property. The first one relates to responsibilities in a society. It partly reads that 'beware everyone is a shepherd and everyone is answerable with regard to his flock (…) A woman is a *guardian over the household of her husband and his children* and shall be questioned about them (as to how she managed the household and brought up the children)…'.[94] The second is about the Prophet's daughter's request for a helper in domestic chores. When she heard that her father had received some female prisoners of war, Fatma asked for one as a maid because she was exhausted and had pains in her hands resulting from the 'hand mill and from grinding' flour.[95] The Prophet told Fatma and her husband that he would teach them something better than the maid's help. He taught them to say Allah Akbar (God is Great) 34 times; alhamdulillah (Praise God) 33 times; and subhana'Allah (Glorified be God) 33 times when they go to bed.

These two sayings show that cooking and caring for a husband and children are part of a wife's role. They may thus not fit in section 2 as part of a non-monetary contribution. Generally, however, Islam will consider the '*urf* (ie, the tradition) of the locality to establish whether these chores are customarily done by wives. If the answer is affirmative, then such chores will be regarded as a married woman's duty. If not, it becomes the husband's duty to get a helper to provide such services. Such an assessment also extends to farm work. However, the management of the family business is a financial contribution. Ordinarily, courts would seek to establish whether the spouse is doing so as an employee (i.e., a manager) or a business partner. In the first scenario, the spouse should draw a salary from the business. And if this is not paid, it remains a debt to the business. In the second scenario, there must be evidence that the spouse contributed to the business's capital.

---

[91] This is known in Arabic as *hadith*, plural *ahaadeeth*.

[92] See Qur'an 30:21 and see also Qur'an 2:187 which metaphorically describes men and women as each other's clothing. The first and second numbers to Qur'anic citations refer to a chapter and a verse respectively.

[93] See Qur'an 4:1 and Qur'an 49:13 which draw the genesis of humankind from Adam and Eve; Qur'an 2:223 identifies women as men's 'tilth'. See also Ali (2001, p. 90).

[94] *Sahih Muslim*, Book 33, Hadith 24.

[95] Al'Bukhari (2007, p. 608).

2.3 Customary Law

In addition to recognising Islamic marital property law, the MPA also permits the application of customary law. Section 11 reads that: 'during the division of matrimonial property between and among spouses, *the customary law of the communities in question* shall, subject to the values and principles of the Constitution, be taken into account'.[96] This provision further identifies some of the applicable customary law tenets as: the law on divorce and termination of a marriage; protection of the rights of future generations to community and ancestral land; and the principles on access and utilisation of ancestral land by a wife or wives or a former wife or former wives. Equally important are section 8 and 6(2) of the MPA. Section 8 is a schema on the property rights of spouses in polygamous marriages. Generally, property acquired by the man and his first wife belongs to both spouses equally; where another wife(ves) joins the union, the property is owned between the man and his wives based on the contributions of each of the parties. Section 6(2) of the Act further excludes property under a customary trust from being regarded as marital property. In *Kiebia v M'lintari & another*,[97] the Supreme Court defined property subject to a customary trust—which is often land[98]—as that land which was before registration in the name of one or more group members and 'always reserved for family or clan uses, such as burials, and other traditional rites'.[99] It could also be that land which was 'reserved for various future uses, such as construction of houses and other amenities by youths graduating into manhood'.[100] The Court was, however, categorical that each case will be determined on its own merit because 'not every claim of a right to land will qualify as a customary trust'.[101] To the Court, what is crucial is:

> the nature of the holding of the land and the intention of the parties. If the said holding is for the benefit of other members of the family, then a customary trust would be presumed to have been created in favour of such other members, whether or not they are in possession or actual occupation of the land.[102]

According to the 2019 Census, Kenya has over 41 ethnic communities.[103] Each of these communities has its own rules of dividing matrimonial property, which are also unwritten. While it is difficult for lawyers and judicial officers to know all these

---

[96] MPA (2013, s. 11) (emphasis added).

[97] *Kiebia v M'lintari & another (Petition 10 of 2015)* [2018] KESC 22 (KLR) (5 October 2018) (Judgment).

[98] Fila et al. (2025, p. 141).

[99] *Kiebia v M'lintari & another (Petition 10 of 2015)* [2018] KESC 22 (KLR) (5 October 2018) (Judgment), para 52.

[100] *Kiebia v M'lintari & another (Petition 10 of 2015)* [2018] KESC 22 (KLR) (5 October 2018) (Judgment).

[101] *Kiebia v M'lintari & another (Petition 10 of 2015)* [2018] KESC 22 (KLR) (5 October 2018) (Judgment).

[102] *Kiebia v M'lintari & another (Petition 10 of 2015)* [2018] KESC 22 (KLR) (5 October 2018) (Judgment).

[103] Kenya National Bureau of Statistics (2019, pp. 423–424).

unwritten customary laws, section 3(2) of the Judicature Act instructs judicial officers to learn about these laws through assessors, expert witnesses, authoritative literature, and judicial notice before making a decision.[104]

Importantly, however, the recognition of these customary law tenets does not oust the application of the MPA. Section 11 simply invokes the consideration of such tenets, such that if these customary laws are in sync with the values and principles of the Constitution, they become the decisive law in a case. Where these customary laws contravene the values and principles of the Constitution, however, the MPA provisions override. The relevant constitutional values and principles are listed in article 10(2)(b), and they include human dignity, equity, social justice, equality, human rights, and non-discrimination.[105]

Some, nonetheless, read this recognition of customary law as a retrograde step in the fight for women's equality,[106] because most customary law seems to discriminate against women by denying them rights to land and matrimonial property.[107] While it is true that the law of some ethnic communities short-changes women, there is a gradual move towards greater equality within these communities and in the courts.[108] Courts are increasingly discounting customary laws which perpetuate discrimination against women.[109] And this is the exact call of section 11, which subjects the consideration of customary law to constitutional values and principles.

In fact, the MPA's inclusion of customary law is not intended to entrench inequalities between the spouses, but to celebrate the law as part of the laws in Kenya. There are still positive aspects to many Kenyan ethnic mores. It is the design of the 2010 constitutional dispensation to restore customary law to its former glory, which was tainted during and immediately after the colonial period. The drafters of the 2010 Constitution lamented this past ill-treatment of the law.[110] That is why they put a provision in the Constitution which values culture.[111] The specific mention of the law in article 2(4) of the Constitution (which voids any law that contravenes the Constitution) is not to disparage it, but to acclaim it as a *bona fide* law in this territory. Similarly, the constitutional recognition of the colonial repugnancy clause in article 159(3) of the Constitution is not an extension of the subjugation of the law to the Victorian mores. Rather, it reflects the identity of an open and democratic society captured in constitutional values and principles, and in article 24(1) of the Constitution (which describes the limitations of the Bill of Rights).

---

[104] See Civil Procedure Act (Cap. 21, Laws of Kenya), s. 87(1) and Evidence Act (Cap. 80, Laws of Kenya), ss. 51, 52, 60(2), (3).

[105] Constitution of Kenya (2010), art. 10(2)(b).

[106] Chan and Mbogoh (2016, pp. 20–21).

[107] Kameri-Mbote and Muriungi (2016, 80).

[108] See Jadeed (2020, p. 220).

[109] *Murungi Kanampiu v Carmen Ithiru Njagi & another* [2016] eKLR.

[110] Constitution of Kenya Review Commission (2003, p. 92).

[111] Constitution of Kenya (2010, arts. 11, 44).

2.4 *Void Marriages, Presumed Marriages, and Property Rights*

When the court declares a marriage invalid or inexistent, it treats related property claims as ordinary property disputes. This conclusion is derived from the recent Supreme Court decision of *MNK v POM* (hereinafter *Mayaka*).[112] After dismissing the claim for a presumed marriage between the parties, the court observed that proprietary interests of cohabitants or former cohabitants are determined by ordinary property rules which apply to strangers.[113] The court reasoned that this approach is necessitated by the fact that the special matrimonial property rules do not extend to cohabiting couples.[114]

According to the Court, such ordinary rules include the law on resulting trusts in cases where the property is registered in the name of one party only. Resulting trusts enable a claimant to acquire an interest in the subject property through the operation of the law. The common intention of the parties that each shall own the property for their common benefit, for example, an intention to make the property a family home or business at the time of purchase, is 'sufficient to give rise to a trust'.[115] According to the Court, this intention is evinced from the conduct of the parties such as contributing to the purchase of the property and/or defraying general housekeeping expenses, such as electricity or water bills.[116]

The presumption of marriage applies in Kenya, but its application is increasingly being called into question. The Supreme Court has explained in *Mayaka* that the presumption should only be applied sparingly.[117] The Court observed that: '…that *the doctrine of presumption of marriage is on its deathbed,* of which reasoning is reinforced by the changes to the matrimonial laws in Kenya.…*[T]his presumption should only be used sparingly* where there is cogent evidence to buttress it'.[118] The Court emphasised that the presumption was not the rule, but rather the exception.[119] Before reaching this conclusion, however, the Court laid down what it termed 'strict parameters' within which a presumption of marriage can be deduced. These are:

a. The parties must have lived together for a long period of time.
b. The parties must have the legal right or capacity to marry.
c. The parties must have intended to marry.
d. There must be consent by both parties.

---

[112] *MNK v POM; Initiative for Strategic Litigation in Africa (ISLA) (Amicus Curiae) (Petition 9 of 2021)* [2023] KESC 2 (KLR).

[113] *MNK v POM* [2023] KESC 2 (KLR), para. 81.

[114] *MNK v POM* [2023] KESC 2 (KLR), para. 81–82.

[115] *MNK v POM* [2023] KESC 2 (KLR), para. 85.

[116] *MNK v POM* [2023] KESC 2 (KLR), para. 85, 88.

[117] See *MNK v POM* [2023] KESC 2 (KLR), para. 65–70.

[118] *MNK v POM* [2023] KESC 2 (KLR), para. 65, emphasis added.

[119] *MNK v POM* [2023] KESC 2 (KLR), para. 70, emphasis Court's own.

e. The parties must have held themselves out to the outside world as being a married couple.
f. The onus of proving the presumption is on the party who alleges it.
g. The evidence to rebut the presumption has to be strong, distinct, satisfactory and conclusive.
h. The standard of proof is on a balance of probabilities.[120]

The court also noted the increasing number of interdependent relationships, that is, long-term 'relationships where couples cohabit with no intention whatsoever of contracting a marriage',[121] and warned against inferring a presumption of marriage in such situations.[122] It called upon Parliament and the Attorney-General to enact a law which spells out the rights and obligations of cohabitees in such relationships.[123]

Therefore, regardless of the nature of the relationship, courts must establish the parties' proprietary rights.[124] For instance, although it did not find a presumed marriage in *Mayaka,* the Supreme Court commended both the Court of Appeal and the High Court for determining the parties' property rights.[125] In a nutshell, if a relationship is presumed to be a marriage, the MPA applies; the interests of the parties in the contested property are adjudged according to their contributions, direct or indirect, financial or in kind, to its purchase or development.[126] Where the property is registered in the name of one partner, there is a rebuttable presumption that the property was held in trust for the other partner.[127] Unless the defendant proves that the property is not matrimonial or that the claimant's contribution was disproportionate, the courts often order an identical division of property between the parties.[128] Where the court finds that there is no presumption of marriage, as in *Mayaka,* courts would divide the property according to ordinary property law.

3 Controversies About the MPA

In addition to the contestations against the recognition of both customary and Islamic laws, critics have also challenged some provisions of the statutory mainstream law. These include section 6 (meaning of matrimonial property); section 7 (ownership based on contribution); and section 2 (recognition of non-monetary contribution like domestic work). This section now presents these criticisms and their alternative views.

---

[120] *MNK v POM* [2023] KESC 2 (KLR), para. 64, emphasis Court's own.
[121] *MNK v POM* [2023] KESC 2 (KLR), para. 66.
[122] *MNK v POM* [2023] KESC 2 (KLR), para. 67.
[123] *MNK v POM* [2023] KESC 2 (KLR), para. 69.
[124] *MNK v POM* [2023] KESC 2 (KLR), para. 76.
[125] *MNK v POM* [2023] KESC 2 (KLR), para. 76.
[126] See MPA (2013, s. 7).
[127] See MPA (2013), s. 14(a).
[128] See *ENM v SNM & another* [2017] eKLR.

3.1 The Meaning of Matrimonial Property

As stated in section 2,the MPA also defines matrimonial property as 'any other immovable property and movable property *jointly owned and acquired during* the subsistence of the marriage'.[129] This definition is found in section 6(1)(c). But critics have attacked this part of section 6 for being insensitive to women. They contend that this clause entrenches the status quo of men's continued land ownership monopoly. Critics argue that in many Kenyan communities, women are often viewed as having transient kinship ties,[130] meaning that daughters rarely inherit their father's land, which typically passes to sons.[131] The MPA, they suggest, perpetuates women's landlessness because sons marry and solely retain such property without a legal requirement to convert the property to matrimonial property.[132]

Critics further opine that the Act entrenches separate property ownership of land (including family land) if it is acquired by the husband and registered in his name only.[133] To critics, this arrangement risks disposal of the land by the husband at will, even when that land is the family's only source of livelihood.[134] Since a majority of Kenyan women are homemakers and/or spend a significant portion of their time in reproductive labour, the critics argue that it is difficult for such women to acquire property jointly with their husbands.[135] The husbands, typically engaged in monetised work, are often the ones able to afford real or tangible property.

Undoubtedly, these are genuine concerns. However, a continued reading of the Act and other related statutes alleviates these discomforts. First, section 7 states that courts can infer ownership if a spouse has contributed to its acquisition. As mentioned earlier, section 2 defines contributions as both monetary and non-monetary.[136] section 2 also provides examples of these non-financial contributions, and it explicitly states that the list is not exhaustive.[137] These types of non-monetary contributions are characteristic of the roles traditionally undertaken by Kenyan wives, as depicted by the Court of Appeal in *Kivuitu v Kivuitu*.[138] It is untrue that section 6 seeks to deny Kenyan wives joint ownership or acquisition of properties with their husbands. Where

---

[129] MPA (2013, s. 2) (emphasis added).

[130] For example, the Luhya, the Taita, the Ameru, the Agikuyu, the Pokomo, the Borana and the Orma. See Jadeed (2020, pp. 149–50) and Chan and Mbogoh (2016).

[131] See generally Jadeed (2020, pp. 153–161) for a discussion on the impact of this concept on women's property rights.

[132] Kameri-Mbote and Muriungi (2016, p. 93).

[133] Kameri-Mbote and Muriungi (2016, p. 93).

[134] Kameri-Mbote and Muriungi (2016, p. 72).

[135] Kameri-Mbote and Muriungi (2016, p. 93).

[136] *EMN v NM* [2018] eKLR, para. 21.

[137] MPA (2013, s. 2). See also Constitution of Kenya (2010), art. 259(4)(b) which instructs that where the term "includes" is used in statutory definitions, it implies that the list is illustrative, not exhaustive.

[138] *Kivuitu v Kivuitu* [1991] KLR 248.

a wife or former wife misses out on the title deed, she can prove her contribution (financial and/or non-financial) to gain an interest in the land.

Aside from the touted limitations of section 6, the remaining concerns about the identity of matrimonial property seem to relate to its exclusion of trust property and the acceptance of prenuptial agreements that demarcate the spouses' matrimonial property.[139] The argument has often been made that recognising prenuptial agreements gives future spouses, especially husbands, an opportunity to exclude tangible property from matrimonial property. And that the power imbalances between men and women, as well as the economic and educational disparities between them, may tilt the agreements in favour of husbands.[140] In the long run, if at all, women will only have access to less important properties. This argument is plausible, as this otherwise bold attempt to respect individual property rights under article 40 could be exploited in ways that ultimately undermine the peaceful enjoyment of property during marriage. The MPA, however, has provided solutions to such an occurrence. Section 6(4) permits a spouse to approach the court to set aside the agreement if the claimant can prove that the agreement 'was influenced by fraud, coercion, or is manifestly unjust'.

The removal of trust land from matrimonial property, on the other hand, has also generated some criticism. The exclusion, it is suggested, omits inherited customary land or other extended family land that a husband may be holding, including that on which the matrimonial home is built.[141] Therefore, upon divorce, women leave empty-handed because they cannot claim this family land.[142] For clarity, section 6(2) reads that 'trust property, *including* property held in trust under customary law, does not form part of matrimonial property'.[143]

The identity of trust property in the MPA is much broader than suggested. It deals with all trust properties; the ancestral land is just one of them. A trust simply confers on the trustee an interest in land, but the trustee holds that interest on behalf of the person creating the trust (the settlor) for the benefit of others (the beneficiaries),[144] sometimes including himself. Therefore, even if the property is registered in the trustee's name, the trustee cannot transfer it to another person to the detriment of the beneficiaries. Doing so is in breach of their trusteeship.[145] In this same vein, a spouse holding title in trust, whether under customary or such other law, cannot pass it as matrimonial property. This is not their property, and one cannot give that which they do not own.

---

[139] MPA (2013), s. 6(2) and 6(3).

[140] Kameri-Mbote and Muriungi (2016, pp. 94–95).

[141] Chan and Mbogoh (2016, pp. 19).

[142] Human Rights Watch and FIDA-Kenya (2020, p. 28).

[143] Human Rights Watch and FIDA-Kenya (2020, p. 28) (emphasis added).

[144] Garner (ed) (2006, p. 734).

[145] *Stephens & 6 others v Stephens & another* [1987] eKLR, p. 4.

3.2 *Linkage of Ownership to Contribution*

As discussed in section II above, section 7 of the MPA predicates a spouse's interest in marital property on their contribution. But some women's rights advocates have raised direct and indirect challenges to section 7. First, section 7 departs from the spousal equality stipulated in the Constitution and ratified human rights treaties.[146] Second, this provision fails to guide courts in quantifying domestic work when assessing contributions.[147] For these reasons, critics have called for the repeal of section 7 and its subsequent substitution with a provision that espouses spousal equality in property division.[148]

3.2.1 Addressing the Difficulties in Quantifying Domestic Work

Critics first challenge section 7 for its inability to guide the courts on how to quantify non-financial contribution, particularly domestic work. Indeed, courts have acknowledged that, despite its significance in a home, domestic work is often non-monetised.[149] The courts have thus surmised that if this work were to be reduced to monetary terms, women's non-financial contributions in the home would be greater than those of men.[150] Thus, in *AWM v JGK*, for instance, the High Court found that the wife's non-monetary contribution to the home was higher than that of the husband.[151] The court considered both her non-financial and financial contributions and ultimately awarded her a 50% beneficial interest in the matrimonial properties, exceeding the 37% share claimed by the husband.[152]

Courts have further attached monetary value to the reproductive labour done by women. Based on the scale of justice, it is not difficult to estimate this non-financial contribution given the peculiar facts of each case. In *MW v AN*, the court surmised that a woman's pregnancy, childbirth, and care counted during the division of marital property.[153] The court also discounted the common Kenyan belief that stay-at-home mums do not work. To the court, 'it is unfair and unjust for one party to be busy just making their money (the 'seen' income) while the other is doing two or three other jobs in the family whose income is 'unseen' and then claim this other one did

---

[146] See IDLO and UN Women (2024, p. 39) and FIDA v Attorney General & another [2018] eKLR, paras. 5–6, 8, 15.

[147] Human Rights Watch and FIDA-Kenya (2020, p. 16).

[148] IDLO and UN Women (2024, p. 40) and UN Committee on the Elimination of all forms of Discrimination Against Women (2017, para. 55).

[149] *AWM v JGK* [2021] eKLR, p. 7 and *MW v AN* [2021] eKLR, paras. 38–39.

[150] See *AWM v JGK* [2021] eKLR, p. 7. See also United Nations Development Programme (1995, pp. 97–98) which indicates that then global value of unpaid work was $16 trillion and women's share was $11 trillion.

[151] *AWM v JGK* [2021] eKLR, p. 7 (emphasis added).

[152] *AWM v JGK* [2021] eKLR, p. 10.

[153] *MW v AN* [2021] eKLR, para. 38.

nothing'.[154] Thus, taking into account that the wife solely cared for and sheltered the children after separation and had previously taken loans to help acquire and develop the matrimonial home, the court awarded her a 50% beneficial interest in the property.

In *EMN v NM*, the court found that the wife made no financial contribution towards the purchase of the different pieces of land. However, she managed the family farm, cared for their children, and gave her husband moral support during their over twenty-year marriage. To the court, these roles were sufficient contributions because they enabled the husband 'to enjoy the comfort and offered a stress-free atmosphere that enhanced his mental and physical capacity to invest, caring less about his ten children since the plaintiff had taken the responsibility'.[155] The court, thus, awarded the wife a 45% beneficial interest in all the properties.

An in-depth look at this post-2013 jurisprudence reveals that courts apply the maxim 'equality is equity' to recognise a former spouse's non-monetary contribution. As the Supreme Court in *JOO v MBO*[156] observed, any substantial direct or indirect contribution is significant.[157] This includes 'contributing to the running of and welfare of the home and easing the burden of the spouse paying for the property'; and 'caring for children and the family at large as the other spouse works to earn money to pay for the property'.[158] To the courts, where both the money-earner and the homemaker and child-carer have contributed identically to the family, their interests are the same.[159] Where a spouse has contributed nothing '(financially or in-kind) to the acquisition of the property',[160] their interest is nil because marriage alone does not confer proprietary rights.

It is based on this same maxim that courts recognise that, often, both parties to a marriage contribute to the welfare of the family.[161] Where this is the case, the courts may apply a rebuttable presumption that if a property is registered in the name of one spouse, then the registered owner holds the property in trust for the other spouse in an unspecified share, which the non-holding spouse must prove. When property is registered in both names, it is presumed to be held in identical shares. However, a party claiming a larger share may present strong evidence demonstrating that, under the circumstances, identical division would be unfair and unconscionable.[162]

The application of this maxim was well explained in *Echaria*.[163] In *Echaria*, the Court of Appeal recalled the application of this maxim in the English case of *Gissing v Gissing* by the House of Lords.[164] While considering the share of a woman who had

[154] *MW v AN* [2021] eKLR, para. 39.

[155] *EMN v NM* [2018] eKLR, *para.* 20.

[156] *JOO v MBO* (Petition 11 of 2020) 4 KLR (KESC 2023).

[157] *JOO v MBO* (Petition 11 of 2020) 4 KLR (KESC 2023), para. 95.

[158] *JOO v MBO* (Petition 11 of 2020) 4 KLR (KESC 2023).

[159] *JOO v MBO* (Petition 11 of 2020) 4 KLR (KESC 2023), para. 96.

[160] *JOO v MBO* (Petition 11 of 2020) 4 KLR (KESC 2023), para. 100 citing Nkhata.

[161] *JOO v MBO* (Petition 11 of 2020) 4 KLR (KESC 2023), para. 103.

[162] *JOO v MBO* (Petition 11 of 2020) 4 KLR (KESC 2023), para. 102.

[163] *Echaria v Echaria* [2007] eKLR.

[164] See *Gissing v Gissing* [1970] 2 All ER 780.

made a substantial but unascertainable contribution to a property registered in the husband's name, the House of Lords employed this maxim to give her identical rights. But the Court added that if 'it is plain, that the contributing spouse has contributed about one-quarter, I do not think *it is helpful or right* for the court to feel obliged *to award either one-half or nothing*'.[165]

This maxim of 'equality is equity' has since been captured by section 14 of the MPA. Incidentally, the same principle was inferred in *Kivuitu v Kivuitu* to assess a wife's non-financial contribution.[166] And the Court of Appeal, four years later, adopted it in *Muthembwa v Muthembwa*. While acknowledging that it was impractical to quantify a couple's respective contributions to the management of a home,[167] the court found that the presumption that the properties registered in the name of the husband were held in trust for the wife had not been rebutted. If anything, the evidence showed that the wife had made a substantial contribution to the acquisition of the property. The court, thus, declined to reduce her share to 10% as pleaded by the husband and upheld the High Court's assessment of 50%.

So, while there may be no strict formula for computing domestic work, the Supreme Court has offered guidance in *JOO v MBO* (Petition 11 of 2020) 4 KLR (KESC 2023). After analysing article 45(3) at length, the court concluded that 'therefore, in the event that a marriage breaks down, the function of any court is to make *a fair and equitable division* of the acquired matrimonial property guided by the provisions of article 45(3) of Constitution'.[168] Put differently, in the case of non-monetary contribution, there must be a substantial contribution by a party to the acquisition of the marital property.[169] It is not enough for the courts to award identical shares merely because the property was acquired during marriage, either in the name of one spouse or both. Such an approach is a wrong application of section 14.[170] The courts must hear the opposing voice keenly. If their evidence dissuades an award of the same rights, it must be upheld. Doing so would uphold the sanctity of property ownership.

3.2.2 Equality Does Not Mean a 50:50 Split

The other contestation, which challenges section 7 as contravening spousal equality, misreads the law because the equality provisions in the Constitution, that is, articles 27 (general equality clause) and 45(3) (spousal equality), do not always stipulate identical treatment of men and women, whether inside or outside wedlock. To this

---

[165] Pearson, LJ in *Gissing v Gissing* [1970] 2 All ER 780, p. 788 (emphasis added).

[166] See *Kivuitu v Kivuitu* [1991] KLR 248, 259.

[167] *Muthembwa v Muthembwa* [2002] 1 EA 186, 194.

[168] *JOO v MBO* (Petition 11 of 2020) 4 KLR (KESC 2023) para 104 (emphasis added).

[169] See *AWM v JGK* [2021] eKLR, p. 10.

[170] *FS v EZ* [2016] eKLR, p. 6.

extent, section 7 does not depart from either article 45(3) or 27 as alleged.[171] Instead, it explains these constitutional provisions as they relate to marital property.[172] That is, a claimant must plead specific contributions, and if the court is convinced, it will award rights commensurate with those contributions, without overriding any established property ownership laws.[173] Simply put, while article 45(3) enshrines marriage as 'a partnership of equals',[174] marriage in itself does not confer proprietary rights.[175] The court must act fairly and in accordance with conscience by evaluating each party's contribution, whether direct or indirect.[176] It must be stressed that the court cannot divest a party of their existing property rights by the fact of marriage only.[177]

In essence, both a holistic reading of the Constitution and a literal interpretation of section 7 divulge several principles on the ascertainment of marital property rights. Incidentally, the relevant superior courts have unequivocally established these rules, and pursuant to the doctrine of *stare decisis*, the law on this subject is settled.[178] Contrary to the claims of some judges and magistrates, the law is neither unclear nor confusing.[179] First, the spousal equality outlined in Article 45(3) reflects a similar enjoyment of fundamental rights and freedoms by the husband and wife.[180] Both parties have similar, not the same, rights in the institution of marriage. Put differently, article 45(3) eliminates the concept of inferiority or superiority between the spouses in a marriage. This first principle rejects the Victorian concept of coverture, where a married woman's legal autonomy was absorbed into that of her husband.

Kiage JA explained this principle succinctly in *PNN,* thus:

> … all that the Constitution declares is that marriage is a partnership of equals. *No spouse is superior to the other.* (…) It is not a case of master and servant. (…) The provision gives equal voice and is meant to *actualize the voluntariness of marriage* and *to hold inviolate the liberty of the marital space.* So in decision making (…) all the way to who shall have custody of children and who shall keep what in the unfortunate event of marital breakdown, *the parties are equal in the eyes of the law.*[181]

The word 'equal' in this pronouncement is used in its substantive form.

Second, this spousal equality does not mean identical entitlement to the properties acquired during marriage. The spouses' beneficial interests can be in 50:50 shares,

---

171 This explanation extends to the argument under article 10 of the Constitution. See Kameri-Mbote and Muriungi (2016, p. 87).

172 *EGM v BMM* [2020] eKLR, p. 5.

173 *JOO v MBO* (Petition 11 of 2020) 4 KLR (KESC 2023) para. 78.

174 *PNN v ZWN* [2017] eKLR, p. 16.

175 *JOO v MBO* (Petition 11 of 2020) 4 KLR (KESC 2023), para. 78.

176 *JOO v MBO* (Petition 11 of 2020) 4 KLR (KESC 2023), paras. 99, 106.

177 *UMM v IMM* [2014] eKLR, para. 21.

178 The relevant superior courts are the High Court, the Environment and Land Court, the Court of Appeal and the Supreme Court. See Constitution of Kenya (2010), art. 162(1).

179 Human Rights Watch and FIDA-Kenya (2020, p. 17).

180 *EGM v BMM* [2020] eKLR, p. 4.

181 *PNN v ZWN* [2017] eKLR, p. 16–17 (emphasis added). See also the High Court decision in *WMM v BML* [2012] eKLR, para. 61.

or one spouse can get more or less than the other.[182] The division depends on their contribution to the acquisition or improvement of the estate.[183] Simply put, article 45(3) or article 27 does not decree automatic equal division of marital property.[184] Kiage JA, still in the *PNN* case, postulated that when a marriage irretrievably breaks down, then:

> … the division and distribution of matrimonial property must be proceeded with on the basis of *fairness and conscience, not a romantic clutching on to the 50:50 mantra.* It is not a matter of mathematics merely as in the splitting of an orange in two, for, as biblical Solomon of old found, *justice does not get to be served by simply cutting up a contested object of love,* ambition or desire *into two equal parts.*[185]

The Supreme Court in JOO v MBO adopted this reasoning and summarised the law thus:

> … the stated equality under article 45(3) means that *the courts are to ensure* that at the dissolution of a marriage, each party to a marriage gets *a fair share* of the matrimonial property *based on their contribution.* This is *best done* by considering *the respective contribution of each party* to ensure no party is *unfairly denied* what they deserve as well as ensuring that *no party is unfairly given more than what he or she contributed.*[186]

The Supreme Court reaffirmed its position by further following the Zambian Supreme Court case of *Nkhata v Nkhata.*[187] This Zambian case forbade limiting the division of marital property to a fixed formula.[188] To the *Nkhata* bench, such division 'should be undertaken on the basis of *fairness and conscience,* not on an *unjustified reference* to 50:50 dogma'.[189] This can only be achieved by deciding each case according to its unique circumstances.[190]

The Kenyan courts have likened the call to a 50:50 division of property, absent consideration of specific circumstances of the parties in relation to the property, as oppressive and a form of pernicious aggrandisement. Mativo J in *FIDA* labelled such a call as 'an open invitation to this Court to open the door for a party to get into a marriage *and walk out of it* in the event of divorce *with more than they deserve'*.[191] Earlier, Tuiyyot J explained this injustice in detail in *UMM v IMM*. He opined that:

> But to hold that Article 45(3) decrees an automatic 50:50 sharing *could imperil the marriage institution.* It would give opportunity to *a fortune seeker to contract a marriage, sit back without making any monetary or non-monetary contribution, distress the union and wait to*

---

[182] *PNN v ZWN* [2017] eKLR, p. 17.

[183] *AWM v JGK* [2021] eKLR, p. 8.

[184] *FIDA v Attorney General* [2018] eKLR para. 60.

[185] *PNN v ZWN* [2017] eKLR, p. 17 (emphasis added).

[186] *JOO v MBO* (Petition 11 of 2020) 4 KLR (KESC 2023), para. 99 (emphasis added).

[187] *Nkhata v Nkhata* [2017] Appeal No. 60/2015 (SCZ/8/017/2015).

[188] *Nkhata v Nkhata* [2017] Appeal No. 60/2015 (SCZ/8/017/2015), p. 21.

[189] *Nkhata v Nkhata* [2017] Appeal No. 60/2015 (SCZ/8/017/2015), p. 21.

[190] *JOO v MBO* (Petition 11 of 2020) 4 KLR (KESC 2023), para. 104.

[191] *FIDA v Attorney General* [2018] eKLR, para. 60 (emphasis added).

> *reap half the marital property*. That surely is oppressive to the spouse who makes the bigger contribution. *That cannot be the sense of equalitycontemplated by Article 45(3)*.[192]

Both these views from the High Court were reiterated by the Court of Appeal and the Supreme Court. Kiage JA in *PNN* discounted that the Constitution sought to convert marriage into a pathway 'to fifty percent wealth regardless of what one does in that marriage.'[193] The Supreme Court found that a 50:50 automatic share would encourage some people to contract marriages, stay comfortably in those marriages without making any financial or non-financial contribution, and then proceed to terminate them as they wait to receive the inevitable 50% share of the property.[194] To the court, such an outcome 'could not have been the intention of our law on the subject'.[195] As all these courts intimate, this is a true extrapolation of article 45(3) and it evinces substantive equality. Therefore, the decisions in *JAO v NA*,[196] *ZWN v PNN*[197] and others, which associated article 45(3) with an obvious 50:50 share of the marital property, are bad law.[198] They misunderstood article 45(3).

The third principle arising from Article 45(3) is that this provision does not concern the redistribution of property rights.[199] In *EGM*, the Court of Appeal held that interpreting this provision to mean that spousal equality entails conferring property rights in an asset registered in the name of the other spouse is both 'textually and contextually' inaccurate.[200] To the court, the equality in this provision simply means that the courts must ensure that both parties get their 'fair share of the property' when the marriage ends. This is done by respecting the parties' contributions.[201] This court's observation partly recaptured its earlier position in *Echaria*. Then, the court held that marriage alone does not entitle one to a beneficial interest in the property of another.[202] And the Supreme Court confirmed this perspective in clear land law semantics in *JOO*. The court declared that:

> Nowhere in the Constitution do we find any suggestion that *a marriage between parties automatically results in common ownership or co-ownership of property* (hence vesting of property rights) and article 45(3) was not designed for the purpose of enabling the court to pass property rights from one spouse to another by fact of marriage only.[203]

---

192 *UMM v IMM* [2014] eKLR, para. 21 (emphasis added).

193 *PNN v ZWN* [2017] eKLR, p. 17.

194 *JOO v MBO* (Petition 11 of 2020) 4 KLR (KESC 2023) para 104.

195 *JOO v MBO* (Petition 11 of 2020) 4 KLR (KESC 2023) para 104.

196 *JAO v NA* [2013] eKLR.

197 *ZWN v PNN* [2012] eKLR, p. 26.

198 *CMN v AWM* [2013] eKLR and *ENM v SNM & another* [2017] eKLR.

199 *EGM v BMM* [2020] eKLR, p. 4.

200 *EGM v BMM* [2020] eKLR, p. 4.

201 *EGM v BMM* [2020] eKLR, p. 4.

202 *Echaria v Echaria* [2007] eKLR, p. 14.

203 *JOO v MBO* (Petition 11 of 2020) 4 KLR (KESC 2023), para. 82 (emphasis added).

3.2.3 Substantive Equality

Substantive equality means treating likes alike and differences differently.[204] It is the fusion of *de jure* and de facto equalities.[205] In other words, substantive equality is the absence of both direct and indirect discrimination.[206] At best, it is the intersection of the equality of outcomes and the equality of opportunities.[207] As relates to sexual equality, substantive equality advances 'concurrent respect[208] for the similarities and differences' of men and women. For the citizens of any given nation, this strand of equality enshrines respect for both individual and group human rights in the laws and the institutions of that country.[209]

Incidentally, substantive equality is visible in all local, regional and international human rights texts. This is traceable specifically in the equality and/or non-discrimination clause or generally in other provisions containing the words 'equal' or 'equality'—unless this general precept qualifies these words to mean 'same' treatment.[210] Often, the specific equality clause explicitly outlaws both direct and indirect discrimination.[211] This proscription can also be captured in words such as 'of itself or in its effect'[212]; or 'the effect or the purpose'.[213] Sometimes, however, the specific equality clause either generally prohibits discrimination or enshrines equality before the law.[214] In such a case, it behoves the courts to interrogate whether any of these dual forms of discrimination exist whenever a claim of discrimination is alleged.[215] It is not enough for the courts to declare the presence or absence of discrimination without this interrogation.

---

[204] Jadeed (2020, p. 56).

[205] Byrnes (2012, p. 55); African Commission on Human and Peoples' Rights (2020) para. 42. The CEDAW Committee limits substantive equality to de facto one, but this thinking does not rhyme the actual application of the principle. The African Commission seemingly gets it right. See African Commission on Human and Peoples' Rights (2020) para. 43.

[206] UN Committee on the Elimination of all forms of Discrimination Against Women (2005, para. 20).

[207] Interights (2011, p. 17).

[208] Jadeed (2020, p. 56).

[209] Kymlicka (1996, p. 6).

[210] Convention on the Elimination of All Forms of Discrimination Against Women (CEDAW), art. 16.

[211] Constitution of Kenya (2010), arts. 27(4)–(5), Constitution of the Republic of South Africa (1996), arts. 9(3)–(4), Constitution of Zimbabwe (2013), art. 56(4).

[212] Constitution of Kenya (1963) (repealed), s. 82(1).

[213] Convention on the Elimination of All Forms of Discrimination Against Women (CEDAW), art. 1.

[214] Canadian Charter of Rights and Freedoms (1982), art. 15; Universal Declaration of Human Rights (UDHR) (adopted 10 Dec 1948), arts. 2, 7, UNGA Res 217 (AIII); International Covenant on Civil and Political Rights (ICCPR) (adopted 16 Dec 1966, entered into force 23 Mar 1976), arts. 2, 3, 26, 999 UNTS 171; African Charter on Human and Peoples' Rights (African Charter) (adopted 27 Jun 1981, entered into force 21 Oct 1986), arts. 2, 3, (1982) 21 ILM 58.

[215] Byrnes (2012, pp. 65–66, 69).

The perspective that the principle of equality in human rights texts refers to its substantive equality is global. Holtmaat, an international human rights lawyer, opines that the meaning of discrimination in article 1 of the CEDAW Convention, for example, transcends the identical treatment conceptions that dominate 'European sex equality law'.[216] A renowned international law scholar, Brownlie posits that group rights are inherent constituents of the 'concepts of equality and human rights'.[217] Meanwhile, almost all the major treaty bodies, such as the CEDAW Committee, the Human Rights Committee and the Committee on Economic, Social and Cultural Rights, share the view that equality in their instruments relates to substantive equality.[218] Various national and international courts have since construed this principle in its substantive sense.[219] These include the Supreme Courts of Canada and the United States, the South African Constitutional Courts, and the European Court of Human Rights.[220]

Basically, substantive equality guarantees justice among the parties involved because it addresses their actual realities or circumstances. Tanaka J, who espoused a classical meaning of substantive equality in his dissenting judgment in the 1966 *South West Case*, observed that:

> … the principle of equality before the law does not mean the absolute equality, namely equal treatment of men *without regard to individual, concrete circumstances*, but it means the relative equality, namely the principle *to treat equally what are equal and unequally what are unequal*. (...) To treat unequal matters differently according to their inequality is not only permitted but required.[221]

Indeed, in para 8 of its General Recommendation 28, the CEDAW Committee asserted that women will not enjoy their CEDAW rights if State Parties concentrate on formal equality.[222] This same view was shared by the African Commission in its General Comment 6 on the Maputo Protocol. The Commission pronounced that:

> At its most basic level substantive equality recognizes that equal treatment in itself *does not and indeed did not guarantee equal outcomes or equalityof opportunities*; as a result, *the law should consider relevant differences that pose disadvantage to an individual or a particular group*. As opposed to the form of laws, its concern is with *the actual enjoyment of a right and unmasking the factors that hinder attainment of equalityin fact*.[223]

In Kenya, substantive equality is found in article 27 of the Constitution, which provision specifically proscribes both direct and indirect discrimination. Substantive equality is also found in other provisions in the Constitution or statutes which

---

216 Holtmaat (2013, p. 99).

217 Brownlie (1985, p. 105).

218 Jadeed (2020, p. 14).

219 Fredman (2016, p. 720).

220 See generally Jadeed (2020, pp. 99–100).

221 *South West Africa (Second Phase)*, Judgment, ICJ Rep (1966) 6, pp. 305–306 (emphasis added).

222 See Jadeed (2020, p. 97).

223 African Commission on Human and Peoples' Rights (2020, para. 42) (emphasis added).

contain the terms 'equal' or 'equality', such as article 45(3). It is wrong, therefore, to ascribe identical treatment to the word 'equal' in article 45(3). So far, a majority of women's rights advocates hold that article 45(3) espouses the same treatment of the spouses before, during and after marriage. On this basis, they argue that upon divorce, the marital property must be shared on a 50:50 basis, irrespective of each party's contribution to the acquisition or improvement of the property. However, as the Court of Appeal held in *PNN*, this understanding is not what our Constitutional drafters had in mind.[224]

3.2.4 Substantive Equality and Islamic Family Law

In line with addressing the concrete circumstances of individuals, substantive equality also postulates justice as plural.[225] As multiculturalists opine, a plural society like Kenya achieves justice when its laws recognise 'both individual and group human rights'.[226] Indeed, while the mainstream law purports to be neutral and beneficial to all, it is neither.[227] This uniform law enacts the values of the majority, whose idiosyncrasies often conflict with those of the minorities.[228] Yet when the law fails to 'reflect people's important values, feelings of betrayal and marginalisation'[229] arise. Justice, therefore, demands that normative structures in a polity must give up their abstract rationality and include minorities' perspectives.[230] The recognition of Islamic marital property law in the Kenyan case, for instance, is one way of achieving this. Doing so does not negate the 'universality of human rights'.[231] It is to appreciate those rights in another fashion, an approach visibly envisioned by the Constitution in its preamble (Kenya has ethnic, cultural and religious diversity), articles 10 (constitutional values and principles), 20(4) (duty of courts to promote the spirit, purport and objects of the Bill of Rights), 21(3) (obligation on State organs and public officers to address the needs of vulnerable groups including members of particular ethnic, religious or cultural communities), and 259(1) (interpretation of the Constitution must promote its purposes, values and principles).

To require Muslims 'to assimilate into dominant and/or secular perspectives that are intolerant of their important religious values' is, therefore, discriminatory. Such insistence perpetuates indirect discrimination. While the clamour is for pursuing

---

[224] *PNN v ZWN* [2017] eKLR, p. 17.

[225] Jadeed (2020, p. 96).

[226] Jadeed (2020, p. 23). For a fuller exposition on the nexus between multiculturalism and the principle of equality, see Jadeed (2020, pp. 80–93).

[227] Fredman (2016, p. 719).

[228] Kymlicka (1996, p. 5).

[229] Jadeed (2020, p. 24).

[230] Jadeed (2020, p. 27).

[231] Jadeed (2020, p. 102).

article 45(3) because critics believe that it dictates identical shares in marital property,[232] the reality is that such a pursuit offends the intimate personal law of Muslim women. As discussed earlier, Islamic law divides matrimonial property in accordance with the spouses' contributions. This conception of marital property, no matter how uncomfortable it is to women's rights advocates, is the law for Muslim women. It behoves them to respect it rather than call for the repeal of section 3 of the MPA. To repeal this provision is to obliterate the multiple consciousnesses inherent in an open and democratic society, like ours.[233] Such an intended repeal would negate the continued demand by some Muslims for the application of their personal law in the realm of marital property. While some Muslims may still opt to employ the mainstream law, such as in the case of *Essa v Essa*,[234] others may not; and it is this latter category that Parliament (a State organ) sought to protect through the MPA.

4 Recommendations

The MPA was enacted in response to the constitutional mandate to enact a law that ascertains and protects matrimonial property, especially the matrimonial home, both during and after marriage. While this law strives to be holistic and inclusive, it has also been challenged for reinforcing men's continued monopoly over titled properties and for reneging on the spousal equality enshrined in the Constitution. This chapter now proposes improvements to both the law and its practical application, aimed at enhancing the enjoyment of the constitutional guarantees of property rights and equality for all.

First, Parliament can amend section 11 of the MPA (recognition of customary law) by linking it to section 3(2) of the Judicature Act, which governs the application of customary law by the courts. This would provide clearer guidance to practitioners on how courts will apply customary law in marital property matters. While section 11 clearly states that the application of customary law in matrimonial property matters must align with constitutional values and principles, this aspect of the provision appears to be overlooked by some practitioners. As such, referring to the general framework for the application of customary law, such as that outlined in section 3(2) of the Judicature Act, can offer meaningful guidance. Establishing this connection to section 3(2) will provide clarity on how courts have dealt with other issues in which customary law has applied.

Second, there is a specific need for the Judiciary and the Law Society of Kenya (LSK) to organise training on the principle of equality, particularly its substantive strand, in one or more of their continuous learning programmes for their members. Through the annual Continuous Judicial Education (CJE), the Kenya Judiciary Academy can offer training to both magistrates and Kadhis on the multiple meanings

[232] See IDLO and UN Women (2024, p. 39) and Kameri-Mbote and Muriungi (2016, p. 88).

[233] Waris (2007, p. 27) and Anaya (1989, p. 837).

[234] *Essa v Essa*, Civil Appeal No. 101 of 1995 (Court of Appeal) (unreported).

of articles 27 and 45(3) of the Constitution, as well as sections 7 and 10 of the MPA. The Academy can organise similar training sessions for the judges during their annual colloquium. Meanwhile, the LSK could also organise similar training sessions for its nationwide membership, as it currently does for other topics in its annual calendar of Continuous Legal Education. When both the bench and the bar are well-trained on the principle of equality, there would be less wrongful understanding of some of the provisions of the MPA. Over time, this shift in conversation will extend beyond legal circles to other court users and non-legal women's rights champions.

5 Conclusion

This chapter has demonstrated that contemporary Kenya's matrimonial property law is largely captured in the Matrimonial Property Act (MPA) and the Constitution. However, the land laws also support the MPA. The Constitution contributes to matrimonial property law through Article 45(3), which enshrines spousal equality. This chapter has highlighted that the confusion surrounding the interpretation of this provision is unwarranted. Article 45(3) does not extend sexual equality to that which did not exist before 2010. Instead, it reiterates the full agency of a man and a woman, before, during, and after marriage. This provision also does not grant spouses property rights they did not have or acquire during marriage. It just emphasises their individual property rights as enshrined in article 40 of the Constitution.

The most important contribution of article 45(3) to the MPA is the clear demarcation of beneficial interests that may arise during marriage. The provision affirms that these rights are equal, not merely as a formal principle but in a substantive sense. This means that each spouse is entitled to marital property relative to their contribution to its acquisition or development. Contributions to matrimonial property need not be exclusively financial, at least under mainstream law. Non-monetary contributions are also recognised. Therefore, the division of matrimonial property may ultimately be 50:50 or allocated in other proportions, depending on each party's specific contributions.

Importantly, however, this chapter has demonstrated that the recognition of customary law and Islamic law on marital property is in tandem with the country's constitutional values of inclusivity and equality. The inclusion of these two laws in the statutory mainstream law is not intended to short-change Kenyan women who subscribe to their ethnic or religious laws. Instead, it is to herald the country as a plural legal system and to allow every Kenyan to enjoy the constitutional benefit of equality, regardless of their ethnic, cultural or religious affiliation.

References

African Commission on Human and Peoples' Rights (2020) General Comment No. 6 on the Protocol to the African Charter on Human and Peoples' Rights on the Rights of Women in Africa (Maputo Protocol): the right to property during separation, divorce or annulment of marriage (Article 7(d))

Al'Bukhari MBI (2007) Al'Bukhari's Sahih: the correct traditions of Al'Bukhari, vol II (trans. Al'Sharif MM). Dar al-Kotob al-Ilmiyah, Beirut

Ali AY (2001) The meaning of the Holy Qur'an, 11th edn. Amana Publications, Beltsville

Anaya SJ (1989) The capacity of international law to advance ethnic or nationality rights claims. Iowa L Rev 75:837–844

Brownlie I (1985) The rights of peoples in modern international law. Bull Aus Soc Leg Philos 9:104–119

Byrnes A (2012) Article 1. In: Freeman MA et al (eds) The UN convention on the elimination of all forms of discrimination against women: a commentary. Oxford University Press, Oxford, pp 55–69

Chan MK, Mbogoh A (2016) Strengthening women's voices in the context of agricultural investments: lessons from Kenya. IIED Land, Investment and Rights Series, International Institute for Environment and Development and Kenya Land Alliance. https://www.iied.org/sites/default/files/pdfs/migrate/12592IIED.pdf. Accessed 29 Oct 2025

Fila AE, Kiage OP, Musembi NC (2025) Partition in life and in death: intestate succession after the Matrimonial Property Act, 2013. Special Issue on Marriage, Property and Equality: Reflecting on a Decade of Family Law Reform in Kenya, E Afr LJ pp. 135–155.

Fredman S (2016) Substantive equality revisited. Int J Cons L 14:712–738

Gaafar R (2014) Women's land and property rights in Kenya. Landesa. https://www.landesa.org/wp-content/uploads/LandWise-Guide-Womens-land-and-property-rights-in-Kenya.pdf. Accessed 29 Oct 2025

Garner BA (ed) (2006) Black's law dictionary (Pocket), 3rd edn. West Group, St. Paul

Holtmaat R (2013) CEDAW: a holistic approach to women's equality and freedom. In: Hellum A, Aasen HS (eds) Women's human rights: CEDAW in international, regional and national law. Cambridge University Press, Cambridge, pp 95–124

Human Rights Watch and Federation of Women Lawyers (Kenya) (2020) Once you get out, you lose everything: women and matrimonial property rights in Kenya. Human Rights Watch, New York

IDLO and UN Women (2024) Strengthening gender equality in law: mapping discriminatory laws against women and girls in Kenya. International Development Law Organisation and UN Women, 24 April 2024. https://www.idlo.int/sites/default/files/2024/publications/documents/240419_un_edl_kenya_web.pdf. Accessed 29 Oct 2025

Interights (2011) Non-discrimination in international law: a handbook for practitioners. Interights, London

Jadeed MA (2020) The inheritance rights of Muslim women in Kenya: reality or rhetoric? Dissertation, University of Nairobi

Jadeed MA (2023) Islamic marriages and divorce in Kenya: ethnocultural diversity. J Com Law 18:211–246

Kameri-Mbote P, Muriungi M (2016) Much ado about nothing: a critical analysis of the matrimonial property in Kenya. Zanzibar Yearbook of Law 6:71–102

Kenya National Bureau of Statistics (2019) 2019 Kenya population and housing census, volume IV: distribution of population by socio-economic characteristics. Kenya National Bureau of Statistics, Nairobi

Kymlicka W (1996) Multicultural citizenship: a liberal theory of minority rights. Clarendon Press, Oxford (Reprint)

LSData (n.d.) Summary Process Definition. LSData. https://www.lsd.law/define/summary-process. Accessed 24 Sept 2025

Norbert C (1977) The Married Women's Property Act, 1882: a study of Victorian reform. MA thesis, Western Kentucky University

Nyamu-Musembi C (2002) Sitting on her husband's back with her hands in his pockets: commentary on judicial decision-making in marital property cases in Kenya. Int Surv of Fam L 2002:229–238

UN Committee on the Elimination of Discrimination Against Women (2005) Concluding comments: Benin. UN Doc CEDAW/C/BEN/CO/1–3

UN Committee on the Elimination of Discrimination Against Women (2017) Concluding observations of the committee on the eighth periodic report of Kenya. UN Doc CEDAW/C/KEN/CO/8

United Nations Development Programme (1995) Human development report 1995. Oxford University Press, New York

Waris A (2007) Making a mountain out of a molehill: the protection of the right to freedom of religion of the Muslim religious minority in Kenya's Constitution. Int J Minor Group Rights 14:25–40

Moza Ally Jadeed is a Lecturer at the Faculty of Law, University of Nairobi. She teaches Equality Law, Gender and the Law, Research Methodology, and Jurisprudence. Her research interests include law and religion, and gender equality. She is an attorney with 20 years of experience and has prosecuted freedom of religion and belief cases up to the Supreme Court of Kenya. She is a Senior Fellow of the Leadership and Advocacy for Women in Africa (LAWA) Fellowship at Georgetown University and a member of the African Consortium for Law and Religion Studies (ACLARS). Jadeed holds a PhD in Law from the University of Nairobi.

The Protection of Women's Property Rights on Dissolution of Marriage in Malawi

Pachalo Nomsa Grace Mwenelupembe

Abstract Malawi's legal response to spousal property rights reflects the country's commitment to harmonising its pluralistic family law framework. With the enactment of the Marriage, Divorce and Family Relations Act (MDFRA) in 2015, the state established a unified legal framework governing the celebration and dissolution of civil, religious, customary, and reputed marriages. The analysis focuses on how the MDFRA, read in conjunction with the Constitution, recognises spouses' rights to acquire property individually and jointly, and to receive an equitable share upon divorce. Particular emphasis is placed on the implications of these provisions for women, especially in customary and informal unions, where legal protection has historically been limited. By examining statutory texts, constitutional guarantees, and judicial interpretations, the chapter reveals persistent gaps between law and practice, particularly in the equitable distribution of property. It further evaluates Malawi's compliance with international human rights norms concerning women's economic rights in marriage. The discussion concludes by identifying areas where the law still falls short in ensuring effective and equal protection of women's property rights and calls for targeted legislative and judicial reforms to address these deficiencies.

1 Introduction

Marriage is an important social institution in Malawi. Although undefined under Malawian law, its characteristics can be parsed from various legal sources, including the Malawian Constitution 1994 ('The Malawian Constitution'), the Marriage, Divorce, and Family Relations Act of 2015 (MDFRA), and applicable customary law principles. Generally, marriage in Malawi is heterogenous and restricted to persons

P. N. G. Mwenelupembe (✉)
University of the Free State, Bloemfontein, South Africa
e-mail: pachalonomsa@gmail.com

A. F. Hammond and P. Batariwah (eds.), *The Law on Marital Property in Africa*, Ius Gentium: Comparative Perspectives on Law and Justice 138,
https://doi.org/10.1007/978-3-032-19358-2_4

eighteen years of age and older.[1] The Constitution of Malawi guarantees the right to marry and start a family.[2] The forms of marriages recognised in Malawi reflect the pluralistic nature of Malawian law. Customary law, for example, has existed in Malawi since time immemorial and has been administered alongside statutory law since the introduction of English common law.[3] Moreover, customary laws have been preserved by section 200 of the Constitution, which provides that, except insofar as they are inconsistent with the Constitution, customary laws in force at the commencement of the 1994 Constitution shall continue to have force of law, as if it has been made in accordance with and in pursuance of the Constitution.

The Constitution thus recognises that marriages may be entered into by law, custom, and repute, or through permanent cohabitation.[4] Four types of marriage are recognised in the MDFRA: civil marriage, religious marriage, customary marriage, and marriage by repute or permanent cohabitation.[5] Before the MDFRA, the entry and dissolution of marriages were guided by different rules, with the entry and dissolution of civil marriages being regulated by the now-repealed Marriage Act of 1903 and Divorce Act of 1905, and the entry of religious marriages being regulated by the repealed African Marriage (Christian Rites) Registration Act of 1923. Customary marriages adhered to the traditions and customs of the communities to which they belonged. The MDFRA has greatly harmonised the law on marriage and family relations by consolidating the rules on the entry into and dissolution of marriage, as well as the distribution of matrimonial property, into a single piece of legislation. While specific formalities must still be followed when contracting a marriage, the dissolution and distribution of matrimonial property largely fall within the ambit of the MDFRA, in addition to some applicable customary law.

The right of women to the fair disposition of property that is held jointly with a husband on the dissolution of marriage in section 24(1)(b)(i) of the Malawian Constitution is the cardinal law on the distribution of matrimonial property. Section 24 of the Constitution of Malawi provides that on the dissolution of marriage, 'howsoever entered', women have the right to a fair disposition of property held jointly with their spouses. The phrase 'howsoever entered' is crucial. It cements the position that all marriages have equal status before the law and that women's property rights will be equally protected regardless of the type of marriage contracted. In proceedings concerning the distribution of property, courts are tasked with ascertaining whether the parties jointly hold property before deciding the question of distribution. Courts have pronounced that the mere fact that the property was acquired during the marriage does not make the property marital property or jointly held property.[6] This is also in line with section 24(1)(a)(ii) of the Constitution, which guarantees women the right to

[1] Constitution of the Republic of Malawi (1994), s. 22(6) and Marriage, Divorce and Family Relations Act (MDFRA) (2015, s. 14).

[2] Constitution of the Republic of Malawi (1994, s. 22[3]).

[3] Wanda (1988, p. 117).

[4] Constitution of the Republic of Malawi (1994, s. 22[4]).

[5] MDFRA (2015, s. 12[1]).

[6] *Sikwese v Banda* [2017] MWHC 37.

acquire and maintain rights in property, independently or in association with others, regardless of their marital status. Section 24(1)(a)(ii) serves a dual function: firstly, it addresses the right of women to own property independently of their husbands, and secondly, it establishes that men and women in marriage unions can own property for their sole use, and such property cannot form part of matrimonial property.[7]

The law, which at a more granular level guides judges in settling property rights between spouses, is the MDFRA. Section 74 of the MDFRA provides that a court shall equitably divide and re-allocate property upon the dissolution of a marriage, taking into account several factors, including the income, financial needs, obligations, age and health of each spouse, the standard of living of the family during the subsistence of the marriage, and the direct and indirect contributions made by either spouse, including the fulfilment of domestic duties. This provision outlines the grounds the court may consider to fairly and equitably distribute property.

This chapter examines the constitutional and statutory provisions governing the settlement of spousal property rights to determine whether they equally safeguard women's property rights upon the dissolution of marriages. The second section of this paper discusses the four types of marriages recognised by Malawian law and their property-related incidents. The third section examines how the concept of matrimonial property is defined by law and interpreted by the courts in Malawi. It also examines the law governing the distribution of matrimonial property and its application to various types of marriages. Section four examines the alignment of domestic law with relevant international human rights treaties and assesses the extent to which prevailing law safeguards women's property rights in various forms of marriage. Section 5 analyses structural and gender-based barriers to women's property rights and advances legal and institutional reforms to address them

2 Legally Recognised Marriages

Malawi has four types of legally recognised marriages: civil marriages, religious marriages, customary marriages, and marriages by repute or permanent cohabitation.[8] The law recognises that each type of marriage has its own set of rules regulating its formation and dissolution.

2.1 Civil Marriages

The MDFRA defines a civil marriage as a marriage celebrated by a registrar in accordance with Part IV and VII of the Act. The defining feature of civil marriage is perhaps that it is celebrated by the Registrar of Marriages according to statutory

[7] *Sikwese v Banda* [2017] MWHC 37.

[8] MDFRA (2015, s. 12).

procedures. Part IV of the MDFRA outlines the law regarding civil marriages. A person intending to contract a civil marriage must first prove, by way of declaration before a registrar, that they are single. Polygamy is prohibited in civil marriages.[9] A prospective spouse must sign and file a notice of the intended marriage in the required form before the Registrar of Marriages. The notice is filed in the jurisdiction where the person ordinarily resides. The notice is then entered into the marriage register and published by affixing it at the door of the Registrar's office, or one's place of work or worship. After 21 days from the date of publication, the Registrar issues a permit if satisfied that the law has been complied with, neither of the parties is married to another person, and no caveat has been filed against the marriage.[10] The parties may then proceed to celebrate their marriage in accordance with Part VII of the Act.

Alternatively, the Minister of Justice can grant a special licence upon proof being presented to the Minister by affidavit that there is no lawful impediment to a proposed marriage. The requirement to give notice and issue the permit by the Registrar is dispensed with, allowing the Registrar to authorise the celebration of the marriage.[11]

2.2 Customary Marriages

A customary marriage is defined as a marriage celebrated in accordance with the customary law rites of one or both of the parties to the marriage.[12] Customary marriages are 'relationships that concern not only the husband and wife but also the family groups to which they belonged before the marriage'.[13] Customary communities in Malawi are generally categorised as patrilineal and matrilineal. Patrilineal customary communities exist among the tribes in the northern and part of the southern regions of Malawi, including the *Tumbuka, Tonga, Sena,* and *Ngonde* tribes. Matrilineal communities exist among the tribes in the central region and most parts of the southern region, including the *Chewa, Lomwe,* and *Yao* tribes.

It follows, therefore, that customary marriages will either be patrilineal or matrilineal. As a rule, all customary marriages, whether matrilineal or patrilineal, are contracted according to the customary law of the prospective spouses. All customary marriage laws recognise that for a marriage to be deemed valid, the parties must have attained the age of puberty, and the woman's parents must consent to the marriage. In patrilineal societies, the bride price (*lobola*) must be paid by a man to the woman's parents or guardians. In matrilineal systems, a traditional ceremony would have been held between a man and an unmarried woman in the presence of their appointed marriage advocates and family members (*chinkhoswe*).[14] Although customary law

---

[9] MDFRA (2015, ss. 17–18).

[10] MDFRA (2015, s. 24).

[11] MDFRA (2015, s. 25).

[12] MDFRA (2015, s. 2).

[13] Bekker (1989), cited in Mwambene (2010, p. 91).

[14] Mwambene (2010, p. 91).

does not specify a precise age for the attainment of puberty or the contracting of marriage, the Constitution stipulates 18 years for all marriages, including customary marriages.[15] Customary marriages are understood as a unity of two families, and not simply the spouses' affair. Thus, the consummation of a customary marriage creates reciprocal rights and obligations between the spouses, for which their respective family groups are collectively responsible.[16]

The procedures preceding the celebration of a customary marriage are governed by the customs or rites of the various ethnic groups. Persons intending to marry under custom are still required to give notice of the intention to marry and fulfil the required marriage customs and rites.[17] The notice is then entered into the marriage register and displayed. After 21 days, a permit authorising the celebration of the marriage is issued. In the case of *Maureen Goodson v Cidrick Chidothi*,[18] the parties had followed customary rites in contracting their marriage. However, they did not comply with the requirement to give notice of intention to marry and to have the notice published. In the lower magistrate court, the court found that there was no valid customary marriage due to non-compliance with section 27. On appeal, the High Court found that there was a customary marriage but did not fault the lower court's holding that section 27 must be complied with and that where a court finds evidence that 'the marriage was not published and no marriage certificate was issued, then the ceremony cannot be considered a valid customary marriage even if all the necessary customs and rights have been followed'.[19]

The court, however, did acknowledge that 'the implications of non-adherence of section 27 by the highest population of marriages means that a lot of customary marriages post-2015 would be rendered null and void'.[20] This is because, prior to the inception of the MDFRA in 2015, customary marriages were not required to be published in the sense required by section 27. The compliance with customary rites and procedures was sufficient to create a valid customary marriage. The High Court lamented that the application of section 27 to customary marriages was discriminatory and made declaratory orders to the Ministries of Justice, Gender and Local Government, among others, to ensure that customary marriages celebrated after 2015 that did not comply with sections 27, 28 and 29 are legalised. This decision was made on 4 October 2024, and as of 2 January 2025, the court's declaratory orders had not been complied with.

[15] Constitution of the Republic of Malawi (1994, s. 22[6]).

[16] Mwambene (2010, p. 91).

[17] MDFRA (2015, s. 27).

[18] *Maureen Goodson v Cidrick Chidothi* [2024] MWHC 50 (High Court).

[19] *Maureen Goodson v Cidrick Chidothi* [2024] MWHC 50, para. 2.8.

[20] *Maureen Goodson v. Cidrick Chidothi* [2024] MWHC 50, para 2.10.

2.3 Religious Marriages

A religious marriage is a marriage celebrated by a cleric in accordance with the recognised rites of a religion, religious body, denomination, or sect to which one or both parties belong.[21] It is estimated that 77.3% and 13.8% of Malawians are Christians and Muslims, respectively; Individuals with no religious affiliation are 2.1%, and 5.6% belong to other religious groups, including Hindus, Baha'is, Rastafarians, Jews, and Sikhs.[22] Interfaith marriages are rare but not uncommon. At the dissolution of a marriage, the court will apply the religious rites adopted by the parties at the time of marriage.

2.4 Marriage by Repute/Permanent Cohabitation

A marriage by repute or permanent cohabitation is a construction of the law. Section 13 of the MDFRA provides that marriage by repute or permanent cohabitation shall only be recognised upon a finding of a court of competent jurisdiction where that court considers, among other things:

1. the length of the relationship, which must be at least 5 years,
2. the fact of cohabitation,
3. the existence of a conjugal relationship,
4. the degree of financial dependence or interdependence and any agreement for financial support between the parties, ownership, use and acquisition of property,
5. the degree of mutual commitment to a shared life, whether the parties mutually have, care for, or support, children; the reputation of the parties in the community as being married and the public display of aspects of their shared relation; and other factors which the court may consider appropriate.

Unlike customary and religious marriages, which are within the jurisdiction of the Magistrates' Courts, the High Court has competent jurisdiction to declare that a marriage by repute or through permanent cohabitation exists. In a recent decision of the High Court declining to dissolve a marriage by repute,[23] the court stated that the reason that marriage by repute or permanent cohabitation is recognised in the first place is to ensure that those who qualify under it benefit from various reliefs ancillary to marriage, such as distribution of matrimonial property and custody and maintenance of children. The court's position cements the view that while a party may not legally set out to contract a marriage by permanent cohabitation, they are nonetheless entitled by law to the reliefs available as if they were validly married.

---

[21] MDFRA (2015, s. 2).

[22] US Department of State (2022).

[23] *Florence Chanika v Joseph Macnewton Mwalilino* (High Court of Malawi Family & Probate Division, 18 April 2024) (unreported).

3 Matrimonial Property

Matrimonial property, also known as marital property or marital estate, refers to property acquired during the subsistence of the marriage and subject to distribution or division at the time of marital dissolution.[24] Under Malawi's common law legal system, matrimonial property refers only to property jointly acquired during marriage. Where title is vested in one party, the court may, in some cases, find a joint intention to use the property for the family's benefit.[25] In the Supreme Court decision of *Sikwese v Banda*, the court expounded on the issue of joint ownership by stating that:

> [W]hether or not in any particular case property is held jointly is a matter of fact, and will depend on the circumstances of the case, including the conduct and intention of the parties in relation to the acquisition of the property; it is not a mere conclusion to be drawn from the existence of marriage. There must be evidence that the property is held jointly.[26]

Thus, the determination of whether property is jointly held depends on the specifics of each case, and the courts must decide, based on the facts and evidence before them, whether it is jointly held. On the other hand, the MDFRA defines matrimonial property as including, 'the matrimonial home or homes, household property in the matrimonial home or homes, any other property whether movable or immovable acquired during the subsistence of a marriage which by express or implied agreement between the spouses or by their conduct is used, treated or otherwise regarded as matrimonial property.'[27]

Two key issues are isolated from the definition in section 2 of the MDFRA; first, the property subject to distribution must be acquired during the marriage, and second, 'it must be treated as matrimonial property'. Only under these conditions can it be subject to distribution. The latter part of the definition, 'that property be treated as matrimonial property' entails that not all property acquired during the marriage may be subject to distribution. A party to a marriage may own property, exclusively. To be considered matrimonial property and eligible for distribution, the property must meet an additional criterion based on the parties' express or implied agreement and conduct. This position is entrenched by section 24(1)(a)(ii) of the Constitution of Malawi, which provides the equal capacity of women to acquire and maintain rights in property, independently and in association with others, regardless of marital status. The law recognises that women, like men, can own property independently, even within a marriage, and that such property is not marital property and is not subject to distribution. Therefore, if a party can demonstrate that, despite a property being acquired during the marriage, the spouse's conduct and intention or treatment of the property disqualifies it from being matrimonial property, then that property

---

[24] Garner (2009).

[25] *Emily Mustafa v Marriam Mustafa* [2021] MWSC 13 (Supreme Court).

[26] *Sikwese v Banda* [2017] MWHC 37 (High Court of Malawi).

[27] MDFRA (2015, s. 2).

will not be subject to distribution. There is thus no general presumption that property acquired during the subsistence of marriage is marital property.

3.1 Rights of Spouses to Matrimonial Property During Marriage

This sub-section discusses the rights of spouses to matrimonial property during the marriage and after its dissolution.

Section 50(1) of the MDFRA provides that spouses have a duty to maintain each other and any children of the marriage. It further provides that each spouse's monetary contribution shall be proportionate to their income. The non-monetary contributions of each spouse are also considered when determining a spouse's contribution to the maintenance of the other spouse or the children of the marriage.[28] Quite crucial is the recognition of non-monetary contributions, which may take the form of domestic household work, including childcare. The law presumes that during the subsistence of a marriage, each party will work towards maintaining the family unit. During this time, a spouse may acquire property independently. Such property may not be considered matrimonial property upon dissolution of the marriage, and the courts will ascertain this by looking at several factors, including the acquisition of the property and the intention and conduct of the parties in relation to such property.

3.2 Rights of Spouses to Matrimonial Property upon Dissolution of Marriage

Women's property rights on dissolution of marriage are protected by section 24(1)(b)(i) of the Constitution, which states that:

> Women have the right to full and equal protection by the law and have the right not to be discriminated against on the basis of their gender or marital status, which includes the right, on the dissolution of marriage, howsoever entered into to a fair disposition of property that is held jointly with a husband.

The courts in Malawi recognise this provision as the foundational law governing the distribution of matrimonial property, that is, property jointly owned by the spouses. This Constitutional recognition and protection of women's property rights applies equally to all marriages. However, at the centre of this provision is the recognition that women are discriminated against based on their gender and that this may manifest itself even in matters concerning matrimonial property.[29] The World Bank reports that although women in Malawi own nearly half of the businesses in the micro, small,

[28] MDFRA (2015, s. 50).

[29] Constitution of the Republic of Malawi (1994, s. 24[1]).

and medium enterprise (MSME) sector, they earn 46% less in sales than their male counterparts.[30] The report states that this stems from having fewer savings to start businesses in the first place than men do. Women also have, on average, fewer years of formal education and carry heavier household work burdens, which limit the time they can devote to starting and growing businesses.[31] Overall, women have fewer opportunities to acquire property in their own right or to contribute financially to property acquisition in marriage. It is, therefore, important for courts to recognise the intersection between gender and the acquisition and subsequent distribution of property acquired during a marriage.

Two issues arise from section 24(1)(b)(i): how does one determine whether property is held jointly with one's husband? How will a court distribute such jointly-held property?

3.3 What Is Jointly-Held Property?

The case of *Sikwese v Banda* is well known for establishing the principle that jointly held property is ascertained by considering the parties' intentions regarding it, as well as their contributions to its acquisition.[32] The parties to this case had been married and acquired considerable property, including real estate. Both parties had maintained jobs and earned income in their own right during the marriage.

The existence of marriage is not conclusive evidence that property acquired during that marriage forms part of matrimonial property. The key is the parties' conduct and intention in acquiring the property. The High Court has applied this reasoning in numerous cases, including in *Chinkono v Chinkono*.[33] In Chinkono, where the court dealt with a dispute over land allegedly acquired by one spouse during courtship and conflicting claims regarding contributions to the construction of a house on that land during the marriage, the court stated that:

> It is not automatic that properties acquired during the subsistence of the marriage belong to both. The court is under obligation to establish the intention of the parties. This is to ensure that all properties which were exclusively acquired by a party belong to him or her whilst properties which were acquired with express or implied intention to be for both parties should be shared between the couple upon dissolution of the marriage based on the financial and other contributions.[34]

The court further stated that 'as understood in property law, the term jointly held property should not be confused with joint ownership of property. In terms of the distribution of matrimonial property, the phrase acquires a watered-down interpretation, which is focused on the conduct and intention of the parties in relation to that

[30] Willman et al. (2022).

[31] Willman et al. (2022).

[32] *Sikwese v Banda* [2017] MWHC 37.

[33] *Olive Chinkono v Simplex Chinkono* [2023] MWHCFam (High Court).

[34] *Olive Chinkono v Simplex Chinkono* [2023] MWHCFam 7 (High Court).

property'. The *Chinkono* court has expounded that the word 'held' is not confined to ownership or possession and that the word 'held' cannot be restricted to the two aspects of ownership or possession. Even if property acquired during the marriage is registered in the name of one party, the position of the court is that the registration of property in the name of one spouse is not conclusive evidence that the property was solely acquired or intended to be for that spouse only. The High Court decision in *Sauti Phiri v Sauti Phiri*,[35] in distributing matrimonial property and in dealing with the issue of whether registration of property in the name of one spouse excludes the other spouse from ownership, the court stated that:

> In matrimonial cases where it is quite possible for the dominant spouse in power relations to register property in his or her name, evidence of registration is not necessarily evidence of intention to own the property exclusively. The Appellant has undoubtedly the rights of legal ownership, but this does not rule out the Respondent's ability to acquire a beneficial interest in the same property. What the court must therefore be satisfied of, is whether the Respondent did acquire a beneficial interest in the property, either through contributions or through some other conduct of the parties.

The court, thus, still interrogates the acquisition of the property and the intention of the parties to ascertain each party's contribution and subsequent interest or share in the property.

The court has had an opportunity to determine whether educational qualifications obtained during the subsistence of the marriage form part of marital property and whether a spouse can claim an interest in the qualifications. In *Tewesa v Tewesa*,[36] the parties had been married for 20 years. During the marriage, the husband had obtained a bachelor's degree and a diploma in education. The wife pleaded that the said qualifications were family property and that she had a beneficial interest in the qualifications, having made contributions towards their acquisition. The court held that there is property in educational qualifications, but that such property vests in the person acquiring the qualifications and thus cannot be distributed. The court further held that a beneficial interest in the qualifications is created and subsists during the marriage, and that, upon dissolution of the marriage, the spouse may be compensated for the loss during the distribution of matrimonial property, taking into account the defendant's future earnings. Despite making this holding, the judgment did not proceed to make computations for compensation in line with the future earnings of the defendant.

Furthermore, the decision did not adequately address the issue of contribution to the acquisition of education qualifications, especially in the context presented by the parties. The court was strongly persuaded by the American decisions cited therein. Apart from the fact of marriage and that the petitioner agreed that the defendant obtain further education, no factual evidence of the petitioner's contribution was presented or discussed by the court. The court relied on the longevity of the marriage to hold that the petitioner had acquired a beneficial interest in the qualifications. The

[35] *Sauti Phiri v Sauti Phiri* [2024] MWHC 62 (High Court), cited in *White v White* [2022] MWHCFam 3.

[36] *Tewesa v Tewesa* [2020] MWHC 28.

decision, however, establishes a precedent that a beneficial interest is created in the educational qualifications of a spouse and that, where such a contribution is proved, a spouse is entitled to compensation at the dissolution of the marriage.

3.4 How Are Property Rights Settled?

Section 24(1)(b)(i) of the Constitution is supplemented by section 74 of the Marriage Divorce and Family Relations Act, which states the following:

> A court shall equitably divide and re-allocate property upon the dissolution of a marriage taking into account:
>
> (a) the income of each spouse.
>
> (b) the assets of each spouse.
>
> (c) the financial needs of each spouse.
>
> (d) the obligations of each spouse.
>
> (e) the standard of living of the family during the subsistence of the marriage.
>
> (f) the age and health of each spouse; or
>
> (g) the direct and indirect contributions made by either spouse, including through the performance of domestic duties.

Of great relevance to women is the recognition of indirect contributions, which includes the performance of domestic duties. The recognition of indirect contributions is crucial for women, who are often burdened with performing domestic work, which affects their economic activities and earning capacities. According to the Supreme Court in *Sikwese v Banda*, several factors are considered to determine each party's contribution. Contribution is also not restricted to financial contributions; the court may consider non-monetary contributions. Non-monetary contribution means:

> ....the contribution made by a spouse for the maintenance, welfare, or advancement of the family other than by way of money, and includes domestic work and management of the home, childcare, companionship, the endurance of the marriage, any other manner or form of contribution as the court may consider appropriate.[37]

However, in circumstances where the extent of that contribution cannot be ascertained with any degree of specificity, the prudent approach is to award each party a 50% share in the property.[38]

The language of equity and fairness in the MDFRA is emphasised as expressed by the African Commission on Human Rights in its General Comment No. 6 on the Protocol to the African Charter on Human and Peoples Rights on the Rights of Women in Africa.[39] Malawi ratified the Protocol in 2005. The Comment expounds as follows:

---

[37] MDFRA (2015, s. 2).

[38] *Sikwese v Banda* [2017] MWHC 37.

[39] African Commission (2021).

> to ensure substantive equality, state parties must fully acknowledge and recognise the many forms of women's contribution to the economic well-being of their families and ensure that this contribution is fully recognised in cases of separation, divorce, or annulment of marriage. This includes wives' contribution to the development of land and property through their unpaid labour as well as childcare.[40]

Section 74 of the Marriage, Divorce and Family Relations Act adopts the principle of fairness and uses the term 'equitable.' Whilst the courts in Malawi have not had the opportunity to interpret equitable sharing of property, the African Commission's General Comment may prove instructive when the courts have an opportunity to pronounce on the principle of equitable sharing in the future. The Comment elaborates that:

> In this vein, this General Comment therefore provides an opportunity for equitable sharing under Article 7(d) of the Maputo Protocol to be interpreted as the apportionment of marital property in excess of half of the property on the basis of awarding material recognition to both the unequal enjoyment of property rights that the woman endured during marriage and the non-monetary contribution of the woman to the household and the family within the context of substantive equality. The objective of this is to avoid injustice and ensure equality between men and women taking into consideration all forms of contribution made towards the acquisition of the marital property.[41]

In other words, equity demands that when sharing property, the unequal position of women in relation to property, the women's endurance during marriage, and the non-monetary contributions to the household and family must be considered. Courts must adopt a wide interpretation of the term 'contribution', especially for women, whose contribution to the acquisition of matrimonial property may not be in black and white, but in less traditional ways. The General Comment goes further to state that:

> The implication of equitable sharing as expounded in this General Comment entails giving due recognition to the reproductive role of women involving the contributions that they make through the time, labor and care giving that they invest in the household. In determining the scope of equitable sharing, account should be given to the duration of the marriage, whether the couple produced children, the cause of the separation, divorce or annulment of marriage and the responsibility that each spouse bears.[42]

The reproductive role is, unfortunately, one which the spouses cannot share. Despite parties to a marriage having equal responsibility towards children and maintaining a home, their roles and responsibilities often differ significantly. Women still bear the sole responsibility for caregiving and homemaking due to their reproductive and maternal roles. These are vital yet overlooked roles for women and should be considered in any judicial orders concerning property distribution.

---

[40] African Commission (2021).

[41] African Commission (2021, para. 43).

[42] African Commission (2021, para 44).

3.5 *Invalid Marriages and Property Rights*

A civil marriage may be declared invalid for various reasons. Once a person has entered into a valid civil marriage, they are prohibited from contracting another marriage while the first remains in effect. Any subsequent marriage entered into under such circumstances is considered void.[43] Additionally, a marriage may become void if the parties are within the prohibited degrees of affinity or kindred. The prohibited degrees of consanguinity and affinity include one's mother and father, whether natural, adoptive, or formerly adoptive; first cousins; as well as the former spouse of one's father or mother.[44] Lastly, a marriage may be declared void if the parties fail to comply with the essential or formal requisites prescribed by law or customary practice for the valid celebration of such marriage.

The parties to an invalid marriage cannot bring themselves within the marital property framework of the Constitution and the MDFRA. In *Phiri v Phiri*,[45] the parties had contracted a civil marriage while another one subsisted. Despite the husband pleading that the petitioner was his second wife, the court declared the marriage null and void and dismissed the petition. As a result, the matrimonial property rules could not apply to the second wife.

However, the MDFRA has introduced, through section 97(1), the concept of *property settlement*. This provision states that, notwithstanding that a marriage has been declared void by the court, the court still has the power to make an order for property settlement. It is important to note that property settlement and the distribution of matrimonial property are treated as distinct remedies under the MDFRA.

The Act, however, does not specify the factors courts should consider when determining property settlement. To date, the courts have not yet interpreted or applied this provision. Nevertheless, women whose marriages have been annulled or declared void may rely on section 97(1) to seek property settlement.

3.6 *Property Distribution in Customary Marriages*

Customary marriages are unique in that they involve an intersection between customary law and statutory law in decisions concerning property distribution. The right to culture is provided for under section 26 of the Constitution, which guarantees every person's right to participate in the cultural life of their choice. However, participation in the cultural life of one's choice is not absolute. It may be limited through section 44(1) of the Constitution, which allows restrictions or limitations on the exercise of any rights and freedoms provided for in the Constitution if the limitations are 'prescribed by law... are reasonable, recognised by international human rights standards and necessary in an open and democratic society'. Harmful cultural

[43] Under MDFRA (2015, s. 18), a party to a civil marriage can only be married to only one spouse.

[44] MDFRA (2015), Third Schedule (Sect. 15).

[45] *Phiri v Phiri* [1980] MWHC 8.

practices are further prohibited under section 5(1) of the Gender Equality Act of 2014. In this regard, cultural practices intending to dispossess women of property acquired during marriage would be unlawful.

There are two main types of customary marriages in Malawi: matrilineal and patrilineal. The matrilineal custom is further grouped into two: matrilocal *(chikamwini)* and patrilocal *(chitengwa)*. In *matrilocal* marriages, the man moves to the wife's village, and lineage is traced through the woman. In *patrilocal* marriages, the woman moves to live in the man's village, but the children still belong to her lineage. In patrilineal marriages, lineage is traced through the father, and residence is typically in the father's village.[46] It is quite crucial for the court to ascertain which cultural system was used at the inception of marriage, 'as each system is replete with its own rules for entry into marriage, grounds for divorce as well as rights and obligations of the parties to the marriage'.[47] Consequently, the distribution of matrimonial property is also affected by the type of customary marriage the parties contracted. As expounded by the court in *Kishindo v Kishindo*,[48] customary marriages under the patrilocal system require that a man build or provide for a house for his wife in his village. In the *matrilocal* system, the obligation is to build a house in the wife's village. At divorce, if the court finds that the husband did not fulfil this obligation, the court may order the husband to do so.

Regarding property distribution in customary marriages, the court in *Kishindo v Kishindo*[49] restated the position in *Kamphoni v Kamphoni*,[50] that the disposal of property at customary law is based on the principles of fairness, reasonableness, comity, proportionality, and solidarity. The court further stated that the principles are wider than those stipulated in section 24(1)(b)(i) of the Constitution and are, therefore, an adumbration of the right, not a limitation. Furthermore, these principles do not conflict with section 24(1)(b)(i) of the Constitution but rather an expansion of the rights under section 24(1)(b)(i) of the Constitution.

Property, especially connected to land, is held not by the spouse but by the family. The courts have recognised that, at customary law and during divorce, the property of the marriage, except for land, is distributed on the principle of fairness. Land issues are already fixed by customary law.[51] In systems where bride price *(lobola)* is paid, also known as the patrilineal system of marriage, the woman moves to live at a man's locality on land owned by the husband and his extended family.[52] In a matrilocal system, the husband relocates to the wife's locality and resides on land that is owned and provided by the wife and her extended family. Consequently, upon divorce, the land remains unaffected, as its ownership was already established at the

---

46 Ngwira (2005).

47 *Rabecca Zimchetera Marion v Masautso Marion*, Matrimonial Appeal No. 4 of 2022 (Unreported).

48 *Kishindo v Kishindo* [2015] MWHC 447.

49 *Kishindo v Kishindo* [2015] MWHC 447.

50 *Kamphoni v Kamphoni* (2012) Matrimonial Cause No 7 (High Court) (PR) (unreported).

51 *Emily Mustafa v Marriam Mustafa* [2021] MWSC 13 (Supreme Court), p. 39.

52 *Emily Mustafa v Marriam Mustafa* [2021] MWSC 13 (Supreme Court), p. 39.

time of marriage.[53] Spouses intending to own land in such a marriage setup must therefore relocate and acquire land elsewhere, and not on the matrimonial homestead. However, with the modernisation of Malawian society, parties to a marriage could be married under custom while residing in cities, thereby disassociating from the customary ownership of land. The obligation to complete certain customary marriage rites remains, as demonstrated in *Kamphoni v Kamphoni*, where the court ordered that the urban house owned by the parties be given to the wife, while the husband was awarded the house built in his village. The court reasoned that the parties had married under the matrilocal system, and the husband had an obligation to build a house in the wife's village, not his own.

Such practices, especially in patrilineal systems, have made women landless. A study found that women who opt to relocate from their maternal land when they marry and settle elsewhere with their husbands, either with their husband's kin or in a neutral place, are the most vulnerable to losing land rights if their marriages dissolve. They are not in a strong position to assert claims to the marital property, and if they return to their maternal home, they are likely to find that their family land has been shared among their siblings, leaving them landless.[54]

4 Application of International Law

The case of *Kishindo v Kishindo* affirmed the application of international law in matters concerning the distribution of matrimonial property. In this matter, upon dissolution of their customary marriage, the court was tasked with distributing the matrimonial property, which comprised two houses and household items. One of the houses was in the wife's name and was in the possession and control of the wife. The wife relied on *Chewa* customary law, arguing that she was entitled to one of the two houses, as her husband had a customary obligation to build a house for her under *Chewa* customary law.

The court stated that in interpreting the word 'held' in section 24(1)(b)(i) of the Constitution, norms of international law and foreign case law must be considered where necessary. The court further stated that under norms of international law, the word 'held' in section 24(1)(b)(i) of the Constitution must refer to all matters in Article (16)(1)(h), of the International Convention on the Elimination of All Forms of Discrimination Against Women which are 'ownership, acquisition, management, administration, enjoyment and disposing of property whether free of charge or for valuable consideration' and that 'consequently, property in marriage, even if "acquired" independently under sections 24(1)(a)(iii) or 28(1) could be jointly 'held' for purposes of section 24(1)(b)(i) because it is during marriage, jointly possessed'.[55]

---

[53] *Emily Mustafa v Marriam Mustafa* [2021] MWSC 13 (Supreme Court).

[54] Matinga (2015).

[55] *Kishindo v Kishindo* [2015] MWHC 447.

The Convention on the Elimination of All Forms of Discrimination against Women (CEDAW) and the Protocol to the African Charter on Human and Peoples' Rights on the Rights of Women in Africa (Maputo Protocol) are key treaties applicable in Malawi. CEDAW was ratified on 17 March 1987, and the Maputo Protocol was ratified on 20 May 2005. The CEDAW directly applies in Malawi by virtue of section 211(2) of the Constitution of Malawi, which provides that binding international agreements entered into before the commencement of the Constitution shall continue to be binding unless otherwise provided by an Act of Parliament. By 1994, when the Constitution of Malawi was enacted, CEDAW had become binding, as it was ratified in 1987. No Act of Parliament has been promulgated ousting the binding nature of CEDAW.

On the other hand, the Maputo Protocol was ratified in 2005 and thus falls within section 211(1) of the Constitution, which provides that any international agreement entered into after the commencement of the Constitution shall form part of the law provided by an Act of Parliament. Therefore, the Maputo Protocol's provisions must be domesticated through an act of Parliament to have direct application in Malawi. The Maputo Protocol, crafted with the lived and unique experiences of African women in mind, encompasses a myriad of women's rights. Malawi's practice so far has been to domesticate aspects of the Maputo Protocol through various pieces of legislation. For instance, health and reproductive rights, as outlined in Article 14, and the elimination of harmful practices, as stipulated in Article 5, are partially domesticated in sections 19 and 5, respectively, of the Gender Equality Act.

Article 7(d) of the Maputo Protocol provides that in case of separation, divorce, or annulment of marriage, women and men shall have the right to an equitable sharing of the joint property deriving from the marriage. This provision is reflected in section 24 of the Malawian Constitution and domesticated through section 74 of the MDFRA, which respectively provide for the distribution of jointly held property in a fair and equitable manner.

Article 16(c) of CEDAW requires state parties to take all appropriate measures to eliminate discrimination against women in all matters relating to marriage and family relations, in particular, to ensure that men and women have the same rights and responsibilities during marriage and at its dissolution. In its General Recommendation number 21, the CEDAW Committee noted some countries disproportionately prioritise financial contributions when dividing marital property, while minimising the significance of non-financial roles such as raising children, caring for elderly family members, and managing household responsibilities. The Committee recognised that such non-financial contributions by the wife enable the husband to earn an income and increase assets, and accordingly recommended that financial and non-financial contributions should be accorded the same weight.[56]

In this regard, the approach must be to balance the duties of a spouse to the marriage and recognise the non-financial contributions of the woman, as she bears the burden of domestic work. This, in essence, echoes the position of the African Commission.

---

[56] CEDAW (1994, para 32).

5 Challenges and Recommendations

At the centre of women's property rights, what remains to be considered by the courts is the gendered aspect of property acquisition, including women's lower earning power, which is due to several factors. The first is gender inequality, which is also prevalent in the workplace. The Gender Equality Act aims to rectify employment inequalities by introducing quotas in public service, requiring appointments to be made in a 60:40 ratio.[57] The government intends to extend these quotas to the private sector, despite the law's current partial implementation.[58] An assessment found that quotas in public service are not usually adhered to during recruitment because the Public Service Act of 1994 and the Malawi Public Service Regulations are not aligned with the Gender Equality Act.[59] The government is yet to implement recommendations for review. Women in Malawi still face gender discrimination in employment, and this affects their earning power and financial contribution to the acquisition of property in marriage, either by themselves or with their spouse.

Second is domestic violence in its various forms. The 2015–16 Malawi Demographic and Health Survey (DHS) found that 34% of women have experienced physical violence since the age of 15, and 20% have experienced sexual violence. Almost half of ever-married women have experienced spousal violence, with the most common type of spousal violence being emotional violence (30%), followed by physical violence (26%), and sexual violence (19%).[60] Domestic violence among married women, including physical, sexual, or emotional abuse by their spouses, is estimated at 42%, surpassing the global average for intimate partner violence.[61] The Prevention of Domestic Violence Act also recognises economic or financial abuse, which could be in the form of refusal to contribute to household costs, misuse of money in joint bank accounts, damaging of property, and denying a spouse from participating in economic activity, including employment.[62] Although limited data is available on the prevalence of economic or financial abuse in Malawi, its presence is undeniable, and its impact on women's acquisition of property must be acknowledged and interrogated. However, such circumstances can only be brought to the court's attention if they are properly pleaded and proved, a process that largely depends on whether women have access to legal representation, particularly by advocates who understand gender dynamics and their implications within the context of marriage. The training of lawyers in gender and property acquisition is therefore crucial and recommended. There must also be increased legal aid provided for women to enable them to ascertain and claim their rights to property in a court of law.

Finally, it is commendable that the constitutional protection of women's property rights, including during the dissolution of marriage, created a benchmark for women's

---

[57] Gender Equality Act (2013, s. 11).

[58] Nation Online (2023).

[59] Boas and Mpazanje (2015, p. 109).

[60] National Statistical Office (2017).

[61] National Statistical Office (2017).

[62] Prevention of Domestic Violence Act (2014, s. 2).

property rights. However, the law, in its application, requires technical expertise that may not be achieved without recourse to legal assistance. The provision of legal aid is therefore essential to the enforcement of women's property rights upon the dissolution of marriage, as legal representation enables the proper articulation of the various factors entitling a woman to a share in the property, particularly in cases where no direct financial contribution to its acquisition is evident. Regarding this, the ACHPR has emphasised that legal aid should be broadly understood to encompass legal representation, legal assistance, legal advice, legal education and information, mechanisms for alternative dispute resolution, and restorative justice processes.[63] Without the intervention of courts and legal aid, the protection of women's property rights, regardless of the type of marriage contracted, shall remain a challenge.

The training of judicial officers is also crucial to ensuring that women have access to the legal remedies provided under the law. The ACHPR requires that state parties should ensure the training of judicial and administrative officers on women's marital property rights as well as women's equal rights within the context of marriage, divorce, separation, and annulment of marriage. The recommendation further ensures that judicial officers are trained on gender equality and its application in judicial or other remedial processes.[64]

All in all, the discussed legal regimes governing property distribution upon the dissolution of marriage in Malawi generally appear gender-neutral, in that both spouses may own property and parties are entitled to a fair distribution of it, taking into account all the circumstances of the case. However, implementation within the social and marital context, against the background of gender roles and relations within the home, tends to place wives at a greater disadvantage compared to their husbands.[65] The recognition of gender and its deep entrenchment in marital relations must be acknowledged in court decisions concerning property distribution. The Constitution of Malawi has recognised gender as a crucial factor in the distribution of matrimonial property.[66] However, the courts have not sufficiently discussed or considered the impact of gender on property acquisition and its subsequent distribution in marriages. To ensure that women's property rights are both legally and in fact protected, gender should be mainstreamed in judicial decisions. The training of judicial officers and the provision of legal aid services are thus essential in protecting women's property rights.

[63] African Commission (2021).

[64] African Commission (2021).

[65] African Commission (2021).

[66] Constitution of the Republic of Malawi (1994, s. 24).

References

African Commission (2021) General Comment No. 6 on Article 7(d) of the Protocol to the African Charter on Human and Peoples' Rights on the Rights of Women in Africa. https://achpr.au.int/index.php/en/documents/2020-03-04/general-comment-no6-article-7d-maputo-protocol-right. Accessed 1 Nov 2025

Bekker JC (1989) Seymour's customary law in southern Africa, 5th edn. Juta, Cape Town

Boas M, Mpazanje F (2015) Women in politics in Malawi. Christian Michelsen Institute. https://www.cmi.no/publications/file/5923-women-in-politics-in-malawi.pdf. Accessed 2 Nov 2025

CEDAW (1994) General Recommendation No. 21: equality in marriage and family relations. UN Doc A/49/38. https://www.refworld.org/legal/general/cedaw/1994/en/61456. Accessed 1 Nov 2025

Garner BA (ed) (2009) Black's law dictionary, 9th edn. West Publishing Company, St. Paul

Matinga B (2015) What's mine? rural women's experiences around property rights in the context of dissolved marriages in matrilineal societies: a case study of Muluwila Village in Kuntumanje Area, Zomba District, Malawi. Dissertation, Stellenbosch University

Mwambene L (2010) Marriage under African customary law in the face of the Bill of Rights and international human rights standards in Malawi. Afr Hum Rights Law J 10(1):78–104

Nation Online (2023) Private sector faces gender quota law. 12 November. Available at: https://mwnation.com/private-sector-faces-gender-quotas-law/. Accessed 1 Nov 2025.

National Statistical Office (2017) Malawi demographic health survey 2015–16. https://dhsprogram.com/pubs/pdf/FR319/FR319.pdf. Accessed 1 Nov 2025

Ngwira N (2005) Women's property and inheritance rights and the land reform process in Malawi. Institute for Policy Research and Analysis for Dialogue Research Paper. https://sarpn.org/documents/d0000585/P522_Malawi_property_rights.pdf. Accessed 1 Nov 2025

US Department of State (2022) 2022 Report on international religious freedom: Malawi. https://www.state.gov/reports/2022-report-on-international-religious-freedom/malawi. Accessed 1 Nov 2025

Wanda BP (1988) Customary family law in Malawi: adherence to tradition and adaptability to change. J Leg Plur Unoff Law 20(27):117–134

Willman A, Puerto M, Wambua VM (2022) An inclusive and resilient economy for Malawi depends on investing in women. https://blogs.worldbank.org/en/africacan/inclusive-and-resilient-economy-malawi-depends-investing-women. Accessed 1 Nov 2025

Pachalo Nomsa Grace Mwenelupembe is a practicing attorney based in Malawi. Her research interests focus on women's rights. Mwenelupembe holds an LLB(Hons) from the University of Malawi, an LLM in Sexual and Reproductive Rights in Africa from the University of Pretoria, and is an LLD candidate at the University of the Free State.

Settlement of Matrimonial Property upon Divorce in Nigeria: The Rights of Spouses, Challenges and Urgent Need for Reforms

Alaba Ibironke Kekere, Itunu Kolade-Faseyi, and Oluwadara Oluwaseun Ajidasile

Abstract Property division during divorce proceedings in Nigeria remains one of the most complex and contentious aspects of matrimonial litigation. The applicable legal rules are shaped by the form of marriage, whether customary, Islamic, or statutory. This pluralism often leads to inconsistent and discretionary outcomes. This chapter critically assesses how judicial reliance on direct financial contributions as the primary measure of entitlement undermines the communal nature of marriage and disproportionately disadvantages women. Many spousal contributions, particularly those of women, are indirect or non-monetary, rooted in care work and emotional labour that rarely translate into legally recognised claims. The analysis also considers the treatment of premarital property, especially in the absence of prenuptial agreements, and examines statutory and judicial approaches to asset division. Highlighting the burden placed on petitioners to prove contribution and the limited attention given to factors such as the duration of the marriage or custodial responsibilities, the chapter underscores the urgent need for reform. It concludes with proposals for a more equitable legal framework that recognises the full scope of spousal contributions and ensures fairer outcomes in matrimonial property settlements.

A. I. Kekere · O. O. Ajidasile
Faculty of Law, Adekunle Ajasin University, Akungba, Nigeria
e-mail: ibironke.kekere@aaua.edu.ng

O. O. Ajidasile
e-mail: oluwadara.ajidasile@aaua.edu.ng

I. Kolade-Faseyi (✉)
College of Law, Caleb University, Imota, Nigeria
e-mail: kolade-faseyi.itunu@calebuniversity.edu.ng

A. F. Hammond and P. Batariwah (eds.), *The Law on Marital Property in Africa*, Ius Gentium: Comparative Perspectives on Law and Justice 138,
https://doi.org/10.1007/978-3-032-19358-2_5

1 Introduction

Whilst marriage, an age-long tradition, is an agreement that is generally expected to last until parties die, it could unfortunately, be terminated by divorce. Therefore, marriage may not be a union for life.[1] When a marriage is dissolved and marital ties severed, the dilemma of who takes what often follows. This situation in Nigeria is quite complex due to the different normative orders that regulate the institution of marriage and its incidence.

The Marriage Act,[2] the principal statute that governs statutory marriages in Nigeria, recognises two kinds of marriage: statutory marriage and marriage under native law and custom, otherwise known as customary law marriage.[3] On the other hand, the Constitution recognises three kinds of marriage: Christian marriage, which is governed by statute; customary law marriage, which is governed by the various native laws and customs; and Islamic marriage, which is governed by Islamic law.[4] Hence, the applicable law for the settlement of matrimonial property would ultimately be determined by the system under which the marriage was contracted.

Determining who gets what upon divorce largely hinges on the judge's understanding of what is equitable. This often involves a consideration of the direct financial contributions of the parties to the acquisition of the property. The petitioner is required to provide clear evidence of the contributions made before the assets can be granted to them. This approach defeats the concept of marriage as a union. Women, especially in Nigeria, while treating marriage as a union of mutual respect and love, are at the receiving end, as their contributions to the acquisition of marital property are usually discreet.

What constitutes marital property is distinguishable from spousal maintenance. Maintenance, commonly referred to as alimony or spousal support in other jurisdictions, is financial support that one spouse is required to provide the other regularly to mitigate the economic impact of the divorce on the less financially stable spouse.[5] This is quite different from a settlement of marital property, which is an ancillary relief granted during divorce as a one-time division of all assets and liabilities acquired during the lifetime of the marriage.

This chapter considers the status of the property owned by one of the parties before marriage, particularly in the absence of a prenuptial agreement, vis-à-vis a critical examination of the statutory provisions on the settlement of property upon divorce and the intrinsic challenges. This chapter also demonstrates that Nigerian laws on the distribution of matrimonial property arguably do not adequately consider or appreciate the role of women in the family and, accordingly, often distribute marital property based on 'who contributes what' without crediting the non-financial

[1] Sagay (1999, p. 1).

[2] Marriage Act (Cap M6) Laws of Federation of Nigeria (LFN) 2004.

[3] By virtue of Marriage Act 2004, ss. 35, 46 and 47, Islamic law marriage is classified under customary law marriage.

[4] Constitution of the Federal Republic of Nigeria 1999 (as amended), See sch. 2, i para 61.

[5] See Byron (2021, p. 293).

contributions of the other party, usually the wife. This approach, in our opinion, is 'union defeatist' (i.e., the woman is in an economically disadvantaged position), and raises the question of whether the approach by the courts in settling matrimonial property needs to be more equitable.[6]

The chapter examines how matrimonial property is settled upon divorce in Nigeria. The discussion centres on the rights of spouses, their challenges, the judicial stance on the treatment of marital property, and the need for reform. The chapter is divided into eight sections. Section 1 is the introduction; Sect. 2 discusses the legal framework regulating the distribution of marital property in Nigeria; and Sects. 3 and 4 examine women's property rights under customary law and Islamic law, respectively. Section 5 discusses the judicial approach to the settlement of matrimonial property in Nigeria. Section 6 explains the legal position of spouses in invalid marriages, while Sect. 7 explores the evidentiary rules on the presumption of marriage. Section 8 concludes the chapter and provides recommendations for reform.

2 Legal Framework Regulating the Distribution of Marital Property in Nigeria

The settlement of matrimonial property upon divorce is governed by a hybrid of laws that provide guidelines for the distribution of marital property and the various rights of spouses. As a general matter, what constitutes marital property or family assets is not specifically defined in any statute. However, the Nigerian courts have espoused definitions of marital property similar to those in the UK. After all, Nigeria inherited a common law system modelled after English law as a result of colonisation. The UK's House of Lords has defined marital property to mean 'property acquired during the marriage other than gifts or inherited property given to only one of the spouses'.[7] Also of note is Lord Denning's well-known definition of marital property, as '...those things which are acquired by one or both of the parties, with the intention that they should be continuing provision for them or their children during their joint lives, and used for the benefit of the family as a whole'.[8] Lord Denning's definition is particularly useful because it provides a test of intention to distinguish between what should be included in the category of marital property and what should be described as separate or individual property belonging to only one spouse. The Nigerian Court of Appeal in *Anieto v Anieto*[9] described marital property as property purchased in the course of the marriage, or where property was purchased before marriage and payment completed after, and in the course of the marriage. Properties that do not

---

[6] Efe and Eberechi (2020, p. 23).

[7] *Miller v. Miller*: McFarlane *v McFarlane* [2006] UKHL 24 (Lord Nicholls).

[8] *Wachtel v Wachtel* [1973] 1 All E.R. 829, 836: Lord Denning calls marital property 'family assets'; *Rimmer v Rimmer* [1953] 1 QB 63.

[9] *Anieto v Anieto* [2019] LPELR-47223.

fall under the definition of separate property (*quod aliqua proprietas non cadit in definitione rerum separatarum*) are described as marital properties.[10]

The major laws like the Constitution of the Federal Republic of Nigeria 1999 (as amended), the Married Women's Property Act 1882, the Violence Against Persons Prohibition Act 2015, the Matrimonial Causes Act 1970, and the African Charter on Human and Peoples' Rights 1981 are examined below:

2.1 Constitution of the Federal Republic of Nigeria 1999 (as Amended)

A Constitution is the organic law of a nation that establishes the conception, character, and organisation of its government and prescribes the extent of its sovereign power and the manner of its exercise.[11] The Nigerian Constitution is the *grundnorm* and fundamental law of the land.[12] All other laws in Nigeria are subject to it and derive their legitimacy from it.[13] It is important to state that customs, practices, principles of law, or laws which derogate from the clear provisions of the Constitution shall not be upheld or allowed to prevail no matter the circumstance.[14] By the provision of section 1 of the Constitution of the Federal Republic of Nigeria (CFRN) 1999 as amended, the Constitution is the supreme law, and any other law inconsistent with the provisions of the Constitution shall be void to the extent of its inconsistency.[15] The Constitution is supreme and binding on all persons subject to it.

The Constitution guarantees every Nigerian the right to own property in any part of the country. Examining the right of every person to own property is important in this discourse because, as would be shown later, some cultural beliefs and practices might encourage the thinking that once a woman gets married, she becomes 'absorbed' by the husband and has no right to own property, either jointly or severally. However, by virtue of section 43 of the Nigerian Constitution, every citizen enjoys the right 'to acquire and own immovable property anywhere in Nigeria'.[16] Immovable property, in this sense, includes lands, houses, buildings, and things affixed to or underneath them.

Similarly, section 42(1)(a), which is the non-discrimination provision of the Constitution, guarantees the right to freedom from discrimination and provides that:

> (1) A citizen of Nigeria of a particular community, ethnic group, place of origin, sex, religion or political opinion shall not, by reason only that he is such a person:-

---

[10] Urhibo (2023, p. 289).

[11] Garner (1999, p. 306).

[12] *AG Abia State v AG Federation* [2002] 6 NWLR 264, 479-480 (Kalgo JSC).

[13] *Musa v INEC* [2002] 11 NWLR 223, 293.

[14] *Okonkwo Timothy v Sunday Oforka and Anor.* [2008] 9 NWLR 204 (Denton-West JCA).

[15] Shehu (2011, pp. 43–72). See also Constitution of the Federal Republic of Nigeria 1999 (as amended), s 1(1).

[16] Constitution of the Federal Republic of Nigeria 1999 (as amended), s 43.

(a) be subjected either expressly by, or in the practical application of, any law in force in Nigeria or any executive or administrative action of the government, to disabilities or restrictions to which citizens of Nigeria of other communities, ethnic groups, places of origin, sex, religions or political opinions are not made subject.

This constitutional provision also applies to a non-Nigerian wife married to a Nigerian husband, provided she subsequently becomes a Nigerian citizen. After being registered as a Nigerian citizen, she can acquire or own immovable property in Nigeria.[17] After the said registration, the erstwhile 'foreign' wife becomes a bona fide Nigerian citizen, subject to the enjoyment of the provisions of the Nigerian Constitution, which includes, but is not limited to, freedom from discrimination on any grounds and the right to own property.

A combined reading of sections 42 and 43 of the Constitution reveals that land acquisition and ownership are not the sole prerogative of any particular gender. It is the fundamental right of every Nigerian, male or female, husband or wife, married or divorced, to acquire and own land in Nigeria.

2.2 *The Married Women's Property Act 1882*

The Married Women's Property Act (MWPA) 1882 is part of the received English law that came with colonialism.[18] It applied to the federating States of Nigeria as a Statute of General Application (SOGA) until the former western region of Nigeria enacted the Married Women's Property Law 1959 (MWPL), which applied to the western and mid-western states in Nigeria.[19] The MWPL is a re-enactment of the MWPA and is in force in the old Western and Midwestern regions of Nigeria. The MWPA still applies to states outside of these two regions.

[17] Constitution of the Federal Republic of Nigeria 1999 (as amended), s 26(2)(a). It is important to state that perhaps because of the patriarchal nature of the Nigerian society, there is no corresponding section in the Nigerian constitution addressing the status of a 'foreign' man married to a Nigerian woman as far as citizenship is concerned. As a matter of fact, a Bill proposing the amendment of the constitution to allow the citizenship conferment on foreigners married to Nigerian women was rejected. It can therefore be inferred that the right of a Nigerian woman to transmit her nationality to her foreign husband is limited by section 26(2); Iroanusi and Fadare (2022).

[18] The Received English Law is one of the sources of Nigerian law. It comprises the English Common Law principles, the Doctrine of Equity and the Statutes of General Application which were enacted in England and were in force before the 1st day of January 1900. See Sanni (2015, p. 126).

[19] In 1959, the Governor of the Western Region enacted a Law which limited the reception of the common law. Some SOGA were reenacted as local legislation, MWPL is one of them. See also Onokah (2003, p. 273).

The MWPA only applies to statutory marriages. It does not accommodate marriages conducted under Islamic law or native law and custom.[20] Section 1(4) of the Act provides that:

> A married woman shall, in accordance with the provisions of this Act, be capable of acquiring, holding and disposing by will or otherwise of any real or personal property as her separate property in the same manner as if she were a *feme sole*, without the intervention of any trustee.

The effect of the above is that a woman marrying after the year 1882 can hold or retain all the property she brought to the marriage or subsequently acquired thereafter as her 'separate property'. By recognising and establishing the doctrine of separate property, spouses, during the subsistence of their marriage, can exercise separate ownership rights to property as if they were not married. They can acquire, hold, alienate, and dispose of property by will without interference from their husbands or any trustee. This removed many of the legal disadvantages that came with coverture.[21] The Act overrules the English common law system that subsumes married women's ability to act autonomously under their husbands' authority or in holding properties.[22] The Act addresses the question of who owns what during marriage, rather than who should receive what upon the dissolution of marriage.[23] Unfortunately, this Act does not regulate the redistribution of marital property in the dissolution of statutory or civil marriages.

Meanwhile, a combined reading of sections 1(3), (4), and (5) of the MWPA reveals that, because women are treated as *feme sole*, their marital status is inconsequential in laying claim to property or having a stake therein. The Act exclusively deals with the interests of parties in property and recognises the contractual rights (including liabilities) of married women with respect to their separate property. In construing provisions of the Act, Nigerian courts ascertain the extent of a spouse's interest in the property of the other spouse.[24] It is also important to state that courts place much emphasis on evidence of a party's financial contribution towards the purchase or development of the said property based on property law rules to give recognition and respect to the property rights of the spouses and to ensure adequate compensation for any loss caused by the marriage, based on what is just and equitable.[25]

---

[20] See section 1(2) of the Act. See also Toyin *Arajulu v James Monday* (HC, 18 February 2019) for a contrary opinion where the court applied provisions of the Married Women Property Law of Oyo State to determine the case of a customarily married spouse.

[21] Coverture was a Common Law doctrine where the existence of a married woman/wife was merged with that of her husband particularly with regard to ownership of property. See Olomola (2021, p. 5).

[22] Olomola (2021, p. 5).

[23] *Pettitt v Pettitt* [1969] 2 All ER 385,393.

[24] Onyi-Ogelle and Nwawulu (2023, p. 117).

[25] See *Toyin Arajulu v James Monday* (HC, 18 February 2019); *Egunjobi v Egunjobi* [1976] 2 FNLR 78.

2.3 *Matrimonial Causes Act 1970*

The Matrimonial Causes Act (MCA) is a federal enactment that governs statutory marriages in Nigeria.[26] This Act is the primary matrimonial law in Nigeria,[27] and includes several provisions that allow a spouse who has entered into a statutory marriage to obtain a property settlement upon the dissolution of that marriage.[28] Specifically, section 72(1) provides as follows:

> The court may, in proceedings under this Act, by order require the parties to the marriage, or either one of them, to make, for the benefit of all or any of the parties to, and the children of, the marriage, such a settlement of property to which the parties are, or either of them is, entitled (whether in possession or reversion) as the court considers just and equitable in the circumstances of the case.

From the provision above, property to be settled (real or personal property) can belong to both spouses or either of them. The settlement typically benefits both parties, either spouse individually, as well as the children of the marriage.[29] It could also be reasonably inferred that the above provision empowers judges who hear the divorce petition to decide how property owned by one or both spouses can be shared. This statutory recognition of the beneficial interest of parties at divorce makes women's right to property very explicit. Their entitlement to claim or call for property settlement upon marital breakdown is clearly stated and not subject to further interpretation.

Notably, the application of section 72 of the Act has come under heavy criticism.[30] The inference of joint ownership of property or the right to call for the settlement of property upon marriage dissolution is not automatic, as a party has to show to the satisfaction of the court evidence of financial contribution for the acquisition of the disputed property.[31] In addition, there is no measuring standard to determine who gets what. The court merely considers what is 'just and equitable in the circumstances of the case'.[32] It is argued that the court's broad discretionary powers risk misuse, as their expansive nature may lead to a slippery slope in which such discretion is exercised arbitrarily. What is 'just and equitable' is subjective and based on the peculiar circumstances of the case, and at the mercy of the court's discretion.[33] This means that what a particular court may find suitable, just, and appropriate in a case may not be equitable or meet the justice of another case. With this, the party with

---

[26] Matrimonial Causes Act (Cap M7) Laws of Federation of Nigeria (LFN) 2004.

[27] Nwogugu (1971, p. 171).

[28] Generally, see Matrimonial Causes Act, ss 72 and 73.

[29] However, no settlement of property would be ordered for the benefit of children who have attained the age of twenty-one (21) years unless the court is of the opinion that special circumstances warrant it. See Cap M7, s 72(3).

[30] Attah (2018, pp. 436–442).

[31] Attah (2018, pp. 436–442).

[32] See *Igbuwe v Igbuwe* (CA, 17 July 2023); *Sunmonu v Sunmonu* (CA, 23 November 2021); *Akinbuwa v Akinbuwa* [1998] 7 NWLR 661, 677.

[33] Onyi-Ogelle and Nwawulu (2023, p. 117).

a better financial standing and evidence of financing the matrimonial property may receive a larger share of the property.[34]

In exercising its general powers under the Act, the court has the authority to order the payment of a lump sum,[35] the execution of any required deed or instrument, the production of title documents, or the completion of any other actions necessary to ensure the effective implementation of an order.[36] Orders for the settlement of property can be discharged when the beneficiary remarries or there is a just cause for such discharge. The same order of the court may be modified, suspended, or revived by the court that issued the first order or by another court.[37]

The settlement of property does not include its redistribution. Such property is merely given for the use and enjoyment of a spouse without the conferment of absolute title on that spouse,[38] because the property can be recalled at any time.[39] A combined reading and analysis of the provisions of the Matrimonial Causes Act (MCA) on the settlement of matrimonial property underscores the discretionary powers of the court based on what is just and equitable, and not necessarily what the party wants. Property can be settled by selling and sharing the proceeds between the parties, conferring ownership of the disputed property on one of the parties, or ordering the payment of a lump sum, while still allowing the recipient the luxury of living in the settled property. This discretionary power of the court has come under severe criticism for being too broad and potentially opening the floodgates to discrimination.[40]

2.4 *Violence Against Persons (Prohibition) Act 2015*

The aim of the Violence Against Persons (Prohibition) (VAPP) Act is to protect all persons (men and women) against all forms of violence in both private and public lives. The focus of the Act is also to prohibit all forms of violence against persons and to provide maximum protection and effective remedies for victims while punishing offenders.[41] The VAPP Act is a federal enactment applicable only in Abuja, the

---

[34] Even though court's discretion is wide, regard is had as to what is fair and equitable based on evidence adduced by parties requesting for the settlement. Standards like interest of children, moral/ and financial contribution of a spouse have been put in place to help judicial officers while exercising their discretion. See below under section 4.0 of this chapter, 'Judicial Approach to Settlement of Matrimonial Property'.

[35] Matrimonial Causes Act, s 73(1)(a-b).

[36] Matrimonial Causes Act, s73(1)(d).

[37] See generally Matrimonial Causes Act, s73(1)(j).

[38] Onyi-Ogelle and Nwawulu (2023, p. 177).

[39] See Matrimonial Causes Act, s73(1).

[40] Ifemeje (2008, p. 175).

[41] See the Explanatory Memorandum to the Violence Against Persons (Prohibition) Act (VAPP Act) 2015.

Federal Capital Territory.[42] Other states in the country will need to enact similar provisions for their states.

Although the VAPP Act does not explicitly deal with or mention the settlement of properties, some of its provisions, which proscribe economic abuse or forced financial dependence,[43] emotional abuse, abandonment of spouses or dependants without sustenance,[44] and the forceful ejection of a spouse from home,[45] can be read into a property settlement. For example, the Act will not accommodate a spouse who lays claim to marital property when the spouse forcefully evicts the other spouse from it or refuses access to it. The offences under the Act are punishable with terms of imprisonment, fines, or both. Criminalising actions that deny a spouse access to marital property is of utmost importance, especially when it can be proven that the spouse being denied access had contributed either in cash or in kind to the acquisition of such property.

2.5 African Charter on Human and Peoples' Rights 1981

The African Charter on Human and Peoples' Rights ('Banjul Charter' or 'ACHPR') is a regional human rights instrument drafted in 1981 but entered into force on 21 October 1986. The Banjul Charter recognises that fundamental human rights flow from the attributes of being human.[46] By virtue of being human, several rights, including the right to property,[47] the dignity of the human person,[48] and equality before the law,[49] amongst others, are assured. These rights are to be enjoyed 'without distinction of any kind such as race, ethnic group, colour, sex, language, religion, political or any other opinion, national and social origin, fortune, birth or other status'.[50] The family is recognised under the ACHPR as the basis of every society, requiring and deserving of State protection.[51] Therefore, State parties are charged with assisting the family in realising its full potential.

Although the provisions of the Banjul Charter are general in nature, with no specific provision on the settlement of marital property, this does not detract from the fact that it serves as a springboard for similar human rights instruments on the continent. Most of its provisions on human rights have been domesticated in national

---

[42] VAPP Act, s 47.

[43] VAPP Act, s 12.

[44] VAPP Act, s 16.

[45] VAPP Act, s 9.

[46] See preamble to African Charter on Human and Peoples' Rights (adopted 27 June 1981, entered into force 21 October 1986) 1520 UNTS 217.

[47] African Charter on Human and Peoples' Rights, art 14.

[48] African Charter on Human and Peoples' Rights, art. 5.

[49] African Charter on Human and Peoples' Rights, arts. 3 and 19.

[50] African Charter on Human and Peoples' Rights, art. 2.

[51] African Charter on Human and Peoples' Rights, art. 18(1).

laws.[52] In Nigeria, for example, with the enactment of the African Charter on Human and Peoples' Rights (Ratification and Enforcement) Act,[53] substantive provisions of the ACHPR are guaranteed and incorporated into national law, and the courts are charged with enforcing its provisions.[54]

3 Property Rights of Women Under Customary Law

Customary law may be described as 'a body of customs and traditions, which regulate the various kinds of relationship between members of the community in their traditional setting.'[55] Obaseki JSC, in *Oyewunmi v Ogunesan*, described customary law as the organic or living law of the indigenous people of Nigeria, regulating their lives and transactions.[56] Nigeria is a heterogeneous and multicultural society with about 350 linguistic groups and over 250 ethnic groups.[57] Each of these groups has its own body of largely uncodified and unique laws that govern the affairs of its members, including their practices regarding marriage, marital breakdown, and incidental matters such as property settlement. Customs are categorised as either ethnic-based or non-ethnic-based; Islamic law is considered a non-ethnic-based custom.

Generally, under customary law, women are regarded as subordinates to their husbands, and as such, their legal identities are subsumed into those of their husbands.[58] Wives have no independent rights apart from those that their husbands allow, and they will require their husbands' consent to dispose of any property they acquire during the subsistence of the marriage.[59] The treatment of a wife as subordinate to her husband is often cited as a foundational element of patriarchy and gender inequality within a marital relationship.[60]

Under customary law, property rights accruing to a man or woman differ from one community to another. In certain customs, the family takes precedence over the marriage union in matters of property. For instance, in *Bini* customs and tradition, the family may take over a deceased husband's property, even when the wife contributed to its acquisition.[61] Under Yoruba customary law, a woman can acquire

---

52 D'Sa (1985).

53 African Charter on Human and Peoples' Rights (Ratification and Enforcement) Act (Cap A9) Laws of the Federation of Nigeria 2004.

54 See *Peter Nemi v AG Lagos State* [1994] 10 SCNJ 1.

55 Okonkwo (2005).

56 *Oyewunmi v Ogunesan* 1990] 3 N.W.L.R 182, 207.

57 See Ministry of Foreign Affairs Nigeria (n.d).

58 Ajayi (2020, p. 10).

59 Onokah (2003, p. 108). See also, Kolade-Faseyi (2023, p. 45) and the case of *Onwuchekwa v Onwuchekwa* [1997] 10 NWLR 5.

60 Schneider (1992, p. 536).

61 Yesufu and Nkomo (2018, p. 9).

property before or during marriage and freely deal with it.[62] This is also the position under *Urhobo* native law and custom.[63] In most *Igbo* communities, however, wives cannot dispose of properties without their husbands' consent.[64] Even where the wife purchased such properties, she must obtain her husband's consent before giving away property acquired during marriage to any person other than her child either during her lifetime or by will.[65] This is because there is an irrebuttable presumption among the *Igbos* that landed properties belong to the husband.[66] After a divorce, a customarily married wife may be forced to leave the matrimonial home, especially if she cannot establish her claim to ownership or other proprietary rights.[67]

A customary law marriage in Nigeria does not grant equal rights to spouses upon the dissolution of their marriage or upon the death of either spouse. Even though case law and enactments proscribe discriminatory practices against women, they continue to exist.[68] An analysis of certain court decisions further demonstrates that women's rights to own property under customary law are more illusory than actual. In *Davies v Davies*,[69] the court, per Buckley J., held that:

> Yoruba native law and custom deprived the widow of inheritance rights in her deceased husband's estate because devolution of property follows the blood. Consequently, unless property given to a wife is proved to be an outright gift during the lifetime of the husband, it will devolve on the husband's death as family property to be inherited by the deceased husband's children or relatives where there are no children.

Thus, under native law and custom, a wife may only be able to claim marital property upon divorce if she can prove that she made a financial contribution to its acquisition. However, establishing such proof may be difficult if she did not keep records of her contributions, particularly as divorce was unlikely to have been anticipated at the time of marriage.[70] The decision of the Supreme Court in *Onwuchekwa v Onwuchekwa*[71] lends credence to this position, as it denied a wife's claim to co-ownership of matrimonial property because she could not provide evidence of her contribution to the property's purchase. Additionally, the court reiterated that, according to custom, the wife and her property are considered the husband's chattel.

---

[62] Onokah (2003, pp. 252–253).

[63] Awhefeada (2011, p. 130).

[64] Awhefeada, U.V., ibid.

[65] Obi (2020, 1977, p. 10).

[66] Egemonu (2017, p. 99).

[67] *Oloko v Giwa* [1939] 15 NLR 31.

[68] See the case of *Ukeje v Ukeje* [2014] 9 NWLR 384. See also sections 41, 42 and 43 of the Constitution of the Federal Republic of Nigeria 1999 (as amended); Articles 2, 5 and 11 of the Convention on the Elimination of All Forms of Discrimination Against Women (adopted 18 December 1979, entered into force 3 September 1981) 1249 UNTS 13; Articles 2 and 3 of the ACHPR.

[69] *Davies v Davies* [1929] 2 NLR 79.

[70] Ojogbo and Edu (2022, p. 236).

[71] *Onwuchekwa v Onwuchekwa* [1997] 10 NWLR 5.

In the case of *Toyin Arajulu v James Monday*,[72] the court considered the issue of joint ownership of property acquired during the subsistence of a customary law marriage. It concluded that the performance of wifely duties, including caring for children and maintaining the home front, was a valuable consideration that could not be quantified in monetary terms.[73] The court, while referring to the non-financial contribution of the petitioner as the 'palm tree principle of justice', relied on it in determining the suit in her favour. The completed building was to be retained as the matrimonial home, with the children as beneficial owners and the petitioner in possession as long as she remained unmarried. The court also ordered that the uncompleted building be sold, the proceeds divided into equal shares, and used for the maintenance of the children.[74] It is important to state that the petitioner/wife's claim was for joint ownership of the property in question. However, it appears the court avoided resolving the question of ownership by granting the petitioner the possessory right to live in the property without defining the nature of the interest conferred on her.[75]

It is essential to note that, although customary law is a significant source of law in Nigeria, customs that do not align with existing laws in the country are repugnant to natural justice, equity, and good conscience are unenforceable.[76] The court in *Alajemba Uke and Anor v Albert Iro,*[77] opined that the *Nneato Nnewi* custom that tends to relegate women and deprive them of their invaluable and constitutionally guaranteed rights is only 'fit for the garbage consigned to history'.[78] Also, customs that discriminate against a woman's right to own property jointly acquired during the subsistence of her marriage contravene existing laws and will be held void to the extent of their inconsistency.[79]

---

[72] *Toyin Arajulu v James Monday* (HC, 18 February 2019) (Abimbola J).

[73] *Toyin Arajulu v James Monday* (HC, 18 February 2019).

[74] *Toyin Arajulu v James Monday* (HC, 18 February 2019) 29.

[75] *Toyin Arajulu v James Monday* (HC, 18 February 2019).

[76] See *Ukeje v Ukeje* [2014] 11 NWLR 384.

[77] *Alajemba Uke and Another v Albert Iro* [2001] 1 NWLR 196.

[78] See *Alajemba Uke and Another v Albert Iro* [2001] 1 NWLR 196, 202 (Pats-Acholonu JCA).

[79] The courts have held such customs to be repugnant to natural justice, equity and good conscience and consequently, have refused to enforce such customary laws and practices. In *Mojekwu v Mojekwu* [1997] 7 NWLR 283, the custom of Nwewi people of Nigeria that gives a brother the right to inherit the estate of his late brother to the exclusion of the deceased's widow and female children was held to be discriminatory and repugnant to natural justice, equity and good conscience and was therefore set aside. Similarly, in *Ukeje v Ukeje* [2014] 11 NWLR 384, the right of a female child to inherit properties was upheld while the Ikwerre native law and custom that stated otherwise was held to be discriminatory and unconstitutional. A major legal reform followed the *Ukeje* judgement as Rivers State Nigeria, the home State of the Ikwerre people, became the first State in Nigeria to promulgate a law that entitled women to share in family property- Rivers State Prohibition of the Curtailment of Women's Right to Share in Family Property Law No 2 of 2022.

4 Property Rights of Spouses Under Islamic Law

Islamic marriages are not accommodated under the Matrimonial Causes Act.[80] Therefore, legal incidents of statutory marriage and privileges accorded to spouses married under the Act are not enjoyed by those married under Islamic rites. In an Islamic law marriage, the husband is duty-bound to provide his wife with reasonable accommodation, clothing, food, and other necessaries.[81] Neither party is obligated to transfer property to the other, and the husband's duty to maintain the wife ceases upon the dissolution of the marriage.[82] Where no reconciliation is effected during the waiting (*iddah*) period, maintenance ceases, and claims to a share of the husband's estate are likely to fail.[83]

A wife in an Islamic marriage can own personal property independently of her husband. Marriage does not transfer ownership of property between spouses under Islamic law.[84] Islamic law does not view marriage as a partnership and prioritises individual property ownership in marital relationships. Consequently, a wife can acquire property with her own funds.[85] In the event of divorce under Islamic law, the wife has the right to exclusive ownership of property she acquired by personal purchase or received as a gift from her parents, including the *mahr*.[86] The wife has a complete and indefeasible property right in the *mahr*. This stands in sharp contrast to the position under customary law, which requires a wife and her family to pay back the dowry upon the dissolution of the customary marriage.

A wife, therefore, has no right to share in the property of the husband. Regarding property jointly acquired during the existence of the marriage, a wife may be able to share in the property if she can prove that she contributed financially towards its acquisition. Proof of financial contribution is a core requirement under Islamic law.[87] A higher contribution concomitantly translates into a larger interest in the property.[88]

The emphasis placed on financial contribution puts homemaker wives at a disadvantage. Their inability to prove financial contribution means that they cannot share in the property acquired by their husbands. Moreover, husbands are legally required to maintain their divorced wives for 3 months from the date of the divorce; if she is pregnant, the maintenance period extends to the delivery of the child.[89] The combination of brief maintenance periods and the exclusion of women from benefiting

[80] See Matrimonial Causes Act, s. 69.

[81] Bani and Pate (2015, p. 104).

[82] Egemonu (2017, p. 87).

[83] Egemonu (2017, p. 99).

[84] See Quran 4:32.

[85] Udoh et al. (2020, p. 4).

[86] The *mahr* is the dower (gift) which by Islamic injunction, the husband is expected to give to his wife as part of the formalities of an Islamic marriage. See Quran 4:4.

[87] Akhtar and Manjoo (2024, p. 77).

[88] Udoh et al. (2020, p. 4).

[89] In Hanafi School of law, a divorced Muslim wife is entitled to maintenance during *Iddah* period whereas in Shefai law, a divorced Muslim wife is not even entitled to maintenance. If after the

from property acquired by their husbands is likely to result in a compounded injustice against divorced women who devoted their time and effort to managing the household, while their husbands earned the family's income.

5 Judicial Approach to Settlement of Matrimonial Property

The settlement of matrimonial property is one of the ancillary reliefs that flow with the dissolution of a marriage. Nigeria has no restrictions on the type of property that can be settled. Although marital property may consist of real or personal property, it does not include mere monetary payments made by one spouse to the other.[90] The courts consider several factors when dividing marital property. These include the parties' income, their financial and housing needs, and more prominently, the contributions made by each party to the marital property.[91] As the Act did not create a compartmentalised system of settlement, courts are at liberty to be guided by these factors or depart from them.[92] The Supreme Court, in *Okotie-Eboh v Okotie-Eboh*,[93] while stressing that its objective is to ensure a fair distribution that caters to the needs and responsibilities of each party, held that its primary consideration in the division of property is the welfare and interests of the children, followed by the interests of the spouses.

The courts often apply stringent property law principles requiring parties to prove legal title by documentary evidence or by direct financial contribution to the acquisition of the property in dispute.[94] Under this system, the courts do not consider a spouse's indirect financial or non-financial contributions to the acquisition of the property.[95] Thus, in *Sodipe v Sodipe*,[96] there was no evidence of direct financial contribution from the wife. As a result, the court concluded that, although the matrimonial property was valued at ten million naira, a token payment of 200,000 naira (approximately 129.69 USD) was to be made to the estranged wife, who had spent forty-three (43) years in the marriage. Additionally, in *Nwanya v Nwanya*,[97] the respondent's wife claimed that she had contributed 6000 naira (approximately 3.89 USD) to the construction of a house in her husband's name. The decision of the lower court granting her a sum of 5400 naira (about 3.48 USD) was set aside on the basis that she could not adduce evidence.

---

expiry of *Iddah* period, she has no means to maintain herself her husband has no liability for her and she is left with nothing. The Iddah period is usually three months.

[90] Byron (2021, p. 293).

[91] Nwogugu (2014, p. 273).

[92] Amucheaz and Nwodo (2022, p. 19).

[93] *Okotie-Eboh v Okotie-Eboh* [1992] 4 NWLR 1.

[94] Efe and Eberechi (2020, p. 7).

[95] Efe and Eberechi (2020, p. 10).

[96] *Sodipe v Sodipe* [1990] 5 WRN 98.

[97] *Nwanya v Nwanya* [1987] 3 NWLR 697.

Furthermore, in *Amadi v Nwosu*,[98] the appellant's husband sold their matrimonial home and moved to another part of the city. The appellant refused to vacate the house, so the respondent/purchaser sued her for a declaration of title, damages for trespass, and an injunction. The appellant could not provide evidence to support her contention that she had an interest in the house. She merely said that she paid for labour and sand to construct the house and made no effort to substantiate her testimony. Under cross-examination, she testified that she did not know when the house was built. Her husband testified that she was not earning money when he built the house, and his testimony that he built the house without any contribution from his wife was not challenged under cross-examination. The Supreme Court dismissed the appellant's claim. Similarly, in *Onabolu v Onabolu*,[99] the wife/petitioner claimed, among other things, that the matrimonial home, which she shared with her husband, should be shared equally between them or sold, and the proceeds of the sale shared equally. The court examined all the pieces of evidence given by the wife/petitioner and the husband/respondent on the joint ownership of the property and found that the evidence of the husband/respondent positively established that he bought the land on which the property was built. The Court of Appeal held that: 'It is settled law that a person who claims to be the joint owner of a property must be able to quantify his contribution. He must give detailed particulars and support them where necessary with receipts of what he bought towards the building of the property...'.

From the above decisions, it can be deduced that in many cases, couples are not treated as joint owners of marital property. The party that can prove title to the property is awarded ownership of it. This undoubtedly results in a rigid and unequal division of property upon the dissolution of marriage. This strict application of property law is unfair to women. Its emphasis on documentary evidence for family agreements or transactions contradicts the principle of family contracts.[100] Since parties typically do not anticipate the breakdown of a marriage, and many women's contributions to the acquisition of marital property are often invisible and non-financial, gathering evidence or obtaining documents to support these contributions may not be readily available.

Aside from the strict property rights approach, there is also the discretionary approach of courts over marital property in cases of marriage dissolution. In *Kafi v Kafi*,[101] the argument of the appellant/husband against the settlement of property was that the wife was not a joint purchaser/developer of the property and that she received monthly maintenance from him. The court ruled against his position and held that evidence of joint ownership or development was not the only condition necessitating a settlement order, but rather, what is 'just and equitable'. The court found it just and equitable to set aside one of the appellant's several properties as a home for the respondent and her children, with the condition that it not be disposed of during the respondent's lifetime.

---

[98] *Amadi v Nwosu* [1992] 5 NWLR 273.

[99] *Onabolu v Onabolu* [2005] 2 SMC 135.

[100] Duson (2021, p. 14).

[101] *Kafi v Kafi* [1986] 3 NWLR 175.

In determining property settlement, the court in *Getrude Mgbeahuruike v Roland Mgbeahuruike*[102] listed factors that should be considered, including whether the property in question was acquired during the course of the marriage. What was the contribution of each party to the cost of the acquisition? What is just, fair, and equitable to do when settling the property? It is important to state that even though there are guiding principles to assist the court in doing justice, they are not set in stone. What is paramount is the interest of the children. The court in *Igbuwe v Igbuwe*[103] opined that section 72(1) of the Matrimonial Causes Act (MCA) should be construed not to apply only to parties but also to their children, as their interest is paramount. The court reasoned that the property in question could be considered the result of the joint efforts of both parties, given that the wife's financial or non-financial contributions were linked to the success of the appellant husband's business.[104]

In *Sunmonu v Sunmonu*,[105] even though the respondent/wife neither owned the property to be settled nor led evidence of her financial contribution to its acquisition or development, the court exercised its discretion in granting her one of the properties in the premises for the duration of her lifetime, provided she does not remarry. The court reasoned that: 'it would be just and equitable for the petitioner to provide a decent roof for his divorced wife and children of the marriage'. It is our opinion that restricting the respondent's possession only to the matrimonial home where she had been living with the children after the husband moved out (and not to the other properties within the premise) meets the justice of the case because the wife did not lead substantial evidence as to contribution but was still granted one of the properties, as the court considered her welfare and that of her children the deciding factor. If she remarries and consequently loses the property granted, her new husband will provide shelter for her and her children.

The court in *Akinbuwa v Akinbuwa*[106] ordered the husband to execute the title document regarding the property settled for the wife. He was to renovate and repair the house and formally hand over the house keys to the Court Registrar, but he remained responsible for the mortgage debt on the apartment. In *Okere v Akaluka*,[107] the husband abandoned his wife and children in the matrimonial home, moved in with his concubine, and sold the matrimonial home. The purported sale to a third party (the appellant) was voided by the court. The court found that the respondent/wife made substantial financial contributions towards the property's purchase, reconstruction, and expansion, and held that the husband cannot rightly dispose of the property without her consent. Even though the property was in the husband's name, the sale

---

[102] *Getrude Mgbeahuruike v Roland Mgbeahuruike* (CA, 4 May 2017).

[103] *Igbuwe v Igbuwe* (CA, 17 July 2023).

[104] See *Ogunbiyi v Ogunbiyi* [2021] LPELR-53497.

[105] *Sunmonu v Sunmonu* (CA, 23 November 2021).

[106] *Akinbuwa v Akinbuwa* [1998] 7 NWLR 674.

[107] *Okere v Akaluka* (CA, 14 November 2014) 1; See *Caroline Aina v Pius Aina* reported in James et al. (2023), pp. 136–137 where a wife successfully challenged the sale by her husband of a matrimonial property where they had lived for more than 30 years.

was still voided on the application of the remedy of constructive trusts.[108] Notably, in all the cases interrogated, the court orders were considered fair, just, and equitable, given the circumstances of each case.

It is important to note that the court's approach to applying the principle of constructive trusts to the settlement of property is gradually receiving legislative backing in Nigeria through the adoption of relevant enactments. For example, in Cross River State, Nigeria, all properties acquired during a marriage that subsisted jointly belong to the parties to the marriage, unless the parties state otherwise in writing. It shall not be a defence that the document evidencing ownership carries the name of one party to the marriage.[109] Under this equity-based approach, establishing ownership of marital property by documentary evidence is discarded.

6 Invalid Marriages and Property

A void marriage produces no legal consequences; it is treated as if it never occurred.[110] The implication is that such a marital relationship is void ab initio.[111] A statutory marriage may be void if: there is a lawful marriage between one of the parties and a third party[112]; the parties are within the prohibited degrees of affinity or consanguinity[113]; there is noncompliance with requirements of the law[114]; the parties' real consent is absent[115]; or one of the parties is below the marriageable age.[116]

Since a void marriage does not confer marital rights or obligations, marital property rights may not arise. However, property settlement may be possible if a party can demonstrate both title and contribution. The presence of such evidence may persuade the courts to recognise the respective interests of the spouses in the property and to order a fair distribution accordingly. In the case of *Oghoyone v. Oghoyone*,[117] the marriage between the parties was void because the appellant was, at the time of the said marriage, lawfully married to another woman. The court declared that it would be unconscionable for either party to claim exclusive ownership of the property they

---

[108] Where title document of a property is conveyed in the name of one of the spouses, it is construed that the spouse is holding same in trust for the benefit of both parties. See *Hussey v Palmer* [1972] 1 WLR 1286 and *Falconer v Falconer* [1970] 1 WLR 1333.

[109] Violence against Persons (Prohibition) Law of Cross River State 2021, s. 11.

[110] *Oghoyone v Oghoyone* (2010) 3 NWLR (pt. 1182) 564.

[111] Olomola (2021, p. 18).

[112] See Matrimonial Causes Act 1970, s. 3(1)(a) and Marriage Act 2004, s. 33(1). See also T*amunomiteim Nola and ors v Duboye Graham-Douglas and anor* (2019) LPELR-48285 (CA).

[113] Matrimonial Causes Act 1970, s. 3(1)(b).

[114] Matrimonial Causes Act 1970, s. 3(1)(c).

[115] Nwogugu (2014, p. 136). See Matrimonial Causes Act 1970, s. 3(1)(d).

[116] Matrimonial Causes Act 1970, s. 3(1)(e).

[117] *Oghoyone v Oghoyone* (2010) 3 NWLR (pt. 1182) 564.

both claim to have contributed to its purchase.[118] The court ordered the sale of the said property and division of the proceeds between both parties in equal shares.

7 Presumption of Marriage and Martial Property Rights

As mentioned, Nigerian law recognises a panoply of different marriage forms: statutory, customary, and Islamic. Where documentary evidence attesting to the celebration of the marriage is absent, the Nigerian legal system encodes principles of evidence that allow the court to infer the existence of a marriage from the parties' conduct. Central to this evidential framework is the presumption of marriage: when a man and woman cohabit and present themselves as husband and wife, Nigerian courts will, in many circumstances, presume a valid and subsisting marriage unless contrary evidence is provided.[119] This presumption is rebuttable and aimed primarily at achieving practical justice where formal proof (for example, a marriage certificate) is absent.

The presumption applies only to Islamic and customary marriages. Section 166 of the Evidence Act 2011 states:

> When, in any proceeding whether civil or criminal, there is a question as to whether a man or woman is the husband or wife under *Islamic or Customary law*, of a party to the proceeding the court shall, unless the contrary is proved, presume the existence of a valid and subsisting marriage between the two persons where evidence is given to the satisfaction of the court of cohabitation as husband and wife by such man and woman.[120]

The statutory presumption is therefore contextual; it operates mainly where the marriage claim stems from customary or Islamic rites and where documentary proof is missing or disputed. Courts regard the presumption as a matter of both convenience and practical reality. Where parties have lived together and held themselves out as spouses, it is more consistent with public policy to treat their relationship as a marriage for legal purposes unless there is clear evidence to the contrary.[121]

If a court concludes, based on the presumption plus any corroborating evidence, that a valid marriage existed, the claimant acquires all the relevant marital rights, including rights to maintenance, potential claims in matrimonial causes proceedings, intestacy rights on the death of a spouse, and the capacity to seek property settlement relief under the Matrimonial Causes Act.

[118] *Oghoyone v Oghoyone* (2010) 3 NWLR (pt. 1182) 584 (Rhodes-Vivour JCA).

[119] *Ekong and anor v Akpan* (2020) LPELR- 49575 (CA). See also Onokah (2003, p. 105).

[120] Evidence Act 2011, s. 166 (our emphasis).

[121] Action4Justice (2025).

8 Conclusion and Recommendations

In the event of an irretrievable breakdown of the marital relationship and the eventual severance of marital ties, it is important that a fair division or settlement of marital property is carried out. This distribution, which contemplates the seemingly invisible and unquantifiable contributions of a spouse, is a better approach that meets the demands of justice. Where principles of fairness and justice are upheld, the divorce process will be less acrimonious, and the dead marital relationship will indeed be laid to rest in peace.

While several factors hinder the equitable division of marital property, a number of factors can safeguard the property rights of spouses. In our opinion, these challenges must be overcome through legal reform. To safeguard the vulnerability of spouses regarding the settlement of marital property, the following recommendations are proposed.

8.1 Amendment of the Matrimonial Causes Act

It is submitted that since the right to property is a constitutionally entrenched right, the right should not be limited to only spouses who contracted a statutory marriage. Section 69 of the Matrimonial Causes Act (MCA) should be amended so that maintenance and property settlement provisions will be extended to spouses married under customary law or Islamic law.

Additionally, the latitude granted under the law for the court's discretionary powers appears too broad. This unfettered discretion is liable to abuse and can lead to injustice. It is recommended that the rules governing the settlement of marital property be clearly defined and should also account for the non-financial contributions of both parties.

Furthermore, for the purpose of clarity and to avoid ambiguity, the Matrimonial Causes Act should be amended to incorporate the definition of marital property. There is no statutory definition of marital property in Nigeria. No Nigerian law itemises what should or should not be classified as marital property, and this needs to change.

8.2 Independent Settlement of Marital Property Rights

It is recommended that the settlement of marital property should not be limited to divorce proceedings as an ancillary relief. A spouse anticipating marital breakdown should be at liberty to bring such suits without it necessarily forming part of divorce proceedings. For instance, where a husband who had contributed much to the acquisition of marital property contemplates marrying an additional wife, his first spouse (if not willing to opt out of the marriage) should be able to approach the court to determine a settlement of their marital property, given prevailing circumstances. If these suits are allowed to proceed independently, individuals married under customary law can also assert their right to a fair distribution of marital property.

8.3 Public Awareness Creation for Married Couples

There is an urgent need to create public awareness about the property rights of spouses. Within the existing legal framework, women who are aware of their rights can enjoy a higher level of protection. For example, provisions of the Constitution, the VAPP Act, and similar enactments that have already been discussed apply to all persons without discrimination. Individuals can always rely on them to assert their property rights regardless of the type of marriage they contracted.

8.4 Legal Aid for Indigent Persons

As a matter of policy, the government should provide legal aid to indigent individuals undergoing divorce to ensure their access to justice. It has been demonstrated that courts have seized the opportunity to set aside repugnant customs through judicial activism; however, this could only occur because those matters were brought before the courts. Unfortunately, individuals, especially women, who end up becoming victims of culture do not have the economic power to assert their rights. Such persons should be granted access to legal aid to enable them to enforce their right to share in marital properties.

References

Action4Justice (2025) Right to exit a marriage. Nigeria, Action4Justice. Available at: https://nigeria.action4justice.org/legal_areas/womens-rights-focusing-on-marriage-rights/right-to-exit-a-marriage/. Accessed 14 Oct 2025

Ajayi MO (2020) Property rights of women married under customary law: review of Arajulu v. Monday 47:(1) EALR 10

Akhtar RC, Manjoo FA (2024) Matrimonial property in Islamic law. In: Briggs M, Hayward A (eds) Research handbook on family property and the law. Edward Elgar, Cheltenham, pp 77–91

Amucheaz CO, Nwodo FA (2022) A contemporary review of financial aspects of divorce. Int J Bus Law Res 10(3):17–21

Attah MO (2018) Divorcing marriage from marital assets: why equity and women fail in property readjustment actions in Nigeria. J Afr Law 62(3):429–442

Awhefeada UV (2011) Married women's property rights in Nigeria: a critical and comparative analysis. DELSU Law Rev. 128–140

Bani LM, Pate HA (2015) The role of spouses under Islamic family law. Int Aff Glob Strategy 37:104–111

Byron IP (2021) Matrimonial causes. In: Olomola OO (ed) Family law and succession in Nigeria. Princeton & Associates Publishing Co. Ltd, Ogun

Obi SNC (1977) The customary law manual: manual of customary laws in Anambra and Imo States. Government Printer, Enugu

Duson NA (2021) Nigerian courts and the adoption of strict property title rights approach in the settlement of property in divorce proceedings relating to statutory marriage: the need to Jettison the approach. Bori Bar J 1(1):1–16

Efe CJ, Eberechi OE (2020) Property rights of Nigerian women at divorce: a case for a redistribution order. Potchefstroom Electron Law J 23:1–39. https://doi.org/10.17159/1727-3781/2020/v23i0a5306. Also available at SSRN: https://ssrn.com/abstract=3919479

Egemonu JN (2017) Critical analysis of laws relating to maintenance and settlement of property upon breakdown of marriage. Crescent Univ Law J 2:83–101

Garner BA (1999) Black's law dictionary, 7th edn. West Publishing Company, Minnesota

Ifemeje SC (2008) Contemporary issues in Nigerian family law. Nolix Educational Publications, Enugu

Iroanusi QE, Fadare T (2022) Nigerian women protest after lawmakers reject bills seeking gender equality. www.citizenshiprightsafrica.org/nigerian-women-protest-after-lawmakers-reject-bills-seeking-gender-equality/?lang=fr Accessed 1 Sep 2025

James TA, Okoro OM, Tsaku DA (2023) An examination of the matrimonial relief of settlement of property under Nigerian law: a need for reform. Niger Bar J 13(1):136–137

Kolade-Faseyi I (2023) Legal framework and institutional mechanisms on domestic violence against women in Nigeria: The case of Ondo state. Dissertation, Adekunle Ajasin University

Nwogugu EI (1971) A critical analysis of the grounds of divorce under the matrimonial causes decree 1970, 4th edn. Butterworths, Oxford

Nwogugu EI (2014) Family law in Nigeria, 3rd edn. Heinemann Educational Books Plc, Abuja

Obi SN (2020) The customary law manual. In: Ajayi MAO (2020) Review of Arajulu v. Monday. East Afr Law Rev 47(1):1–32

Ojogbo S, Edu O (2022) Comparing maintenance and property rights in marriage under customary law and statutory law in Africa. Oxf Univ Commonwealth Law J 22(2):229–252

Okonkwo CO (ed) (1979) Introduction to Nigerian law (Sweet & Maxwell, London) cited in Asein JO (2005) Introduction to Nigerian legal system, 2nd edn, Ababa Press Ltd, Lagos

Olomola OO (2021) Introduction into Nigerian family law. In: Olomola OO (ed) Family law and succession in Nigeria. Princeton & Associates Publishing Co. Ltd, Ogun

Onokah MC (2003) Family law in Nigeria. Spectrum Publishers, Enugu, p 108

Onyi-Ogelle OH, Nwawulu A (2023) An appraisal of the legal framework for the protection of women's proprietary rights in marriages in Nigeria. Afr J Law Hum Rights 7(2):114–118

Sagay IE (1999) Nigerian family law, principles, cases, statutes and commentaries. Malthouse Press Limited, Lagos

Sanni AO (ed) (2015) Introduction to Nigerian legal method, 2nd edn. Obafemi Awolowo University Press Limited, Ile-Ife

Schneider EM (1992) Particularity and generality: challenges of feminist theory and practice in work on woman abuse. N Y Univ Law Rev 67:520–569

Shehu AT (2011) Judicial Review and Judicial Supremacy: a paradigm of constitutionalism in Nigeria. Int Comp Law Rev 11(1):43–72

Udoh OD, Folarin SF, Isumonah VA (2020) The influence of religion and culture on women's rights to property in Nigeria. Cogent Arts & Humanities 7:1–10. https://doi.org/10.1080/23311983.2020.1750244

Urhibo K (2023) Marital property under customary law in Nigeria: a critical appraisal of robbing the Nigerian woman of her right. J Legal Stud Res 9(1):283–303

Yesufu S, Nkomo T (2018) Women, and land and property rights in Benin City, Nigeria. South Afr J Soc Work Soc Dev 3(30):1–18

Alaba Ibironke Kekere is a senior lecturer at the Faculty of Law, Adekunle Ajasin University, Akungba-Akoko, and Head of the Department of Private and Property Law. Her research interests include family law, criminal law, and the criminal justice system. Kekere has served as Coordinator of Entrepreneurship Studies and Sub-Dean of the Faculty of Law and previously worked in the Ondo State Judiciary as Rent Tribunal Chair and Magistrate. She is a member of the Nigerian Bar Association (NBA) and the National Association of Law Teachers (NALT). Kekere holds an LLB from the University of Ado-Ekiti, a BL from the Nigerian Law School, an LLM from Obafemi Awolowo University, and an LLD from North-West University, South Africa.

Itunu Kolade-Faseyi is a Senior Lecturer at the College of Law, Caleb University, Lagos State, Nigeria. Her research interests include family law, criminal law, and gender and the law, with a focus on women's and children's rights. She teaches Family Law, Criminal Law, and Nigerian Legal Method and has contributed extensively to legal development through publications in reputable law journals. Kolade-Faseyi has also worked with NGOs and advocacy bodies to promote the rights of vulnerable groups. She is the Head, of the Department of Public Law at Caleb University. She holds an LLB and BL from the Nigerian Law School and an LLM and PhD in Law.

Oluwadara Oluwaseun Ajidasile is a legal practitioner and scholar whose research focuses on family law, property law, and the rights of women and children. She is a Barrister and Solicitor of the Supreme Court of Nigeria with over 12 years of post-call experience, combining practical expertise with academic insight. Ajidasile teaches Family Law, Law of Torts, and Constitutional Law at Adekunle Ajasin University, Akungba-Akoko. Her research explores the intersection of law and social justice, aiming to strengthen legal frameworks for vulnerable and marginalized groups. She advocates for reforms that promote equitable access to justice and empower women and children. Ajidasile is currently a doctoral candidate at a leading Nigerian university.

Marital Property Rights During and After the Dissolution of Marriage in Tanzania

Veronica Buchumi

Abstract Marital property rights in Tanzania are shaped by a formal legal framework that appears clear in principle but proves far more complex in practice. While statutory provisions govern the ownership and division of property during and after marriage, social and cultural dynamics continue to complicate their application, particularly upon divorce. This chapter analyses the legal regime in Mainland Tanzania, focusing on how property rights are understood and contested in the context of a marriage dissolution. It examines the role of the courts in navigating ambiguities and adapting the law to shifting realities, including economic changes, evolving gender roles, and changing family structures. Despite legal recognition of spousal equality, implementation often falls short, with many women encountering structural barriers to claiming a fair share of matrimonial property. Drawing on statutory analysis and judicial practice, the chapter highlights the disjuncture between law and lived experience and identifies key gaps in enforcement, access to justice, and legal awareness. In response, it proposes reforms to strengthen the protection of property rights for all spouses, ensuring that the law is not only formally equitable but also substantively fair in its outcomes.

1 Introduction

Marriage is both a social and legal institution. It alters not only the personal status of individuals but also their property rights, depending on the legal framework governing marriages in a given jurisdiction. While the question of property rights between spouses may not be a major issue during the subsistence of marriage, it becomes complex when the marriage ends, whether due to death, divorce, separation, or annulment. Different jurisdictions, including Tanzania, establish legal frameworks and social justice principles to regulate the ownership and control of properties between spouses during and after marriage.

V. Buchumi (✉)
University of Dar es Salaam School of Law, Dar es Salaam, Tanzania
e-mail: buchumi.veronica@udsm.ac.tz

A. F. Hammond and P. Batariwah (eds.), *The Law on Marital Property in Africa*, Ius Gentium: Comparative Perspectives on Law and Justice 138,
https://doi.org/10.1007/978-3-032-19358-2_6

This chapter analyses the law governing property rights in marriage and the division of matrimonial properties after a divorce in Mainland Tanzania.[1] The laws regulating marriage and property rights between spouses seem unambiguous. In practice, however, the changing economic, social, and cultural dynamics of the Tanzanian community have complicated the law, prompting the courts to continually interpret, challenge, and reshape the laws to promote equality and fairness between spouses. The chapter critically assesses the intersection between law, practice, and the lived experiences of those navigating divorce in Tanzania. It highlights the legal provisions governing property distribution while addressing gaps and challenges in their implementation. Finally, it proposes reforms to address these issues.

This chapter is divided into seven sections. Following the introduction, Sect. 2 discusses the plurality of Tanzania's legal framework on marriage and matrimonial relations, highlighting the interplay among statutory law, customary law, and religious law in regulating marriage. Section 3 evaluates the provisions of the LMA, specifically its definition of matrimonial property, the rights it grants spouses during marriage, and its implications for spousal rights upon the termination of marriage and the distribution of matrimonial assets. Section 4 discusses the rules governing the presumption of marriage, bigamous marriages and surrounding property rights. Section 5 explores the influence of human rights legislation on Tanzania's matrimonial property law. Section 6 provides recommendations for filling the existing gaps in the legislative framework, and Sect. 7 concludes the chapter.

2 A Synopsis of the Law Regulating Marriages and Matrimonial Relations

Marriages in Tanzania are regulated by the Law of Marriage Act (LMA),[2] enacted in 1971 to unify and harmonise the multiple legal regimes existing after independence. Before the LMA, several legal regimes regulated marriages, including statutory, religious, and customary laws. For instance, the then Marriage Ordinance (Chapter 109), the Matrimonial Causes Ordinance (Chapter 364), and the District Courts (Separation and Maintenance) Ordinance (Chapter 274) regulated all matters concerning civil marriages that mainly applied to Christian and monogamous marriages.[3] African customs and traditions regulated marriages among Africans. The customary laws of the African communities were largely uncodified until 1963, when a series of Customary Law Declarations were adopted to codify the customary laws of specific communities. Marriages between Muslims were regulated by the Islamic rites described in the Quran and other religious edicts authorised by the Marriage, Divorce and Succession (Non-Christian Asiatics) Ordinance. However, African traditions and customs still regulated marriages and related matters between Muslims of

[1] References to Tanzania in this chapter should be taken to mean Mainland Tanzania.

[2] Law of Marriage Act, Cap 29 (Revised Edition 2019) (Tanzania) (Act No 5 of 1971).

[3] Mtengeti-Migiro (1990, p. 521).

African origin.[4] These separate regimes had different rules and modalities to deal with spouses' property rights during and after marriage.

The parallel existence of the varying legal regimes regulating marriages often clashed and frequently perpetuated the unequal treatment of spouses depending on the applicable regime. Consequently, through White Paper No. 1 of 1969, the government proposed unifying the laws regulating marriages, leading to the enactment of the LMA in 1971. In the White Paper, the government contended that its intention was not to disregard the differences between the various legal regimes but rather to recognise, unify, and grant equal importance/status to all marriages in their varying forms.

Apart from recognising the various forms of celebrating marriages in Tanzania, including civil, customary, and religious marriages, the LMA sets common standards that apply to all forms of marriages in Tanzania without distinction. Besides, the LMA establishes common and general standards to be adhered to in officiating marriages regardless of the form of marriage celebration. Certain conditions and requirements must be observed, including the minimum marriage age, a 21-day notice of intention to marry, and marriage registration, regardless of whether the marriage is civil, customary, or religious.[5] Likewise, questions relating to property rights in marriage are primarily, or ought to be, governed by the LMA.

In Tanzania, customary and Islamic laws apply under the authority of the Judicature and Application of Laws Act.[6] However, the application of customary and religious rites in regulating the property rights of spouses is superseded by the LMA. Section 12(4) of the Judicature and Application of Laws Act prohibits customary and Islamic laws from being applied to matters regulated by the LMA. Nevertheless, the limited knowledge and awareness among Mainland Tanzanians, along with the deeply ingrained nature of customary and religious rites in people's lives, render the applicability of the LMA in many aspects of marriage largely ineffective. Unless individuals are involved in disputes which compel them to seek the involvement of courts of law or other related authorities, religious and customary laws continue to dominate individuals' matrimonial lives.

The pluralistic nature of the legal framework governing matrimonial issues in Tanzania is unique. While statutory law acknowledges the role and significance of customary and religious marriage rules, their application is limited and subject to the cross-cutting provisions of the LMA. These customary and religious rules only apply to the extent that they do not conflict with the Constitution or other statutory laws.

Conversely, customary and religious rules hold significant weight in matters of succession and inheritance rights among spouses and their families. For example, if Islamic law governs the administration of a decedent's estate, the distribution will follow the inheritance rules outlined in Islamic law. Likewise, if the law applicable to the decedent's estate is customary law, then customary law applies to the distribution of the deceased's estate to the extent that it does not contravene the constitutional

---

[4] Read (1972, p. 19) and United Republic of Tanzania (1969).

[5] Law of Marriage Act (Revised Edition 2016), ss 13, 18 and 43.

[6] Judicature and Application of Laws Act, Cap 358 (Revised Edition 2002).

provisions on equality and non-discrimination. There have been instances where courts have declared certain customary rites discriminatory against women, particularly due to restrictions on female inheritance of clan land and the limited inheritance rights of widows from their husbands' estates.[7]

Given the interplay between statutory law on the one hand and religious or customary law on the other, the discussion on the plurality of legal frameworks in this chapter serves a comparative purpose. Applying customary or Islamic law to regulate marital property is more a matter of practice than a legal requirement, as outlined earlier. The following section explores the LMA, focusing on the provisions that govern property issues between spouses during and after marriage, particularly when the marriage is dissolved through divorce.

3 Overview of the Legal Framework on Spouses' Property Rights

The LMA primarily regulates spouses' property rights during and after the dissolution of marriage through divorce or separation. Part IV of the LMA (Property, Rights and Liabilities and Status) contains specific provisions (sections 56, 58, 59, and 60) relating to the spouses' property rights during the marriage's subsistence. Additionally, section 114 of the LMA governs the division of matrimonial properties following separation or divorce. Overall, the LMA provisions on property rights reflect article 24 of the Constitution of the United Republic of Tanzania, which guarantees every person's right to own and protect their property. The LMA grants each spouse the right to independently acquire, own, and dispose of property during the marriage. These provisions align with the government's proposal in the white paper, which suggests that the law should explicitly state that either spouse may own separate property, whether acquired before or during the marriage.[8] Sections 58 and 60 of the LMA emphasise the separate ownership of properties between spouses, implicitly suggesting a modified separate property matrimonial regime in Tanzania (see Part 3.2 below for more details).[9]

[7] *Mwile Mugisha Mgallah (Administrator of the Estate of Daniel G. Mgallah) v Bertha J. Wandi & Idda Daniel Mgallah (Administratrix of the Estate of Daniel G. Mgallah)* (High Court of Tanzania, 2020); *Hyasintha Kokwijuka Felix Kamugisha v Deusdedith Kamugisha* [2020] TZHC 954; *Leonance Mutalindwa v Mariadina Edward* [1986] TLR 120; *Angelo Bisiki v Antonia Bisiki and Others* [1989] TLR 225.

[8] United Republic of Tanzania (1969, p. 12).

[9] Rwezaura (1984, p. 183).

3.1 Definition of Matrimonial Property (Marital Property)

The LMA does not define or interpret the phrase matrimonial assets/properties. Its meaning has been developed through case law since 1983. The Court of Appeal has defined matrimonial assets/properties in the case of *Bi Hawa Mohamed v Ally Sefu* to include:

> Those things which are acquired by one or other or both of the parties, with the intention that there should be continuing provision for them and their children during their joint lives, and used for the benefit of the family as a whole.[10]

The Court of Appeal adopted the definition of family assets from Halsbury's Law of England, 4th Edition, in formulating its interpretation of matrimonial assets. The Court argued that the term 'family asset' is essentially equivalent to 'matrimonial assets'. Given the application of the doctrine of precedent in Tanzania, all courts have consistently adopted this definition when determining what constitutes matrimonial property. For instance, in *Habiba Ahmadi Nangulukuta & Others v Hassani Ausi Mchopa & Another*,[11] the Court of Appeal sitting in Mtwara noted:

> In our jurisdiction, issues of matrimonial properties are governed by the Law of Marriage Act. However, the said law has not specifically defined the term 'matrimonial assets'. Unlike other jurisdictions like India, the term 'matrimonial assets' is defined under section 4(1)(a) of the Matrimonial Property Act...the definition given above, is not far from what this Court stated in the famous case of *Bi. Hawa Mohamed... they refer to those properties acquired by one or other spouse before or during their marriage, with the intention that there should be continuing provisions for them and their children during their joint lives.*[12]

In the absence of a statutory definition of matrimonial assets/properties, courts have resorted to definitions established in other jurisdictions, as indicated above. However, the question arises regarding how well the above definition aligns with the property rights provisions outlined in sections 58 and 60 of the LMA. The definition seems to erode the possibility of separate property ownership under sections 58 and 60 of the LMA discussed below. Arguably, the adopted definition is too broad, as it includes all properties owned by spouses, whether solely or jointly, provided such properties are intended for the continuing provision of the family during the subsistence of the marriage. Moreover, given the nature of a marriage relationship, it is difficult for spouses to demonstrate that the properties they own were not intended for the provision of the family.

In the case of *Salum Ramadhani v Amina Ramadhani*,[13] the respondent wanted an equal share of the property acquired during the subsistence of the marriage. The appellant was not willing to let the respondent have any of the property, most of

---

[10] *Bi Hawa Mohamed v Ally Sefu* [1983] TLR 32, 5.

[11] *Habiba Ahmadi Nangulukuta & Others v Hassani Ausi Mchopa & Another* [2022] TZCA 156.

[12] Emphasis added; See, *Gabriel Nimrod Kurwijila v Theresia Hasani Malongo* (Court of Appeal of Tanzania, 2018) where the court had also previously reiterated the definition of matrimonial properties.

[13] *Salum Ramadhani v Amina Ramadhani* (High Court of Tanzania, 2021).

which he contended was his personal property acquired before the marriage. This is one of the few cases attempting to challenge the definition of matrimonial properties provided above. The issue for determination was whether the respondent was entitled to any share in the property she listed as being matrimonial property or property jointly acquired during the subsistence of their marriage. The High Court noted:

> The property to which each party/spouse should be entitled is that property which the parties chose to call home and to which they jointly contribute. They may also include property of the parties generated during marriage otherwise than by external donations. In other words, it is the matrimonial home plus property acquired during the marriage otherwise than by gifts or inheritance. However, not every property acquired by either spouse during the subsistence of the marriage constitutes matrimonial property... In the absence of a statutory provision, there can be no suggestion that the status of marriage per se results in any common ownership or co-ownership of property.

While borrowing a definition of matrimonial assets or properties from other jurisdictions is not inherently problematic, it is crucial to consider the differences in laws regulating property rights in marriage across various jurisdictions. The definition of matrimonial assets in a country with a community property system would differ from that of a country with a separate property system or one that does not specifically define a matrimonial property regime. For example, in Kenya, which follows a system similar to Tanzania's, section 6 of the Matrimonial Property Act defines matrimonial property as follows:

> 6. Meaning of matrimonial property
>
> (1) For the purposes of this Act, matrimonial property means—
>
> (a) the matrimonial home or homes;
>
> (b) household goods and effects in the matrimonial home or homes; or
>
> (c) any other immovable and movable property jointly owned and acquired during the subsistence of the marriage.
>
> (2) Despite subsection (1), trust property, including property held in trust under customary law, does not form part of matrimonial property.
>
> (3) Despite subsection (1), the parties to an intended marriage may enter into an agreement before their marriage to determine their property rights.
>
> (4) A party to an agreement made under subsection (3) may apply to the Court to set aside the agreement and the Court may set aside the agreement if it determines that the agreement was influenced by fraud, coercion or is manifestly unjust.

In Tanzania, the definition of matrimonial assets/properties should be influenced by the interpretation of sections 58, 59, and 60 of the LMA, which in turn must determine the extent to which the courts in Tanzania can borrow and apply definitions from other jurisdictions. The interpretation of section 114 of the LMA on the division of matrimonial assets should be read in the context of the sections regulating property rights between spouses during marriage. The High Court in *Salum Ramadhani's case* constructively interpreted LMA provisions on property rights and revealed the complexities of defining matrimonial properties.[14] The Court further stated that 'the

[14] *Salum Ramadhani v Amina Ramadhani* (High Court of Tanzania, 2021) p. 6.

principle of equal ownership of matrimonial property between husband and wife is a matter of policy and cannot be inferred by courts'.[15] Basing its reasoning on the wording of section 60 of the LMA, the Court rightly stated that not every property acquired by either spouse during the subsistence of marriage constitutes a matrimonial property.

3.2 Spouses' Property Rights During Marriage

As indicated above, the enactment of the LMA, to an extent, subsumed the role of other legal regimes regulating marriages in Tanzania. Sections 58 and 60 of the LMA regulate property rights between spouses during marriage, implying a separate property matrimonial regime in Tanzania. For easy reference, the two principal provisions are reproduced below.

> Section 58 (Separate property of husband and wife)
>
>> Subject to the provisions of section 59 and to any agreement to the contrary that the parties may make, a marriage shall not operate to change the ownership of any property to which either the husband or the wife may be entitled or to prevent either the husband or the wife from acquiring, holding and disposing of any property.
>
> Section 60 (Presumption as to property acquired during marriage)
>
>> Where during the subsistence of a marriage, any property is acquired—
>> (a) in the name of the husband or of the wife, there shall be a rebuttable presumption that the property belongs absolutely to that person, to the exclusion of his or her spouse; or
>> (b) in the names of the husband and wife jointly, there shall be a rebuttable presumption that their beneficial interests therein are equal.

From the above provisions, save for the exceptions provided in section 59 of the LMA regarding a matrimonial home (to be discussed shortly), marriage does not deprive either spouse of the ability to own, acquire, and deal with their properties in a manner they deem fit. Thus, unless parties have agreed otherwise, properties acquired before marriage continue to be in the ownership and full control of the spouse who owned the properties. Additionally, a spouse is not prohibited or prevented from acquiring property by any means in their individual capacity.

A brief analysis of the second proviso to section 58, '*subject to... and any agreement to the contrary that the parties may make...*' shows that though individuals in a marriage have a right to continued separate ownership of properties acquired before or during marriage, they can agree otherwise. Arguably, spouses can agree to alter or adjust the nature of their rights in properties acquired before and during marriage to fit their needs and wishes. This implies that potential spouses or spouses can make prenuptial and post-nuptial agreements to determine the management of properties they acquire before and during the marriage. However, in practice, the

[15] *Salum Ramadhani v Amina Ramadhani* (High Court of Tanzania, 2021) p. 8.

legality of such agreements in Tanzania is uncertain, resulting in various interpretations regarding their status. There is no legislation or provision governing pre- and post-nuptial agreements other than section 60(b), which provides a basis for inferring their applicability.

While section 60 of the LMA demonstrates the possibility of solo and co-ownership of properties by spouses, it is not without ambiguities. Paragraph (a) provides absolute ownership of the property acquired in one spouse's name. Superficially, this entails that legal and beneficial interests vest in the spouse in whose name the property is acquired unless proven otherwise. On the other hand, in paragraph (b) on properties acquired jointly by the spouses, the presumption is that they have equal beneficial interests. It is unclear why the emphasis is on beneficial interest rather than legal interest in the property, where all spouses are deemed to have equal and undivided shares in the property jointly acquired.

In the absence of a provision clarifying the term 'jointly' in the phrase 'any property acquired is acquired in the names of the husband and wife jointly', ambiguities remain as to whether the intention was for common occupation, joint occupation, or joint efforts. In addition, many properties owned by spouses lack proper title documentation, which creates challenges in identifying the rightful owner and determining the type of ownership held between the spouses. Section 60 is limited in its scope, as it mainly focuses on registrable properties, such as real estate, vehicles, and business entities, which may not always accurately reflect the names of the actual owners. Apparently, it is challenging to prove whether properties in a marriage are acquired jointly or solely by the spouses.[16]

The Land Act also affirms the possibility of spouses co-owning property, explicitly recognising their right to hold land either as joint occupiers or as occupiers in common.[17] Section 60 of the LMA raises a critical point regarding the documentation and registration of properties between spouses. For properties expected to have titles as to ownership, the names appearing on the title play a crucial role in determining property ownership.[18] As such, a spouse who, for instance, financially contributes to the acquisition of the property but has their name excluded from the title may struggle to assert their contribution unless there is proof to support it.[19] Theoretically, a prudent approach would be for the names of both spouses to appear

---

[16] See the following judgments: *Dr. Olivia Michael Kimaro v Dr. Derick David Nyasebwa* [2023] TZHC 17407, *Bibie Mauridi v Mohamed Ibrahim* [1989] TLR 162, and *Elizabeth Watson Nyingi v Wilberd Bandola* [2022] TZHC 815.

[17] Land Act 2019, s 159(1), (2) & (8).

[18] *Gabriel Nimrod Kurwijile v Theresia Hassani Malongo* (Court of Appeal of Tanzania, 2018) where the court refused to recognise a house whose title was in the parties' child's name as a matrimonial property and *Flora Thomas Mongáteko v. Juma Morega Tagenda* [2024] TZHC 8460, where the court refused to recognise a car whose title was in a third party's name as a matrimonial property.

[19] *Miki Abasi Kipa v Rehema Steven Mwankusye* [2023] TZHC 16328, where the appellant failed to prove his contribution in properties whose title was in the respondent's name, and the court ruled that the properties were separate properties of the respondent.

on the title or any other relevant documents, for example, contracts related to the acquisition of such properties to which they jointly contributed during the marriage.

The separate property approach adopted under the LMA is not without qualifications. When property owned by one spouse is used as the matrimonial home, the other spouse is deemed to acquire an interest in it by virtue of its use, and this interest may be protected through the registration of a caveat. The other qualification emanates from a spouse's contribution to improving a property separately owned by the other spouse.[20] If one spouse solely owns a property to which the other spouse contributes by way of development or improvement, the contributing spouse acquires an interest in the property that can be claimed or compensated for upon the dissolution of the marriage. Nevertheless, the law is silent on how to prove or quantify the other spouse's contribution, making it a challenging issue during divorce proceedings. The subsequent part explores the provisions relating to spouses' property rights or interests in a matrimonial home, which the law recognises as having a *sui generis* status regardless of who owns the home.

3.2.1 Matrimonial Home and Ensuing Spouses' Rights and Interests

Section 2 of the LMA, which is in *pari materia* with section 112(2) of the Land Act,[21] defines a matrimonial home as:

> The building or part of a building in which the husband and wife ordinarily reside together and includes—
>
> (a) where a building and its curtilage are occupied *for residential purposes only*, that curtilage and any outbuildings thereon; and
>
> (b) where a building is on or occupied in conjunction with agricultural land, any land allocated by the husband or the wife, as the case may be, to his or her spouse for her or his exclusive use.

In *National Bank of Commerce Ltd v Nurbano Abdallah Mulla*,[22] the Court, attempting to differentiate between a matrimonial home and matrimonial property, contended that the phrase 'matrimonial home' should be confined to the house where the spouses ordinarily reside. In the case of *Habiba Ahmadi Nangulukuta & Others v Hassani Ausi Mchopa & Another*,[23] the appellants (wives), after realising that their late husband had sold a property, deemed a matrimonial home, requested the Court to declare the house a matrimonial property and the sale void. The Court stated that:

> it is also clear that the suit property was not a matrimonial property or even a matrimonial home/dwelling house, as the appellants in their own evidence testified that they were not

[20] Law of Marriage Act (Revised Edition 2016), s 114(3).

[21] Land Act 2019, s 112(2).

[22] *National Bank of Commerce Ltd v Nurbano Abdallah Mulla* [2020] TZCA 238.

[23] [2022] TZCA 156.

living in that house and were not even aware that the said house was purchased by the second respondent.[24]

This understanding of what constitutes a matrimonial home can also be inferred from paragraph (a) of the quoted definition above. It is only an estate used for residential purposes that is regarded as a matrimonial home. As such, the LMA contains special provisions to protect spouses' interests in such a home, as the spouses are deemed to have acquired an interest by residing in the property. The interest acquired by a non-owning spouse in a matrimonial home is beneficial.

As noted above, section 59 of the LMA establishes the first automatic exception to the separate property regime as set out in sections 56 and 60 of the Act. Suppose the estate or interest in a matrimonial home is owned by one of the spouses, the non-owning spouse is deemed to have an interest in the home, which said interest can be protected by caveat, caution, or any other means possible under any given law related to registration of titles or deeds.[25] The law further prohibits the alienation of such property interests, whether by sale, gift, lease, mortgage, or otherwise, without the consent of the other spouse.[26] Thus, a non-owning spouse secures a protected beneficial interest in the property interests of the other spouse, provided such landed property is their marital residence.

However, section 59(2) of the LMA implies that the interest acquired by the non-owning spouse is viable if the marriage subsists. The provision stipulates that if any spouse in a marriage alienates their estate or interest in the matrimonial home to a third party, such alienated interest is subject to the right of the other spouse to continue residing therein until the marriage is dissolved or the court, on a decree for separation or an order for maintenance, orders otherwise. A third party is only protected if they can demonstrate that they had no knowledge of such an interest, or that the interest could not have come to their attention even if they had exercised reasonable due diligence.[27]

3.3 Dissolutions of Marriage and the Division of Matrimonial Properties

The discussion under this part focuses on the implications of the dissolution of marriage by divorce or separation and the subsequent division of matrimonial properties. Thus, it does not examine what happens to matrimonial properties when a marriage dissolves due to the death of one spouse.

Section 114 of the LMA governs property rights between spouses upon the dissolution of marriage through divorce or when the court issues a separation decree.

---

[24] *Habiba Ahmadi Nangulukuta & Others v Hassani Ausi Mchopa & Another* [2022] TZCA 156, p. 19.

[25] Land Act 2019, s. 161(3) on the protection of land owned by one spouse for the interest of both.

[26] Land Act 2019, s. 114 provides special conditions for mortgages involving a matrimonial home.

[27] Law of Marriage Act (Revised Edition 2016), s 59(2).

Section 114(1) grants courts the authority to order the division of assets, or to direct the sale of properties and the distribution of the proceeds between the spouses. The properties or assets to be divided between the spouses are those acquired during the marriage through their joint efforts or those acquired before the marriage by one spouse but substantially improved during the marriage by the other party or through their joint efforts.[28] In *Bi Hawa's case*,[29] the court stated that there are three conditions to be determined by courts in exercising the vested jurisdiction:

> It is apparent from the citation and the wording of section 114 that the assets envisaged thereat must firstly be matrimonial assets, and secondly, they must have been acquired by them during the marriage and (thirdly) by their joint efforts.

The above three conditions have since been applied consistently by courts in Tanzania in settling claims for the division of matrimonial properties following a divorce or separation decree. Thus, after issuing a divorce or separation decree, the court in the same divorce or separation proceedings or subsequent proceedings brought by an interested party, must determine:

> i. The existence of matrimonial assets;
>
> ii. If the identified matrimonial assets were acquired during marriage or before marriage but substantially improved by the other party; and
>
> iii. Finally, the contribution made by both parties in acquiring the identified matrimonial properties.

The LMA further provides factors to guide courts in exercising the vested power to divide the assets. Such factors include:

> a. the customs of the community to which the parties belong;
>
> b. the extent of the contributions made by each party in money, property or work towards the acquiring of the assets;
>
> c. any debts owing by either party which were contracted for their joint benefit; and
>
> d. the needs of the children, if any, of the marriage....[30]

As the courts consider these factors, the law emphasises the inclination towards equality in dividing the assets. Courts have held that the principle of equality does not require a strict 50/50 division, but rather a distribution based on each party's contribution to the acquisition of the property.[31]

As stated in Part 3.1 above, the LMA does not define the term *matrimonial property* or marital property. Although the marginal note to section 114 is labelled, 'Power of court order division of matrimonial assets' the word 'matrimonial assets' is not

---

[28] Law of Marriage Act (Revised Edition 2016), s 114(3).

[29] *Bi Hawa Mohamed v Ally Sefu* [1983] TLR 32, 5.

[30] Law of Marriage Act (Revised Edition 2016), s 114(2).

[31] *Bibi Maulidi v Mohamed Ibrahim*, [1989] TLR 162 and *Yesse Mrisho v Sania Abdul* (Court of Appeal of Tanzania, 2016).

used in the actual provision. Apart from sections 67,[32] 108(b),[33] and 114, no other sections mention matrimonial assets/properties in the LMA. Although phrases like 'joint efforts' and 'substantially improved' are used in section 114, and are central to the implementation of the section, they are not defined in the law. Thus, their interpretation is left to the wide discretionary powers of the courts.

Comparatively, the application of Islamic law and customary law in matters relating to property in marriage has been affected by the LMA. For instance, ordinarily, under Islamic rites, the question of distributing properties upon dissolution of marriage would not arise. Traditionally, the concept of matrimonial property does not exist in Islam, as each spouse is entitled to their own property, and the husband is obligated to maintain his wife in all respects. Besides, a husband, whether during subsistence or after dissolution of marriage, is not expected to benefit from or control the properties of his wife or wives. However, Islamic rules regulating marriage continue to be affected by the calls for equality between men and women through various international and regional human rights principles.[34]

Upon divorce, a woman would only be entitled to a specified sum of money as prescribed in the Quran, without any claim to the distribution of property. However, in practice, these rules are not strictly adhered to. Courts, when handling divorce proceedings involving Muslim spouses, have gone further to distribute properties identified and proven to be matrimonial assets, applying the principles established under section 114 of the LMA. In the *Bi Hawa Mohamed's case,* where the parties were married according to Islamic rites, the Court of Appeal opined that, in addition to the parting gift that the wife received from her husband following a divorce decree, she was entitled to a distribution of the matrimonial properties to the extent of her contribution.[35] However, *Bi Hawa Mohamed* did not receive a share of the identified matrimonial assets, as the evidence showed that she mismanaged the assets.

Regarding the applicability of customary law, though the Judicature and Application of Laws Act prohibits customary law in matters guided by the LMA, section 114(2)(a) of the LMA requires courts to consider the customs of the community to which the parties belong. While courts are required to consider the customs of the parties, the consideration of such customs is influenced by several factors, including the requirement that these customs not be inconsistent with statutory law and that the parties originate from the same community. In *Pulcheria Pundugu v Samwel Huma Pundugu,*[36] the High Court was of the view that when the court considers the question of division of matrimonial assets under section 114(1) of the LMA and where the parties are of different customs, a non-traditional mode of life

[32] Section 67 of the LMA relates to spouses' agreement to live apart and in making such an agreement they could include provisions relating to, among others, matrimonial property.

[33] Section 108(b) deals with duties of court in a petition for separation or divorce imposed a duty on courts to inquire into the arrangements made or proposed as regard the division of any matrimonial property and to satisfy itself that such arrangements are reasonable.

[34] Akhtar and Manjoo (2024).

[35] *Bi Hawa Mohamed v Ally Sefu* [1983] TLR 32, 5.

[36] *Pulcheria Pundugu v Samwel Huma Pundugu* [1985] TLR 7.

may be assumed, in which case section 114(2)(a) may not be invoked. The Court further stated:

> It may have been Sukuma custom that a divorced wife is not entitled to a share of matrimonial assets jointly acquired during the subsistence of marriage, but with due respect...customary law is no longer valid after the enactment of the LMA. Of course, section 114(2)(a) says that in dividing assets under section 114(1), the Court shall have regard to the customs of the community to which the parties belong. But that does not mean the petitioner is not entitled to a share in the assets.

Over time, the customs and traditions of most communities in Tanzania have been blamed for perpetuating inequalities and discriminatory tendencies between spouses, as women had limited property rights not only in marriage but at different levels of the community. In its reasoning to include domestic duties or household chores in determining spousal contribution to the acquisition of assets, the Court of Appeal in the *Bi Hawa Mohamed* case reiterated that 'the Act seeks to liberate married women from such exploitation and oppression by reducing the traditional inequality between them and their husbands insofar as their respective domestic rights and duties are concerned'.[37]

Tanzania has over 125 tribes, each with its own diverse customs and traditions, many of which are not necessarily codified. Thus, not all customary laws or rules are known by the courts. This is the justification for having assessors sit with judges and magistrates in certain proceedings to assist courts in determining issues related to customs and traditions within a given community. In 1963, efforts were made to codify certain customs and traditions, culminating in the adoption of several Local Customary (Declarations) Orders applicable to specific listed communities. For instance, the first schedule of the Local Customary Law (Declaration) Order[38] contains rules regarding the maintenance rights of a divorced woman. The rights and entitlements of such a woman depend on several factors, including the husband's employment status or economic activities, as well as whether the woman is considered a defaulter.

For instance, a wife whose husband is a farmer would receive a quarter of the agricultural products of the divorce year or the products accumulated in storage in the year of divorce.[39] A woman whose husband is a peddler or self-employed would be entitled to a one-time payment of 150 Tanzanian shillings (equivalent of 0.056 USD).[40] A woman whose husband is a farmer, peddler, or self-employed would be entitled to the crops and the specified monetary payment.[41] If the husband is an employee, then the wife would be entitled to a month's salary of the husband.[42]

---

[37] *Bi Hawa Mohamed v Ally Sefu* [1983] TLR 32, 5, 26.

[38] Local Customary Law (Declaration) Order, Government Notice No 279 of 1963, published in the *Tanzania Government Gazette*, commenced on 1 August 1963.

[39] Local Customary Law (Declaration) Order, para. 71(A).

[40] Local Customary Law (Declaration) Order, para. 71(B).

[41] Local Customary Law (Declaration) Order, para. 71(C).

[42] Local Customary Law (Declaration) Order, para. 71(D).

However, the woman's employment status is irrelevant in determining her entitlements after divorce. An employed, divorced woman would still be entitled to her maintenance rights regardless of her employment status, as it is assumed to be the husband's responsibility to maintain his wife.[43] Remarriage is a ground to vitiate the entitlement of a divorced woman; any unpaid amount cannot be claimed if the woman remarries.[44] If the woman is found to be at fault, the man would not be obligated to pay the maintenance.[45] Unsurprisingly, in all divorce circumstances, the wife is expected to retain all her belongings, including the properties she brought from her parents' home, inherited assets, and gifts given by her husband, friends, or relatives on both sides.

It is evident that, under customary law, a divorced woman is entitled only to a one-time maintenance payment, with no claims to the division of matrimonial property. It can therefore be argued that, similar to Islamic law, the concept of matrimonial assets is foreign to customary law. As indicated in Part 2 above, the LMA was enacted to ensure equality and reduce discriminatory rules that were prevalent at that time. As long as the parties approach the courts of law to seek divorce and the subsequent distribution of assets, the LMA will be applied, with limited consideration of customary or Islamic rules that appear discriminatory from a human rights perspective.

3.4 Challenges in Assessing Parties' Contribution to the Matrimonial Assets

As described above, once the court grants a divorce or separation decree, the question of dividing property between spouses may arise in the same or subsequent divorce or separation proceedings. Furthermore, a division of the properties occurs when the court is satisfied that there are matrimonial assets between the spouses. Otherwise, property division may still occur if one party has made a substantial contribution to the improvement of the properties belonging to the other party, acquired before or during their marriage. The determination of the division process is guided by section 114(2) of the LMA, as explained above. Of the four factors, the most challenging, which has received massive interpretation by courts, is the need to consider the extent of the contributions made by each party.

In Tanzania, marriage alone is not enough to warrant a share in what has been identified as matrimonial assets following a divorce or separation decree. Beyond the marriage, the spouse claiming a share in the property bears the burden of establishing the extent of their contribution to assist the court in reaching a decision on the division

---

[43] Local Customary Law (Declaration) Order, para. 75.

[44] Local Customary Law (Declaration) Order, para. 73.

[45] Local Customary Law (Declaration) Order, para. 74.

of assets between the spouses.[46] In the case of *Yesse Mrisho v Sania Abdul*,[47] the issue before the Court of Appeal was whether there was a need to establish joint efforts in acquiring the matrimonial property. The Court of Appeal contended that proof of marriage is not the only factor for consideration in determining the contribution of a spouse towards the acquisition of the identified matrimonial property. This departed from the High Court's decision that since the parties were married, they were entitled to an equal distribution of the properties acquired during their marriage.

On several occasions, courts have emphasised the need for evidence to prove spousal contribution in acquiring or improving the matrimonial assets owned by one spouse before or during the marriage. For instance, in *Joyce Hamidu Mtambo v. Joseph Burton Mwasakanile*,[48] the Court restated that:

> It is a trite law that the fundamental principle guiding the division of matrimonial property is the contribution of each spouse towards the acquisition of the property. That is, if the parties acquired together any asset or property it will be subject to division based on proof of one's contribution.[49]

In determining the extent of the contribution, the court relies on the evidence adduced by the parties. Based on section 110 of the Evidence Act, the one who alleges a share in the matrimonial asset has the burden of proving their contribution.[50] In *Mohamed Abdallah v Halima Lisangwe*,[51] the Court reiterated that 'the principle under the division of property under section 114 of the LMA is one of compensation'.[52] The same principle was stated in a prior case, *Pulcheria Pundugu v Samwel Huma Pundugu*. Thus, one must convince the court by presenting evidence of one's contribution or effort in order to be compensated for the property in question. In determining the extent of contribution, the issue of providing evidence raises two questions that courts continue to grapple with: what constitutes joint efforts and what evidence is most effective in demonstrating the contribution to a matrimonial union.

The question of what constitutes joint efforts under Section 114(1) of the LMA remained unresolved until 1983, when the case of *Bi. Hawa Mohamed* finally settled the long-standing issue. While there was no dispute regarding the monetary or direct contribution in acquiring or improving the matrimonial properties, the same was not the case for the domestic work or chores performed by stay-at-home wives. The challenge in determining what constitutes spousal contribution or joint efforts ensued from the absence of the interpretation or determination criteria under the LMA.

Thus, judges and magistrates exercised discretion in interpreting and ruling on what could or could not be considered joint efforts or contributions. Two conflicting

---

[46] *Habiba Ahmadi Nangulukuta v Hassani Ausi Mchopa* [2022] TZCA 156.

[47] *Yesse Mrisho v Sania Abdul* (Court of Appeal of Tanzania, 2016).

[48] *Joyce Hamidu Mtambo v Joseph Burton Mwasakanile* (High Court of Tanzania, 2022), p. 8.

[49] *Joyce Hamidu Mtambo vs Joseph Burton Mwansakanile* (High Court of Tanzania, 2022), pp. 8-9.

[50] *Dr. Olivia Michael Kimaro v. Dr. Derick David Nyasebwa* [2023] TZHC 17407 where the court stated that mentioning the properties without proving their existence and ownership of the same is not enough.

[51] *Mohamed Abdallah v. Halima Lisangwe* [1988] TLR 197.

[52] Rwezaura (1984, p. 183).

positions were developed. Some judges adopting a narrow view ruled that wives' domestic duties could not amount to a contribution, as they were mere conjugal obligations that were obvious for wives to perform in a marriage. On the other hand, another group of judges adopted a broader interpretation, that domestic or household chores constituted joint efforts to be counted as contribution, entitling a spouse performing them to a share of the matrimonial assets upon divorce or separation.[53]

In 1983, the Court of Appeal, in the case of *Bi Hawa Mohamed v. Ally Sefu* sided with those who adopted the broader view and ruled that domestic or household chores constituted joint efforts to consider in the division of matrimonial properties. The Court of Appeal's reasoning was based on the need to cure or rectify the traditional exploitation and oppression of married women by their husbands and enhance the equality of men and women in marriages.[54] Though it is now established that performing domestic duties or household chores are contributions to the acquisition or improvevent of marital assets, the question remains: how much can be accommodated under the phrase 'domestic duties or work'?

Courts in Tanzania continue to modify the nature and meaning of spousal contribution or joint efforts to ensure that parties in matrimonial proceedings do not leave a marriage with empty hands. Love, care, affection towards spouses and, in extreme cases, sex, which are ideally the pillars upon which marriage is built, are also regarded as factors to consider in determining spousal contribution. However, these factors are, in most cases, considered when determining the effort of a wife, rather than that of the husband. For instance, in *Tumaini M. Simonga v Leonia Tumaini Balenga*,[55] the husband challenged the High Court's decision to allocate a share in a property acquired by him based on the indirect or non-monetary contribution of a salaried wife. The husband's main argument was that since the wife earned a salary, the Court should have considered only her monetary contribution, not her domestic or indirect efforts. The Court of Appeal upheld the decision of the High Court and stated:

> In essence, the extent of contribution made by each spouse is not restricted only to material or monetary contribution, it can extend to either matrimonial obligation or work or intangible considerations such as love, comfort and consolation of a wife to her husband, the peace of mind and the food prepared by the wife for her husband as observed by the High Court.[56]

On the second question, what evidence should spouses produce to prove their contribution to the identified matrimonial assets? As discussed above, it is the responsibility of the party claiming a share in the matrimonial properties to present evidence demonstrating their contribution, from which the court will determine the appropriate compensation. The question of proving contribution in acquiring matrimonial assets is complicated by several factors, including the nature of the marriage relationship,

[53] See a detailed discussion on the conflicting position before the case of *Bi. Hawa Mohamed* in Mtengeti-Migiro (1990, p. 521) and Rwezaura (1984, p. 183).

[54] Mutiso (2019, p. 121).

[55] *Tumaini M Simonga v Leonia Tumaini Balenga* [2023] TZCA 249.

[56] *Tumaini M. Simoga vs Leonia Tumaini Balenga* [2023] TZCA 249, p. 13.

which is primarily built on love and trust. In most cases, when married life is peaceful, the focus is hardly on accumulating evidence of every contribution spouses make when properties are acquired. There are many instances where spouses contribute to acquiring properties, but such properties are registered in only one spouse's name.[57] Unless the spouse whose name is not on the title can provide convincing evidence to the court, it may be difficult for the court to award compensation based on mere claims alone.

Spouses often lack documentary or tangible evidence to substantiate their contribution claims and instead heavily rely on oral accounts of their marital life and conduct. For example, in the case of *Elizabeth Watson Nyingi v Wilberd Bandola*,[58] the appellant challenged the trial court's distribution, which awarded her 30% and the respondent 70%. She argued that, as a public servant, she was entitled to an equal share, as her contribution went beyond just performing domestic chores. In determining the issues in the appeal, the High Court stated:

> Being a public servant does not necessarily mean the appellant contributed towards the acquisition of the property in dispute. With nothing more to indicate, the appellant used her earnings as a public servant to the acquiring of disputed matrimonial home. I take the appellant's assertion to be mere words as there were no exhibits to back up her assertion, and worse enough, the appellant testified that she did not even remember how much she took as a loan or how much was apportioned in the construction of the disputed house, the appellant was supposed to prove what she alleged…

Further, in *Dr. Olivia Michel Kimaro v Dr. Derick David Nyasebwa*,[59] the High Court insisted on the importance of evidence by stating:

> Mentioning the properties without proving their existence and ownership of the same is not enough. I say so because the appellant did not tender any document showing proof of joint or sole ownership of the alleged matrimonial properties by the parties. It could be lucky on her part if the respondent admitted the existence and ownership of the alleged matrimonial properties.[60]

In the aforementioned case, apart from the appellant's own testimony, no other witnesses were summoned to testify on her behalf, nor were any documents produced. She claimed that the documents were in the respondent's custody, but the respondent denied the existence of such properties.

While the reasoning and decisions of different matrimonial cases cannot be generalised due to differing circumstances and contexts, the above extracts demonstrate some evidentiary challenges or hurdles in proving one's contribution to claimed matrimonial properties. It is apparent that without solid evidence from a party claiming a share in a property, it is difficult for courts to order its division.

---

[57] In *Bahati Boniface Kazuzu v Ruth Alex Bura* [2021] TZHC 10170, the appellant claimed personal ownership of a property to which the wife had made a monetary contribution, although the title was in the appellant's name. The wife contended that she allowed her husband's name to appear alone on the title because they were spouses.

[58] *Elizabeth Watson Nyingi v Wilberd Bandola* [2022] TZHC 815.

[59] *Dr. Olivia Michael Kimaro v Dr. Derick David Nyasebwa* [2023] TZHC 17407.

[60] *Dr. Olivia Michael Kimaro v Dr. Derick DavidNyasebwa* [2023] TZHC 17407.

The requirement to produce sufficient evidence to justify the division of matrimonial properties implicitly calls for spouses to maintain records of any acceptable contributions to properties acquired during the marriage. In the case of *Miki Abazi Kipa v Rehema Steven Mwankusye*,[61] where the respondent (wife) could adduce documentary evidence (titles to the properties in her name and purchase receipts) of properties acquired before marriage, the appellant husband's claim for division of the identified properties was unsuccessful for failure to adduce concrete evidence regarding his contribution. In this case, the husband received no share, and even his intangible efforts were not considered because he did not claim them in court.

Furthermore, it is more difficult to prove indirect or non-monetary contributions made by spouses to the acquisition of assets because of the court's expansive interpretation of these contributions, which includes things like love, solace, and peace of mind. The courts' methods for determining whether the person making the claim truly loved or expressed affection are unclear. Besides, how such intangible contributions can be proven and quantified remains unanswered. While including domestic work or household chores is a justified and welcome step to address the historical marginalisation of married women, it remains unclear whether this should extend to the love, affection, and comfort spouses provide each other.

4 The Presumption of Marriage, Bigamous Marriages, and Property Rights

There is a presumption of marriage in Tanzanian law. If parties have lived together for two or more years and 'acquired the reputation of being husband and wife', the law presumes them married.[62] The presumption remains rebuttable, and a party can adduce sufficient evidence to show, for instance, that one of the parties is in a subsisting marriage and lacks the capacity to contract a subsequent marriage.[63] If the presumption is effectively rebutted, the court, under section 160(2) of the Law of Marriage Act, is vested with the power to make or grant orders, including orders pertaining to the division of matrimonial property as the court would have done if it had issued a divorce or separation order.

Furthermore, Tanzanian law voids marriages concluded by a person who has previously contracted a valid monogamous marriage with a third party.[64] The same principle applies if a person, having contracted a polygamous marriage, purports to contract a subsequent monogamous marriage.[65] However, legislation remains unclear about the property rights of such void marriages. In the meantime, the High Court

---

[61] *Miki Abazi Kipa v Rehema Steven Mwankusye* (High Court of Tanzania, 2022).

[62] Law of Marriage Act (Revised Edition 2016), s. 160(1).

[63] *Amina Ally v Ibrahim Nicolous Lyakurwa*, Civil Appeal No. 8 of 20212 [2014] TZHC 2626 (3 June 2014), p. 5–6.

[64] Law of Marriage Act (Revised Edition 2016), s. 15(1).

[65] Law of Marriage Act (Revised Edition 2016), s. 15(2).

has held in *Amina Ally v Ibrahim Nicolous Lyakurwa*,[66] held that where parties have jointly acquired property, such property shall be divided between them notwithstanding that the marriage is void. The judicial practice is to recognise void marriages as concubinages and apply section 160(2) of the Law of Marriage Act to the property acquired by the spouses.

5 Human Rights Law Impact on the Law on Matrimonial Property

The impact of international and domestic human rights law on the legal framework governing the ownership of matrimonial property and its distribution upon divorce is substantive. Although the LMA was enacted in 1971, when Tanzania's human rights law framework was still in its conception, the provisions of the LMA on spousal property rights and the division of matrimonial properties upon divorce were crafted to reduce inequalities and discrimination in customary and Islamic marriages.

The enactment of the LMA preceded the enactment of the 1977 Constitution of the United Republic of Tanzania. Even then, it was not until 1984 that the Bill of Rights was introduced into the Constitution, where the right to equality and non-discrimination, on the one hand, and the right to own property and to protect that property, on the other hand, were recognised and protected.[67] Besides, Tanzania became a party to most international and regional human rights instruments years after the enactment of the LMA.[68] Thus far, the provisions of the Law of Marriage Act (LMA) that promote equality, prohibit discrimination within marriage, and safeguard the property rights of both men and women are generally in alignment with the global and regional human rights instruments ratified by Tanzania. Section 11(4) of the Judicature and Application of Laws, which limits the application of customary and Islamic laws in matters covered by the LMA, reflects the indirect influence of human rights law on marriage-related issues, including the division of matrimonial property upon divorce.

In practice, as shown above (parts 3.3 and 3.4), human rights principles on equality and non-discrimination have influenced the Courts in Tanzania's progressive journey to give meaning to the LMA provisions on matrimonial properties and associated rights upon dissolution of marriage. A good example of such influence is the recognition and inclusion of domestic work to determine parties' contributions. This approach was adopted to salvage the marginalisation of homestay wives whose

[66] Civil Appeal No. 8 of 20212 [2014] TZHC 2626 (3 June 2014), p. 15.

[67] The Constitution of the United Republic of Tanzania 1977, arts. 13 and 24.

[68] Tanzania acceded to the 1966 International Covenant on the Civil and Political Rights and the 1966 International Covenant on Economic and Social Cultural Rights on 11 June 1976; ratified the 1979 Convention on Elimination of all Forms of Discrimination against Women on 20 August 1985; ratified the 1981 African Charter on Human and Peoples' Rights (ACHPR) on 18 February 1984, and ratified the 2003 ACHPR Protocol on the Rights of Women in Africa on 03 March 2007.

household chores were likely to go unnoticed in distributing identified matrimonial properties upon dissolution of marriage by divorce.[69]

Besides, the courts' broad definition of matrimonial properties constitutes another apparent example of the influence of women's rights and empowerment on the LMA. As indicated above, though the LMA provides for the possibility of separate property in marriage, the definition of matrimonial property discussed in Part 3.1 above blurs this possibility, which only becomes apparent if a party fails to prove their contribution in the acquisition of the claimed matrimonial property. The customs and traditions of most communities in Tanzania are designed so that most properties are likely to be owned by the husband, even when the wife contributes to their acquisition. Thus, the courts' broad definition of matrimonial property, which includes all assets regardless of whether they are owned by the husband or wife, as long as they are used to support the family, ensures equality and fairness between men and women in marriages.

6 Recommendations

While property rights between spouses during marriage may not present complex determination issues, the same cannot be said for property rights when the marriage is dissolved through divorce or separation. Parties to marriages in Tanzania retain the power and right to acquire, own, and dispose of property as they please, either solely or jointly, during the subsistence of the marriage. However, the absence of a definition of marital property, coupled with the broad provisions governing property during and after marriage, has left the determination of spousal property interests and rights to the courts' discretion. Thus, the division of properties following divorce or separation in Tanzania is based on the principle of compensation. A party claiming an interest in what may be designated as marital property must provide evidence of their contribution in order to receive a share. Courts in Tanzania continue to play a significant role in cautiously interpreting the provisions of the LMA on the division of matrimonial properties. However, due to the changing social, cultural, and economic context surrounding the institution of marriage, the 1971 Law of Marriage Act is struggling to withstand the test of time, highlighting the need for reforms to address the evolving nature and needs of marriage.

Any attempt to propose possible ways to overcome the identified hurdles and complications in the division of matrimonial properties is an ambitious mission. While it is possible to draw lessons from other jurisdictions with relatively progressive legal frameworks on similar matters, the cultural, social, and economic context of a given country is crucial in determining the appropriate approach to regulating the division of matrimonial property upon dissolution of marriage. Besides, in a

[69] *Salum Ramadhani v Amina Ramadhani* (High Court of Tanzania, 2021). See also, *Lawrence Mtefu v. Germana Mtefu* (HC, 2000) where the court refers to art. 13 of the Constitution in justifying why women's indirect contribution counts.

society with a diverse population in terms of development and culture, it is generally difficult to have an approach that fits all community members without shortcomings or disadvantages, at least for one party to the marriage.

For instance, the Tanzanian courts' current approach, which appears to be guided by the principle that the division of matrimonial properties is based solely on compensation, seems fair on the face of it. Intrinsically, the principle reduces marriage to a mere commercial or business union, where a party only reaps what they have sown. Ordinarily, the relationship between a husband and wife is based on the agreement of both parties to unite and jointly share their social, economic, and sometimes even political lives, making it a *sui generis* contract whose regulation cannot be fully grounded in the usual economic principles. Additionally, due to the low value often assigned to domestic efforts (as case law suggests, typically 20–40% of the identified matrimonial assets), a spouse who stays home and takes care of the household is at a disadvantage, as their compensation is likely to be lower.

While the courts' discretionary powers concerning the division of matrimonial property are essential to allow for a specific determination of the unique facts of each case, the need for reform cannot be overemphasised or overlooked. The current law has outlived the dynamics of contemporary society, particularly in marriage relationships, forcing courts to adapt its application to the nature of each case and the issues arising. Some of the proposed reforms are discussed below. The proposed reforms could be implemented by enacting a specific law regulating property rights between spouses during and after marriage, as has been done in countries such as Kenya,[70] Rwanda,[71] South Africa,[72] and England and Wales.[73] The other option is to amend the LMA and include comprehensive provisions on spousal property rights. Below are possible reforms that should feature in the legal framework regulating marital property rights and their division.

6.1 Interpretation of Matrimonial Properties/Assets

Introducing a provision to define the phrase 'matrimonial properties/assets' is one aspect that requires legislative clarity rather than relying on court-developed definitions. As mentioned earlier, the definition adopted by the courts is broad, which undermines the concept of separate property between spouses in marriage. The main criterion is based on whether the property plays a role in sustaining the family. Technically, unless one can demonstrate that a property owned separately was not used to meet the family's needs, all properties of the spouses are likely to be classified as matrimonial properties. Thus, having a provision in the law stipulating what

---

[70] The Matrimonial Property Act, Cap 152, Revised Edition 2022, Laws of Kenya.

[71] Law Governing Matrimonial Regimes, Donations & Successions, Law No 27 of 2016, Official Gazette No 31, published 1 Aug 2016.

[72] Matrimonial Property Act 88 of 1984, Government Gazette No 9322, 25 July 1984.

[73] Matrimonial Causes Act 1973, c 18, Public General Acts, United Kingdom.

constitutes matrimonial property in light of the provision regulating property rights in marriage reduces the apparent risk of having a definition that is too broad or too narrow, detached from the core provisions regulating property in a marriage.

6.2 The Need for Choice in Matrimonial Property Regimes

Borrowing from Rwanda and South Africa, Tanzania should consider the possibility of parties to a marriage choosing or determining how they want to manage their properties during the marriage and upon its dissolution. This approach grants the parties in a marriage complete freedom and control over their property rights. For example, the Law Governing Matrimonial Regimes, Donations, and Successions in Rwanda offers couples three regimes to choose from when marrying. These regimes allow them to create a contract that outlines the management of properties in the marriage. The three regimes include the community of property regime, the limited community of property regime, and the separate property regime.[74] Article 19 of that Law requires the Civil Status Registrar to guide the prospective parties in selecting the appropriate regime at least seven days before the marriage.

In South Africa, parties to a marriage can enter into pre- and post-nuptial agreements to govern their property rights during and after marriage. In addition to the agreements entered into by the parties, the Matrimonial Property Act establishes two systems to govern property rights in marriage: the accrual system and marriages in community of property.[75] The latter is a default matrimonial regime in South Africa that is applied when spouses have not decided on property management.[76]

Although the approaches of Rwanda and South Africa place considerable autonomy in the hands of spouses to manage their property rights and interests, in jurisdictions that still strongly adhere to the idea of marriage as a sacred union founded on love and affection, the adoption of such an approach is likely to face criticism. Moreover, the systems requiring parties in a marriage contract to select a system applicable to them entail a clear understanding of the law. Much needs to be done to raise public awareness of key issues and the implications of each choice.

6.3 Determining a Spouse's Contribution

If Tanzania deems it necessary to retain the current provisions on the division of matrimonial property under section 114 of the LMA, then appropriate amendments should be made to clearly define and expand the factors to be considered in the division of matrimonial assets. As discussed above, only two of the four factors

---

[74] Law No 27 of 2016 (Rwanda), art 4, ss 1–3.

[75] Matrimonial Property Act 88 of 1984 (South Africa), ch. 3.

[76] Jong and Pintens (2015, p. 551).

provided under section 114(2) of the LMA have received considerable consideration. Moreover, determining the extent of each party's contribution to the acquisition of matrimonial property remains a complex issue. The current legal framework provides only a limited set of factors, which may not fully capture the diverse and nuanced realities of married life. In light of this, Tanzania might benefit from considering provisions similar to those found in section 25 of the Matrimonial Causes Act 1973 of England and Wales, a statute that has influenced Tanzanian law due to its colonial legacy.

In addition to considering the welfare of any minor child of the family, courts in England also consider several other factors. These include the financial needs, obligations, and responsibilities of each party to the marriage, both current and those that are likely to arise in the foreseeable future. The standard of living enjoyed by the family before the breakdown of the marriage is also considered. The courts consider the age of each party, the duration of the marriage, and any physical or mental disability that either party may have.

Furthermore, the contributions made by each party, or those they are likely to make in the future, to the family's welfare are considered, including contributions such as caring for the home or family. The conduct of each party may be relevant, especially if it would be inequitable for the court to disregard it. Lastly, in divorce or annulment proceedings, the court assesses the value of any benefit each party stands to lose as a result of the dissolution or annulment of the marriage.[77] The above factors, reproduced from section 25 of the Matrimonial Causes Act of England, refute the principle of compensation as developed by courts in Tanzania.

In an ideal marriage, both parties give and take in a way that makes the notion of compensation based solely on direct or indirect contributions to the marriage seem inadequate. As such, focusing purely on the extent of each party's contribution to acquiring matrimonial property may not be sufficient in all cases. It is crucial to consider additional factors that could affect the lives of the parties beyond their financial or material contributions to property acquisition.

For example, the matrimonial home holds profound significance for both spouses, serving not only as a place of residence but also as a place of shelter. Given this, it may be more appropriate to allocate equal shares to both parties, as each entered the marriage with a legitimate expectation of cohabiting for a substantial period. While this approach might appear unjust to a party who made greater financial contributions toward acquiring the home, it is important to recognise that the other spouse may have relinquished their own residence to join in the marital union, with the expectation of building a life together. This justifies the expectation of equal sharing, as the sacrifices and commitment made by one party in building a shared life should be duly considered.

[77] Matrimonial Causes Act 1973 (England), s. 25(1)–(2).

7 Conclusion

This chapter has attempted an explanation of the property rights of spouses. It has explained how the matrimonial property regime in Tanzania, the separate property regime in the LMA, is increasingly being rendered nugatory because of the broad definition of matrimonial property by the Tanzanian courts. The legal position of the matrimonial home as a form of marital property in a class of its own has also been explained. Evidently, spouses have a stronger claim to an interest in the matrimonial home than other assets acquired by the spouses.

This chapter has further elaborated on the legal principles applied by the courts in the division of property between spouses. In general, the law governing the division of matrimonial property upon the dissolution of marriage through divorce in Tanzania primarily considers the actual contributions of each party, including the domestic efforts of a stay-at-home spouse, in the acquisition of matrimonial properties. Although the inclusion of domestic work as a legitimate non-monetary contribution is a progressive step, assessing its scope and assigning it an objective value for the purpose of equitable division has proven to be a complex and contentious issue.

This chapter concludes by offering recommendations on how the legal framework may be reformed. It advocates for a clearer definition of matrimonial property, an expanded list of factors to guide courts in making decisions on the division of matrimonial property, and a shift away from compensation as the primary yardstick for division.

In conclusion, amidst the identified uncertainties and complexities, it is undeniable that the law needs reform to include specific and clear provisions on property rights and the division of these upon the dissolution of marriage. This chapter nonetheless adds one caveat: any reforms should be based on public views and draw lessons from the positive practices of other jurisdictions, while considering the changing relations and roles of spouses in contemporary marriages in Tanzania.

References

Akhtar RC, Manjoo FA (2024) Matrimonial property in Islamic law. In: Briggs M, Hayward A (eds) Research handbook on family property and the law. Edward Elgar, pp 77–91

De Jong M, Pintens W (2015) Default matrimonial property regimes and the principles of European family law—a European-South African comparison (Part 2). S Afr Law J 3:551–566

Mtengeti MR (1990) The division of matrimonial property in Tanzania. J Mod Afr Stud 28:521–526

Mutiso B (2019) Getting to equal: Resolving the judicial impasse on the weight of non-monetary contribution in Kenya's marital asset division. Mich J Gend Law 26:121–173

Read JS (1972) A milestone in the integration of personal laws: The new law of marriage and divorce in Tanzania. J Afr Law 16:19–39

Rwezaura BA (1984) Division of matrimonial assets under the Tanzania marriage law. Verfass. Recht Übersee 17:177–193

United Republic of Tanzania (1969) Government proposal on uniform law of marriage, government white paper No. 1 of 1969

Veronica Buchumi is a Lecturer at the University of Dar es Salaam School of Law. She teaches Family and Child Law and conducts research on family and child rights, with a focus on strengthening legal frameworks for their protection and enforcement in Tanzania. She collaborates with both state and non-state actors to advance legal protections and contributes to research on forced displacement as a member of the University's Research Chair on Forced Displacement. Buchumi's work emphasises the intersection of law, social justice, and vulnerable populations. She holds an LLD from the University of Bayreuth and LLM and LLB degrees from the University of Dar es Salaam.

Marital Property Settlement after the Dissolution of Marriages in Nigeria and Uganda: A Comparative Appraisal

Omolade Olunike Olomola

Abstract Family law rules on marital property settlement do more than redistribute assets. They also signal how the law conceptualises marriage, whether as a contract or a status-based institution. This chapter undertakes a comparative analysis of Nigeria and Uganda, two jurisdictions that treat marriage as an institution of status and share a common law heritage rooted in British colonialism. Despite these shared foundations, the chapter reveals important distinctions in the cultural, social, and legal treatment of property division upon divorce. Differences in socioeconomic conditions and gender norms have shaped divergent practices, particularly in how contributions to marital property are assessed and how rights are enforced. The analysis explores both statutory frameworks and judicial approaches, highlighting areas where each system upholds or undermines fairness and equality between spouses. In an era of increased cross-border marriages, this comparative study offers valuable insights for navigating family law across African contexts. The chapter concludes by identifying best practices for achieving just outcomes in marital property settlements and encourages the use of amicable resolution mechanisms to minimise conflict and uphold the dignity of separating spouses.

1 Introduction

A marriage may end because of irreconcilable differences between the parties. When a marriage ends, the settlement of property is usually among the most important issues that must be addressed to effectively disentangle the parties from each other's affairs. In the past, marriage was regarded as a union based on mutual love, care, and support.[1] The increasing prominence of property settlement issues at the time of marriage dissolution over other equally important issues, such as alimony, child

[1] Attah (2016, p. 163).

O. O. Olomola (✉)
Department of Private and Property Law, University of Ibadan, Ibadan, Nigeria
e-mail: oo.olomola@ui.edu.ng

A. F. Hammond and P. Batariwah (eds.), *The Law on Marital Property in Africa*, Ius Gentium: Comparative Perspectives on Law and Justice 138,
https://doi.org/10.1007/978-3-032-19358-2_7

custody, or child support, suggests an emphasis on the pecuniary benefits a party may derive from a marriage.

However, the applicable family law rules on property settlement have far-reaching consequences. The rules not only effectively realign the parties' property rights but also reflect the legal system's endorsement of marriage as an institution, whether contractual or status-based. Ordinarily, a situation in which the parties are allowed to make their own arrangements would presuppose that they are free agents, independent, and capable of deciding their own rights.[2] This strategy would involve separation, pre-nuptial, and post-nuptial agreements. This procedure is not a common practice in Nigeria. In Nigeria, the prevailing approach is for parties to share property equally or through an alternative formula. Sharing in the Nigerian way views the relationship as a partnership where each party has an equal claim to the assets.[3] The position is similar in Uganda. Generally, the guiding principle in determining the share of the parties to the marriage is the spouses' tangible financial contribution, direct or indirect, which is clearly provable in relation to the acquisition of the disputed property. In both jurisdictions, parties can still enter into private contracts and arrangements regarding their property.

In this chapter, the legal regimes for the settlement of marital property in Nigeria and Uganda will be examined to identify the similarities and differences. This comparative work between Nigeria and Uganda is essential because the appraisal will provide deep insights into the different approaches to property division in these two African countries. It is important to note that the two countries were formerly British colonies, and as a result of this shared history, they have similar legal frameworks regarding family law and the rules of inheritance established by common law. The common law heritage in Nigeria and Uganda emphasises judicial precedent and the application of general principles to specific cases. However, the two countries' different socio-cultural and socioeconomic circumstances present some differences in the cultural attitudes towards marriage and property sharing. With increasing mobility and cross-country marriages, understanding the approaches to property division in different countries can help individuals and families navigate complex family law issues.

By comparing the marital property rights after the dissolution of marriage in Nigeria and Uganda, this chapter hopes to foster a deeper understanding of the complexities of family law in Africa and identify best practices for promoting fairness, justice, and human rights. In addition, there is a general recommendation for the amicable settlement of marital property.

This chapter is divided into eight sections. Following the introduction, section 2 discusses the various forms of marriage recognised in the two countries. Section 3 examines the laws governing the dissolution of the recognised forms of marriage, as well as recent reforms proposed under the Marriage Bill 2024. Section 4 analyses the concept of matrimonial property in Uganda and Nigeria, drawing on judicial definitions and leading cases. Section 5 evaluates the legal framework for the division

---

[2] Probert (2009, p. 161).

[3] Probert (2009, p. 161).

of matrimonial property in both countries, emphasising constitutional guarantees of equality and judicial approaches to equitable distribution. Section 6 explores the key differences and similarities between the two countries regarding marital property distribution. Section 7 offers recommendations for harmonising Uganda's plural legal systems, implementing pending legal reforms, and promoting gender equality in the division of matrimonial property. Section 8 concludes the chapter.

2 The Forms and Types of Marriage in Nigeria and Uganda

Nigerian law recognises monogamous and polygamous marriages. Each form of marriage has different laws and incidents that regulate the parties' rights, obligations, duties, and privileges. While a monogamous marriage is a marriage to one wife or husband at a time, a polygamous marriage is a multi-spousal marriage which permits a person to marry more than one spouse.

A monogamous marriage in Nigeria is similar to that in England, permitting a person to be legally married to only one spouse at a time.[4] The laws which govern the celebration and incidents of monogamous marriage, on the other hand, are found principally in the Marriage Act (Cap M6 Laws of the Federation of Nigeria, 2004) and the Matrimonial Causes Act (Cap M7 Laws of the Federation of Nigeria, 2004). Hence, a monogamous marriage may be described as a statutory marriage. Item 61 of the exclusive legislative list in the Constitution of the Federal Republic of Nigeria, 1999 (as amended) recognises the power of the National Assembly to legislate on the 'formation, annulment and dissolution of marriage other than marriage under Islamic Law and customary Law, including matrimonial proceedings relating thereto'. Therefore, by virtue of section 4(2) and (5) of the 1999 Constitution, no State House of Assembly can legislate monogamous marriages. Other forms of marriage are within the legislative competence of the states. The most common form of polygamy in Nigeria is polygyny, which involves the marriage of a man to more than one woman. Polygamous marriages are acceptable forms of marriage under Nigerian customary and Islamic laws.[5] It should be noted that Islamic marriages in Nigeria are classified as customary marriages. From the discussion above, the types of marriage under Nigerian law are statutory, customary, and Islamic marriages.

Uganda is unique because its Constitution not only raises the marriageable age to eighteen but also prohibits same-sex marriages.[6] Five types of marriage are recognised in Uganda: church marriages, civil marriages, Mohammedan (Islamic) marriages, customary marriages, and Hindu Marriages.[7] A church marriage is

[4] Standley and Davies (2013, p. 23).

[5] Ambali (2014).

[6] Constitution of Uganda 1995, art 31.

[7] The Marriage Act Cap 251 of Uganda does not explicitly provide for the recognised types of marriages. Each of the recognised types of marriage is governed by different legislation. Church and civil marriages are governed by the Marriage Act CAP 251, and Islamic marriage by the

conducted when a man and a woman marry in accordance with the Christian faith within any of the recognised Christian churches. This includes Orthodox Catholics, Anglicans, Seventh Day Adventists, and Pentecostals. In Uganda, Christian marriages are considered civil marriages and are governed by the Marriage Act, which regulates matrimonial remedies and the solemnisation of marriage.[8] A civil marriage is a marriage conducted by the Registrar General (commonly known as the Registrar of Marriages) or their agents, such as the Chief Administrative Officer at the district level. An Islamic marriage is celebrated according to the Islamic faith, otherwise known as '*Nikah*'. This kind of marriage is potentially polygynous.[9] A customary marriage is celebrated according to the customs of the community/ethnic group to which the parties belong. The various ethnic groups in Uganda, such as the Baganda, Banyankole, Luo, Karamojong, Iteso, and Langi, have distinct marriage customs and traditions. In Uganda, the law does not recognise cohabitation as marriage, regardless of the length of cohabitation, the children born out of the relationship or the property acquired.[10]

3 Overview of Divorce Laws in Nigeria and Uganda

3.1 Statutory Marriage

In Nigeria, the Matrimonial Causes Act of 1970 has established the procedure for divorce by a court of competent jurisdiction, provided it is satisfied that the parties find it intolerable to live together as husband and wife and that the marriage has irretrievably broken down.[11] Prior to 1970, the Nigerian law on divorce was based on the matrimonial offence theory.[12] Nigeria has since introduced no-fault divorce, a result of which is the introduction of 'irretrievable breakdown' as the sole ground for divorce.[13] However, the old fault-based factors, such as adultery and desertion, remain relevant.[14] In Nigeria, marriage under the Act can be dissolved in the High Court of any state in the Federation. A petition for the dissolution of the marriage can

---

Marriage and Divorce of the Mohammedans Act, Cap 252. Hindu marriage is governed by the Hindu Marriage and Divorce Act, Cap 250, and customary marriage is governed by the Customary Marriage (Registration) Act.

[8] Marriage Act (Cap 251, Laws of Uganda).

[9] Polygyny is a practice where a man is married to more than one woman. It is often referred to as polygamy.

[10] *Baryamureeba James v Kabakonjo Abwooli and Others* (High Court of Uganda, 20 January 2020).

[11] Matrimonial Causes Act 1970, ss 15–16.

[12] See, for example, the English Matrimonial Causes Act 1965, which applied in Nigeria before 1970.

[13] Olomola and Olatunbosun (2017, pp. 133–135).

[14] Matrimonial Causes Act 1970, s 15(1)–(2) and Olomola and Olatunbosun (2017, pp. 133–135).

only be instituted by either the husband or the wife. According to the Matrimonial Causes Act, 1970, section 15(1):

> A petition under this Act by a party to a marriage for a decree of dissolution of the marriage may be presented to the court by either party to the marriage upon the ground that the marriage has broken down irretrievably.

Thus, in the case of *Ekrebe v Ekrebe*,[15] the court held that the appellant could not be heard since the phrase 'the marriage has broken down irretrievably', as required by section 15(1), was not included in the petition, even though the petition itself contained the words *'cruelty, desertion and adultery'*. The court ruled that these factors are relevant considerations but do not serve as grounds for dissolution.[16] Also of interest is the case of *Ezirim v Ezirim,*[17] where Nnaemaka Agu J. C, delivered the unanimous opinion of the court:

> It is necessary to bear in mind the fact that although the Act created only one ground of divorce, to wit; that the marriage has irretrievably broken down; yet that the facts which may lead to the marriage breaking down irretrievably are categorized under sub-sections (a) to (h) of section 15(2). Only those facts can suffice to found a petition for divorce. In other words, a court hearing a petition for divorce ought not to hold that the marriage has irretrievably broken down unless the petitioner or cross-petitioner, as the case may be satisfies the court on one or more of the … facts.[18]

This case emphasises the omnibus ground for divorce under section 15(2)(h) of the Matrimonial Causes Act of the Laws of the Federation of Nigeria (2004), often referred to as the "irretrievable breakdown" clause. It provides a catch-all provision for granting divorce, allowing the court to consider the overall circumstances of the marriage and determine whether it has indeed broken down irretrievably.

Divorce in Uganda is generally governed by the Divorce Act, Cap 249 (now Cap 144) Laws of Uganda, which lays down the procedure to be followed in divorce proceedings. The Divorce Act provides for requirements that should be met by both parties for a divorce decree to be granted. Previously, the Divorce Act permitted a husband to rely on the sole ground of his wife's adultery.[19] However, a wife had to prove that:

> (a) her husband has changed his profession of Christianity for the profession of some other religion, and gone through a form of marriage with another woman; or (b) has been guilty of—(i) incestuous adultery; (ii) bigamy with adultery; (iii) marriage with another woman with adultery; (iv) rape, sodomy or bestiality; (v) adultery coupled with cruelty; or (vi) adultery coupled with desertion, without reasonable excuse, for two years or upwards.[20]

The different legal expectations of spouses, based on gender, are reflective of the double standard of old English divorce law. However, in the case of *Uganda Association of Women Lawyers and ors v Attorney General (Constitutional petition)*

---

[15] *Ekrebe v Ekrebe* [1993] 3 NWLR 514; see also *Labode v Labode* [1972] NMLR 195, 197.

[16] *Ezirim v Ezirim* 17 NWLR (Pt. 902) 611 (CA).

[17] *Ezirim v Ezirim*Ezirim 17 NWLR (Pt. 902) 611 (CA).

[18] *Ezirim v Ezirim* (2004) 17 NWLR (Pt. 902) pp. 623–624.

[19] Divorce Act 1971 (Cap 144), s 4(1).

[20] Divorce Act 1971 (Cap 144), s 4(2).

Uganda,[21] the Constitutional Court of Uganda held that the sections in the Divorce Act that stipulated different grounds for divorce for men and women were unconstitutional and effectively nullified them. This means a husband can rely on the same grounds for divorce available to a wife. Although the judgement has taken effect as a precedent, the Divorce Act is yet to be amended. It should be noted that according to Article 31(1) of the Constitution of the Republic of Uganda (1995), '[m]en and women of the age of eighteen years and above, have the right to marry and to found a family and are entitled to equal rights in marriage, during marriage and at its dissolution'. This provision guarantees spouses equal rights during and at the dissolution of marriage, irrespective of gender.

There is a Marriage Bill 2024 currently before Parliament that aims to resolve the challenges related to property distribution. The bill introduces significant reforms focused on equal property rights and child protection, marking a major update to Uganda's marriage laws. This is not the first time such a bill has been presented to Parliament. In December 2009, the Marriage and Divorce Bill was introduced to modernise Uganda's marriage laws. It sought to recognise various forms of marriage, define marital rights and responsibilities, and establish clear guidelines for divorce. Among its most contentious provisions are the prohibition of bride price returns and the ban on widow inheritance. Despite the ongoing discussion, the Marriage Bill has yet to be enacted into law.

3.2 Islamic Marriages

The processes for dissolving an Islamic marriage in Nigeria and Uganda are the same, as the religion is universal and its tenets follow the injunctions of the Holy Quran. In Uganda, the Marriage and Divorce of Mohammedans Act of Uganda Cap 252 is the primary legislation that covers this area. Section 2(15) of Uganda's Divorce of Mohammedans Act provides that all marriages between persons professing the Mohammedan religion shall be valid if celebrated according to the customary rites and observances of that religion. It further states that all divorces from such marriages must also follow these rites and be registered in accordance with the provisions of the Act. In Nigeria, which predominantly follows the Maliki Islamic Law School,[22] there is no Statute or specific legislation which governs the dissolution of Islamic marriages in Nigeria. A heavy reliance is placed on the Holy Quran, Hadith, and the jurisprudence of the Maliki Islamic School.

[21] *Constitutional Petition No 2 of 2003* [2004] UGCC 1.

[22] Sherifat and Kolade-Faseyi (2021, p. 136).

3.3 The Hindu Marriages

Section 8(16) of the Hindu Marriage and Divorce Act, Cap 250 of Uganda,[23] is to the effect that the Divorce Act shall apply to marriages and matrimonial causes relating to marriages celebrated under the Hindu Marriage and Divorce Act. In addition to the grounds for divorce mentioned in the Divorce Act, a divorce petition may be presented by either party to a marriage on the ground that the respondent has ceased to be a Hindu because of conversion to another religion. Divorce can also be sought if the respondent has renounced the world by entering a religious order and has remained in that order apart from the world for at least three years immediately preceding the presentation of the petition. Furthermore, a wife may petition for divorce if her marriage was solemnised before the commencement of this Act, and her husband was already married at that time or married again before the Act's commencement, with the other wife still alive when the petition was filed. This provision is unique to Uganda, as Nigerian law has no equivalent.

3.4 Customary Marriages

Marriage under customary law in Nigeria is seen as a lifelong contract which may not be broken. Marriage is not just a union between a man and a woman, but between two families. Culturally, divorce is frowned upon and is rarely resorted to. Unlike a statutory marriage, which can only be dissolved in court, a Customary law marriage may be dissolved without judicial pronouncement or intervention.[24] According to Nwogugu, non-judicial divorce remains an important aspect of customary law matrimonial cases. Therefore, it is incorrect to assert that all customary law marriages must be dissolved by a competent customary court.[25]

A customary law marriage in Nigeria may be dissolved extra-judicially, judicially or upon the death of one of the parties. In Nigeria, technically, no reason need be given for the dissolution of a marriage, as divorce can be granted by mutual consent of both spouses.[26] Among the *Idomas*[27] and *Igalas*,[28] no reason must be given to a court by a

[23] Hindu Marriage and Divorce Act 1961 (Cap 250).

[24] Nwogugu (2014, p. 213).

[25] Nwogugu (2014, p. 214).

[26] Nwogugu (2014, p. 217).

[27] The *Idomas* are a major ethnic group in Benue State and parts of Nasarawa, Cross River, Enugu, and Kogi States. They speak *Idoma*, a language in the Benue-Congo branch of the Niger-Congo family. They are an ethnic group native to the middle belt region of Nigeria.

[28] The *Igala* people are one of the major ethnic groups in Nigeria, predominantly found in Kogi State, particularly in the eastern part of the state. Like the *Idomas*, they are also from the middle belt region of Nigeria, but they are specifically located in Kogi State. Their language is *Igala* which belongs to the Kwa branch of the Niger-Congo family. *Idomas* and the *Igalas* have a lot in common.

spouse seeking a divorce.[29] Customary law focuses more on the fact that a marriage has irretrievably broken down, rather than assigning individual responsibility to a spouse for the failure of the marriage. However, a party's fault may be relevant in determining when the bride price is repayable.[30] The grounds for divorce in a customary law marriage may be outlined in a statutory provision, as is the case in some parts of Nigeria.[31]

In Uganda, the termination of a customary marriage depends on the customs of the tribe to which the parties belong. The customs, however, must be fair and just. It can also be terminated by a court of law, using procedures applicable to church or civil marriages, to the extent possible. In *John Tom Kintu Muwanga v Myllious Gafabusa Kintu*,[32] Justice S.B. Jossa stated that when parties choose to be governed by customary law in their marriage, they will be governed by the same rules. The rules are subject to the rights guaranteed by the Constitution.

The Customary Marriages Act is silent on how customary marriages are dissolved. In Uganda, customary divorce is often concluded through the return of the bride price, as established in the case of *Bisanga v Bisanga*.[33] In this case, the court ruled that once a customary law marriage is dissolved, the husband is entitled, under Teso customs, to claim the return of the dowry. The formal divorce may take a long time after the separation; it is signified by the actual return of the dowry or by an order for its return. The return of the bride price is evidence that the marriage has been dissolved. The husband can claim the full value of the bride price, irrespective of the years the couple had been married, the number of children produced, or whose fault led to the breakup of the marriage. However, the decision of *Mifumi (u) Ltd and others v Attorney General* provided a new twist in customary marriages and divorces, as discussed above.[34] In this case, the court held that the bride price constituted a gift which should not be returned. The court held that the demand for the return of the bride price after the dissolution of a customary law marriage devalues the worth, respect, and dignity of a woman and therefore violated Article 31(1) of the 1995 Uganda Constitution on the equal rights of both men and women to found a family and exercise equal rights in the marriage and on its dissolution.

---

[29] Anyebe (1985, p. 91).

[30] Izunwa (2015, p. 77).

[31] Nwogugu (2014, p. 217); for example, section 7 of the Marriage, Divorce and Custody of Children Adoptive By-Law Order 1958, which applies to parts of Ogun, Oyo, Ondo, and Bendel, states the following grounds for divorce: 'betrothal under marriageable age; refusal by either party to consummate the marriage; harmful diseases of a permanent nature which may impair the fertility of a woman or the virility of a man; impotency of the husband or sterility of the wife; conviction of either party for a crime involving a sentence of imprisonment of 5 years or more; ill-treatment, cruelty or neglect of either party for 3 years or more; venereal disease contracted by either party; lunacy by either party for 3 years or more; adultery; leprosy contracted by either party; desertion for a period of 2 years or more.'

[32] [2001] UGHC 46.

[33] *Bisanga Ahmed Bisanga v Zaituni Musseti Ng'ariba and Another* [2020] TZHC 4204.

[34] *Mifumi (U) Ltd & Anor v Attorney General & Anor* [2015] UGSC 13.

4 The Concept of Matrimonial Property in Uganda and Nigeria

4.1 Uganda

The 1995 Constitution of Uganda recognises equality in marriage and provides for equal rights for a man and a woman at the time of contracting marriage, during marriage, and at its dissolution.[35] Uganda has further affirmed its commitment to equal marital rights by ratifying the Convention on the Elimination of all Forms of Discrimination Against Women (CEDAW), which, among other things, advances appropriate measures to eliminate discrimination against women in all matters relating to marriage and family relations.

The decision to divorce is simpler than the consequences and resolutions that follow. The more vexed issues pertain to marital property acquired by the parties. Usually, parties have no express agreement on how to distribute such properties upon divorce.

It is important to note that not every property acquired either individually or jointly before or during the subsistence of marriage constitutes matrimonial property to be shared equally upon divorce. In *Muwanga v Kintu,* the Supreme Court of Uganda, per Bbosa J, in an attempt to define matrimonial property stated as follows:

> There is always property which the couple chose to call home. There may be property which may be acquired separately by each spouse before or after marriage. Then there may be property which a husband may hold in trust for the clan. Each of these should be considered differently. The property to which each spouse should be entitled is that property which parties chose to call home and which they jointly contribute to.[36]

This assertion was reiterated in *Rwabinumi v Bahimbisomwe,*[37] where the Ugandan Supreme Court recognised that 'matrimonial property is understood differently by different people'. Thus, for any property to constitute matrimonial property, the couple must have contributed to acquiring the property during their marriage. In *Kivuitu v. Kivuitu,* Mwangusya, J. observed as follows:

> Our courts have established a principle which recognises each spouse's contribution to acquisition of property, and this contribution may be direct, where the contribution is monetary or indirect where a spouse offers domestic services. When distributing the property of a divorced couple, it is immaterial that one of the spouses was not as financially endowed as the other, as this case clearly showed that while the first respondent was the financial muscle behind all the wealth they acquired, the contribution of the petitioner is no less important than that made by the respondent.[38]

---

[35] Constitution of the Republic of Uganda 1995, art. 31(1).

[36] *Muwanga v Kintu* (High Court, 1997).

[37] *Rwabinumi v Bahimbisomwe* [2013] UGSC 5.

[38] *Kivuitu v. Kivuitu* (1991) HCB 135 at p.139.

The law in Uganda stipulates that matrimonial property should strictly apply to persons who are or were legally married.[39] However, this position of the law overlooks the harsh reality that, in 2011, over 28 per cent (or more) of 'couples' in Uganda were merely cohabiting, a figure considerably lower than recent statistics.[40] According to the 2016 Uganda Demographic and Health Survey (UDHS), 27 per cent of women and 15 per cent of men aged 15–49 were cohabiting. This is a consistent figure; the practice is common among young people. A study conducted in 2020 projected that 53.8 per cent of young people were cohabiting, and this trend is considered a threat to the institution of marriage in Uganda.[41]

According to Kainamura J in *Basheija v Basheija & Anor*,[42] the property of spouses belongs to one or more of the following clusters:

- Cluster A includes properties acquired during the subsistence of marriage, to which the parties jointly contributed.
- Cluster B includes the matrimonial home of the couple.
- Cluster C includes property in joint names.
- Cluster D includes property acquired by each party before marriage.
- Cluster E includes property whose ownership is disputed or held in trust for others.

Accordingly, properties in Clusters A, B, and C are marital properties that the parties have contributed to either directly or indirectly and should be put in a pool to be shared equally. Even when any property in these categories is sold, the party who sold the property should compensate the other party with half the sale proceeds.[43]

4.2 Nigeria

Matrimonial property refers to all property acquired by either spouse during the marriage. Marital property includes real estate and other assets a couple acquires together during their marriage, such as a home or investment property, cars, boats, furniture, or artwork, when not acquired by either spouse as separate property.[44] It also includes other assets such as investments, savings, and personal property. It is important to state that the definition of marital property is not explicitly provided for in a single statute but can be inferred from various legal provisions and judicial interpretations. Section 72 of the Matrimonial Causes Act provides guidance on property settlement in divorce proceedings. While it does not directly define 'marital property', it allows courts to distribute property acquired by either party during the marriage based on the contributions made by both spouses. Under the Nigerian

[39] *Case v Ruguru* [1970] EA 55.

[40] Kes et al. (2011).

[41] Uganda Law Reform Commission (2020, p. 3).

[42] *Basheija v Basheija & Anor* [2013] UGHCFD 9.

[43] Kes et al. (2011).

[44] Olomola and Olatunbosun (2017, pp. 133–135).

Matrimonial Causes Act, marital property typically includes assets acquired by either spouse during the marriage, such as houses, cars, investments, bank accounts, and jointly owned businesses.

Before the introduction of English law in Nigeria and the enactment of statutes regulating spouses' property rights, customary law marriages (including Islamic marriages) were the usual practice in Nigeria. The capacity of a wife married under customary law to acquire and own property is dependent on the tribe or village into which she marries, because there are different customs in Nigeria. In *Igbo* culture, a woman married under customary law is not permitted to acquire and own property independently of her husband.[45] This means that a woman could only acquire property jointly with her husband. This stemmed from the historical perspective that a woman was considered a chattel owned by her husband, with very limited rights. The justification for this is that during the pre-colonial period, both the capital with which a woman traded and her income were regarded as her husband's.[46] The wife's right to acquire and own real estate was subject to the husband's prior consent and overall control, and a married woman was not entitled to the settlement or transfer of property, other than her personal effects, at divorce.[47] Some cultures, like the *Idoma* community, permit the customary law wife to own both personal and real property. The *Idoma* community allows women to own properties separate from their husbands; invariably, they can inherit family property at divorce. Although women can own property, it is believed that whatever property they own belongs to the heirs of both the husband and wife.[48]

The combined provisions of the Constitution of the Federal Republic of Nigeria 1999 (as amended) and the Matrimonial Causes Act (MCA) 1970 now assert a woman's right to own property. Section 43 of the Constitution gives a solid background on the right to acquire property, stating that '[e]very citizen of Nigeria shall have the right to acquire and own immovable property anywhere in Nigeria'. Citizens of Nigeria, regardless of gender or socioeconomic status, are free to acquire and own immovable property, including fixed assets such as land and factories. The situation is different for a marriage celebrated under the Act, otherwise referred to as statutory marriage, which allows a woman to own property as an individual or jointly with her husband. Usually, the court exercises its discretion to ensure that family properties are divided equitably and fairly.

The legal framework for marital property distribution in Nigeria has evolved from its colonial influences to incorporate customary laws and modern statutory provisions. Uganda's legal system, on the other hand, has been shaped by its colonial past and post-independence reforms, with significant influences from customary practices and international human rights principles.

---

[45] Obi (1977, para 321).

[46] Onokah (2003, pp. 251–252).

[47] Ashiru (2007, pp. 320–321) and Edu and Ojogbo (2022, pp. 229–252).

[48] Native Authority (Declaration of Idoma Native Marriage Law and Custom) Order 1959, s 14.

5 Legal Frameworks and Gender Inequality in Marital Property Distribution After Dissolution of Marriage

5.1 Nigeria

The major legal framework on marital property distribution after dissolution of marriage is provided for in the Matrimonial Causes Act (MCA) 1970. Customary law also significantly influences the distribution of marital property upon the breakdown of a marriage. Section 72 of the Matrimonial Causes Act (MCA)[49] provides for the division of property acquired during the marriage based on the contributions of both parties. The Act emphasises the equitable distribution of property, considering both spouses' financial and non-financial contributions.[50] It is important to pay attention to the wording of section 72 of the MCA, as it provides for the settlement of property, not its redistribution between the two parties. Nigerian courts do not order the redistribution of property between spouses, and the existing law provides no guidelines for such redistribution. This is because section 72 of the MCA grants the court the power to make a property settlement.

Property settlement is commonly defined as the sharing of the properties of a marriage by the parties or by the court on the dissolution of the marriage.[51] It is also defined as an agreement entered into by a husband and a wife in connection with a divorce that provides for the division of their assets.[52] It is important to note that this relief must be claimed in the petition or the respondent's cross-petition for the court's consideration. This is based on the principle of law that a court cannot grant what is not claimed by a party to a suit. In several cases,[53] Nigerian courts have held that where a spouse, in most cases, the wife, does not contribute financially towards the acquisition of a property, their claim for an interest in such property purchased by the other spouse will fail on divorce. The courts have held that the property rights between married spouses are completely separate. For a spouse's application for a property right to succeed, they must prove, on a preponderance of probabilities, that they are a joint owner of the property in question or that their financial contribution towards the purchase or development of the property was substantial.[54] The High Court and Customary Courts both have jurisdiction over marital property disputes, with the High Court applying statutory laws and the Customary Courts applying customary laws.

Traditionally, in Nigeria, most ethnic groups do not share matrimonial property with a wife on divorce. The property is perceived as belonging to the man, and he is not required to give any of it at the end of the marriage. It is also doubtful if he

[49] Matrimonial Causes Act, Cap M7, Laws of the Federation of Nigeria 2004.

[50] Matrimonial Causes Act 1970, s 72(1).

[51] Aniche (2024).

[52] Vocabulary.com (n.d.).

[53] *Nwanya v Nwanya* [1987] 3 NWLR (Pt 62) 697; *Sodipe v Sodipe* [1990] 5 WRN 98.

[54] *Amadi v Nwosu* [1992] UJBT 1, 4.

can give her anything of value. In the event of the dissolution of a customary law marriage, a woman often goes away empty-handed; she is not entitled to financial compensation in the event of divorce. Igbo Customary law denies women the right to their deceased husbands' or their fathers' landed property. In *Ejiameka v Ejiameka*,[55] the court held that a widow had no right to her deceased husband's estate. The Onitsha native law and custom provides that a married woman, on the death of her husband without a male issue, may use the deceased husband's property subject to the consent of her husband's family. Her rights to the property are limited, as she cannot assume ownership of it as her own. If the family does not consent to her use of the property, then she cannot touch or use it. However, her right to occupy the building or a part of it is subject to good behaviour.[56]

5.2 Uganda

The 1995 Constitution of Uganda prohibits discrimination based on gender. It accords men and women the same status and rights, and also provides for the right of everyone to own property.[57] In Uganda, property interests are not acquired or lost by marriage as per the Succession Act.[58] The Succession Act (Cap 162) of Uganda specifically provides that marriage does not affect either spouse's ownership or interests in property. This provision emphasises the principle of separate property ownership in Uganda, where each spouse retains control and ownership of their individual property, regardless of their marital status. This provision is significant, as it protects the property rights of individuals, particularly women, who may have acquired property before or during marriage.[59]

Additionally, in Uganda, the separate property rule applies to all recognised marriages. It is important to state that neither the Marriage Act nor the Divorce Act sets out guidelines for regulating property sharing during divorce or judicial separation. The Marriage Act (Cap 251) and the Divorce Act (Cap 249) of Uganda do not provide specific guidelines for regulating property sharing in the event of divorce or judicial separation. Instead, the courts in Uganda have developed a body of case law that guides the distribution of property in divorce and judicial separation proceedings. The courts consider various factors, including the length of the marriage,[60] the contributions of each spouse,[61] and the needs and interests of each spouse and any children.[62]

---

[55] *Ejiameka v Ejiameka* [1972] East Central State Law Report 68.

[56] *Nezianya v. Okagbue* [1963] 1 All Nigerian Law Report 352.

[57] Constitution of the Republic of Uganda 1995, arts. 21, 26.

[58] Succession Act, Cap 162, s 39 (Uganda) and Succession (Amendment) Act 2022 (Uganda).

[59] Succession Act, Cap 162, s 39 (Uganda) and Succession (Amendment) Act 2022 (Uganda)

[60] *Ambayo v Aserua* [2022] UGCA 272.

[61] *Kagga v. Kagga* [1969] EA 643 (EACA).

[62] *Rwabinumi v Bahimbisomwe* [2013] UGSC 5.

Additionally, the Succession Act (Cap 162) provides some guidance on the distribution of property upon divorce or death, but it does not provide a comprehensive framework for property sharing in divorce or judicial separation. In *Kakooza v Kakooza*,[63] the Court of Appeal of Uganda held that '...the law as it stands at the moment does not provide for the sharing of property on divorce. The court has to rely on decided cases and such other principles as may be applicable to achieve a just and equitable solution'.[64]

This case highlights the lack of clear guidelines regulating property sharing in Uganda and the need for the courts to rely on case law and other principles to achieve a just and equitable solution. The Ugandan Supreme Court has noted that, 'joint property between husband and wife should be shared equally on divorce, irrespective of who paid for what and how much was paid'.[65] In sharing marital properties after divorce, the Ugandan courts have adopted an approach that places judicial value on direct, indirect, monetary, or non-monetary spousal contributions towards the acquisition of marital property. Thus, in the case of *Ambayo v Aserua*,[66] the court held that equality does not automatically mean equity, and that a claim for half of the property must be backed by facts to succeed. In this case, the Court of Appeal held that the facts did not justify an equal division of the property. Thus, the wife was entitled to only 20 per cent of the property, as she did not contribute to the purchase of the family home or its upkeep. In Uganda, the High Court and Family Division handle marital property disputes, focusing on applying statutory and constitutional provisions to ensure fair outcomes.

There is also the Marriage Bill in Uganda, which, though not yet enacted, proposes comprehensive reforms to protect women's property rights and ensure equitable distribution of marital property. The Marriage Bill is the product of a multifaceted approach that examined various factors, including legal norms, cultural practices, social and developmental elements, and political and economic changes that influence individual communities and national perceptions about domestic relations in the changing Ugandan society.[67] In the case of *Julius Rwabinumi v Hope Bahimbisomwe*,[68] the court emphasised the importance of considering both parties' contributions to marital property, thus advocating for gender equality in property distribution. The court also stated the importance of non-financial contributions and awarded the wife a fair share of the property. The bill proposes significant changes in women's legal status within the institutions of marriage and succession. The bill's provisions address historical inequalities in matrimonial property rights, particularly benefiting women whose non-financial contributions have often been undervalued. By legally recognising domestic work and child-rearing as valuable contributions, the bill seeks to ensure fair property distribution upon dissolution of marriage.

---

[63] *Kakooza v Kakooza* [2005] 2 ULR 605.

[64] *Kakooza v Kakooza* [2005] 2 ULR 605.

[65] *Rwabinumi v Bahimbisomwe* [2013] UGSC 5.

[66] *Ambayo v Aserua* [2022] UGCA 272.

[67] Uganda Law Reform Commission (1996, p. 17).

[68] *Rwabinumi v Bahimbisomwe* [2013] UGSC 5.

Additionally, the proposed penalties for demanding the return of spousal gifts and the establishment of a National Marriage Register are intended to reduce disputes and enhance transparency in marital relations. Overall, the Marriage Bill of 2024 represents a progressive step towards equitable matrimonial property rights in Uganda, reflecting contemporary societal values and the need for legal recognition of all forms of spousal contributions.

5.3 Islamic Marriages and Marital Property Rights in Nigeria and Uganda

Islamic law favours the individual ownership of property.[69] Where property is jointly acquired during the subsistence of a marriage, whether through a joint business venture or other forms of investment, the determination of ownership is guided by an assessment of each party's respective financial and non-financial contributions. Islamic law recognises both partnerships (*musharakah*) and contracts that clarify the parties' property arrangements. In the Nigerian case of *Musa v. Musa*, the Court affirmed that under Islamic law, property acquired by spouses remains individually owned unless jointly purchased.[70] The principles of Islamic family law apply similarly in Nigeria and Uganda. However, the judicial structure for the administration of these principles differs slightly. In Nigeria, there is a Sharia Court of Appeal. Though the structure of the court varies from state to state, it ultimately has jurisdiction over matrimonial property disputes under Islamic law. In Uganda, however, the Islamic courts envisaged under the Constitution, which are to have jurisdiction over matters of Islamic law, such as marriage, divorce, inheritance, guardianship, and custody, have not yet been established. Thus, in many instances, claims under Islamic law are settled through secular courts or by local religious authorities.

---

[69] Qur'an 4:7—"For men is a share of what they have earned, and for women is a share of what they have earned." This is the foundation for separate property ownership and economic independence.
[70] *Musa v Musa* (2007) 7 NWLR (Pt. 1032) 152.

6 Key Similarities and Differences Between Nigeria and Uganda in the Distribution of Marital Properties after Divorce

6.1 Similarities

6.1.1 Constitutional Protections and Gender Equality

As noted earlier, the Nigerian Constitution guarantees every citizen's right to acquire and own immovable property anywhere in the country. This right, when read together with Section 42, which prohibits discrimination based on gender, provides a constitutional basis for gender equality in property rights, including the right to marital property upon dissolution of marriage. Similarly, the 1995 Constitution of Uganda contains robust provisions for gender equality and property rights. The Constitution ensures the equality of men and women in marriage and guarantees the right to own property. These constitutional protections show Uganda's commitment to gender equality in sharing marital properties after divorce. Both constitutions serve as the supreme law, and any customary or statutory law that contradicts these provisions would be considered void to the extent of its inconsistency.[71]

6.1.2 Consideration of Both Financial and Non-Financial Contributions

Under Section 72 of the Matrimonial Causes Act (MCA), the Nigerian courts consider both financial and non-financial contributions when determining property settlements. Non-financial contributions such as household management, raising children, and supporting the spouse's career are taken into account to ensure an equitable settlement. The principle of considering both financial and non-financial contributions is also recognised in Uganda. The Ugandan landmark case of *Julius Rwabinumi v Hope Bahimbisomwe*[72] emphasised that non-financial contributions, such as domestic work and emotional support, are critical in determining the division of marital property. Ugandan courts have repeatedly reinforced this approach in subsequent cases, ensuring a more equitable distribution of property.

[71] Constitution of the Federal Republic of Nigeria 1999, s. 1(3) and Constitution of the Republic of Uganda 1995, art. 2(2).

[72] *Rwabinumi v Bahimbisomwe* [2013] UGSC 5.

6.1.3 Judicial Emphasis on Fairness and Equity

Both Nigeria and Uganda's judicial systems are increasingly moving towards equity-based decisions in property distribution cases. Ugandan courts have actively interpreted constitutional provisions and international legal instruments to promote fairness in the division of matrimonial property, particularly by recognising non-financial contributions made by spouses.[73] In *Kagga v Kagga*,[74] the ruling clarified that a spouse must prove contributions, reinforcing the principle that marriage does not automatically entitle both parties to equal property division. In another instance, the court struck down traditional practices that disproportionately affected women, aligning its ruling with international human rights principles.[75]

Nigeria's courts have taken bold steps in inheritance rights,[76] but property division remains largely conservative, preferring financial contributors. Future judicial activism in both countries may focus on further protecting women's rights, particularly through constitutional and international human rights frameworks.

In Nigeria, the distribution of matrimonial property upon divorce or judicial separation is governed primarily by the Matrimonial Causes Act (MCA) of 1970. However, the Act does not explicitly provide for how matrimonial property should be shared, leaving courts with *discretion* to determine fair distribution based on evidence and contributions. On its part, the equitable principles applied by Uganda's judiciary reinforce the courts' role in ensuring fairness in property settlements, irrespective of the form of marriage contracted.

It is worth noting that, in cases where a marriage is void on any number of grounds —for example, when one of the parties to a monogamous marriage contracts a second marriage without dissolving the first—the Nigerian and Ugandan courts invoke principles of equity and fairness. Under Nigerian law, a void marriage does not prevent a court from exercising its discretion under section 72 of the Matrimonial Causes Act to order property settlement in favour of the parties and any children. The discretion can be invoked in matrimonial causes, including nullity cases. A similar statutory power does not exist in Uganda; therefore, courts rely on principles of equity, considering both the financial and non-financial contributions of the parties, as well as the nature of their relationship, in determining the division of property between them.

---

[73] *Rwabinumi v Bahimbisomwe* [2013] UGSC 5.

[74] *Kagga v. Kagga* [1969] EA 643 (EACA).

[75] *Mifumi (U) Ltd & Anor v Attorney General & Anor* [2015] UGSC 13.

[76] *Ukeje v Ukeje* [2014] 11 NWLR 384.

6.2 Differences

6.2.1 Statutory Guidelines on Marital Property Distribution

Nigeria has a more established statutory framework for marital property distribution, primarily governed by the Matrimonial Causes Act.[77] Section 72 of the MCA provides clear guidelines on property settlement, emphasising the consideration of both spouses' contributions during the marriage. However, it is important to note that the MCA focuses on the 'settlement' of property rather than 'redistribution', meaning that the courts can only settle property disputes based on what is claimed, rather than actively redistributing assets. In contrast, Uganda lacks a specific statutory framework for dividing marital property upon divorce. The Marriage and Divorce Acts do not provide detailed guidelines for property sharing, leaving the matter largely to judicial interpretation and discretion. The Marriage Bill, which proposes comprehensive reforms to protect women's property rights, remains unenacted, creating a gap in statutory protection for the equitable distribution of marital property.

6.2.2 Influence of Customary Law

Customary law plays a significant role in marital property distribution in Nigeria, particularly where statutory law is silent or cultural practices are deeply rooted. Customary practices often favour men, limiting women's rights to property after divorce. For example, under Igbo customary law, women traditionally have limited property rights.

However, the Nigerian courts have started challenging these practices by applying equitable principles from statutory laws, as seen in *Nwosu v Nwosu*,[78] where it was held that any property acquired by a woman before marriage and independently during the marriage remains her separate property. She is free to manage or dispose of the property as she deems fit without undue interference from her husband. This right is guaranteed under the three types of marriages in Nigeria. The right of independent property ownership applies to all types and forms of marriages in Nigeria.[79] In the same vein, the court in *Okere v Akaluka*[80] held that it would be most unconscionable to deprive a woman and her children of the right to a property to which she contributed substantially to its acquisition and development. The court also expressed the view that the indirect contributions of wives to the matrimonial property should grant them a beneficial entitlement to the property on the basis that '... it was the performance of their functions as wives that enabled their husbands... to perform theirs'.[81]

---

[77] Matrimonial Causes Act 1970, s. 72(1).

[78] *Nwosu v. Nwosu* [2012] 8 NWLR 1.

[79] *Nwosu v. Nwosu* [2012] 8 NWLR 1.

[80] *Okere v Akaluka* [2014] LPELR-24287 1, 60–61.

[81] *Okere v Akaluka* [2014] LPELR-24287 1, 60–61.

Customary law in Uganda also influences property division. In the case of *Kakooza v Kakooza,* the High Court of Uganda considered the distribution of property following the dissolution of a customary marriage.[82] The court held that, in the absence of a written agreement or evidence of a contrary intention, the distribution of property should be guided by customary law. The court applied customary law principles, emphasising the importance of family and communal property ownership. The court held that the property in question should be distributed in accordance with customary law, with a significant portion going to the family and community. This case illustrates the influence of customary law on property distribution. However, the Ugandan courts have been more proactive in upholding women's property rights. The Ugandan Constitution provides strong protections against gender discrimination, which has allowed courts to overrule customary practices that deny women equitable rights to marital property.

6.2.3 Settlement Versus Redistribution of Property

The concept of 'settlement' under Nigerian law, particularly in the context of Section 72 of the Matrimonial Causes Act, limits the courts to resolving property disputes based on the claims brought before them. The law does not mandate an active redistribution of property, meaning that unless a party claims a specific form of relief, the court cannot order the redistribution of assets. This has been a point of contention in ensuring equitable outcomes, as seen in Nigerian courts' interpretation of this section.

By contrast, Ugandan courts have exhibited a proactive approach to property redistribution to achieve equitable outcomes, even in the absence of explicit statutory enactments. Judicial activism in this respect is commendable and prepares an optimistic ground for the application of the Marriage Bill, if it is eventually passed into law. In the *Julius Rwabinumi v Hope Bahimbisomwe* case,[83] the court advocated for equal sharing of jointly acquired property, regardless of the initial ownership or financial contribution. This proactive redistribution approach aims to achieve a more balanced outcome, particularly in cases where one spouse's contributions are non-monetary.

In Nigeria, despite the statutory provisions, gender biases persist due to the strong influence of customary law. On the other hand, the Constitution in Uganda promotes gender equality; however, customary practices still pose significant challenges. In addition, both Nigeria and Uganda face socioeconomic challenges, such as poverty and limited access to legal resources, that hinder the equitable distribution of property. Cultural norms in both countries often prioritise men's property rights, leading to unequal outcomes for women. These challenges underscore the urgent need for comprehensive reforms that transcend legal changes and address the social and cultural barriers that hinder true gender equality in property rights.

---

[82] *Kakooza v Kakooza* [2005] 2 ULR 605.

[83] *Rwabinumi v Bahimbisomwe* [2013] UGSC 5.

7 Recommendations

7.1 Inconsistencies in Marriage Laws and Harmonisation

In Nigeria, there is a need to harmonise statutory and customary laws to ensure consistent and equitable outcomes. Nigeria is a legally pluralistic society, meaning multiple legal systems coexist, including customary law, Islamic law (Sharia), and statutory law. This pluralism significantly impacts marriage laws, as different legal traditions govern different types of marriages. Statutory law prohibits polygyny (otherwise known as polygamy), but customary and Islamic laws permit it. Divorce rules differ significantly across systems, leading to jurisdictional disputes. Some customary and Islamic laws limit women's property rights upon divorce. Under most customary marriages, despite the rights to equal treatment and to own property provided under the Constitution, wives are not considered legally capable of owning property. When allowed to own property, they are deemed to hold it in trust for their husbands or heirs, leading to an unequal distribution of property upon divorce. This is in sharp contrast with statutory marriages, where women are recognised as having the right to own property and, therefore, receive an equitable share of the property on divorce. Thus, there is a need for the harmonisation of the two laws to ensure equal protection of women under both marriages. Legal reforms and improved enforcement of human rights laws could help address these issues, while the preservation of cultural and religious traditions should be encouraged.

7.2 Non-Registration of Customary and Islamic Marriages in Nigeria

The issue of non-registration of customary and Islamic marriage is another challenge. This results in legal uncertainty, especially concerning matters such as property distribution. The lack of registration can also result in unequal treatment of those in non-registered marriages compared to those married under the Marriage Act, further complicating issues of spousal rights and entitlements.

7.3 Codification of Customary Law Rules/Legislative Reforms

There is an immediate need to codify Islamic and customary laws in Nigeria to address contemporary realities. Non-codification gives room for inequality through the arbitrary application of the rule. In Uganda, there is a need to strengthen the implementation of statutory and constitutional provisions to protect women's property rights. In addition, the Parliament needs to take positive steps to pass into law the Marriage Bill, which is long overdue. This will effectively address the socioeconomic barriers and imbalances that hinder equitable property distribution in Uganda. Granting judges wide discretion to determine the value of a spouse's non-monetary contribution is problematic, as it can lead to inconsistent and subjective outcomes.

7.4 *Creation of Awareness and Education*

It is also of contingent necessity to promote awareness and education on gender equality and property rights. Promoting awareness and education about marriage law reforms in Nigeria and Uganda is crucial for ensuring compliance, protecting vulnerable individuals, and fostering gender equality. A combination of legal literacy campaigns, school education, media outreach, and community engagement can help bridge the gap between legal provisions and societal practices.

8 Conclusion

The comparative analysis of the allocation of marital properties after the dissolution of marriage in Nigeria and Uganda reveals both similarities and differences in the legal frameworks and practices. While both countries strive for equitable distribution, the influence of customary laws and socioeconomic factors poses significant challenges. By addressing these challenges and promoting gender equality, both countries can enhance the protection of property rights and achieve more equitable outcomes for all parties involved.

As both countries continue to evolve in their legal practices, it is essential to monitor the impact of these differences on the protection of women's rights and the equitable distribution of marital property. The ongoing efforts to reform domestic relations laws in Uganda, particularly through the Marriage Bill, may provide a more robust framework for addressing these issues in the future.

Marital property settlement after the dissolution of marriage in Nigeria and Uganda reflects the complexities of legal pluralism, gender dynamics, and evolving judicial interpretations. While both countries recognise statutory, customary, and religious marriages, significant differences exist in how marital property is distributed upon divorce.

In Nigeria, statutory marriages are governed by the Matrimonial Causes Act, which aims for equitable distribution based on contribution, while customary and Islamic laws often favour male ownership of property. In contrast, Uganda has made strides toward gender equality through judicial pronouncements and legal reforms, such as the Succession (Amendment) Act and the Marriage and Divorce Bill, which seek to ensure fairness in property division.

Despite these efforts, both countries face challenges, including cultural resistance, a lack of legal awareness, and weak enforcement mechanisms. Women, in particular, often struggle to claim their rightful share of matrimonial property due to societal norms and legal loopholes. For equitable marital property settlements, Nigeria and Uganda must strengthen legal frameworks, enhance public awareness, and improve judicial enforcement. A balance between statutory regulations and customary practices is necessary to ensure fair, just, and gender-sensitive outcomes in marital property division after divorce.

References

Ambali MA (2014) The practice of Muslim family law in Nigeria. Tamaza Publishing Co Ltd, Kano

Aniche A (2024) Settlement of property after divorce in Nigeria. https://lawclinicpro.com/settlement-of-property-after-divorce-in-nigeria/. Accessed 1 Sept 2025

Anyebe AP (1985) Customary law: the war without arms. Fourth Dimension Publishing Co. Ltd, Benin

Ashiru MOA (2007) Gender discrimination in the division of property on divorce in Nigeria. J Afr Law 51:316–331

Attah M (2016) Family welfare law in Nigeria. Ambik Press, Benin

ConstitutionNet (2024) Constitutional history of Uganda. https://constitutionnet.org/country/uganda. Accessed 16 Aug 2025

Edu OK, Ojogbo SE (2022) Comparing maintenance and property rights in marriage under customary law and statutory law in Africa. Oxf Univ Commonwealth Law J 22:229–252

Izunwa MO (2015) Divorce in Nigerian statutory and customary marriages: a comparative critique of grounds, procedures and reliefs attaching thereto. Peak J Soc Sci Humanit 3(6):77–83

Kes A, Jacobs K, Namy S (2011) Gender differences in asset rights in Central Uganda. International Center for Research on Women (ICRW). https://www.icrw.org/wp-content/uploads/2016/10/Gender-Land-and-Asset-Survey-Uganda.pdf. Accessed 2 Sept 2025

Nwogugu EI (2014) Family law in Nigeria, 3rd edn. HEBN Publishers Plc, Ibadan

Obi SNC (1977) The customary law manual: a manual of customary laws obtaining in the Anambra and Imo states of Nigeria. Government Printer, Lagos

Olomola O, Olatunbosun AI (2017) Settlement of matrimonial property and the rights of housewives. Manag Ind Law J 7:133–135

Onokah MC (2003) Family law. Spectrum Books, Ibadan

Probert R (2009) Cretney and Probert's family law, 7th edn. Sweet & Maxwell, London

Sherifat M, Kolade-Faseyi I (2021) Revisiting the dissolution of marriage under Islamic law in Nigeria. MUNFOLLIJ 1:130–136

Standley K, Davies P (2013) Family law, 8th edn. Palgrave Macmillan, London

Uganda Law Reform Commission (1996) A study report on the reform of the law on domestic relations. Uganda Law Reform Commission, Kampala

Uganda Law Reform Commission (2020) Study on cohabitation in Uganda. https://www.ulrc.go.ug/projects/study-on-cohabitation-in-uganda/. Accessed 16 Aug 2025

Vocabulary.com (2024) Property settlement. https://www.vocabulary.com/dictionary/property%20settlement. Accessed 1 Sept 2025

Omolade Olunike Olomola is a Professor at the Department of Private and Property Law and alternate Director of the Women's Law Clinic at the University of Ibadan, Nigeria. She teaches Family Law, Social Justice, Clinical Legal Education, and Gender and Reproductive Health Rights

Law. Her research focuses on family law, gender justice, reproductive health rights, and international humanitarian and human rights law. She was acting Dean of Law at Elizade University (2017–2019) and the immediate past Dean of Law at Cavendish University, Uganda. She holds an LLB, LLM, and PhD from the University of Ibadan, in addition to a certificate in International Humanitarian Law from the University of South Africa.

Ownership of Marital Property in Zambia

Annie Kangwa Chewe

Abstract The distribution of marital property in Zambia reflects the tension between dual legal systems, customary and statutory law, that often produce divergent outcomes upon the dissolution of marriage. While property ownership is seldom questioned during the subsistence of marriage, divorce frequently triggers disputes, with each spouse seeking exclusive control over assets. This chapter interrogates the principles governing the ownership of marital property in both legal regimes, paying particular attention to the gendered challenges women face in asserting their rights. It traces the historical and cultural evolution of women's property rights and critiques prevailing legal doctrines that permit individualised claims in what is inherently a collective marital enterprise. The chapter contends that marriage constitutes a unit of existence in which both spouses contribute, whether directly or indirectly, to the acquisition of assets. Upon divorce, this unit dissolves and should give way to an equal or equitable division of marital property. Through doctrinal and contextual analysis, the chapter advocates for reform of Zambia's family law framework to ensure that property division upon divorce better reflects the principles of unity, equity, and recognition of all forms of spousal contribution.

1 Introduction

Ownership of marital property, whether during or at the end of a marriage, remains a contentious matter worldwide, especially in jurisdictions with multiple legal paradigms and differing rules. Zambia operates a dual legal system in which

A. K. Chewe (✉)
University of Zambia School of Law, Lusaka, Zambia
e-mail: annie.chanda@unza.ac.zm

A. F. Hammond and P. Batariwah (eds.), *The Law on Marital Property in Africa*, Ius Gentium: Comparative Perspectives on Law and Justice 138,
https://doi.org/10.1007/978-3-032-19358-2_8

customary law and statutory law, both valid legal systems, are applied side by side.[1] Marriages are contracted under both systems of law and are regulated as such. Statutory law marriages are contracted pursuant to the provisions of the Marriage Act,[2] while customary law marriages are contracted according to the various traditions and customs of the 73 ethnic groupings in Zambia. Furthermore, some people also contract religious marriages under various religious doctrines. Therefore, there are basically three types of marriage practised in Zambia. Statutory and customary law marriages are recognised under the laws of Zambia,[3] while religious marriages are recognised under the rules of the respective religious doctrines.

Upon marriage, spouses exist as a unit and act collaboratively in pursuit of their mutual well-being. To this end, married couples acquire various types of property during the subsistence of their marriages. These may include real property, such as land and houses, or household chattels, like furniture. Sometimes, couples jointly acquire property, especially land, and register the property in both their names. Joint ownership, as legally understood, does not necessarily apply to other movable chattels. However, even though property may not be jointly acquired as legally understood, property acquired by a couple during their marriage is generally understood to belong to both of them and used for their collective well-being. The question of ownership of such property between the parties is not often discussed while the marriage subsists. However, at divorce, property sharing and ownership are hotly contested between the parties, with each claiming ownership of property individually to the exclusion of the other party.

This chapter argues that marriage creates a unit of existence which inherently prevents spouses from making individual claims to property ownership while the marriage subsists. The chapter argues further that upon divorce, when this unit is dissolved, the parties should share equally in the property acquired during the marriage. This argument is premised on the understanding that the couple's combined resources, whether monetary or in-kind, embody the principles of unity and equality within marriage. This chapter, therefore, discusses the ownership of marital property by parties to a marriage, whether statutory or customary, with a specific focus on the plight of women in Zambia. This aims to validate the argument that parties to a dissolved marriage should share property equally, or at least equitably, upon divorce.

This chapter comprises seven sections, beginning with an introduction. Section 2 explores the historical evolution of women's property rights, concentrating on the initial subjugation of women and the role of courts in altering the status quo. Section 3 examines the various forms of marriage in Zambia and their legal implications

[1] The Constitution of Zambia in arts. 1(1) and 7 recognise customary law and customary practices as long as it does not contradict the Constitution and any other written law. Several other laws like the High Court Act Chapter 27 (s. 14), the Subordinate Courts Act Chapter 28 (s. 16) and the Local Courts Act Chapter 29 of the Laws of Zambia (s.12(1)) also recognise the existence of customary law as a valid system of law in Zambia as long as it is not repugnant to natural justice and good conscience and does not contradict the written law.

[2] Marriage Act Chapter 50 of the Laws of Zambia, ss. 6–28.

[3] Marriage Act Chapter 50 of the Laws of Zambia, s. 34 recognises the validity of statutory and customary law marriages in Zambia.

for spousal rights. Section 4 analyses the influence of both domestic and international human rights instruments on women's ownership of matrimonial property. Section 5 reviews the statutory and customary law frameworks governing property rights during marriage and after divorce. Section 6 offers recommendations to address the shortcomings in Zambia's marriage laws, and section 7 concludes the chapter.

2 Historical Context of Women's Property Rights

Before delving into the issue of ownership of marital property and property settlement in Zambia, a brief overview of the historical situation of women regarding their status as married women is necessary to provide the context in which ownership of marital property, including property settlement, has been viewed over the years. A commentary by Blackstone provides insight into how women have been and continue to be considered in certain sections of society. Looking at marriage and the bond created by the marriage between the parties, Blackstone,[4] when discussing the doctrine of coverture[5] stated that:

> the very being or legal existence of the woman is suspended during the marriage, or at least is incorporated and consolidated into that of the husband under whose wing, protection, and cover she performs everything...Upon this principle of a union of persons in husband and wife, depend almost all the legal rights, duties, and disabilities that either of them acquires by marriage.[6]

This chapter argues that this commentary and other similar beliefs or sentiments are at the root of women's subordinate position in society, including gender violence against women in various contexts. Although the doctrine of coverture, as espoused by Blackstone, was not directly introduced in Zambia, the country's practices indicate that, by and large, people have behaved in ways that reflect Blackstone's account of the doctrine. Although recent years have seen some progress, traditional dynamics persist in many households, with men in paid employment and women primarily engaged in unpaid domestic duties. Therefore, what Blackstone stated long ago remains valid to this day, at least in Zambia: women are still regarded in some sections of society as property owned by men and, as such, are often seen as having no legal entitlements. In traditional Zambian society, a man is expected to provide for a woman, and in return, he acquires exclusive rights over her.[7] During the process of contracting marriages, men pay a bride price to seal the marriage contract and make

[4] Blackstone (1768, p. 449).

[5] The doctrine of coverture refers to the legal status of a married woman considered to be under her husband's protection and authority.

[6] Cretney et al. (2002, p. 70).

[7] Chuulu et al. (1999, p. 28).

the marriage valid.[8] Within marriage, men may perceive themselves as superior and often assert authority over their wives. In the same light, the man is presumed to own all the property acquired during the marriage because he is often the one in gainful employment. This subordination affects women across all divides and is rooted in traditional practices across tribes in Zambia.

Even with so much advancement, especially in human rights, some sections of society still view a woman as a man's property with no independent existence of her own. As a result, family resolution of disputes is often biased against women and in favour of men who have exclusive rights over their wives.[9] A woman is typically not entitled to a share of the property acquired during the marriage in the event of a divorce. The same dynamic often persists when a man dies, leaving behind a widow. Studies have shown that widows are frequently mistreated and deprived of property that rightfully belongs to them.[10] Generally, the deceased man's family is supposed to continue caring for the widow through the practice of widow inheritance as provided by law. This customary law practice, known as levirate marriage, involves the obligation of the brother of a deceased man to marry the widow, primarily to preserve the deceased's lineage.[11]

In Zambia, progress in realising women's property rights has been made through the enactment of legislation and the delivery of court decisions that have primarily examined the reasonableness of customary law, applying the principles of equity and equality in the division of marital property.[12] For example, in 2024, the High Court refused to recognise and apply an *Ndebele* custom which sought to deny a woman custody of her children and a share in the matrimonial property upon divorce, because the man had paid a bride price and a sum of money termed '*lobola*', at the time the marriage was contracted.[13]

[8] See *Fenias Mafemba v Esther Ngula Sitali* [2007] ZR 215, where Mafemba's claim as surviving spouse was denied in the absence of a valid customary marriage. Mafemba lived with Inonge the daughter of Esther Sitali for 14 years and had two children but never paid bride price. At Inonge's death, Mafemba was not recognised as a surviving spouse of Inonge Sitali.

[9] Colson (1958).

[10] Chuulu et al. (1999, p. 28). See also Banda (2008).

[11] Deceased Brother's Widow's Marriage Act, Chapter 57 of the Laws of Zambia, s 3.

[12] See for example the Anti-Gender Based Violence Act, No.1 of 2011 and the Gender Equity and Equality Act, No. 22 of 2015, *Chibwe v Chibwe* [2000] ZMSC 59, where the Supreme Court stated that the court is vested with wide powers in re-adjusting the financial position of the parties to the divorce. Although there are no hard and fast rules in making awards on property adjustment, the court is guided by the principle of doing justice taking into account the circumstances of the case. The court also stated that in Zambia, courts must invoke both the principles of equity and law concurrently.

[13] See *Julius Sibanda v Flat Mooyo* [2024] ZMHC 77.

3 Forms of Marriage and Their Legal Consequences

A logical starting point for defining marital property in Zambia is the validity of the marital union,[14] as the recognition of a valid marriage is fundamental to determining what qualifies as marital property.[15] As noted above, Zambia recognises two types of marriage under the law: statutory and customary marriages. A statutory law marriage is a marriage contracted between one man and one woman to the exclusion of all others. This definition is implicitly captured by the provisions of the Marriage Act as follows:

> Any person who is married under this Act or whose marriage is declared by this Act to be valid, shall be incapable during the continuance of such marriage of contracting a valid marriage under any African customary law, but, save as aforesaid, nothing in this Act contained shall affect the validity of any marriage contracted under or in accordance with any African customary law, or in any manner apply to marriages so contracted.[16]

Statutory law marriages are monogamous, riding on the definition provided by Lord Penzance in the celebrated case of *Hyde v Hyde and Woodmansee,* in which his Lordship, when defining a marriage, looked at marriage '…as the voluntary union for life of one man and one woman to the exclusion of all others'.[17] The court's reasoning incorporated Christian values, which only allow marriage between one man and one woman. Polygamous unions, in this scenario, are invalid. However, in Zambia, as can be seen from Section 34 of the Marriage Act, customary law marriages are recognised as valid. These marriages are contracted according to the various customs and traditions of the Zambian people. Some tribes practice polygamy while others do not, but generally, there is no impediment to contracting a customary union subject to the conditions set by the law.[18] The most common and acceptable form of polygamy in Zambia is polygyny. In other words, a man can marry more than one wife.

Irrespective of the form of marriage, the parties must comply with the necessary formalities to validate their marriages. These include family introductions, marriage payments and kitchen parties among others.[19] The incidents of each marriage depend on the system of law under which the marriage was contracted.

Parties may contract a marriage under the Marriage Act before the Registrar of Marriages at the Civic Centres dotted across the country. This is conducted pursuant

[14] See *Fenias Mafemba v Esther Sitali* [2007] ZR 215 where a claim as surviving spouse was denied in the absence of a valid customary marriage.

[15] See *Mathews Chishimba Nkhata v Esther Dolly Mwenda Nkhata* (SC, 28 November 2017, pp. 17–19).

[16] Marriage Act, Chapter 50 of the Laws of Zambia, s 34.

[17] *Hyde v Hyde and Woodmansee* [1866] L.R 1 P&D 130.

[18] See Marriage Act Chapter 50 of the Laws of Zambia, s. 34. Under Zambian law, polygamous unions may be contracted and they have been reported to be quite widespread in the nation.

[19] During kitchen parties which are also known as bridal showers, the bride is presented with gifts such as stoves, fridges, pots, plates and pans to help her start her home. The bride's mother and other older and more experienced women share their wisdom on marriage with the new bride.

to the provisions of the Marriage Act, particularly Sections 6 to 28. Parties could also choose to marry in church. If they do so, the solemnisation of the marriage by a recognised religious minister, along with the signing of the marriage certificate, creates a valid marriage. The process at Civic Centres and in churches results in a valid civil or statutory marriage.

Parties may also decide to marry purely under customary law. It is mandatory for all applicable processes, particularly the payment of the bride price, to be undertaken; otherwise, there is no marriage. In the case of *Fenias Mafemba v Esther Sitali*,[20] the Supreme Court upheld the High Court's decision that the payment of the bride price sealed the marriage contract and no length of cohabitation by the parties could constitute a valid customary law marriage.

Generally, it appears that the same couple marries three times: first, under customary law, with the payment of a bride price to seal the marriage; second, according to church rules, when they take their vows; and finally, by signing the marriage certificate, resulting in a statutory marriage. Controversy sometimes arises when parties undergo purely religious ceremonies and take their marital problems to court. These marriages are not regulated by law. If parties can show some form of customary law, custom, or tradition that they followed during the process, the marriage may be treated as a valid customary law marriage.

In addition, there is no presumption of marriage under Zambian law. The Supreme Court in *Fenia Mafemba v Esther Sitali* held that no length of cohabitation can constitute a valid marriage.[21] The Appellant and Inonge Sitali, the daughter of the Respondent, cohabited for 14 years and had two children. When Inonge died, the Appellant alleged that he was the surviving spouse and should therefore be entitled to inherit a part of her estate under intestacy laws. The claim failed because he was unable to establish the existence of a valid marriage between himself and the deceased.

4 Human Rights and the Ownership of Marital Property in Zambia

Notably, Zambia has made positive strides in domesticating international instruments, particularly the Convention on the Elimination of All Forms of Discrimination Against Women (CEDAW), to allow citizens to benefit from its provisions. The Anti-Gender-Based Violence Act,[22] for instance, was enacted in 2011 to provide civil remedies to abused men, women, and children. Further, in 2015, the government enacted the Gender Equity and Equality Act[23] to ensure equality between men and women in all spheres of life.

[20] *Fenias Mafemba v Esther Sitali* [2007] ZR 215.

[21] *Fenias Mafemba v Esther Sitali* [2007] ZR 215.

[22] Anti-Gender Based Violence Act No. 1 of 2011.

[23] The Gender Equity and Equality Act No. 22 of 2015.

The CEDAW is particularly important. According to Munalula,[24] the CEDAW seeks to eliminate discrimination against women to ensure they can fully access and enjoy their human rights. Munalula states that much of the discrimination addressed in the Convention is systemic and considered an integral and natural part of most societies. Therefore, the CEDAW seeks to ensure the equal participation of men and women in all aspects of life to realise equal human rights.

In 2016, the Constitution of the Republic was amended to recognise, among other things, the equal worth of men and women in the preamble in the following words: 'We, the People of Zambia confirm the equal worth of women and men and their right to freely participate in, determine and build a sustainable political, legal, economic and social order'.[25] The Constitution contains the Bill of Rights under Part III. Article 11 provides as follows:

> It is recognised and declared that every person in Zambia has been and shall continue to be entitled to the fundamental rights and freedoms of the individual, that is to say, the right, whatever his race, place of origin, political opinion, colour, creed, sex or marital status, but subject to the limitations contained in this part, to each and all of the following, namely;
>
> a. Life, liberty, security of the person and the protection of the law;
>
> b. Freedom of conscience, expression, assembly, movement and association;
>
> c. Protection of young persons from exploitation;
>
> d. Protection for the privacy of his home and other property, and from deprivation of property without compensation

Article 11 is the general guarantee of human rights applicable to everyone. However, the rights are not absolute but are subject to limitations designed to ensure that the enjoyment of the said rights and freedoms by any individual does not prejudice the rights and freedoms of others or the public interest. Articles 16 and 17 protect the right to property and privacy, respectively. Of importance to this chapter is article 23 on non-discrimination. According to article 23(1), 'no law shall make any provision that is discriminatory either in itself or in its effect... '. Article 23(4)(c) and (d) provides that clause (1) shall not apply to any law so far as that law makes provision '(c) 'with respect to adoption, marriage, divorce, burial, devolution of property on death or other matters of personal law and (d) for the application in the case of members of a particular race or tribe, of customary law with respect to any matter to the exclusion of any law with respect to that matter which is applicable in the case of other persons'.

The Constitution has been criticised for fueling discrimination and promoting harmful customary practices against women, as Article 23 (4) (c) and (d), reproduced above, excludes customary law from constitutional scrutiny and therefore permits discrimination in the private sphere.[26] The Constitution is also presumably said to permit the existence of bad customary practices and personal laws, such as those relating to marriage, divorce, burial, and the devolution of property.[27] To help

---

[24] Munalula (2005, p. 17).

[25] Preamble to the Constitution Amendment Act No 2 of 2016, para 6.

[26] Munalula (2005, p. 86); Nthani (2014); Ndulo (2011, pp. 87–120).

[27] Munalula (2005, p. 86); Nthani (2014); Ndulo (2011, pp. 87–120).

neutralise the discrimination contained in article 23(4)(c) and (d), the 2016 amended Constitution provides for the supremacy of the Constitution in article 1(1), thereby bringing customary law and customary practices under constitutional scrutiny. Therefore, even if customary law is a valid justice paradigm, the practices and customs thereunder are subject to the Constitution, and all those customs and practices which contravene the Constitution shall be declared null and void. However, the question that begs an answer is the effect of this supremacy clause on article 23, which is an entrenched provision in the Bill of Rights. Despite this, courts have used the supremacy provision to declare and refuse to uphold bad customary practices.[28]

5 Regulation of Ownership of Marital/Matrimonial Property in Zambia

The above discussion of the legal framework for human rights, with its emphasis on equality and non-discrimination, sets the tone for the discussion of ownership of marital property in Zambia. The legal framework governing property settlement in Zambia is the Matrimonial Causes Act No. 20 of 2007 for statutory marriages, while customary marriages are governed by the distinct traditions and customs of Zambia's 73 tribes.

In terms of actual statutes regulating ownership of marital property, the primary statute is the Matrimonial Causes Act (MCA) No. 20 of 2007. Additionally, the Zambian Constitution, particularly the 2016 Constitution amendment, is relevant. There are also the Local Courts Act (Chapter 29 of the Laws of Zambia), the Subordinate Courts Act (Chapter 28 of the Laws of Zambia), and the High Court Act (Chapter 27 of the Laws of Zambia). The Matrimonial Causes Act deals with property settlement for dissolved statutory law marriages, while the other laws listed above deal with property settlement arising from customary law marriages. The Local Courts have original jurisdiction over customary law matters,[29] while the subordinate courts (Magistrate Courts), the High Court, the Court of Appeal, and the Supreme Court deal with such matters on appeal.[30] Therefore, the dissolution of marriage and property settlement is governed by Zambia's dual system of law.[31]

However, the dual system is not watertight, and there have been cases in which courts have applied the provisions of the MCA to customary law marriages rather than the specific traditions and customs applicable to such marriages. In the case of

[28] See *Julius Sibanda v Flat Mooyo* [2024] ZMHC 77; *Maureen Muyoba v Godwin Muyoba* [2018] ZMHC 369.

[29] See Local Courts Act Chapter 29 of the Laws of Zambia, s. 12.

[30] See *Ann P. Nkhoma v Smart Nkhoma* [2004] ZMHC 1 in which after dissolution of the parties' customary marriage, the applicant Ann P Nkhoma issued originating summons in the High Court claiming an equal share of the matrimonial property. The High Court held that since the matter did not come before it by way of appeal, it had no jurisdiction to hear the application and dismissed it.

[31] Munalula (2005, p. 86).

Lizzy Musauka v Mpasi Solomon Dube,[32] the parties' customary law marriage was dissolved by the Local Court. On an appeal in respect of property settlement, the Supreme Court held that 'in line with Section 55 of the Matrimonial Causes Act, in any property settlement after divorce, whether customary or statutory marriage, the interest of the children of the family must be considered as well'. The court did not establish the specific customary practices regarding property sharing but instead applied statutory law to resolve the matter.

Customary law is a valid legal paradigm and can only be set aside if it is found to be repugnant or contrary to the written law. It is argued that the court fell into error by applying statutory law to a customary law issue without ascertaining the existence of the custom or practice. In the case of *Chibwe v Chibwe,* the Supreme Court established that customary law should be applied unless it is repugnant to natural justice or contradicts the written law. The application of statutory law to customary law matters also flies in the face of Section 3 of the MCA, which restricts the application of the provisions of the MCA to statutory marriages. The courts should, therefore, instruct parties to clearly disclose the customary law under which their marriage was conducted. This will enable the court to resolve property settlement issues after divorce within the relevant justice paradigm, with customary law being judged against the repugnancy clause. The approach in *Noah Bwalya and Fredrick Mutale v Idah Namwalizi*[33] is instructive. The Supreme Court ordered a retrial of the case because, although the marriage between the parties was said to be customary, neither the trial court nor the appellate courts determined which specific customary law governed the marriage.

5.1 Ownership of Marital Property During Marriage

Under the Zambian family law system, when parties enter into a marriage, they create a unit in which the two persons exist as equals. Similarly, it is generally understood that the property acquired by the couple during the marriage is for their mutual benefit. In determining what amounts to marital or matrimonial property, the general rule is that everything acquired by the parties to the marriage during its subsistence is matrimonial property and, therefore, available to be shared should the parties decide to divorce. This includes both movable and immovable property, as long as it is acquired by the couple during the marriage or brought into the marriage with the intention that it be used for their joint benefit and comfort.[34]

---

[32] *Lizzy Musauka v Mpasi Solomon Dube* (SC, 21 December 2017).

[33] *Noah Bwalya and Fredrick Mutale v Idah Namwalizi* (SC, 13 June 2016).

[34] The Zambian courts rely on the English case of *Wachtel v Wachtel* [1973] 1 ALL E.R 829 where Lord Denning defined family property as 'items acquired by one or the other party to the marriage with the intention that those should be continuing provision for them and the children during their joint lives and are for the use of the family as a whole. That family property includes those capital assets such as the matrimonial home, furniture and income generating assets such as commercial properties'; Zambia is a common law country and regularly draws inspiration from

During the subsistence of the marriage, it is understood that the parties to the marriage do not acquire individual property but acquire family property, which they use together without distinguishing between what belongs to the man and what belongs to the woman.[35] In the case of *Annette Chilima v Peter Chilima,*[36] concerning the distribution of marital property in the absence of a divorce, Justice Muzyamba held that:

> when a man and woman join in holy matrimony, they become one body, one flesh and during the subsistence of their marriage, they acquire and own property jointly and indivisibly, and until the marriage is put asunder, none of them should be heard to say he owns this or that property. It follows that the court is not competent to order distribution or share of matrimonial property between the parties where a marriage is still subsisting. This is so even where the parties are on separation. To hold otherwise would not only be striking a death nail in a principle which is sacrosanct, but would also be opening a Pandora's box in this era of greed for wealth. This would inevitably lead to unstable marriages.[37]

What is clear from the *Chilima* decision is that property division cannot occur while a marriage is still legally subsisting, even if the spouses are separated. As long as the marriage has not been formally dissolved, all property is considered jointly and indivisibly owned, and the court lacks the authority to divide it between the parties. However, a new perspective on this position appears to have been introduced by the Court of Appeal in February 2024 in the case of *Yammie Zimba and Margaret Zimba v Cynthia Zimba.*[38] In this case, the respondent, Cynthia Zimba, was judicially separated from the deceased, Kanyuka Zimba, whom she married on 23 April 1994. They were granted a decree of judicial separation on 8 May 2014. Kanyuka Zimba died intestate on 26 April 2015. Upon his death, Cynthia and her child were excluded from inheriting any property by the appellants, who were the administrators of the late Kanyuka Zimba's estate, claiming that Cynthia was not a surviving spouse.

The High Court, relying on Section 35 of the Matrimonial Causes Act, held that because the marriage was not dissolved and the parties were merely separated, the Respondent Cynthia Zimba was the surviving spouse and therefore entitled to a share under the Intestate Succession Act.[39] This section states that, 'A decree of Judicial Separation relieves the petitioner from the obligation to cohabit with the other party to the marriage while the decree remains in operation, but except as provided by this

---

English statutes and case law. The English legal system still informs the Zambian legal system in a material particular. For example, the 2007 MCA is modelled on the 1973 MCA of England, with some provisions being verbatim. See *Mathews Chishimba Nkhata v Esther Dolly Mwenda Nkhata* (SC, 28 November 2017).

[35] This idea of mutual benefit and joint or communal property was recently dislodged by the Supreme Court in *Nkhata v Nkhata* (SC, 28 November 2017) when it stated that parties to a marriage could have some personal property for their individual benefit separate from the other spouse.

[36] *Annette Chilima v Peter Chilima* [2000] ZMSC 23.

[37] *Annette Chilima v Peter Chilima* [2000] ZMSC 23.

[38] *Yammie Zimba and Margaret Zimba v Cynthia Zimba* [2024] ZMCA 10.

[39] Section 5 of the Intestate Succession Act Chapter 59 of the Laws of Zambia gives 20% of the estate to a surviving spouse.

Part, does not otherwise affect the marriage or the status, rights and obligations of the parties to the marriage.'

The administrators of the estate appealed the decision. The Court of Appeal, relying on Section 36(1) of the Matrimonial Causes Act and holding it superior to Section 35, ruled in favour of the administrators. According to Section 36(1), "Where a party to a marriage dies intestate as to any property while a decree of judicial separation is in operation, that property shall devolve as if that party had survived the other party to the marriage." Thus, the Respondent, Cynthia Zimba, was legally presumed to have died before her husband, Kanyuka Zimba, and was therefore excluded as a beneficiary of his estate.

It should be noted that while Section 35 preserves the marriage and prevents property division during judicial separation, under Section 36(1), if one spouse dies while judicial separation is in effect, the surviving spouse is legally treated as having predeceased the other. As a result, the separated spouse loses all inheritance rights, even though the marriage has not been dissolved and property has not been divided, as happened in the *Zimba* case, where all the matrimonial property of the spouses remained with Kanyuka Zimba. The Court of Appeal's decision in the *Zimba* case is inconsistent with the reasoning in the *Chilima case* because, while *Chilima* held that property cannot be shared during a subsisting marriage, even when spouses are separated, *Zimba* treats judicial separation as a legal fiction of death, disqualifying the surviving spouse from inheriting, despite the marriage not being dissolved. This inconsistency unjustly denies a surviving separated spouse their property rights when the other dies intestate.

Until appealed against, *Zimba* remains the law, and, by the doctrine of stare decisis, binds all lower courts handling similar matters. A question arises as to whether the court would have reached a different decision had it used the purposive interpretation of the two sections and invoked the principles of equity and law concurrently. It is unjust that a party who has contributed to the acquisition of matrimonial property is completely denied a share of it because the other spouse dies intestate while the two are judicially separated. These laws must be reconciled through an amendment. If the reasoning of the Court of Appeal is anything to go by, the proposed legislative reform should require property settlement when a decree of judicial separation is made under Section 35.

The issue of individual property always arises in divorce, with each party claiming that some of the property is theirs alone, to the exclusion of the other. This contradicts the long-established principles of the family unit, as seen in the case of *Annette Chilima v Peter Chilima*,[40] cited above. However, the Supreme Court seemed to validate this individualistic thinking when it stated in the case of *Mathews Chishimba Nkhata v Esther Dolly Mwenda Nkhata* that:

> our own understanding is that it is possible for parties to a marriage to acquire property during the subsistence of the marriage, which is not intended to be for the provision of the family as a whole. And therefore, in the face of property settlement, it would defeat the justice of the case to hold such property as the parties designated as extra personal investment, as

---

[40] *Annette Chilima v Peter Chilima* [2000] ZMSC 23.

> amenable to property adjustment merely because it was acquired during the subsistence of the marriage.[41]

Clearly, this means that parties in a marriage are free to own individual property. This then validates the thinking that matrimonial property is property acquired through the joint efforts of the parties and intended by them to be for the joint benefit of the family as a whole. The same principle applies to property brought into the marriage by one or both parties. The parties must make it clear how the property should be treated. The reasoning in the *Nkhata* case could destabilise marriages on property lines, as parties will start to lead separate lives within the marriage.

5.2 Property Settlement After Divorce

5.2.1 Under Statutory Law

When a marriage breaks down, the court has extensive power over both spouses' capital assets and future earnings. The said powers are to be exercised after considering 'all the circumstances of the case so as to place the parties as far as is practicable in the financial position in which they would have been had the marriage not broken down…'.[42]

The parties to a dissolved marriage are expected to share the matrimonial property equally or equitably at divorce. Munalula argues that marriage under statutory law is said to give women better entitlements upon divorce in terms of property settlement.[43] This is because the law governing property settlement is clearly defined in the Matrimonial Causes Act 2007. This law draws inspiration from the English system and its subsequent developments. It can safely be assumed that property settlement could be 50/50 between the parties. However, courts in Zambia have not been implementing the 50/50 rule. They share property in different percentages for various reasons, as seen in the cases discussed in this chapter. The Matrimonial Causes Act 2007 provides in Section 55 that:

> the court may upon granting a decree of divorce … make (a) an order that a party to the marriage shall transfer to the other party … such property as may be specified in the order, being property to which the first mentioned party is entitled either in possession or reversion; (b) an order that settlement of such property as may be specified, being property to which a party to a marriage is entitled, be made to the satisfaction of the court for the benefit of the other party to the marriage …[44]

From the wording of this provision, there seems to be a latent suggestion that parties to a marriage can claim individual ownership of property during the subsistence of

[41] *Mathews Chishimba Nkhata v Esther Dolly Mwenda Nkhata* (SC, 28 November 2017, pp. 23–24).

[42] Cretney (1973, pp. 653–656).

[43] Munalula (2005, p. 86).

[44] Matrimonial Causes Act No. 20 of 2007, s. 55.

the marriage; however, the court can order that such property be settled for the benefit of the other party. It may also mean that the property is registered in the name of one of the parties, but is not to be owned solely by that party. Indeed, marital property can be registered in the names of one of the parties, but that does not necessarily mean the property is owned exclusively by that party. In the case of *Lizzy Musauka v Mpasi Solomon Dube*,[45] the Supreme Court stated that it did not matter in whose name the property was registered. What was important was that the property in question qualified as matrimonial property to be shared on divorce.

The court is guided by the provisions of the law in dividing the property between the parties to the dissolved marriage. These provisions are based on the English law principles established in the case of *Wachtel v Wachtel,*[46] where Lord Denning held that '..., a party to divorce proceedings provided he or she has contributed either directly or in kind (that is, looking after the home) has a right to financial provision. The percentage is left in the discretion of the court, taking into account all the circumstances of the case'.[47]

In line with the principles in *Wachtel v Wachtel,* courts in Zambia have made decisions on property settlement considering the parties' contributions. The bottom line, as can be discerned from the discussion thus far, is that the parties must provide proof of contribution. In the case of *Fabian Ponde v Charity Bwalya*,[48] the Supreme Court stated that, 'it does not matter that financial contribution was not made by both spouses to the acquisition or development of family assets, what matters is that the parties to the marriage made contributions either materially or in kind towards those assets'.[49] Usually, husbands claim they bought all the properties because they typically have the financial muscle between the two; on the other hand, wives also claim that what they bought with their own money is theirs alone. Times have changed, and women who were traditionally not in gainful employment and often depended entirely on their husbands are now emancipated and sometimes even earn more than their husbands. This means that women's contributions extend far beyond the traditional roles of tending to the home and performing domestic chores, which they have been associated with for years.

Regarding how the parties view property settlement, the Supreme Court stated in the case of *Mathews Chishimba Nkhata v Esther Dolly Mwenda Nkhata* that:

> regrettably, property settlement in this country, as in many others, seems to proceed on the premises which, we must state, now resides in a bygone era, that it is the responsibility of the man in a marriage to fend for the family and that the woman's role is confined to performing domestic chores. If the basis for sharing of family property is that both spouses contributed to its purchase or its creation, it should follow that where it can be demonstrated that one spouse invested nothing either financially or in kind, in the acquisition of the property, they should technically not be entitled to a share only on the basis of having entered into the marriage. Our view is that property settlement should be undertaken on the basis of fairness and conscience,

[45] *Lizzy Musauka v Mpasi Solomon Dube* (SC, 21 December 2017).

[46] *Wachtel v Wachtel* [1973] 1 ALL E.R 829.

[47] *Wachtel v Wachtel* [1973] 1 ALL E.R 829.

[48] *Fabian Ponde v Charity Bwalya* [2020] ZMSC 123.

[49] *Fabian Ponde v Charity Bwalya* [2020] ZMSC 123.

> not on an unjustified reference to a 50:50 dogma. In our view, property sharing should not reside in a fixed formula in law. It should not be a matter of mathematics. Each case should be determined in terms of how much each party contributed and an appropriate percentage apportioned on that basis.[50]

In all the decisions on property settlement, the reasoning of the courts is that for a party to claim a share of the matrimonial property, that party must show their contribution, whether in kind or cash. Any person in a valid marriage where property has been acquired through the joint efforts of both spouses is entitled to a share of that matrimonial property upon dissolution of the marriage, unless a valid reason is provided to justify their exclusion. What remains in the discretion of the court is the actual percentage or nature of property awarded to each of the parties to the dissolved marriage. No comfort should be derived merely from being married, and as stated by the Supreme Court in the *Nkhata* case, a marriage is not and should never be regarded as the reason for equal sharing of matrimonial property.[51] Each party's actual contribution must be demonstrated and established.

5.2.2 Under Customary Law

Under customary law, there is a general belief that all the property belongs to the man as the breadwinner and the head of the family. It is noted that 'in most rural and peri-urban areas of Zambia, land is considered to be owned by the male head of the household and few women have their names on land documents or consider themselves to be land owners'.[52] A 2011 study conducted in the *Chibombo* and *Namwala* districts of Central and Southern Provinces of Zambia revealed that both men and women understood matrimonial property to belong to the man and his family, and that at divorce, it is up to the husband to decide what he would give to his ex-wife.[53] As a result, women tend to be disadvantaged after divorce, for the men claim everything or assert that a larger portion of the property belongs to them.

Many people fail to recognise a woman's contribution in kind, such as taking care of the home, as sufficient for the acquisition of matrimonial property. This perspective has resulted in significant hardship, especially when a husband passes away, as his family often challenges the widow's rights to the property. The situation is further complicated by customary law, which lacks clearly defined and uniformly established rules regarding the division of property in the event of divorce. It is acknowledged that some tribes recognise women in the sharing of property. Among the *Ushi* of Luapula province, for example, a woman is entitled to a reasonable share

[50] *Matthews Chishimba Nkhata v Esther Dolly Mwenda Nkhata* (SC, 28 November 2017, pp. 22–24).

[51] *Matthews Chishimba Nkhata v Esther Dolly Mwenda Nkhata* (SC, 28 November 2017, p. 21).

[52] See also Kalinda, Chirwa, and Thankian (2022).

[53] Chanda (2011).

of the matrimonial property.[54] This is probably true for many other tribes but except the *Lozis*, who insist that a woman is not entitled to any share of the matrimonial property.

The case of *Sanikonda Phiri v Elestina Zulu*[55] illustrates how men often attempt to get the lion's share of the matrimonial property on divorce. The Matero Local Court dissolved the 54-year-old marriage between the parties and ordered the sharing of the matrimonial property. During their marriage, the couple acquired various properties, including five houses, a farm, one bare plot, two shops, a bar and tavern, two trucks, one car and three sewing machines. The local court ordered that the woman be given one house, a shop, a tavern, and two sewing machines. The court also ordered joint ownership of the farm. The man appealed against the decision, arguing that some of the properties belonged to his uncle. He further claimed that two of the houses had been given to his sons, while the other properties had been sold. The man argued that he had already given his former wife a house, a shop and a sewing machine and that these items were sufficient to fulfil his obligations. These sentiments resonate well with the findings from the study conducted in *Chibombo* and *Namwala,* referred to above, where men claimed that it was for them to decide what to give to the women at divorce. The High Court held that the woman was entitled to an equal share of the proceeds from the properties the man sold after the marriage was dissolved. She was also entitled to a one-third interest in the farm. The local court award of a house, a shop, a tavern and two sewing machines was upheld. In this case, it is evident that the man was determined to deny his former wife an equitable share of the property they acquired during their 54 years of marriage. While such trends to deny women equal shares are common, they are rarely pleaded as customs.

Local Courts have original jurisdiction to hear and determine divorce cases involving customary law marriages, as well as other matters involving customary law.[56] These courts are widely spread across the country, and their importance cannot be ignored, as they provide access to justice in many communities. Additionally, there are few appeals from their decisions. It is unclear whether this is due to ignorance or satisfaction with the decisions made. In any case, the local courts handle a huge volume of work in Zambia's urban and rural areas. The future of the local courts within the court system in Zambia is quite secure, and they are well recognised by the Constitution in article 120, which, in part, provides that local courts shall progressively become courts of record, like all other courts.[57] Writing in 1990, Coldham stated that although it was the ultimate goal of the government to have a fully professionalised judiciary, it recognised that local courts still had an important role to play in the administration of justice, particularly in rural areas. He further stated that if

---

[54] See *Rosemary Chibwe v Austin Chibwe* [2000] ZMSC 59 where the court recognised the *ushi* customary law as valid. The evidence from the assessors showed that under that custom, a woman was entitled to a reasonable share of property at divorce.

[55] *Sanikonda Phiri v Elestina Zulu* (HC, 5 September 2012).

[56] The Local Courts Act s. 12(1) provides that '... a local court shall administer (a) the African customary law applicable to any matter before it in so far as any such law is not repugnant to natural justice or morality or incompatible with the provisions of any written law'.

[57] Constitution Amendment Act No. 2 of 2016, art. 120(2).

the amount of business transacted by the local courts and the paucity of appeals from their decisions indicated their popularity and effectiveness, they had then proven their worth.[58] This statement stands true today, and local courts remain more accessible to the people than any other court in the country.

Additionally, local courts have adopted new approaches to property division after divorce, as demonstrated in several cases. For instance, in the case of *Fabian Ponde v Charity Bwalya,*[59] the Chilenje Local Court, upon dissolving the marriage, ordered the defendant to pay K15,000.00 to the plaintiff as compensation and instructed that all household goods be shared equally between the parties. The court, however, did not make a specific order relating to the two houses acquired during the subsistence of the marriage. On appeal before the Supreme Court, the appellant (Fabian Ponde, the man) argued that the property on which the two houses were built was too small to be shared. The Supreme Court held that no property was too small to be shared by a former husband and wife, and that the claim that the plot was too small was not a good reason to prevent fair sharing of the property. The Supreme Court did not disturb the local court's order for compensation and custody of children.

In *Muyoba v Muyoba,*[60] the Chelstone Local Court ordered the sharing of the property acquired by the parties during the subsistence of the marriage and awarded a house to the wife. The husband appealed the decision, stating that the house did not belong to him but to the children. However, he failed to prosecute the appeal. In the meantime, he took possession of the property awarded to him by the Local Court but prevented his wife from taking possession of hers. The High Court held that there was no justification for the respondent to refuse to give effect to the Local Court's decision and accordingly awarded the vesting order. In the case of *Julius Sibanda v Flat Mooyo,*[61] the Chelstone Local Court, after dissolving the marriage, ordered that 'the plaintiff (Flat Mooyo) gets the farm in Chisamba and a plot on title, while the defendant was to remain with the house and get the car. The parties were to share the cattle equally'. On appeal to the High Court, the appellant, Julius Sibanda, argued that under the Ndebele custom, a divorced person, in this case the wife, was not entitled to a share of the property acquired during the marriage nor to the custody of the children of the family. The High Court held that 'enforcement of a custom which wholesomely deprived a spouse of any entitlement to a share of the property or the custody of the children should be tested against the provisions of article 1 (1) of the Constitution'.[62] The court further stated that in determining the case, it would be guided by the need to do justice as established in *Chibwe v Chibwe*.[63] The court indicated that 'a man's cultural right, whatever the culture, which overrates him on account of having paid *lobola,* is inhuman and unjustifiable'.[64] In the end,

[58] Simon Coldham (1990).

[59] *Fabian Ponde v Charity Bwalya* [2020] ZMSC 123.

[60] *Maureen Muyoba v Godwin Muyoba* [2018] ZMHC 369.

[61] *Julius Sibanda v Flat Mooyo* [2024] ZMHC 77.

[62] *Julius Sibanda v Flat Mooyo* [2024] ZMHC 77.

[63] *Chibwe v Chibwe* [2000] ZMSC 59.

[64] *Julius Sibanda v Flat Mooyo* [2024] ZMHC 77.

the court shared the property equitably between the parties. These cases demonstrate that local courts have been more receptive to ensuring fairness, equity, or equality in the division of marital property. Their decisions are rarely upset in their entirety by superior courts.

In some cases, applying the tradition under which the parties contracted their marriage can be unjust and unfair to women. In a 1977 case of *Mwiya v Mwiya*,[65] the Mulobezi Local Court dissolved the marriage contracted under *Lozi* customary law between the parties. It made no order regarding property sharing because no *Lozi* custom allowed a man to share his property or maintain his former wife for the rest of her life after divorce. On appeal by the woman, the subordinate court upheld the Local Court's decision. On a further appeal to the High Court, the judge sitting with assessors held that there was no *Lozi* custom requiring a husband to share property with his wife on divorce, nor was there any custom requiring him to maintain her for life. This decision is an affront to human rights, especially the rights of women. The *Lozi* custom is repugnant to natural justice, equity, and good conscience because it is unfair that the woman should walk out of the marriage with nothing and her contribution not be regarded at all.

In the landmark decision of *Rosemary Chibwe v Austin Chibwe*,[66] the Supreme Court provided sufficient guidance to courts on the application of the principles of law and equity concurrently in divorce cases arising from customary law unions. In the *Chibwe* case, the husband, with the intention of defeating the course of justice, transferred a number of capital assets and real properties into the names of companies while divorce proceedings were pending. During the hearing of the matter before the local court, he pleaded that the properties did not belong to him, so his divorced wife could not benefit from them. The woman appealed all the way to the Supreme Court, which ruled that the respondent's transfer of property ownership could not evade the court's authority to order a fair distribution of all the assets. This particular case involved the *Ushi* custom, which entitles a woman to a reasonable share of the marital property upon divorce.

Questionable practices, such as the Lozi custom seen in *Mwiya v Mwiya*, have no place in modern Zambia, despite the courts not having overruled the decision, which continues to be cited as authority in property settlement cases. One thing worth noting is that the courts are willing to strike down harmful or repugnant customary laws and practices which are injurious to the welfare of women and children.

5.2.3 Bigamous Marriages and Property Rights

A person who marries a third party without previously dissolving any validly contracted pre-existing monogamous marriage does not have the capacity to contract the second marriage. The second marriage is, therefore, void. No special property rights exist between the parties, and property jointly acquired will be divided between

---

65 *Mwiya v Mwiya* [1977] ZR 113.

66 *Chibwe v Chibwe* [2000] ZMSC 59.

them based on their respective contributions towards the property's purchase and development. In *Walker v Walker*,[67] the court did not find an existing marriage between the applicant and the deceased because the deceased was already married to a third party, a marriage he had not dissolved at the time of the second marriage. While the applicant was unable to inherit a portion of the estate in her capacity as s surviving spouse, the court invoked the equitable principle of a constructive trust to award her 50% of the farm on which she lived based on her contribution. Her contribution to the development of the property included, among other things, 'stay[ing] at the farm alone, stamping the land, and plan[ting] a banana plantation'.[68] She even went as far as selling 'fresh fish from the Zambezi river to raise money' and 'chasing elephants away from the land'.[69] In another case of bigamous marriages, the court treated the spouse to the second marriage as a dependent for the purposes of inheritance.[70]

6 Recommendations

This chapter begins with the argument that married couples exist as a single unit and that upon divorce, the couple should share the property acquired through their combined resources equally or equitably. The discussion above has shown that property settlement is often a contested issue, with problems persisting in certain areas. This chapter, therefore, makes the following recommendations:

6.1 Amendment of Relevant Laws (Law Reform)

It is recommended that laws with contradictory applications be either amended or repealed to ensure they operate in harmony. Examples include sections 35 and 36(1) of the MCA. As demonstrated in the *Zimba* case, the current inconsistency unjustly denies a surviving judicially separated spouse any claim to matrimonial property upon the other's death, despite Section 35 preserving the legal status and rights within the marriage. Reconciling these provisions is necessary to prevent such unjust outcomes and to preserve the intended purpose of judicial separation within Zambia's legal framework.

Further, article 23(4)(c) and (d) of the Constitution, which appear to sanction discrimination by removing customary law from constitutional scrutiny in matters of a personal or private nature, should also be amended to ensure the proper enforcement of the non-discrimination provision.

---

[67] *Walker v Walker* (HP 9 of 2010) [2011] ZMHC 52.

[68] *Walker v Walker* (HP 9 of 2010) [2011] ZMHC 52, p. 14.

[69] *Walker v Walker* (HP 9 of 2010) [2011] ZMHC 52, p. 14.

[70] *Charity Oparaocha v Winfridah Murambiwa* (2004) ZR 142.

The amendments and/or repeal of these provisions, along with the enactment of new provisions, will contribute to uniform practices and the consistent application of the law, regardless of whether the parties are married under customary law or statutory law.

6.2 Amendment of the Bill of Rights

The Bill of Rights should be strengthened by firstly, incorporating economic, social, and cultural rights, and secondly, explicitly ensuring equality in all aspects, including property ownership and distribution between couples.

There is also a need to define the components of the repugnancy clause. Although the courts are utilising this clause, there appears to be a lack of literature clearly defining its constituent elements. As a result, each court handling a case in which customary law or a customary practice is invoked must rely on its professional judgment to accept or reject the pleaded custom. This approach may lead to inconsistency in the application of the repugnancy clause, which might undermine the stability and predictability of the legal system.

6.3 Promotion of the Dual Legal System in Zambia

Zambia operates a dual legal system, comprising statutory and customary law, as valid justice paradigms. Therefore, courts seized with matters where customary law is pleaded should not shy away from promoting customary law and establishing standards that should be of general application and followed by everyone. This is based on the understanding that customary law is living law, capable of changing and adapting to new trends, just like statutory law, which can be amended from time to time. Courts make law as they interpret it, and therefore should contribute to law reform in this sense.[71]

In addition, concerted efforts should be made to establish minimum standards codified in areas of personal law where customary law is actively applied and relied upon by the people. This is not an insurmountable task, as it has been done before. For example, in 2023, the government amended sections 2, 33, and 34 of the Marriage Act to allow for the voiding of any marriage where one party is a child. This is irrespective of the type of marriage entered into. A child is defined in the Constitution as a person below the age of 18 years. This amendment addresses the issue of child marriages,

---

[71] Kaaba (2019). In this article Kaaba criticized the Supreme Court for failing or shying away from making a proper determination in a novel succession issue. He stated that the court had an opportunity to create uniform standards to guide the people going forward and that customary law is living law capable of changing.

which have been prevalent under customary law, particularly in the absence of a specified age of majority for contracting a marriage.

Other critical areas, such as the equal sharing of property and the abolition of repugnant customs, should also be addressed similarly by establishing standards that apply universally, regardless of the type of marriage entered into. This approach will foster uniformity and reduce the challenges parties face in divorce proceedings.

Additionally, the government should conduct sensitisation campaigns to educate communities on the enjoyment of human rights and the equitable sharing of property among divorced couples. This human rights initiative should encompass both men and women to ensure its effectiveness and foster broader societal acceptance.

7 Conclusion

This chapter has examined the question of property ownership within marriage and upon divorce in Zambia. It has been found that during marriage, ownership claims are often not there because parties tend to operate under the belief that marriage is a lifelong commitment, with all property acquired being intended for the collective good and benefit of the family as a whole. It has also been established that fierce contestations characterise property settlement cases, with men trying by all means to deny women equal or equitable shares in the property acquired by the parties during the marriage. Despite these problems, it has been established that courts in Zambia have often ruled in favour of equality and equity in property settlements, provided that both parties contributed to the acquisition of the property in question. Contributions to the acquisition of marital property are not limited to monetary forms but can also be made in kind or through other material support. This recognition has alleviated some of the suffering that women experience during divorce.

This chapter began with the argument that marriage creates a unit of existence, which inherently means that there can be no individual claim to marital property while the marriage subsists. Upon divorce, when this unit is dissolved, the individual parties should share the property acquired during the marriage, either equally or at least in an equitable manner. This argument is grounded in the understanding that the resources contributed by the parties as a couple, whether monetary or in kind, are pooled together, symbolising unity and equality. The discussion in this chapter has established that parties often make individual claims to marital property, especially during divorce. However, the law and court decisions have shown that parties to a marriage are entitled to a share of the property they acquired during the marriage. Further, the chapter has established that the validity of a marriage and the contributions of the parties should be considered in determining property settlement cases. The paper has also highlighted the unfortunate presence of contradictory provisions in certain statutes, such as the MCA, where a woman was denied property rights because she was judicially separated at the time of her husband's death, resulting in an unjust outcome. The chapter has further established that, although there are discriminatory, bad, or repugnant customary practices among some tribes, customary law is not inherently bad. There are some good practices which should be harnessed. It is hoped that the recommendations made in this paper will be embraced to help alleviate the plight of women, particularly in the sharing of matrimonial property on divorce.

References

Banda TM (2008) Silent tears: the continued violations of widows' inheritance rights in Zambia. A study of widows' experience in Kitwe, District of the Copperbelt Province of Zambia. Master's Thesis, University of Zimbabwe

Blackstone W (1768) Commentaries on the Laws of England, vol 1. Clarendon Press, Oxford

Chanda AC (2011) The customary practices of the Lenje of Chibombo and the Ila of Namwala Districts of Zambia. Unpublished Research Report, Directorate of Research and Graduate Studies—University of Zambia

Chuulu MB, Chileshe PM, Ntalasha HM, Chanda AW (1999) Justice in Zambia: myth or reality: women and the administration of justice. Women and Law in Southern Africa Research Trust, Harare

Coldham S (1990) Customary marriage and the urban local courts in Zambia. J Afr Law 34(1):67–75

Colson E (1958) Marriage and family among the Plateau Tonga of Northern Rhodesia. Manchester University Press, Manchester

Cretney SM (1973) Financial provision after Wachtel v Wachtel. Mod Law Rev 36(6):653–656

Cretney SM, Masson JM, Bailey-Harris R (2002) Principles of family law, 7th edn. Sweet and Maxwell, Mytholmroyd

Kaaba OB (2019) Kilolo Ng'ambi v Opa Kapijimpanga Appeal No 210/2015 (Judgment of 9 October 2018). SAIPAR Case Rev 2(1):19–22 https://scholarship.law.cornell.edu/cgi/viewcontent.cgi?article=1025&context=scr. Accessed 25 Oct 2025

Kalinda R, Chirwa M, Thankian K (2022) Women and land tenure in Zambia: Legal and customary challenges for women. Arch Curr Res Int 22(8):60–70. https://doi.org/10.9734/acri/2022/v22i8548

Munalula MM (2005) Women, gender discrimination and the law: cases and materials. UNZA Press, Lusaka

Ndulo M (2011) African customary law, customs and women's rights. Indiana J Glob Legal Stud 18(1):87–120

Nthani EM (2014) An investigation into adultery as a ground for divorce under customary law in patrilineal marriages in Zambia. Dissertation, University of Zimbabwe

Annie Kangwa Chewe is a legal practitioner of 27 years and Dean of the School of Law at the University of Zambia. Her research focuses on family law, human rights, and public law. She practised extensively at the National Legal Aid Clinic for Women, where she later became Executive Director (1999–2010). Chewe has served as Chair of the Student Board of Discipline since 2008, Vice Chair of the Lusaka District Education Board, and member of national legal committees, including ZIALE and the Council of Law Reporting. She also chairs the Training and Curriculum Development Committee of ZIALE and served as Vice Chapter President of Transparency International Zambia (2020–2023). She holds an LLB (Zambia), LLM (Lund University), and PhD (Africa Research University).

Civil Law Traditions: Côte d'Ivoire, Ethiopia, Morocco

Ivorian Matrimonial Property Law Reform: Between Resurgence and Emergence

Alfred Kouakou Kouassi

Abstract The 2019 reform of Ivorian family law introduced significant changes to Côte d'Ivoire's matrimonial property regimes, responding to shifting social dynamics and the growing importance of equality within marriage. Previously governed predominantly by the community of property regime, Ivorian matrimonial law has evolved to offer spouses new legal options, including the separate property regime and the ability to execute customised matrimonial agreements. This chapter examines the legal framework and impact of these reforms, employing a diachronic legal analysis to determine whether the changes represent a continuation or a transformation of past practices. It examines legislative texts, case law, and comparative insights from other jurisdictions to evaluate the principles, mechanisms, and limitations introduced by the reform. The findings reveal that while the reform promotes the principles of spousal equality and contractual freedom, it also imposes regulatory limits grounded in public policy and morality. Notably, the inclusion of the notary as a key actor in matrimonial contracts reflects the formalisation and state oversight of private marital arrangements. The chapter recommends further reform, including codified conflict-of-law rules and premarital legal education, to strengthen the legal certainty and practical effectiveness of Ivorian matrimonial property law in an increasingly transnational context.

A. K. Kouassi (✉)
Université Des Lagunes, Abidjan, Côte d'Ivoire
e-mail: alfred.kouassi@ulagunes.com

A. F. Hammond and P. Batariwah (eds.), *The Law on Marital Property in Africa*, Ius Gentium: Comparative Perspectives on Law and Justice 138,
https://doi.org/10.1007/978-3-032-19358-2_9

1 Introduction

'In many cases, a reform is simply the replacement of old disadvantages which everyone knows about, by new disadvantages which are not yet suspected, and the nature and extent of which practice then reveals'.[1]

The ideal of human rights is beginning to take hold in black Francophone Africa. This, at least, is reflected in the various international human rights instruments ratified by states. To ensure coherence within national legal systems, incorporating international instruments into domestic law may necessitate amending existing national legislation to align with the ratified agreements.[2] According to the legislature, this need for legal alignment was among the key factors that led to the adoption of Law No. 2019–570 of 26 June 2019, on marriage.[3]

This law introduces new perspectives on marital relationships, addressing both the personal aspects of marriage and the associated financial implications, particularly in relation to matrimonial property regimes. In this respect, the Ivorian matrimonial regime now stands in stark contrast to the past, as the legislature has decided to offer spouses an *à la carte* matrimonial regime, designed to respond more adequately to the interests of each family. However, it is the promotion of the principle of equality between spouses in the management of household assets that, above all, undoubtedly constitutes the major innovations of this reform, and which this study sets out to analyse.

Matrimonial property regimes are usually understood as the:

> set of property rules governing, during and at the dissolution of marriage, spousal property (as regards ownership, disposition, administration and enjoyment) and all pecuniary matters of the household, both as between the spouses and in their relations with third parties, including the rules of the primary matrimonial property regime.[4]

This shows the influence of marriage on spousal property rights, as the law provides a framework for the ownership, management, and distribution of property between spouses during marriage and at its dissolution.[5] Against this background, this study explores the question: What has been the impact of the 2019 marriage law reform on the regulation of matrimonial property in Côte d'Ivoire? More specifically, what provisions concerning matrimonial property regimes has the reform introduced into Ivorian positive law? Does this legal development represent a substantive shift in the framework governing matrimonial property, or does it largely reflect a continuation of existing legal paradigms?

An attempt to answer this question may begin with an examination of the legislative provisions set out in Chapter 8 of the Act, which outlines the legal framework for

---

[1] Planiol (1904, p. 955), quoted in Guedje (2018, p. 111).

[2] See Explanatory Memorandum to Law no. 2019–570 of 26 June 2019 relating to Marriage.

[3] Law no. 2019–570 of 26 June 2019 relating to Marriage.

[4] Cornu (2016, p. 880).

[5] Caparros (1965–1966, p. 292).

organising the property relations between spouses. It is titled 'The pecuniary effects of marriage'. Under the terms of Article 58:

> The matrimonial property regime governs the property consequences of the marriage in relations between the spouses and in relation to third parties. The spouses may enter into any agreements with respect to their property that they deem appropriate, provided that such agreements are not contrary to morality, public policy or the provisions of this Act. All matrimonial agreements shall be drawn up by notarial act before the marriage ceremony and shall only take effect from the date of the ceremony.

Article 59 establishes that, unless the spouses have made a specific agreement regarding the financial effects of their marriage, their union automatically results in either a community of property regime or a separation of property regime. Under Article 60, spouses are not allowed to modify or override the rights and obligations that arise from the matrimonial property regime they have selected, even by mutual agreement. According to Article 101, spouses who choose the separation of property regime are permitted to structure their financial relations through a formal agreement, which must either be approved by the president of the competent court or authenticated by a notary.

The relevant articles indicate that marriage has a direct effect on the legal characterisation of spousal property, by specifying the manner in which the assets of the spouses are to be organised. In this context, while the community and separation of property regimes, already recognised under prior laws, remain available to spouses, the reform also introduces a new alternative: the conventional matrimonial regime, which is now emerging as a central option in structuring spousal property relations.

As can be seen, rather than confining itself to offering a regime of community of property with an option for separation of property, as was the case in the past,[6] the Ivorian legislature has now introduced an *à la carte* matrimonial property regime grounded in contractual principles. In so doing, a triptych of matrimonial property regimes can be observed in Côte d'Ivoire. A joint analysis of articles 58, 59, 60, and 101 of the Ivorian law on marriage will therefore focus on the resurgence of regimes of community or separation of property, on the one hand, and the emergence of contractual matrimonial property regimes, on the other.

This chapter is divided into seven sections. Sections two and three trace the development of matrimonial property law in Côte d'Ivoire and situate the 2019 reform of the Ivorian matrimonial property regimes as a significant legal shift away from male-dominated marital structures toward formal equality between spouses. They specifically discuss the community and separate property regimes, highlighting the gradual introduction of these concepts into Ivorian law. The sections also introduce a new regime, the contractual regime, advanced by recent reforms in Ivorian family law. Section four examines how the State regulates agreements between spouses,

---

[6] Under the terms of art. 69 (new) of Law no. 64–375 of 7 October 1964 relating to marriage, as amended by Law no. 83–800 of 2 August 1983, Marriage has the effect of creating a community of property between the spouses unless they expressly declare that they opt for the regime of separation as to property. See also Article 70 (new) of the same law which states that: 'The option results from their joint declaration before the civil registrar when the marriage is celebrated'.

with particular emphasis on judicial oversight and the legal standards contracts must meet to be considered valid and enforceable. Section five discusses the consequences of bigamous marriages. The sixth section provides recommendations, drawing on approaches taken by similarly placed countries. Section seven concludes the chapter.

Before proceeding, it is important to note that this chapter addresses only the legal consequences of civil marriages in Côte d'Ivoire because 'only marriages celebrated by a civil registrar have legal effect'.[7] Thus, Ivorian law does not recognise customary and Islamic marriages. As customary and Islamic marriages are potentially polygamous, their non-recognition means that polygamous marriages have no legal validity.

2 The Resurgence of Traditional Matrimonial Property Regimes

Before 1964, Ivorian law favoured a single matrimonial regime, then the community of property regime.[8] A new option, the separate property regime, was introduced in 1983.[9] Today, article 59 of the 2019 Ivorian law on marriage, which states that 'marriage creates between the spouses either the regime of community of property or that of separation of property', reaffirms the two matrimonial regimes that were already in effect before the law's enactment. These two property regimes are well known in many legal systems.[10] However, both then and now, the legal regime of community of property remains highly relevant in Côte d'Ivoire, as does the continued existence of the separation of property regime, particularly because

[7] Law no. 2019–570 of 26 June 2019 relating to Marriage, art. 14.

[8] See Dumetz (1975, pp. 265–266), where it reads, 'The option in favour of a single community matrimonial regime only came to light late in the drafting of Ivorian laws. Thus, the draft law provided that the spouses would have a choice between two regimes—community of acquests and separation as to property [...]. [At the end of the preparatory work, which had taken place in the presence of all the MPs, a meeting was to be held in the presence of the Head of State, President Houphouët-Boigny. Until then, there was no attempt to discuss the choice that the bill left to the spouses. [...] At the end of the ensuing discussions on this particular point, it was decided to amend article 68 of the Marriage Act, giving it the form it had in the [then] wording: 'marriage has the effect of creating between the spouses a community of property, governed by the following provisions". This text therefore seems to have expressly excluded the possibility of adopting a regime other than that of community of property.'

[9] This is stated in article 69 (new) of Law no. 64–375 of 7 October 1964, relating to marriage, amended by Law no. 83–800 of 2 August 1983 as: 'The essence of marriage is to create between the spouses a community of goods unless they expressly declare to opt for the regime of separation of property'.

[10] See Caparros (1965–1966, p. 292), who states that, '[i]n the area of economic relations between spouses, there are two major contradictory ideas: the idea of independence of each spouse vis-à-vis the other, and the idea of solidarity between them. Depending on the legal system, one of these ideas may be the thesis, the other the antithesis'.

many spouses still do not formalise their asset arrangements through a contractual agreement.

2.1 The Decline of Community of Property as a Common Law Matrimonial Property Regime

History shows that the concept of community of property between spouses has existed for more than a thousand years; for example, this system is known in countries with a Roman-Germanic tradition or a Common Law tradition. In Ivorian law, by providing in 1964 that 'marriage has the effect of creating between the spouses a community of property, governed by the following provisions',[11] the Ivorian legislature was fully in line with this tradition.

However, when the community of property regime was enshrined in Ivorian family law in 1964, the legislature took care to exclude the possibility of spouses adopting a matrimonial property regime other than the single community regime.[12] Consequently, spouses were prohibited, from the outset, from adopting the separation of property regime, especially by agreement.[13] In fact, as one author observes,

> since it had prohibited the adoption of the regime of separation of property by agreement, the Ivorian legislature had a duty to prohibit any modification of the legal regime by agreement. Otherwise, it was feared that the spouses would attempt to modify the communal logic by specific provisions included in the marriage contract. For this reason, any modification by agreement of the unique Ivorian legal regime was prohibited.[14]

This is how the community of property regime came to be the exclusive matrimonial regime accepted by Ivorians, with the corollary of the regime's immutability.[15]

The first dent made in the exclusivity of the community of property regime came with the 1983 Marriage Amendment Act, article 69, which provided that: 'marriage has the effect of creating a community of property between the spouses unless they expressly declare that they opt for the separation of property regime'. Thus, nineteen years had sufficed for the legislature to introduce the separation of property regime alongside the regime of community of property, with future spouses then having the option to choose between these two regimes.[16]

Now, although the introduction of the option in favour of the regime of separation of property had clearly marked a decline in the exclusivity of the community regime

---

[11] Law no. 64–375 of 7 October 1964 relating to Marriage, art. 68.

[12] Dumetz (1975, p. 269).

[13] Dumetz (1975, p. 270).

[14] Dumetz (1975).

[15] The immutability of the matrimonial property regime refers to the principle whereby 'once the marriage has been celebrated, the spouses may not make any change to their matrimonial property regime; it remains a rule that such a change may only result from a judgment [...] in the cases specified by law'. See Cornu (2016, p. 523).

[16] Lohoues-Oble (2023, p. 214).

by the 1983 reform, it was still accepted by that reform that if the spouses 'fail to opt before [the civil registrar] on the day of the marriage for the regime of separation of property, they will be united under the regime of community of property'.[17] Clearly, by granting spouses the right to opt for the regime of separation of property, the legislature had conferred on the provisions of the community regime the character of suppletive provisions, that is, those applied in the absence of specific choices made by the spouses.

Regarding the value of suppletive legal provisions, one author states that, through such provisions,

> the legislator takes into account not only the probable will of the persons concerned, but also a whole range of social, economic and historical considerations, which do not originate in the supposed thoughts of the persons concerned. Based on these data, it forges a model, i.e. a standard solution that seems best suited, all factors considered, to the social environment for which it is intended.[18]

The 1983 reform of matrimonial property regimes clearly signals the legislature's preference for the community of property model, which is viewed as 'an extension of the monogamous conception of the family: *duo in una carne*'.[19] This preference also underscores the legislature's circumspection towards customary traditions since the 1964 Marriage Act, given that customary practices for managing matrimonial property between spouses were based on a separatist conception of ownership.[20]

Today, thirty-six (36) years after the 1983 reform of the marriage law, a new landscape has emerged in Ivorian matrimonial property law, with the effective decline of the community of property as the default legal regime. Indeed, the 1983 reform's preference for the community of property regime, as a suppletive provision, has now given way to the equal standing of the community of property and separation of property regimes.[21] This new situation already signals a shift in the traditional conception of the community of property regime.

2.2 The Establishment of a New Concept of the Community of Property Regime

As we have just seen, the 1964 Ivorian law on marriage instituted the unique community of property regime, limited to acquests, as a necessary consequence of marriage.[22] Under this regime, each spouse retained ownership of assets acquired before the marriage, as well as any property inherited or gifted from their family;

---

[17] Law no. 64–375 of 7 October 1964 relating to Marriage as amended by Law no. 83–800 of 2 August 1983, art. 23 (new).

[18] Cornu (2008, p. 328).

[19] Planiol and Ripert, p. 13.

[20] Dumetz (1974, p. 266).

[21] See Law no. 2019–570 of 26 June 2019 relating to Marriage, art. 59.

[22] Lohoues-Oble (2023, p. 214).

these properties remained separate from the joint marital estate. Consequently, the marital estate consisted mainly of property acquired for valuable consideration during the marriage. Any property thus acquired is termed 'acquest'.[23]

As for the management of this community property, it was conceived under the prism of the patriarchal model. According to Jacqueline Lohoues-Oble,

> the management of this community was attributed to the husband. He was the 'master and lord', head of the family (art. 58 of the Marriage Act) and head of the community (art. 71 of the same Act). In this capacity, he was responsible for the administration of joint property and his wife's own property (art. 79 of the aforementioned law). He could, without her consent, sell, alienate and mortgage joint property. It was only with regard to his wife's personal property that the law required him to obtain her consent (art. 81 of the aforementioned law).[24]

In reality, this form of community property, an expression of the inequality between husband and wife in the management of household assets, was simply a reflection of the legal status attributed to women at the time.[25] It was, in fact, a widespread concept both within the colony of Côte d'Ivoire and in the former French metropolis. In this respect, some authors argued at the time that recognising the equal powers of wife and husband, or the full capacity of a married woman, would be incompatible with the regime of community of property.[26] Others, on the other hand, felt that, logically, a woman's capacity should require the abandonment of the community of property regime,[27] in the sense that there could only be one captain in a ship.

However, things have since changed, as evidenced by the progressive changes made to women's rights globally.[28] Since then, the powers of married women in

---

[23] Simler (n.d.), p. 3.

[24] See Lohoues-Oble (2023, p. 216).

[25] See Piatowski (1960) who states that, 'It was clearly noted at the 2nd International Congress of the Association Henri Capitant pour la culture juridique française that the general problem of the current evolution of the status of spouses raises three essential questions. The first is that of the management of the family and the household; the second, that of the capacity of the wife; the third, that of the general economy of matrimonial property regimes'.

[26] Vasseur (1955, p. 434), quoted by Piatowski (1960, p. 503).

[27] Ancel (1956, pp. 58–59), quoted by Piatowski (1960, p. 503).

[28] See Bucher (2000, p. 20). See also Piatowski (1960), who noted,'One of the most powerful factors behind this development has been the emergence of the social and political role of women and the enshrinement of their fundamental right to equality with men. This development should not be viewed solely from a legal perspective. It was made possible by an economic and social situation that made it essential for women to be fully integrated into the functioning of society and the economy. From another angle, this integration can be seen as a liberation movement, aimed at the full development of both women and men'. Piatowski again observed in 1960, '[...] The socialist countries have implemented in their legislation the principle of equal rights and, of course, equal powers for men and women in family life in the most consistent way, it seems to us. But this principle is also gaining increasing ground in the legal systems of other countries. It has been accepted for many years in the Scandinavian systems. In the Netherlands, it would be difficult, after the 1956 reform, to demonstrate what this "head of the family" status, recognised in the husband under Article 159 of the Dutch Civil Code, actually consists of. A similar question may arise in France in relation to article 213 of the Civil Code following the forthcoming adoption of the bill on the reform of matrimonial property regimes'.

managing the household have changed significantly. The 1983 reform of family law in Côte d'Ivoire echoed this by introducing greater involvement of women in the management of the community,[29] to the point of granting them rights similar to those of their husbands over their own property and reserved property.[30] However, it was not until 36 years later, with the reform of the marriage law in 2019, that the legal rights, duties, and privileges of husbands and wives were substantially modified. In the management of joint property, the husband could not, 'without the consent of the wife, dispose of these assets *inter vivos* free of charge; dispose of or encumber with rights in rem, immovable property, businesses or holdings belonging to the community; and bequests made by him may not exceed his share in the community'.[31] In the past, the husband, as head of the family, exercised 'alone all acts of administration or disposal of the joint property'.[32] Things had now changed, and presently, married women have the 'status of a co-responsible person' in the management of the community of property.[33]

The new idea of equal powers between spouses is reflected in their shared authority over household decisions. Whereas in the past, the husband's opinion generally prevailed, unless the wife had recourse to the courts in the cases provided for by law,[34] the situation is now different. Today, joint property other than the spouses' earnings and income is administered by one or the other of the spouses,[35] just as the agreement of both spouses is required[36] for acts of alienation or disposal of joint property.

In its current composition, community assets remain unchanged, in that they still consist of the spouses' common property and their own property, and the system is supplemented by a presumption of common property: 'Any property is presumed to be common, if one of the spouses does not prove that it belongs solely to him/her'.[37] The removal of the reference to the wife's 'reserved property' in the new wording of

---

[29] See Lohoues-Oble (1984–1985, p. 62), who observed in 1984 that, 'The state of legal incapacity in which the 1964 community regime placed women cannot be accepted in today's Ivorian society, where women increasingly engage in activities that provide them with the means of relative independence.'

[30] See Lohoues-Oble (2016, p. 216). In Côte d'Ivoire, as in other legal systems, the "reserved property" of a married woman refers to property she acquires through her work or through income separate from that of her husband. Such property is left to the administration and disposal of the married woman, even in a community property regime.

[31] Law no. 64–375 of 7 October 1964 relating to Marriage as amended by Law no. 83–800 of 2 August 1983, art. 81 (new).

[32] Law no. 64–375 of 7 October 1964 relating to Marriage as amended by Law no. 83–800 of 2 August 1983, art. 81 (new).

[33] Simler (n.d., p. 3).

[34] See in particular Law no. 64–375 of 7 October 1964 relating to Marriage as amended by Law no. 83–800 of 2 August 1983, art 82 and 87.

[35] Law no. 2019–570 of 26 June 2019 relating to Marriage, art. 82(1).

[36] Law no. 2019–570 of 26 June 2019 relating to Marriage, art. 82(2).

[37] Law no. 2019–570 of 26 June 2019 relating to Marriage, art. 74.

community property clearly reflects the advancement of egalitarian principles in the updated law governing community property.

With regard to the liquidation of the community,[38] the mechanisms for calculating 'rewards' are more clearly and effectively articulated in the 2019 reform.[39] However, the most significant contribution of the reform undoubtedly lies in the improvement of the surviving spouse's assets upon dissolution of the community.[40]

3 The Survival of the Regime of Separation of Property

Unknown in Ivorian legislation since 1964, the regime of separation of property was introduced into Ivorian law in 1983, due to the influence of both tradition[41] and modernity.[42] While opting for this regime means that 'each spouse retains the administration, enjoyment and free disposal of his or her personal property',[43] the 2019 reform raises the question of the innovations made to the regime of separation of property. The answer to this question can be found in the content and scope of the new regime of separation of property.

---

[38] See Law no. 2019–570 of 26 June 2019 relating to Marriage, arts 90–94.

[39] See Buat-Menard (2010, p. 15), where it reads that rewards are 'claims compensating for movements in value between the community property and a spouse's own property, i.e. resulting in the enrichment of the community property and the corresponding impoverishment of the spouse's own property, or vice versa'.

[40] Law no. 2019–570 of 26 June 2019 relating to Marriage, art. 96.

[41] See Lohoues-Oble (1984–1985, pp. 54–55), who noted that, 'In traditional Ivorian societies, while the community spirit was very strong among members of the same lineage, to the point of creating a common heritage (the lineage heritage, over which all members of the lineage have rights), this was not the case for spouses. Most of the time, they were married under the regime of separation of property, which reflected a dual principle. The principle of the conservation of property within the lineage had to be respected […]. […] In addition, the concept of marriage accepted by these societies was that a man had an obligation to provide for his wife even if she had property. It is therefore because the system traditionally adopted was that of separation of property that most African legislations have retained it as the legal system'.

[42] See Lohoues-Oble (1984–1985, p. 54), who writes, 'The introduction of the regime of separation of property into Ivorian law in 1983 was "a consequence of the evolution of Ivorian society. […] It cannot be disputed that many spouses intend to make their union conditional on maintaining in their hands the free administration and disposal of all their property, whether acquired before or during the marriage'.

[43] Law no. 64–375 of 7 October 1964 relating to Marriage as amended by Law no. 83–800 of 2 August 1983, art. 103.

3.1 The Content of the Regime of Separation of Property

Understood as a regime that maintains the separatist division of the pecuniary interests of the spouses,[44] the history of the regime of separation of property could be presented, in certain respects, as that of the stone initially rejected by the builders that became the cornerstone. Indeed, traditionally, in Europe, both in civil and common law legal systems, the acceptance of the separate property regime was not unanimous.[45]

In Black Francophone Africa, unlike in France, traditional practices did not disregard the system of separation of property.[46] More specifically, in the Ivorian context, the practice of separation of property in traditional societies was essentially based on a principle of customary law: 'the conservation of property within the lineage'.[47] Unlike the community of property system, only the separation of property regime can ensure consistent application of this principle, especially in cases involving exogamy.

Admittedly, it was in 'the evolution of Ivorian society' that, according to the explanatory memorandum to the 1983 Ivorian law on marriage, the Ivorian legislature admitted having found the basis for the adoption of the regime of separation of property. However, today, both in Europe and Africa, the separation of property regime is recognised for its virtues. Indeed, given the economics of this matrimonial regime, which leads to resources being allocated to household expenses while maintaining the autonomy of each spouse's assets,[48] the separation of property is generally recommended in the interest of certain households where one spouse carries on a so-called high-risk activity, such as a liberal profession or commercial enterprise.[49] This arrangement enables the family to protect its property interests from the financial risks that may arise during the marriage due to one spouse's activities.

With their assets thus delimited, each spouse 'retains administration, enjoyment and free disposal of them'.[50] On this point, the difference between the present community of property regime and the *status quo ante* is less pronounced to the extent that the 2019 reform has reinforced spousal equality. Under the new rules, each of the spouses alone administers their earnings and income from the exercise of their professional activity.[51] However, unlike the community of property regime, the separation of property regime seems, in theory, the least altruistic, since sharing the enrichment of each spouse does not seem to be the main inclination.

---

[44] Lohoues-Oble (1984–1985, p. 54).

[45] See Caparros (1965–1966, p. 293).

[46] See Lohoues-Oble (1984–1985, p. 55). It is 'because traditionally the regime adopted was that of separation of property that most African legislations have retained it as the legal regime. This is the case in Senegal, Mali and Togo [...]'.

[47] Lohoues-Oble (1984–1985, p. 54).

[48] Law no. 2019–570 of 26 June 2019 relating to Marriage, art. 98.

[49] Lohoues-Oble (1984–1985, p. 59).

[50] Law no. 2019–570 of 26 June 2019 relating to Marriage, art. 98.

[51] Law no. 2019–570 of 26 June 2019 relating to Marriage, art. 81.

Regarding their own assets, Article 99 of the 2019 law provides that spouses may prove by any means that they have exclusive ownership of a specific movable asset.[52] As for exclusive ownership of immovable property, this is easy to prove as a notarial deed is always required in such cases.

The fact remains that the absence of community, as defined by the separation of property, does not necessarily mean that spouses subject to this regime have no shared ownership. Property or a mass of undivided property may exist in the case of separation of property, hence, the assumption expressed by the legislature as follows:

> Property over which neither spouse can prove exclusive ownership is deemed to belong to them jointly, each for half. However, according to their nature and purpose, movable property of a personal nature and rights exclusively attached to the person, are presumed to belong to one or the other. Proof to the contrary may be adduced by any means.[53]

Clearly, it follows from this provision that property for which the spouses cannot justify exclusive ownership is subject to this particular form of property management known as 'joint ownership'.[54] From this perspective, the indivision thus established could even be used by spouses under a separation of property regime to 'technically constitute a lasting organisation of the collective ownership of certain property' belonging to them.[55] However, it must be acknowledged that such a view might appear to contradict the spirit of the separation of property regime.

However, in the absence of proof to the contrary 'produced by any means',[56] the Ivorian legislature accepts that, 'according to their nature and purpose, movable property of a personal nature' is presumed to belong exclusively to one or other of the spouses. An example often cited in legal literature is clothing: legally, it is classified as personal property. This is because property is considered personal when it is used solely by the individual concerned and serves only their personal interest.[57] In addition, the legislature goes on to say that such a presumption of exclusive ownership is permitted for 'rights that are exclusively attached to the person',[58] such as the right of claim, which is the creditor's personal right to require the debtor to perform a certain service or abstain from performing a certain act; or an intellectual right, which is the right held by a person over a work of the mind.

In addition to the mechanism of joint ownership (indivision), the use of mandates has also been introduced to allow one spouse to manage certain property on behalf of the other within the separation of property regime, to the extent that:

> if, during the marriage, a spouse entrusts the other with the administration of their own property, the rules of mandate apply. When one of the spouses manages the other's own

[52] Law no. 2019–570 of 26 June 2019 relating to Marriage, art. 99.

[53] Law no. 2019–570 of 26 June 2019 relating to Marriage, art. 110.

[54] Ghestin (2000, pp. 529–530).

[55] Ghestin (2000, pp. 529–530).

[56] Ghestin (2000), pp. 529–530).

[57] Rakotovahiny (2015).

[58] Law no. 2019–570 of 26 June 2019 relating to Marriage, art. 100(2).

property without opposition from the other, they are deemed to have received a tacit mandate covering only acts of administration.[59]

3.2 *The Scope of the Regime of Separation of Property*

In addition to determining the content of the regime of separation of property, it is necessary to identify its scope. In this respect, just like the community of property, the separation of property regime is subject to what is commonly referred to as the basic or primary regime. These are provisions of public order, independent of the variety of regimes, and which affect in one way or another the economic relationships of the spouses, as a manifestation of the need 'to ensure the essential allocation of property to the family'.[60] Under the heading of 'provisions common to matrimonial property regimes',[61] six (6) articles form the core of the primary regime in Ivorian family law.

The general idea is that the spouses should be closely involved in the day-to-day running of the household. The legislature stipulates that while 'each of the spouses receives his or her earnings and income', they 'may not dispose of them freely unless he or she has paid the household expenses'.[62] In prosaic terms, the way in which the contribution is made may consist of one of the spouses periodically paying a fixed sum or a share of their income. This obviously requires a family budget that is as transparent as possible. Clearly, the smooth running of a household requires a certain number of routine legal acts intended to govern the day-to-day existence of the spouses as a household, a common home.[63] In this respect,

> Each of the spouses has the right to engage in any contract that pertains to household maintenance, support and education of children. Any debt thus contracted by one jointly obliges the other. However, solidarity does not apply to expenses manifestly excessive in view of the standard of living of the household or the utility of the transaction. The absence of solidarity is not enforceable against third-party contractors acting in good faith.[64]

In addition to the household debt management regime thus envisaged, the primary regime also considers the banking autonomy of the spouses. To this end, each spouse may open any deposit or securities account in their own name without the consent of the other. The spouse holding the account is deemed, vis-à-vis the depositary, to have free administration of the funds and securities in deposit. Lastly, the legislature has introduced habilitation[65] or authorisation[66] mechanisms to address potential conflicts

[59] Law no. 2019–570 of 26 June 2019 relating to Marriage, art. 85.

[60] Caparros (1965–1966, p. 303).

[61] Law no. 2019–570 of 26 June 2019 relating to Marriage, art. 66–71.

[62] Law no. 2019–570 of 26 June 2019 relating to Marriage, art. 67.

[63] Carbonnier (1993, p. 487).

[64] Law no. 2019–570 of 26 June 2019 relating to Marriage, art. 71.

[65] Law no. 2019–570 of 26 June 2019 relating to Marriage, art. 69.

[66] Law no. 2019–570 of 26 June 2019 relating to Marriage, art. 70.

between spouses in managing the household, subject to the supervision of the judge. From this point of view, the basic regime serves as a limit to the separation of property regime, as it defines the extent of the rights that spouses under separation of property have in the 'administration, enjoyment and free disposal' of their own property.[67]

However, in addition to this limitation on the autonomy of spouses governed by a separate property regime, the legislature has just given these spouses the option of contractually adjusting the extent of their autonomy over the 'administration, enjoyment and free disposal' of their separate property. This is the most significant innovation introduced by the 2019 reform relating to the separation of property, contained in article 101 of the said Act. This text provides that 'spouses who opt for the regime of separation of property may, by an agreement approved by the president of the competent court or executed by a notary, organise their property relations'. From now on, separation of property may be agreed upon, allowing spouses to make certain adjustments, particularly to their autonomy, under the legal regime of separation of property. However, such a liberal approach is subject to the formalities of an authenticated deed. The separation of property may also be judicial. A practical example might be where the spouses are married under the community of property regime and one of them turns out to be a 'disastrous administrator'. In such a case, the other spouse could, in anticipation of a change in the regime adopted,[68] request the dissolution of the community of property regime to 'protect his or her interests from the wreckage',[69] and subsequently, have the household live under a regime of conventional separation.

Overall, in addition to the restrictions that the basic regime imposes on the autonomy of spouses under the separation of property regime, spouses can modify the extent of this regime to benefit the family.

3.3 *The Emergence of a New Matrimonial Property Regime*

Traditionally, matrimonial agreements under Ivorian law were kept on the 'shelf of explosives', far beyond the reach of spouses. However, when it became apparent that the rigidity of the legal basis for matrimonial property regimes was sometimes contrary to the family's interests, the legislature adjusted its approach. Beyond the interstices to which it was initially confined, the contract can now be widely used by the spouses in the management of their assets. Does this mean that the State has relinquished its traditional hold on the organisation of family relationships? Such abandonment is unimaginable, given that the family plays too decisive a role in the construction of social reality.[70]

---

[67] Law no. 2019–570 of 26 June 2019 relating to Marriage, art. 98.

[68] Law no. 2019–570 of 26 June 2019 relating to Marriage, art. 62.

[69] Carbonnier (1993, p. 487).

[70] Lemouland (2012, p. 730).

The 2019 reforms indicate that matrimonial agreements are not left to the sole discretion of the spouses, as evidenced by the involvement of a notary in their drafting, but, more fundamentally, that State regulation of such agreements reflects an attachment to the family as a protected institution.

4 State Regulation of Agreements

The regulation of matrimonial agreements in Ivorian law reflects a contrast. While today it reflects the tendency to respect individual autonomy, which must be protected, it nonetheless embodies a particular conception of public policy in matrimonial matters.[71] In this respect, although the 2019 reform initially gave the impression that matrimonial agreements had unlimited scope, it soon became clear that this view required qualification. While the freedom to enter into matrimonial agreements is recognised, it is accompanied by limitations on the spouses' autonomy in organising their matrimonial property regime.

4.1 Freedom of Marital Agreements Enshrined

Dominated for a long time by a prohibitive public order, the family had a status in which individual wills, and *a fortiori,* the spirit of contract, had very little influence in family matters. This hermetic approach can be explained by the traditional emphasis on the group over the individual. However, various factors, including a certain social and moral neutrality toward the different family models as they are actually experienced,[72] would encourage a breakthrough in the contractual spirit in family relations.[73] In doing so, among the new trends identified in comparative family law, the general movement towards contractualisation has not gone unnoticed,[74] since contractual arrangements have been accepted in areas where they were previously prohibited, leading to 'an adaptation of family law to concrete situations'.[75]

---

[71] In this case, the concept of public policy is understood to mean 'a peremptory norm from which individuals may not deviate either in their behaviour or in their agreements; a directive norm which, whether or not expressed in a law, corresponds to all the fundamental requirements (social, political, etc.) considered essential to the functioning of services, the maintenance of security or morality (in this sense, public policy includes morality), the running of the economy (economic public policy) or even to the protection of the environment.) considered essential to the functioning of services, to the maintenance of security or morality (in this sense public policy includes morality), to the functioning of the economy (economic public policy) or even to the safeguarding of certain overriding particular interests (public policy of individual protection)'. See Cornu (2016), p. 720.

[72] Bucher (2000, p. 20).

[73] Pousson-Petit (2013, p. 155).

[74] See Cornu (2016, p. 257).

[75] Lemouland (2012, p. 742).

Although evocative, the expression of this development in terms of contractualisation may be questionable in light of the classic definition of a contract.[76] This is because the purpose of matrimonial agreements is usually broader and more diverse than 'obliging a person to give, do, or not do something'.[77] Be that as it may, by now providing that 'the spouses may enter into any agreements concerning their property as they see fit',[78] the Ivorian legislature is contributing to the development of relations between spouses, which is part of the broader development of family law.[79]

For spouses, the freedom of matrimonial agreements is analysed in terms of the freedom to enter into or refrain from entering into a marriage contract. Spouses retain the freedom to forgo a marriage contract by choosing to follow one of the legal matrimonial regimes. However, they may just as well decide to enter into a 'marital contract',[80] making adjustments to one or other of the legal matrimonial property regimes. Granting spouses the option of a marital contract obviously meets the need to adapt the matrimonial property regime more closely to their specific situation. However, the question remains as to what the content of such marital agreements should be, especially as Ivorian law, unlike other legal systems, does not provide spouses with any premarital information on this matter.[81]

In determining the content of the marital contract, given that the purpose of contractual arrangements is to adapt the law to the concrete situation of the spouses, at least two (2) objectives could be assigned to such contracts. A marital contract could aim to protect or benefit the spouses. To this end, the spouses may modify the community of property as provided for in its legal form. If, for example, they wish to make the couple owners of all their property, the spouses can extend the community assets to 'all movable and immovable property already owned by them on the date of the marriage,[82] as well as that which they will receive [individually] at a later date by succession or gift'.[83] In this respect, a separation of property regime may be balanced by clauses designed to protect a spouse who is not expected to benefit from the other's financial gains, such as a homemaker not engaged in income-generating activities. This is because:

> Can we not consider that by remaining at home, the wife has contributed more than her share to the household expenses and that, as such, the husband will have to pay her a balance on

---

[76] French Civil Code 2006, art. 1101.

[77] Lemouland (2012, p. 745).

[78] Law no. 2019–570 of 26 June 2019 relating to Marriage, art. 58(2).

[79] Lamarche and Lemouland (2009, pp. 3–4).

[80] Law no. 2019–570 of 26 June 2019 relating to Marriage, art. 17.

[81] See, in French law, Décret n°2002-1556 du 23 décembre 2002.

[82] According to the 2019 reform, these community assets comprise, in addition to the spouses' own property (article 73) and property presumed to be common property (article 74), the following other property: '(1) the spouses' earnings and income; (2) property acquired by the spouses for valuable consideration during the marriage, excluding the property referred to in article 73; (3) property bequeathed or given jointly to the two spouses'.

[83] Carbonnier (1993, p. 490).

> the dissolution of the marriage? This balance would compensate for the inequality in the services provided by the spouses. Its basis is the restoration of justice.[84]

As the underlying theme in this case is generosity between spouses, particularly in matters of community of property, future spouses, or persons initially married under the separation of property regime and who wish to change matrimonial property regime, 'after two years of application of the regime adopted',[85] may make adjustments to the fate of a surviving spouse's patrimony, as legally defined.[86] From this point of view, a *préciput*[87] clause, commonly included to avoid joint inheritance and, in principle, revoked *ipso jure* in the event of divorce, is an effective way to protect the rights of the surviving spouse to their living environment (home and furnishings) or enable the entrepreneur who is the beneficiary to become the sole owner of their work tools.[88]

Furthermore, a marital contract could be more resolutely aimed at protecting the assets of the spouses vis-à-vis third parties, including the creditors of either spouse. It should be noted that even when they 'do not relate to the needs and expenses of the household',[89] debts contracted by each of the spouses with joint property may be pursued,[90] not only 'against the own property of the spouse who contracted them', but 'in the event of insufficiency, against the joint property'.[91] This clearly exposes the income of one spouse to the pledge of the other spouse's creditors. This is why the regime of separation of property is recommended in such cases, to the extent that each of the spouses' assets is independent of the other, and the assets of one of the spouses would not suffer from the other's bad affairs.

4.2 *The Existence of Reservations to the Autonomy of Spouses Regarding Marital Agreements*

Paragraph 2 of article 58 of the above-mentioned Law of 2019 provides that: 'The spouses may enter into any agreements with respect to their property that they consider appropriate, provided that they are not contrary to morality [...]'. If there

[84] See Lohoues-Oble (1984–1985, p. 60).

[85] Law no. 2019–570 of 26 June 2019 relating to Marriage, art. 62.

[86] See Law no. 2019–570 of 26 June 2019 relating to Marriage, art. 96.

[87] The préciput is a 'matrimonial advantage conferred by marriage contract or an amending agreement on a surviving spouse, consisting, for its beneficiary in the right to deduct from the joint estate, before any division and outside any share, at the time of the dissolution of the community, a specific asset or a sum of money'. See Cornu (2016, p. 787 and 791).

[88] Lonne-Clement (2014).

[89] Law no. 2019–570 of 26 June 2019 relating to Marriage, art. 76(3).

[90] As *regards a fortiori* debts relating to the needs and expenses of the household, article 76 provides that they may be pursued 'against joint property and the private property of either [spouse]'.

[91] Law no. 2019–570 of 26 June 2019 relating to Marriage, art. 76.

is a concept linked to natural law,[92] like that of equity,[93] or natural obligation,[94] to which this text seems firmly attached, it is obviously that of 'good morals',[95] used in this case.

Remember the provisions of article 6 of the Ivorian Civil Code,[96] which provide that morality is an obstacle to absolute and unlimited freedom of contract.[97] From this perspective, paragraph 2 of article 28 of the 2019 family law reform demonstrates the Ivorian legislature's intention to introduce a moral dimension into the regulation of matrimonial property regimes by applying the concept of good morals, a notion well established in the civil law tradition.[98] The result is for the judge to assess such marital contracts against the yardstick of 'good morals'—that set of values whose translation into legal terms has traditionally given rise to various rules of conduct formulated by Roman and doctrinal traditions. This set of values is rendered in particular terms relating to or connected with loyalty, probity, conscience, decency, and honesty. It tends to moralise, in this case, matrimonial relationships both between spouses and towards third parties.

In addition to this reservation against the illegality of marital agreements, the Ivorian legislature prohibits, again by virtue of paragraph 2 of article 58, marital agreements that are contrary to 'public policy or the provisions of this law'. Thus, in addition to moral values, the Ivorian legislature has enshrined the imperative to protect other values and objectives essential to protecting the family's interests. For, *mutatis mutandis*, as one author explains:

> within the unitary notion of public policy, two different aspects can be distinguished, as was emphasised in particular in the thesis by Mr Benjamin Remy. On the one hand, there are values expressed in principles. For example, the prohibition of all discrimination based on race or religion. And on the other hand, objectives, relating, for example and in particular, to the organisation of the economy; an objective that police laws aim to achieve. Competition law, for example. Even when police laws are involved, public policy is always at work.[99]

Finally, among the other reservations made by the Ivorian legislature to the freedom of matrimonial agreements are the provisions of article 60 of the new law. This provides that 'the spouses may not, by agreement, derogate from the duties or rights arising from the matrimonial regime they have chosen'. We must therefore agree with Dean Jean Carbonnier that, 'speaking of duties rather than obligations', this provision of the new Ivorian law on marriage 'suggests that morality is more important here than technical dryness, and placing duties before rights, it seems to invite each spouse to

---

[92] See Dabin (1928, pp. 418–421).

[93] See Bergel (2003, p. 49) and Seriaux (2014, pp. 91–92).

[94] Seriaux (2014, p. 22).

[95] See Domat (1828–1830, p. 397), quoted in Géraud-Llorca (2013, pp. 69–70).

[96] Ivorian Civil Code 2005, art. 6.

[97] Géraud-Llorca (2013, pp. 69–70).

[98] Géraud-Llorca (2013, pp. 69–70).

[99] Mayer (2008).

be demanding of himself rather than of the other. It is through duties, not rights, that marriage is best defined'.[100]

4.3 The Notary's Involvement in Drafting Matrimonial Agreements

Under the provisions of paragraph 3 of article 58 of the Ivorian law on marriage, 'all matrimonial agreements shall be drawn up by notarial act before the marriage is celebrated and shall only take effect from the date of the celebration'. In addition to the marginal role left to the judge in the organisation of property relations,[101] the notary now appears to be a key figure among the authorities required to seal matrimonial agreements, since the legislature has given the notary the function of drawing up matrimonial deeds. It is therefore worth investigating why marriage contracts are subject to this notarial formalism. Such formalism, while highlighting the classic function of the notary, nonetheless raises the question of the responsibility of this professional in the exercise of such a mission.

4.3.1 Reasons Why Marriage Contracts Must Be Notarised

'One binds oxen by their horns and men by their words, and a simple promise or agreement is worth as much as the stipulations of Roman law'.[102] You only have to read this famous phrase by Loysel to realise that the principle of consent as the basis for contractual rights and duties predates Napoleon's Civil Code. In fact, the Middle Ages, under the influence of canonists who attached great importance to contractual promises, placed consensual contracts at the top of Gaius's classification of contracts.[103] Indeed, 'in addition to their moral value, the principle according to which all agreements are binding, regardless of how they are made, presents a clear economic advantage by facilitating transactions as far as possible'.[104] However, the purely consensual nature of a contract can sometimes make it difficult to prove good faith if it is not a value shared by the parties.

Seen in this way, the principle of contract as consent, which is not to be understood as an absence of form, but rather as implying freedom of form,[105] was, it seems,[106] so well established in France under the Old Law that it was not thought useful to

[100] Carbonnier (1993, p. 441).

[101] Law no. 2019–570 of 26 June 2019 relating to Marriage, art. 101.

[102] Loysel (1607, p. 2).

[103] Gaius (1988, pp. 89–90). See also Seriaux (2006, p. 34).

[104] Seriaux (2006, p. 34).

[105] Flour (1950, p. 96).

[106] See Nuyten and Lesage (1998, p. 502) and Planiol and Ripert (1952, p. 100).

enshrine it expressly in the aftermath of the French Revolution.[107] Thus, although such a principle is nowhere explicitly stated in the *travaux préparatoires* of the Civil Code, the Code nevertheless implicitly endorses it, as the principle of contract as consent is more directly implied in certain provisions of the 1804 version of the French Civil Code, which is applicable in Ivorian law.[108] In this respect, the provisions of Ivorian family law claim to be based on contract as consent, since article 4 of the 2019 Ivorian law on marriage expressly states this.[109]

However, the consensual nature of Ivorian law on matrimonial property regimes does not grant freedom of form for marriage contracts, as matrimonial agreements must comply with a formal framework that clearly distinguishes them from private deeds. They must be 'drawn up by notarial act before the marriage takes place and will only take effect from the date of the marriage'.[110] Since a marital contract is not merely a statement of the spouses' intentions, but an act that must offer security and protection to the spouses, their children and third parties, the seriousness of such a contract requires that it be formalised by a public officer[111] vested with public authority, the notary.[112] In this regard, the requirement for a notarised marital contract serves to protect spouses because the legislature intends to shield them from the risk of making commitments without fully considering the consequences. This is especially important since Ivorian law, unlike other legal systems, does not

[107] The concept of Ancien Droit simply boils down to a distinction between two major areas: the north of France applied customary law, based on usages and privileges that were often the work of centuries; the south of France was subject to Roman law, which was often codified.

[108] See French Civil Code 2006, art. 1583 which states that: 'It is complete between the parties, and ownership is acquired as of right by the buyer with respect to the seller, as soon as the thing and the price have been agreed upon, although the thing has not yet been delivered or the price paid'.

[109] Law no. 2019–570 of 26 June 2019 relating to Marriage, art. 4.

[110] Law no. 2019–570 of 26 June 2019 relating to Marriage, art. 58(3).

[111] See Law no. 69–372 of 12 August 1969 on the status of notaries, as amended and supplemented by. Law No. 97–513 of 4 September 1997, art 1 to the effect that notaries are public officers appointed to receive deeds and contracts to which the parties must or wish to give the character of authenticity attached to acts of public authority, and to ensure the date, keep the deposit, issue first authentic copies.

[112] See Zehouri (2016), who reports that, 'the notary's office arrived in Côte d'Ivoire in the suitcases of white or western settlers who were concerned about securing the land they had appropriated or exploited without owning it. They also intended these public officers to authenticate the commercial or civil transactions they were preparing to conclude in all fields. Aware that the era of colonisation would sooner or later be over to the benefit of national actors, the colonists did not want to expose their possessions to expropriation without compensation. In order to be compensated for the loss of real or personal property, a notarised deed serves as irrefutable proof for the claimant, up to the point of forgery. As the years went by, the colonists signed notarial deeds with the nascent state of Côte d'Ivoire, but also with Ivorians, who thus discovered the ministry of the notary and its benefits in the areas of legal advice, authentication of deeds, collection of duties on behalf of the state, and publication and conservation of notarial public deeds. However, as in continental France, the interest of the notary's office is confirmed in Côte d'Ivoire in the formidable sector of property transactions. As part of the public authority tasks delegated to notaries by the State (law no. 71–74 of 16 February 1971), the legal protection of property transactions accounts for 40% of notaries' activity, far ahead of inheritance and gifts, companies and businesses, notarial legal advice, etc.'

provide premarital information[113] to help spouses understand the full scope of their contractual obligations.

In any event, in its classic conception, the notarial marriage deed is intended to authenticate the marital contract, which confers on it a particular force that is not recognised in private deeds.[114] Thus, placed at the top of the hierarchy of evidence, the notarised marriage certificate 'is endowed with a special legal weight comparable only to that of a judicial judgment. Its preservation by the notary preserves the recognised rights, because a right that cannot be proven is a right that does not exist'.[115] Accordingly, the legislature mandates the use of the notarial marriage record as evidence, as the notary's official findings are presumed authentic, unless and until proven to be forged. In this respect, legal doctrine calls for a distinction to be made between the probative value of the various entries made in the notarial deed. For example, the system of 'statements that correspond to the personal observations of the public official',[116] differs from that of 'statements in the notarial deed that relate what the parties have declared to the public official'.[117] For, while the latter 'are only authentic until proven otherwise', the fact remains that 'the personal findings of the public official are authentic until a forgery is discovered'.[118] In short, if the Ivorian legislature requires pre-constituted proof for marital contracts, it is undoubtedly because this aligns with the common law principles governing all matters related to civil status, of which marriage is a fundamental component.

---

[113] See in French law, Decree n°2002–1556 of 23 December 2002 implementing Article 22 of Law n° 2001–1135 of 3 December 2001 relating to the rights of the surviving spouse and illegitimate children and modernizing various provisions of inheritance law and modifying Decree No. 74–449 of May 15, 1974 relating to the family record book. https://www.legifrance.gouv.fr/affichTexte.do%3bjsessionid=739E302CD2155D6CA2FF50FF7B6BA7A5.tpdjo10v_3?cidTexte=LEGITEXT000005633781&dateTexte=vig.

[114] See French Civil Code 2006, art. 1317 which states: 'An authentic instrument is one which has been received by public officers empowered to draw up such instruments at the place where the instrument was written and with the requisite formalities'.

[115] Conseil Supérieur du Notariat (n.d., p. 25).

[116] See Ghestin and Goubeaux (1994, pp. 582–583). According to these authors: 'this enhanced authority attaches only to the personal findings of the public official, which fall within the scope of his powers. This is the case, for example, in a notarial deed, where the deed states that the parties were present or that they signed, the date of the deed, the fact that a payment was made in the sight of the notary (...) On the other hand, where the statements in the deed relate to facts that do not fall directly within the competence of the public official, it is not necessary to have recourse to forgery to combat them. Thus, the mention in a deed by which the notary affirms that the testator affirms that the testator is of sound mind leaves open the possibility of demonstrating by any means the testator's insanity of mind'.

[117] Ghestin and Goubeaux (1994, pp. 582–583).

[118] Ghestin and Goubeaux (1994, p. 587).

4.3.2 The Responsibility of the Notary Who Draws up a Marriage Contract

There are mainly two views on the nature of the notary's liability: the contractual nature of notarial liability and the tortious or quasi-tortious nature of the notary's liability. Authors who support a tortious view base their argument on the unsuitability of the rules of contractual liability law for notarial liability claims.[119] From a contractual perspective, it is generally believed that notarial liability is no different from the contractual liability of other professionals, such as lawyers, doctors, and auctioneers. After all, 'it[notarial liability] is based on a contract (generally the contract of mandate) or a quasi-contract for business management'.[120]

However, a third view, parsed from emerging case law, avoids the doctrinal parochialism which attempts to pigeonhole the notary's liability into either contract or tort.[121] In fact, as soon as the notary was vested with a function that he exercised by delegation of public authority, case law began to view this as the basis for his liability, one characterised as professional civil liability.[122] Such a conception of the basis of notarial liability is not unknown in Ivorian law, as revealed by the observations of one author, in the following terms:

> notaries are public officers instituted to receive deeds and contracts that the parties must or wish to give the character of authenticity validated by the exercise of public authority, and to ensure their date, keep their deposit, and issue documentation and undertakings. They are required to exercise their office with the most scrupulous probity and the greatest diligence. A notary's professional civil liability may be incurred in the following cases: a breach of the rules governing his professional status that causes damage to others; a tort or quasi-tort; or a fault committed in the performance of a mandate entrusted to him by a client.[123]

Accordingly, in matters of professional civil liability, a notary who drafts marital agreements may be held liable for a notarial fault if that fault results from a breach of professional duty. When such liability arises from the notary's failure to fulfil obligations inherent to their official role, for example, a violation of a specific professional duty, it does not necessarily constitute liability in tort. This is why a more refined analysis of the notary's professional civil liability suggests that 'notarial liability is a functional liability',[124] arising from the notary's function as a public official.

In his capacity as a public official, the notary traditionally serves as an authenticator of deeds. When acting as the drafter of matrimonial agreements, as provided under the 2019 Ivorian law on marriage, the notary remains subject to obligations of

[119] See in particular Mazeaud and Tunc (1983, p. 600). See also Poulpiquet (2009–2010, p. 22).

[120] See Poulpiquet (2009–2010, p. 23). See also Durry (1986), quoted in Poulpiquet (2009–2010, p. 23).

[121] Poulpiquet (2009–2010, p. 28).

[122] Poulpiquet (2009–2010, p. 28).

[123] Komoin (2002, p. 14).

[124] Poulpiquet (2009–2010, p. 29).

personal[125] and territorial competence,[126] limitations of competence,[127] and formal requirements.[128]

Furthermore, in addition to their role as drafters of deeds, notaries also have a general advisory role, which extends beyond their function as authenticators of deeds. In fact, since the notary is not a 'mere scribe, a passive witness to contractual agreements',[129] the task of drafting deeds not only requires the notary to give authentic form to the parties' agreements, but also to advise his clients. This view is not new, having been confirmed by a ruling of the French Court of Cassation on 21 July 1921:

> Notaries, who have been appointed to give the parties' agreements the legal form and authenticity that this entails, also have the task of informing their clients of the consequences of the commitments they enter into; as they are liable under article 1382 of the Civil Code, they cannot stipulate that they are immune from liability and consequently decline the principle of their liability by alleging that they have confined themselves to giving the parties' agreements authentic form.[130]

In addition to its history, the argument regarding the notary's duty to provide information and advice on matrimonial agreements remains extremely topical, as comparative law demonstrates. A case concerning the professional liability of a notary who drafted a marriage contract for future spouses illustrates this point. The clients, who later faced financial difficulties due to one spouse's liberal profession, sued the notary claiming that he failed to adequately advise them on the risks of their chosen matrimonial property regime. On 3 October 2018,[131] the First Civil Chamber of the French Court of Cassation dismissed the notary's appeal on the grounds that:

> the notary responsible for drawing up the contract chosen by the future spouses is obliged not to inform them in the abstract of the consequences of the various matrimonial property regimes, but to advise them specifically with regard to their situation, by informing them

[125] See Law no. 69–372 of 12 August 1969 on the status of notaries, as amended and supplemented by. Law No. 97–513 of 4 September 1997, art 5–6.

[126] Law no. 69–372 of 12 August 1969 on the status of notaries, as amended and supplemented by. Law No. 97–513 of 4 September 1997, art. 17 states that, 'a notary must reside in the locality designated as the seat of the office, failing which he will be deemed to have resigned'.

[127] Law no. 69–372 of 12 August 1969 on the status of notaries, as amended and supplemented by. Law No. 97–513 of 4 September 1997, art. 16 states that, 'Notaries may not receive deeds in which their parents or relatives, in the direct line at all levels and in the collateral line up to and including the level of uncle and nephew, are parties, or which contain provisions in their favour'.

[128] Law no. 69–372 of 12 August 1969 on the status of notaries, as amended and supplemented by. Law No. 97–513 of 4 September 1997, art. 26 states that, 'Notaries' deeds are, under their responsibility, either handwritten, typed or printed using indelible ink. In all cases, they are written in a single context, legibly, without abbreviations, blanks, overwriting, additions to the body of the document, gaps or line spacing. Words that have been overwritten, interlined or added are void. Words that must be crossed out are done so in such a way that their number can be seen in the margin of the corresponding page or at the end of the deed and are approved in the same way as cross-references written in the margin'.

[129] Poulpiquet (2009–2010, p. 54).

[130] Cass. civ. 21 Jul 1921, *D. 1929, I, p. 29.*

[131] Cour de cassation, 1re Ch. civ., 3 Oct 2018, no. 16–19.619, ECLI:FR:CCASS:2018:C100924.

> and drawing their attention, in a complete and detailed manner, to the scope, effects and risks of the matrimonial property regimes that may meet their concerns; [...] by noting that, at the time the marriage contract was concluded, Mrs Y[one of the spouses]... was practising a liberal profession and had incurred debts in order to set up in business, thus demonstrating that this activity involved a financial risk, and in holding that, in view of the situation the notaries did not show that the future spouses had informed them of any particular reasons that might encourage them to choose a matrimonial property regime similar to that of universal community, nor that they had given them advice tailored to their specific professional situation, the Court of Appeal characterised, without showing any bias, the failure of the notary who drafted the document to fulfil his obligation to provide information and advice.[132]

The Ivorian legislature's decision to designate the notary as the drafter of marital agreements is a promising development for the future of family law in Ivorian courts. While the judiciary has yet to clarify its position on the liability of notaries in this context, one can only extend best wishes to the Ivorian notary in fulfilling his mission to advise and support families.

5 The Effects of Bigamous Marriages

Under Ivorian law, the second marriage of a spouse who is already married must be annulled by a judge.[133] The annulment does not alter the legal effects of the marriage before its dissolution, meaning the marriage remains valid until formally annulled.[134] However, if both spouses acted in bad faith in contracting the marriage, the marriage is deemed never to have existed.[135] Where only one party exercised bad faith, the marriage is considered to have existed solely in favour of the innocent spouse.[136] In any event, the innocent party will be able to enforce the chosen matrimonial regime against the guilty party, particularly with respect to property rights, financial obligations, and any benefits accrued during the union.

6 Recommendations

Unlike the legislation of certain states, such as Senegal or Benin, which have adopted conflict-of-law solutions in matters of matrimonial property regimes, the Ivorian reform of matrimonial property law has remained silent on this subject. Yet, the inclusion of such conflict-of-law provisions would have enhanced the predictability and credibility of the reform. By omitting this dimension, the Ivorian legislature has

---

132 Cour de cassation, 1re Ch. civ., 3 Oct 2018, no. 16–19.619, ECLI:FR:CCASS:2018:C100924.

133 Law no. 2019–570 of 26 June 2019 relating to Marriage, art. 26.

134 Law no. 2019–570 of 26 June 2019 relating to Marriage, art. 26.

135 Law no. 2019–570 of 26 June 2019 relating to Marriage, art. 37.

136 Law no. 2019–570 of 26 June 2019 relating to Marriage, art. 38.

shown a lack of realism, particularly given the increasing cross-border movement of individuals and the legal complexities such mobility inevitably brings.

Admittedly, by remaining silent on the issue of the law applicable to matrimonial property regimes in conflict-of-law situations, the legislature seems to have deferred to the traditional approach, leaving it to judges or notaries to identify the relevant conflict-of-law rule. However, this approach introduces uncertainty, as Ivorian law lacks codified conflict-of-law rules in this area, and relevant case law remains scarce and difficult to access.[137] Without explicit guidance on which law applies in cross-border situations, future conflicts are both foreseeable and inevitable.

Furthermore, as previously noted, a marriage contract is not merely a declaration of the spouses' intentions, but a legal instrument intended to provide security and protection for the spouses, their children, and third parties. Given its significant legal consequences, it is essential to protect future spouses from making uninformed commitments. To this end, raising awareness at an early stage, such as by incorporating premarital education on matrimonial property regimes into the secondary school curriculum, would be a prudent and proactive measure. Such education would empower individuals to make informed decisions, thereby strengthening the stability and fairness of marital relationships from the outset.

7 Conclusion

It would be recalled that the primary focus of this chapter has been to examine the influence of Ivorian Law No. 2019–570 of 26 June 2019 on the institution of marriage. This analysis has consequently explored the extent to which the reform has contributed to the evolution of matrimonial property law in Côte d'Ivoire. Ivorian law on matrimonial property regimes has evolved considerably both over time and in form. However, the legislature has overlooked the perspective of private international law. The development of Ivorian law on matrimonial property regimes over time has been driven by these major principles, which now underpin Ivorian family law. First, in response to the increasing emphasis on human rights, the traditional legal inequality between spouses has been replaced by the principle of equality, which governs both the community of property and the separation of property regimes. Second, the principle of protecting family interests has expanded the application and flexibility of the separation of property regime. The malleability of the separatist matrimonial property regime has been made possible largely by principles grounded in consent, which, subject to morality and public policy, now occupy a more prominent place in Ivorian matrimonial property law than in the past. This novelty in Ivorian matrimonial property law is also evident in the notary's entry into the realm of matrimonial agreements, indicating that formalism has become a significant aspect of matrimonial property in Ivorian law.

---

[137] Kouassi (2020, p. 50).

From this point onward, we may symbolically extinguish the lanterns guiding this study by acknowledging, as Planiol observed at the outset of this chapter, that: 'in many cases, a reform is only the replacement of old inconveniences, which everyone knows, by new inconveniences, which one does not yet suspect, and whose practice then reveals the nature and the extent'.[138]

References

Bergel J-L (2003) Théorie générale du droit. Dalloz, Paris

Dabin J (1928) La notion du droit naturel et la pensée juridique contemporaine. Rev Néo-Scolastique Philos 30(20):418. https://www.persee.fr/docAsPDF/phlou_0776-555x_1928_num_30_20_2521.pdf. Accessed 31 Oct 2025

De Poulpiquet J (2009–2010) Responsabilité des notaires. Civile—disciplinaire—pénale. Dalloz, Paris

Domat J (1828–1830) Œuvres complètes. New edn by Rémy J, FIRMIN-DIDOT, Paris, vol 4, Tome 1, Title XVIII, section IV, § 1

Flour J (1950) Quelques remarques sur l'évolution du formalisme. In: Le droit privé français au milieu du XXe siècle. Etudes offertes à Georges Ripert, vol I. LGDJ, Paris

Ghestin J (dir.) (2000) Traité de droit civil : Les biens. LGDJ/Montchrestien, Paris

Ghestin J, Goubeaux G (1994) Traité de droit civil—Introduction générale, Le contrat. LGDJ, Paris

Guédj L (2018) Les droits successoraux du conjoint survivant dans les États francophones de l'Afrique de l'Ouest. Rev Béninoise Sci JuridS Adm 40:111

Kouassi A (2020) Le juge ivoirien et la loi étrangère. University of Parakou, Thesis

Lamarche M, Lemouland J-J (2009) Mariage (4° effets). Répertoire de Droit Civil, Dalloz

Lonne-Clément A-L (2014) Régimes matrimoniaux: aménagements des conventions permettant d'adapter les règles du Code civil à la situation des parties. Compte-rendu de la réunion du 23 Janvier 2014 de la Commission Famille du barreau de Paris. https://www.lagbd.org/index.php?title=R%C3%A9gimes_matrimoniaux_:_am%C3%A9nagements_des_conventions_permettant_d%27adapter_les_mod%C3%A8les_du_Code_civil_%C3%A0_la_situation_des_parties_(fr)&veaction=edit&mobileaction=toggle_view_mobile. Accessed 31 Oct 2025

Mazeaud H, Tunc A (1938) Traité théorique de la responsabilité civile, Tome 1, 6th edn. Montchrestien, Paris

Mayer P (2008) La diversité des aspects de l'impérativité en droit international des affaires. In: Colloque sur L'impérativité en droit international des affaires : questions d'actualité, Cour de Cassation, Paris. https://univ-droit.fr/recherche/actualites-de-la-recherche/manifestations/25420-l-imperativite-en-droit-international-des-affaires-questions-d-actualite. Accessed 31 Oct 2025

Nuyten B, Lesage L (1998) Formation des contrats: regards sur les notions de consensualisme et de formalisme. Rép. Defrénois, p. 502, n° 16

Planiol M (1904) In: Sorel A (ed), Le Code civil: 1804–1904. Le livre du centenaire, vol 2. A. Rousseau, Paris

Planio M, Ripert G (1952) Traité pratique de droit civil français, t. VI, Obligations, 2nd edn by Eismein. LGDJ, Paris

Rakotovahiny M-A (2015) Le vêtement, un bien particulier. In: Pousson A (dir), Le vêtement saisi par le droit. Travaux de l'IFR, LGDJ, n°8. https://books.openedition.org/putc/1468?lang=fr#authors. Accessed 31 Oct 2025

Sériaud A (2006) Manuel de droit des obligations, 2nd edn. PUF, Paris

---

[138] Planiol and Sorel (1904, p. 955) et seq.

Sériaud A (2014) Manuel de droit des obligations. PUF, Paris
UN Human Rights Committee (2000) CCPR General Comment No. 28: Article 3 (The Equality of Rights Between Men and Women), CCPR/C/21/Rev.1/Add.10, 29 March 2000. https://www.refworld.org/legal/general/hrc/2000/en/38892. Accessed 31 Oct 2025
Zehouri PA-B (2016) Le notariat en Côte d'Ivoire. https://news.abidjan.net/h/592910.html. Accessed 31 Oct 2025

Alfred Kouakou Kouassi is a Lecturer and academic researcher at the Université des Lagunes in Abidjan. He teaches Private International Law, the Law of Contracts, and Mediation. His research focuses on the decoloniality of law, legal positivism, and legal naturalism. Kouassi holds a PhD in Private Law.

Marital Property Division Under the Ethiopian Family Law

Terefe Gebreyesus

Abstract Ethiopia's complex federal system has resulted in a pluralistic family law landscape, with the Revised Family Code (RFC) of 2000 applying only to the federal cities of Addis Ababa and Dire Dawa. Rooted in a civil law tradition, the RFC establishes a default community property regime that presumes equal ownership of property acquired during marriage, irrespective of formal title. This chapter examines the structure and practical application of the community property regime, including distinctions between personal and marital property, rules on marital debt, and the legal treatment of property upon divorce. It analyses judicial interpretation of key provisions and how courts handle marital contracts, spousal agreements, and court-ordered property division. Special attention is given to the challenges posed by polygamous unions and how Ethiopian courts have pragmatically responded to such cases to avoid unjust enrichment or exclusion of one spouse from proprietary interests. Despite clear statutory goals of equality and marital unity, implementation varies widely, and jurisprudence remains inconsistent. The chapter argues that while the RFC aims to protect both spouses, particularly women, its effectiveness is hampered by gaps in judicial reasoning, uneven enforcement, and social practices beyond the law's reach. Continued jurisprudential development is essential to ensure that the legal framework delivers on its promise of equality and empowerment in the division of marital property.

1 Introduction

Marriage is one of the enduring and fundamental relationships of humanity. In many societies, it is regarded as a 'cornerstone of a society'.[1] In the Ethiopian context, one scholar has described marriage as follows: 'although entered into by way of an

T. Gebreyesus (✉)
Griffith Law School, Griffith University, Brisbane, QLD, Australia
e-mail: t.gebreyesus@griffith.edu.au

[1] Robinson (2022, pp. 488–489)_.

A. F. Hammond and P. Batariwah (eds.), *The Law on Marital Property in Africa*, Ius Gentium: Comparative Perspectives on Law and Justice 138,
https://doi.org/10.1007/978-3-032-19358-2_10

agreement, Ethiopian marriage is not a contract but an institution'.[2] When individuals establish this institution, it affects their lives in many ways: socially, personally, and financially.

One of the essential effects of marriage is its pecuniary effect on the spouses, their children, and even the broader society. There are two economic effects of marriage: marital property and marital debt. Regarding marital property, there are two broad systems in the world: 'community property regimes and separate (personal) property regimes'.[3] In community property regime countries, after marriage, 'the husband and wife generally have joint ownership of all the property acquired after the marriage'.[4] On the other hand, in countries with separate property regimes, marriage does not automatically trigger the communality of property. Instead, each spouse can maintain separate ownership of the property.[5] Countries that follow the civil law legal tradition tend to have community of property regimes, while countries with the common law legal tradition tend to have separate property regimes.[6] Since the Ethiopian legal system is generally a civil law legal system, it has a community property regime.

This chapter is divided into six sections. Section one introduces the subject by situating marriage within Ethiopian society as a foundational institution and outlining the dual social and legal significance of marital property. Section two provides a historical and legal overview of family law in Ethiopia, tracing the evolution from the 1960 Civil Code to the Revised Family Code (RFC) of 2000, and discussing the federal structure that gives rise to multiple legal systems, including religious and customary laws. Section three examines the content of the RFC regarding marital property, distinguishing between common and personal property, and detailing the management of marital assets and liabilities. Section four addresses the division of marital property upon divorce, analysing three primary mechanisms—marital contracts, mutual agreement, and judicial determination—and highlighting interpretative challenges through case law. Section five explores broader challenges in the application of marital property rules, including the legal treatment of bigamous marriages, disparities in enforcement, and the continuing influence of customary and religious practices. The chapter concludes in section six by evaluating the effectiveness of Ethiopia's family law in promoting gender equality and unity, while underscoring the importance of consistent judicial interpretation and improved jurisprudential clarity.

---

[2] Krzeczunowicz (1964, p. 176).

[3] Parkinson (2023, p. 404).

[4] Parkinson (2023, p. 404).

[5] Parkinson (2023, p. 404).

[6] Waggoner (1994, p. 24).

2 Family Law in Ethiopia

Ethiopia's history is debatable. Many cultural and ethnic societies that are part of present-day Ethiopia have existed for thousands of years. However, the country's present-day boundaries result from political developments in the late 19th and early twentieth centuries. In addition, Ethiopia is a country with more than eighty different languages and cultures.[7] Despite Ethiopia's complex political history and its ethnic, cultural, and linguistic diversity, family and marriage have remained central social institutions in the country.

The country's ethnic and cultural diversity is reflected in the various types of marriages and rituals associated with them.[8] As a result of these cultural differences, the principles that govern family relationships also differ from culture to culture.[9] Some of these societies' principles, rituals, and customs were inconsistent with international human rights instruments such as the Universal Declaration of Human Rights. For instance, in many ethnic groups, marriage customs did not require the consent of the spouses.[10] Consequently, as will be seen in the following paragraphs, Ethiopia started to *modernise* its laws by introducing foreign, mainly Western family laws and principles. In this regard, the Ethiopian experience is different from that of many other African countries, where Western family laws and principles were introduced primarily through colonialism. In Ethiopia, however, it was a wilful legal transplant or legal import that occurred in the 1950s and early 1960s.[11] During this period, Emperor Haile Selassie introduced several substantive legal Codes, including the Civil Code and the Criminal Code.

The Civil Code was imported from France in 1960.[12] The Code is a comprehensive and written national law that regulates private relationships. Marriage and family-related matters are some of the issues covered in the Civil Code. The legal provisions in the Civil Code that regulate marriage and family matters are not entirely of European origin. Some provisions in the family law were reformative, while others codified the existing social beliefs about marriage and family.[13] The Civil Code recognises various kinds of marriages: civil marriages, marriages before an officer of civil status, religious marriages, and customary marriages.[14]

Some argue that it introduced elements of modernity into Ethiopian family law.[15] Enforced for four decades, from 1960 to 2000, its full implementation nationwide remains uncertain. In practice, the law was primarily applied in urban centres, with limited reach in rural areas. In most parts of the country, marriage and family issues

---

7 Marcus and Mehretu (2025).

8 For some brief descriptions of differences in marriage practices, see Augustyniak (2009).

9 For some brief descriptions of differences in marriage practices, see Augustyniak (2009).

10 Sisay (2015, p. 87).

11 Beckstrom (1973, p. 559).

12 Beckstrom (1973, p. 559).

13 Belay (2016, p. 244).

14 Ethiopian Civil Code 1960, art. 577.

15 See Teshome (2002, p. 154) and see also Gizaw (2007, p. 36).

have been governed by local, ethnic, and cultural rules and customs. The Civil Code does not define what constitutes marital property. It does not clearly outline the rules governing the partition of marital property.[16]

In 1991, significant political changes occurred in Ethiopia. This political change affected Ethiopian family law in two ways. First, it initiated the adoption of a new federal family law. In the 1960s, a student-led revolution started in Ethiopia, ultimately leading to the overthrow of Emperor Haile Selassie by a military regime that assumed power. A 17-year war was waged by militia groups opposed to the military regime, culminating in the victory of a faction that later evolved into the political party known as the Ethiopian People's Revolutionary Democratic Front (EPRDF). This group assumed power in 1991 and introduced reforms, as well as ratified international human rights instruments that proclaim equality between men and women. In 1995, a new constitution was also adopted, guaranteeing equality between men and women, including marriage equality.[17] This, along with other factors, contributed to the adoption of new family codes nationwide.

The second relevance of this political change to family law in Ethiopia is the restructuring of the country into ethnic-based federal states, which grants the various ethnic groups their own state or autonomous administrative unit. Based on this federal structure, there are eleven states and two special cities, namely Addis Ababa and Dire Dawa.[18] The federal government administers the cities, and the federal parliament has the power to make private laws for them. Each state has its own legislative, executive, and judicial branches of government. After a controversy regarding whether the federal or the state parliaments have the power to make laws on family law issues, it was resolved that states have the authority to legislate on family law matters for their residents, while the federal parliament retains the power to enact family laws for the residents of the two special cities.[19]

Accordingly, except for the new states (one state, Southhern Nations, Nationalities and Peoples disintegrated into four news), all other states have their own family laws. The federal parliament enacted the Revised Family Code (RFC) in 2000 for the two special cities. The RFC constitutes is a pioneering legislative instrument in several respects. First, its making was fairly participatory. Second, many of the States' family laws are copies of the federal revised family law. The regional state courts have the power to apply state family laws and to decide issues arising under them. However, the Federal Supreme Court retains the authority to adjudicate family law cases that have been decided by the state courts. The court decides on States' family law matters

[16] See Ethiopian Civil Code 1960, arts 669 ff.

[17] Federal Democratic Republic of Ethiopia Constitution 1995, arts 34–35.

[18] The Constitution recognised nine Regional States. Now there are 12 regional states. Three of the states were created out of the State of Southern Nation, Nationalities and Peoples Region since 2020.

[19] Belay (2016, pp. 248–250).

in its capacity as a cassation division.[20] The Federal Supreme Court decides these cases by applying the state laws in which the cases originate.

2.1 Overview of the RFC

The RFC comprises 323 articles. It is a codified law that provides comprehensive coverage of family matters. The main reason for revising the Civil Code was that some of its concepts were outdated and discriminatory against women. For instance, the Civil Code stipulated that the husband is the head of the family and is responsible for administering marital property.[21] It also incorporates the practice of betrothal which the Revised Family Code does not incorporate.[22] A few states' family laws incorporated this practice with a significant modification to its definition under the Civil Code.[23] The RFC also introduced no-fault divorce, whereas the Civil Code only allowed fault-based divorce for serious grounds such as adultery and long-term absence of one of the spouses.[24]

Generally, the conceptions of family and marriage underlying these two laws are of Western origin, even though the drafters attempted to incorporate some indigenous and Ethiopian concepts of family and marriage. The Ethiopian conceptions of marriage also share important aspects with those of the Western legal systems. This is because in the West and in many parts of Ethiopian society, Christianity has a significant influence on ideas regarding marriage.[25] However, it is also important to note that Ethiopia has a substantial Muslim population, and this means that Islam has also influenced the ideals and practices of marriage and family.

This chapter focuses mainly on the content and practice of the RFC. It recognises two types of affinal relationships: Marriage and irregular unions. Even though the RFC acknowledges these two relationships, they have different legal consequences. The Family Code fully recognises and regulates both the personal and financial aspects of marriage, while it only partially recognises and governs the financial aspects of irregular unions.[26] Although federal and state family laws do not define

[20] A cassation division is a division of the Federal Supreme Court that has the mandate of correcting 'basic or fundamental error of law'. See the Federal Courts Proclamation no. 1234/2021, arts 2(4), 10.

[21] Hallward-Driemeier and Gajigo (2015, p. 262).

[22] See Ethiopian Civil Code 1960, art. 560 which provides that betrothal is an agreement between two families agreeing that two persons of that family will marry.

[23] Under both the Amhara and the Oromia Family Codes, betrothal is an agreement between the future spouses. See Amhara Family Code 2003, art. 1 and Oromia Family Code 2004, art. 9.

[24] Ethiopian Civil Code 1960, arts 669–670.

[25] Choudhry and Herring (2019, p. 4).

[26] Revised Family Code (RFC) 2000, arts 48 ff and 98 ff.

marriage,[27] they recognise its various forms, namely civil, religious, and customary unions. A civil marriage is a marriage that is concluded before an officer of civil status.[28] A religious marriage is one concluded according to religious rules, and a customary marriage is one concluded through the community's custom.[29] The RFC also acknowledges and grants full legal efficacy to marriages validly celebrated in accordance with the law of the place of celebration.[30] Article 71 of the RCF stresses that 'the causes and effects of dissolution of marriage shall be the same whichever the form of celebration'.[31]

Nonetheless, the Constitution acknowledges this plurality of laws, stating, 'this Constitution shall not preclude the adjudication of disputes relating to personal and family laws in accordance with religious or customary laws, with the consent of the parties to the dispute'.[32] The State and Federal Parliaments can also make laws to establish or recognise religious and customary courts.[33] Parties may elect to exclude the application of the RCF regime in favour of their customary or religious laws. Following the constitutional mandate, the federal government and many states established Sharia courts that were similarly structured to the formal federal and state courts. The Sharia courts apply Sharia law regarding marriage and division of marital property. However, the main sources of Islamic law, the *Sharia* and *Sunnah*, do not have comprehensive legal principles regarding the division of matrimonial property.[34] In the Ethiopian context, this has resulted in conflicting judicial decisions.[35]

The availability of multiple forums leads to forum shopping, in which individuals choose one court over another, believing that one will advance their interests more effectively.[36] In *Weyzero Jieto Yasin Shibeshi v Ato Hassen Mehammed*, the Cassation Bench of the Federal Supreme Court addressed this issue. In that case, one of the parties petitioned before the religious Sharia court after the formal court had decided on the divorce of their marriage. The Supreme Court held that such approach is illegal and unconstitutional.[37] In most situations, the women plaintiffs prefer to go to the formal courts because they believe that these courts treat them equally to men.[38]

---

[27] Other jurisdictions define what marriage is. See, for example, the Australian Marriage Act 1961 (Cth), s. 5 which defines marriage as 'the union of two people to the exclusion of all others, voluntarily entered into for life'.

[28] Revised Family Code 2000, art. 22.

[29] Revised Family Code 2000, arts 2–4.

[30] Revised Family Code 2000, art. 5.

[31] See Revised Family Code 2000, art. 74. Other regional/state family codes have similar provisions.

[32] Federal Democratic Republic of Ethiopia Constitution 1995, art. 34(5).

[33] Federal Democratic Republic of Ethiopia Constitution 1995, art. 78(5).

[34] Akhtar and Manjoo (2024, p. 77).

[35] Abod (2011, p. 90).

[36] Seidel (2019).

[37] *Weyzero Jieto Yasin Shibeshi v Ato Hassen Mehammed,* Cassation File No. 93779 (Jan 2013).

[38] Seidel (2019, p. 151).

3 Marital Property Under the Revised Family Code

Under the federal and state family laws, the conclusion of marriage creates common property between the spouses, unless they have a marital contract stating otherwise. The RFC describes the types of property that become the common property of the spouses and the types of property that remain each spouse's personal property. The states' family laws have similar provisions.[39]

3.1 Marital Property

The RFC stipulates that, in principle, all property acquired after marriage is considered the common property of the spouses. Specifically, it states that proprietary interests acquired by spouses through their personal effort and from their personal or common property are considered common property of the spouses.[40] This means that all wages earned by each spouse, as well as all income derived from investment properties belonging to either spouse or both, become common property as long as these incomes are acquired after marriage. It also stipulates that unless there is a contrary declaration, all property acquired by an onerous title and through donation to both spouses is also common property.[41] The proprietary interests acquired by onerous title are property interests that spouses acquire through transactions, such as purchases and leases.[42] These provisions are one of the pillars of marital property definitions. However, they must be understood in conjunction with other provisions that define and explain the personal property of each spouse. The RFC recognises two'forms' of personal property. The first is proprietary interests that the spouses acquired before marriage. The second ones are properties acquired during marriage, but they remain personal properties of each spouse. These are properties that one spouse inherits or when someone donates to the spouse personally.[43]

Two justifications can be identified to explain why the RFC emphasises the creation of common property in marriage. First, creating a common property regime increases unity between spouses because married couples are less likely to compete to alienate their property. In other words, it 'decreases parties' incentive to view their marriages individualistically' and encourages them to invest in common goods and common goals.[44] Second, in a marital relationship, it is difficult to quantify each spouse's contribution; that is, their contributions to the marital relationship are equal.

---

[39] See Amhara Family Code 2003, art. 73, Oromia Family Code 2004, art. 78 and Tigray Family Code 2004, art. 83.

[40] See Revised Family Code 2000, art. 67(1). Even though the provision talks about'ownership', it does not seem logical to limit this legal principle to'ownership'.

[41] Revised Family Code 2000, arts 62(2) and (3).

[42] See Explanatory Minutes to the Revised Family Code, p. 17.

[43] Revised Family Code 2000, art. 57.

[44] Frantz and Dagan (2004, p. 104).

This means their contributions to the economic aspect of the relationship are deemed equal, and it is not the court's role to investigate the spouses' financial or non-financial contributions. Therefore, the presummtion that states a proprietary interest is aquired in the marriage is common property reduces courts involvement in determining the ownership of a properiatary interest aquired in marriage.

These provisions and other similar provisions have been proven to be litigious. These cases pose some level of complexity in implementing these rules. In the following paragraphs, we examine several cases as examples, highlighting the issues that frequently arise under these laws. In *Ato Bezuneh Cherke v Weyzero Meaza Engidaye*, the issue was whether the compensation paid to one of the spouses was marital property.[45] In this case, one of the disputed homes was built using compensation awarded to one spouse (the respondent). The compensation was received by her personally following the death of her daughter, which resulted from the wrongdoing of another party. The house was constructed during the marriage with the applicant, using those funds. The respondent maintained that since the compensation was paid directly to her, it should be treated as her separate property rather than marital property.[46] The issue for the court was whether the compensation paid to the respondent constituted marital property. The court reasoned that, regardless of the reasons for the compensation, such compensation constitutes income acquired while the applicant and respondent were in a valid marrriage. Arguably, one of the main issues here is that the applicant's contribution to acquiring this "income" is insignificant.

Regarding marital debt, not every debt incurred during the marriage is marital debt. A marital debt is one incurred 'in the interest of the household'.[47] The Code also defines what constitutes 'in the interest of the household'. These are debts incurred to fulfil the livelihood of the spouses and their children, debts incurred to fulfil an obligation of maintenance by which one or both spouses are bound, and other debts that the court may recognise to be in the interest of the household.[48] Two somewhat contradictory implications can be inferred. First, such a formulation has a significant evidentiary effect. When spouses dispute the characterisation of a particular debt, the burden of proof rests on the spouse asserting that the debt is marital debt. In practice, men are typically the administrators of marital property. This imposes a burden on husbands to prove that a debt they incur is indeed in the household's interest. This, in turn, protects the interests of women because if husbands cannot prove that the debt was indeed in the household's interest, it would be considered a personal debt of the husband, which he would be required to pay from his share of the common property. The potential problem with this position is that, in some circumstances, it may be very difficult to prove that the money is actually spent in the best interest

[45] *Ato Bezuneh Cherke v Weyzero Meaza Engidaye*, Cassation File No. 26953 (Federal Supreme Court, 2008).

[46] Even though this appellate case is not clear, it is reasonable to assume that the deceased daughter, who was the reason for the compensation seems to be the child of the respondent only. If she were the child of both spouses, the applicant would have been paid the compensation as well.

[47] Revised Family Code 2000, art. 71.

[48] Revised Family Code 2000, art. 71.

of the household. Proving this may require serious record keeping, and especially in the Ethiopian social and cultural context this might be a bit challenging. In the absence of proof, the court may readily conclude that a debt incurred in the interest of the household to be personal debt of the husband.

The second implication concerns the position the court took in *Weyzero Nun Sentayehu Guz v Ato Tesfaye Woldemichael*.[49] In this case, the wife borrowed a significant amount of money from a staff credit union while married. She claimed that she and her husband bought a house and a car with the money. As nearly half of the money was outstanding and unpaid, she asked the court to classify the unpaid balance as marital debt. The husband, on the other hand, argued that the debt was not marital debt and that the money was not spent in the interest of the household. The court held that the debt was a marital debt. The court reasoned that from the 'content and spirit' of Article 71 of the RFC, it could be inferred that a debt that is incurred while the marriage subsisted was presumed to be spent in the interest of the household. The court further articulated that this presumption could be rebutted by adducing evidence that proved otherwise. Since the husband failed to produce evidence, the court held that the debt was a marital debt to be paid from the common property of the spouses. The problem with this position is that it renders Article 71 almost useless, as this provision dictates that the spouse claiming a debt as marital debt must prove it by adducing evidence. The good thing about this position is that it might avoid complexities that I have raised in the previous paragraph regarding unavailability of evidence. One can also argue that this interepretation does not align with the intention of the legislature. If the legislature had intended for all debts incurred by a spouse to be automatically presumed marital, it could have expressly provided for this in the law. At the very least, such an interpretative choice requires thorough justification, which the court failed to offer.

One significant exception is that spouses can regulate the pecuniary effects of their marriage through a marital contract.[50] Theoretically, spouses in Ethiopia can use any system or regime of marital property. In their marital contract, they can state that all past and future earnings remain personal property. That is, spouses can agree to keep property separate. In this regard, the Ethiopian law provides for a separate personal property regime.

The Family Code also provides rules governing the management of marital property. For the purpose of managing marital property, the family law divides the common property into 'earnings' and common property.[51] It provides that each spouse should manage their respective 'earnings'. This does not mean that 'earnings' are not marital property; this provision simplifies their use. It can be argued that where neither spouse controls their own earnings, or where one spouse transfers control of their earnings to the other, that spouse may become subject to the economic control and manipulation of the other.

---

[49] *Weyzero Nun Sentayehu Guz v Ato Tesfaye Woldemichael*, Cassation File No. 56184 (Nov 2010).

[50] Revised Family Code 2000, arts 42–48.

[51] Revised Family Code 2000, arts 64–66.

3.2 Personal Property

The RFC also recognises the personal property of the spouses. The primary category of personal property is the property that a spouse possesses on the day of marriage. The general principle of the RFC is that any proprietary interest that spouses have before marriage is their personal property, unless both spouses agree to convert it into marital property.[52] Additionally, property that a spouse acquires after marriage by succession or gift is also considered personal property.[53] One of the main rationales underlying the distinction drawn by the lawmaker between marital and personal property is the idea of effort and contribution in acquiring the property.[54] If one examines the properties classified as personal property, namely those acquired by either spouse before marriage, by donation, or by succession, it becomes evident that the other spouse's contribution to their acquisition is minimal or nonexistent.

The law also recognises that any property acquired by a spouse during the marriage remains personal property if it is obtained through the exchange of their personal assets, purchased with their personal funds, or acquired using proceeds from the sale of their personal property.[55] However, this rule is applicable only if a spouse who acquires property in this manner applies to a court for recognition and the court determines that the property indeed qualifies as personal property.[56] The Supreme Court applied this principle in two similar cases.[57] In both cases, one of the spouses bought property by either selling their personal property or using compensation paid by a public authority for the acquisition of their personal property. They bought the disputed property while they were married. However, they failed to apply to the court for a declaration that these new properties were indeed personal property, having been purchased with the proceeds from their personal property. In both cases, the court held that, because the applicants failed to comply with the law, their personal property was considered marital property.[58]

In another case, the wife acquired the land on which a house was built, and she initiated construction of the house three months before her marriage to the applicant.[59] The construction of the house was completed after the marriage, with money the wife borrowed from the bank. However, it was being paid from their common income in the

---

[52] Redaei (2017, p. 81).

[53] Revised Family Code 2000, art. 57.

[54] *Weyzero Senya Sheh Temam v Weyzero Belaynesh Matebo, Cassation File No. 43988 (Federal Supreme Court, 2003).*

[55] Revised Family Code 2000, art. 58(1).

[56] Revised Family Code 2000, art. 58(2).

[57] *Mrs Yeshi Teshome v Mr Mesfin Hailu*, Cassation File No. 95680 (Federal Supreme Court, 6 October 2014) and *Shambel Basha Gezahegn Dilnesaw v Weyzero Tewabech Demeke*, Cassation File No. 37275 (Federal Supreme Court, 28 October 2018).

[58] The first case, namely *Mrs. Yeshi Teshome v Mr Mesfin Hailu*, Cassation File No. 95680 (Federal Supreme Court, 6 October 2014) was a case decided under one of the State's family laws while the second was decided based on the RFC. Both family laws have identical rules on the matter.

[59] *Ato Mekonin Belachew v Alemitu Adem*, Cassation File No. 25005 (Federal Supreme Court, 2008).

marriage. The court held that the house was marital property. The court found that the house was built during a valid marital relationship, and that both parties contributed to repaying the money borrowed to build it. To use the court's expression, 'the house became a house' when the marriage was intact. Since the Family Code stipulates that any property acquired by spouses during their marriage is considered marital property, the construction of the house was completed when the marriage was intact and thus became 'marital property'.

One of the significantly influential provisions of the RFC is the provision relating to proof of personal or marital property. Art 63 (1) provides, 'All property shall be deemed common property even if registered in the name of one of the spouses unless such spouse proves he is the sole owner thereof.' It can be argued that this provision was primarily included to protect women's proprietary interest. In the Ethiopian context, men are typically the primary breadwinners and the main administrators of common property.[60] However, in the course of managing such property, husbands may not always act in a manner that reflects its marital nature. For example, they may register property solely in their name or present themselves as the exclusive owners. In such situations, it becomes challenging to produce evidence that clearly establishes the marital character of the property.

Additionally, husbands, due to their control over marital property, may attempt to convert it into personal property through various means. Consequently, it is challenging for the court to determine that a particular property is marital property. This may force the court to rule that marital property is the husband's private property. As a result, registration of the property in a spouse's name is not enough to prove that a given property is not marital property. Rather, it is usually the husband, and theoretically the wife, who must provide additional evidence demonstrating that the property is indeed private.

4 Divorce and Division of Marital Property

According to the RFC, there are three grounds for the dissolution of marriage: death or absence of one of the spouses, dissolution by a court due to a violation of one of the essential conditions of marriage, or divorce.[61] When a marital relationship ends in either death/absence or divorce, the determination and division of marital property becomes an important issue. The RFC provides three ways in which the proprietary effects of marriage may be liquidated: by marital contract, by mutual consent upon divorce, or by court determination and apportionment. The following subsections examine these mechanisms.

---

[60] Legally, the Civil Code provides that marital property 'shall be administered by the husband' but this provision is repealed by RFC.

[61] Revised Family Code 2000, art. 75.

4.1 Marriage Contracts

The RFC provides somewhat detailed explanations and requirements of a marital contract. However, it can be argued that the RFC does not explicitly specify all the conditions necessary for a legally binding marital contract. It states that the marital contract cannot override the mandatory provisions of the law.[62] This statement can be interpreted in two ways. First, the mandatory provisions referred to here are those found in the Code itself. For instance, article 7 provides that the minimum age for marriage is sixteen years.[63] Some provisions stipulate that marriage should be conducted with the consent of both spouses. However, it is arguable that this provision applies to marital contracts. It is possible to imagine a scenario in which spouses freely agreed to marry but sign a marital contract under duress. Or a woman may be willing to marry a man but would not have signed a marital contract regarding the marital property, but for the man's deceit. In such cases, one might argue that the marital contract remains valid because it does not violate the mandatory provisions of the Family Code.

The second interpretation is that the 'mandatory provisions of the law' should be taken to mean any relevant provisions of the law. That is to say, in addition to mandatory provisions found in the RFC, the relevant mandatory provisions of other laws, especially mandatory rules of contract law, also apply to marital contracts. This line of interpretation seems plausible. It is also imperative to recognise that in jurisdictions such as Australia, the enforceability of such contracts is determined by the rules governing the enforceability of contracts generally.[64] One can argue that a marital contract cannot be valid if it violates the general mandatory provisions of contract law. It should also be noted that a marital contract should not be comprehensive in its consideration of the pecuniary effects of marriage. It can cover only some aspects of the financial relationship between spouses. In such circumstances, any other aspects not covered by the marital contract will be regulated by the provisions of the RFC.

A marital contract should also be attested by two witnesses of each of the spouses.[65] When a marital contract that regulates the pecuniary effects of marriage is validly made, the contract becomes the primary source of rules governing the creation, regulation, and division of marital property in the event of divorce.

However, it is difficult to argue that the RFC addressed all relevant questions regarding marital contracts. The courts typically grapple with issues such as whether a contract or agreement between spouses constitutes a marital contract and, interpretation of marital contracts. In *Mrs Tsehay Tessema and Mrs Alemnesh Tessema v Amanual Wondwosen*, the Cassation Bench of the Federal Supreme Court considered

---

[62] See Revised Family Code 2000, art. 42(3). The Amharic version is also similar in meaning.

[63] In principle, a person has to attain the age of 18 to validly conclude marriage. However, in a very exceptional case, a Minister of Justice may allow 16 years old to marry.

[64] Paterson et al. (2016, p. 125).

[65] Revised Family Code 2000, art. 44.

how to correctly classify contracts.[66] In this case, the deceased husband and wife amended their 'contract of marriage'. The amendment gave the wife the exclusive right to use the house at the husband's death. The house was the marital property of the spouses. The court unanimously determined that this agreement was not a marital contract, but rather, a donation contract.[67] The court, while not providing a comprehensive explanation, noted that the contract did not impose any obligation on the husband, and that the right conferred by the contract was only enjoyable upon the husband's death.[68] The court then concluded that these facts demonstrated the true nature of the contract to be a donation contract, and that the pertinent provisions of the Civil Code must therefore be applied. From this argument, we can infer the nature of the marital contract. Based on this reasoning, a marital contract imposes obligations on both parties. Especially, it must impose a duty or some consideration on the spouses during the subsistence of the marriage. The second inference might be that when one spouse gives a proprietary interest to another, it cannot be considered a marital contract. Obviously, these inferences seem logical from the court's reasoning. But it is difficult to justify them based on the provisions of the RFC, which defines a marital contract as 'a contract that regulates the pecuniary effects of marriage'.[69] Contrary to the court's opinion, it seems that the house was marital property because it was one of the pecuniary effects of the marriage. The amended marital contract concluded by the spouses is the instrument through which their marital proprietary interests are regulated.

Another important case decided regarding marital contracts concerns their interpretation. In *Mr Biruk Haile Yesus v. Mrs Fanaye Abebe,* the spouses signed a marital contract regarding a house owned by the husband before marriage.[70] In the contract, the spouses listed three properties as 'sources of livelihood ',[71] namely, the house, the husband's salary, and 10,000 Ethiopian Birr in cash. The expression they used in Amharic is መተዳደሪያችን *(metedaderiachin).* This expression essentially suggests that these properties are essential for their day-to-day living. The spouses utilised these properties and income, and they lived together for 11 years before their marriage ended in divorce.[72] The issue was whether this expression would mean that the spouses intended to make the house marital property.

The court assumed that the marital contract is interpreted in accordance with the rules of general contract interpretation stipulated in the Civil Code. The court then proceeded and stated the following (similar description):

[66] *Mrs Tsehay Tessema and Mrs Alemnesh Tessema v Amanual Wondwosen,* Cassation File No. 5617, Fed. Sup. Ct. Cassation Bench Judgements, Vol. 11, pp. 55–58 (translated from Amharic to English by the author).

[67] *Mrs Tsehay Tessema and Mrs Alemnesh Tessema v Amanual Wondwosen,* p. 57.

[68] *Mrs Tsehay Tessema and Mrs Alemnesh Tessema v Amanual Wondwosen,* p. 57.

[69] Revised Family Code 2000, art. 42(1).

[70] *Mr Biruk Haile Yesus v Mrs Fanaye Abebe*, Cassation File No. 38544, Federal Supreme Court Cassation Bench Judgements, Vol. 10, pp. 2–3.

[71] This is the author's translation.

[72] *Mr Biruk Haile Yesus v Mrs Fanaye Abebe*, p. 2.

> The spouses used the cash and the house as their economic means of living for the past eleven years. Accordingly, considering the circumstances when they signed the contract of marriage, and the fact that they agreed to make the house 'metedaderiachin', we could not find any reason not to believe that the spouses intended to use the word metedaderiachin to convert the listed property into marital property.[73]

In short, the court concluded that the spouses agreed to convert the house into marital property. The court assumed that the marital contract was to be interpreted in accordance with the rules of general contract interpretation stipulated in the Civil Code. The court then started its analysis from the principle that if the terms of a contract are clear, the court should not depart from them.[74] It can be argued that the word *metedaderiachin* is not ambiguous. If it is ambiguous, it means that one can equally give one of the following meanings to the word. First, it might mean the creation of common property, or it might also mean a temporary means of livelihood. It is difficult to argue that the word can mean the creation of common property.

The second rule of interpretation is that if the terms of the contract are ambiguous, the court needs to seek the common intention of the parties.[75] This is achieved by considering the general conduct of the parties before and after the contract is made.[76] The court did not provide which general conduct of the spouses it considered. What the court emphasised is the fact that 'cash' was listed as *metedaderiachin.* The court appeared to suggest that when cash is listed in this manner, it becomes common property as long as the marriage remains intact. Even though the court did not expressly state the rationale for this conclusion, it appears to be that cash, by its nature, is consumable, and if the spouses intend to consume it, they thereby treat it a marital asset. The court also seemed to further presume that when parties to a contract list consumables and real property together as *metedaderiachin*, it means that they intend to make the non-consumable house marital property. This is a far-fetched argument. The court, for reasons not stated, placed limited emphasis on the husband's salary, notwithstanding the fact that it was included in the list. Due to its nature, it is difficult to say that the husband's salary is common property after the dissolution of marriage.

These cases illustrate the debates and issues related to the use of marital contracts in regulating the proprietary effects of marriage. It is essential to note that at least for now, marital contract is not the primary means of regulating marital property.[77]

---

[73] *Mr Biruk Haile Yesus v Mrs Fanaye Abebe*, p. 3. This is the author's translation.

[74] Ethiopian Civil Code 1960, art. 1733.

[75] Ethiopian Civil Code 1960, art. 1734.

[76] Ethiopian Civil Code 1960, art. 1734.

[77] Even though there are no empirical data to support this, the author observed this when he was a family bench judge at the Federal First Instance Court.

4.2 Agreement

The RFC also allows the spouses to determine their proprietary relationship by agreement other than a marital contract.[78] Article 77 provides the procedures governing this. It says, 'where the spouses have agreed to divorce by mutual consent, such agreement shall be submitted to the court'. Such agreements may also address the division of their marital property. The court then has the power to ascertain whether the divorce is indeed their true desire, and whether the spouses freely agree with the detailed division of property.[79] If the court determines that this is the case, it approves the agreement for divorce and the division of marital property. However, the court also has the power to give an order instructing the parties to correct the marital property division if it finds that the agreement 'adversely affects' the interests of one of the spouses.[80] This requirement is very difficult to implement. If the court ascertains that the parties agreed without any duress or misstatement and if the parties' agreement is not against law and societal morality, then it can reasonably be concluded that the party that forfeited their interest has done so voluntarily. If that is the case, it is difficult to see why the court would force the one who voluntarily renounces their proprietary interest to reconsider it. Alternatively, on what basis would the court say that the agreement is against the interest of one of the parties? It seems the lawmaker assumed that if the agreement is unfair to one of the spouses, there was a defect in the process of making it. However, this is not always the case.

4.3 Division by the Court

The third scenario is when there is neither a marital contract nor an agreement regarding marital property. In such a situation, the parties file a petition with the court for divorce and division of marital property, or for division of marital property only.[81] When one spouse petitions the court for these reasons, the court may require the parties to reach an agreement on how to divide their property, either directly or through arbitration.[82] If all these efforts fail, the court will liquidate the spouses' pecuniary relations. The law provides that before the court divides marital property, the spouses must first take their personal property.[83] The court further orders that any third party claims be satisfied prior to the division of marital property. After all these, the court divides what is left of the marital property equally to both spouses and their heirs.

[78] Revised Family Code 2000, art. 85.

[79] Revised Family Code 2000, art. 80.

[80] Revised Family Code 2000, art. 80(3).

[81] Revised Family Code 2000, arts 83(1)-(2). Procedurally, the parties may ask the court for division of marital property only or divorce and marital property in one claim.

[82] Revised Family Code 2000, arts 83(1)-(2).

[83] Revised Family Code 2000, art. 86.

4.4 Presumption of Marriage and Proprietary Interest

The presumption of marriage may take two forms. First, a couple may assert that they are validly married while being unable to produce their marriage certificate. If the couple can establish that 'they mutually consider themselves and live as spouses and... are considered and treated as such by their family and the community',[84] then the law may recognise their marriage and the established rules on marital property will apply to them. The second form of presumption arises when a man and woman live together without entering into a valid marriage.[85] If the couple cohabits for a minimum of three years, the marriage is deemed to create common property, and the established rules governing property rights will apply.[86] In other words, the law treats an irregular union as a marriage for the purpose of dividing common property.

5 Challenges

There are a few challenges to applying the division and administration of property rights. One of these challenges is the practice of bigamy or polygamy. Ethiopia is one of the countries that are located in the 'polygamy belt' in sub-Saharan Africa.[87] However, polygamy is more prevalent in rural areas of the country than in the major cities. A survey conducted in 2011 indicated that rural areas of Somali, Afar, Benshangul-Gumuz, and Oromia, have high rates of polygamous marriage.[88] Polygamy is not prevalent in the City of Dire Dawa or in Addis Ababa, where the Revised Family Code is applicable. Nonetheless, it remains important to address the challenges it poses concerning the division of marital property in Ethiopia.

The marital property rules of all family laws in Ethiopia are designed on the assumption that marriage in Ethiopia is typically between a man and a woman. Generally, bigamy or polygamy is prohibited in Ethiopia.[89] The RFC particularly prohibits bigamous marriage. It states that 'a person shall not conclude marriage as long as he/she is bound by the bonds of a preceding marriage'.[90] Bigamy is also a criminal offence under the Federal Criminal law.[91] The criminal law provides an exception that concluding a bigamous marriage in conformity with traditional or religious practices and recognised by law is not a criminal offence. However, there

[84] Revised Family Code 2000, art. 96.

[85] Revised Family Code 2000, art. 98.

[86] Revised Family Code 2000, art. 102.

[87] Jacoby (1995, p. 939).

[88] Ethiopian Central Statistical Agency and ICF International (2012).

[89] Polyandry, the practice of one women having multiple husbands, does not exist in Ethiopia.

[90] Revised Family Code 2000, art. 11. Technically and somewhat unrealistically it can be argued that one can circumvent this by concluding marriage with two spouses.

[91] Criminal Code of the Federal Democratic Republic of Ethiopia 2005, art. 650(1).

is no particular law that recognises bigamy.[92] However, it is very difficult to think that the lawmakers were unaware of the existing societal practice.

The difference between societal practices and the country's family laws creates a challenge. When a marriage is dissolved, the court divides the common property equally to between the spouse or their heirs. Division of common property in a bigamous marriage is problematic. Three cases reflect this problem. The first case concerns a situation in which a husband had two wives, and one of them sought divorce and the liquidation of property.[93] The husband lived in Saudi Arabia with one of his wives. He later travelled to Ethiopia and married another woman, promising to take her to Saudi Arabia, a promise he could not keep. During this period, a house was built in Ethiopia. The wife living in Ethiopia asserted that the house was built solely through her and her husband's efforts and claimed that the wife residing in Saudi Arabia did not contribute to its construction. The court acknowledged that both the federal and the state family laws do not address the issue of resolving property division in a bigamous/polygamous marriages, as these laws prohibit bigamous marriages.[94] The court then acknowledged that when communities engage in a practice that the law prohibits, courts should approach such issues in a manner that does not create societal chaos.[95] The court decided that the wife, who lived in Saudi Arabia with her husband, was entitled to a 50% share of the house's value, mainly because the wife in Ethiopia had, in fact, contributed 50% towards the house's construction.

In a similar case, a disagreement arose between the Federal Supreme Court and the Amhara State Supreme Court regarding the appropriate solution in such cases.[96] According to the State Court, the law should not recognise the proprietary interest of the second wife who married the husband after the first wife. This is because it affects the interests of the first valid marriage. However, the Federal Court disagreed with this approach, stating that it was not a fair solution. The court also reasoned that when there is a bigamous marriage, the spirit of family law is not to enrich one spouse by the hard work and efforts of the other, thereby depriving one of the spouses of the benefit of their hard work and contribution towards acquiring the property. The court also laid down the principle of partition. It stated that if there is evidence that one of the wives has contributed more to the acquisition of the property than the other, that spouse might have a greater proprietary entitlement. Following this principle, the court apportioned two houses located in different cities using a differing ratio. That is, the wife who lived in one city got 50% of the property found in that city and 25% in another.

---

[92] The exception is the Harari State Family Code which recognizes bigamous marriage based on religious grounds. See Harari Region Family Code 2005, art. 111(2).

[93] *Zeynaba Kelifa v Kedija Siraj* (Cassation File No 50489/2010) FSC Cassation Decision Vol 11 (2011) 2–5.

[94] *Zeynaba Kelifa v Kedija Siraj* (Cassation File No 50489/2010) FSC Cassation Decision Vol 11 (2011) 2–5.

[95] *Zeynaba Kelifa v Kedija Siraj* (Cassation File No 50489/2010) FSC Cassation Decision Vol 11 (2011) 2–5.

[96] *Aminat Ali v Fatuma Wubet* (Cassation No 45548/2010) (Fed Sup Ct) Vol 13 (2012), pp. 167–170.

In another case, the husband had two wives.[97] His marriage to both women was terminated because of his death. The case concerned a house built during the time the husband was married to both women. The trial court decided that the house (proceeds from its sale) should be divided in half, with one half going to the surviving son and the other half to the two wives. The court stated that the law presumed a property acquired by spouses during a valid marital relationship to be marital property. The court found that no evidence rebutted this presumption, and therefore, the second wife also had a proprietary interest in the house.

What makes these cases similar is that the court recognises that a bigamous marriage creates a proprietary interest for all spouses involved if the property is acquired during a valid marriage. However, the apportionment scales differ. This difference has attracted the attention of a few writers.[98] The main principle that the court seems to follow in dividing marital property in a bigamous marriage is the contribution principle. Evidence of the level of contribution towards earning or building a given marital property determines the ratio of apportionment. If one of the wives contributed more to acquiring that property, this determines the ratio of her portion. In the first case, the distribution pattern reflects this and appears to constitute a sensible and equitable approach. Without such evidence, the court divides the property equally between the husband and the two wives.[99] Some have argued that this violates the equality of the spouses, stating that marital property should be divided equally among the three.[100] Overall, though, it is difficult to say that the court's approach is discriminatory, especially in cases where there is evidence showing the spouses' contributions towards acquiring marital property.

The Ethiopian approach to marital property division in bigamous marriages, which is discussed, reveals a phenomenon in which the law seeks to transform society, yet a portion of society still engages in the practice. As we have seen, bigamous marriages have both cultural and religious aspects, and the practice is prevalent in many societies in the country. In such a situation, the court must balance the desire for social transformation with the protection of innocent individuals, usually women who enter into marriage without knowlege of laws prohibiting bigamous marriage.

The other challenge relates to the applicability of the family laws. The Revised Family Code is directly applicable only to the two cities. It is also difficult to say that the States' laws have applicability in all areas of the country. Still, customary and religious laws are applicable. The evidence for this conclusion is the prevalence of underage and bigamous marriages. Ethiopia is still one of the countries in which

---

[97] *Weyzero Sayad Ahmed v Weyzero Rahma Ali* (Cassation File No 24625, Federal Supreme Court Cassation, Nov 2007).

[98] Ashagre (2012) and Hirko (2019).

[99] This is the case in which the court did not address the contribution of the spouses to the creation of the property.

[100] Ashagre (2012).

underage marriage is prevalent, regardless of all family laws prohibiting the practice.[101] Similarly, the provisions of the law that relate to the pecuniary effects of marriage may not be applicable with full force.

6 Conclusion

Ethiopia has a plurality of family laws. These family laws are customary, religious, and formal laws. The federal and state parliaments have made formal family laws since the 2000s. These laws are similar to the state family laws, which are based on the Federal Revised Family Code. Consistent with other civil law systems, Ethiopian family law provides that any property acquired during the marriage is regarded as common property. Spouses have equal rights to use the common property throughout the marriage and to share it equally upon the dissolution of the marriage. In principle, spouses can alter these rules by agreement. Additionally, family laws stipulate that spouses have equal rights to manage marital property. Spouses also have equal access to their respective earnings, thereby providing women with an independent economic resource that enhances their empowerment. A study concluded that the implementation of the Revised Family Code (RFC) significantly contributed to women's economic empowerment in regions where the RFC and comparable legislation were enacted.[102]

A similar point can be made regarding the specific laws regulating marital property. Generally, the family law provisions governing the creation and division of marital property are practical and effective. They appear to be designed with the aim of promoting spousal equality and preserving the unity of marriage. That is, the legal provisions that deal with marital property are designed to further the marital bond and unity.

Overall, the interpretation and application of these provisions do not seem to cause injustice and inequality. It is difficult to conclude that the court's application of these provisions is systematically erroneous. However, it does not mean that there are no inconsistencies here and there. Communal practices such as bigamy or polygamy also pose a challenge to the application of the rules adopted in the family laws. The primary issue with the Ethiopian courts, particularly the Cassation Division, is that they do not clearly explain their interpretations and decisions. The cases we have seen in this chapter are examples of such practices. The function and purpose of the Cassation Division is to create uniformity in the interpretation and application of law. The best way to create such uniformity is through jurisprudential development. Jurisprudence in family law develops when court decisions are supported by clear, thorough, and well-reasoned legal analysis. As these laws are increasingly applied by courts and legal professionals across a relatively wider part of the country, the body of jurisprudence surrounding them will continue to grow and improve.

---

[101] Liang et al. (2021, p. 7).

[102] Hallward-Driemeier and Gajigo (2015, p. 260).

References

Abod M (2011) Legal pluralism, Sharia courts and constitutional issues in Ethiopia (2011). Mizan Law Rev 5(1):72–104
Akhtar RC, Manjoo FA (2024) Matrimonial property in Islamic law. In: Briggs M, Hayward A (eds) Research handbook on family property and the law. Edward Elgar, pp 77–91
Ashagre A (2012) The effect of bigamous marriage on distribution of marital property in Ethiopia. J Ethiop Law 25(2):236–253
Augustyniak Z (2009) Marriages in Ethiopia. Stud Afr Lang Cult 43:99–113
Beckstrom JD (1973) Transplantation of legal systems: an early report on the reception of the Western laws in Ethiopia. Am J Comp Law 21(3):557–583
Belay M (2016) Public consultation toward Ethiopia's family law reform and the revised code's response. Mizan Law Review 10(1):244–264
Choudhry S, Herring J (2019) Introduction. In: Choudhry S, Herring J (eds) The Cambridge Companion to Comparative Family Law. Cambridge University Press, Cambridge, pp 1–18
Ethiopian Central Statistical Agency, ICF International (2012) Ethiopia Demographic and Health Survey 2011. Addis Ababa and Calverton
Frantz CJ, Dagan H (2004) Properties in marriage. Columbia Law Rev 104(1):75–133
Gizaw TS (2007) Judicial implementation of the revised family code in Addis Ababa. Dissertation, Old Dominion University
Hallward-Driemeier M, Gajigo O (2015) Strengthening economic rights and women's occupational choice: the impact of reforming Ethiopia's family law. World Dev 70:260–273
Hirko SB (2019) The disputed constitutionality of the precedent practice of the Federal Supreme Court and its implications for Oromia family law: the case of bigamous marriage in Ethiopia. J Afr Law 63(2):193–203
Jacoby HG (1995) The economics of polygamy in sub-Saharan Africa: female productivity and the demand for wives in Cote d'Ivoire. J Political Econ 103(5):938–971
Krzeczunowicz G (1964) The nature of marriage under the Ethiopian Civil Code. J Afr Law 11(3):175–180
Liang M, Simelane S, Chalasani S, Snow R (2021) New estimations of child marriage: evidence from 90 low-and middle-income countries. PLoS ONE 16(10):1–17. https://doi.org/10.1371/journal.pone.0258378
Marcus HG, Mehretu A (2025) Ethiopia. Encyclopaedia Britannica. https://www.britannica.com/place/Ethiopia/Relief. Accessed 23 Oct 2025
Parkinson P (2023) Australian family law in context: commentary and materials, 8th edn. Thomson Reuters, Sydney
Paterson J, Robertson A, Duke A (2016) Principles of contracts. LawBook Co., Sydney
Redaei M (2017) The federal family law content and its application. Kaleab Printers, Addis Ababa
Robinson JA (2022) The evolution of the concept of marriage in South Africa: the influence of the Bill of Rights in 1994. Obiter 26(3):488–504
Seidel K (2020) Constitutional recognition of Islamic family law and Shari'a courts in Ethiopia: governmental strategies to co-regulate the plural family law arena. Verfassung und Recht in Übersee / Law and Politics in Africa, Asia and Latin America 53(2):140–171
Sisay MG (2015) Departure of Ethiopian family laws: the need to redefine the place of societal norms in family matters. Haramaya Law Rev 4(1):81–105
Teshome T (2002) Reflections on the revised family code 2000. Int Surv Family Law 153
Waggoner L (1994) Marital property rights in transition. Miss Law Rev 59(1):21–104

Terefe Gebreyesus is a lecturer at Griffith Law School, Australia. His teaching and research interests include family law, Australian constitutional law, comparative constitutional law, and public international law. Before pursuing graduate study, he practised as a federal prosecutor and served as a federal judge in Ethiopia, specialising in criminal and family law. He holds an LLB, JD, LLM, and PhD.

An Economic Interpretation of Morocco's New Family Code of 2004: Divorce and Marital Property

Hicham Hafid

Abstract The 2004 introduction of Morocco's New Family Code (NFC), also known as *Moudawana al-usra,* marked a significant shift in the country's family law, aiming to balance Islamic principles with universal human rights values. Against the backdrop of rapid socio-economic transformation, characterised by rising female education, labour force participation, and access to paid employment, this chapter presents an economic analysis of two key legal reforms that impact marital stability: women's access to divorce and the matrimonial property regime. It explores how the NFC empowers women to seek divorce on grounds such as *chikak* (irreconcilable differences), even in the absence of fault, thereby altering traditional gender dynamics. At the same time, it critically evaluates the law's reaffirmation of the Islamic principle of separate property while allowing for contractual arrangements between spouses concerning jointly acquired assets. The chapter examines the practical role of the Adoul (notary) in formalising such contracts and argues that while property agreements may promote economic agency for working women, they often fail to protect housewives and lower-income women who lack bargaining power or the ability to accumulate assets during marriage. The analysis concludes that, although the NFC offers greater autonomy and legal equality, structural inequalities continue to limit its transformative potential for economically vulnerable women.

1 Introduction

In Morocco, the family is based on the legal bond of marriage. This institution has historically been inextricably linked to society. However, the profound changes that the country has undergone in recent years, driven by factors such as economic development, girls' education, women's participation in the labour market, and their access

H. Hafid (✉)
Institute of African Studies, Mohammed V University, Rabat, Morocco
e-mail: hichamhafid.iea@gmail.com

Moroccan Association of Economic Sciences (AMSE), Rabat, Morocco

A. F. Hammond and P. Batariwah (eds.), *The Law on Marital Property in Africa*, Ius Gentium: Comparative Perspectives on Law and Justice 138,
https://doi.org/10.1007/978-3-032-19358-2_11

to paid employment, have resulted in the institution of the family being crossed by contradictory currents. These currents have transformed the family into a battleground between tradition and modernity, between the values of the past and those of the present. Historically, Moroccan women were primarily confined to the home and engaged in domestic chores. However, they now participate in economic and political life alongside their husbands. They sometimes share family expenses with their husbands, and legal provisions have been introduced to protect their property and ensure justice. Since then, Moroccan legislation has focused on issues of great importance in the relationship between spouses, such as property acquired during the marriage, whether owned by the husband, the wife, or shared between them.

It is important to note that this interest in the wife's right to family property is not a recent phenomenon. In fact, it has been a long-standing concern within Islamic *Shari'ah* law, which has historically recognised the right of both parties to own their share of work and activity. Similarly, Arab family law, except in Tunisia,[1] has consistently upheld the principle of separation of property. The principle has long historical antecedents grounded in Muslim law. Under Article 35 of the old Family Code (1957-58), spouses were subject to the legal regime of separation of property.

The New Family Code (NFC), also known as the *Moudawanaal-usra*, was introduced in Morocco in 2004 to reconcile religious standards with human rights values. The NFC draws inspiration from both Islamic guidelines and universal human rights standards. It is commonly regarded as the Code of Personal Status and Successions. The *Moudawana* is regarded as a symbol of resolution between sacred religious texts and the constraints of the modern era. The *Moudawana* represents a revolutionary change in the position of Moroccan women, conferring upon them equal status with men in marriage. The minimum age for marriage has been set at 18 for both spouses, rather than 15.[2] Polygamy remains possible, but the new family law restricts the grounds for divorce.[3] In the event of divorce, child custody can revert to the mother or father.[4] Finally, spouses can enter into a contract for the administration of acquired property.[5]

This chapter examines two significant family law reforms from an economic perspective that are directly related to marital stability. The first concerns the ease with which a wife can obtain a divorce, regardless of whether her husband is at fault (*chikak*).[6] The second concerns the matrimonial property regime (separation of property), which the NFC has reaffirmed. This regime allows spouses to conclude contracts regarding property acquired during marriage.

---

[1] In Tunisia, the so called 'Spouses' Jointly Shared Property System' has been established by law 94 of 1998. According to some Tunisian researchers, the current form of matrimonial property in the Tunisian law is a voluntary system that spouses agree on when contracting the marriage or even after it; it is independent from the marriage contract and its documents are separate from the marriage documents. See Attounissia Blog (2006).

[2] Moroccan Family Code (*Moudawana*) (2004), art. 19.

[3] Moroccan Family Code (*Moudawana*) (2004), arts. 40-46.

[4] Moroccan Family Code (*Moudawana*) (2004), art. 171.

[5] Moroccan Family Code (*Moudawana*) (2004), art. 49.

[6] Moroccan Family Code (*Moudawana*) (2004), arts. 94–97.

In light of the aforementioned considerations, the economic analysis of these two components represents a novel scientific approach that has been and continues to be debated between legal experts and economists specialising in family economics. Two reasons justify my choice. First, I seek to assess the sensitivity of these issues in Morocco, a country undergoing significant economic and legal transformations. Secondly, I aim to identify avenues for reflection that can enrich the debate on matrimonial property regimes and, consequently, eliminate confusion and ambiguity surrounding this subject. The socio-cultural dynamics of Moroccan society also justify our choice. Technically, an economic interpretation of these issues is very rare.

The methodology adopted is an analytical quantitative approach, consisting of analysing official documents (the Constitution and the *Moudawanna*) and reports and studies by academics (sociologists, jurists, economists). This chapter cross-references data from various national and international bodies, including the Ministry of Justice, the High Commission for Planning, and the World Bank report.

This chapter is divided into six sections. Following this introduction, Section two explores the ideological, legal, and socio-economic changes that have shaped family law reform in Morocco. It explores the historical tensions between conservative and progressive forces, the role of the monarchy in shaping reform, and the impact of shifting social dynamics, including increased female education, labour force participation, and evolving gender norms, on the institution of marriage and marital stability. Section three discusses the matrimonial property regime, focusing on the principle of separation of property under Islamic and Moroccan law, the challenges surrounding property division contracts, evidentiary burdens in court, and the limited legal protections available to economically dependent spouses. Section four examines the economic rationale behind the marriage contract, applying household bargaining theories and addressing issues of opportunism, inequality in asset accumulation, and the undervaluation of domestic labour. Section five proposes legal and institutional reforms to enhance awareness, procedural fairness, and gender equity in matrimonial property arrangements, particularly through the revision of Article 49. The chapter concludes in section six by reflecting on the broader need for inclusive development and socio-legal reform to fully realise the transformative promise of Morocco's family law.

2 The Reform of the Family Institution in Morocco: Between Muslim Tradition and Modernity of Moroccan Society

For over three decades, the question of reforming the institution of the family has been a subject of significant debate and controversy between two opposing groups. On the one hand, some advocate for modernity, the removal of religious influence from family law, and the abolition of all domestic legal norms that do not align with the human rights philosophies espoused by international conventions. On the other hand, some defend Muslim tradition and consider marriage to be a fundamental institution. The latter refers to the Moroccan Constitution, which designates Islam as the state religion. In the event of disagreement, royal arbitration resolves the impasse because of the Monarch's prerogative under the Constitution as Commander of the Faithful (Amir Al Mouminine) and Head of State.[7]

It is important to recall that the initial reform of the *Moudawana* in 1993 gave rise to social tensions between supporters and opponents. The main demands of the former were to establish the equality of spouses within the family, abolish matrimonial guardianship, ban polygamy, enshrine judicial divorce as the sole means of dissolving the marital bond, and guarantee women's rights with regard to alimony, child custody, and the marital home. To ease social tensions, the late Hassan II, in his 27 July 1992 speech, stated:

> I have heard and listened to complaints about the Moudawana or its application. I want you to know, my dear daughter, a Moroccan woman, that the Moudawana is first and foremost a matter for me. I am responsible for the Moudawana. Moroccan women are encouraged to contact the Royal Cabinet, women's associations, or the King of Morocco directly to share their observations, criticisms, grievances, and any other concerns regarding the Moudawana and its implications for women and their future. As the "Amir Al Mouminine,"[8] the King of Morocco is well-positioned to apply and interpret religion.[9]

On 29 September 1992, following the constitutional referendum held on 9 September, the late Hassan II reassured a group of women:

> Your concerns are valid, and we cannot prohibit what God has permitted nor make lawful what He has forbidden. (…). I will convene a group of "Ulemas" to whom I will request to prepare an answer and to suggest modifications to the points raised in your reports. Specific proposals will be presented to you, and if both parties can reach an agreement, we will then proceed to the necessary amendment of the articles of the Moudawana in order to achieve a better situation. In the absence of this agreement, it is unlikely that you will meet again, as this would be perceived as a failure to reach a consensus. If you do not reach an agreement, then I will take responsibility as "Amir Al Mouminine", who respects religion and the sunnah.[10]

In October 2003, King Mohamed VI initiated the formation of a commission to oversee the renovation of the former *Moudawana*. In his instructions to the commission preparing the text, he made it clear that he was bound by the principles of the Muslim religion and that he could not 'authorise what God has prohibited, nor prohibit what he has authorised'.[11] The values considered in this reform are those of tolerant Islam, which adopt Islam as the main reference point, without denying the relevance of human rights. In the event of silence or insufficiency of the written rule, the legislator invites the judges to refer to the prescriptions of the Malekite Rite and the jurisprudential effort. Article 400 states that:

[7] Moroccan Constitution (2011), arts. 41-42.

[8] Commander of the faithful and protector of religion.

[9] Benradi (2006), p. 31.

[10] Benradi (n.d.).

[11] Family Code of 2004, Official Bulletin number 5358 du 2 Ramadan 1426 (6 Oct 2005), p. 667.

> In the event that a specific issue has not been addressed in this Code, it is recommended that reference be made to the prescriptions of the Malekite Rite and/or the conclusions of the jurisprudential effort (Ijtihad) in order to provide concrete expression to the values of justice, equality, and harmonious coexistence in everyday life, as espoused by Islam.[12]

2.1 Legal and Socio-economic Changes Influencing the Family Institution in Morocco

The legal and socio-economic reforms adopted by the Kingdom of Morocco in recent years have introduced a significant transformation in the family structure and the labour market. The traditional family model, where the male partner is the primary breadwinner and the female partner is primarily responsible for domestic duties, is gradually being supplanted by a new model where, in most cases, especially in urban areas, both spouses are engaged in remunerative activities outside the home. Moreover, the Kingdom of Morocco is dedicated to the principles of equality and democracy, as evidenced by its ratification of numerous international conventions and treaties that promote women's rights.[13] Over the years, it has implemented a series of legal and institutional reforms, culminating in the enactment of the new family code in 2004 and the constitutional reform in 2011.[14]

2.2 Legal Reforms and Marital Stability

The 2004 Family Code established equal rights for men and women regarding the minimum marriage age. The Code stipulates that both sexes must be at least 18 years of age.[15] Previously, the minimum age for women was 15 years. Furthermore, the Code permits adult women to marry without the involvement of a matrimonial guardian.[16] Another significant alteration in the new *Moudawanna* pertains to the dissolution of marriage. The Moroccan legislature has made considerable strides in facilitating women's access to divorce by authorising unilateral divorce (*chikak*).[17] This novel form of dissolution, as described in the French translation, is divorce 'for reasons of discord'. If a woman seeks to dissolve her marriage, she must file a divorce

---

[12] Moroccan Family Code (*Moudawana*) (2004), art. 19, art. 400.

[13] See e.g. the Universal Declaration of Human Rights; Convention on the Political Rights of Women, International Covenant on Economic, Social and Cultural Rights, Convention on the Elimination of All Forms of Discrimination Against Women, Protocol to the International Convention on Political and Civil Rights, Protocol to the Convention on the Elimination of Discrimination Against Women, Optional Protocol to the Convention against Torture and the Paris Climate Agreement (2016).

[14] Moroccan Constitution 2011, art. 19.

[15] Moroccan Family Code (*Moudawana*) (2004), art. 19.

[16] Moroccan Family Code (*Moudawana*) (2004), art. 24.

[17] Moroccan Family Code (*Moudawana*) (2004), arts. 94–97.

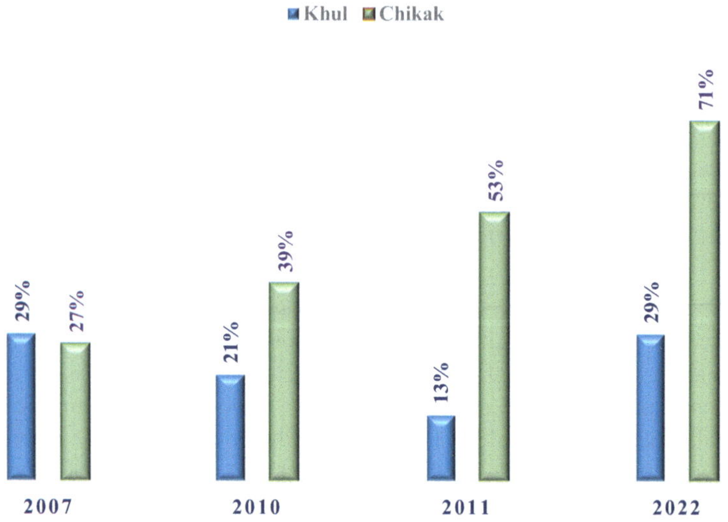

Fig. 1 Evolution of divorce grounds in per cent from 2007 to 2022. (Department of Justice, 2024, author's compilation)

application with the court. In this case, the court is obliged to accept and pronounce the divorce within a maximum period of six months from the date of the application. This period is contingent upon an assessment of each party's relative fault in order to assess the compensation due to the aggrieved spouse.[18] Indeed, the liberalisation and simplification of the legal rules of divorce provided spouses with the opportunity to opt for divorce more easily if the continuation of life with two no longer brought them the expected satisfaction. This legal revolution led to an increase in the divorce rate and upset the stability of the Moroccan family, which plays a crucial role in the balance of economic and social systems.[19]

As Fig. 1 illustrates, since the implementation of this reform, *chikak* divorces have proved popular. This can be attributed to a more favourable divorce modality for women, as evidenced by the data from the Ministry of Justice. Indeed, data from the Ministry of Justice indicates that the *chikak* divorce rate increased from 27 per cent in 2007 to 71 per cent in 2022. Concurrently, other forms of divorce, less favourable to women, for instance, *khul*,[20] declined.

Nevertheless, the existence of a 'right to divorce' is not the sole factor contributing to this increase. The socio-economic changes that Morocco has experienced in recent

---

[18] Moroccan Family Code (*Moudawana*) (2004), art. 97.

[19] Wolcott and Hughes (1999).

[20] A divorce by *Khul* is a separation agreement that allows spouses to set certain conditions, provided that they respect family law and the interests of the children; See Moroccan Family Code (*Moudawana*) (2004), art. 114, which states that Khul is a legal procedure through which a woman may petition for a divorce in exchange for the return of her husband's dowry.

years have, in part, undermined the objectives of the family institution and, consequently, marital stability. In its 2012 report, the World Bank states that the increase in the divorce rate in Morocco is strongly linked to economic, technological, and social changes.[21] The participation of women in economic and political life, along with their increased level of education, has resulted in a reduction in the benefits of marriage and an increase in the likelihood of divorce. This observation is corroborated by several theorists, including Heckert et al., who posit that:

> when women contribute more than 50 per cent of the couple's income, the probability of divorce is higher compared to "traditional" couples. When the female contribution is less than 25 per cent, the difference is not statistically significant. However, the risk of divorce is significantly higher when the woman's contribution is between 25 per cent and 50 per cent of the couple's income.[22]

Rogers identifies an inverted U-shaped relationship between a woman's contribution share of a couple's total income and the likelihood of seeking divorce.[23] Becker posits that an increase in labour supply increases the probability of divorce, as the reduction in investments specific to marriage (e.g., children, knowledge of the spouse's habits) would lead to a higher divorce rate.[24] The advantage of this occupational specialisation is less pronounced for highly engaged women in the labour market (with high income). Schwartz and Han demonstrate that the divorce rate is higher among couples with disparate levels of education and income, particularly if the woman's level of education surpasses that of her spouse.[25]

2.3 *The Impact of Socio-economic Factors on Traditional Norms of Marriage*

The socio-demographic data provided by the High Commission for Planning (HCP) demonstrate the profound transformations that have altered Morocco's economic, social, and political profile. These data indicate that the activity of women has increased significantly in recent years. They have gained a more prominent role in the labour market and have become more economically self-sufficient than before. The employment rate increased from 13 per cent in 1994 to 25 per cent in 2004 and is currently at 23 per cent. This expansion of female employment reflects the growth of the tertiary sector and the decline in employment in agricultural and industrial sectors for men. Further detail is provided in the following table, which shows changes in the employment rate between 2012 and 2022 according to gender and sector of activity.

[21] See El Fethouni and Hamelin (2016), p. 20, citing World Bank Morocco data.

[22] Heckert et al. (1998, p. 690).

[23] Rogers (2004, p. 59).

[24] Becker et al. (1977).

[25] Schwartz and Han (2014, p. 605).

Table 1 Employment rates by gender and sector of activity. (High Commission for Planning (HCP), 2023, les femmes marocaines en chiffres, author's compilation)

	2012		2022	
	Woman	Men	Woman	Men
Managers, executives, professionals	2,5	2,7	9,2	4
Technicians and intermediate professionals	7,5	3,7	6,7	2,4
Employees	7,8	9,1	13,2	11,7
Retailers, commercial and financial intermediaries	1,7	7,9	2,3	11,3
Farmers, fishermen, foresters and hunters	11,6	15	6,9	12,4
Artisans and qualified workers (except agricultural workers)	9,6	20,3	10,6	22,1
Farmers and fishermen (including qualified workers)	48,2	16,3	34,6	13,3
Plant and machine operators and assemblers	0,3	5	1,4	5,9
Non-agricultural workers, warehousemen and small tradesmen	10,9	17,9	15,1	16,9

While Table 1 depicts notable improvements in the female employment rate, suggesting progress toward resolving women's employment issues, women still experience higher long-term unemployment than men across all occupational categories. The political field has remained particularly closed to women for decades. The representation of women in legislative and executive institutions has progressed slowly, but it remains significant compared to the 2000s.

Figure 2 illustrates the evolution of the proportion of 'elected' positions held by women in the deliberative bodies of local councils, disaggregated by level and type of local council. In regional councils, the participation rate of women reached 38.5 per cent in 2021, a notable increase from 2.21 per cent in 2009. A similar pattern can be observed in the case of prefecture and provincial councils, where women's participation increased from 2.25 per cent in 2009 to over 35 per cent in 2021.

Moreover, in the field of education, notable advancements have been made, including an increase in the number of female students across all educational levels and improvements to school and university social services. In 2022, the proportion of women in higher education was 58.4 per cent, and the feminisation rate of graduates of the normal cycle of higher education exceeded 50 per cent in several fields. The proportion of women in these fields is as follows: 66 per cent in dentistry, 66.9 per cent in commerce and management, 61.7 per cent in medicine and pharmacy, 57.4 per cent in law and economics, and 56.1 per cent in technology.[26]

The socio-economic and political developments of recent decades have profoundly altered the traditional values and norms associated with marriage.[27] Couples increasingly expect one another to assume responsibility for a range of family matters, including managing children, social security contributions, household chores, and other domestic responsibilities.

[26] High Commission for Planning (2023).

[27] High Commission for Planning (2023).

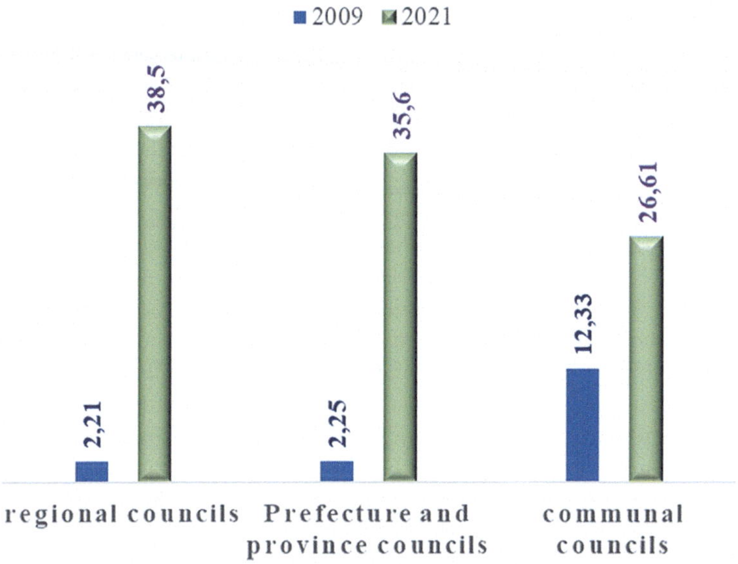

Fig. 2 Evolution of women's electoral representation in 2009 and 2021 (in per cent) (HCP, 2024, author's compilation)

Additionally, they are placing greater demands on one another regarding their professional careers and the ability to benefit from domestic economies of scale. Indeed, through her salaried work, the Moroccan woman has acquired autonomy. Aside from her economic independence, her social status is now defined by her profession rather than her husband's. This has implications for the institution of marriage, as it no longer has to guarantee the stability of the union.[28] The most recent report from the HCP corroborates this shift, indicating that the number of marriage certificates issued decreased from 307,000 in 2008 to 252,000 in 2022, representing a decline of over 22 per cent.[29] Additionally, the report highlights that while the number of marriages in younger generations has decreased, the remaining unions are more likely to result in divorce. The report indicates that the number of divorces has continued to increase since the adoption of the NFC, rising from 55,000 in 2008 to over 88,000 in 2022, a 60 per cent increase.

It is acknowledged that the participation of women in the labour market is not the primary factor driving the transformations of the couple. However, the increase in the participation rate of women in education, politics, and the labour force, which has occurred alongside a rise in their wage-earning capacity, and the increase in their enrollment rate and, consequently, their level of education, are among the significant contributing factors. These two phenomena are interrelated. The acquisition of a

[28] Forsé (1986) notes that some unmarried women, typically with a high level of education, are reluctant to enter into marriage, viewing it as an obstacle to their career strategy. However, they do not abandon the project of raising a child, and in this case, the one-child model is predominant.

[29] High Commission for Planning (2023)

diploma serves as an incentive for women to pursue employment opportunities. Concurrently, the growing participation of women in the labour market has prompted parents to educate their daughters in a manner that differs from previous generations. This often entails encouraging them to continue their studies for longer periods.[30]

The economic theory of the family posits that the higher the woman's level of education, the greater the risk of divorce.[31] Education allows women to better understand their obligations and rights.[32] If women feel that they are not respected in the relationship, education helps them enhance their critical thinking skills and stand up for their rights. Consequently, marriage is no longer the sole avenue for social advancement for women. In the majority of cases, it is now paid work that fulfils this role. Consequently, there is a potential for marriage to be marginalised, as it is only required to provide emotional 'comfort', which is a significant departure from its former social role.[33] Rootalu notes that when spouses are more educated, they have better socio-economic opportunities, making them more independent and able to support themselves.[34] Thus, unlike highly educated Estonian couples who tend to divorce less,[35] research has shown that couples from developing countries with higher levels of education tend to divorce more.

2.4 *Overview of Marriages in Morocco*

In Morocco, the only recognised marriage is a religious civil marriage that complies with the provisions of the *Moudawana.* A religious civil marriage combines religious and civil elements. All other forms of marriage are either not recognised or governed by stringent conditions.

Polygyny is permitted in Morocco, subject to several conditions. A man seeking to marry a second wife must establish, before a court of competent jurisdiction, exceptional and objective justifications for the second marriage[36] and the ability to treat both wives with absolute justice and fairness.[37] He must also demonstrate compliance with the requirement to inform his first wife of his intention to marry a second wife, as she reserves the right to stipulate in her marriage contract a provision that allows her to divorce her husband if he takes on another wife.[38] Notwithstanding the fulfillment of the stated conditions, the ultimate decision rests with the judge. In the event that an investigation is conducted pursuant to a request to marry a second

[30] High Commission for Planning (2023)

[31] Becker et al. (1977, pp. 1141–1187).

[32] King et al. (2008, pp. 907–922).

[33] Forsé (1986).

[34] Rootalu (2010).

[35] Rootalu (2010).

[36] Article 41 of the NFC; reasons could include illness or sterility of one's spouse.

[37] Article 41 of the NFC.

[38] Article 45 of the NFC.

wife, the authorities retain the prerogative to categorically reject authorisation of a polygynous marriage if they determine that the criteria for justice and fairness have not been satisfied, or are unlikely to be satisfied in the future. In practice, obtaining judicial authorisation for polygyny is highly challenging. The property rights of spouses in polygynous marriages follow the rules set out in the *Moudawana.*

Unregistered customary marriages have severe consequences: the parties cannot seek a divorce through the courts, cannot inherit from each other's estates, and the woman cannot receive spousal support during the waiting period. For children of such unions, however, the law recognises and legitimises them, entitling them to child support and inheritance rights. Paternity can be established through voluntary acknowledgement or evidentiary proof.

Generally, there is no presumption of marriage regardless of the duration of cohabitation. In very rare circumstances where the parties have gone through the marriage formalities but for some reason the marriage contract was not registered, a judge can retroactively ratify the marriage if the parties can prove the existence of the marriage contract and explain why it was not registered. Once the marriage is recognised, the matrimonial property rules discussed in this chapter will apply to the spouses.

3 Matrimonial Property in Moroccan Law

3.1 The Context of Islamic Law

Islamic law does not recognise any specific form of matrimonial property regime. The concept of matrimonial property is not present in Islamic law. The only known regime is the separation of property: each spouse is entitled to retain the disposition of all their property.[39] A woman is entitled to receive a dowry[40] (sadaq or mahr) and maintenance (nafaqa), according to a conception that corresponds to the patriarchal structure of the Muslim family. Islamic law has long recognised women as full-fledged civil persons, with the absolute freedom to dispose of their money and property. Like men, they are also entitled to financial independence to meet their social and economic needs. Wives are not required to disclose their income to their husbands. Husbands are not entitled to demand a share of their wives' income to contribute to household expenses, which are entirely the wives' responsibility.[41]

---

[39] Moroccan Family Code (*Moudawana*) (2004), art. 49.

[40] Moroccan Family Code (*Moudawana*) (2004), arts. 26-27. Article 26 defines *sadaq* as the financial contribution made by the husband to signify his willingness to marry and build a stable family. Article 27 allows the amount of *sadaq* to be agreed after consummation.

[41] There are four major schools of Sunni Islamic jurisprudence: Hanafi, Maliki, Shafi'i, and Hanbali; with differences and similarities between them in terms of marital requirements, prohibitions, etc. While Hanafism maintains a presence in Tunisia and Algeria, which were previously under Ottoman rule, Mâlikism remains the most prevalent school of Islamic jurisprudence in the region, and the only one officially recognised in Morocco.

Islamic law stipulates that a woman receives one-quarter of the inheritance if the deceased had no children and one-eighth if the deceased had children.[42] Furthermore, the husband also inherits from his wife. He inherits half of his deceased wife's estate if she bore no children and a quarter if she died with children. In practice, the spouses are treated as if they were separated from their property during their marriage.[43] The system of property separation is in place during marriage to protect spouses from unforeseen life events. This allows them greater freedom to invest, protects each spouse against their respective debts, and mitigates the consequences of such debts. However, upon the dissolution of the marriage, the original and final property holdings are compared to determine the extent to which each spouse was enriched during the marriage.

3.2 The Context of the New Moudawana

Article 35 of the former Moroccan *Moudawana* (1957 Personal Status Code) is explicit in this regard. The situation remains unchanged in the New *Moudawana*. Article 49 of the new code adopted this religious principle of separation of property and provides that 'both spouses have their own property'.

Spouses may, however, choose a community of acquests regime, as the law permits future spouses to enter into a separate marriage contract. This allows them to jointly manage the property acquired during the marriage and distribute it if necessary. Consequently, 'the spouses are permitted to agree upon the conditions for the acquisition and distribution of property acquired during their marriage'.[44]

3.3 Regime of Separation of Property in Morocco

The principle of separation of property applies to all Moroccan spouses, except Moroccans of the Jewish faith, who are subject to the rules of personal Hebrew Moroccan status.[45] Under this regime, each spouse's property is distinct from that of the other. Each spouse retains the administration, enjoyment, and free disposition of their personal property, whether acquired before or during the marriage or property derived from an inheritance, bequest, or gift. Each spouse is required to provide evidence of their respective property.

---

[42] Qur'an 4:11-12.

[43] Leroy (1983, p. 56).

[44] Moroccan Family Code (*Moudawana*) (2004), art. 49. *Adouls* must notify both spouses of the applicable property provisions at the time of marriage. If no agreement exists, courts apply general evidentiary rules, considering each spouse's contributions. *Adouls*, regulated under Law No. 16.03, are justice auxiliaries responsible for authenticating marriage, divorce, and inheritance documents. Since 2018, women have been permitted to practise as *Adouls*.

[45] Moroccan Family Code (*Moudawana*) (2004), art. 2.

This overview of the property separation regime reveals three major findings:

- **Protection of the spouse's property:** The separation of property is a legal mechanism that serves to preserve and protect the property of all individuals against the debts of another. When a spouse engages in commercial, artisanal, or liberal activities, the separation of property allows for the protection of the other spouse's property. This ensures that the creditors of the entrepreneurial spouse cannot seize the other spouse's property to obtain payment of the professional debts of the former.
- **Wealth autonomy:** This principle would permit each spouse to retain the administration, enjoyment, and free disposition of their personal property acquired before the marriage and to develop it independently of the property of the other spouse, with the consequences and the attendant effects. In the absence of invoices or deeds of ownership, there is a presumption of ownership of acquests corresponding to the traditional use that is made of the property by the man or the woman.[46] The significance of establishing the principle of the separation of property is to guarantee that neither spouse may exploit the other for their own benefit or use the institution of marriage to enrich themselves by deviating from the moral values set forth in the marriage contract.

In contrast, this system can have certain disadvantages, particularly for spouses who contribute to their children's education but have no income of their own. In the event of marital dissolution, whether by divorce or the death of the spouse, these individuals may find themselves lacking in resources due to the absence of community property. This can complicate the determination of property ownership. Since the enactment of the revised Family Code in 2004, spouses have the option of supplementing the separation of property with a separate agreement, distinct from the marriage certificate, in which the spouses 'may agree on the conditions for the growth and distribution of the property they have acquired during their marriage'.[47]

3.4 Invalid Marriage and Property Rights

Where a man enters into a subsequent marriage without complying with the polygyny requirements, the matrimonial property framework will not apply. The property rights of the parties to the subsequent marriage will be adjusted based on common law property principles. The wife of the first marriage reserves all her rights, including the right to seek a divorce resulting from her husband's bigamy. Harm is automatically

---

[46] Moroccan Family Code (*Moudawana*) (2004), art. 34. Property brought by the wife into the household under Jihaz or Chouar (e.g. wedding keychain and furniture) remains hers. In ownership disputes, general rules of evidence apply. In the absence of evidence, the husband's sworn statement prevails for items typically used by men, the wife's oath for those used by women, and joint-use items are divided after both swear oaths—unless only one is willing, in which case their statement prevails.

[47] Moroccan Family Code (*Moudawana*) (2004), art. 49.

recognised, and she is entitled to compensation. On the other hand, the second wife faces significant legal vulnerability, lacking meaningful legal protections. Her only recourse to recover any invested funds is to initiate legal action based on proof of her specific financial contributions. This process is characterised by its protracted nature, substantial financial demands, and an element of uncertainty.

However, as with a customary marriage, the children from this union are protected. The paternity of these children can be legally confirmed,[48] typically through the father's acknowledgement of his parental role. Consequently, they are entitled to receive child support and inherit from their father under certain circumstances.[49]

3.5 Marriage Contracts: Confusion and Misunderstanding

A prenuptial agreement is a contract between two individuals who are about to marry. It is a consensual deed that can be drawn up by the *Adouls*[50] at the time of drafting or after the marriage. It is introduced by article 49 of the Family Code, which requires the spouses to agree on the content of the clauses of the contract. These clauses must not be contrary to the fundamental objectives of the marriage. The spouses may opt for joint management of the property acquired during the marriage, with the stipulation that, in the event of dissolution of the marriage, the property will be shared equally between them. Since the *Moudawana* came into force in 2004, the number of contracts on the division of property at the time of marriage has been insignificant. For instance, in 2015, out of more than 301,000 marriage certificates, only 611 contracts were recorded (see Fig. 1). A similar trend was observed in 2019. Of 275,477 marriage certificates, only 699 were accompanied by a property division contract, a rate of 0.25%.[51]

The failure to draw up a contract for the division of property at the time of marriage calls into question the viability of Article 49. Two major contradictions are identified. Firstly, the provisions relating to the method of growth and distribution of property

---

[48] Moroccan Family Code (*Moudawana*) (2004), art. 154, 158-162.

[49] Under the 2004 *Moudawana*, where a marriage is declared invalid, paternal filiation (*nasab*) may nonetheless be established if the union was entered into in good faith (*shubha*), if there was cohabitation suggesting a marital relationship, or if the father acknowledges paternity (*iqrār*) or it is judicially proven, including through DNA testing. In such cases, the child retains full rights to maintenance and inheritance. See Moroccan Family Code (*Moudawana*) (2004), arts. 142-162.

[50] The *Adoul* is a person who exercises a liberal profession according to the specialisations and conditions defined by law no. 16.03 relating to the profession of *Adoul* and the specific legislative texts. This profession is one of the auxiliary professions of justice. *Adouls* are responsible for authenticating contracts that the Moroccan Family Code requires to be authenticated, such as marriage and repudiation contracts, as well as handling divorce and inheritance cases. *Adouls*' offices bear a resemblance to those of notaries and notaries public, though with minor distinctions. Historically, this profession was exclusively male, however, in 2018, a historic shift occurred as women were granted permission to practise and authenticate marriages, divorces and other legal documents for the first time.

[51] Ministry of Justice and Liberties (n.d.).

acquired during the marriage remain ambiguous and challenging to apply. This is especially evident in cases where family property is registered solely in the husband's name, and the wife is unable to prove that her salary has been used to cover household expenses. Secondly, the property division contract is an optional act, and the *Adouls* do not systematically inform spouses about the issue when they sign the marriage contract.

3.5.1 The Entitlement to a Proportion of the Family Property

In instances where a contract has not been established and a dispute over the ownership of property acquired during the marriage or its subsequent distribution, the spouses may resort to legal recourse, as outlined in the final paragraph of article 49 which states, that 'recourse shall be had to the general rules of evidence, while taking into account the work of each of the spouses and the efforts they have made and the burdens they have assumed with a view to the development of family property'.[52] Thus, the evaluation of these efforts and the work accomplished is a matter for a competent court, which must assess their importance, nature, and effects on the profits made during the marriage. However, in cases where the wife is unable to prove her claim against her husband, who, in most cases, has title to the property in dispute because it is solely in his name, case law is strict on the issue. Moroccan judges consider that all forms of evidence are admissible, provided they are sufficient and clear.

They refuse to use their power to make up for the lack of evidence. They decline to mandate an expert evaluation or initiate an investigation to ascertain each spouse's share of the family property. The onus, therefore, falls upon the plaintiff wife to prove her entitlement, and the court is not obliged to use its discretion to ascertain the veracity of the matrimonial property in question.[53] This failure to obtain recognition of the right to a share in the husband's assets is evidenced by the majority of actions brought by Moroccan women in such cases. As demonstrated in several cases referenced in academic works, this issue is complex and characterised by significant divergences among Moroccan courts.

In a case before the Family Court of Tangier, the wife petitioned for a 50% share of the property's value, which was under the husband's name. The couple had been married for some 35 years. The wife asserted that she had contributed to the construction of the property through her salary and a loan in her name. The Family Court of Tangier dismissed the wife's claim, citing insufficient evidence to substantiate her assertion. The loan contract in question did not provide evidence that the borrowed funds had been used to build the property in question.[54]

---

[52] Moroccan Family Code (*Moudawana*) (2004), art. 49.

[53] Cour suprême, Morocco, case no. 2276, judgment of 5 March 1997 (unpublished), cited in Le régime matrimonial en droit marocain, Cahiers du Larden 7, p. 219.

[54] Tangier Family Court, case no. 832/07/33 (02 Jan 2008), *Revue Justice de la Famille* no. 4, p. 241, cited in Darkaoui (2021).

In another case before the Casablanca Family Court, the wife asserts that she is entitled to 50% of the fortune accumulated by her husband during their marriage (millions of Moroccan dirhams). The parties had been married for 50 years. It was established by witnesses and the husband's confession that the wife had always worked alongside her husband on the farm. After declaring that the wife had indeed participated in the growth of her husband's funds, the Family Court of Meknes, however, specified that this material improvement of the husband was not due solely to the wife's participation and estimated a modest share, amounting to DH60,000 (equivalent to 6,000 US dollars), to the wife.[55]

Whilst the aforementioned rulings are rigorous in terms of establishing proof of the wife's participation in the growth of the family assets, the courts are more considerate and flexible in other cases. For instance, the Supreme Court, in a ruling dated 21 October 2009,[56] asserted that a wife who has contributed to the enhancement of the family's resources is entitled to demand compensation from her husband. Consequently, the supervision of construction projects and the collection of rent can be regarded as contributions to the family's assets, for which the wife must be compensated.

In another ruling issued on 21 February 2008, the Casablanca Family Court awarded the wife compensation for her domestic work. The court found that the wife's contribution to the husband's assets through her domestic labour constituted an active participation in their development. As a result, the court ruled that the wife was entitled to financial compensation for the work she had performed.[57]

Other rulings by courts in the south of Morocco take into account the efforts made by the wife alongside her husband during the marriage.[58] This is a form of customary law[59] to which judges often refer in disputes over the division of matrimonial property. This rule of division is closely aligned with a marital property regime that strongly favours the sharing of property acquired during the marriage. It is prevalent in certain regions of southern Morocco under the Arabic designation 'cadwasia' ya'[60] or the Berber appellation 'tamazzelte'. It recognises the wife's share, which varies from case to case, in the property acquired during the marriage, regardless of her other property rights against the husband in the event of the dissolution of the marriage or what she may inherit in the event of the husband's death. While the

---

[55] Meknes Family Court, case no. 516/04/5 (27 Sep 2007), *Revue Justice de la Famille* no. 4, p. 235, cited in Darkaoui (2021).

[56] Supreme Court, case no. 80/2/1/2008 (21 Oct 2009), *Almajala almaghribia lidirasat alkanouniya walqadaeya* (The Moroccan Review of Legal and Judicial Studies) no. 2 (Feb 2010), available at Jurisprudence.ma.

[57] Casablanca Family Court (21 Feb 2008), quoted in Achtibi (2010), p. 108, as cited in Darkaoui (2021).

[58] Marrakech Court of Appeal, case no. 1346/83 (30 Mar 1984), unpublished, cited in Loukili and Zirari-Devif (2004).

[59] The judge assesses the wife's contribution in accordance with Islamic legal principles pertaining to evidence, including testimony and oaths. His power to evaluate the consideration to be allocated to the wife was not constrained.

[60] This practice is not limited by the general rules of evidence.

Table 2 Components of the property each spouse enjoys separately.

Wife	· Property acquired before the marriage contract. · Debts owed to third parties. · Gifts, inheritance, wills, or personal compensation. · Endowments and gifts given by the husband at the engagement and conclusion of the marriage contract. · Furniture, luggage, jewellery, and other objects brought to the marital home.
Husband	· Property acquired before the marriage contract. · Debts owed to third parties. · Gifts, inheritance, wills, or personal compensation.

system provides for the wife's share, each spouse also retains certain categories of property individually. A summary of these categories is provided in Table 2.

3.5.2 Role of *Adouls* in the Awareness of Spouses

The contract for the management and distribution of property is an optional agreement that can be drawn up at any time, even during the marriage. However, it is during the conclusion of the marriage contract that the '*Adouls* inform both parties'[61] of the possibility of concluding the contract. As legal professionals and drafters of the marriage contract, the *Adouls* are the primary actors influencing the choice of regime.[62] However, in practice, few *Adouls* advise couples on the specifics of this contract at the time of marriage certificate issuance. The Family Code does not impose penalties on *Adouls* who limit this information, making it difficult for couples to prove they were not informed.

Furthermore, the *Adouls* often include the phrase 'both parties have been notified of the provisions of section 49' in the marriage certificate, which may lead to confusion. This informational failure can be explained from a psychological perspective. Typically, the marriage certificate is concluded during the festivities. At this juncture, the *Adouls* tend to avoid discussing with spouses the possibility of the dissolution of the relationship,[63] and the implications this may have for the division of property. The spouse can perceive this as a negative signal. Moreover, the celebratory atmosphere and the significant presence of families and relatives are not conducive to serious, open, and amicable discussions regarding the management of shared assets. From an economic perspective, selecting a marriage contract entails a financial cost, as it necessitates drafting a separate contract from the marriage certificate. This contract will only be granted if the anticipated benefit of sharing property outweighs the associated costs on the day of the marriage.

[61] Moroccan Family Code (*Moudawana*) (2004), art. 49.

[62] Cornu (1985, p. 30).

[63] Casman (1991, p. 458).

4 Is the Marriage Contract Economically Justified?

Despite its economic significance, the decision to enter into a marriage contract has received limited attention in economic literature.[64] In 1981, unit household models posited that couples behaved like a single entity.[65] In this context, the marriage contract is not necessary because the rules of resource allocation do not influence household choices. In Becker's model, the individual is rational and chooses to marry when the optimal utility of withdrawing from the marriage exceeds that of remaining alone.

While Becker's studies provide a valuable foundation for research into the economics of marriage and divorce, it is important to note that these studies were conducted when most women were not yet participating in the labour market. In this context, a new model of collective households has been developed,[66] which posits that the marriage contract can influence the behaviour of couples. The contract may favour a more or less equal sharing of resources within the household and encourage or discourage specialisation within the relationship. In other words, spouses negotiate their marriage contract to define their shares, and the outcome depends on the bargaining power of each spouse, which is influenced by 'distribution variables'.[67]

A third-generation model developed emphasises the importance of laws governing divorce, which interact with laws on the type of marital regime.[68] It is their combined action that influences the choices of individuals. This concept is further elucidated by Cigno, who posits that marriage serves as a means for couples to reciprocally compensate the individual who invests in intangible capital (e.g., education of children and domestic work).[69] This interdependence between the economy and the law implies that the law largely governs the conjugal relationship, as the spouses are unable to terminate it without first obtaining a judicial decree. State intervention in marriage circumvents the high transaction costs associated with the formation of a marital union between a man and a woman.[70]

As with any long-term contract involving specific investments, the marriage contract exposes the parties to a risk of opportunism. One of the problems with this long-term contractual relationship is that the investments made by the spouses in the context of marriage would generate gains whose distribution is asymmetrical over time. This asymmetry would render the husband's promise to fulfil his long-term maintenance role ineffective, thereby undermining the efficacy of the marriage assurance for the wife. The potential for conflict arises from the possibility that one spouse may adopt a strategic approach that encourages him to breach the contract

---

[64] Becker (1973), Becker et al. (1977) were among the first researchers to explore the nexus between marriage and divorce economics.

[65] Becker (1981).

[66] Chiappori et al. (2002, pp. 37–72).

[67] Chiappori et al. (2002, pp. 37–72).

[68] Clark (1999, pp. 41–54).

[69] Cigno (2012, pp. 193–213).

[70] Allen (1990, pp. 171–191).

when the other spouse is entitled to the largest share of the surplus generated by the marriage. The husband's optimal strategy is to leave his wife without compensation once she has made her contribution to the marriage.[71]

4.1 *Forms of Opportunism In Marriage*

Opportunism is revealed when one of the parties can terminate the relationship without fulfilling the obligations that were agreed upon at the beginning of the marriage. Two distinct categories of opportunism have been identified:[72] the green grass effect (also known as the greener grass effect) and the black widow effect (also known as the Black Widow effect). Schematically, the 'greener grass elsewhere' effect leads affluent men to abandon women from disadvantaged backgrounds. In this case, the husband initiates the dissolution of the marriage if the potential gains of a new marriage (or celibacy) exceed the potential gains of the first marriage. This is because he is not required to compensate his first wife for the losses she suffers as a result of the divorce. The "black widow" effect refers to the opposite situation where the financial compensation that the wife can claim makes it advantageous for her to initiate the dissolution of the marriage and enter into a new relationship whose net profits would have been lower in the absence of compensation.

Opportunism may be defined as the appropriation of quasi-annuities from the marriage contract by one of the parties involved. Cohen[73] posits that the quasi-annuity of a married individual, regardless of gender, corresponds to the difference between the gains they receive from marriage and the gains they should receive to maintain the union, once their investments in marriage are made. According to the same author, virtual annuities can have different sources, related to the reasons why people marry and the types of damages that the breach of the contract would impose on them. Spouses may receive quasi-annuities from investments in specific marital assets, such as children. Similarly, since women are supposed to 'depreciate' faster than men in the marriage market, they will be able to receive a quasi-annuity. The question thus arises as to how the beneficiary of these quasi-annuities may be protected from the potential destruction by their spouse?

For instance, one spouse may be compelled to suspend their professional career, or at least pursue it on a part-time basis, in order to dedicate themselves fully to domestic duties and the education of children.[74] This results in two consequences: first, the spouse's income within the household is diminished, and second, the spouse active in the labour market and thriving professionally accumulates wealth for their own benefit.[75] This concept encompasses the notion of 'patrimonial harm related to

[71] Geddes and Zak (2002, pp. 119–137).

[72] Dnes (1999, pp. 533–552).

[73] Cohen (1987, pp. 267–303).

[74] Baugniet (2012, pp. 1–8).

[75] Baugniet (2012, p. 375).

married life,' which is divided into two components: the first component is 'unpaid economic collaboration and its impact on professional career and earnings prospects after marriage.'[76] The second component is 'the unintended confusion of wealth and its impact on the capital of each partner during the marriage'.[77]

Another common example is the assisting spouse who invests and helps her husband's business grow, especially his wealth, for free most of the time.[78] This arrangement carries significant risk, as in the event of divorce, the assisting spouse may have contributed to the growth of the other spouse's assets, particularly where a business is involved, without any legal entitlement to the resulting benefits. The business-owning spouse ultimately retains the gains, to the detriment of the contributing spouse who invested without compensation. In the absence of a legal mechanism available to the injured spouse, the only recourse for financial compensation may be the doctrine of unjust enrichment. This legal principle permits the economically disadvantaged spouse, who has suffered impoverishment to the benefit of the economically strong spouse without just cause, to seek restitution for the loss incurred.

It is important to note that one of the primary goals of the new *Moudawana* is the establishment of a novel legal framework for the administration of wealth procured during marriage. The reforms advance a vision of fairness that rebalances the quasi-annuities and ensures that each spouse obtains a fair proportion of property jointly acquired. Perhaps the most significant improvement is the classification of housework by women as a form of contribution capable of growing the family assets. Furthermore, upon the death of one spouse, the surviving spouse is entitled to retain the marital residence, subject to the specific regulations prescribed by law. However, with a long-term contract, it is unlikely that women will benefit as the generous property relations framework in the *Moudawana* may cease to apply to them in the absence of a strong basis on which courts may disregard contracts to protect women.

5 Recommendations

As demonstrated above, the 2004 Family Code established the principle of equality between spouses. Nevertheless, legal and socio-economic shortcomings persist, underscoring the need for a comprehensive and inclusive reform approach to address the socio-economic needs of wives, particularly in rural areas, and to ensure adequate protection in the event of marital dissolution. In light of these considerations, this chapter explores three avenues for reflection, namely:

---

[76] Leleu (2018, p. 67).

[77] Leleu (2018, p. 67).

[78] Baugniet (2012, pp. 1–8).

5.1 *Legal Reforms Must Be Part of an Inclusive Development Process*

The sharing of family property is not an end in itself in terms of meeting women's expectations, as the benefits of marriage can never, with rare exceptions, save women from poverty if they have wealthy spouses. Improving the situation of women and demanding equality between men and women cannot be achieved without at the same time promoting social equality in general. It is a lamentable fact that in 2023, Morocco will be ranked 120th in the Human Development Index (HDI), as determined by the United Nations Development Programme (UNDP). This classification is predicated on a multitude of criteria, including social inequality, poverty, educational attainment, and the efficacy of the healthcare system, among others. In this sense, it is imperative that legal reforms be incorporated into a comprehensive global development process, encompassing a robust educational system, adequate employment opportunities, and the enhancement of economic conditions for women, particularly rural women. These measures are crucial to ensure that women are equipped with the necessary resources to cope with the potential dissolution of their marriage.

5.2 *Reinforcing Procedures to Promote Understanding of the Rights and Obligations Associated with Marriage*

While it is indeed the case that the *Moudawana* grants a greater number of rights to women, the inadequacy of the means for publicising and raising awareness of the law has not enabled Moroccans, and particularly Moroccan women, to properly grasp their new rights. Improving knowledge of the new provisions and legal procedures in the *Moudawana* requires a wide-ranging campaign to raise awareness and popularise the rights and obligations of spouses. Furthermore, field surveys are necessary to gauge public perceptions of the matrimonial property regime, property division contracts, and other related matters. The purpose of this approach is to facilitate the establishment of mechanisms by competent authorities for assessing the effort made by the wife in building up the family assets.

5.3 *Review the Applicability of Article 49 of the Moudawana Regarding the System of Proof in the Absence of a Property Division Contract*

It is important to acknowledge that, despite the efforts made to draw up a contract for the division of property between spouses, article 49 of the NCF remains ambiguous and difficult to apply, particularly in cases where the family property is registered solely in the husband's name and the wife is unable to prove her participation in the growth of the family assets. This difficulty constitutes a significant obstacle to the assessment and safeguarding of the injured wife's pecuniary rights, insofar as the Moroccan courts adopt a stringent stance with regard to the applicable evidence regime. This has resulted in a certain degree of divergence among the various courts in Morocco. While some rulings take into account the efforts made by the wife within the family home when calculating compensation for her participation in household chores, others are rigorous about the wife's contribution to the family's assets. To address the asymmetry of information between spouses and to establish a certain degree of social and financial justice between them, it would be wise to consider the following measures:

- New assessment mechanisms, including expert appraisals and surveys, should be employed to determine the respective shares of each spouse in the family assets.
- Provide the family justice system with sufficient, qualified human resources and equipment to improve the application of article 49 of the NFC.
- Opening up to other disciplines encompassing sociology, economics and anthropology to correctly assess each spouse's share and do justice to the injured party.

6 Conclusion

This chapter has presented an economic interpretation of two significant legal reforms included in the *Moudawana*, which are directly related to marital stability. The first reform pertains to divorce proceedings, while the second concerns the issue of marital property during and at the end of marriages. These reforms appear to be the inaugural step in a legal and social process that seeks to enshrine gender equality and women's rights within the family institution. It permits women to apply for the dissolution of marriage, regardless of their husband's fault. It also protects the economic rights of wives in the event of the dissolution of the conjugal bond by introducing the principle of division of property acquired during the marriage.

This chapter has observed that twenty years after the new *Moudawana* came into force, a series of malfunctions have occurred, some of which may be unexpected or undesirable and incompatible with today's society. These include a remarkable increase in the divorce rate. Moreover, in addition to its limited use, the marriage contract has faced significant challenges in establishing a clear and comprehensive legal framework. Issues persist regarding spouses' awareness of their rights and obligations, the fair distribution of property acquired during the marriage, and protection against the opportunistic termination of the contract. These shortcomings have led to increased scrutiny of Article 49 of the New Family Code, particularly in relation to the division of property.

More reforms are therefore needed. In the King's speech on the occasion of the Feast of the Throne in 2022, he called for the constitution of a body responsible for renewing the 2004 Family Code. As a religious leader, HM the King reiterated in his address that he is unable to 'authorise what God has prohibited, nor prohibit what he has authorised'.[79] This stance provoked a strong response from various societal actors, including political parties and civil society organisations.

On 30 March, 2024, a report on the proposed amendments to the 2004 Family Code was submitted to the Head of Government for submission to HM the King. These amendments will undoubtedly impact the legal provisions on marriage and divorce, as well as the protection of children's interests, while ensuring equity between men and women in their respective rights and obligations.

The King then referred proposals concerning religious texts to the Supreme Council of Ulemas, the body with a monopoly on fatwas (religious opinions), of which he is President. Following a six-month period, on 24 December 2024, the Authority submitted to the Sovereign a report on its activities, presented in two volumes. The initial volume addressed 'proposals relating to the Family Code', while the subsequent volume addressed 'proposals of a general nature' that were not directly associated with the Code's text, but rather contingent on its optimal implementation. The Forum submitted a total of 139 amendment proposals, categorised into seven books of the Code.

In the context of the property separation regime, two main proposals are worthy of mention. Firstly, the introduction of a novel framework for managing property acquired during the marital relationship, with the wife's domestic labour being recognised as a contribution to the development of that property. Secondly, it is proposed that the husband or wife be granted the right to retain the marital residence in the event of the death of the other, subject to the stipulated legal conditions.

References

Allen D (1990) An inquiry into the state's role in marriage. J Econ Behav Organ 13:171–191

Attounissia Blog (2006) Participation in Property between Spouses (17 December 2006). Available at: https://attounissia.blogspot.com/2006/12/. Accessed 3 Nov 2025

Baugniet N (2012) La séparation de biens avec participation aux acquêts: rêve d'un régime matrimonial idéal? In: Taymans J-F (ed) Liber Amicorum Jean-François Taymans. Editions Larcier, Bruxelles, pp 1–8

BeckerGS(1973) Atheoryofmarriage:PartI. J Political Econ81(4),813–846.

Becker GS, Landes EM, Michael RT (1977) An economic analysis of marital instability. J Political Econ 85(6):1141–1187. https://www.jstor.org/stable/1837421

Becker GS (1981) A treatise on the family. Harvard University Press, Cambridge

Benradi M (n.d.) Les révisions du code du statut personnel: quels acquis pour les femmes marocaines? Faculté de Droit Rabat Souissi

Benradi M (2006) Dynamique sociale et évolution des statuts des femmes au Maroc. Rapport Prospective Maroc 2030, Haut Commissariat au Plan.

Casman H (1991) Équité et bonne foi dans les relations patrimoniales entre époux—Réflexions sur l'élaboration d'un contrat de mariage juste. Revue trimestrielle de droit de la famille 4:450–462

[79] King Mohammed VI (30 July 2022), Discours à la Nation à l'occasion de la Fête du Trône, Le Matin. Available at: https://lematin.ma/express/2022/sm-roi-adresse-samedi-discours-nation-loccasion-fete-tro/379159.html.

Chiappori P-A, Fortin B, Lacroix G (2002) Marriage market, divorce legislation, and household labor supply. J Political Econ 110(1):37–72
Cigno A (2012) Marriage as a commitment device. Rev Econ Househ 10(2):193–213
Clark S (1999) Law, property, and marital dissolution. Economic Journal 109(454):41–54
Cohen L (1987) Marriage, divorce, and quasi rents; or, "I gave him the best years of my life". J Leg Stud 16(2):267–303
Cornu G(1985) Lesrégimesmatrimoniaux.7éme.Éd.,Paris,P.U.F. p.30.
Dnes AW (1999) Applications of economic analysis to marital law: concerning a proposal to reform the discretionary approach to the division of marital assets in England and Wales. International Rev L & Econ 19:533–552
El Fethouni Y, Hamelin N (2016) The effect of media and economics on the change of divorce rate in Morocco. Int J Acad Res Reflect 4(3):20–30
Forsé M (1986) Le recul du mariage. Observations et diagnostics économiques: revue de l'OFCE 16:217–234. https://doi.org/10.3406/ofce.1986.1068
Geddes R, Zak P (2002) The rule of one-third. J Leg Stud 31:119–137
Haut-Commissariat au Plan (2023) Les femmes marocaines en chiffres. https://www.hcp.ma/region-agadir/docs/docs/La%20femme%20marocaine%20en%20chiffres,%202023.pdf. Accessed 1 Nov 2025
Heckert DA, Nowak TC, Snyder KA (1998) The impact of husbands' and wives' relative earnings on marital disruption. J Marriage Fam 60(3):690–703
King K, Fogle L, Logan-Terry A (2008) Family language policy. Lang Linguist. Compass 2(5):907–922. https://doi.org/10.1111/j.1749-818X.2008.00076.x
Leleu Y-H (2018) La réforme des régimes matrimoniaux par la loi du 22 juillet 2018: présentation, évaluation. In: La réforme du droit des régimes matrimoniaux. Editions Larcier, Bruxelles, p 67
Leroy J (1983) Perspectives sur le devenir du régime de la séparation de biens. Revue trimestrielle de droit civil
Loukili M, Zirari-Devif M (2004) Le Nouveau Code marocain de la Famille: une réforme dans la continuité. Dans Yearbook of Islamic and Middle Eastern Low Online. Brill
Loukili M (2016) Le régime matrimonial en droit marocain. Cahiers du LADREN 7(1):216–220
Rogers S (2004) Dollars, dependency, and divorce: four perspectives on the role of wives' income. J Marriage Fam 66:59–74. https://doi.org/10.1111/j.1741-3737.2004.00005.x
Rootalu K (2010) The effect of education on divorce risk in Estonia. Trames 14(1):21–33. http://www.kirj.ee/public/trames_pdf/2010/issue_1/trames-2010-1-21-33.pdf. Accessed 21 Oct 2025
Schwartz CR, Han H (2014) The reversal of the gender gap in education and trends in marital dissolution. Am Sociol Rev 79(4):605–629. https://doi.org/10.1177/0003122414539682
Wolcott I, Hughes J (1999) Towards understanding the reasons for divorce. Working Paper No. 20. Australian Institute of Family Studies, Melbourne. https://aifs.gov.au/research/research-reports/towards-understanding-reasons-divorce. Accessed 21 Oct 2025

Hicham Hafid is a Professor-Researcher at Mohammed V University, Rabat, within the Institute of African Studies (IEA), and Vice-President of the Moroccan Association of Economic Sciences (AMSE). His research interests include family law, regional integration, trade policy evaluation, and economic development in Africa. He has authored books and reports on governance and immigration, published articles in leading academic journals, and participated in international conferences on development. Hafid has conducted field missions across East, West, and Central Africa. His current research focuses on strengthening Afro-African cooperation and enhancing the continent's productive capacities. He holds a PhD from the University of Aix Marseille III, obtained in 2010.

Bijural System: Cameroon

The Resolution of Disputes Over Ownership of Marital Property Under the Common Law System in Cameroon

Fomchang Valery

Abstract Ownership of marital property remains a major source of litigation between spouses in Cameroon, particularly where the title to matrimonial property is held in one spouse's name. Despite the evolution of spousal roles and contributions, courts and legal commentators have historically attributed ownership to the party named on the title deed, often to the exclusion of the non-titled spouse. Against this backdrop, and within the context of Cameroon's bijural legal system, this chapter investigates how the courts determine ownership and resolve disputes over jointly and separately owned marital property. The chapter focuses on the forms of marital property ownership under the common law system, the determination of property rights before, during, and after marriage, and the legal principles governing the distribution of property. This chapter notes the courts' use of ancillary relief mechanisms, such as lump sum orders and property adjustment orders, to address economic disparities following divorce or separation. The chapter recommends the codification and clarification of judicially developed equitable principles to harmonise practice across jurisdictions and ensure that marital property rights reflect the lived realities of marriage, as well as the values of fairness and gender equality.

F. Valery (✉)
Faculty of Law and Political Science, University of Bertoua, Bertoua, Cameroon
e-mail: evangval1@yahoo.fr

A. F. Hammond and P. Batariwah (eds.), *The Law on Marital Property in Africa*, Ius Gentium: Comparative Perspectives on Law and Justice 138,
https://doi.org/10.1007/978-3-032-19358-2_12

1 Introduction

Cameroon is a country of rich natural, cultural, linguistic, and legal diversity. Located in Central Africa, Cameroon spans an area of approximately 475,442 square kilometres, stretching from the Atlantic coast in the southwest to the Lake Chad basin in the north. The country encompasses a diverse range of landscapes, including coastal plains, dense rainforests, savannas, and mountainous highlands. Cameroon's total population is estimated to be over 27 million, with more than 250 ethnic groups and languages.[1]

Cameroon's legal system is especially distinct on the African continent. While the legal system of many countries is dominated by one legal tradition substantially altered or modified to meet the socio-economic needs as well as the social and cultural aspirations of their people, Cameroon's legal system is constructed on the scaffolding of two major legal traditions: the French civil law tradition and the English common law tradition. This is unsurprising when considering the country's history. Formerly a German territory, Cameroon was governed by the French and English until its independence in the 1960s. Its status as the paradigmatic bijural legal system in Africa goes in lockstep with its status as a bilingual country, with French and English recognised as its official languages.

The diversity of Cameroon has resulted in a multiplicity of customary laws and statutory laws governing marriage, divorce, and spousal property rights. In the interstices lies Islamic law, which exerts some influence among Muslims. This chapter does not intend to explore the full scope of Cameroon's pluralism in family law, however. Apart from statutes that apply generally, Cameroon's bijural legal system does not mean that civil law and common law apply to everyone irrespective of their geographical location. The application of any system of law is defined and limited to certain geographical locations. Thus, the civil law system is applicable to the French areas, and the common law is limited to Anglophone Cameroon. This chapter examines marital property rights within this bijural legal system, noting the place of the English principles on property within the system and the extent of their application as a way of managing conflict between the two legal traditions. It should, however, be noted that this discussion substantially relies on English law, as Anglophone Cameroonian law generally follows the prevailing practice in England at any given point in time.

This chapter is divided into five sections. Section 1 is the introduction. Section 2 discusses Cameroonian legal pluralism both generally and in the specific context of family law. It concisely identifies the matrimonial property regimes recognised in Cameroon. Section 3 examines marital property rights in Anglophone Cameroon, highlighting the promotion of equality through constitutional recognition and the ratification of key international instruments, including the Convention on the Elimination of All Forms of Discrimination Against Women (CEDAW) and the Protocol to the African Charter on Human and Peoples' Rights on the Rights of Women in Africa (Maputo Protocol). Section 4 addresses the property rights of spouses in customary

[1] CIA (2024).

marriages. Section 5 makes recommendations for change, specifically calling for the introduction of independent legal frameworks for marital property rights in England that are not wholly dependent on English and French legal development, as exists in the status quo.

2 Legal Pluralism in Cameroon

The introduction of the English common law and civil law systems into Cameroon was first guaranteed by the League of Nations under Article 22 of its Covenant, which gave the former German Cameroon to Britain and France as a mandated territory.[2] Secondly, article 9 of the League of Nations Mandate Agreement with France and Britain granted Britain and France the authority to administer and legislate in accordance with their laws, contingent on modifications to accommodate local conditions.[3] When Cameroon became a Trust Territory, article 9 was replaced in 1946 by articles 4 and 5 of the Trusteeship Agreements with France and Britain, respectively.[4] Article 5(a) relating to Britain provided that Britain shall have 'full powers of legislation, administration and jurisdiction in the Territory' to be administered in accordance with its laws, subject to modifications necessitated by local conditions and subject to the United Nations Charter and the Trusteeship Agreement. Article 4(1) of the Agreement relating to France was similarly worded, except that it did not require French law to be modified to accommodate local conditions. This history explains why Cameroon has remained a bijural state. That is, one in which both the rules of English law[5] and the civil law are applicable.

Customary law in Cameroon occupies a paradoxical space. It is recognised in principle but often marginalised in practice.[6] Its status is shaped by a complex interplay of colonial legacies, constitutional provisions, and tensions between legal pluralism and state centralism.[7] The 1996 Constitution of Cameroon acknowledges traditional values that conform to democratic principles, human rights, and statutory law.[8] Historically rooted in the traditions and practices of over 250

[2] Ngoh (2001, pp. 1–2).

[3] Fuashi (2012, p. 62).

[4] United Nations General Assembly (1946).

[5] This explains the application of the English Common Law and the English Law of Property Act of 1925 in Cameroon. As to the frequency with which the Cameroonian courts will apply the English common law, see the provision of Section 11 of the Southern Cameroon High Court Law 1955 that provides: 'Subject to the provision of any written law and in particular this section and of section 10, 15 and 22 of this law: The common law, the doctrines of equity and the statute of general application which were in force in England on the first day of January 1900, shall in so far as they relate to any matter with respect to which the legislature of the Southern Cameroons is for the time being competent to make laws, be in force within the jurisdiction of the court'.

[6] Kiye (2021, p. 2).

[7] Gebeye (2017).

[8] Constitution of Cameroon 1996, art. 1(2).

ethnic groups, customary law was the dominant legal system prior to colonial rule. However, the Germans, French, and British introduced civil and common law systems that marginalised indigenous legal norms.[9] Post-independence efforts to unify Cameroon's legal system have further complicated the status of customary law, often relegating it to a subsidiary role despite its continued relevance in rural communities and among traditional authorities.[10] The 1996 Constitution of Cameroon provides limited recognition of customary law. Article 1(2) authorises the state to "recognize and protect traditional values that conform to democratic principles, human rights and the law."[11] This conditional endorsement reflects a philosophical tension: while customary law is acknowledged as part of Cameroon's multicultural heritage, its legitimacy is contingent upon alignment with modern legal and human rights standards. This has led to the selective incorporation of customary norms, particularly in areas such as marriage and land tenure, where recent legislation has sought to formalise traditional practices.[12] Under Law No. 2024/016 of 23 December 2024, the status of customary unions is elevated to that of civil marriages on the condition that they are declared and transcribed into the civil register, thereby affording couples married under customary rites the same legal protections and rights previously reserved for civil marriages.[13]

The fragmentation of Cameroon's legal system between civil, common, and customary law has led to legal pluralism, but not parity. Customary courts, once central to dispute resolution, have seen their jurisdiction curtailed, especially in criminal matters. The Judicial Organisation Ordinance of 2006 and the Criminal Procedure Ordinance of 2005 effectively removed criminal jurisdiction from customary courts, further diminishing their role.[14] This reflects a philosophical shift toward legal uniformity and centralisation, often at the expense of community-based justice systems.

Despite these challenges, customary law remains resilient in practice. In rural areas, traditional leaders continue to administer justice based on local customs, particularly in matters of family law, succession, and land rights.[15] The persistence of customary law underscores its philosophical foundation in communal values, restorative justice, and social cohesion. However, without comprehensive reform and more precise integration mechanisms, customary law risks further marginalisation.

[9] Fombad (2015).

[10] Kiye (2021, p. 3).

[11] Constitution of Cameroon 1996, art. 1(2).

[12] An instance of this is the recent enactment of Law No. 2024/016 of 23 December 2024, which formally recognises customary marriages and integrates traditional practices into the national legal framework.

[13] See Law No. 2024/016 of 23 December 2024 Organising the Civil Registration System in Cameroon, art. 49; see also Law Library of Congress (2025).

[14] See Judicial Organization Ordinance No. 2006/015 of 29 December 2006 and read with Criminal Procedure Code, Law No. 2005 of 27 July 2005. These statutes reorganized the judicial system and centralized criminal jurisdiction under formal courts such as the Courts of First Instance and High Courts, thereby limiting the role of customary courts to civil and family matters.

[15] See generally, Ndeh (2020, pp. 1–11).

2.1 Family Law in Cameroon

Cameroon's family law is a multifaceted legal structure shaped by its colonial past, cultural diversity, and modern legal developments.[16] It draws from four distinct systems: civil law, common law, customary law, and Islamic law.[17] Each system holds sway depending on geographic location and the nature of the dispute.[18] Civil law, rooted in French colonial influence, dominates family matters in Francophone regions, while British-derived common law governs similar issues in Anglophone zones, such as the North West and South West.[19] Customary law, rooted in the traditions of various ethnic communities, plays a significant role in regulating marriage, inheritance, and family responsibilities, although it often raises concerns about gender equity and human rights.[20] In areas with Muslim majorities, Islamic law regulates personal status matters, including marriage and divorce, offering yet another legal dimension within Cameroon's pluralistic framework.[21]

Marriage in Cameroon is legally recognised through three distinct forms: civil, customary, and religious. Civil marriage, conducted under the Civil Code, requires formal registration and typically assumes monogamy, unless parties explicitly agree otherwise.[22] Customary marriages is more fluid, governed by local traditions that often permit polygyny and place heavy emphasis on familial negotiation and bride price.[23] Under Islamic law, marriages are potentially polygynous. Regardless of the type of marriage, the law mandates mutual consent and a minimum age of 18 for both parties to safeguard personal autonomy and prevent child marriage.[24]

Divorce proceedings reflect the dual legal structure of the country. Under civil and common law, divorce may be granted on grounds such as adultery, abandonment, mutual consent, or irretrievable breakdown of the marriage.[25] Customary law provides its own procedures, which vary by ethnic group and can sometimes prioritise communal and patriarchal interests over individual rights.[26] When deciding child

---

[16] See generally, Fombad (2015).

[17] Fombad (2007).

[18] Fombad (2007).

[19] Ngwafor (1993, p. 122).

[20] It has been noted by Ngwafor for instance, the varying forms of customary law in Cameroon have a commonality of denying women property ownership rights. In traditional societies in Cameroon, she is also looked upon as her husband's property. See Ngwafor (1990, pp. 297–298).

[21] Generis Global (2024). These regions include the North Region, the Adamawa Region and part of the West Region especially among the Bamoun people of Foumban.

[22] Civil Status Registration Ordinance No. 81/02 of 29 June 1981, s 49. Section 49 of the CSRO requires that parties to a civil marriage declare their choice of marital regime either monogamy or polygamy at the time of registration. This statute is the legal foundation for civil marriage procedures in Cameroon.

[23] Ndangoh (2022, pp. 1–11).

[24] Civil Status Registration Ordinance No. 81/02 of 29 June 1981, s. 52(1).

[25] Matrimonial Causes Act 1973, s. 1(2).

[26] Kiye (2015, p. 75).

custody, courts consistently apply the principle of the child's best interests, and both parents retain legal authority unless compelling reasons dictate otherwise.[27]

It must be noted that when a marriage is declared null and void in Cameroon, the law treats the union as invalid. Nonetheless, under the Cameroon Civil Code, the marriage may still produce civil effects for a spouse and children born of the union if the spouse entered into the marriage in good faith.[28] In such circumstances, a court may consider the property rights of the innocent spouse and children and apply partition or succession rules to divide jointly-held or undivided property equitably, taking into account the spouse's good-faith status and contribution.[29]

In Anglophone Cameroon, divorce proceedings are governed by the prevailing divorce law in England.[30] This means that any amendments or reforms to English divorce law automatically affect the legal framework in Anglophone Cameroon, regardless of the underlying motivations for those changes.[31] Presently, the applicable statute is the Matrimonial Causes Act 1973, which outlines the grounds and procedures for divorce.[32]

Conversely, the legal regime in Francophone Cameroon remains unchanged. It continues to apply the French divorce law as it existed before Cameroon's independence in 1960.[33] Specifically, the operative legislation is the French Divorce Law of 1884, which reflects the principles and provisions of French civil law from that era.[34] Unlike its Anglophone counterpart, this legal framework has not evolved in tandem with contemporary French reforms, resulting in a more static and historically anchored approach to divorce.[35]

2.2 *Marital Property Regimes in Cameroon*

In Cameroon, marital property regimes are governed by statutory law and influenced by customary practices, with couples typically choosing between the community property and separate property regimes.[36] These regimes determine how assets are

[27] See Law No. 2006/015 of 29 December 2006 and read with Civil Status Registration Ordinance No. 81/02 of 29 June 1981 and Matrimonial Causes Act 1973, s. 71.

[28] See Cameroon Civil Code 2005, arts. 201–202.

[29] See Cameroon Civil Code 2005, arts. 815 et seq.

[30] Southern Cameroons High Court Law 1955, s. 15 states, 'The jurisdiction of the High Court in probate, divorce and matrimonial causes and proceedings may, subject to the provision of this law and in particular of section 27, and to rules of court, be exercised by the court in conformity with the law and practice for the time being in force in England', and Ghogomu (2018, p. 51).

[31] Ghogomu (2018, p. 51).

[32] Ghogomu (2018, p. 182).

[33] Ghogomu (2018, p. 26).

[34] Ghogomu (2018, p. 26).

[35] Ghogomu (2018, p. 26).

[36] Tamfu (2013).

owned, managed, and divided during marriage and upon dissolution.[37] To prevent disputes over the ownership of marital property, Section 49 of the Civil Status Registration Ordinance of 6 May 2011[38] mandates that the marriage certificate must specify the matrimonial property regime chosen by the parties. This means that the couple must indicate whether they have opted for a community property or a separate property arrangement in their marriage agreement.

Under the community property regime, all assets acquired during the marriage are jointly owned by both spouses, regardless of who earned or purchased them.[39] Each spouse has equal rights to manage and dispose of these assets.[40] However, property acquired before marriage, received through inheritance, or given as a gift remains separate unless it is explicitly merged into the community estate.[41] Upon divorce, community assets are generally divided equally, unless the couple agreed otherwise in a prenuptial contract.[42] This system promotes economic unity and is often preferred by couples who wish to pool resources and responsibilities.[43]

Conversely, the separate property regime allows each spouse to retain ownership and control over their individual assets. Property acquired before or during the marriage remains the exclusive property of the acquiring spouse, and there is no automatic sharing of income, investments, or debts.[44] Upon divorce, each spouse keeps their own property, and only jointly acquired assets are subject to division.[45] This system is favoured by couples who wish to maintain financial independence or protect personal or family wealth.[46]

In Anglophone Cameroon, which includes the North West and South West regions, the separate property system is more commonly applied. This reflects the influence of English common law traditions, which emphasise individual ownership and contractual freedom.[47] Unless explicitly stated in a marriage contract, the default assumption leans towards separate ownership.[48] In formal civil marriages registered under the law, the chosen property regime must be declared and documented to ensure legal clarity.[49] As this chapter focuses on the law of Anglophone Cameroon, the discussion is limited to the legal framework applicable in that region, which is largely derived

---

[37] Tamfu (2013).

[38] Law No. 2011/011 of 6 May 2011 to amend and Supplement Certain Provisions of Ordinance no 81/02 of 29 June 1981 to Organize Civil Status Registration and Various Provisions relating to the Status of Natural Persons.

[39] Law No. 2011/011 of 6 May 2011.

[40] Law No. 2011/011 of 6 May 2011.

[41] Ngwafor (2001, p. 174).

[42] Tabe (2000, p. 703).

[43] Matrimonial Causes Act 1973 (Cameroon), s. 1(2).

[44] Matrimonial Causes Act 1973 (Cameroon), s. 1(2).

[45] Matrimonial Causes Act 1973 (Cameroon), s. 1(2).

[46] Kiye (2016, p. 273).

[47] See generally, Boldeman (2007, ch. 9).

[48] Matrimonial Causes Act 1973 (Cameroon), s. 1(2).

[49] Djoupoyang (2023, p. 190).

from English law. Unless otherwise indicated, any reference to Cameroon hereafter refers specifically to Anglophone Cameroon.

3 Forms of Marital Property Rights Disputes Under Cameroonian Law

Tensions of ownership of marital property may be categorised differently. From the standpoint of the moment of the acquisition of the property, three types of disputes often emerge: disputes relating to property acquired before the celebration of the marriage; second, clashes on who owns property acquired during the marriage; and disputes over ancillary reliefs. Each of these disagreements is resolved differently under Cameroonian law.

Before addressing these specific issues, it is essential to define marital property. Cameroonian courts generally adopt the definition of marital property in the English case of *Wachtel v Wachtel*.[50] Therein, the court held that family assets, which are the same as marital property, refer to 'those things, which one, other or both parties acquire, with the intention that there should be a continuing provision for them and their children during their joint lives, and used for the benefit of the family as a whole'. The tenor of this definition suggests that marital property governs several significant issues. These issues include (a) things acquired (b) by one, other, or both parties in the marriage, and (c) with the intention that they should be used for the benefit of the family.

3.1 Co-Ownership at Common Law

3.1.1 Joint Tenancy

There are two forms of co-ownership that correspond to what is known in common law as joint tenancy and, in civil law systems, tenancy in common. It is essential to note that the term' joint tenancy' can have varying meanings depending on the legal discipline or context in which it is used. From the legal point of view, Section 1(6) of the Law of Property Act 1925 refers to a legal estate as one 'not capable of substituting or of being created in an undivided share in land or of being held by an infant'.[51] This definition is minimally useful. There is, however, general agreement among

[50] [1973] EWCA 10.

[51] Similarly, s. 36(2) of the Law of Property Act provides that, 'no severance of a joint tenancy of a legal estate, so as to create a tenancy in common in land, shall be permissible whether by operation of law or otherwise, but, this subsection does not affect the right of a joint tenant to release his interest to the other joint tenants, or the right to sever a joint tenancy in an equitable interest whether or not legal estate is vested in the joint tenants'.

scholars on what the term "joint tenancy" means. With some variations, virtually all authorities accept that joint tenancy is 'a tenancy with two or more co-owners who take identical interests simultaneously by the same instrument and with the same right of possession'.[52] Each of the elements of this definition is important.

First and foremost, it is elementary that joint tenancy is an agreement reached by the consent of two or more persons. Another fundamental attribute is that, in a 'joint tenancy', the parties agree to take identical interests in a property. A third defining trait is that the instrument binding the party's interest produces the same right of possession over the property. That is, both parties have an equal right to the property in a joint tenancy.

For the present purpose, it should be underscored that, under a joint tenancy, each joint tenant is entitled to the benefit of the entire property. Thus, in *Goodman v Gallant*,[53] a husband and a wife were joint beneficial tenants in their home. She and a third party together purchased her husband's interest, with the conveyance declaring that they held the property 'upon trust to sell until sale upon trust for themselves as joint tenants'. The wife issued a notice to sever her share and sought a declaration that she held a three-quarter interest in the house. She equally argued that, upon severance of a joint tenancy, the parties' shares were not necessarily equal but depended on their intentions. The third party argued that they owned the house as joint tenants and thus held the sale proceeds in equal shares. The court held that they owned the house as joint tenants and thus ordered that the sale proceeds be divided equally. It is evident from this case that, although the property was contributed in unequal shares, it was conveyed to them as joint tenants, and a claim that it was a tenancy in common failed. The rationale for this decision was that, in a joint tenancy, no tenant owns a specific share of the property. Any transfer of the legal title must be done by all the joint tenants together.

According to Bray, the two main features of a joint tenancy are the right of survivorship and unities of possession, interest, title, and time.[54] The most important element is that the right of survivorship in a joint tenancy is guaranteed under section 1(6) of the Law of Property Act 1925. The right of survivorship carries both legal and practical implications. Legally, it ensures that when a couple jointly holds title to property, such as a home or land, upon the death of one spouse, the title automatically transfers to the surviving spouse. This transfer of property occurs regardless of who made the mortgage payments. Similar to the deed designation of joint tenancy, this mechanism bypasses court proceedings. This salient feature of survivorship requires that, on the death of one of the joint tenants, the estate remain with the surviving joint tenants. Thus, any attempt to pass an interest in a joint tenancy under a will is unenforceable because the joint tenant has no share to leave the property under their will. Lastly, since the legal estate vests in the other joint tenants automatically, there is no need to formally vest the legal title in the survivors.

---

[52] Garner (1993, p. 1477).

[53] (1986) Fam 106.

[54] Bray (2007, p. 51).

Another basic objective of the right of survivorship is that, if the couple divorces or obtains a legal separation, all of the property in the joint tenancy is divided evenly between the couple. Each spouse retains ownership of their separate property. In contrast, a few limitations aim to restrict the equal division or automatic transfer of marital property to the surviving spouse. The most significant of these limitations concerns situations where a legal estate cannot exist in divided shares. This aspect of the joint tenancy process is intended to enable the property to be awarded solely to one spouse. It is particularly common in cases involving the marital home or jointly owned land. Given that dividing a matrimonial home will not be feasible, the court commonly awards the house to one of them. The other spouse receives assets equivalent to half the value of the home.

3.1.2 Tenancy in Common

According to Black's Law Dictionary, a tenancy in common is a 'tenancy by two or more persons in equal or unequal undivided shares, each person having an equal right to possess the whole territory but no right to survivorship'.[55] It also refers to 'one or two or more tenants who hold the same land by unity of possession but by separate and distinct title, with each person having an equal right to possess the whole property but no right to survivorship'.[56] The main remark here is that a joint tenant differs from a tenancy in common in that each joint tenant has a right of survivorship to the other's share. It also means that, under a tenancy in common, the co-owners hold specific shares in the land or a proportional share.

Although each tenant can claim a share, he cannot physically separate the property and claim exclusive possession of his share. Each tenant in common must claim rights over the entire property. The main difference with the joint tenancy is that the doctrine of survivorship does not operate on the death of a tenant in common, and as such, the share can pass under a valid will or intestacy. Unlike joint tenancy, tenancy in common requires only one unity—the unity of possession—between the co-owners.

3.2 Resolving Disputes of Ownership of Marital Property Before the Marriage

One of the leading causes of tension in marriage relates to properties that spouses acquire before the marriage. Such properties include engagement gifts, dowries, and properties acquired through inheritance.

The rule regarding engagement gifts is outlined in Section 2 of the Law Reform (Miscellaneous Provisions) Act 1970. According to Subsection 1:

---

[55] Garner (1993, p. 1478).

[56] Garner (1993, p. 1479).

> a party to an agreement to marry who makes a gift of property to the other party to the agreement on the condition (express or implied) that it shall be returned if the agreement is terminated shall not be prevented from recovering the property by reason only of his having terminated the agreement.

The phrase 'shall not be prevented from recovering the property' is the clause that settles any eventual dispute between the parties. It requires that, if the marriage is not celebrated, the engagement gift be considered the donor's property. In contrast, section 3(2) of the Act states that: 'the gift of an agreement ring shall be presumed to be an absolute gift; this presumption may be rebutted by proving that the ring was given on the condition, express or implied that, it should be returned if the marriage did not take place for any reason'. It follows from this that the ring, except otherwise provided, should be considered the woman's personal property.

In addition, a dispute may arise between the couple regarding the ownership of the dowry paid by the husband before the marriage celebration. In the event of the union's breakdown, the primary issue for the parties is determining ownership of the dowry. Section 77 of the Civil Status Registration Ordinance of 2011 has settled this dispute by providing that, in the event of the non-celebration of the wedding, the parents of the woman must reimburse the amount paid by the prospective husband. This implies that the money paid as dowry is considered a surety paid by a prospective husband to the parents of the prospective wife, who assure him of the marriage. Therefore, if the marriage does not take place, the parents are obligated to refund the dowry.

Beyond these specific gifts provided by legislation, it is important to state that women are no longer a legal disability which inhibits their ability to own property. Previously, as Rabiatu observes, until the passage of the Married Women's Property Act of 1870, English common law dictated that most property a wife owned as a *feme sole* was placed under her husband's control upon marriage.[57] This implies that although the wife retained legal ownership of the property, she could neither manage nor control it. Again, she could not sell, rent, or mortgage her real property without her husband's consent. Equally, she had no right to rent from her real property. A married woman's personal property was vested in the husband absolutely under the common law, and consequently, he could dispose of it as he wished. The basis for this treatment of common law was the doctrine of coverture.

This English position appears consistent with the framework influencing the regulation of married women's property rights in Cameroon. The Cameroonian Constitution, although not explicitly focused on married women, provides a robust framework for protecting property rights and promoting gender equality. The Constitution provides in article 16 that, 'Men and women of full age, without any limitation due to race, nationality or religion, have the right to marry and to found a family. *They are entitled to equal rights as to marriage, during marriage, and at its dissolution*'.[58]

---

[57] Rabiatu (2010, p. 63).

[58] Constitution of Cameroon 1996, art. 16 (emphasis added).

Article 17 also emphasises the right of 'everyone' to own property. To these provisions can be added the equality and non-discrimination clause of the Constitution.[59]

Clearly, the Constitution establishes a foundational guarantee of property rights and non-discrimination applicable to all citizens, including married women. Cameroon has further reinforced these principles by ratifying key international instruments: the Convention on the Elimination of All Forms of Discrimination Against Women (CEDAW) on 23 August 1994, and the Maputo Protocol, the Protocol to the African Charter on Human and Peoples' Rights on the Rights of Women in Africa, on 13 September 2012. Both treaties obligate Cameroon to eliminate gender-based discrimination and uphold women's rights to property, dignity, and equality. The Maputo Protocol, in particular, calls for legislative and policy measures to ensure women's equal access to property and inheritance, as well as to protect them from harmful practices and economic exclusion.[60] These commitments, when read in conjunction with domestic constitutional guarantees, provide a robust legal foundation for advancing married women's property rights in Cameroon.

3.3 Resolving Disputes of Ownership During the Marriage

Case law and legal writers have developed various approaches to resolving issues related to the ownership of marital property. According to Ngwafor, couples face two forms of dispute: arguments over the ownership of properties acquired during the marriage and those over the ownership of the matrimonial home.[61] This section explores key tensions regarding couples' rights to marital property during marriage. These disputes often revolve around ownership, division, and control of property within the marriage.

3.3.1 Disputes of Ownership of Properties Bought Out of Housekeeping Allowance

One of the primary disagreements couples face in marriage concerns the ownership of property purchased by the wife with housekeeping money. Ngwafor notes that, traditionally under common law, if a husband provided his wife with an allowance for housekeeping expenses, any property purchased with that money would be considered his property.[62] Nevertheless, according to Ngwafor, this common law position

---

[59] Constitution of Cameroon 1996, art. 7 states, 'All are equal before the law and are entitled without any discrimination to equal protection of the law. All are entitled to equal protection against any discrimination in violation of this Declaration and against any incitement to such discrimination'.

[60] Protocol to the African Charter on Human and Peoples' Rights on the Rights of Women in Africa (adopted 11 July 2003, entered into force 25 November 2005) art. 7(d).

[61] Ngwafor (1993, pp. 177–186).

[62] Ngwafor (1993, pp. 177–186).

does not reflect the current position of the law.[63] Section 1 of the UK's Married Women's Property Act 1964 states the current position of the law as follows:

> If any question arises as to the right of a husband or wife to any money derived from any allowance made by the husband for the expenses of the matrimonial home or for similar purposes, or to any property acquired out of such money, the money or the property shall in the absence of any agreement between them to the contrary, be treated as belonging to the husband and wife in equal shares.

It flows from this rule that any property bought by a wife from housekeeping money given to her by her husband is presumed to belong to them both in equal shares. Considering that Section 11 of the Southern Cameroon High Court Law limits the applicability of English statutes to only pre-1900 statutes, it is most likely that it does not represent the law in this country.

Nonetheless, there will clearly be exceptions to this generalisation in particular cases. The first exception to the equality principle is that this section does not apply if the parties have already agreed on the balance of funds or property purchased with such an allowance. Moreover, this rule applies only when the husband provides the allowance. Ngwafor, a prominent scholar on Cameroonian law, notes that it is reasonable to conclude that where the wife provides the allowance, the remaining funds or property belong to the wife. In England today, the truth about the legal position of property bought by the husband from an allowance provided by the wife is settled by section 200 of the Equality Act 2010, which amends this provision so that it refers to housekeeping money given by either spouse to the other, not just husbands to wives.

3.3.2 Disputes Over Properties Purchased by a Spouse Out of Their Personal Income

Another problem couples face in marriage, besides those that accrue from housekeeping allowances, is determining ownership of properties purchased by a spouse from their personal income. The rule of law in this area is that when both spouses are employed, property acquired using one spouse's income is considered the exclusive property of that spouse.[64] For example, if a husband buys shares, then, subject to any contrary intention, he is considered to own them. Similarly, if a wife buys a car, she owns it. So, in *Moussi v Moussi*,[65] the court held that property bought by the wife with her personal income belonged exclusively to her. The rationale for this view is that, in section 74(1) of the Civil Status Registration Ordinance,[66] a married woman may exercise a trade different from that of her husband, in which case she will be entitled to a personal income. The divorce court may decide otherwise. However,

---

63 Ngwafor (1993, pp. 177–186).

64 Ngwafor (1993, p. 182).

65 *Moussi v Moussi*, Suit No. HFC/115mc/87 (High Court, 6 June 1988) (unreported).

66 Law No. 2011 of 14th December 2011 amending Ordinance No. 81 of 29th June 1981 relating to the Civil Status Registration.

the presumption at law is that if a husband opens an account in the wife's name, the money belongs to her. In *Body Lawson v Body Lawson,*[67] a husband was prevented from laying claim to money in an account he had opened for his wife in appreciation of her kindness to him when he was sick.

3.3.3 Disputes of Ownership of Gifts Made to Married Couples

Finally, an essential battle over ownership of marital property concerns gifts made to married couples. Each spouse presumptively owns any gift, such as a birthday present given to them personally. This means that upon the termination of the marriage, the spouse to whom the gift was made owns it. If the gift was merely made to the couple because of the marriage, it would be logical that it should rightfully revert to the giver at the end of the relationship. This was the court's position in the case of *Adeline Njohzoh Fanwi Ferim v Ivo Laris Tamajong*.[68] Here, on the termination of the marriage by a decree absolute, the court held that the two buses given to the couple by Mr Fred Ferim did not form part of the couple's marital property and should be returned to the gift-giver. Nevertheless, if a gift is given to them as a married couple, it is presumed to be a gift to both of them. This may include a gift of financial assistance to help them acquire a home.

3.3.4 Resolving Disputes of the Ownership of the Matrimonial Home

The legal principle is that ownership of the matrimonial home is determined by the person whose name appears on the land title.[69] The courts are hesitant to change the title deed on land titled documents. An example that illustrates this view is *Leake v Brussi*,[70] where the court ruled that it would not alter the title or grant ownership to a party whose name does not appear on the conveyance deed.

However, the courts have always been anxious to prevent an unscrupulous defendant from using the title deed to deny a spouse whose name is not on the title deed the right to ownership of the matrimonial home in instances in which it would be grossly unfair to the plaintiff to do so. The courts have, therefore, developed a number of exceptional circumstances to enable a spouse whose name is not on the title deed to benefit from the property. Under what circumstances will a party whose name is not on the deed be considered the owner of the matrimonial home? One of the main exceptions to the rule that the title deed is the sole determinant of the ownership of a matrimonial home, as highlighted by Ngwafor,[71] is the wife's contribution. A notable

[67] *Body Lawson v Body Lawson*, Suit No. HCF/128Mc/86 (unreported).

[68] *Adeline Njohzoh Fanwi Ferim v Ivo Laris Tamajong* (High Court, 2017).

[69] Ngwafor (1993, p. 71).

[70] *Leake v Brussi* [1974] 2 All ER 186.

[71] Ngwafor (1993, p. 186).

English law example applicable in Cameroon is *Cook v Head*,[72] where, although the title deed was in the husband's name, the court found that the wife's contributions to the family budget were crucial in acquiring the property. As a result, the court ruled that the husband was holding the property in trust for both of them in equal shares.

In addition, Ngwafor explains that the ownership of the matrimonial home may also rest on the indirect contribution of one spouse.[73] This mostly happens when the wife does not contribute directly to the mortgage instalment but donates part of her income to cover joint household expenses, thereby enabling the husband to pay the mortgage with his income. Judicial and legislative developments in English law have progressively acknowledged the equitable interest of spouses in property acquired or improved during marriage. In *Fribance v Fribance* [1957] 1 WLR 384, Lord Denning LJ laid the groundwork for this recognition by observing that 'the whole of the [spouses'] resources were expended for their joint benefit... and the product should belong to them jointly. It belongs to them in equal shares'. His judgment underscored the principle that joint financial or domestic contributions, regardless of who held legal title, should confer joint beneficial ownership. This judicial philosophy was later reinforced by Section 37 of the Matrimonial Proceedings and Property Act 1970, which provides that where a husband or wife contributes in money or money's worth to the improvement of real or personal property, the contributing spouse acquires a beneficial interest in the property, as the court deems just in the circumstances. Together, these authorities establish an equitable framework that safeguards the financial interests of both spouses and acknowledges the value of shared contributions to matrimonial property.

Finally, the ownership of the matrimonial home may accrue to the spouse who carries out construction work on land belonging to the other spouse. In this case, the applicant may argue that, although the respondent owns the land, the applicant was responsible for constructing the house. In such instances, section 24 of the Matrimonial Causes Act 1973 empowers UK courts to make property adjustment orders in the context of divorce, nullity, or judicial separation proceedings. These orders may include the transfer or settlement of property between spouses or for the benefit of a child, the variation of nuptial settlements (excluding pensions), or the extinguishment of a party's interest under such arrangements. Section 24A of the Matrimonial Causes Act 1973 allows the court to order a sale to give effect to any property adjustment order made under Section 24. Together, these provisions enable equitable redistribution of matrimonial assets to promote fairness during the dissolution of marriage.

In the case of *H v H*,[74] Lord Denning MR held that in the enumerable and infinitely various disputes as to property which may occur between husband and wife, the judge should have a free hand to do what is just.[75] It will be in the interest of justice for

[72] *Cook v Head* [1972] 1 WLR 518.

[73] Ngwafor (1993, p. 186).

[74] *H v H* [1947] 63 TLR 645.

[75] By so deciding, he was citing verbatim the provision of section 17 of the Married Woman's property Act 1882 that provides "In any question between husband and wife as to the title to or

the court to rely on the following equitable maxims: 'equity will not suffer a wrong to be without a remedy' and 'equity is equality'.[76] These maxims pray the court to issue an order directing the sale of the matrimonial home and the equal sharing of the proceeds between the parties. Nevertheless, to succeed, the applicant must furnish the court with documents related to the house they want to sell. Equally, the court cannot order the sale of the house without examining the building permits, land certificates, and other documents related to the said house. It was pursuant to the absence of the foregoing that, in the Cameroonian case of *Enow Mbomg Judith v William Acha Fonge,*[77] the court refused to entertain and grant the applicant's second prayer that the matrimonial home be sold.

The legal implications of this, as noted by Ngwafor, are that it prevents a husband who abandons his wife and children in a home he purchased solely in his name from selling the property to a third party or evicting them from the home. Legal protections against spousal eviction are enshrined in both UK and Cameroonian law, reflecting a shared commitment to safeguarding residential rights within marriage. In the UK, Section 1(1) of the Matrimonial Homes Act 1983 confers upon a spouse in occupation of the matrimonial home the statutory right not to be evicted or excluded by the other spouse without a court order, regardless of proprietary entitlement. This provision ensures continuity of residence and shields vulnerable spouses during marital disputes. Similarly, Cameroon's Penal Code, under Section 358-1, criminalises the unlawful eviction of a spouse from the matrimonial home. It stipulates that any spouse who, outside judicial proceedings and without legitimate reason, expels the other from the home is liable to imprisonment for three months to one year and a fine ranging from 50,000 to 500,000 Central African CFA francs. The law further prescribes harsher penalties—up to five years' imprisonment—if the victim is pregnant, if the eviction involves violence or destruction of personal property, or if it is perpetrated by someone other than the spouse. These provisions underscore the legal systems' recognition of the matrimonial home as a protected space and their efforts to deter coercive or abusive displacement within domestic relationships.

3.4 Resolving Disputes of Ownership of Marital Property Through Ancillary Relief

According to Burton Frances, an ancillary relief refers to the acquisition of marital property through financial orders following a decree of divorce, judicial separation

possession of property, either party may apply by summons or otherwise in a summary way to the High Court or a County Court and the court may, on such an application (which may be heard in private) make such order with respect to the property as it thinks fit."

[76] See also the Nigerian case of *Egbuna v Egbuna* [1989] 2 NWLR 773 and also the English case of *Gissing v Gissing* [1970] UKHL.

[77] *Enow Mbomg Judith v William Acha Fonge* (High Court, 2024).

or the death of one of the spouses of the marriage.[78] Similarly, Curzon conceptualises ancillary relief to mean an incidental relief which is auxiliary to a divorce action or suit, issued in favour of a party to the marriage or a child of the family and includes maintenance pending a suit; financial provision orders; property adjustment orders; and property sale orders.[79] This section examines two forms of ancillary reliefs: financial provisions orders and property adjustment orders.

At common law, without court involvement, most separating couples can enter into an agreement to settle all substantive issues arising from their marriage. Typically, this agreement outlines the terms of property division, child custody, and spousal support that the couple has agreed upon. However, upon the dissolution of the marriage, if the couple cannot reach an amicable agreement on how to divide the marital property, it becomes necessary to involve the courts. In court, most couples seek an order for both property adjustments and a lump-sum payment.

3.4.1 Lump Sum Payment

A key substantive issue in divorce proceedings is the applicant's request for a lump-sum order against the respondent. In the case of *Enow Mbomg Judith v William Acha Fonge*,[80] the applicant's first prayer was for an order requiring the respondent to pay a lump sum of 10,000,000 CFA. In contrast, in *Epey Samuel Mbeng v Epey Nee Oben Miriam,*[81] the petitioner appealed against the decision of the Fako High Court, ordering him to pay the respondent 20,000,000 CFA Francs as a lump sum. A concept of central importance to the trial process is the legal basis of the award.

The main law that governs lump sum payments is the provision of section 23(1)(c) of the UK's Matrimonial Causes Act 1973, which empowers the High Court to order a party to the marriage to make a lump sum payment to the other party. It provides as follows:

> On granting a degree of divorce, a degree of nullity of marriage or a degree of judicial separation or at any time thereafter whether in the case of a degree of divorce or a nullity of marriage before or after the degree is made absolute, the court may make any one or more of the following orders, that is to say, an order that either party to the marriage pay to the other such lump sum or sums as may be specified.

Section 25(1)(a) to (g) of the UK's Matrimonial Causes Act 1973 provides a list of factors that the courts must take into consideration in deciding whether to exercise their power under section 23(1)(c) of the MCA 1973. Such factors include, but are not limited to, the income, earning capacity, property, and other financial resources each party currently has or is likely to have in the foreseeable future, as well as their financial needs, obligations, and responsibilities, both present and future. A party's

---

[78] Burton (2003, p. 124).

[79] Curzon (2001, p. 63).

[80] *Enow Mbomg Judith v William Acha Fonge* (High Court, 2024).

[81] *Epey Samuel Mbeng v Epey Nee Oben Miriam*, Suit No. CAS/22/2012, *SOWECAM Law Report*, Vol. 9, pp. 139–147.

inability to comply with these requirements will lead to the rejection of their plea. It is to this effect that, in *Enow Mbomg Judith v William Acha Fonge*,[82] being unaware of their various incomes, earning capacities, and other financial resources, the court could not proceed to make an order for the lump payment of 10,000,000 CFA francs requested by the applicant from the respondent.

Similarly, in *Epey Samuel Mbeng v Epey Nee Oben Miriam*,[83] the Fako Court of Appeal held that the trial court erred by considering only the petitioner's property when granting the lump sum of 20,000,000 CFA francs. The law requires both parties to provide property and financial declarations so that the court can assess all relevant evidence and make a decision that reflects the justice of the case. The Court of Appeal emphasised that, in determining the lump sum, the court should have considered, among other things, the respondent's educational background—the fact that the respondent had graduated from Higher Teacher Training College and had worked about a year after marriage—as well as the petitioner's position as a senior staff member at National Refining Company Limited (SONARA) with a substantial salary of 1,600,000 CFA francs.

3.4.2 The Procedure to Apply for an Ancillary Relief of a Lump Sum Payment

By section 30 of the Matrimonial Causes Act 1973, the applicant begins the proceedings for an ancillary relief/financial order of a lump sum by application through a conveyancing counsel in the due form A. The applicant submits Form A to the High Court and serves it on the other party. Both parties must then simultaneously exchange their financial statements in Form E with each other and submit them to the court. Both parties go through amicable proceedings before a judge of the High Court. Where the parties do not agree, the High Court designates another judge for the final hearing.

On its part, Section 2.69E of the Family Proceedings (Amendment No. 2) Rules 1999, tagged 'Open proposal' of the UK Family Proceedings Rules 1999 states:

> (1) No less than 14 days before the date fixed for the final hearing of the application for ancillary relief, the applicant must (unless the court directs otherwise) file with the court and serve on the respondent an open statement which sets out concise details, including the amounts involved, of the orders which he proposes to ask the court to make.

The phrase 'before the date fixed for the hearing', as used in the above provision, suggests that 'the procedure is ancillary or subsidiary to proceedings for divorce, nullity for marriage or judicial separation'.[84] As such, the applicant for an ancillary relief for a lump sum must apply when making the petition or the answer thereto.

[82] *Enow Mbomg Judith v William Acha Fonge* (High Court, 2024).

[83] *Epey Samuel Mbeng v Epey Nee Oben Miriam*, Suit No. CAS/22/2012, *SOWECAM Law Report*, Vol. 9, pp. 139–147.

[84] *Epey Samuel Mbeng v Epey Nee Oben Miriam*, Suit No. CAS/22/2012, *SOWECAM Law Report*, Vol. 9, p. 139, per His Lordship Lord Justice Theophilus Tayi Tatsi.

Finally, Section 2.69E in its subsection 2 of the 1999 law provides that: 'not more than 7 days after service of a statement under paragraph (1), the Respondent must file with the Court and serve on the Applicant an open statement, which sets out concise details including, the amounts involved of the order, which he proposes to ask the Court to make'. Based on this, in *Epey Samuel Mbeng* v *Epey Nee Oben Miriam*,[85] the Court of Appeal of Fako rejected the petitioner's application, stating that there was no evidence in the proceedings to show that the parties had made the mandatory application or completed the required forms with their financial declarations, including the necessary valuations of the properties of each or both spouses. In finding no basis for the trial judge to award a lump sum of 20,000,000 CFA francs to the respondent, the court reasoned that no expert had properly evaluated the property of the spouses. It should be noted that it is not the court's responsibility to value the spouses' assets, as suggested by the trial court in its judgment.

3.4.3 Property Adjustment Order

In addition to seeking an order compelling the respondent to pay a lump sum, the applicant also seeks a property adjustment order, which constitutes another significant point of contention. On the strength of Section 24 of the Matrimonial Causes Act 1973, the court is empowered to make property adjustment orders after granting a decree absolute of divorce. It states: 'property adjustment orders may be made in favour of a spouse or child of the family, or any person for the benefit of such child, on the grant of a decree nisi or at any time following'. Like an order for a lump sum, the applicant must comply with the provisions of Section 25, which outline matters the court must consider when deciding whether to make a property adjustment order. These matters include, but are not limited to, the income, earning capacity, property, and other financial resources each party has or is likely to have in the foreseeable future, their financial needs, obligations, and responsibilities, the standard of living enjoyed by the family before the marriage breakdown, and the contributions made by each party to the welfare of the family, among other factors. Should the applicant fail to furnish the court with any of the above-mentioned information, no such order will be made in their favour.

4 Property Distribution in Customary Marriages

Under Cameroonian customary law, property relations in polygynous unions are organised around the concept of separate "houses" or households. Each wife and her children form a distinct unit, which is reflected most clearly in succession practice, where a deceased man's estate is divided *per stirpes*, that is, between the branches

[85] *Epey Samuel Mbeng v Epey Nee Oben Miriam*, Suit No. CAS/22/2012, *SOWECAM Law Report*, Vol. 9, pp. 139–147.

represented by his wives and their children.[86] Although this principle arises in the context of inheritance, it illustrates the broader customary understanding that each wife and her household possesses distinct property interests during the marriage, reflecting the husband's moral and customary obligations toward each family unit.[87] This principle is reflected in the emerging Family Code,[88] which provides that polygamous marriages shall be governed by the separate ownership regime.[89] The Code further states that in polygamous marriages, the husband and each wife form a separate matrimonial family, and no spouse is obliged to provide for the needs of her co-spouses or those of their children.[90] Within the Cameroonian legal framework, the concept of customary law encompasses native law, customs, and Muslim law. Accordingly, matters relating to marriage, property relations, and succession under this head fall within the jurisdiction of customary courts in non-Muslim cases, while similar matters involving Muslim parties are adjudicated before the Alkali Courts, which apply Muslim law in accordance with the applicable legal framework.

5 Recommendations

5.1 Harmonisation of Family Law Across Jurisdictions

The legal dualism inherited from Cameroon's colonial past, with English common law prevailing in the Anglophone regions and French civil law in the Francophone regions, continues to generate inconsistency in the treatment of marital property. It is recommended that Cameroon initiate efforts toward harmonising family law, particularly provisions relating to marital property, divorce, and inheritance. Such reforms should adopt best practices from both systems while ensuring alignment with Cameroon's constitutional guarantee of gender equality. In doing so, it must be recognised that the continued reliance on law as in force in France and England to govern spousal property rights results in the foreign influence of domestic law in Cameroon without due regard to the context within which such marriages are contracted and consequently dissolved in Cameroon, particularly the economic, cultural, and social context of Cameroon. Such a unified system must thus take into consideration the peculiarities of the Cameroonian legal framework, particularly its bijural nature.

[86] Ebi (2008, pp. 218–221).

[87] See Ebi (2008, pp. 218–221); see also Ngwafor (2006, pp. 127–128).

[88] Also known as the Draft Code of the Person and the Family.

[89] Ngwafor (2006, p. 127). See also Draft Code of the Person and the Family, s. 749.

[90] Draft Code of the Person and the Family, s. 365(1)-(2).

5.2 *Codification of Marital Property Rights*

There should be a comprehensive codification of marital property rights within a unified family code, reflecting both statutory and judicial interpretations of these rights, as well as the evolving principles underlying them. This code should clearly define marital property, outline each spouse's rights regardless of formal ownership documentation, and provide enforceable protections for indirect financial or domestic contributions made during the marriage.

6 Conclusion

This chapter has examined the legal framework for marital property in Anglophone Cameroon. It has revealed the nuanced interplay between statutory provisions, equitable principles, and judicial discretion. The increased use of ancillary relief mechanisms, such as lump-sum payments and property adjustment orders, reflects a judicial effort to redress economic imbalances and uphold fairness upon marital dissolution. It explains how disputes arise regarding marital property. The meaning of marital property as distinguished from separate property, the special significance of the matrimonial home, and the use of ancillary reliefs to readjust property rights after a divorce are also covered in this chapter.

References

Boldeman L (2007) The doctrine of freedom of contract. In: The cult of the market: economic fundamentalism and its discontents, ch. 9. ANU Press

Bray J (2007) Key facts: land law, 3rd edn. Hodder Education, London

Burton F (2003) Family law, 1st edn. Routledge-Cavendish. https://doi.org/10.4324/9781843145004

CIA (2024) The World Factbook: Cameroon. https://theodora.com/wfbcurrent/cameroon/cameroon_people.html. Accessed 18 Sept 2025

Curzon LB (2001) Briefcase on family law, 2nd edn. Cavendish Publishing, London

Djoupoyang IG (2023) Matrimonial agreements: Solutions to the perennial problem of matrimonial regimes in Cameroonian law. Law Pol Rev 161–191

Ebi JN (2008) The Structure of succession law in Cameroon: Finding a balance between the needs and interests of different family members. PhD thesis, University of Birmingham

Fombad CM (2007) Researching Cameroonian Law. Globalex, June/July. https://www.nyulawglobal.org/globalex/Cameroon.html. Accessed 20 Sept 2025

Fombad CM (2015) Managing legal diversity: Cameroonian bijuralism at a critical crossroads. In: Vernon VP, Mohamed YM (eds) Mixed legal systems, east and west. Routledge, New York

Fuashi NT (2012) Statehood and the law-making process in Cameroon: from bifurcation to unification. Fundamina 18(2):59–77

Garner BA (1993) Black's law dictionary. Cavendish Publishing, London

Gebeye BA (2017) Legal theory in Africa: Between legal centralism and legal pluralism. Queen Mary Law Journal. https://www.academia.edu/34195081/Legal_Theory_in_Africa_Between_Legal_Centralism_and_Legal_Pluralism. Accessed 18 Oct 2025

Generis Global (2024) Understanding marriage and divorce regulations in Cameroon. https://generisonline.com/understanding-marriage-and-divorce-regulations-in-cameroon/. Accessed 17 Sept 2025

Ghogomu DL (2018) The complexities and inequalities of the laws of divorce in Cameroon and how these can be overcome. PhD thesis, University College London

Kiye ME (2015) Conflict between customary law and human rights in Cameroon: the role of the courts in fostering an equitably gendered society. Afr Study Monogr 36(2):75–100

Kiye ME (2016) The harmonisation of family law in Cameroon: a critical appraisal. J Afr Law 60(2):273–290

Kiye ME (2021) Customary law in Anglophone Cameroon and the repugnancy doctrine: an insufficient complement to human rights. J Afr Stud 42(2):1–22. https://escholarship.org/uc/item/3jm9186m. Accessed 9 Nov 2025

Library of Congress (2025) Cameroon: Law enacted to provide legal recognition of customary marriages. Global Legal Monitor, 7 January. https://www.loc.gov/item/global-legal-monitor/2025-01-07/cameroon-law-enacted-to-provide-legal-recognition-of-customary-marriages/. Accessed 9 Nov 2025

Ndangoh ML (2022) Bride price and marriage under Cameroonian family law. Synsto Journals 1(1). https://www.synstojournals.com/law/article/download/23/55/57. Accessed 16 Oct 2025

Ndeh MS (2020) Traditional justice system and conflict resolution: exploring the pre-colonial institutional frameworks in Mamfe and Bakweri lands of Cameroon. Eur J Soc Sci Stud 1–11. https://eajournals.org/wp-content/uploads/Traditional-Justice-System-and-Conflict-Resolution-Exploring-the-Pre-Colonial-Institutional-Frameworks-in-Mamfe-and-Bakweri-Lands-of-Cameroon.pdf. Accessed 15 Sept 2025

Ngoh VJ (2001) Southern Cameroons, 1922–1961: a constitutional history. Ashgate Publishing Co, Surrey

Ngwafor EN (1990) Cameroon: property rights for women—a bold step in the wrong direction. J Fam Law 29(2):297–302

Ngwafor EN (1993) Family law in anglophone Cameroon, 1st edn. The University of Regina Press, Regina

Ngwafor EN (2001) Family law in anglophone Cameroon: practice and procedure. Presses Universitaires d'Afrique

Ngwafor EN (2006) The family code: a satisfactory gestation period. Int Surv Fam Law 120–129

Rabiatu ID (2010) A practical guide on the OHADA uniform act on securities in bijural Cameroon, 2nd edn. Symbolic Graphics, Cameroon

Tabe ST (2000) Property adjustment after divorce in Cameroonian statutory law: a rapprochement civil and common law systems? Afr J Int Comp Law 12(4):703–717

Tamfu NR (2013) Matrimonial regime in Cameroon. Légavox, 9 May. https://www.legavox.fr/blog/tamfu-ngarka-richard/matrimonial-regime-cameroon-11589.pdf. Accessed 14 Sept 2025

United Nations General Assembly (1946) Trusteeship Agreement for the Territory of the Cameroons under British Administration, UN Doc A/RES/63(I), 13 December 1946. https://digitallibrary.un.org/record/3995996. Accessed 16 Oct 2025

Fomchang Valery is a senior lecturer at the Faculty of Law and Political Science, University of Bertoua, Cameroon. He previously served as an Assistant Lecturer at the University of Yaoundé II, Soa, holding various teaching and administrative posts, before pioneering the English Law Department at the newly established University of Bertoua. His research interests include family law, company law, medical law, arbitration, investment law, mining law, and commercial law. He holds a Ph.D. in Business Law from the University of Yaoundé II, Soa.

Mixed Legal Systems: eSwatini, Mauritius, Seychelles, South Africa, Zimbabwe

Proprietary Consequences of Marriage in eSwatini

Dumsani Dlamini

Abstract Eswatini's plural legal system gives rise to overlapping and, at times, conflicting regimes that govern the proprietary consequences of marriage. This chapter provides a comprehensive analysis of matrimonial property systems during the subsistence of a marriage and upon its dissolution by divorce, examining how both Roman-Dutch law and eSwatini customary law operate under the supremacy of the 2005 Constitution. It outlines the distinctive rules governing civil marriages in and out of community of property, including recent reforms such as the abolition of marital power and the introduction of the accrual system under the draft Matrimonial Property Bill. The analysis also explores the evolving rights of women in customary marriages, the classification of personal and joint property, and the legal status of property situated on eSwatini Nation Land. By drawing on case law, proposed legislation, and international human rights norms, the chapter demonstrates how courts have incrementally dismantled patriarchal norms embedded in family law. It concludes by advocating for further legal clarity, especially regarding dual marriages, spousal consent for juristic acts, and equitable recognition of contributions in cohabitation and polygamous unions.

1 Introduction

This chapter examines the proprietary consequences of marriage in eSwatini, both during the subsistence of a marriage and upon its dissolution by divorce. To this end, the chapter analyses the legal framework governing the different types of matrimonial property systems recognised in eSwatini.

Owing to the plural legal system of eSwatini, it is inevitable that, at some point, there will be tension between the 'legal regimes' regulating the matrimonial property systems. As a result, the chapter highlights some of the points of tension between the legal regimes and illustrates how the legal system addresses these tensions. The

D. Dlamini (✉)
Department of Law, University of eSwatini, Kwaluseni, Eswatini
e-mail: dcdlamini@uniswa.sz

A. F. Hammond and P. Batariwah (eds.), *The Law on Marital Property in Africa*, Ius Gentium: Comparative Perspectives on Law and Justice 138,
https://doi.org/10.1007/978-3-032-19358-2_13

use of the expression ‘legal regimes’ as opposed to ‘legal systems’ is most preferred in this context as it is inspired by Chaskalson P., who, writing in the context of South African law, stated that there is only one system of law in the Republic of South Africa.[1] It is moulded by the Constitution, which serves as the supreme law; all laws, including the common law, owe their existence or force to the Constitution and are subject to constitutional control.[2] The same could be said of eSwatini. It has a single mixed legal system comprising various sources of law, all subject to the Constitution of the Kingdom of eSwatini Act 1 of 2005 (2005 Constitution), the supreme law of eSwatini.

Eswatini is predominantly a patriarchal society, evidenced by the embodiment of some patriarchal precepts in the rules governing the matrimonial property systems.[3] Accordingly, this chapter also illustrates how the courts have used international and national human rights law to integrate the notion of equality of spouses in marriage during the subsistence of marriage and on its dissolution by divorce. It is apposite, perhaps, to touch briefly on legal pluralism in eSwatini before we examine the different matrimonial property systems. This is because these systems are regulated by the different legal regimes that constitute the legal system of eSwatini.

This chapter is divided into ten sections. Section 1 introduces the subject by examining the proprietary consequences of marriage in eSwatini, both during marriage and upon divorce, within the context of the country’s plural legal regime. Section 2 explains the nature and implications of legal pluralism in eSwatini, especially the interplay between Roman-Dutch law and eSwatini customary law under the 2005 Constitution. Section 3 discusses the matrimonial property systems governed by Roman-Dutch law, including marriages in and out of community of property, with attention to the legal nature and content of community of property, reforms introduced by case law and legislation, and the implications of the proposed Matrimonial Property Bill. Section 4 focuses on the abolition of marital power and the administration of the joint estate, analysing key court decisions and proposed legislative reforms that aim to ensure equal authority of spouses over matrimonial property. Section 5 examines the proprietary consequences of divorce for spouses married in community of property, including rules governing division, issues of forfeiture of benefits, and the treatment of property situated on eSwatini Nation Land. Section 6 turns to marriages out of community of property, exploring the rationale behind antenuptial contracts, the implications of complete separation, and the proposed accrual system introduced by the bill. Section 7 discusses property rights under eSwatini customary marriages and explores the proposed reforms under the Matrimonial Property Bill of 2022. Section 8 examines the legal approach to invalid marriages and the resulting implications for property rights. Section 9 offers detailed recommendations for reform

---

[1] *Pharmaceutical Manufacturers Association of South Africa & Another: In re Ex Parte President of the Republic of South Africa & Others* (CCT 31/99) [2000] ZACC 1; 2000 (2) SA 674; 2000 (3) BCLR 241 (25 February 2000), para 44.

[2] *Pharmaceutical Manufacturers Association of South Africa & Another* (CCT 31/99) [2000] ZACC 1; 2000 (2) SA 674; 2000 (3) BCLR 241 (25 February 2000), para 44.

[3] For example, the common law doctrine of marital power.

to ensure that the law meaningfully reflects the realities and rights of all spouses in eSwatini, and Sect. 10 concludes the chapter.

2 Legal Pluralism in eSwatini

Legal pluralism in eSwatini consists primarily of Roman-Dutch common law (Roman-Dutch law) and eSwatini customary law as reinforced by the 2005 Constitution.[4] As the 2005 Constitution is the supreme law of eSwatini, the application of both Roman-Dutch law and eSwatini customary law is subject to its provisions.[5] To the extent that any other law is inconsistent with the 2005 Constitution, that other law shall be void.[6]

Surprisingly, neither the 2005 Constitution nor the statutory law defines eSwatini customary law, despite its recognition as part of the law of eSwatini.[7] Even court cases which involve eSwatini customary law do not shed light on its meaning.[8] In the absence of legislative interpretation of eSwatini customary law, one may seek guidance on its meaning from Ronald Thandabantu Nhlapho, who defines it as the body of traditional practices and customs of the people of eSwatini, which have been part of the culture of eSwatini since the inception of the eSwatini State in the late eighteenth century.[9] eSwatini customary law applies to the extent that it does not contradict the 2005 Constitution or statutory law.[10] An eSwatini customary law marriage is governed by eSwatini customary law. The rules governing the proprietary consequences of an eSwatini customary law marriage during its subsistence and on its dissolution by divorce cannot be established, as there are hardly any court cases that enunciate these rules. Furthermore, no legislation governs eSwatini customary law marriages, which could be a possible source of these rules.

Roman-Dutch law is the common law of eSwatini and applies to the extent that it does not conflict with the 2005 Constitution or statutory law.[11] Roman-Dutch law regulates two types of matrimonial property systems. These are civil law marriages, known as marriage in community of property and of profit and loss, commonly referred to as marriage in community of property. There are also marriages out of community of property, with or without the exclusion of community of profit and loss, commonly referred to as marriage out of community of property.

In a marriage in community of property, the spouses become tied co-owners in undivided and indivisible half-shares of all the assets and liabilities both parties had

[4] For a brief discussion of legal pluralism in eSwatini, see Dlamini (2023, pp. 285–287).

[5] Constitution of the Kingdom of eSwatini 2005, s. 2(1).

[6] Constitution of the Kingdom of eSwatini 2005, s. 2(1).

[7] Dlamini (2023, p. 440).

[8] Dlamini (2023, p. 440).

[9] Dlamini (2023, p. 440).

[10] Dlamini (2023, p. 440) and Constitution of the Kingdom of eSwatini 2005, s. 252(3).

[11] Constitution of the Kingdom of eSwatini 2005, s. 252(1).

at the moment of the conclusion of their marriage,[12] as well as of all the assets they acquire and the liabilities they incur during the subsistence of the marriage.[13] In contrast, parties who conclude a marriage out of community of property keep their own separate estates made up of all the assets and liabilities they acquired before and during the subsistence of the marriage.[14] Each spouse can alienate or deal with their assets as they please without seeking the other spouse's consent.

The legal system of eSwatini permits a couple to contract a marriage in both its customary and civil forms.[15] In the so-called 'double or dual marriage', both marriages have the same legal status.[16] A double or dual marriage occurs when parties who are already married under civil law contract a marriage under eSwatini customary law, or when spouses married under eSwatini customary law contract a civil marriage with each other.[17] Considering that marriage is a personal choice, it is difficult to ascertain why a couple would choose to marry under different legal regimes.[18] What is certain, though, is that a double or dual marriage gives rise to a conflict of laws problem between eSwatini customary law and Roman-Dutch as the two legal regimes vie for dominance, requiring the court to make a proper choice of law.[19] The conflict can be resolved by categorising the issues for determination as civil or customary and invoking the applicable legal regime.[20]

In the absence of statistics, it is difficult to state with certainty which of the marital regimes between civil and eSwatini customary law marriages is the most favoured in eSwatini. The general observation, however, is that not many parties contract dual or double marriages. Regarding civil marriages, it may be noted that the general trend is to contract a marriage in community of property. Put differently, marriage in community of property is the most common form of civil marriage. Recently, couples are increasingly opting for marriage out of community of property. One plausible explanation for couples favouring marriage in community of property is that a civil marriage is often associated with Christianity. To a certain extent, couples who contract a civil marriage subscribe to the Christian faith. In the Christian faith, it is accepted that once parties are married, they cleave to each other and become one.[21] Therefore, it would be contrary to the principles of the Christian faith for a couple to enter into a marriage agreement where they maintain separate property instead of a joint estate. The succeeding sections consider the matrimonial property systems recognised in eSwatini's hybrid legal system.

---

[12] Singh (2019, p. 318) and *Estate Sayle v Commissioner for Inland Revenue* 1945 AD 388.

[13] Heaton and Kruger (2015, p. 62).

[14] Human et al. (2010, p. 100).

[15] *Dlamini v Dlamini* (33 of 2017) [2017] SZSC 58 (10 November 2017).

[16] *Dlamini v Dlamini* (33 of 2017) [2017] SZSC 58 (10 November 2017).

[17] Marriage Act 1964, s. 7(1).

[18] Dlamini (2023, p. 446).

[19] Dlamini (2023, p. 447).

[20] Dlamini (2023, p. 447).

[21] Erhlich (1970, pp. 291–311).

Before proceeding, it is worth noting that the status of Islamic marriages in eSwatini is unclear. The only case which has come before a superior court is *Precious Phylicia Latiff* v *The Ministry of Home Affairs* & 2 *Others*.[22] In that case, the High Court was asked to rule on whether Islamic marriages are valid under the laws of eSwatini. The applicant had instituted proceedings seeking an order that would, among other things, dissolve her marriage to the respondent, award custody of the minor child to her, and forfeit the respondent's proprietary rights. The parties were alleged to have married in accordance with what they referred to as Sunni Islamic law. Unfortunately, the matter was dismissed on procedural grounds, leaving the substantive question unresolved.

It is undisputed that married members of the Muslim community may encounter challenges when they approach courts in relation to divorce and proprietary rights matters. Although the 2005 Constitution recognises the right to freedom of religion,[23] seemingly, this freedom does not extend to family law insofar as couples married under Islamic law are concerned. The Marriage Act of 1964, a pillar of civil marriages, requires marriages to be solemnised by, among others, ministers of religion appointed by the Minister who adhere to the stipulated formulas, whether civil or religious. This legal framework does not cover Islamic marriages solemnised solely in line with Sunni or other Islamic rites, as there is no provision for the automatic appointment of imams as marriage officers unless they apply and qualify under the Act.

It must also be pointed out that the 2005 Constitution recognises what it terms common law husband and wife and mandates Parliament to enact legislation to regulate the property rights of common law husband and wife. A common law husband and wife relationship depicts a de facto relationship of persons who are cohabiting and are in a conjugal relationship that lacks legal recognition as a marriage. As Parliament has not yet enacted the relevant legislation, the courts have not yet had occasion to determine the property rights of common-law husbands and wives. In the absence of the legislation envisaged by the 2005 Constitution, the inescapable conclusion is that the courts may decide the proprietary consequences of common law husband and wife on basis of the concept of tacit universal partnership.

3 Matrimonial Property Systems Governed by Roman-Dutch Law

As mentioned in the introduction, Roman-Dutch law governs the matrimonial property systems concerning both marriages in community of property and marriages out of community of property.

---

[22] *Precious Phylicia Latiff* v *The Ministry of Home Affairs* & 2 *Others* (607 of 2013) [2017] SZHC 107(7 June 2017).

[23] Constitution of the Kingdom of eSwatini 2005, s. 23.

3.1 Marriage in Community of Property

Regarding civil marriages, a marriage in community of property is the default matrimonial property system in eSwatini. This means that spouses are regarded as being married in community of property when they contract a civil marriage, unless certain circumstances exist that disprove the assumption that the marriage is in community of property. In cases where the spouses have entered into a valid antenuptial contract that explicitly excludes community of property and community of profit and loss,[24] or where the husband is domiciled in a jurisdiction whose laws stipulate that marriages are out of community of property at the time of the marriage,[25] the marriage cannot be classified as being in community of property. Additionally, a marriage contracted by a minor without the consent of their legal guardian is typically considered invalid unless the establishment of a community of property arrangement benefits the minor.[26] In such instances, the marriage would not be deemed to be in community of property.

3.2 The Legal Nature of Community of Property

Community of property is created the moment a marriage is solemnised,[27] and brings about a universal economic partnership.[28] The spouses become tied co-owners in undivided and indivisible half-shares of all the assets and liabilities they had at the moment of concluding their marriage formalities, as well as of all the assets they acquire and the liabilities they incur during the subsistence of the marriage.[29] Upon conclusion of the marriage, the separate estates of the spouses are automatically merged into one joint or shared estate for the duration of the marriage.[30] Both spouses hold equal shares irrespective of the value of the contribution of either of the spouses to the joint estate.[31] Upon termination of the marriage, all liabilities are settled from the joint estate, and the balance of the joint estate is shared equally between the spouses.[32] The legal implications of this matrimonial property system are that it has the potential to place the spouses in a financially precarious position because, upon the solemnisation of the marriage, the parties are jointly liable and thus not protected against each other's creditors.[33] Secondly, considering that the executor has an obligation to liquidate some, or even all, of the assets belonging to the joint

[24] Human et al. (2010, p. 80).

[25] Human et al. (2010, p. 80).

[26] Human et al. (2010, p. 80).

[27] Singh (2019, p. 318).

[28] Singh (2019, p. 318).

[29] Heaton and Kruger (2015, p. 62).

[30] Human et al. (2010, p. 81).

[31] Singh (2019, p. 318).

[32] Singh (2019, p. 318).

[33] Heaton and Kruger (2015, p. 67).

estate to satisfy the claims of creditors, liquidity issues might be experienced upon the death of one of the spouses.[34] The surviving spouse may still encounter liquidity challenges because the executor is authorised to liquidate part, or even the entire joint estate, to satisfy the claims of heirs when their inheritances become due and payable.[35]

3.3 The Content of Universal Community of Property

3.3.1 Assets that Generally Fall into the Community

Upon solemnisation of the marriage, all assets, movable or immovable, corporeal or incorporeal, that either spouse owned before the solemnisation of the marriage automatically become common in terms of ownership and legal possession.[36] Ownership of the assets is transferred automatically to the joint estate by operation of law. As a result, delivery of movable property, registration of immovable property, and cession of rights are not necessary.[37] Thus, immovable property brought into the joint estate by either spouse on solemnisation of the marriage remains registered in that spouse's name. However, regardless of the name in which the property is registered, it is part of the joint estate.[38] This begs the question: What is the legal position of registration of immovable property and other real rights in immovable property which the husband and the wife acquire during the subsistence of the marriage? However, it should be noted that in the past, registration of the property in the joint names of the spouses was not automatic. Before 2010, the law prohibited the transfer or cession to, or registration of, immovable property and other real rights in the name of a woman married in community of property, unless the property or real rights were excluded from the community by law or by a condition of a bequest or donation.[39] The property could be registered only in the husband's name, even if the deed of sale showed the names of both spouses as purchasers. It took the intervention of the courts for the Parliament of eSwatini to amend the law to allow women married in community of property to register immovable property and other real rights jointly with their husbands.

In *Aphane v Registrar of Deeds & Others*,[40] the applicant, a woman married in community of property, and her husband sought to register immovable property in their joint names. In terms of section 16(3) of the Deeds Registry Act of

---

[34] Denson (2020, p. 747).

[35] Denson (2020, p. 747).

[36] Denson (2020, p. 746).

[37] Heaton and Kruger (2015, pp 63–64).

[38] Heaton and Kruger (2015, pp. 63–64).

[39] Deeds Registry Act 1968, s. 16(3).

[40] *Aphane v Registrar of Deeds & Others* (383 of 2009) [2010] SZHC 29 (23 February 2010).

1968, the property could be registered in the sole name of the husband. The applicant approached the High Court for an order invalidating the limitation imposed by section 16(3) for its want of compliance with sections 20 and 28 of the 2005 Constitution. Section 20 provides for equality before the law and prohibits discrimination based on gender. Section 28 provides that women have a right to equal treatment with men and that the right includes, among other things, equal opportunities in economic activities. The court held that section 16(3) was discriminatory against women married in community of property and declared it to be unconstitutional.

On appeal,[41] the Supreme Court confirmed the declaration of invalidity and ordered the registration of immovable property, bonds, and other real rights in the joint names of husbands and wives married in community of property pending the enactment of legislation by Parliament. Parliament has enacted the amending law,[42] and it (the amending law) states without equivocation, in its long title, that it seeks to provide for the equality of natural persons to own property. This aspiration of Parliament finds expression in the substantive provisions of the amending Act, as they provide that a deed registered in respect of immovable property for a married person shall state the full names of the spouse, the type of marriage (civil or customary), and whether it is a marriage in or out of community of property.[43] A possible interpretation of this provision is that the law now allows either spouse in a marriage in community of property to register immovable property in their own name. This registration, however, does not detract from the fact that the property is co-owned, as the deed registered will indicate that the marriage is in community of property. Further, the parties may register the property in their joint names if they are both purchasers. This represents a clear departure from section 16(3) of the old legislation, which prohibited women married in community of property from registering immovable property in their own names or jointly with their husbands.

The proprietary consequences of civil marriages are largely regulated by Roman-Dutch law. Of course, other statutes, such as the Deeds Registry Act of 1968 (Deeds Registry Act), have a bearing on the proprietary consequences of civil marriages. The amendment of the Deeds Registry Act has overridden some of the principles of the common law.[44] In interpreting the 2005 Constitution, the courts have also issued decisions that abolish some common law principles applied in the administration of the matrimonial property of spouses married in community of property.[45] Also significant is the introduction of the Matrimonial Property Bill of 2022 (the bill). The bill is part of the process to implement section 34 of the 2005 Constitution, which mandates Parliament to enact a law to regulate the property rights of spouses. Consequently, it seeks to regulate the property rights of spouses in respect of all

[41] *Attorney-General v Aphane* (12 of 2009) [2010] SZSC 32 (27 May 2010).

[42] Deeds Registry (Amendment) Act 2012.

[43] Deeds Registry (Amendment) Act 2012, s. 16(1)(b)(i)-(iii).

[44] See, for example, Deeds Registry (Amendment) Act 2012, s. 16(3).

[45] See, for example, *Sacolo & Another v Sacolo & Others* (1403 of 2016) [2019] SZHC166 (30 August 2019), which abolished the marital power of the husband in marriages in a community of property.

types of marriages recognised in eSwatini. Although the bill is not law, it shall be considered in this discussion alongside the existing law to the extent that it seeks to introduce certain reforms to the law governing the existing matrimonial property systems. In this part, the bill is considered as it relates to a marriage in community of property.

One of the concepts the bill defines is matrimonial property, which means matrimonial home or homes[46]; household goods and effects in the matrimonial home or homes[47]; or any other immovable and movable property jointly owned and acquired during the subsistence of the marriage.[48] The matrimonial home is any property that either spouse or both spouses own or lease, is occupied or used by one or both spouses as their principal residence, and includes any other attached property.[49] The bill recognises that matrimonial property consists of property jointly owned or owned by either spouse and acquired during the marriage. This reinforces the common law principle that in a marriage in a community of property, the spouses' estate is a joint estate, and both parties enjoy equal ownership.[50]

The bill lists the protection of the matrimonial home as one of its objects.[51] With this end in view, it prohibits the mortgaging or leasing of the matrimonial home without the written and informed consent of both spouses.[52] Unless a court issues an order of eviction, neither spouse shall be evicted from the matrimonial home by or at the instance of the other spouse while the marriage subsists.[53] The bill lists three lawful instances in which any person may evict a spouse from the matrimonial home.[54] The provisions on the definition and protection of the matrimonial home and matrimonial property are progressive, particularly insofar as they affect women married in community of property. Before abolishing the husband's marital power, the husband could dissipate the joint estate's assets without the wife's consent or knowledge. Some dishonest husbands could even go to the extent of selling the matrimonial home without the wife's consent. The proposed law implies that the husband will no longer be able to unilaterally deal with the matrimonial property and the matrimonial home without the wife's consent, as was the case in the era of the husband's marital power. The common law doctrine of marital power and its impact on women married in community of property is discussed later in the chapter.

The bill provides that immovable property which forms part of the matrimonial property but is not yet registered shall be registered in the names of the husband and the wife.[55] In relation to the registration of immovable property in the names

[46] Matrimonial Property Bill 2022, s. 4(1)(a).

[47] Matrimonial Property Bill 2022, s. 4(1)(b).

[48] Matrimonial Property Bill 2022, s. 4(1)(c).

[49] Matrimonial Property Bill 2022, s. 2.

[50] Singh (2019, p. 318).

[51] Matrimonial Property Bill 2022, Memorandum of objects and reasons, para (f).

[52] Matrimonial Property Bill 2022, s. 6.

[53] Matrimonial Property Bill 2022, s. 7(1).

[54] Matrimonial Property Bill 2022, s. 7(2).

[55] Matrimonial Property Bill 2022, s. 4(3).

of married persons, this provision of the bill is more explicit than the provisions of the Deeds Registry Amendment Act of 2012, as it clearly and without any doubt permits the registration of immovable property in the joint names of spouses married in community of property. Notably, the registration of the property in the joint names of the husband and wife is peremptory. This means there is a statutory obligation on the Registrar of Deeds to register the property in the names of both spouses if they are married in community of property. Contravening any provision of the bill is an offence. On conviction, the offender shall be liable to a term of imprisonment not exceeding two years or a fine not exceeding E10,000.00 or both.[56]

The bill further provides that immovable property deemed matrimonial property and registered in the name of one of the spouses shall, notwithstanding any law to the contrary, be regarded as matrimonial property.[57] This stipulation seeks to reinforce by statutory provision the common law principle that immovable property brought into the marriage by either spouse becomes part of their joint estate by operation of law. As a result, no transfer is required, and regardless of the name under which the property is registered, it shall be considered part of the joint estate.

There are exceptions to the general rule that all assets owned by the spouses at the end of the marriage, or acquired by them during the marriage, become part of their joint estate. The next section examines the exceptions to the rule.

3.3.2 Assets Excluded from the Joint Estate

Assets Excluded by Antenuptial Contract

An antenuptial contract is an agreement concluded between the prospective spouses that prescribes the terms and conditions by which their marriage shall be governed.[58] It is executed before the solemnisation of the marriage and comes into effect immediately the marriage is solemnised.[59] Spouses married in community of property may exclude certain assets from the joint estate by means of an antenuptial contract.[60] The effect of executing an antenuptial contract is that the joint estate coexists with a separate estate or estates consisting of the excluded assets.[61] Unless the proceeds or fruits of the excluded assets are also explicitly excluded in the antenuptial contract, they form part of the joint estate.[62] The recognition of separate assets is a common law principle. The bill reinforces this principle by providing a legislative basis for it, prohibiting a spouse married in community of property from instituting legal proceedings against another person or defending legal proceedings without the other

---

[56] Matrimonial Property Bill 2022, s. 36.

[57] Matrimonial Property Bill 2022, s. 4(3).

[58] Singh (2019, p. 318).

[59] Singh (2019, p. 318).

[60] Heaton and Kruger (2015, p. 64).

[61] Human et al. (2010, p. 82).

[62] *Blatchford v Blatchford's Executors* (1861) 1 EDC 365.

spouse's written consent, unless the proceedings concern the spouse's separate property.[63] The bill defines separate property as property that does not form part of the joint estate.[64]

Assets Excluded by Will or Donation

At common law, a third party may make a bequest or a donation to a husband or wife with the proviso that the asset shall not form part of the joint estate.[65] If the testator or donor does not explicitly exclude the fruits of the asset from the joint estate, they will become part of it.[66]

Fideicommissum or Usufruct

There is a common law rule that assets subject to a fideicommissum or fideicommissary property are not part of the joint estate but are part of the proceeds of the property.[67] Similarly, usufructuary property is excluded from the joint estate of the spouse married in community of property, but the proceeds become part of the joint estate.[68] The most plausible reason for the rule that the proceeds of assets subject to a fideicommissum or usufruct do not fall into the joint estate is that these assets belong to a category of property and rights that the beneficiary cannot alienate, as they are of a personal nature.[69]

Jocalia (Small Gifts or Engagement Gifts)

The engagement ring and small gifts that the spouses give each other in anticipation of marriage are excluded from the joint estate and become part of the separate estate of the spouse who receives the gift.[70]

Costs Awarded in Matrimonial Proceedings

If a couple married in community of property is embroiled in matrimonial proceedings against each other and the marriage is not dissolved, any order as to costs granted

---

[63] Matrimonial Property Bill 2022, s. 11(1)(a).
[64] Matrimonial Property Bill 2022, s. 2.
[65] Heaton and Kruger (2015, p. 64).
[66] Human et al. (2010, p. 82).
[67] *Barnet v Rudman* 1934 AD 203.
[68] Heaton and Kruger (2015, p. 64).
[69] Human et al. (2010, p. 83).
[70] Heaton and Kruger (2015, p. 65).

in favour of either of them does not fall into the joint estate.[71] The claim to costs falls into the separate estate of the spouse who has been granted the claim.[72]

Replacing Assets

The general rule is that assets that are excluded in an antenuptial contract fall into separate estates of the spouses. Thus, an asset that replaces an asset that was excluded in an antenuptial contract does not become part of the joint estate.[73]

Having ascertained which property falls into the joint estate and in whom ownership of such property vests, it is helpful, perhaps, to determine who is charged with the administration of the matrimonial property of spouses married in community of property. It is to that discussion that we now turn.

4 Abolition of Marital Power and the Administration of the Joint Estate

4.1 Abolition of Marital Power

In *Sacolo & Another v Sacolo & Others*, a full bench of the High Court defined the common law doctrine of marital power as:

> ...the right of the husband to rule over and defend the person of his wife, and to administer her goods in such a way as to dispose of them at his own will, or at any rate to prevent his wife dealing with them except with his knowledge and consent.[74]

As a consequence of the marital power:

> the husband assumes the office of administrator of the joint estate, and the wife finds herself subordinated to his guardianship, bereft of active legal capacity save where common law or statutory dispensations have been grudgingly granted. The husband's power to administer the joint estate as he pleases – buying, selling investing, donating or squandering its assets – is fettered at common law only by the rule that transactions in fraud of the wife will be set aside at her instance, and by the remedies of interdiction and *boedelscheiding* (both of which are available in severe cases of maladministration).[75]

Before the commencement of the 2005 Constitution, there was no legislation in eSwatini that restricted the operation of marital power. As shown above, marital power not only restricted the legal capacity of women married in community of

[71] Heaton and Kruger (2015, p. 66).

[72] *Comerman v Comerman* 1938 TPD 220.

[73] *Ex parte Lelie* 1945 WLD 167.

[74] *Sacolo & Another v Sacolo & Others* (1403 of 2016) [2019] SZHC166 (30 August 2019), para 9.

[75] *Sihlongonyane v Sihlonganyane* (4070 of 2013 A)[2013] SZHC 144 (18 July 2023), para 15.

property to act but also infringed on their right to dignity as it rendered them inferior to their husbands.[76] After the coming into force of the 2005 Constitution, the first court case in which the husband's marital power was tested for its constitutional validity was *Sihlongonyane v Sihlongonyane*.[77] This case concerned the constitutionality of the husband's marital power insofar as it denied women married in community of property *locus standi* to sue and be sued in their own name. The court held that denying *locus standi* to women married in a community of property violated the constitutional right to equality of all persons before the law, as guaranteed in sections 20 and 28 of the 2005 Constitution. This case interfered with marital power insofar as it restricted women married in community of property from suing or being sued without their husbands' assistance. It did not completely abolish it. The Court order also made it clear that the abolition of the restriction took effect from 12 November 2013, meaning that from this date, married women who were subject to their husbands' marital power enjoyed the right to sue and be sued in their own names. It can be safely concluded that the right which married women enjoyed from 12 November 2013 did not alter the legal consequences of any act or omission that took place before the abolition of the restriction that the marital power had on the capacity of women to sue or be sued.

To justify its reasoning that the marital power of the husband amounted to unfair discrimination based on sex, affecting women in a specific type of marriage while not impacting men in the same way, the court referenced the United Nations Human Rights Committee's interpretation of the right to equality.[78] The court observed that eSwatini was a state party to the International Covenant on Civil and Political Rights and that, in enacting sections 20 and 28 of the 2005 Constitution, the State was fulfilling its obligations under that instrument. The *Sihlongonyane* case provides a clear example of a case in which the High Court relied on national and international human rights law to protect and promote women's rights, particularly women married in a community of property.

The case of *Sacolo* completely abolished marital power. At common law, if consent to marry is granted on behalf of a minor who has not reached the age of majority, the minor attains majority status once they get married. In the *Sacolo* case, the applicant argued that, in the administration of the joint estate, the existence of marital power rendered a woman married in community of property a minor, even if she had attained majority status. This is because she can deal with the matrimonial property only if the husband knows and has given consent. On the contrary, the applicant contended that the husband can deal with the property without the wife's knowledge and approval. The applicant further contended that, in practice, the marital power conferred upon the husband is prone to abuse, often to the detriment of the other spouse.

It is possible to restrict the husband's marital power through an antenuptial contract that excludes community of property. The antenuptial contract enables each party

---

[76] Heaton and Kruger (2015, p. 70).

[77] *Sihlongonyane v Sihlongonyane* (4070 of 2013 A)[2013] SZHC 144 (18 July 2023).

[78] United Nations Human Rights Committee (2000), art. 3.

to a marriage out of community of property to retain their separate property, which they can alienate or deal with as they please without seeking the other spouse's consent. The applicant argued that the availability of this option did not eliminate the discrimination to which marital power subjected women who intended to contract a civil law marriage in community of property. According to the applicant, the reason was that an antenuptial contract served both spouses equally, yet marital power restricted the rights of married women only. The applicant argued that marital power was inconsistent with the equality provisions of the 2005 Constitution and that it was a violation of the right to dignity to which women were entitled under the 2005 Constitution, as it perpetuated the minority status of women within marriage.

Although much of the applicant's argument was premised on international human rights law, the court, in making its judgment, found it unnecessary to rely on international law, as, according to the court, the matter could be conclusively and effectively determined according to national law. It is submitted that the court should not have avoided drawing inspiration from international human rights law; it could still have used international law to support its reasoning, already informed by other grounds.[79]

The court held that the applicant's arguments had merit and issued an order declaring the common law marital power unconstitutional, as it was discriminatory against women. The court ruled that women married in community of property under the Marriage Act of 1964 have the same capacity and authority as their husbands to administer marital property. It is worth mentioning that the bill also seeks to abolish the husband's marital power over his wife's person and property.[80] An inference that can be drawn from this provision is that the bill seeks to eliminate marital power in all its manifestations, not just one aspect of it, as was the case when the High Court intervened in the *Sihlongonyane case*. This aspiration is more vivid in section 3(2) of the bill, which states that the abolition of marital power is intended to remove the limitations that marital power places on the wife's capacity to contract and to litigate. In this respect, the bill apparently gives legislative endorsement to the *Sacolo case*, which clearly abolished marital power. Once the bill is enacted into an Act of Parliament, it will abolish any marital power a husband has over the person and property of his wife immediately before the Act's commencement.[81] It is not clear from the bill what "immediately before" means and how it is to be determined. In the *Sacolo case*, the abolition of marital power was unconditional, suggesting that abolition took effect on the date of judgment. The bill was drafted years after the court's judgement and does not follow the court's approach, as it does not state that the abolition will take effect on the date of commencement of the Act. By placing this qualification 'immediately before', the bill gives the impression that the drafters intended that the law should also cover or apply to a certain period before its commencement. It remains uncertain what ills the bill's drafters envisaged would result in the unqualified abolition of marital power, prompting them to specify that the abolition must be 'immediately before' to address the concern. To avoid any doubt regarding

---

[79] Dlamini (2021, pp. 68–69).

[80] Matrimonial Property Bill 2022, s. 3(1).

[81] Matrimonial Property Bill 2022, s. 3(3).

this period, the drafters should have stated the period in clear terms or given an interpretation of 'immediately before'.

However, the abolition of marital power shall not affect the legal consequences of any act of commission or omission that occurred before the abolition.[82] This means that women will continue to experience some of the negative consequences of exercising marital power before its abolition. By not extending the abolition to the legal consequences of actions taken under marital power while it was in effect, it is presumed that the drafters aimed to avoid the disruption that would arise from invalidating transactions that were lawful when made and entered into under the marital power. The bill shall govern all marriages in community of property once it becomes law, regardless of when the marriage was contracted.[83] A plausible justification for this is that the bill aims to reform the law governing the various existing matrimonial property systems.

As discussed below, the abolition of marital power has affected the administration of the property of spouses married in community of property.

4.2 The Equal Administration of the Joint Estate

Before the judgment of the Supreme Court in the *Aphane* case, the Deeds Registry Act of 1968 provided that the husband of a woman to whom he is married in community could alone deal with immovable property registered in the wife's name.[84] This was an incident of the marital power of the husband. The woman could deal with the property only if a court order had granted her authority. The Deeds Registry (Amendment) Act, which was promulgated after the *Aphane* case, stipulates that neither spouse in a marriage in community of property may deal with immovable property or other real rights that are part of the joint estate without the written consent of the other spouse or court authorisation.[85]

It may be argued that the amending provision was intended to integrate the principle that spouses have equal capacity and authority to administer matrimonial property. The application of this provision is illustrated in the case of *Ntshalintshali v Mthethwa & Others*,[86] in which the fourth respondent, a woman married in community of property, successfully objected to the sale of land belonging to the joint estate. She argued that the sale agreement concluded by her husband and the applicant was unenforceable because her written consent had not been sought and obtained before the sale of the land. The court ordered the husband of the fourth respondent to pay the applicant's costs of the proceedings because he had been reckless in dealing with the

---

[82] Matrimonial Property Bill 2022, s. 3(5).

[83] Matrimonial Property Bill 2022, s. 3(4).

[84] Deeds Registry Act 1968, s. 16(4).

[85] Deeds Registry (Amendment) Act 2012, s. 16(3).

[86] *Ntshalintshali v Mthethwa & Others* (1547 of 2007) [2017] SZHC111(9 June 2017).

property. Similarly, in *Rautebach v Rautebach & Others*,[87] the applicant, a woman married in community of property, successfully sought an order setting aside a deed of sale over immovable property that was part of the joint estate, which had been concluded by her husband and the respondents without her written consent. Again, the court ordered the applicant's husband to pay the costs of the proceedings because he had no authority to alienate the property without the applicant's written consent. In totally abolishing marital power, the court ordered, in the *Sacolo* case, that husband and wife married in community of property and, in terms of the Marriage Act of 1947, had equal capacity and authority to administer matrimonial property.

In keeping with the changes introduced by the amending legislation and the decided court cases, the bill reinforces the principle of equal management of the joint estate. As a starting point, the bill recognises the equality of powers of spouses married in community of property.[88] In this regard, upon the bill coming into force, a wife married in community of property will have the same authority as the husband had before the bill regarding the disposal of assets and management of the joint estate.[89] It should be remembered that under the old law, a married woman who was subject to the husband's marital power did not enjoy the same power her husband had in the alienation of the assets and the management of the joint estate.

The bill outlines the extent of the capacity of spouses married in community to act regarding the management of the assets of the joint estate.[90] Either spouse may not perform any juristic act pertaining to the joint estate without the other spouse's consent.[91] As the bill explicitly outlines the juristic acts that shall not be performed without the written consent of either spouse, it may be argued that not all juristic acts require written consent. Some, particularly those not specifically listed, require other forms of consent, which may be oral or tacit.[92] Unfortunately, the bill does not list the juristic acts that do not require written consent for their performance.

Apparently, the bill does not permit independent management of the joint estate. Independent management entails that either spouse has the capacity to perform certain juristic acts binding on the joint estate without the consent or knowledge of the other spouse.[93] The principle of independent management of the joint estate is established by statute. However, the same statute may provide exceptions to limit its application, thereby protecting the interests of both spouses and third parties.[94] A statute may provide for independent and concurrent management of the joint estate by the husband and the wife.[95]

---

[87] *Rautebach v Rautebach & Others* (68 of 2014) [2020] SZHC 69 (28 April 2020).

[88] Matrimonial Property Bill 2022, s. 8.

[89] Matrimonial Property Bill 2022, s. 8.

[90] Matrimonial Property Bill 2022, s. 9(2)–(3).

[91] Matrimonial Property Bill 2022, s. 9(1).

[92] Heaton and Kruger (2015, p. 73).

[93] Human et al. (2010, pp 88–89).

[94] Human et al. (2010, pp. 88–89).

[95] Human et al. (2010, pp. 88–89).

Seemingly, the bill requires joint management of the joint estate and attaches equal importance to all juristic acts, mandating the written consent of both spouses for their valid performance. Notably, unlike the era of marital power, where only the wife's legal capacity was restricted, the bill proposes limitations on the legal capacity of both spouses. While it is understandable that the provision requiring the written consent of both spouses for the valid performance of all juristic acts pertaining to the joint estate is meant to protect the interests of both spouses, this arrangement can potentially impede the spouses' participation in commercial activities.[96] This is the result of the failure of the bill to divide the juristic acts into different categories, that is, those that are binding on the joint estate but do need the consent of both spouses because they do not unreasonably prejudice the other spouse and those that need the consent of both spouses because they are very important and that the consequences flowing from unilateral action could have a drastic effect on the joint estate or the other spouse. For example, the bill prohibits either spouse from alienating marital property, such as livestock and jewellery.[97] A spouse who sells a chicken from a flock of chickens without the other spouse's consent would not unreasonably prejudice the other spouse or the joint estate. Similarly, a wife who sells some of her jewellery, which the husband may not know of or even be interested in, may not necessarily prejudice the joint estate.

On the other hand, neither spouse may conclude a transaction regarding any matrimonial property from which the family derives sustenance unless the other spouse gives written and informed consent.[98] There is merit in requiring the other spouse's written consent before a transaction of this kind is carried out. It would drastically prejudice the other spouse and the joint estate if one spouse, for example, could unilaterally lower the rental fee charged on leased premises, which is a source of livelihood for the family, without the written and informed consent of the other spouse.

The bill provides a comprehensive list of the juristic acts that neither spouse shall perform without the other spouse's written consent.[99] Examples of these acts are as follows:

- The alienation, mortgaging, and burdening with a servitude of immovable property.[100]
- The conclusion of a contract for the alienation, mortgaging, and burdening with a servitude of immovable property.[101]

---

[96] Heaton and Kruger (2015, p. 71).

[97] Matrimonial Property Bill 2022, s. 9(2)(d).

[98] Matrimonial Property Bill 2022, s. 5.

[99] Matrimonial Property Bill 2022, s. 9.

[100] Matrimonial Property Bill 2022, s. 9(2)(a).

[101] Matrimonial Property Bill 2022, s. 9(2)(b).

- The alienation, pledging, or hypothecating of any livestock, motor vehicle, any jewellery, coins, stamps, paintings, or any other assets forming part of the joint estate[102];
- Receipt of money due or accruing to the other spouse or the joint estate. The source of the money could be remuneration, earnings, bonus, an allowance, royalty, a pension, or a gratuity resulting from services rendered by the other spouse,[103] or inheritance, legacy donation,[104] or income derived from the other spouse's separate property.[105]

The consent required for certain juristic acts may be granted through ratification within a reasonable period after the act has been performed.[106] Ratification has the same effect as prior consent. As the juristic acts for which ratification may be granted are different in nature, there appears to be a glaring omission in the bill in that it does not prescribe the form that the subsequent ratification must take with respect to each of the juristic acts. Although the bill insists on the principle of equal administration of the joint estate by requiring both spouses' consent to perform juristic acts, it envisages the possibility that either spouse may unreasonably withhold consent to the prejudice of the estate or the other spouse. In this respect, the bill permits a spouse to apply to the court for leave to conclude a transaction if the other spouse unreasonably withholds consent.[107] The import of this provision is that a spouse's consent is not absolute; the court can order that it be dispensed with if it is unreasonably withheld. Community of property ceases on the dissolution of the marriage by divorce. The succeeding section examines the proprietary consequences of a marriage in community of property on its dissolution by divorce.

5 Proprietary Consequences of Divorce for Spouses Married in Community of Property

5.1 Division of the Joint Estate

One of the aspects of the patrimony of the husband and wife that the consequences of divorce mostly affect is the division of their assets.[108] It should be remembered that the spouses own the joint estate in equal, undivided and indivisible shares during the subsistence of a marriage in community of property. On dissolution of the community by divorce, the general rule is that a spouse married in community of property is

[102] Matrimonial Property Bill 2022, s. 9(2)(c).
[103] Matrimonial Property Bill 2022, s. 9(2)(g)(i).
[104] Matrimonial Property Bill 2022, s. 9(2)(g)(iii).
[105] Matrimonial Property Bill 2022, s. 9(2)(g)(iv).
[106] Matrimonial Property Bill 2022, s 9(3).
[107] Matrimonial Property Bill 2022, s 10(1).
[108] Singh (2019, p. 317).

entitled to half of the net value of the joint estate as the shares become determinate and divisible.[109] The practice is that the spouses draw up an agreement or deed of settlement providing, among other things, for the division of the assets of the joint estate[110]; the divorce is concluded, and the deed of settlement is made an order of the court.[111]

It is worth mentioning that in some cases, the issue of potential conflict of laws has arisen regarding the division of property of spouses married in community of property whose matrimonial home is not on a title deed land but on eSwatini Nation Land. Eswatini Nation Land is land held by *iNgwenyama* in trust for the nation of eSwatini. The *iNgwenyama* is the hereditary and traditional head of the State of eSwatini.[112] The eSwatini traditional government is administered according to eSwatini customary law, and the *iNgwenyama* is one of the institutions that serve as a pillar of the eSwatini traditional government.[113] The distinction between a person whose name is registered in a title deed and a person who has been allocated eSwatini Nation Land is that the person who holds a title deed can claim title to or ownership of the land registered in the deed. On the other hand, a person who has been allocated eSwatini Nation Land cannot claim ownership of the land they occupy. The proprietary rights of such a person are restricted to use and occupation only.

In *Nxumalo v Nkambule & Another*,[114] the applicant, a woman, sought an order interdicting and restraining the first respondent, her former husband, from visiting her home. The applicant and the respondent were once married in community of property and later divorced. After the divorce, the applicant stayed in the matrimonial home, and the respondent resided elsewhere. The deed of settlement, agreed upon by both parties and made an order of court, stipulated that the applicant would retain the matrimonial home as her sole and exclusive property. The house was situated on eSwatini Nation Land, which the respondent had acquired according to the eSwatini traditional system of *kukhonta*. The *kukhonta* custom is the mechanism by which a chief, who is the local head of a traditional community or chiefdom, allocates land to *eMaswati* from other chiefdoms who wish to reside in his area.[115]

Before the adoption of the 2005 Constitution, women did not have the capacity to acquire eSwatini Nation Land without the assistance of a male person. Generally, they could acquire it through kukhonta, involving a father, husband, or son. It was also stated in the settlement deed that the applicant shall have a life usufruct in and to the matrimonial home without any interference from the respondent. This arrangement entitled the applicant to live in, rent, mortgage, and do as she wishes with the property, except for selling it. Regarding the settlement deed, the applicant was required to obtain the respondent's consent if she intended to mortgage the matrimonial home.

---

[109] Human et al. (2010, p. 152).

[110] *Nxumalo v Nkambule & Another* (1154 of 2017) [2018] SZHC 11(13 February 2017).

[111] *Nxumalo v Nkambule & Another* (1154 of 2017) [2018] SZHC 11(13 February 2017), para 4.

[112] Constitution of the Kingdom of eSwatini 2005, s. 4(1) and s. 228(1).

[113] Constitution of the Kingdom of eSwatini 2005, s. 227.

[114] *Nxumalo v Nkambule & Another* (1154 of 2017) [2018] SZHC 11(13 February 2017).

[115] *Mahlalela v Dlamini & 2 Others* (17 of 2013) [2013] SZHC 40 (2013), para 21.

The permission of the respondent was not to be unreasonably withheld. The applicant could not sell the property because, under eSwatini customary law, a person or persons allocated land for dwelling and cultivation cannot claim land ownership. The reason is that their 'proprietary rights over such land is that of use or occupation only. The land does not belong to them. It belongs to the King of Swaziland and the Nation at large.'[116]

In this case, the applicant sought an interdict against the respondent for entering her premises without her knowledge or permission, in violation of the deed of settlement. The respondent contended that he had the right to visit the homestead, as the local traditional authorities considered it his homestead, being situated on eSwatini Nation Land. He further argued that he still owed allegiance to the local authorities who had allocated him the land and that he was responsible for ensuring no misconduct occurred at the homestead. He further submitted that the applicant could not claim an exclusive right over the homestead, as he was the one who had given her the right to use and enjoy the property.

The court granted the interdicting order, having determined that the deed of settlement had conferred on the applicant the right to occupy and enjoy the usage of the homestead without any disturbance from the respondent. It noted that the applicant enjoyed a right to privacy that the respondent could not violate, even though he remained accountable to the local traditional authorities. The court rejected the respondent's claim that he owned the homestead by virtue of being the male who had acquired the land through the *kukhonta* custom. The court acknowledged that, before the enactment of the 2005 Constitution, this custom prevailed; however, with the adoption of the 2005 Constitution, the prevailing order was that women had equal access to eSwatini Nation Land for normal domestic purposes.[117] The court remarked that common decency dictated that the respondent should politely approach the applicant if he wished to discuss anything regarding the homestead. This remark suggests that the respondent still had a 'link' with the homestead.

The case involves a situation where both common law and eSwatini customary law had to be applied in the division of the spouses' matrimonial property, despite their marriage being governed by common law. Customary law was applicable in the division of the joint estate as the matrimonial property was situated on eSwatini Nation Land. Seemingly, the spouses did not approach the traditional authorities to settle the question of who would retain exclusive and sole possession and occupation of the matrimonial home before they drafted the settlement deed. Now that the 2005 Constitution grants women equal access to eSwatini Nation Land, the better view is that the spouses should have approached the traditional authorities to inform them of their divorce and mutual agreement to allow the applicant to retain the matrimonial property as her sole and exclusive property. By this arrangement, the traditional authorities would now regard the applicant as the sole person with exclusive rights over the occupation and use of the property, and the respondent would cease to have

[116] *Spintex Swaziland (Pty) Ltd. v Motsa & Others* (2142 of 2012) [2013] SZHC 97 (30 April 2013), para 19.

[117] Constitution of the Kingdom of eSwatini 2005, s. 211(2).

any right over the homestead. In applying customary law, the traditional authorities must consider the applicable constitutional law provisions. It is argued that had the spouses consulted the traditional authorities, the settlement deed would have been drafted to exclude the respondent's claimed rights over the property. It defies logic that the respondent still retained an unjustified semblance of "control" over property that was allocated as the applicant's share during the division of the matrimonial property.

If spouses married in community of property fail to reach an agreement on the division of the estate, the court may exercise its discretion and order a division it considers just or appoint a liquidator to sell the assets, settle all liabilities of the joint estate, and divide the balance equally between the spouses.[118] Equal division of the joint estate may not occur if the court has granted an order for the forfeiture of benefits.

5.2 Forfeiture of Patrimonial Benefits

Upon dissolution of the marriage, a spouse may forfeit their patrimonial benefits if it is found that they acted irresponsibly in dealing with the joint estate. The basic principle regulating the forfeiture of patrimonial benefits is that a spouse must not benefit financially from a marriage for which they are responsible for its break-up.[119] An example of a case that illustrates the application of this principle is *Nyembe v Nyembe*,[120] in which the plaintiff had asked the court, in divorce proceedings, to issue an order depriving the defendant of his proprietary benefits in the remaining joint estate because he was responsible for the dissolution of the marriage. The plaintiff alleged that the defendant had committed adultery, which had caused the marriage to fail, and that he had failed to properly manage the assets of the joint estate, such as immovable property. In granting the order sought, the court observed that the defendant had dissipated the marital assets, exercising his marital power in a manner that was not in the best interest of the joint estate in anticipation of an order that might be made against him in the divorce proceedings.[121] The court has no discretion to withhold an order of forfeiture if the injured spouse prays the court for it.[122]

If the court grants a forfeiture order against one of the spouses, the spouse against whom the order has been granted will be entitled to receive only the assets he or she brought into the joint estate.[123] The order of forfeiture of benefits does not deprive a spouse of the assets they contributed to the joint estate, but invalidates a claim

[118] *Dhanwanthi v Shanduth* 1961 (2) SA 692 (N).
[119] *Murison v Murison* 1930 AD 157.
[120] *Nyembe v Nyembe* (1604 of 2008) [2008] SZHC 233 (11 December 2008).
[121] *Nyembe v Nyembe* (1604 of 2008) [2008] SZHC 233 (11 December 2008), para 33.
[122] *Murison v Murison* (n 117).
[123] Human et al. (2010, p. 155).

that they have to the other spouse's assets.[124] In other words, the forfeiture only affects benefits accrued to a spouse flowing from the marriage, which they would not have had otherwise.[125] Other than entering into a marriage in community of property, prospective spouses may decide to enter into a marriage out of community of property excluding community of profit and loss, or a marriage out of community of property with retention of community of profit and loss.

6 Marriage Out of Community of Property

A marriage is classified as out of community of property if the prospective spouses execute a valid antenuptial contract excluding community of property before entering the marriage.[126] Similarly, if, at the time of the marriage, the husband was domiciled in a state where the legal system treats marriage as being out of community of property, the marriage is considered out of community of property, even if no antenuptial contract was entered into.[127] This can be explained based on the marriage domicile, which is the legal system governing the matrimonial property system.[128] The spouses cannot later change it even if they relocate to another state, as it is fixed when the marriage is entered into.[129]

6.1 The Rationale of an Antenuptial Contract

By concluding an antenuptial contract, the spouses primarily seek to avoid being subjected to all or some of the common law or statutory rules governing the matrimonial property consequences of marriage.[130] An antenuptial contract enables the spouses to control the patrimonial consequences of the marriage, such as the matrimonial property system.[131]

[124] Heaton and Kruger (2015, p. 130).

[125] Human et al. (2010, p. 155).

[126] Denson (2020, pp. 746–747).

[127] Heaton and Kruger (2015, p. 61).

[128] Human et al. (2010, p. 80).

[129] Human et al. (2010, p. 80).

[130] Heaton and Kruger (2015, p. 83).

[131] Denson (2020, p. 747).

6.2 Proprietary Consequences of a Marriage Out of Community of Property Excluding Community of Profit and Loss During the Subsistence of the Marriage

The matrimonial property system of spouses who have entered into a marriage which is out of community of property and community of profit and loss is called 'complete separation of property'. The proprietary consequences of a marriage out of community flow from the terms of the spouses' antenuptial contract. The spouses keep their own separate estates comprising all the assets and liabilities they acquired before and during the subsistence of the marriage.[132] Each spouse can alienate or deal with their assets as they please without seeking the other spouse's consent.

6.3 Proprietary Consequences of a Marriage Out of Community of Property Excluding Community of Profit and Loss on Dissolution by Divorce

On dissolution of the marriage, unless there is an agreement to the contrary, the spouses keep their separate estates.[133] There is another variation of a marriage out of community of property, which is discussed below.

6.4 Marriage Out of Community of Property with Retention of Community of Profit and Loss

This rare form of marriage out of community of property is another option available to prospective spouses, although it appears that few choose to pursue it. The reluctance of most prospective spouses to choose this matrimonial property system could be explained, perhaps, on the ground that, in so far as ownership of assets by the spouses is concerned, the position is similar to the system called 'complete separation of property'. What distinguishes the two matrimonial property systems is the effect of the retention of the community of profit and loss. It may be reasonably argued that, by entering into a marriage out of community of property and expressly excluding community of profit and loss, spouses intend to avoid the legal and financial consequences associated with the retention of community of profit and loss.

A marriage out of community of property with retention of community of profit and loss means that each spouse keeps the assets and liabilities they had before

[132] Human et al. (2010, p. 100).

[133] Human et al. (2010, p. 157).

the conclusion of the marriage formalities.[134] A spouse who receives donations, bequests, and inheritances during the subsistence of the marriage keeps them as separate property.[135] The effect of retaining community of profit and loss is that profit and loss attained during the marriage's subsistence turn into joint profit and loss and form a joint estate in which each spouse owns an undivided half-share.[136] The profits and losses are shared during the subsistence of the marriage.[137] Upon dissolution of the marriage by divorce, the spouses retain their respective estates, which are two separate estates. The bill introduces a new variation of marriage out of community of property that is subject to the accrual system.

6.5 Marriage Out of Community of Property with the Accrual System

6.5.1 The Meaning of the Accrual System

A marriage out of community of property and community of profit and loss results in a complete separation of property. This is detrimental to the spouse who fails to grow their estate. The bill has introduced the accrual system to address the potential prejudicial effect of having a complete separation of property. This is in recognition of the fact that the accumulation of a spouse's estate during marriage may be attributed to the direct or indirect contributions of both spouses.[138] A spouse may be fully occupied with certain chores or activities that benefit the whole family and be unable to grow their own estate because the spouse's resources, such as time and energy, are channelled towards increasing the other spouse's estate. In this respect, the bill recognises that a spouse may make non-monetary contributions for the family's maintenance, welfare, advancement, and endurance.[139] These contributions include domestic work and management of the matrimonial home[140]; child care[141]; companionship during the subsistence of the marriage[142]; management of family business or property[143]; farm work[144]; and any other matter that the court may regard as a non-monetary contribution.[145] Surely, it would be unfair to deny a spouse who made

[134] Heaton and Kruger (2015, p. 91).
[135] Heaton and Kruger (2015, p. 91).
[136] Heaton and Kruger (2015, p. 91).
[137] Heaton and Kruger (2015, p. 91).
[138] Human et al. (2010, p. 108).
[139] Matrimonial Property Bill 2022, s. 2.
[140] Matrimonial Property Bill 2022, s. 2(a).
[141] Matrimonial Property Bill 2022, s. 2(b).
[142] Matrimonial Property Bill 2022, s. 2(c).
[143] Matrimonial Property Bill 2022, s. 2(d).
[144] Matrimonial Property Bill 2022, s. 2(e).
[145] Matrimonial Property Bill 2022, s. 2(f).

any of these contributions a legal claim to the accumulation of the estate of the other spouse, as it is undeniable that the spouse who lays a claim would have contributed either directly or indirectly to the increase of the other spouse's estate. Upon dissolution of the marriage, these contributions should be taken into account to enable the spouses to benefit from or share in the accumulation of each other's estates, even if there is no joint estate.[146] The accrual system has been described as 'a type of postponed community of profit'.[147] This is because the marriage is out of community of property and community of profit and loss during its existence. However, upon its termination, it resembles a community of profit in the sense that the parties share in the accrual of the estates they have acquired during the subsistence of the marriage.[148]

To highlight the importance the legislature places on reforming the system of complete separation of property, as discussed above, the bill stipulates that the accrual system will automatically apply to all marriages out of community of property and community of profit and loss that are concluded after the bill becomes law.[149] Unlike in the case of all marriages in community of property to which the bill shall apply once it has come into effect, regardless of the date of commencement of a particular marriage, the accrual system shall not apply to marriages out of community of property that were concluded before the bill obtained the force of law.

Considering the gap that the accrual system seeks to fill in the existing law, the better view is that the legislature should have made provision in the bill stipulating a period within which spouses who concluded a marriage out community before the coming into force of the bill could by way of a notarial contract apply the accrual system to their marriage if they so wished. The bill could further permit the parties to stipulate in the notarial contract whether the accrual shall apply from the date of the execution of the contract or retroactively, that is, from the date of the conclusion of their marriage. This approach was followed in the South African legal system when the law governing marriage out of community of property was reformed.[150] Although a marriage out of community of property subject to the accrual system is the default matrimonial system for parties entering this marital regime, spouses who marry out of community of property and community of profit and loss after the bill becomes law are free to exclude the accrual system from their matrimonial property arrangement.[151]

It is important to note that the bill stipulates that the accrual system may only be excluded expressly in an antenuptial contract.[152] Failure by the parties to follow this procedure will render the marriage out of community of property subject to the accrual system. By executing an antenuptial contract excluding the accrual system,

---

146 Human et al. (2010, p. 108).

147 Heaton and Kruger (2015, p. 92).

148 Heaton and Kruger (2015, p. 92).

149 Matrimonial Property Bill 2022, s. 12.

150 Marriage and Matrimonial Property Law Amendment Act 3 of 1988, s. 21(2)(b).

151 Marriage and Matrimonial Property Law Amendment Act 3 of 1988, s. 21(2)(b).

152 Marriage and Matrimonial Property Law Amendment Act 3 of 1988, s. 21(2)(b).

parties will consciously opt into the system of complete separation of property with its attendant prejudicial consequences. Spouses intending to marry have a right to enter into an antenuptial contract to determine their property rights.[153] A spouse who is a party to an antenuptial contract may approach a court for an order to set aside the contract.[154] The court may grant the order if it determines that the antenuptial contract was procured through fraud, coercion, or is manifestly unjust.[155]

6.5.2 The Accrual Claim

Upon dissolution of the marriage by divorce, the spouse whose estate shows a smaller or no accrual is entitled to claim against the estate of the other spouse for an amount equal to half of the difference between the accrual of the respective estates.[156] The practical effect of this provision is that it will also elevate the spouse whose estate shows small growth or no accrual to a favourable position. This provision of the law, to an extent, bears out the observation that the accrual system is a type of postponed community of profit.

It is worth noting that the bill distinguishes between the accrual claim and the right to accrual sharing.[157] While the right to share in the accrual exists during the life of the marriage, the claim to which a spouse is entitled in respect of the estate of the other emerges only on the dissolution of the marriage.[158] The right of a spouse to share in the accrual is protected in the sense that a spouse may apply to a court for the immediate division of the accrual in terms of the accrual system or on other grounds as the court deems just.[159] The court will grant the order if it is satisfied that the conduct of the other spouse is seriously jeopardising the right of the applicant to share in the accrual upon dissolution of the marriage or that the planned conduct of the other spouse is seriously jeopardising the right of the applicant to share in the accrual and that the application will not prejudice other persons.[160] Either spouse cannot transfer their right in the accrual, or creditors who proceed against the spouse cannot attach the right during the subsistence of the marriage.[161] The right to share in the accrual does not form part of the insolvent estate of a spouse.[162] The accrual of a spouse's estate is the amount by which the net value of that estate at the dissolution of the marriage exceeds its net value at the commencement of the marriage.[163] The

---

[153] Matrimonial Property Bill 2022, s. 13.
[154] Matrimonial Property Bill 2022, s. 13(2).
[155] Matrimonial Property Bill 2022, s. 13(2).
[156] Matrimonial Property Bill 2022, s. 14(1).
[157] Heaton and Kruger (2015, p. 93).
[158] Matrimonial Property Bill 2022, s. 14(2).
[159] Matrimonial Property Bill 2022, s. 19(1).
[160] Matrimonial Property Bill 2022, s. 19(1).
[161] Matrimonial Property Bill 2022, s. 19(1).
[162] Matrimonial Property Bill 2022, s. 14(2).
[163] Matrimonial Property Bill 2022, s. 15(1).

bill lists assets that are not to be considered when determining the accrual of the estate of a spouse.[164]

While the accrual system has some advantages in the sense that the spouses can still keep their separate property, the calculation of the accrual upon dissolution of the marriage looks complicated. Apart from the different matrimonial property systems that are recognised in marriages governed by civil law, there is also another property arrangement system for married persons regulated by eSwatini customary law.

7 Property Rights Under Eswatini Customary Marriage

Writing in the context of the proprietary consequences of marriage in eSwatini in the mid-80 s, Nhlapho observed that eSwatini's customary approach to matrimonial property was neither similar to the community of property nor the separation of property.[165] He noted that it is difficult to determine the detailed rules of eSwatini customary law pertaining to property and that this was a problem common to customary systems everywhere.[166] The Supreme Court, as a court of last resort, undertook a judicial excursion primarily to bring clarity to and provide authoritative guidance to other courts on the issue of dissolving an eSwatini customary marriage.[167] The court's decision was highly significant because it introduced a new judicial approach to determining whether divorce exists under eSwatini customary law.[168]

It is unfortunate that although the courts of eSwatini, including the Supreme Court, have dealt with a plethora of cases involving the dissolution of an eSwatini customary marriage, none have had occasion to ventilate in depth the rules governing the proprietary consequences of an eSwatini customary law marriage during the subsistence of the marriage and on its dissolution by divorce. The reason, perhaps, is that in most cases, the applicants have approached the courts for an order to delete or expunge entries regarding the marriage in the marriage registry. Before a court may grant the order, it must determine whether the requirements for dissolution of an eSwatini customary law marriage have been complied with. None of the cases have turned on the proprietary consequences of the marriage on its dissolution by divorce. There is also a dearth of recent academic literature on this subject.

Nhlapho argued that certain components of eSwatini customary property law could be recognised. The first was that the husband had the final word in all matters relating to his household, including property.[169] Although Nhlapho made this assertion long before the enactment of the 2005 Constitution, which advocates for the

[164] See Matrimonial Property Bill 2022, s. 15(2)(a)(b) and s. 16(1)(2).

[165] Nhlapho (2010, p. 8).

[166] Nhlapho (2010, p. 11).

[167] *Hlawe v Seyama* (50 of 2016) [2017] SZSC 41 (08 October 2017).

[168] Dlamini (2023, p. 297).

[169] Nhlapho (2010, p. 12).

equality of all before and under the law and for other women's rights, his point of view cannot be entirely dismissed solely on the basis that we are now governed by the 2005 Constitution. To some extent, it can be argued that certain aspects of the husband's marital power, such as dealing with certain matrimonial property without the wife's consent, still exist under eSwatini customary law. Moreover, patriarchal biases are more pronounced under customary law. None of the court cases in which marital power was interfered with and ultimately abolished involved parties who were married in accordance with eSwatini customary law. The husband's marital power in an eSwatini customary law marriage has not been tested for its constitutional validity. In the absence of a court case dealing with it or statutory law that explicitly abolishes it, one cannot determine with certainty the extent to which the equality provisions of the 2005 Constitution and other provisions on women's rights have interfered with it.

The second component that Nhlapho mentioned pertains to two beasts known as liphakelo and insulamnyembeti, respectively. *Liphakelo* is 'a cow given to the wife by her husband when she has been with her new family for some time'.[170] Traditionally, newlywed wives are prohibited from openly consuming milk and sour milk in the family.[171] The gift of this cow marks an end to the prohibition and signifies full acceptance or integration of the wife into the extended family, which entitles her to eat these foods openly.[172] This is an ancient custom, and it is doubtful whether most modern e*Maswati* still follow it. The other beast *insulamnyembeti* 'is a female cow given to the bride's mother in appreciation for raising her from childhood.'[173] This cow is given by the groom's family and is kept as the personal property of the mother of the bride.

The significance of these beasts in the context of marital property is that they belong to the wife. Nhlapho asserts that:

> So strong are the wife's rights over these cattle (and their increment) that they cannot be attached to satisfy a court order against the husband for a fine or compensation. On the death of a polygamist, this property would devolve upon the special heir of the wife's house, not the deceased's general heir.

According to traditional custom in eSwatini, on the rare occasions when the dissolution of a customary marriage is permitted, the wife's belongings are typically packed and placed outside her hut, and a designated person is assigned to escort her, along with her possessions, back to her parental home.[174] Historically, it may have been simpler to identify and separate the wife's belongings, as the husband was typically the primary breadwinner and the main contributor of assets to the marital estate. Today, notwithstanding that the matrimonial property system under eSwatini customary law neither resembles community of property nor separation of property,

[170] Nhlapho (2010, p. 12).

[171] Nhlapho (2010, p. 12).

[172] Nhlapho (2010, p. 12).

[173] *Mhlanga v Mhlanga* (16 of 2014) [2014] SZSC 51 (03 December 2014).

[174] *Hlawe v Seyama* (16 of 2014) [2014] SZSC 51 (03 December 2014), para 36.

the distribution mechanism of the property between the spouses has to be rational so as not to prejudice either spouse given that the accumulated assets which may include movable and immovable property and money may be the result of the joint effort of both parties or either of them.

Conscious of the need to reform the matrimonial property system governed by eSwatini customary law, the government has proposed several reforms to the existing law to serve the demands of current times. The proposed reforms are expressed in the bill as shown below:

7.1 Abolition of Marital Power

It was stated in the discussion on civil law marriages that the bill abolishes the marital power of the husband in all its manifestations. It is assumed that the abolition, which undoubtedly is underpinned by the equality provisions of the 2005 Constitution and other women's rights provisions guaranteed in 2005, also extends to eSwatini customary law marriages. There is no clear reason for holding that eSwatini customary law marriages are exempt from abolition. This is because the principles of eSwatini customary law are applicable to the extent that they do not conflict with a statute or the 2005 Constitution,[175] the supreme law of eSwatini.

There is an indication that the bill intends to abolish the marital power in customary law marriages[176] as it entitles spouses involved in more than one customary law marriage to joint and equal ownership and other rights over the matrimonial property[177] and equal rights of management and control over the matrimonial property. It should be remembered that an eSwatini customary law marriage is potentially a polygamous marriage. It is possible for the husband to have a matrimonial home and matrimonial property for each of his wives. The envisaged joint, equal ownership and proprietary rights and equal rights of management and control over the matrimonial property shall be exercised by the husband and each of his wives in relation to the matrimonial home and the matrimonial property belonging to the husband and that wife.[178] It is submitted that this reform introduces to customary law marriages some elements of a marriage in community of property. It is impossible to reconcile equal ownership and equal rights of management and control over matrimonial property by the spouses and the marital power of the husband, unless one argues that marital power, as practised in eSwatini customary law marriages, differs markedly from that under common law.

Some traditionalists blindly argue that in eSwatini customary law marriages, a wife has significant status or recognition because the husband cannot deal with certain matrimonial property without consulting her. The traditionalists fail to distinguish

[175] Constitution of the Kingdom of eSwatini 2005, s. 252(3).

[176] Matrimonial Property Bill 2022, s. 23(1)(b).

[177] Matrimonial Property Bill 2022, s. 23(1)(a).

[178] Matrimonial Property Bill 2022, s. 23(2).

between consulting or reporting to a person and obtaining consent from that person. A married man under eSwatini customary law may consult or report to his wife before dealing with the matrimonial property, but that does not mean he is seeking consent from the wife. The proprietary consequences relating to equal ownership and management of matrimonial property shall apply to every eSwatini customary law marriage entered into before the bill comes into force.[179] Although the spouses shall have joint and equal ownership and control over the matrimonial property, each spouse shall retain exclusive rights over personal property.[180] Unfortunately, the bill does not define 'personal property'. The bill also refers to separate property under eSwatini customary law.

7.2 Separate Property

During the subsistence of an eSwatini customary law marriage, a spouse may acquire and keep separate property.[181] The bill classifies certain property as separate property.[182] In the context of the wife, this classification is helpful as it clarifies other assets that may form part of a wife's separate property other than *liphakelo* and *insulamnyembeti*. The bill provides a statutory basis for recognising *liphakelo*[183] and *insulamnyembeti*[184] as separate property. Separate property in an eSwatini customary law marriage also includes household utensils, livestock, a dowry for a daughter, and land allocated for dwelling or cultivation purposes.[185] Regarding land allocated for dwelling or cultivation purposes under eSwatini customary law in eSwatini Nation Land, neither spouse may claim ownership of it, as they only have the right to use and occupy the land.

Property acquired by a spouse before marriage, or obtained through bequest, devise, inheritance, or as a gift from someone other than the spouse, may also be considered separate property.[186] If the giver or testator has explicitly stated that the income or fruits of these assets are to be excluded from the spouse's joint property, they shall remain that spouse's separate property.[187] A spouse's separate estate can also be formed by property that a spouse acquires as a gift or inheritance from a third party after the conclusion of the marriage.[188] A spouse may retain as separate property damages or a right to damages arising from personal injuries, nervous

[179] Matrimonial Property Bill 2022, s. 23(1).
[180] Matrimonial Property Bill 2022, s. 23(3).
[181] Matrimonial Property Bill 2022, s. 24(1).
[182] Matrimonial Property Bill 2022, s. 24(2).
[183] Matrimonial Property Bill 2022, s. 24(2)(a).
[184] Matrimonial Property Bill 2022, s. 24(2)(b).
[185] Matrimonial Property Bill 2022, s. 24(2)(c).
[186] Matrimonial Property Bill 2022, s. 24(e).
[187] Matrimonial Property Bill 2022, s. 24(g).
[188] Matrimonial Property Bill 2022, s. 24(f).

shock, mental distress or loss of guidance, care and companionship suffered by the spouse or the part of a settlement representing those damages.[189] If a spouse is paid a lump sum provided under a personal injury or similar plan, that lump sum shall be kept as separate property for that spouse.[190] Proceeds or rights to proceeds of an insurance policy to which a spouse is entitled, and which are payable on the death of the insured person, qualify as separate property of that spouse.[191] Property that the spouses have agreed should not be included in the joint estate shall be separate property.[192] Separate property also includes property that the parties have agreed upon as separate property.

The bill does not stipulate the mechanism by which assets, such as property that a spouse acquired before marriage, property that the spouses have agreed should not be included in the joint estate, and property that the parties have agreed is separate property, shall be excluded from the joint estate. It is assumed that the procedure commonly followed in civil law marriages will be applied, meaning the parties will enter into an antenuptial contract. Writing in the context of the separation of property by antenuptial contract, Nhlapho made an interesting observation which should motivate spouses married according to eSwatini customary law to embrace this concept. He said:

> The truth of the matter is that if the parties are working towards the same goal, individual control of separate assets and incomes can become no more than a convenient division of labour, enabling each spouse to contribute in his or her own way. The important ingredient is agreement. There is no automatic control of one's property by someone else. If we accept that in a well-run household, all major decisions should be by mutual agreement anyway, we can hardly criticise a regime which, by its very nature insists on such consensus before the decision is taken.[193]

Separate property in customary law marriage is also recognised in the Marriage Bill of 2022, which requires a spouse in a polygamous marriage to maintain and update an inventory of the property they own in consultation with the other spouse and in a timely manner.[194] The spouse shall register the inventory with the Registrar or Chief.[195] A man who is a party to a subsisting customary marriage and intends to marry a subsequent wife must apply to a Chief, indicating, among other things, that he has made an inventory of property owned separately from that of the spouse in the subsisting relationship.[196] The Chief may decline to grant the application if this condition has not been satisfied. This requirement is intended to protect the spouse's separate property in the subsisting marriage. In addition to the matrimonial property

---

[189] Matrimonial Property Bill 2022, s. 24(h).
[190] Matrimonial Property Bill 2022, s. 24(i).
[191] Matrimonial Property Bill 2022, s. 24(j).
[192] Matrimonial Property Bill 2022, s. 24(k).
[193] Nhlapho (2010, p. 9).
[194] Marriage Bill 2022, s. 26.
[195] Marriage Bill 2022, s. 26.
[196] Marriage Bill 2022, s. 25(1)(c).

systems found in civil and customary law marriages in eSwatini, the Matrimonial Property Bill regulates property in cohabitation relationships.

7.3 Property in Cohabitation Relationship

There is no dispute that the frequency of cohabitation is increasing worldwide.[197] A couple may cohabit because there are legal restrictions preventing certain categories of persons from marrying each other.[198] Young people also view cohabitation as a 'trial marriage' as they are discouraged from committing themselves to formal marriage by the high divorce rate.[199] Cohabitation may also be appealing to older couples who want to avoid a second divorce.[200]

The Marriage Bill of 2022, a proposed law that seeks to reform existing laws relating to marriages and provide for other matters incidental to marriage, states that cohabitation shall not, by itself, constitute a marriage or give rise to a presumption of marriage in terms of the proposed legislation.[201] By cohabiting, parties do not get automatic entitlement to property rights but can rely on the law of contract, property, and unjustified enrichment to enforce rights to each other's property.[202] Although a cohabiting couple shall not be regarded as married, one or both of the spouses may, during the subsistence of the cohabitation, register the particulars of any monetary and non-monetary contribution each party may have made during the cohabitation with the office of the Registrar of Marriages.[203] The rights of the parties shall not be affected by their failure to register, but the party alleging that there was cohabitation or that certain contributions were made shall bear the burden of proving the existence of these facts.[204] The court may distribute the property equitably if it is satisfied that the parties cohabited and that they made some contributions.[205]

Upon cessation of cohabitation, either or both parties may apply to the court for an order to distribute the property proportionate to the amounts each party has registered.[206] Only persons with the legal capacity to marry each other under the terms of the Marriage Bill may claim entitlement to the rights conferred by the bill on cohabiting parties.[207] For example, the Marriage Bill prohibits a couple from marrying

[197] Sinclair (1996, p. 271).

[198] Sinclair (1996, p. 272).

[199] Sinclair (1996, p. 272).

[200] Sinclair (1996, p. 272).

[201] Marriage Bill 2022, s. 7.

[202] Sinclair (1996, p. 274).

[203] Marriage Bill 2022, s. 7(2)(a).

[204] See Marriage Bill 2022, s. 7(2)(c) and Matrimonial Property Bill, 2022, s. 28(2).

[205] Marriage Bill 2022, s. 7(d) and Matrimonial Property Bill, 2022, s. 28(3).

[206] Marriage Bill 2022, s. 7(2)(b) and Matrimonial Property Bill, 2022, s. 28(1).

[207] Marriage Bill 2022, s. 7(4).

each other because they are related within the forbidden degrees of relationship.[208] Such parties may not cohabit and claim entitlement to the rights conferred on cohabiting parties in terms of the Marriage Bill. In line with the Marriage Bill of 2022, the Matrimonial Property Bill also allows for an agreement between parties who intend to cohabit or are already cohabiting regarding the ownership of each party's separate property,[209] property which the parties acquire during the cohabitation,[210] and the distribution of property acquired during the cohabitation.[211]

There is no doubt that the proposed law seeks to provide legal protection to cohabiting parties. A question may be raised as to whether it is the business of the law to regulate the consequences of cohabitation. Many arguments have been advanced for or against using the law to protect cohabitants. An argument that stands out for its persuasiveness is couched in the following language:

> A better argument for intervention is that marriage is most often distinguishable from cohabitation only by the piece of paper that testifies to its existence. The nature of the human relationship is ubiquitously identical; children are often the result; and women are notoriously left financially at risk when the relationship fails. Marriage and cohabitation create similar emotional involvements, dependencies and complex issues of finance and property. A concern for the victims of the breakdown of all intimate relationships suggests that non-interference is unjust, callous.[212]

8 Invalid Marriages and Property Rights

Prior to 2019, the courts did not adjudicate any case pertaining to the property rights of spouses in bigamous marriages.[213] This changed in 2022 when the Supreme Court suggested in *Zwakele Ntshangase v Duduzile Annah Ntshangase*[214] that bigamous marriages could in some cases amount to tacit universal partnerships, a consequence of which would be the equal division of property between the spouses. In that case, the appellant, a woman, had married her deceased husband as his second wife in accordance with eSwatini customary law. The deceased husband had a subsisting civil law marriage with another woman, which had not been dissolved at the time he married the appellant, a fact which was unknown to the appellant. The second marriage of the deceased husband to the appellant was unlawful, given that section 7 of the Marriage Act of 1947 bars any individual already married under the Act from

---

[208] Marriage Bill 2022, s. 11.

[209] Matrimonial Property Bill 2022, s. 27(1)(a).

[210] Matrimonial Property Bill 2022, s. 27(1)(b).

[211] Matrimonial Property Bill 2022, s. 27(1)(c).

[212] Sinclair (1996, p. 293).

[213] *Ex parte Ginindza* 1979–81 S.L.R. 361. See also *Dlamini v Dlamini* [1989] SZHC 15 (21 April 1989), *Mkhatjwa v Matsebula and Others* [1999] SZHC 112 (27 July 1999), and *Simelane v Simelane and Others* [1997] SZHC 69 (6 June 1997).

[214] *Zwakele Ntshangase v Duduzile Annah Ntshangase* (57/2021)[2022]SZSC 47(20 September 2022).

contracting another marriage with anyone other than the lawful spouse during the subsistence of the first marriage. Upon the distribution of the assets of the deceased husband, it was argued that the appellant could not benefit from the estate of the deceased as her marriage to the deceased was null and void.

The Supreme Court acknowledged that the marriage of the appellant to the deceased was bigamous and void as the deceased was already married in accordance with civil law when he married the appellant. This fact alone, the Court determined, was not sufficient to exclude the appellant from laying claim to the property of the deceased.[215] The Court reasoned that the union between the appellant and the deceased constituted a putative marriage. By definition, a putative marriage is a marriage solemnised according to the prescribed formalities, which one or both parties entered into in good faith.[216] Relying on the writings of jurists, the Court stated that if spouses in a putative marriage have lived together as husband and wife for a considerable length of time, it was competent for a court to order that their combined property be shared equally between them or their heirs.[217] Further, the Court observed that jurists generally agree that when one party enters into a marriage in good faith, a community of property arises if it benefits the innocent party.[218] In the circumstances of this case, the Court concluded that a tacit universal partnership had been established between the appellant and the deceased. On this basis, the appellant, as the innocent party, was entitled to lawfully claim a half share of the deceased's estate before any distribution to the deceased's heirs.[219]

This case stands out for a number of reasons. First, the Court went beyond simply finding that the eSwatini customary law marriage was bigamous; it also considered the circumstances of the marriage and determined that it was a putative marriage with proprietary consequences. The appellant, who had lived with the deceased for about 37 years, was on the verge of losing her matrimonial home, having lost the case in the High Court on the basis that her marriage to the deceased was bigamous and that she had failed to establish the existence of a tacit universal partnership between herself and the deceased.

Second, the Court highlighted the distinction between a tacit universal partnership and a partnership by contract. The latter comes into being when two or more persons in writing or orally undertake that each of them will contribute, whether in the form of labour or capital, to a lawful business which is to be conducted for their joint benefit

---

[215] *Zwakele Ntshangase v Duduzile Annah Ntshangase* (57/2021)[2022]SZSC 47(20 September 2022), para 42.

[216] *Zwakele Ntshangase v Duduzile Annah Ntshangase* (57/2021)[2022]SZSC 47(20 September 2022), para 43.

[217] *Zwakele Ntshangase v Duduzile Annah Ntshangase* (57/2021)[2022]SZSC 47(20 September 2022), para 44.

[218] *Zwakele Ntshangase v Duduzile Annah Ntshangase* (57/2021)[2022]SZSC 47(20 September 2022), para 44.

[219] *Zwakele Ntshangase v Duduzile Annah Ntshangase* (57/2021)[2022]SZSC 47(20 September 2022), para 50–53.

and with the aim of generating a profit to be shared among them.[220] According to the Court, the intention to establish a tacit universal partnership must be inferred from the conduct alleged to establish the partnership.[221] The Court stated that a universal partnership must not be asset-targeted; it should be informed and motivated by the particular facts of a case.[222] In the Court's view, a partner who claims a particular asset under a tacit universal partnership need not have contributed financially towards the acquisition of that asset.[223] The Court reasoned further that it was enough that the partners had lived together as husband and wife, whether legally or merely in name.[224] The Court opined that the concept of a tacit universal partnership was a mechanism designed to compensate spouses who stood to lose from a relationship whose validity and terms of engagement were mistakenly assumed to be legitimate.[225] It was through this pragmatic approach, in which the Court considered the circumstances of the case, that the appellant succeeded in her claim.

9 Recommendations

The discussion on the proprietary consequences of marriage in eSwatini, both during the marriage's subsistence and upon its dissolution by divorce, revealed significant weaknesses in the existing legal framework. Draft bills have been developed to introduce reforms to the existing law. The bills confirm the recommendations for reforming the law. However, additional recommendations are made due to certain omissions in the draft bills.

9.1 Enactment of a Divorce Act

It is recommended that a comprehensive Divorce Act be enacted to regulate divorce and provide for related incidental matters. Although both the common law and the draft bills address divorce, there is a strong case for enacting a comprehensive Divorce Act that fully addresses all aspects of divorce.

---

[220] *Zwakele Ntshangase v Duduzile Annah Ntshangase* (57/2021)[2022]SZSC 47(20 September 2022), para 57.

[221] *Zwakele Ntshangase v Duduzile Annah Ntshangase* (57/2021)[2022]SZSC 47(20 September 2022), para 57.

[222] *Zwakele Ntshangase v Duduzile Annah Ntshangase* (57/2021)[2022]SZSC 47(20 September 2022), para 66.

[223] *Zwakele Ntshangase v Duduzile Annah Ntshangase* (57/2021)[2022]SZSC 47(20 September 2022), para 66.

[224] *Zwakele Ntshangase v Duduzile Annah Ntshangase* (57/2021)[2022]SZSC 47(20 September 2022), para 66.

[225] *Zwakele Ntshangase v Duduzile Annah Ntshangase* (57/2021)[2022]SZSC 47(20 September 2022), para 43.

9.2 Division of Juristic Acts into Categories

The juristic acts outlined in the Matrimonial Property Bill should be categorised into two types. First, those binding on the joint estate but not requiring both spouses' consent, as they do not unduly affect the other spouse. The second category includes acts that require the consent of both spouses, as unilateral actions could significantly impact the joint estate or the other spouse.

9.3 Listing of Juristic Acts that Require Oral or Tacit Consent

It is presumed that while the bill requires the consent of both parties for the performance of all juristic acts, not all acts require written consent. This observation is premised on the fact that the bill explicitly lists the juristic acts that require the written consent of both spouses. It is recommended that the bill explicitly enumerate the juristic acts for which written consent is not required, but which may be validly concluded with oral or tacit consent.

9.4 Interpret the Phrase 'Immediately Before'

The bill must provide an interpretation of the phrase "immediately before" to guide how the period covered by the phrase will be determined.

9.5 Prescribe the Form that the Subsequent Ratification Must Take with Respect to Each of the Particular Juristic Acts

It is recommended that the bill specify the required form for ratifying juristic acts performed without the consent of one spouse. Since the juristic acts vary, it is inevitable that the methods of ratification will also differ.

9.6 Address the Question of a Dual Marriage and Its Proprietary Consequences

The courts have determined that, in the context of a dual marriage, the marriage in respect of which a divorce decree has not been granted continues to subsist. The draft bills should stipulate how the property of spouses who are parties to a double or dual marriage shall be distributed on the dissolution of either of the marriages.

9.7 Amendment of Marriage System to Include the Accrual System

Parliament should provide a limited period for spouses who concluded a marriage out of community of property before the Matrimonial Property Bill obtains the force of law to amend their marriage to include the accrual system.

10 Conclusion

There is no doubt that the law governing the matrimonial property systems needs to respond to or address the needs of the society in which it applies. It has emerged from the discussion that interventions to align the governing law with the 2005 Constitution have been made by the courts, resulting both in the abolition of common law principles which offended the principle of equal administration of the joint estate and the amendment by Parliament of certain laws to integrate the principle of equality of spouses. An interrogation of the legal framework regulating the issues under review revealed some gaps in the law. Attempts are being made to address the weaknesses in the law, as evidenced by the Marriage Bill and the Matrimonial Property Bill. The draft Bills have set the stage for reforming certain aspects of the marriage law of eSwatini, and wide consultations are ongoing pending their promulgation into law. There is a case for further research on the proprietary consequences of marriage in eSwatini, and this will become more feasible once the draft bills are enacted into law.

References

Denson R (2020) A comparative exposition of the law of husband and wife in terms of Islamic law, South African law and the law of England and wales–part one. Obiter 41(4:747

Dlamini D (2021) The implementation of public international law in eSwatini with reference to comparative jurisdictions. Dissertation, University of Johannesburg

Dlamini D (2023) The marriage law of eSwatini. In: Hammond AF, Adegbite FR, Mensa-Bonsu MYA, Batariwah P (eds) Family law in Africa: perspectives on selected systems of marriage. Talbot Publishing, Clark, NJ

Erhlich RJ (1970) The indissolubility of marriage as a theological problem. Scott J Theol 23(3):291–311

Heaton J, Kruger H (2015) The variable consequences of a civil marriage: marriage in community of property. In South African Family Law 61–82

Human S, Robinson JA, Smith B (2010) Marriage in community of property. In: Skelton A, Carnelley M (eds) Family law in South Africa. Oxford University Press Southern Africa, Cape Town

June S, Heaton J, Hahlo HR (1996) The law of marriage. Juta, Cape Town

Nhlapho T (2010) Proprietary consequences of marriage in Swaziland: law versus culture and the effect on women's rights. University of Swaziland, No. 86/0410

Sinclair JD (1996) Cohabitation. TheLaw of Marriage. p. 271.

Singh PP (2019) Law of persons, family law and law of succession. In: van Besouw K (ed) Introduction to South African law. Pearson Publishing, Cape Town
UN Human Rights Committee (2000) General Comment No. 28: Article 3 (the equality of rights between men and women). CCPR/C/21/Rev.1/Add.10, 29 March 2000. https://www.refworld.org/legal/general/hrc/2000/en/38892. Accessed 30 Oct 2025

Dumsani Dlamini is a lecturer and Head of the Department of Law at the University of eSwatini, where he teaches Administrative Law, Public International Law, Jurisprudence, and Aspects of Law for Health Practice. He also teaches Constitutional Law, Disciplinary Procedures, Public International Law and Criminal Law part-time at the Matsapha Police Academy. His research interests include family law, human rights law, public international law, and administrative law. He holds an LLD from the University of Johannesburg, an LLM in Human Rights and Democratisation in Africa from the University of Pretoria, and an LLB from the University of eSwatini.

An Overview of Matrimonial Property Rights in Mauritius

Rajendra Parsad Gunputh

Abstract Mauritius operates a mixed legal system, drawing on both French civil law and English common law. This hybridity is most evident in the area of matrimonial property rights, where the substantive rules derive from the Mauritian Civil Code (*Code Civil Mauricien*), while the procedural aspects reflect the English legal tradition. This chapter examines the matrimonial property regimes available to spouses, including the community property system, the separate property regime, and notarial marriage contracts, and evaluates how these regimes govern the ownership and distribution of assets during and after marriage. Particular attention is given to the classification of community and personal property, the duties of spouses concerning household expenses, and the evolving role of women in the financial and professional domains. The chapter also addresses the legal protection of the family home, including restrictions on its alienation without spousal consent, and analyses relevant jurisprudence that interprets these safeguards. Drawing from French doctrine and Mauritian case law, it traces the gradual shift toward greater autonomy for married women and the growing recognition of their financial contributions. The chapter concludes with reform proposals aimed at clarifying the scope of marital and personal property and empowering spouses in separate property marriages to challenge transactions involving the family home.

1 Introduction

Mauritius' legal system combines elements of English common law and French civil law. Influenced by different waves of colonialism, particularly by the French and English, Mauritian law draws heavily from the French Civil Code (1715–1810), with a few traces of English law (1810–1968) in the fields of civil and private law. Although the interests of its former colonial powers did not always align, there is no evidence of any real conflict between French and English law. This interaction

R. P. Gunputh (✉)
Faculty of Law and Management, University of Mauritius, Moka, Mauritius
e-mail: rpgunput@uom.ac.mu

A. F. Hammond and P. Batariwah (eds.), *The Law on Marital Property in Africa*, Ius Gentium: Comparative Perspectives on Law and Justice 138,
https://doi.org/10.1007/978-3-032-19358-2_14

between French and English law is very fluid. Legislative efforts have preserved the coexistence of these two systems of law through the Treaty of Capitulation in 1810, following the defeat of the French by the British Empire. In Mauritian courts today, the Civil Code, which is primarily applied in disputes before the courts, is of French inspiration, both in terms of doctrine and judicial precedents; however, judgments are handed down in English. As such, Mauritian matrimonial property regimes and inheritance are inspired by the French Civil Code, while marital procedures follow English law. Better known as the Mauritian Civil Code or the *Code Civil Mauricien* (CCM), the former Napoleonic Code that was applicable on the island has undergone profound amendments. The CCM was amended in 2007, 2011, and 2018,[1] in line with the evolving needs of Mauritian society in various spheres of the law, such as family law, property law, and co-ownership regimes. Local courts are influenced by decisions of the French Court of Cassation (Cour de Cassation), while the written Constitution of Mauritius, adopted in 1968,[2] retains the Privy Council[3] of the King of England as the court of last resort.

This introduction is followed by an analysis of the legal consequences of the dissolution of marriage on marital property. It then examines the various marital property regimes applicable between spouses and the rules governing property distribution upon marital breakdown. It further comments on the influence of international human rights on gender equality and ownership of marital property. The chapter offers recommendations for reform and concludes with a summary of key findings. Relevant Mauritian case law, legal doctrines, and reforms are integrated throughout to reflect the country's mixed legal system.

1.1 Forms of Marriages Under Mauritian Law

In Mauritius, only civil marriages have legal effect.[4] Mauritians, though, enter into other forms of marriage, such as customary or religious marriages, because there is no legal prohibition on contracting such extra-legal marriages. A religious marriage may be valid if it is celebrated by a priest or minister authorised to celebrate civil marriages, or the marriage is solemnised in the presence of a Civil Status Officer. Once such marriages are registered, they have the legal effect of civil marriages. For the avoidance of doubt, customary marriages are not recognised, and Islamic marriages are valid only if solemnised in the same manner as religious marriages with civil effect. Polygamous marriages are impermissible under Mauritian law and have penal consequences. Section 257 of the Criminal Code criminalises polygamy, stating that 'Any person, who being married, marries another person before the

[1] The Code Civil Mauricien (Amendment) Act 2007; The Code Civil Mauricien (Amendment) Act 2011; The Code Civil (Amendment) Act 2018.

[2] Constitution of Mauritius 1968, s. 8 provides only for the right to property.

[3] Constitution of Mauritius 1968, s. 81.

[4] Gunputh (2023, p. 509).

dissolution of the first marriage'. 'Marriage' is defined broadly to include both civil marriages and religious marriages with civil effect.[5]

Where a party contracts a subsequent marriage without dissolving the first, the subsequent marriage is void. Only the first marriage will be recognised. This means that the property rights provisions described in this chapter apply only to the parties of the first marriage. Similarly, the non-recognition of Islamic marriages implies that the property rights of parties in an Islamic marriage with civil effect will be governed by the same matrimonial property rules.

Regarding a presumption of marriage, Mauritian law provides a sophisticated response. The CCM, heavily influenced by French civil law, does not formally recognise unmarried relationships or cohabitation. Thus, cohabitation does not create any automatic legal rights or duties between the partners. However, the English common law applicable to Mauritius recognises a presumption of marriage if the parties, having lived together and borne children, enter into a civil marriage, with or without a subsequent religious ceremony.[6] In the absence of contrary evidence, the court will presume that they have met the necessary prerequisites for marriage and, therefore, are validly married.[7] According to Justice Barnard in the case of *Russel v AG*, where there is evidence of a marriage ceremony having been performed, followed by the cohabitation of the parties, the validity of the marriage will be presumed in the absence of conclusive evidence to the contrary.[8]

2 Brief Overview of Property Rights During Marriage

The way property is classified, managed, and administered before divorce, particularly under different matrimonial régimes, directly shapes the rights and obligations of each spouse at the point of separation. Understanding the distinctions between common and personal property, and how these are treated during the marital relationship, provides the necessary context for analysing post-divorce property disputes. This brief preliminary discussion lays the legal and conceptual foundation for a more accurate and comprehensive understanding of property rights after divorce.

Once the formalities of marriage are observed, the CCM governs the legal framework that defines the rights and duties of spouses. It establishes a set of rights and obligations between the spouses,[9] as well as the duties of the spouses[10] towards their children[11] and even towards their sons-in-law and daughters-in-law.[12] These rights

[5] Mauritian Criminal Code 1838, 257(3).

[6] *Morris v Miller* (1767) 98 E.R. 73.

[7] *Re Taplin* [1937] 3 All E.R. 105 (6 May 1937).

[8] *Russel v AG* [1949] P 391.

[9] Code Civil Mauricien 1974, arts 203–211.

[10] Code Civil Mauricien 1974, arts 212–226.

[11] Code Civil Mauricien 1974, arts 204 and 205.

[12] Code Civil Mauricien 1974, art 206.

and duties, which include, inter alia, assistance, loyalty, relief, and education, are mutual, and spouses are under an obligation to live together in a community of life. The family home is to be established at a place chosen by mutual agreement.[13] If the spouses are married under the legal community of goods (Articles 1401–1420 CCM), one of the spouses cannot sell the family home and its furniture without the consent of the other.[14] Consequently, the sale will be null and void.[15] However, no action for nullity of such a sale will be entertained before a court of law if brought after the statutory period of more than one year following the dissolution of the marriage.[16]

Conversely, if the spouses are married under the separate property regime, either spouse is free to sell the family home and its furniture without the consent of the other.[17] Each spouse is also free to contract alone for the maintenance of the marriage and the education of their children without the authorisation of the other, except in the case of "excessive expenditures," for which the non-contracting spouse is not liable.[18] A Judge in Chambers may intervene to prescribe all necessary measures in the best interest of the family,[19] even to prevent the sale of property belonging to one spouse to persons acting in bad faith. These measures may not exceed three years[20] in duration and, if necessary, must be published in a local newspaper to inform third parties.[21] While such protective measures aim to safeguard the family's interests, parallel legal developments were taking place in the commercial sphere, particularly regarding the status of married women.

Properties used for commercial purposes underwent significant reforms in France until married women attained the status of traders. The French spouse was considered a minor[22] until the French laws of February 18, 1938 (*la loi française du 18 février* 1938) and September 22, 1942 (*la loi française du 22 Septembre* 1942) were enacted, granting her full civil capacity. From then on, she held the status of a trader without needing her husband's authorisation, especially following the French law of July 13, 1965 (la loi française du 13 juillet 1965). This legislation was later incorporated into both the Mauritian Commercial Code (*Code de Commerce Mauricien*)[23] and the CCM,[24] reflecting the Mauritian legislator's intention for married spouses to fully enjoy legal capacity in matters of trade. As a result, a married woman may now trade and open a bank account without her spouse's consent. Upon dissolution of the marriage, each spouse remains the owner of any sums deposited in their respective

13 Code Civil Mauricien 1974, 215.

14 Code Civil Mauricien 1974, art 216(1).

15 Code Civil Mauricien 1974, art 216(2).

16 Code Civil Mauricien 1974, art 216(2).

17 Code Civil Mauricien 1974, art 216(3).

18 Code Civil Mauricien 1974, art 221.

19 Code Civil Mauricien 1974, art 221.

20 Code Civil Mauricien 1974, art 221(3).

21 Code Civil Mauricien 1974, art 222–2.

22 Peterka (2008).

23 Code de Commerce Mauricien 1809, art. 5.

24 Code Civil Mauricien 1974, art. 233.

accounts.[25] She may also, in her capacity as a trader, sell her personal property for the purposes of her business,[26] or to manage and dispose of her personal assets.[27]

Additionally, under the legal community property system, a married woman may sell not only her own property but also that of her husband, regardless of ownership, as stipulated in Article 1420 of the CCM.[28] If one spouse is unable to give consent due to a lack of legal capacity (such as insanity or dementia) or acts contrary to the best interest of the family, a Judge in Chambers may authorise the other spouse to act alone.[29] Such authorisation is binding on the spouse who refuses to consent. Regardless of the matrimonial regime, one spouse may grant the other a mandate to represent them, which may also be revoked at any time.[30] Having briefly examined property rights within marriage, a few key points are noted regarding the loss of spousal status, the implications of legal separation, and the recognition of foreign divorce judgments, laying the foundation for how property is shared in Mauritius.

Divorced persons are no longer considered spouses, even after a de facto reconciliation. According to a strict interpretation of articles 251, 252, and 253 of the Napoleonic Code, one or both spouses may lose or revoke all gifts and matrimonial benefits.[31] Under article 229 of the CCM, divorce by mutual consent is now legally recognised. Even before this reform, in practice, a divorce by mutual consent could proceed in the absence of a counterclaim to the principal claim.[32] This is in line with the Divorce and Judicial Separation (Miscellaneous Provisions) Act 2011 (Act No. 2 of 2011), which follows the same procedure set out under the Divorce and Judicial Separation Act 1981 (Act No. 20 of 1981), namely by way of petition, counterclaim, and cross-petitions.[33]

It should be noted that the Supreme Court held in *Carrim v. Carrim,*[34] that Mauritian law does not prevent a foreign judgment granting divorce by mutual consent from taking effect in Mauritius. Legal separation does not affect inheritance rights, as it merely loosens marital ties. The spouses remain legally bound, and only the party at fault, where the legal separation is ordered solely against them, is deprived of inheritance rights.[35] Since *Dookun v. Dookun*,[36] Mauritian case law has followed

---

[25] Code Civil Mauricien 1974, art. 217(2–3).

[26] Code de Commerce Mauricien 1809, art 6.

[27] Code Civil Mauricien 1974, art. 225.

[28] Article 1420 has been repealed by Act 26 of 1980, s 14 and Act 26 of 1999, s. 24.

[29] Code Civil Mauricien 1974, arts. 218 and 220.

[30] Code Civil Mauricien 1974, art. 219.

[31] Since a ruling by the Cour de cassation, civ. 1re, 4 February 1992; *X v Mme Y* (Administrative Court of Appeal of Nantes, 6 March 2020), holding that gifts made during the marriage are revocable even with regard to the innocent spouse, the divorce being granted to the exclusive detriment of one of the spouses.

[32] Code Civil Mauricien 1974, art 238(3): but this option requires a joint agreement and can be pursued after the marriage has lasted at least 24 months.

[33] Divorce and Judicial Separation Act 1981, s. 4.

[34] *Carrim v Carrim* [1976] MR 216.

[35] Napoleonic Code, art 274.

[36] *Dookun v Dookun* [1994] SCJ 287.

French jurisprudence on de facto separation. In the event of one spouse's death, the surviving spouse automatically inherits, as personal obligations persist.

3 Matrimonial Property Regimes Between Spouses

It is a well-established principle in Mauritius that spouses are free to choose the matrimonial regime of their preference, as provided for under the CCM and further elaborated in the relevant provisions of Title Five.[37] Before their marriage, the future spouses may have a marriage contract drawn up by a public notary establishing the matrimonial system by which they wish to be governed and containing all the relevant stipulations considered desirable for the spouses and their children.

The core of the matrimonial regime in Mauritius lies in the specific system chosen by the spouses at the time of marriage,[38] as this choice determines the legal and financial consequences that will apply, especially in the event of a marital breakdown.[39] The chosen legal regime has a significant impact on how courts determine property ownership within marriage. Thus, Mauritian courts rely on relevant provisions of the CCM,[40] which establish explicit and relevant rules distinguishing between common properties[41] (*biens communs*[42]) and personal property[43] (*biens propres*[44]), the latter being excluded from the community of property.[45] For instance, to resolve

---

[37] Code Civil Mauricien 1974, art 1393.

[38] Civil Status Division, 7th Level, Emmanuel Anquetil Building, Port-Louis, Mauritius.

[39] Under the legal system of separation of property (*régime des separation des biens*), properties they have acquired belong to each spouse only, in the event of the dissolution of the marriage. Under the legal system of community of goods (depending on two main types of properties: properties which either belong to a spouse before marriage (termed as *des biens propres*), or properties which the spouses have acquired during their marriage (termed as *des biens communs* or community of goods).

[40] Code Civil Mauricien 1974, art 1401 provide for properties which are common properties and properties which belong to either spouse only.

[41] The mass of the common property consists of 'acquisitions', that is, the whole of the property, either movable or immovable, acquired as from the date of the marriage by either of the spouses and which the law does not expressly consider as personal property. It consists mainly of property purchased with money derived from the incomes or salaries of the spouses.

[42] Remuneration of the spouses is a common property. Indeed, all properties are common properties unless the other spouse may prove on a balance of probabilities that it is a personal property—Code Civil Mauricien 1974, art 1402.

[43] Personal properties include immoveable property which belonged to either of the spouses prior to the marriage or which accrued to that spouse by succession or donation after the date of the marriage. It will remain the exclusive property of the spouse to whom it belonged or to whom it accrued by way of inheritance or donation.

[44] Clothes, indemnities in case of an accident, properties obtained by successions and donations are personal properties. See Code Civil Mauricien 1974, arts 1404–1405.

[45] The legal community of goods as provided by the Code Civil Mauricien is a community reduced to 'acquisitions' characterised by the following characteristics: the main one, as regards the ownership of property between the spouses, is the existence of a mass of property which is common to both of

civil disputes between spouses over property claims in cases of divorce or judicial separation,[46] the property remains under the administration of either the husband[47] or the wife,[48] depending on whether it is common property or personal property. It is worth noting that the courts draw inspiration from French doctrine and jurisprudence in applying these distinctions.[49]

Under the new section 59 of the Civil Status (Amendment) Act No. 30 of 1979, spouses in Mauritius may choose among three matrimonial regimes: the community property system, which is the most common among Mauritian spouses, the separate property regime, or the parties can enter into a marital contract to regulate their property rights. Of these forms, the community property system is the most common. Marital contracts, on the other hand, are quite rare and not a popular choice among Mauritians.

3.1 Community Property System

The CCM distinguishes between community property (*des biens communs)* and personal property (*des biens propres*).[50] The distinction between the two is not always clear.

Earnings and salaries of a spouse are classified as community property.[51] Other products resulting from labour also constitute community property as they are listed

---

them (*biens communs*) and which differs from the property belonging personally to either of them (*biens propres*).

[46] During the marriage, common property remains in a state of indivision, held in co-ownership by both spouses. In the event of divorce or judicial separation, this property is equally divided between them. If the marriage is dissolved by the death of one of the spouse or both spouses the common property is divided between the surviving spouse and their heirs of the deceased spouse or between the respective heirs of both spouses as the case may be following the Code Napoléon (Amendment) Act 1980 which amended some sixty articles of the Code Civil Mauricien where, henceforth, the surviving spouse is a heir like his/her children. See Code Civil Mauricien 1974, art 78.

[47] For spouses married under the legal community of goods, the Code Civil Mauricien 1974, art 1421 provides for the administration of properties by the husband, but the consent of his spouse is mandatory for all transactions; otherwise, they would be null and void.

[48] Under the legal system of the legal community of goods, the administration of personal property differs from the administration of common property; that is, each spouse has the usufruct and free disposition of his/her personal property, and each spouse has the power to administer the common property which has been obtained from his/her work. For example, the wife freely administers her common property, which is derived from her gains, emoluments, and profits, whereas the husband administers all the other common property.

[49] The articles of the Code Civil Mauricien (CCM), on matrimonial regimes, are *in toto* similar to those of the Code Civil Français (CCF) and it is trite law that the doctrine and judicial precedents which prevail in France would exactly the same.

[50] Code Civil Mauricien 1974, art 1401–1418.

[51] Code Civil Mauricien 1974, art 233.

as profits made for the community. Debts,[52] income,[53] and severance allowances received following a dismissal are all forms of community property. Other forms of property, such as clothes, damages obtained in a car accident, pensions, insurance, and money obtained from a lease, are, however, properties that are strongly attached to a spouse and, as such, do not fall under community property.[54] They are personal property.[55]

Lastly, article 1424 of the CCM specifies that spouses may not, without the consent of the other, alienate or encumber with real rights the immovable property, businesses, and holdings belonging to the community. It is worth noting that the legal rules governing the disposal of jointly owned matrimonial property have evolved. While article 1424 of the Napoleonic Code prohibits one spouse from disposing of community property without the other's consent, earlier interpretations, such as in *Jhollun v. Canarapen*,[56] allowed such sales if done without fraud, especially for marriages that predated new legislation, such as Act 26 of 1980. However, Justice Matadeen clarified that the legislature intended these newer rules to apply retroactively.[57] French case law supports this view, confirming that the 1965 reforms (Law of July 13 1965) govern both the power to alienate and administer joint property, regardless of the date of marriage.[58] Cases like *Gunnoo*,[59] and *Barry v Barry*[60] further reflect this evolution, with courts now strictly applying the law and recognising both spouses as having full legal capacity.

Article 1441 of the CCM lists the various ways in which a matrimonial relationship may be impacted. These include the absence of a spouse, divorce, separation of property and spouses (corps), and in some cases, the modification of the pre-existing matrimonial regime. Once the matrimonial relationship is affected, the CCM provides for the sharing of the community property between the spouses.[61] Each spouse is entitled to a half share,[62] as well as their individual property.[63] If the court finds that it is necessary for one of the spouses to receive a reward (*récompense*[64]) for losses incurred during the marriage, a sum of money will be allocated to the spouse who

---

[52] Code Civil Mauricien 1974, art 1409–1418.

[53] Code Civil Mauricien 1974, art 1403.

[54] Code Civil Mauricien 1974, art 1404.

[55] *André v Regnard* [1954] MR 122.

[56] *Jhollun v Canarapen* [1995] SCJ 205.

[57] The intention of the legislator, as can be culled from the text of the statute, was that the new articles 1400 to 1474 shall apply with effect from the commencement of that Act to the matrimonial regimes of spouses who were married under the legal regime of community of goods and property even before the commencement of that Act.

[58] Cass. civ. 15 April 1970 (D 1971 143, note Ponsard); T.G.I. Seine, March 11, 1966, D. 1966, Somm. 93.

[59] *Babboo v Gunnoo* [1992] SCJ 143.

[60] *Barry v Barry* [1937] MR 187.

[61] Code Civil Mauricien 1974, arts 1450–1464.

[62] Code Civil Mauricien 1974, art 1458.

[63] French Civil Code, art 1467.

[64] Code Civil Mauricien 1974, art 1451.

incurred the loss. For example, a spouse is entitled to a fair share of the proceeds from a community property if the other spouse sells it and refuses to share the gains. While the wife's reserved property, although separately managed by her, was deemed to form part of community property,[65] this is no longer the case in either Mauritius or France.

It must be pointed out, though, that in Mauritius, jurisdiction over family matters, including divorce, permanent separation, alimony, custody of children, and dissolution of the matrimonial regime, lies solely with the Supreme Court (Family Division), with a right of appeal to the Court of Civil Appeal[66] under the Civil Appeal Act, and ultimately to the Judicial Committee of the Privy Council as the final appellate court.[67] In the absence of a specific Mauritian law on evidence, English law of evidence applies by virtue of section 162 of the Courts Act 1945, as confirmed in *Jhundoo v Jhuree*.[68] In civil cases, the burden of proof lies with the plaintiff, who must prove their case on a balance of probabilities.

3.2 Separate Property Regime

Another matrimonial regime, but less common than the community property system, is the separate property regime.[69] The Mauritian legislator has adopted only a limited number of provisions from the French Civil Code.[70] Specifically, Chapter Three of Title Five of the Mauritian Civil Code outlines the separate property regime, which spouses may choose in accordance with section 59 of the Civil Status (Amendment) Act No. 30 of 1979, provided the marriage was celebrated before an Officer of the Civil Status.[71]

To be governed under the separate property regime, the spouses must clearly express their wish accordingly in a contract of marriage concluded before the celebration of the marriage.[72] The spouses each retain ownership of the property they possessed prior to the marriage, as well as any property acquired during the marriage.[73] Either spouse may administer such property and dispose of it freely

[65] Former Napoleonic Code, art. 1401(2), now abolished by Act No. 26 of 1999, stated, 'The reserved property of the wife, although subject to separate management by virtue of article 217, forms part of the acquests'.

[66] A division of the Supreme Court—Constitution of Mauritius 1968, s 80.

[67] Constitution of Mauritius 1968, s 81.

[68] [1981] MR 111.

[69] Code Civil Mauricien 1974, arts 1475–1478.

[70] Only four articles, i.e., art.1475–1478 of Code Civil Mauricien 1974 are present in the CCM, whereas in the French Civil Code, there are articles 1536 to 1543.

[71] Code Civil Mauricien 1974, arts 1475–1478.

[72] *Jourdain v Hily* [1877] MR 23.

[73] *Arnal v Arnal* [1863] MR 73.

without the intervention of the other spouse as if they had not been married.[74] In the event of a divorce or legal separation, either spouse is entitled to reclaim their personal property. If the marriage is dissolved by death, the property of the deceased accrues to their heirs. There is no partition of property.

If the parties have opted for this regime, they are still required to comply with article 214 of the CCM, which obligates the parties to contribute to expenses incurred during the marriage according to their respective means. In addition to the legal requirement to contribute towards household expenses, each spouse has the right to administer, enjoy, and dispose of their personal property as if they were not married.[75] In Mauritius, under civil and private law, parties to a suit may prove, by all means (including title deeds, witnesses, and presumptions), that the property in dispute is their personal property.

3.3 Contract of Marriage by Notarial Deed

The CCM contains two relevant articles[76] concerning marriage contracts, which are applicable when spouses choose to enter into a marriage contract by notarial deed.[77] However, the clauses in the notarial deed must not be against public order and morality. Given the contractual liberty and diversity of regimes available, it is not feasible for the Mauritian Government to predefine or recommend the specific content of such contracts. Therefore, prospective spouses are encouraged to seek appropriate legal advice on the options available to them.

4 Pecuniary Relationships and Personal Relationships

The pecuniary and personal relationships between spouses are provisions of public order, and the parties may not derogate from them, regardless of whether they married under any regime. Under the terms of article 226 of the Napoleonic Code, 'The provisions of this chapter, on all points where they do not reserve the application of matrimonial agreements, are applicable, by the sole effect of marriage, whatever the matrimonial regime of the spouses'. These are, therefore, mandatory obligations as well as a series of measures that apply to everyone and are intended to regulate, among other things, the family home and the spouses' contribution to household expenses. For clarity and convenience, they are grouped, as we will see below, under two main obligations: personal relations and financial relations.

---

[74] *Collet v Rosse* [1865] MR 95.

[75] Code Civil Mauricien 1974, art 1476.

[76] Code Civil Mauricien 1974, arts 1479–1480.

[77] Code Civil Mauricien 1974, arts 1479–1480.

These personal relationships are set out in articles 212 to 217 of the Napoleonic Code. Article 212 of the Napoleonic Code provides that spouses owe each other mutual fidelity, help, and assistance. The interpretation of Article 212 of the Napoleonic Code was widely discussed in the case of *Dookun Jadoo Hermann v. Dookun Catherine Ahnee*,[78] where the Court held that,

> This obligation differs from a simple maintenance obligation in that it goes beyond the satisfaction of strict maintenance needs and is not subordinated to the spouse's state of need. It is intended to cover the costs of maintaining the household and bringing up the children, in which case law includes all lifestyle expenses, including purely pleasure expenses (holidays, travel, or even expenses relating to) the installation of the family home.[79]

Mutual fidelity, support, and assistance include the provision of adequate and physical support when the other spouse is in ill health. In *Baligadoo v. Baligadoo,* for instance, the Supreme Court refused to dissolve a marriage simply because the plaintiff wife saw her husband as a depressive. The Court affirmed the principle that spouses provide each other with all necessary moral and physical support, regardless of the age and health of the spouses.[80]

The maintenance obligation also imposes an obligation to cohabit. If the spouses do not cohabit, the obligation of maintenance does not arise. In *Morel v. Morel*,[81] the Supreme Court affirmed that if the plaintiff/wife refuses to cohabit because a religious marriage had not been performed and made it a condition *sine qua non* for her request, her application for maintenance would not be granted.

According to the French Court of Cassation (*Cour de Cassation*), the obligation to cohabit may cease in certain cases of de facto separation, where the fault is attributable to the husband due to ill-treatment, violence suffered by the wife, or a failure of one spouse to maintain the other. However, in *Jokhoo v Jokhoo*[82] and *Khodadin v Khodadin*,[83] the refusal to cohabit with one's husband and parents-in-law did not constitute a serious insult. It is also settled case law that amicable separation agreements are absolutely null and void because, according to the obligations arising from the marriage contract, no agreement can release the spouses from their duty to cohabit.[84]

---

[78] *Dookun Jadoo Hermann v Dookun Catherine Ahnee* [1994] SCJ 287.

[79] Benabent (2014, p. 139).

[80] It should also be noted that this moral and physical support is also financial, and one of the spouses will provide this support in proportion to his or her means. In this regard, the *Lalouette v. Lalouette* case, in which, under article 208 of the Napoleonic Code, the Supreme Court, using the powers conferred on it, can reduce alimony because both the creditor and the debtor are in need.

[81] *Morel v Morel* [1941] MR 13.

[82] *Jokhoo v Jokhoo* [1973] MR 282.

[83] *Khodadin v Khodadin* [1954] MR 175.

[84] (Court of Cassation, 2 January 1907); (Court of Cassation, 26 January 1938).

4.1 The Family Home

The spouses must have a family home that they have chosen mutually, and where they have elected to live together with their children.[85] The family home must be different from other secondary residences.[86]

The safety and protection of spouses remain paramount; therefore, legal penalties are imposed if the marital home is disposed of without the consent of one of the spouses. Under the old article 213 of the Napoleonic Code, the wife was required to live with her husband and 'follow him wherever he sees fit to reside'. The husband no longer has this legal privilege. Paragraph 2 of the new article 215 of the Napoleonic Code provides that the family residence is the place chosen by mutual agreement. Admittedly, disputes may arise over the choice, especially when spouses have multiple separate residences.[87]

In some limited cases, a judge in chambers can authorise one of the spouses to perform an act[88] in respect of the family home, without the consent of the other spouse. The judge typically gives his authorisation, provided that the two criteria are met: one of the spouses is unable to express their wishes, or unreasonably withholds consent contrary to the interests of the family. Furthermore, under Mauritian law, Act of July 13 1965 gives the judge in chambers the power to act if one of the spouses seriously fails in their duties and jeopardises the interests of the family.

In France, it is the responsibility of the trial courts to determine the location of the family home, which must be protected at all costs, even when the spouses are legally separated.[89] In Mauritius, the family home is distinct from a separate residence, and this distinction is important in the event of divorce, as the surviving spouse has a right of usufruct over the main dwelling house. Furthermore, in the best interest of the family, the Supreme Court strictly applied the provisions of article 216 of the CCM in *Murugan v. Murugan.*[90] Under article 216 of the CCM, spouses may not dispose of the rights by which the family home is secured, nor of the furniture with which it is furnished, even if the husband is the owner of the family home or if it is the property of one of the spouses. Article 216 of the CCM has not undergone any new changes, as its purpose remains the same: to largely ensure the protection and security of married women. According to Professor R. Garron, who was the architect of the great legislative reform of 1982:

> In theory, article 216 establishes the primacy of the interests of the family over the particular interests of the spouses. Even if the dwelling belongs to a particular spouse, he or she can no

---

[85] Code Civil Mauricien 1974, arts 215 and 768.

[86] A. Weil, Droit Civil, Précis Dalloz, no 64: "Domicile, résidence et habitation" (no information available on this article on the web).

[87] In the event of a dispute, the main residence is the marital home.

[88] But what is the act in question? The Court of Cassation, Civ.1re of 17 November 1981, Bull. Civ. I, no 340 considers that all acts of disposal are covered, i.e. sales, renunciations, right to remain on the premises, constitution of a mortgage, constitution of a pledge, but this list is not exhaustive.

[89] Peterka and Guiguet-Schielé (2022).

[90] *Murugan v Murugan* [2003] SCJ 169.

> longer dispose of it freely if it has been assigned to a family purpose. This derogation from the rule of free disposal of one's own property, which is now the general rule in all legal matrimonial property regimes, is a remarkable illustration of the influence of the purpose for which the property is used on its legal status. Because a spouse's own property now has a family purpose, its legal status ceases to be that of a sole property and becomes, in terms of disposition, that of a joint property. Both spouses must cooperate in this act of disposal.[91]

However, the facts in *Murugan* show that the action was brought outside the statutory time limit. An action filed by a spouse more than one year after becoming aware of the deed is considered time-barred.[92] Both local courts and those influenced by French legal tradition agree on this point: the action must be initiated within one year from the date the spouse became aware of the deed.[93] A ruling by the French Court of Cassation (*Cour de Cassation*) dated April 6 1994 confirms that, in the event of a dispute regarding the time limit, the burden of proof lies with the party invoking the expiration.[94]

Article 216 of the CCM does not distinguish between personal property and community property, ensuring that the family home is protected for both spouses, even if it is personal property. This means that a married woman may not find herself without a roof over her head. She may even seek to have a deed transferring the property to a third party declared null and void if she has not given her consent,[95] even if the property in question is not hers. The consent of both spouses, married in a community property regime, is therefore required for acts of disposal.[96]

According to the courts, a surety bond or mortgage falls into this category of acts of disposal. Therefore, a house cannot be seized for default if the spouse who took out the mortgage failed to obtain the consent of the other spouse.[97] The exception to this general rule is that a family home may be seized in case of fraud.[98] In fact, in *Sondhoo v. HSBC*,[99] the Court ruled that a family home mortgaged without a spouse's consent could not be seized, unless the transaction was tainted by fraud. In

---

[91] Garron (1980, p. 16).

[92] See Code Civil Mauricien, art 216(2); According to a decision of the Court of Paris, 11 February 1981.

[93] It's easy to see why: article 216 of the CCM is a perfect reproduction of the provisions of article 215, paragraph 3 of the French Civil Code.

[94] (Court of Cassation, 6 April 1994).

[95] Under the terms of art. 216, para 2, 'Either spouse who has not consented to the deed may apply for its annulment. The action for nullity is open to him or her within one year of the day on which he or she became aware of the deed, but may never be brought more than one year after the matrimonial property regime was dissolved'.

[96] According to the Cour de cassation, 1re, 17 Nov. 1981: Bull. Civ. 1, No. 337: 'The undertaking as guarantor of a married woman is valid, no fraud being established or alleged, provided that this undertaking is distinct from the assignment given as security, which, relating to the property used to house the family, was annulled for having been granted without her husband's consent'.

[97] *Sondhoo v The Hong Kong & Shanghai Banking Corporation Ltd and Mr Sondhoo* [1999] SCJ 358.

[98] (Court of Cassation, 18 June 1985).

[99] [1999] SCJ 358.

Paw Chin Chan Chiang v. Ramburn Basdeo,[100] the Supreme Court extended article 216's protection to tenants.

However, the provisions of article 216 of the Napoleonic Code do not apply to the legal regime of separation of property,[101] as affirmed in *Aubeelock v. Aubeelock*,[102] where the court nullified a sale made under the legal community of goods regime to protect the family home.

4.2 Pecuniary Relations

4.2.1 Rise of Women's Autonomy

Previously, men dominated the matrimonial space to the detriment of women. Decisions regarding the household's financial management were primarily made by men. Things have changed in a rapidly changing society. Married women now play a more significant role in financial matters than in personal relationships.

In addition to the duty of support and addressing the unequal sharing of household expenses, the Napoleonic Code (Amendment No. 2) Act 1980 introduced reforms regarding the professional independence of married women, household powers of spouses, the opening of bank accounts, and the power to dispose of furniture. These changes apply solely by virtue of the marriage, regardless of the spouses' matrimonial regime, and spouses cannot contract out of these statutory rules through the use of matrimonial agreements.[103] In developing these reforms, Mauritian law draws liberally from French law.

France's law of September 22 1942, enshrined the woman's role in household expenses. The contribution to household expenses is associated with the duty to help. However, France's Law of July 13 1965, is also intended to protect one of the spouses against excessive expenditure by the other and against certain acts that are not jointly and severally binding on the spouse who performed them.[104] Under the terms of article 214 of the CCM, matrimonial agreements do not regulate the spouses' contribution to the expenses of marriage. Spouses contribute in proportion

[100] [2003] SCJ 120.

[101] Napoleonic Code, art 216(3).

[102] *Aubeelock v Aubeelock* [1999] MR 199. According to Peeroo J., the provisions of article 216, paragraph 1 of the Napoleonic Code apply even if the family home is the separate property of one spouse, unless the spouses are governed by a matrimonial regime of separation of property as provided in our article 216 paragraph 3......'There is no doubt that, as regards the separate property of a spouse, that spouse remains the sole owner; however, they may not exercise the right to dispose of such property without the consent of the other spouse where it is used as the family home'.

[103] Napoleonic Code, art 226.

[104] Above all, according to the (Court of Paris, 3 June 1975), certain loans are not considered binding on the household where they are not incurred for its needs.

to their respective faculties.[105] It should be noted that under the provisions of the former article 214 of the CCM, the husband had to provide the wife with necessaries according to her faculties and condition. This seemed normal at first, since the husband was also regarded as 'lord' and 'master' of the marriage, and it was up to him to assume this responsibility. Spouses are now jointly and severally liable for certain expenses and household acts.[106]

Article 223 of the CCM further provides that each spouse may exercise a profession, receive their earnings and wages, and dispose of them after paying the costs of the marriage. The triumphant arrival of France's Law of July 13 1965, granted married women broad rights over their earnings, salaries, and property acquired through their own professional work, independent from their husbands; however, the law's impact was less satisfactory, and its success was not as popular as initially expected. Banks, in particular, were suspicious of married women, as it was up to them to prove that they had a profession separate from their husbands and that their salaries and other earnings came from this activity. In France, recognition of the emancipated woman was a relatively slow process. Despite the old law's continued denial of her legal capacity, a few laws such as that of July 10 1850 on the publicity of marriage contracts and that of February 13 1889 on the legal mortgage of married women, the law of May 31 1854 abolishing civil death and the law of April 9 1881 supplemented by the law of July 20 1895 authorising married women to open a bank account without the assistance of their husband, regardless of their matrimonial status. These laws enabled married women to engage in independent activities and to have greater legal capacity. But the real change was that a married woman could exercise a profession without her husband's authorisation. The laws of February 18 1938, and September 22 1942, which were deemed to discriminate against women by subjecting their capacity to exercise a commercial profession to their husband's permission, were quickly replaced by the laws of July 13 1965, and December 23 1985, on the equality of spouses in matrimonial property regimes.

The French laws of February 18 1938, and September 22 1942 retained certain provisions rooted in the outdated concept of marital power. Mauritian law has reflected similar principles, as seen in the *Ireland Fraser v. Madame Vial* decision. In that case, the Supreme Court, drawing directly on the French laws of 1938 and 1942, addressed a married woman's request to engage in commercial activity. Although the Court acknowledged that she had been effectively 'abandoned' by her husband, it held that his authorisation remained necessary, except in cases where tacit authorisation could be inferred. It was based on this tacit consent that the woman was permitted to continue her commercial profession. The Act of July 13 1965, has had very positive repercussions in Mauritian law for married women: not only do they

[105] The amount of the spouses' contribution in proportion to their respective means will be subject, in the event of litigation, to the sovereign assessment of the trial judge, in (Court of Cassation, 29 January 1971).

[106] Do instalment purchases of household appliances constitute household acts? The Cour de cassation answers in the affirmative: (Court of Cassation, 13 December 1965).

enjoy complete freedom to exercise a profession, but they also enjoy unrivalled independence in managing their affairs. For example, article 223 of the CCM states that every wife has the right to exercise a profession without her husband's consent, to receive her earnings and wages and to dispose of them after paying the marriage debts.[107]

4.2.2 Spouses in Commercial Partnerships

Under article 1382–1 of the Napoleonic Code, spouses may, alone or with other persons, be partners in the same company and participate together in its management if the following conditions are met: (1) contributions are pooled, (2) participation in profits and losses and (3) the existence of '*affectio societatis*'. Mutual assistance alone is not enough to establish a de facto partnership. In a judgment dated February 17 1976,[108] the Court ruled that no de facto partnership existed between the spouses, rejecting the wife's creditor's attempt to hold the husband liable based on such a partnership.

Publication is required in the event of a change in the matrimonial property regime for the change to be enforceable against third parties. This option is only available if neither spouse is indefinitely and jointly and severally liable for the company's debts. It is therefore important for third parties to know the matrimonial property regime of the trader or traders with whom they are doing business. In many cases, the assets subject to commercial debts depend on the type of matrimonial property regime chosen by the trader.[109] Where a spouse has opted for a separate property regime, the spouse must issue a notice informing third parties. The notice, as well as any decision pronouncing a divorce, legal separation or separation of property between spouses, shall be published in two Mauritian daily newspapers, one of which shall be published by the Registrar of Companies or any other person authorised for that purpose. Commercial spouses who choose a matrimonial property regime other than the legal community must notify third parties through a notice, similar to the one used for the separation of property regime.The spouses may freely opt for a new matrimonial property regime every five years, but this free choice may lead the spouses to make disguised gifts,[110] or in some cases, commit fraud. Mindful of the dangers involved, the legislature has imposed strict publicity measures to ensure that such agreements can be relied on as against third parties. Under article 69 of the

[107] The former art. 223 of the Code Civil Mauricien 1974 states: 'A woman has the right to exercise a profession without the consent of her husband, and she may always, for the needs of this profession, alienate and obligate alone her personal property in full ownership'.

[108] (Court of Cassation, 17 February 1976).

[109] Code de Commerce Mauricien 1809, title IV, Publicity of Matrimonial Property Regimes, para 17.

[110] According to the Napoleonic Code, art. 1099: 'Spouses may not give to each other indirectly beyond what is permitted by law'. Paragraph two adds that: 'Any gift disguised as a gift, or made to an intermediary, shall be null and void'.

Mauritius Commercial Code, the change of matrimonial property regime will only be effective against third parties if these formalities have been duly completed.

5 Key Issues in Marital Property Law

This discussion addresses several important topics related to the sharing of property on divorce and the promotion of equality in marriage. Specifically, it covers the meaning of household debt, the married woman's right to work, the concept of a wife's reserved property, challenges of excessive expenditure and insolvency, and the opening and management of bank accounts. Each of these issues plays a crucial role in ensuring a fair and equitable division of property between spouses.

5.1 Meaning of 'Household Debt'

Understanding what constitutes household debt is essential in the context of sharing matrimonial property upon divorce, as it directly impacts how liabilities are divided between spouses.

There is a challenge regarding whether loans obtained by a spouse qualify as household debt. The French Court of Cassation has held that loans repeatedly taken to cover daily household expenses are considered household acts. Under article 220 of the French Civil Code, enacted by the Act of July 13 1965, each spouse can independently incur household debts, making both jointly and severally liable for any such obligations.[111] Some authors have questioned whether married women remain jointly liable for debts contracted before the law's enactment.[112] It is generally accepted that wives are still jointly liable for pre-law debts, ensuring the law's mandatory effect is preserved.

5.2 A Married Woman's Right to Work

It is important to clarify the legal status and classification of each spouse's earnings and assets during the marriage. The evolution of articles 223 and 225 of the Napoleonic Code shows how the law now recognises the independent financial identity of each spouse, particularly salaried women.

[111] Even though the husband had written bad cheques and had abandoned his wife for several years, she was still ordered to pay them because of the solidarity rule!

[112] Patarin and Morin (1966).

The new article 223 of the Napoleonic Code[113] stipulates that each spouse may freely exercise a profession, receive their earnings and wages, and dispose of them after paying household expenses. In contrast, the former article 223 of the Napoleonic Code states that a woman has the right to pursue a profession without her husband's consent and may independently manage, alienate, and dispose of her personal property fully owned by her for professional purposes. In addition, and pursuant to article 225 of the new Napoleonic Code, each spouse administers, obliges, and disposes of their personal property alone, demonstrating the special attention paid by the Mauritian legislator to salaried women. This is one of the reasons why article 225 of the Napoleonic Code has been amended. The former article 225 of the Napoleonic Code stated that when a woman engaged in a profession, the property she managed, specifically, her earnings and wages, was considered part of the community property. As a result, even if she incurred obligations unrelated to her profession, those obligations could still bind the community through her reserved property.

5.3 A Wife's Reserved Property

The legal treatment of a wife's earnings has evolved under community property regimes in both Mauritius and France. While the wife's reserved property, although separately managed by her, was deemed to form part of community property,[114] this is no longer the case in either Mauritius or France. Under French law and its judicial precedents (Case No. 16–11.599, February 1, 2017), earnings and salaries are considered property belonging to the legal community of goods. Judges have discretionary power to address situations where one spouse exceeds their fair share of household expenses through professional activities. However, such disputes primarily arise after the dissolution of the marriage or in cases of de facto separation, where one spouse may have financially enriched the other. In these circumstances, claims of unjust enrichment can be made. This is less common in community property regimes, where the value of the defendant's work is typically considered part of the joint estate from which they have benefited.

5.4 Insolvency

The question arises regarding the role of the married woman in the event of the husband's insolvency, especially since she is legally considered to represent him. French case law has established that, in such cases, the wife is obligated to contribute

---

[113] This is Act No. 26 of 1999 (The Napoleonic Code Amendment Act 1999).

[114] Article 1401 of the former Napoleonic Code, paragraph 2, now abolished *by Act No. 26 of 1999*, answers in the affirmative: 'The reserved property of the wife, although subject to separate management by virtue of article 217, forms part of the acquests'.

to household expenses and to pay household debts. Before the 1965 law, French courts tended to interpret the wife's financial responsibilities narrowly, often ruling she was not personally liable for certain debts. The law of July 13 1965, changed this by formally recognising the wife's role in financial matters, making the responsibilities and rights of spouses more balanced and equitable.

5.5 Excessive Expenditure

Financial decisions and debts incurred by one spouse can legally bind both spouses, even if only one of them approved the expense.

Under article 221, paragraph 1 of the French Civil Code, each of the spouses has the power to enter into contracts on his or her own for the upkeep of the household or the education of the children, and any debt contracted by one of them obliges the other jointly and severally. These obligations are primarily practical in nature, and the spouses are jointly and severally liable.[115] However, the real aim of the legislator is to ensure the autonomy of the spouses. For example, either spouse may enter into contracts for the maintenance of the household[116] or the education of the children without the other spouse being present, but the debts incurred bind the other spouse jointly and severally. However, these rules do not apply to 'manifestly excessive expenditure.' In such cases, the contract is invalid, and only the spouse who incurred the expense is responsible for payment, while the other spouse is not obliged to pay. We cannot compile a list of scenarios in which the spouse is not obliged to pay the debts or expenses. The provisions of the Civil Code do not specify a threshold figure. Accordingly, it is up to the courts to determine whether the expenses are excessive and should be paid by only the spouse who incurred them, relieving the other spouse of any financial responsibility for those costs. This will be a quantitative assessment, given that joint and several liability does not apply to instalment purchases and loans if they have not been entered into with the consent of both spouses.

5.6 Opening and Managing Bank Accounts

The financial independence of married women has evolved, especially regarding their ability to open and manage bank accounts. Historically, under the 1942 law, married women could open accounts but with restrictions.

The development and use of cheques, as well as commerce in general, have certainly benefited married women, who can now open a bank account in their name.

---

[115] A decision of the Court of Paris, dated 11 December 1943, even accepted the existence of a joint and/or several obligation between spouses separated by property for household debts.

[116] As well as loans, provided they are not excessive (Court of Cassation, 24 March 1971). See also Abitbol (1985, p. 1) and *Tribunal de Rouen*, 22 Dec 1970, *Dalloz 1971*, p. 429.

The law of September 22 1942, permitted married women to open a current account in their own name, using their signature, on behalf of their husband, subject to certain conditions: the bank was required to notify the husband when the account was opened, and the wife could not overdraw the account without his prior permission. However, the reforms of July 13 1965, through article 221 of the French Civil Code and article 217 of the Napoleonic Code, aimed to establish full equality between spouses by allowing each to open deposit and securities accounts in their name without needing the other's consent.

Articles 221–1, 1426, and 1427 of the Napoleonic Code provide safeguards in cases where one spouse proves the other is incapacitated, committing fraud, or unable to express their will. In such situations, the capable spouse may request the judge's permission to act alone on behalf of the other, exercising the same powers that the incapacitated or absent spouse would have had. In practice, however, it is rare, but not impossible, for one of the spouses to jeopardise the family's interests. In the case of *Madame Nirupa Ramtale v Barclays Bank Ltd*,[117] the plaintiff-wife was surprised when the bank refused to allow her to withdraw a certain sum because her husband had recommended that she be prohibited from making any bank withdrawals. The Supreme Court found that banks had developed a number of procedures enabling a husband wishing to protect himself from his spouse's profligacy by limiting their shared financial responsibility.[118] The wife's action was dismissed on the grounds that articles 1426 and 1427 of the Napoleonic Code are remedies for fraudulent management of the community by the other spouse. In other words, the court rejected the wife's claim because the legal protections under articles 1426 and 1427 only apply when one spouse fraudulently mismanages the shared marital property. Since the husband did not fraudulently manage the community property, the law did not support the wife's case.

6 The Impact of International Human Rights Law on Marital Property and Gender Equality in Mauritius

International human rights law, particularly the European Convention on Human Rights of 1950, has played a significant role in shaping Mauritius' legal frameworks to ensure equal rights and protections for spouses.

Several reforms enacted in France, such as the laws of August 30, 1947, July 13, 1965, February 18, 1938, and September 22, 1942, were subsequently adopted into Mauritian domestic law. These reforms transformed the legal status of married women, who had previously been treated similarly to minors, granting them full legal capacity to engage in commerce and to open bank accounts independently, without requiring their spouse's authorisation.

---

[117] *Madame Nirupa Ramtale v Barclays Bank Ltd* [1998] SCJ 176.

[118] Dupuis (1988, p. 39).

The Code Napoléon (Amendment) Act 1980 significantly reformed the management of common property, traditionally administered by the husband under article 1421 CCM. However, the new article 1421(5) CCM limits these rights if the husband abuses them. Furthermore, article 217(2) CCM establishes that the husband has no claim over the wife's personal property, which she manages and administers independently and autonomously.

Following reforms inspired by the French law of December 3 2001, the Mauritian legislator guaranteed that the surviving spouse has full rights to enjoy the family home after the death of the other spouse, granting them equal heirship status alongside other heirs. This change, enacted under the Code Napoléon (Amendment) Act 1980, included the wife in the succession as provided by articles 767 and 768 CCM. Prior to this important reform, the wife was not considered an heir.

The development and application of the different marriage regimes are not isolated from global human rights frameworks. International human rights law plays a significant role in promoting fairness, equality, and the protection of rights within marriage. Mauritius is party to several key instruments, including the Convention on the Elimination of All Forms of Discrimination Against Women (CEDAW), the International Covenant on Civil and Political Rights (ICCPR), and the Universal Declaration of Human Rights (UDHR).[119] These instruments impose obligations on the state to uphold gender equality, prohibit discrimination, and protect the rights of spouses in marital relationships.[120]

CEDAW is particularly impactful in the context of matrimonial property sharing. Article 16(1)(h) of CEDAW requires state parties to guarantee equal rights for spouses regarding ownership, acquisition, and management of property. Mauritius ratified CEDAW in 1984, and subsequent reviews by the Committee on the Elimination of Discrimination Against Women have assessed the country's progress.

In its 2018 concluding observation (CEDAW/C/MUS/CO/8), the Committee noted certain positive developments but expressed concerns over limited integration of CEDAW provisions into national law and insufficient judicial reliance on the Convention in resolving matrimonial property disputes.[121]

---

[119] Mauritius is party to several core international human rights instruments that impose binding obligations to uphold gender equality and protect the rights of individuals in marriage and family life. Specifically, Mauritius acceded to the Convention on the Elimination of All Forms of Discrimination Against Women (CEDAW) on 9 July 1984, to the International Covenant on Civil and Political Rights (ICCPR) on 12 December 1973 (along with its First Optional Protocol), and it upholds the principles of the Universal Declaration of Human Rights (UDHR), which, though not a treaty subject to ratification, has informed the country's legal and policy frameworks on equality and non-discrimination. See United Nations Treaty Collection (2025).

[120] See CEDAW (1979), arts 1–16 which collectively establishes a comprehensive framework for achieving gender equality. They require states to define and eliminate all forms of discrimination against women through legal, policy, and institutional reforms; ensure the full development and advancement of women; dismantle gender stereotypes and cultural norms that perpetuate inequality; and guarantee equal rights in all aspects of marriage and family life, from entry into marriage to its dissolution.

[121] CEDAW Committee (2018), para 10.

Domestically, Mauritius has enacted legislation that complements its international obligations. The Equal Opportunities Act 2008 prohibits discrimination based on gender, marital status, and family responsibilities, strengthening legal protections for women in marriage.[122] The Protection from Domestic Violence Act 2016 further supports vulnerable spouses, particularly women, by addressing abuse and creating avenues for redress.[123] The Constitution of Mauritius also guarantees equality and prohibits discrimination under sections 3 and 16, establishing a foundational basis for interpreting matrimonial property laws in line with human rights principles.[124]

Nonetheless, challenges persist. Reports from organisations such as Musawah highlight limited visibility of CEDAW in the judicial reasoning of Mauritian courts.[125] Women may contribute indirectly to marital wealth through unpaid domestic labour, which is not always recognised under strict legal interpretations.[126]

Judicial remedies are available, with constitutional challenges under sections 17 and 18 of the Mauritian Constitution providing potential relief where matrimonial property laws infringe on human rights.[127] The National Human Rights Commission and the Equal Opportunities Commission serve as institutional pillars tasked with enforcing equality and investigating complaints.[128] However, these bodies face limitations in terms of accessibility, enforcement power, and public awareness.[129]

---

[122] Equal Opportunities Act (2008), Mauritius.

[123] Protection from Domestic Violence (Amendment) Act (2016), Mauritius.

[124] See Constitution of Mauritius (1968), ss 3 and 16. Section 3 affirms the existence of fundamental rights and freedoms without discrimination based on race, origin, political opinion, colour, creed, or sex. Section 16 explicitly prohibits discriminatory laws and practices, reinforcing the constitutional commitment to equality.

[125] Musawah (2018, p. 9).

[126] See UN Women (2024, p. 3). This brief highlights that Mauritian women spend significantly more time on unpaid domestic and care work than men. In Mauritian matrimonial property law, strict adherence to legal regimes such as séparation de biens has often led to the exclusion of non-financial spousal contributions, particularly domestic labour performed by women, from asset division during divorce. A notable example is *Albert v Albert* (MA 39/2019 (arising in DV 97/2018)) [2020] SCSC 590, where the Supreme Court of Seychelles applied Mauritian law to deny a wife's claim for property division after 43 years of marriage. Despite her substantial unpaid contributions, including managing family businesses and raising children, the court ruled that she had no legal entitlement under the chosen regime.

[127] See Constitution of Mauritius (1968, ss. 17–18). Section 17 provides for the enforcement of protective provisions, allowing individuals to seek redress in the Supreme Court when their constitutional rights are violated. Furthermore, section 18 outlines derogations from fundamental rights during emergencies, but also reinforces the limits of such derogations, preserving core human rights protections.

[128] See Equal Opportunities Commission (2025), About the Equal Opportunities Commission.

[129] See National Human Rights Commission (2025), *Annual Report 2024*, p. 9. The National Human Rights Commission Annual Report 2024 highlights in Chapter I (pages 3–4) that the Commission's Human Rights Division lacks jurisdiction over private entities and is unable to investigate complaints older than two years. These limitations stem from its statutory mandate under the Protection of Human Rights Act 1998 and considerably restrict its accessibility for certain complainants seeking redress. There are limited public engagement and sensitisation campaigns, as noted in Chapter III (pages 73–77).

In conclusion, Mauritius has made commendable strides in aligning matrimonial property sharing with international human rights law, especially through legal reforms and institutional mechanisms. Still, full realisation of these rights requires deeper integration of international norms into domestic jurisprudence, enhanced judicial training, and broader public education to ensure spouses, particularly women, understand and can assert their property rights.

7 Recommendations

7.1 Clearer Classification of Assets

Mauritius could greatly benefit from a clearer and more precise classification of assets. Specifically, it should be easier to distinguish between community property and personal property. By clearly defining which assets are genuinely joint, the legal framework would avoid the blanket 50/50 division of all assets, including salaries, that frequently results in unfair or inequitable outcomes. Such a refined system would better balance the protection of individual ownership rights with recognition of the mutual financial contributions made during a marriage.

7.2 Protecting the Family Home

Legal disputes also arise when one spouse takes a loan from a bank by mortgaging the family home without the other spouse's consent and subsequently defaults on the mortgage. As noted, a suit instituted by an aggrieved spouse whose consent was not obtained can be dismissed if it is brought more than one year after the alleged offence. Spouses whose marriages are contracted under the separate property regime are, however, precluded from instituting similar actions to challenge the validity of transactions involving the family home. Mauritian courts have generally upheld the validity of transactions involving the matrimonial home in separate property marriages.[130] Inevitably, spouses, children and in some cases, entire families are rendered homeless simply because the spouse who is not a party to a transaction cannot challenge it in a court of law. The Mauritian legal system should develop reforms which extend the protections afforded to spouses in community property marriages to those in separate property marriages. The enhanced protections will better secure the family home.

---

[130] See for instance, *Bouton v Mauritius Commercial Bank Ltd* [2005] SCJ 60.

7.3 Spousal Autonomy and Financial Accountability

While husbands typically administer common properties, personal properties acquired through inheritance or donations,[131] as well as usufruct rights, remain under the autonomous management of each spouse. However, in practice, cases have emerged where one spouse accumulates excessive debts. Under Mauritian matrimonial law, both spouses are generally liable for debts incurred unless the other spouse can prove, on the balance of probabilities, that these debts were manifestly excessive and unrelated to family maintenance. Since salaries and earnings are considered common property, this regime may inadvertently encourage one or both spouses to spend money excessively. Nonetheless, Mauritian law grants spouses full independence in managing their professional and commercial activities,[132] which further complicates financial accountability within marriages.

In light of these challenges, reforms should aim to balance spouses' autonomy with protections against financial mismanagement, thereby promoting fairness and stability within marital property relations.

8 Conclusion

Mauritius's legal system stands as a unique interplay between two historically divergent traditions, French civil law and English common law, artfully stitched into a mixed jurisdiction that defines the nation's legal character. The Code Civil Mauricien (CCM), modelled on the Napoleonic Code, sets the substantive framework for family law, succession, and matrimonial property regimes, while English procedural principles govern the practical implementation of justice. This dual structure, although intellectually rich, presents interpretive and operational challenges, particularly in areas such as divorce settlements and asset division.

This chapter has introduced the various matrimonial property regimes in Mauritius and the issues that arise when a marriage dissolves. The dominant community property system distinguishes between marital property and personal property, a distinction that is not always clear in every instance. Nonetheless, this chapter has noted the equal division of community property. This chapter has also explained the pecuniary effects of marriage and observes the strong fetters Mauritian law places on the family law with a view to protecting both spouses. The chapter equally praises the personal effects of marriages to the extent that it uplifts women and prioritises their equality. It is hoped that the recommendations stated above, especially on clarifying marital and personal property, will go a long way towards strengthening marital property rights in Mauritius.

[131] Code Civil Mauricien 1974, art. 1405(1).

[132] Code Civil Mauricien 1974, art 223.

References

Abitbol E (1985) Contribution to marital expenses and its deferred litigation. In: Essays in Honour of Raynaud. Dalloz/Sirey, pp 1–25

Benabent A (2014) Droit de la famille, 3rd edn. LGDJ, Paris

Committee on the Elimination of Discrimination Against Women (2018) Concluding observations on the eighth periodic report of Mauritius, CEDAW/C/MUS/CO/8, 14 Nov 2018. https://humanrights.govmu.org/Documents/Convention%20Corner/CEDAW/CEDAW%20COR_2018.pdf. Accessed 30 Oct 2025

Convention on the Elimination of All Forms of Discrimination Against Women (CEDAW) (1979) United Nations General Assembly Resolution 34/180, adopted 18 Dec 1979, entered into force 3 Sep 1981. https://www.ohchr.org/en/instruments-mechanisms/instruments/convention-elimination-all-forms-discrimination-against-women. Accessed 30 Oct 2025

Dupuis M (1988) Une institution dérogeant aux règles des régimes matrimoniaux: le compte bancaire joint. Dalloz, Chron., pp 39–46

Equal Opportunities Commission (2025) About the Equal Opportunities Commission. https://eoc.govmu.org/eoc/. Accessed 30 Oct 2025

Garron R (1980) The Reform du Code Napoléon with respect to successions and family law. Henry & Cie, Les Pailles

Gunputh RP (2023) The law of marriage and divorce in Mauritius. In: Hammond AF, Adegbite FR, Mensa-Bonsu MY, Batariwah P (eds.) Family law in Africa: comparative perspectives on systems of marriage in selected African countries. Talbot Publishing, Austin, pp 509–522

Musawah (2018) Thematic Report on Mauritius, CEDAW 71st Session, October 2018. https://www.musawah.org/resources/musawah-thematic-report-on-mauritius-2018/. Accessed 31 Oct 2025

National Human Rights Commission (2025) Annual Report 2024 (28 March 2025). https://www.ohchr.org/sites/default/files/documents/hrbodies/spt-opcat/npm/npm-mauritius-2024.pdf. Accessed 31 Oct 2025

Patarin J, Morin G (1966) La réforme des régimes matrimoniaux: Étude de la loi n° 65–570 du 13 juillet 1965 (Vol. I, 3e éd.). Répertoire du Notariat Defrénois

Peterka N (2008) Matrimonial regimes. Dalloz HyperCours, Paris

Peterka N, Guiguet-Schielé Q (2022) Régimes matrimoniaux, 7th edn. Dalloz, Paris

UN Women (2024) Labour-Market Inequalities in Mauritius: Gender Pay Gap and Unpaid Domestic Work, March 2024. https://africa.unwomen.org/sites/default/files/2024-03/brief-gender_pay_gap_and_labour_market_inequalities_in_mauritius.pdf. Accessed 31 Oct 2025

United Nations Treaty Collection (2025) Chapter IV: Human Rights. https://treaties.un.org/Pages/Treaties.aspx?id=4&subid=A&lang=en. Accessed 1 Nov 2025

Rajendra Parsad Gunputh is a Professor of Law with a Personal Chair in International Comparative Law at the University of Mauritius and former Dean of the Faculty of Law & Management (2020–2023). His research interests include family law, international humanitarian law, labour law, media law, and ethics. He has authored over 200 articles, several treaties on Mauritian law, and numerous books and manuals. He has served as a visiting professor at Gujarat National Law University and is Honorary Professor at the University of Xiangtan, China. He was Editor-in-Chief of *Just Africa* and serves on several editorial boards. Gunputh holds double PhDs in Public and Private Law from l'Université Paris V-René Descartes and l'Université de la Réunion (both with first-class distinctions), an HDR from l'Université de la Réunion, a PGCE in Higher Education from the University of Mauritius, and a Post-Doctorate in Public Law from l'Université Paris X-Nanterre.

Marital Property in Seychelles

Cédric Tuyau

Abstract Rooted in a mixed legal heritage shaped by both French civil law and British common law influences, Seychelles' approach to marital property division reflects a unique blend of legal traditions and local customs. This chapter explores the legal framework governing property distribution upon divorce, highlighting its evolution, practical application, and broader social and legal implications. Unlike systems that impose rigid statutory guidelines, Seychelles relies heavily on judicial discretion and the expressed or implied intentions of the spouses. While this flexibility enables courts to tailor outcomes to the specific facts of each case, including consideration of contributions, conduct, and agreements between the parties, it also leads to unpredictable and inconsistent results. The chapter examines this tension between flexibility and certainty, comparing Seychelles' approach with more structured systems such as those in the United Kingdom and Sweden. It concludes by proposing reforms that would enhance equity, transparency, and coherence in the adjudication of matrimonial property disputes, without unduly restricting judicial adaptability.

C. Tuyau (✉)
University of Seychelles, Victoria, Seychelles
e-mail: cedric.tuyau@unisey.ac.sc

A. F. Hammond and P. Batariwah (eds.), *The Law on Marital Property in Africa*, Ius Gentium: Comparative Perspectives on Law and Justice 138,
https://doi.org/10.1007/978-3-032-19358-2_15

1 Introduction

The history of Seychelles, from its colonisation in 1756, has been shaped by its physical geography and strategic position in the western Indian Ocean.[1] First colonised by the French, Seychelles became a British colony in 1810. The legal legacy of Seychelles' colonial past is reflected in its hybrid legal system. While civil law is heavily influenced by the French civil law tradition,[2] criminal law and procedure is shaped by the English common law tradition.[3]

Seychelles' approach to divorce has been influenced by its colonial past, specifically the French and British influences. The French Civil Code, which was applicable during French colonial rule, laid the foundation for the regulation of marriage and divorce through codified principles.[4] The subsequent British administration introduced legal concepts and statutes that reflected English matrimonial law, the influence of which will be further discussed in this article.

Examining the legal framework for property division in Seychelles reveals both distinct features of the Seychellois legal system and opportunities for law reform. Although statutory laws establish a framework for fair distribution, gaps in implementation and differences in court approaches hinder the achievement of equitable outcomes, especially for women. The legal rights of spouses to marital property, both during marriage and after divorce, are influenced by conflicts between statutory law and traditional customs. This calls for a careful, sophisticated approach to amending the law.

This chapter, therefore, aims to explore the intricate aspects of property division after divorce in Seychelles. Like many other countries, Seychelles has a complex system for dividing marital assets that combines statutory laws, traditional customs, and evolving international human rights standards. This study examines the legal frameworks that regulate property division, considering their societal consequences and the transformative impact of international norms on shaping these laws.

This chapter is divided into five sections. The first section serves as an introduction, followed by the second, which examines the legal regime governing marriages in Seychelles. Section 3 provides an assessment of the legal framework for property distribution upon divorce, emphasising the influence of human rights conventions on the provisions of the New Civil Code. Section 4 offers suggestions for reforms based on issues highlighted throughout the chapter, while section 5 concludes the chapter.

---

[1] Allen (2022, p. 1).

[2] Twomey (2017).

[3] *Gardette v R* [1959] SLR 179.

[4] Mujuzi (2023, p. 237).

2 Legal Framework

The Civil Code of Seychelles Act 2020 ("CSS" or "new Code") came into effect on 1 July 2021, following the conclusion of a thorough, all-encompassing legal reform process that began in 2013. The CCS more accurately reflects contemporary Seychellois societal needs and puts the country on par with most countries. The CSS replaced the Civil Code of Seychelles Act (1975 Code), which became effective on 1 January 1976, a few months before Seychelles' independence from Britain on 29 June 1976.[5] The 1975 Code was strongly influenced by the Napoleonic Code introduced in 1808. However, unlike its Mauritian counterpart, which still has its code in French, the Seychellois Code was translated into English.[6] That said, the Code's evolution over three centuries demonstrates the country's willingness to adapt its laws to reflect societal needs.

Marriage and divorce were initially governed by the Code Civil of 1808, which contained all the tenets of marriage, from conception to termination and its possible consequences.[7] However, over the years, the country moved towards more specific laws, such as the Civil Status Act,[8] the Status of Married Women Act,[9] and the Matrimonial Causes Act,[10] the latter two of which were modelled on English law. With the introduction of the new Code, the consolidation of laws on marriage and divorce led to the repeal of the individualised laws governing different aspects of marriage and divorce. The consolidation of these laws in the new Code was intended to improve clarity, efficiency, and accessibility of the legal aspects of marriage and divorce, and to simplify legal procedures. Furthermore, the new Code implemented progressive measures to protect children's rights, recognise domestic relationships and clarify the status of marriages and divorces in the country.

2.1 Matrimonial Regimes in Seychelles

Seychelles' legal framework for marriage is primarily centred on civil marriages governed by the CCS. Therefore, the Courts do not recognise religious marriages, like Islamic marriages, when deciding on the validity of a union between two people.[11] Customary marriages and other forms of polygamous marriages are also not recognised. There is no presumption of marriage in Seychelles.

Seychelles' legal system does not observe a 'community of property' regime, in contrast to other African countries like Mauritius, which share a common or similar

[5] Civil Code of Seychelles Act 1975.

[6] Halpérin (2005, p. 229).

[7] Code Napoléon par arrêté Decaen, N ° 168 du 21 Avril 1808.

[8] Civil Status Act 1893.

[9] Status of Married Women Act 1948.

[10] Matrimonial Causes Act 1992.

[11] *Majah v Majah* (2010) SLR 327.

colonial and legal heritage with Seychelles. Although both Seychelles and Mauritius have mixed legal systems[12] and use civil codes to govern family law, Mauritius uses a default community property system under which any assets acquired during a marriage are regarded as shared property, irrespective of individual contributions or ownership during the marriage.[13] When a marriage ends, the assets are usually split equally between the spouses, reflecting the shared ownership and partnership perception.[14]

In Seychelles, the CCS does not clarify the type of matrimonial property regime applicable. Furthermore, although it has been considered that the principle of separation of property was the default matrimonial property regime, case law and the new Code may have blurred the distinction between the principles. For instance, Article 259(1)(a), 259(2) and 259(4) of the CCS provide that:

> 259.(1) (a) The parties to a qualifying relationship which has subsisted for at least seven years will, where the relationship ends inter vivos, share equally the property which has been acquired by each during the relationship in the context of the relationship, other than property acquired by one of the parties on succession or from a third party by way of a gift inter vivos or by will.
>
> (2) It is presumed for the purposes of paragraph (1) that all property held by each of the parties at the termination of the relationship was acquired during the relationship in the absence of evidence to the contrary.
>
> (4) A party whose name property is held may retain title subject to paying the other party the sum necessary to give effect to the requirements of this article.

The articles mentioned above are comparable to the 'community regime' observed in France and Mauritius, where properties acquired during the marriage are considered part of the 'common assets' of the parties.[15] It is also understood that parties who have been married for less than seven years would generally retain separate ownership of assets acquired prior to the marriage, consistent with the position previously established under the Matrimonial Causes Act. However, with the introduction of Article 295(5) of the Civil Code, the court is now empowered, in cases where the qualifying relationship has lasted fewer than seven years, to make orders concerning any property of either party. This includes property acquired during the marriage, provided that the court, taking into account all relevant circumstances—such as each party's contribution to the relationship, their qualifications, and financial means—considers it just to do so for the benefit of either party or any child of the relationship.

Thus, matrimonial property in Seychelles can be defined as any asset(s) jointly owned by spouses or acquired during the marriage through their combined efforts. Properties considered separate assets of individual spouses are excluded from this definition. When the matrimonial property is registered solely in one spouse's name,

[12] Bogdan (1989).

[13] Code Civil Mauricien, art. 1401.

[14] Code Civil Mauricien, art. 1402.

[15] Gunputh (2008, p. 885).

the court presumes ownership in favour of that spouse. This presumption is consistent with common law principles, which traditionally prioritise legal title when determining ownership.

Parties may, however, still opt for prenuptial agreements.[16] These agreements establish explicit provisions concerning the allocation of assets, financial obligations, and other aspects of the marriage. They enable couples to tailor their marital arrangements to their preferences and specific circumstances, establishing a legal structure for resolving conflicts or issues during the marriage.[17] Likewise, prenuptial agreements reduce conflict and uncertainty by establishing clear guidelines and expectations, thereby providing spouses with a better understanding and assurance of their rights and responsibilities within the marriage.

Moreover, Seychelles' legal system is continually evolving to adapt to shifting societal norms and global trends. Although the separation of property regime is currently the dominant standard for civil marriages, there is potential for future reforms or amendments to accommodate different marital arrangements, such as community property or other models that emphasise economic equality and partnership between spouses. These advancements would necessitate a thorough examination of the cultural, legal, and financial consequences, as well as extensive discussions with stakeholders and experts in Seychelles' legal space.

Before examining the rules on property division, it is important to note that where a marriage is declared null and void ab initio, the parties are regarded as never having been married. Each party retains ownership of property acquired in their individual name, both before and during the purported marriage. Notwithstanding, a spouse who has made demonstrable financial or material contributions toward property registered in the other's name may seek reimbursement or compensation, subject to satisfactory proof before the court.

3 Division of Property

3.1 The Legal Framework Governing the Process of Property Settlement

Prior to the repeal of the Civil Code of Seychelles Act 1976 on 1 July 2021, and its replacement by the CCS, matrimonial matters, including those involving matrimonial property, were dealt with under the Matrimonial Causes Act 1992 and the Matrimonial Causes Rules, 1993. With the enactment of the CCS, which came into effect on 1 July 2021, the Matrimonial Causes Act was repealed, and some of its

[16] Code Civil Seychelles Act 2020, art. 160(2).

[17] *Leonil v Leonil* [1998] SCSC 16.

provisions were imported into the Civil Code 2020 with modifications. Hence, matrimonial causes and matters involving matrimonial property, which were filed as of 1 July 2021, are now dealt with under the Civil Code 2020.

Section 9(2) of the Civil Code of Seychelles (Consequence of Enactment) Act 2021 further provides that:

> [s]ubsidiary legislation made under the Matrimonial Causes Act in force at the commencement of this Act will continue in force under the Civil Code of Seychelles Act 2020 (Act 1 of 2021) in relation to matrimonial and en menage causes.

Hence, the Matrimonial Causes Rules, 1993, remain applicable unless they are inconsistent with any provision of the Code, as provided for in Article 4 of the Civil Code, 2020. In other words, the Matrimonial Causes Rules continue to be in force as if made under the Civil Code of Seychelles.[18]

Section 20 of the Matrimonial Causes Act gave the court extensive discretionary authority to issue property adjustment orders. These orders encompassed the conveyance of assets, disbursement of fixed amounts, or any other suitable remedy deemed essential by the court. The court exercises its discretion based on several factors, including the parties' financial resources, their respective contributions to the marriage, and the well-being of any children.

The courts and the Seychelles community faced difficulties dealing with the property implications of ending long-term domestic partnerships for an extended period. The 1975 Code did not include provisions for the division of property belonging to domestic partners during their lifetime. In the case of married couples, the courts utilised the authority granted by the Matrimonial Causes Act to issue *in rem* property orders to divide matrimonial property in the event of a termination of the marriage during the lifetime of the parties involved. However, there was no similar legal provision in place regarding long-term domestic relationships. In a failed domestic relationship, one party usually has the option to pursue a restitutionary right, specifically unjust enrichment, through personal legal action.[19] To establish a contribution to the domestic property, it was necessary to provide evidence of contributions, such as mortgage payments.[20]

The changes in the law regarding the division of domestic property were motivated by concerns about the material well-being and property imbalance that arose from the legislation outlined in the 1975 Code. Most domestic relationships in Seychelles are not formalised through marriage, and typically, the significant assets of the relationship are registered under the male partner's name. Consequently, women often encountered difficulties after the dissolution of their relationship, as demonstrated by the legal precedents.

These modifications also align Seychelles with its obligations under international law, particularly Articles 2 and 5 of the Convention on the Elimination of All Forms of Discrimination Against Women (CEDAW), which require State Parties to eliminate

---

[18] *Rose v Richmond* [2024] SCSC 24.

[19] *Labiche v Ah-kong* [2010] SCCA 6.

[20] *Michel Larame v Neva Payet* [1987] SCA 4.

discrimination through legislative measures and address social and cultural practices that perpetuate gender stereotypes. Additionally, communications such as *A.T. v Hungary,*[21] by the CEDAW Committee, emphasise the obligation of States to ensure effective legal protections against gender-based violence, further underscoring Seychelles' legislative amendments.

3.2 Nature and Purposes of Property Adjustment Orders

Article 26 of the Constitution, alongside Articles 544 and 545 of the Civil Code, establishes the absolute and exclusive right of an owner over immovable property, provided that such rights are exercised within the bounds of the law. Interference with property rights is permitted only in narrowly defined circumstances as prescribed by law, for example, in divorce cases. Upon divorce, the court is tasked with determining a fair adjustment of immovable property acquired by spouses during the marriage.[22] The courts strive to balance the fundamental right to property with equitable considerations arising from the parties' shared contributions. The legal principles ensure that adjustments are guided by fairness while respecting the sanctity of property ownership as enshrined in constitutional and civil law provisions.

The law emphasises the concept of equity and aims to prevent one party from being unfairly disadvantaged due to the termination of the marriage. Article 259(1)-(3) of the CCS contains the most salient principles on the division of matrimonial property as follows:

> 259.(1) (a) The parties to a qualifying relationship which has subsisted for at least seven years will, where the relationship ends inter vivos, share equally the property which has been acquired by each during the relationship in the context of the relationship, other than property acquired by one of the parties on succession or from a third party by way of a gift inter vivos or by will.
>
> (b) In cases to which sub-paragraph (a) refers, the court may, having regard to all the circumstances of the case, make such order as the court thinks fit relating to the property that is shared for the benefit of a child of the relationship.
>
> (2) It is presumed for the purposes of paragraph (1) that all property held by each of the parties at the termination of the relationship was acquired during the relationship in the absence of evidence to the contrary.
>
> (3) The court may, in exceptional circumstances where it would be repugnant to justice to apply paragraph (1), make such orders as it thinks fit for the division of the property of the parties, having regard to all the circumstances of the case and in particular each party's contribution to the relationship.

Generally, property adjustment orders aim to prevent one party from being unfairly impoverished while the other party prospers after a marriage dissolution.[23] The

[21] *A.T. v Hungary* (2005) Communication No 2/2003, UN Doc A/60/38.

[22] *Rouillon v Valmont* [2024] SCCA 11.

[23] *Finesse v Banane* [1981] SLR 103.

court's mandate is to ensure that both parties are financially restored to a position similar to what would have been maintained if the marriage had continued and that each party diligently fulfils its financial responsibilities.[24] This principle, deeply ingrained in Seychellois family law, goes beyond the immediate context of divorce and emphasises the ongoing importance of ensuring fair financial arrangements after the marriage ends.

It is worth noting that there is usually a tendency to divide assets equally, as observed in England and Wales.[25] This equitable framework ensures that neither party is left in a disproportionately disadvantaged position following the dissolution of a marriage. However, the concept of equitable division extends beyond the mere classification of assets as matrimonial property. Courts are empowered to make orders concerning any property owned by one or both parties, regardless of whether it qualifies as matrimonial property, provided such orders serve the broader interests of justice and the well-being of the parties or any relevant child.

This expansive judicial discretion reflects the need to adapt to diverse circumstances and ensure a just outcome. For instance, the legal framework does not solely focus on the timing or specific nature of property acquisition. Instead, it evaluates whether the property is subject to a financial or property order designed to address the financial needs and rights of the involved parties. This principle is particularly relevant when one party seeks to shield assets from equitable distribution. The case of *Pillay v Lablache,*[26] provides a compelling illustration. In this case, the court scrutinised Mr. Pillay's deliberate attempt to place property in a company and then assert a usufructuary interest. Such manoeuvres, aimed at frustrating Ms. Lablache's claims, highlight the necessity of anti-avoidance principles under the MCA.

The legal rules, therefore, prevent individuals from undermining equitable outcomes through strategic asset transfers, emphasising the court's role in safeguarding fairness. The judgment in *Pillay* aligns with the landmark UK decision in *Prest v Petrodel,*[27] where the Supreme Court reinforced the principle that properties controlled by a party, even if not legally owned, could be subject to ancillary relief orders. This decision underscores the obligation of courts to examine transactions designed to evade financial relief claims and ensure justice in matrimonial disputes. By addressing attempts to obscure the true ownership of assets, courts ensure that the principles of fairness and equity prevail, reflecting the overarching aim of matrimonial property division laws.

The court's ability to exercise fair and just powers allows it to consider various factors, such as each spouse's financial contributions, their individual needs and circumstances after the divorce, and any other pertinent considerations deemed necessary for the fair allocation of assets.[28] The influential *Desaubin v Periol,*[29]

[24] *Edmond v Bristol* [1982] SLR 353.
[25] *M v M* [2013] EWHC 2534 (Fam).
[26] *Pillay v Lablache* [2024] SCSC 30.
[27] *Prest v Petrodel* [2013] UKSC 34.
[28] *Lau-Tee v Lau-Tee* [2021] SCSC 26.
[29] *Desaubin v Periol* [1996] SLR 90.

for instance, clarifies the crucial significance of the contributions made by both parties to the marriage when determining property division outcomes. In that case, the court examined the connection between financial and non-financial contributions and how they affect the division of assets, strengthening the principle of fairness that guides property adjustment laws.[30] The court held that prioritising monetary input alone would be unjust, thereby affirming that both tangible and intangible efforts must be considered to achieve a fair division. This reinforced the principle that fairness underpins property adjustment laws and called for comprehensive assessments that consider the totality of each party's contributions to ensure a just and equitable outcome.

Significantly, the development of legal principles regarding property adjustment orders in Seychelles reflects a more substantial movement towards comprehensive evaluations of the parties' situations, as exemplified in *Alcindor v Alcindor*.[31] Section 25 of the UK Matrimonial Causes Act 1973 involves a comprehensive approach that includes income, earning potential, property, and other financial assets when determining property adjustments. While not binding, this provision has exerted persuasive influence on Seychellois jurisprudence. In *Alcindor*, the court referred to analogous reasoning found in UK family law to support its holistic analysis of both financial and non-financial contributions. This demonstrates that Seychellois courts, while rooted in their mixed legal tradition, do draw inspiration from foreign legal sources such as the UK, thereby enriching their interpretative approach with comparative and cosmopolitan insights.

In addition, the Seychellois courts highlight the importance of prioritising the well-being of the children involved when making decisions about property adjustments. In *Serret v Serret*,[32] the court emphasised the importance of evaluating housing availability for minor children, thus incorporating child-focused viewpoints into property adjustment analyses. In line with the principle of utmost importance in family law, this comprehensive approach emphasises the merging of child well-being and ownership rights, representing the intricate and multifaceted nature of property adjustment law in Seychelles.

Overall, the legal framework concerning property adjustment orders in Seychellois family law is a complex combination of legal principles, precedents, and foreign influences. Indeed, the property adjustment jurisprudence in Seychelles reflects the evolving principles of fair justice in family law by carefully considering contributions, international legal norms, and perspectives that prioritise children's well-being. The following sections explain these considerations more fully.

---

[30] *Samori v Charles* [2012] SLR 371.

[31] *Alcindor v Alcindor* [2010] SCSC 53.

[32] *Serret v Serret* [2012] SLR 112.

3.2.1 Asset Allocation

The process of dividing marital property is based on the principle that jointly owned assets should be divided equally, as stated in Article 295 of the Civil Code. This assumption is based on the belief that both spouses make equal contributions to obtaining and preserving marital assets, and it forms the basis for property division proceedings.[33]

Notably, Article 815 of the Civil Code states that, 'co-ownership arises when property is held by two or more persons jointly'. Nevertheless, Seychellois courts have the authority to depart from this presumption in light of the particular circumstances of each case. This was confirmed in *Charles v Charles*,[34] where the Court of Appeal held,

> In my view, both parties are vested with absolute ownership of the house in question. In my judgment, it follows that such ownership is in equal shares, as this would accord with the intention of the parties. Commenting on the parties' intention, the court added, "Bearing in mind that they registered the property in question during the height of their love affair, probabilities are overwhelming, in my view, that the parties intended co-ownership in equal shares. In this regard, it must always be borne in mind that what matters is the intention of the parties at the time when they registered the matrimonial property and not at the time of divorce.[35]

The above establishes a standard for future legal understandings of jointly owned property in marital conflicts in Seychelles. The rationale is similar to that observed in the UK, as seen in the case of *Stack v Dowden*,[36] where the House of Lords ruled that the ownership shares of property should be determined based on the parties' intentions at the time of purchase. This highlights the importance of the initial intention and the mutual agreement recorded during property registration in determining ownership shares.[37] This principle promotes equity and consistency in distributing assets when relationships end, emphasising the importance of clearly documenting ownership intentions to prevent future conflicts.

The case of *Maurel v Maurel*[38] emphasises the intricate character of property ownership in marital relationships. It acknowledges that simply registering a property under one spouse's name does not conclusively establish exclusive ownership, especially if the other spouse can prove a mutual intention regarding the property. The legal principles stated in Article 815 of the Civil Code emphasise the significance of intention and circumstances in establishing property ownership. Although the law assumes that co-owners have equal rights, it is adaptable to account for the intricacies of personal relationships, especially within marriage.[39] The legal framework ensures

---

[33] *Florentine v Florentine* [1990] SLR 141.

[34] *Charles v Charles* [2005] SCCA 13.

[35] *Charles v Charles, as quoted in Nancy v Nancy*(MA130/2018) [2020] SCSC 288 (22 May 2020), para. 76.

[36] *Stack v Dowden* [2007] UKHL 17.

[37] *Jones v Kernott* [2012] 1 AC 776.

[38] *Maurel v Maurel* [1998] SCCA 5.

[39] *Figaro v Figaro* [1982] SLR 200.

fairness and equity in property relations by prioritising the parties' intentions. This promotes stability and harmony within familial and societal contexts.

3.2.2 Contributions to the Marital Property

Contributions to marital property encompass not only financial inputs but also non-financial contributions, such as domestic labour, caregiving, and support. This expanded comprehension of contributions acknowledges that both partners play essential roles in acquiring and preserving marital assets. In *Chetty v Emile,*[40] the court dismissed the notion of marriage being a business partnership where careful tabs are kept on contributions to the marriage. The court noted that doing so would be:

> to deny marriage the love, affection and the sanctity that goes with it[marriage]...To look into the monetary contribution that goes into the acquisition of the matrimonial property and make an award purely on that consideration would mean to leave the other party who toiled and sweated to keep the home fires burning, destitute.[41]

As noted, an integral aspect of the division of matrimonial property involves establishing the definition of matrimonial property. Although jointly owned assets are typically divided equally, categorising property acquired during the marriage as either marital or separate can significantly impact the division process. When determining the status of assets, Seychellois courts consider several factors, including the timing of the acquisition, the source of funds, and the parties' intentions. Additionally, their respective contributions to the acquisition of the property can significantly impact the property division outcomes.

Furthermore, Seychellois legislation acknowledges the significance of considering the future needs and circumstances of the parties involved in property division proceedings. Although the principle of equal shares is the initial basis, the courts can modify the distribution, considering factors such as age, health, earning potential, and childcare obligations. This comprehensive approach ensures an equitable division of property, taking into account each party's ability to meet their financial needs post-divorce.

In *Lesperance v Lesperance*,[42] the court analysed a scenario where the assets acquired during the marriage were registered solely in the respondent's name. However, the court recognised the petitioner's substantial contributions to obtaining and maintaining the property. The contributions encompassed manual labour in construction and administrative support, which enhanced the respondent's financial capacity to obtain the property. This case highlights that contributions to acquiring and maintaining marital property go beyond financial investments and can encompass different types of support and effort.

---

[40] *Chetty v Emile* [2008-2009] SCAR 65.

[41] *Chetty v Emile, as quoted in Faure v Sinon* (Civil Appeal SCA 23/2021) [2023] SCCA 11 (Arising in /ppMA 290/2018 out of DV 159/2017) SCSC 462 (26 April 2023) para. 30./p.

[42] *Marie Hortense Lesperance v Ralph Armand Lesperance* SCA 3 of 2003.

In addition, the court cited an earlier case, *Lesperance v Lesperance*[43] (a different case with the same name), highlighting the significance of equal treatment in resolving similar cases. In the previous instance, the court had required an equitable division of marital assets, considering similar conditions. Nevertheless, the analysis also emphasises a warning from the *Charles* case: while equality is an important principle, it should not overshadow the court's discretionary authority as specified in statutory provisions. The court stressed the importance of achieving equality but highlighted the necessity of considering individual circumstances when making property settlements.

3.2.3 Non-Financial Contributions

Matrimonial property law is a complex and disputed field within family law, characterised by its contentious and multifaceted nature. Dividing assets during divorce or separation necessitates a careful equilibrium between legal principles, fair considerations, and the practicalities of marital relationships. The courts believe that a party's contribution to the marital property is one aspect that will be considered when examining 'all the circumstances of the case'. In the *Esparon v Esparon*,[44] the court did not consider 'financial contributions' to the acquisition of the property as a significant factor. Instead, it emphasised the relevance of 'contributions of each party to the welfare of the family, including housework and care roles'. This case underscores the significance of acknowledging non-financial contributions, such as affection, assistance, and child-rearing, in determining the distribution of marital assets.

Thus, in Seychelles, the distribution of assets in divorce cases requires a careful evaluation of both legal ownership and the contributions made by each partner. Although legal title initially determines ownership, a spouse's substantial contributions towards acquiring or maintaining the property can override this presumption. As a result, the provisions of the then Matrimonial Causes Act, along with established judicial precedents, can lead to a fair and equitable distribution. In *Chetty v Emile*,[45] the court noted that:

> Contributions towards matrimonial property cannot be measured in purely monetary terms, in hard cash. As stated earlier, the love and sweat and long hours of vigil to bring up a family by the spouses all have a role to play in the accumulation of matrimonial property. The cooking, the sweeping, the cleaning, the sewing, the laundering, tending to the children and the many other nameless chores in a home are not things a value can be put on, but certainly contribute towards the build up of matrimonial property. We also find it difficult to accept that once a party makes a choice of his or her partner and decides to live together as husband and wife one party cannot be heard to say that I had the better job or I am the person who brought in more money, when the relationship goes sour.... The position certainly would be different if there is evidence to the effect that one party squandered the wealth or deliberately

---

[43] *Lesperance v Lesperance* [2001] SCCA 19.

[44] *Esparon v Esparon* [2012] SLR 39.

[45] *Chetty v Emile* [2008-2009] SCAR 65.

> omitted to do what is reasonably expected of that party as a spouse. That is not the situation in the present case.[46]

The Seychelles Court of Appeal's ruling appropriately recognises the indispensable contribution made by spouses in managing a household and fostering a family. Although the court acknowledges the importance of non-financial contributions, it fails to establish a specific framework for assessing and measuring them. The inherent challenge lies in the subjective nature of quantifying tasks such as cooking, cleaning, and childcare in monetary terms. Although these contributions undeniably enhance the overall worth of marital assets, their value must be accurately determined. The focus on intangible elements, such as emotional support and companionship, also obscures the practical aspects of acquiring and owning assets. Therefore, although *Chetty v Emile* emphasises the importance of acknowledging non-financial contributions, the difficulties of including them in property division proceedings remain to be resolved.

The cases need to provide a clear, organised system for assessing and comparing these contributions. The ambiguous nature of non-financial contributions presents a substantial obstacle for courts when resolving property disputes, as it complicates the determination of each party's rights and entitlements. In the absence of explicit criteria for evaluating non-financial contributions, there is a risk of inconsistency and subjective decision-making in asset distribution.[47]

In *Boniface v Malvina,*[48] the Court of Appeal confronted the question of whether a property registered solely in one spouse's name, but acquired during a period of cohabitation before marriage, should be treated as matrimonial property. The court rejected the traditional approach of strictly classifying assets as either 'matrimonial' (acquired during the marriage) or 'non-matrimonial' (acquired before the marriage or individually). Instead, it adopted a more purposive and equitable approach by considering the shared intentions of the parties and the contributions, both financial and non-financial, made during the relationship. This effectively blurred the distinction between pre-marital and post-marital property by allowing assets acquired before the formal union to be redistributed based on the dynamics of the relationship. While this progressive move reflects an effort to modernise family law and acknowledge diverse relationship structures, it simultaneously raises concerns about predictability and legal certainty. By moving away from clearly defined categories without establishing concrete criteria for assessing joint ownership or contribution, the ruling introduces ambiguity that could lead to inconsistent outcomes and diminish protections for individuals with pre-marital assets.

It seems Seychelles can be said to have a property distribution that is similar to that of the UK. This represents a significant deviation from its origins, which are based on civil law.

---

[46] *Lesperance v Lesperance* [2001] SCCA 19.

[47] *Ho Peng v Ho Peng* [1993] SLR 71.

[48] *Boniface v Malvina* [2020] SCCA 11.

4 Recommendations

4.1 Clarifying the Definition of Matrimonial Property

It is recommended that clearer legislative guidance be provided to support the courts in exercising their discretion when modifying and distributing property registered solely in one spouse's name, as highlighted in *Desaubin v Periol*.[49] While Section 20 of the Seychelles Matrimonial Causes Act 1992 granted broad judicial powers to apportion assets based on each party's contributions, the current framework leaves significant room for subjective interpretation. This can result in inconsistent outcomes, particularly when assessing non-financial contributions or navigating complex ownership arrangements.

While intended to ensure fairness, Seychelles' current legal framework for the distribution of assets in cases of divorce or separation has several weaknesses and areas that could be improved when compared to systems in other jurisdictions. The Seychellois approach, characterised by substantial judicial discretion and emphasis on the parties' original intentions, frequently results in inconsistent and unpredictable outcomes. Seychelles can improve its system by learning from other countries to achieve a fairer and transparent distribution of assets. It was observed that a more precise statutory definition would improve the concept of 'matrimonial property' in Seychelles.

That said, Article 259(2) of the CCS suggests that all property owned by each party at the end of the relationship was obtained during the relationship unless proven otherwise. Still, the seven-year requirement is arbitrary and excludes property that would otherwise have fallen into the category of matrimonial property had contribution and intention been the most important factors. While this assumption simplifies asset division, it may need to account for the intricate circumstances surrounding property acquisition. For example, the Family Law Act of 1975 in Australia takes a comprehensive approach by explicitly considering each party's contributions, including both financial and non-financial contributions, as well as each party's future needs.[50] Seychelles can achieve a fairer distribution by implementing a comparable strategy that considers the complexities of each party's contributions and future situations.

4.2 Reducing the Discretionary Powers of the Courts

In addition, the discretionary power granted to Seychellois courts to issue property orders, while allowing flexibility, can lead to inconsistent results. To address this issue, the Seychelles could consider adopting the United Kingdom's Section 25 of the Matrimonial Causes Act 1973, which provides a comprehensive framework

---

[49] *Desaubin v Periol* [1996] SLR 90.

[50] Parkinson (2003, p. 1).

to guide judicial decision-making.[51] This section thoroughly analyses the factors to be considered, including income, potential earnings, property ownership, and other financial assets.[52] Enforcing comparable legal principles in Seychelles would provide judges with clearer instructions, resulting in more predictable and equitable rulings in property adjustment cases. Seychelles can establish rules to incorporate these considerations, ensuring that all pertinent factors are consistently and fairly considered in every case.

Cases like *Miller v Miller*[53] and *McFarlane v McFarlane*[54] in the UK highlight the significance of fairness, needs, compensation, and sharing in matters related to marriage dissolution. These principles establish a systematic framework for courts to adhere to, guaranteeing a fair evaluation of monetary and non-financial contributions to the marriage.[55] The structured approach mentioned here starkly contrasts with Seychelles' dependence on judicial discretion and the parties' intentions during property registration. Furthermore, applying the principles of equity and parity in the distribution of assets, as exemplified in Sweden, provides valuable insights.[56] In Sweden, the system guarantees that any property obtained during the marriage is divided equally, regardless of the individual in whose name it is registered.[57] This approach inherently appreciates the collaborative efforts of both partners and streamlines the process of dividing assets.

However, unlike the UK approach, the Swedish model leaves minimal room for judicial discretion in the face of exceptional circumstances. In the UK, while equality is a guiding principle, courts retain the flexibility to depart from an equal division where necessary to achieve fairness, particularly when issues of needs, compensation, or non-matrimonial property are at stake. Therefore, although the Swedish model promotes certainty and formal equality, it may lack the adaptability of the UK system, which allows for a more context-sensitive resolution. If Seychelles were to adopt a model similar to Sweden's, it would need to carefully consider whether the lack of discretionary leeway could lead to rigid outcomes in atypical or high-need cases. Nonetheless, the Swedish approach still offers a valuable perspective on how formal equality can secure recognition for the non-owning spouse's contributions and reduce the likelihood of unjust disadvantage.

Article 259(3) of the CCS could benefit from further refinement in addressing exceptional circumstances. In certain exceptional cases, the existing provision permits judges to exercise discretion and deviate from the principle of equal sharing. Nevertheless, the absence of explicit criteria for defining exceptional circumstances can result in inconsistent implementations. Seychelles can adopt more explicit criteria to guide judicial discretion, drawing lessons from jurisdictions like New Zealand,

[51] *Charman v Charman* [2007] 1FLR 1246.

[52] Miles and Hitchings (2018, p. 1).

[53] *White v White* [2006] UKHL 24.

[54] *McFarlane v McFarlane* [2004] UKHL 24.

[55] Welstead (2012, p. 209).

[56] Perry (2022, p. 379).

[57] Karlsson (2011, p. 443).

where the Property (Relationships) Act 1976 permits deviations from equal sharing only in situations deemed 'repugnant to justice'.[58] This would aid in ensuring more consistent and fair results.

The consideration of the parties' original intentions, as emphasised in Seychelles' legal precedents, should also be counterbalanced by considering the tangible contributions made during the marriage. The UK's *Stack v Dowden*[59] case prioritises the parties' intentions during property acquisition and presents a nuanced perspective. Nevertheless, it is enhanced by a comprehensive evaluation of the contributions and circumstances throughout the marriage. Seychelles gains from implementing a comparable and equitable strategy, considering initial intentions and subsequent contributions when dividing property. Although cases such as *Chetty v Emile*[60] have acknowledged the significance of these contributions, a better framework for evaluating them still needs to be developed.

Seychelles could adopt a more systematic method of assessing non-financial contributions, drawing inspiration from countries like the UK and New Zealand. This would ensure that all types of contributions are acknowledged and valued fairly. On the other hand, France exemplifies an informative model with its community property regime, wherein assets obtained during the marriage are automatically regarded as jointly owned.[61] This system inherently prioritises the collaborative contributions of married partners, making the asset division process more accessible and ensuring that non-financial contributions are acknowledged without requiring complicated assessments.[62] Seychelles could enhance the accuracy of marital partnerships by implementing a community property regime that mirrors the actuality of both partners contributing in various ways to the acquisition and upkeep of assets.

Moreover, the emphasis on parties' intentions during property registration, as demonstrated in cases such as *Charles v Charles,*[63] can frequently result in unfair or unjust outcomes. This approach needs to sufficiently consider the changing nature of marital contributions as time progresses. On the other hand, the UK approach considers both parties' needs and contributions during the marriage, providing a more flexible and fair method of dividing assets. To achieve a fair and equitable distribution of assets, Seychelles should prioritise both parties' actual contributions and needs throughout the marriage rather than solely focusing on the initial intentions.

[58] Property (Relationships) Act 1976, s. 13(1).

[59] *Stack v Dowden* [2007] UKHL 17.

[60] *Chetty v Emile* [2008-2009] SCAR 65.

[61] Frémeaux and Leturcq (2023, p. 115).

[62] Frémeaux and Leturcq (2019, p. 145).

[63] *Charles v Charles* [2005] SCCA 13.

4.3 Removing Procedural Barriers

In *Udwadia v Udwadia*,[64] the Seychelles Supreme Court refused to grant Mrs. Beryl Udwadia leave to file for a matrimonial property adjustment order outside the two-month statutory time limit prescribed under Rule 34(1) of the Matrimonial Causes Rules. This case highlighted the procedural rigidity within the matrimonial legal framework, even when fairness and equity might have supported the applicant's cause. The respondent's counsel successfully argued that the affidavit was defective and that the applicant's failure to comply with mandatory timelines amounted to a disregard for procedural law.

The court agreed, relying on precedent that stresses strict compliance with court rules, including *Lablache De Charmoye v Lablache De Charmoye*,[65] where courts insisted that rules must be followed and cannot be set aside for convenience. Thus, *Udwadia v Udwadia* demonstrates that procedural barriers—particularly statutory deadlines—are applied with little flexibility, even in sensitive family law matters where equitable considerations and attempts at amicable settlement might otherwise justify a more discretionary approach. The case illustrates how procedural rigidity can frustrate substantive justice, especially when applicants are unaware of technical requirements or genuinely attempt settlement outside the court.

By comparison, the United Kingdom's legal framework, as outlined in the Matrimonial Causes Act 1973, adopts a more flexible approach, allowing financial relief claims, including property adjustments, to be filed long after divorce. Cases like *Wyatt v Vince*,[66] where a claim was allowed decades post-divorce, highlight the UK's focus on fairness and equitable outcomes, with courts considering factors such as financial changes and child welfare when delays occur. France adopts a middle-ground approach, with Article 2224 of the Civil Code requiring property claims to be initiated within five years of divorce. This strikes a balance between procedural deadlines and fairness, ensuring that spousal rights are protected while maintaining legal certainty.

Seychelles could benefit from reforming its rigid procedural deadlines to better align with international standards. Extending the current two-month period to six months or a year, as in France, would provide claimants more time to prepare while preserving legal certainty. Incorporating judicial discretion for exceptional circumstances, similar to the UK's approach, would further ensure fairness without undermining procedural integrity. Such reforms would modernise Seychelles' matrimonial property laws, making them better equipped to address the complexities of matrimonial disputes and promoting a balance between certainty and justice.

In addition, Seychelles' reliance on judicial discretion, while providing flexibility, often leads to unpredictability and subjective assessments. On the other hand, the UK has a well-organised legal system that offers a more defined route for courts, helping them evaluate contributions and guaranteeing more uniform and equitable results. Introducing precise criteria for assessing non-financial contributions in Seychelles

[64] *Udwadia v Udwadia* [2024] SCSC 9.

[65] *Lablache De Charmoye v Lablache De Charmoye* [2019] SCSC 34.

[66] *Wyatt v Vince* [2015] UKSC 14.

would decrease the reliance on personal judgment and improve the ability to anticipate judicial rulings. Implementing this approach would bring Seychelles in line with jurisdictions that have effectively achieved a balance between flexibility and clarity. This would ensure that all contributions, regardless of type, are equitably acknowledged and valued when dividing marital assets.

5 Conclusion

Seychelles' approach to property division after divorce is intricately intertwined with its historical context and current legal developments. The legal framework, based on French civil law and influenced by British legal traditions, encompasses a system characterised by judicial discretion and a commitment to honouring the intentions of the parties involved. The Seychellois courts have considerable discretion in determining the division of marital assets, taking into account the unique circumstances and agreements of the spouses.

In contrast to the inflexible systems observed in nations such as the United Kingdom and Sweden, where statutory guidelines or community property principles determine asset distribution, Seychelles' approach allows for more nuanced, case-specific decision-making. The flexibility in Seychelles' legal system, which reflects its distinctive legal heritage, can result in different outcomes that may seem inconsistent to those observing from the outside. In addition, the legal framework of Seychelles has developed in parallel with socio-economic transformations, such as its shift towards a multiparty democracy and its increasing reliance on tourism. These factors influence current deliberations on potential reforms to achieve a more equitable alignment between established legal principles, changing societal expectations, and global standards of justice.

Seychelles' legal system's flexibility is both advantageous and problematic, especially when it comes to matters of gender equality and the recognition of non-financial contributions in marriage. Although the system aims to achieve fairness and equality, judicial discretion requires a thorough examination of each case's specific circumstances to ensure fair outcomes for all parties. Seychelles' legal approach to property division after divorce reflects its historical development and its dedication to adapting to modern challenges. Seychelles aims to uphold the principles of justice and to adapt its legal framework to meet the diverse needs and circumstances of its population when distributing marital assets, while carefully navigating these complexities.

References

Allen RB (2022) History of the Seychelles. Oxford Research Encyclopedia of African History, Oxford

Bogdan M (1989) The law of Mauritius and Seychelles: a study of two small mixed legal systems. Juristförlaget i Lund, Lund

Frémeaux N, Leturcq M (2019) Individualisation du patrimoine au sein des couples: quels enjeux pour la fiscalité ? Rev OFCE 161:145–175

Frémeaux N, Leturcq M (2023) Les formes légales de vie en couple et leurs conséquences sur le partage du patrimoine et des ressources entre conjoints en France. Rech Fam 20:115–133

Gunputh RP (2008) Les limites d'adaptation—Interprétation du code civil français dans la synthèse du droit mixte Mauricien—Coexistence et influence dans les mascareignes. Rev Int Droit Comp 60:885–925

Halpérin J-L (2005) Deux cents ans de rayonnement du code civil des Français? Cah Droit. 46:229–251

Karlsson Sjögren Å (2011) Matrimony, property and power: marriage settlements in Sweden 1870–1920. Scand J Hist 36:443–461

Miles J, Hitchings E (2018) Financial remedy outcomes on divorce in England & Wales: not a "meal ticket for life." Aust J Fam Law 31:43–80

Mujuzi JD (2023) Marriage by cohabitation (common law marriage) in Seychelles: emerging issues. In: Blair SL, Zhang Y (eds) Cohabitation and the evolving nature of intimate and family relationships. Contemporary perspectives in family research, vol 24, Emerald Publishing Limited, Leeds, pp 237–267

Parkinson P (2003) Quantifying the homemaker contribution in family property law. Fed L Rev 31:1–55

Perry ES (2022) Sweden: harmonising family law across borders in Europe. In: Wilson RF, Carbone J (eds) International survey of family law, pp 379416

Twomey M (2017) Legal metissage in a micro-jurisdiction: the mixing of common law and civil law in Seychelles. City Print

Welstead M (2012) Miller v Miller; McFarlane v McFarlane [2004] UKHL 24. Denning L.J. 18(1):209–219. https://doi.org/10.5750/dlj.v18i1.315

Cédric Tuyau is a lecturer in Civil Law at the University of Seychelles, specialising in international contract drafting. He teaches and develops curricula that equip students with analytical skills to address complex legal challenges and foster precision in legal reasoning. His research critically examines civil law frameworks and their application in practical contexts. Tuyau has extensive professional experience, including as a former Money Laundering Reporting Officer. He is a Fellow of the Higher Education Academy and holds a Doctor of Laws (LL.D) as well as a Postgraduate Diploma in Higher Teaching and Learning, reflecting his commitment to both scholarly and pedagogical excellence.

A Critical Analysis and Overview of the South African Legal Framework on Matrimonial Property Rights and Divorce

Untalimile Crystal Mokoena and Zamokuhle Mopai

Abstract This chapter aims to provide an overview of the developments of matrimonial property rights in South Africa in the past three decades of a democratic society based on human dignity, equality, and freedom. The Constitution and international human rights instruments in South Africa have significantly transformed matrimonial property rights. Spouses now enjoy equal rights and capacities to own, acquire, and distribute matrimonial property according to their preferred matrimonial property system. This transformation is even more guarded during the dissolution of marriages and is evidenced through many judicial decisions discussed in this chapter. With three types of marriages legally recognised, namely, civil marriages, customary marriages, and civil unions, the distribution of matrimonial property, particularly in customary marriages, has received significant judicial and scholarly attention in South Africa. Case law and literature are indicative of how laws governing matrimonial property have developed to the current applaudable state where gender equality is recognised. This contribution explores the meaning, consequences, and implications of the property rights of spouses both during and after the dissolution of marriages, especially customary marriages, and examines the practicality of the application of some of the legal developments to the matrimonial property rights in marriages in South Africa.

U. C. Mokoena · Z. Mopai (✉)
School of Law, University of Venda, Thohoyandou, South Africa
e-mail: zama.mopai@univen.ac.za

U. C. Mokoena
e-mail: crystal.mokoena@univen.ac.za

A. F. Hammond and P. Batariwah (eds.), *The Law on Marital Property in Africa*, Ius Gentium: Comparative Perspectives on Law and Justice 138,
https://doi.org/10.1007/978-3-032-19358-2_16

1 Introduction

South Africa currently recognises three types of marriages: civil marriages,[1] customary marriages,[2] and civil unions.[3] All these types of marriages produce serious legal consequences and can be dissolved either by death or an order of the court through a divorce decree. However, in certain instances, the marriages can be annulled by being set aside due to their invalidity or voidability from the outset.[4] It should be noted that Islamic marriages are not legally recognised, but simply acknowledged for proprietary consequences only, especially upon the death of one of the spouses or divorce. This chapter focuses on two things: the matrimonial property systems governing these different types of marriage, and the consequences of divorce on matrimonial property rights.

Importantly, the grounds and procedures for divorce are set out in statutes governing each marriage. However, the procedure and consequences of judicial dissolution are the same and are set out in the Divorce Act 70 of 1970. Extrajudicial dissolution is not recognised in South Africa.[5] Therefore, no marriage can be validly dissolved without a judicial decree of divorce from a competent court.[6] This chapter provides an overview of the matrimonial property systems available and applicable in South Africa. Furthermore, the chapter examines the divorce process for each of these marriages, including the legal consequences and challenges associated with divorce, particularly regarding matrimonial property. The chapter focuses on the South African matrimonial legal context, with special attention to customary marriages, given their unique nature compared to civil marriages and civil unions.

In terms of structure, this chapter is divided into nine sections. Following this introduction, Sect. 2 provides a brief overview of marriages in South Africa. Section 3 offers a synopsis of the dissolution of marriages, while Sect. 4 presents a general overview of South Africa's matrimonial property systems. Section 5 is dedicated to analysing the matrimonial property system governing customary marriages. Section 6 introduces recent updates on the property rights of spouses in Islamic marriages. Section 7 briefly interrogates the applicability of a presumption of marriage under South African law. Section 8 offers recommendations for improving the legal framework of the matrimonial property system in South Africa, and Sect. 9 concludes the chapter.

[1] Civil Marriages Act 25 of 1961.

[2] Recognition of Customary Marriages Act 120 of 1998.

[3] Civil Unions Act 17 of 2006.

[4] See Mopai and Mokoena (2023, p. 267).

[5] Moore and Himonga (2015).

[6] USLegal (n.d.).

2 A Brief Overview of Different Marriages in South Africa

South African law recognises three types of marriages: civil marriages, civil unions, and customary marriages. These marriages are regulated by different statutes. Civil marriages are governed by the Marriage Act,[7] and are defined as a voluntary union between one man and one woman to the exclusion of others.[8] Civil unions, on the other hand, are unions allowing for the solemnisation of marriages for both same-sex and opposite-sex partners.[9] They are regulated by the Civil Unions Act.[10] The third and last type of marriage in South Africa is the customary marriage. A customary marriage is one entered into under customary law.[11] This type of marriage can either be monogamous or polygamous.

Since this chapter focuses on divorce and matrimonial property rights, we discuss how these marriages are dissolved. This is significant, considering that many property-related challenges often arise upon the dissolution of marriages. Therefore, the following section provides an overview of the legal framework for dissolving different types of marriage in South Africa.

3 Dissolution of Marriages

There are different ways in which a marriage can be terminated or dissolved in South Africa.[12] A marriage may be dissolved through death, nullity, or divorce.[13] The first two occur automatically, as they are determined by the circumstances surrounding the marriage rather than initiated by the parties themselves. For example, when one of the parties dies, it is understood that the marriage cannot continue. Similarly, if the marriage was not legally compliant for any reason, the marriage and all consequences arising from it would have to be set aside through a court order.[14] However, the third method, which is divorce, is a voluntary dissolution initiated by either party or by mutual consent, on the grounds that the relationship between the spouses has irretrievably broken down with no prospect of reconciliation.[15] It should be noted that divorce applies only to legally valid marriages.[16] For all three recognised marriages

---

[7] The Marriage Act 25 of 1961.

[8] See Heaton (2010).

[9] Rautenbach (2022) and Bakker (2017, p. 121).

[10] Civil Unions Act 17 of 2006.

[11] Recognition of Customary Marriages Act 120 of 1998, s. 1.

[12] For further study on South African divorce law, see Heaton (2014).

[13] See Skeleton and Carnelley (2014).

[14] However, the nullity of the marriage will be made effective by a court order upon application for such a marriage to be declared null and void due to its invalidity.

[15] Divorce Act 70 of 1979, s. 4(1).

[16] [16]According to s. 1 of the Divorce Act 70 of 1979, the High Court or Regional Courts have jurisdiction to grant a divorce decree.

in South Africa, divorce can only be obtained through a decree of divorce from a competent court.[17]

The divorce process is provided for in the Divorce Act 70 of 1979, and it applies to all marriages, including customary marriages. The court must satisfy itself that the marriage has irretrievably broken down, with no prospects of restoration.[18] Once the divorce is granted, the parties return to their initial status as unmarried individuals and are free to remarry.[19]

4 General Overview of the Legal Framework Governing the Matrimonial Property Systems of Marriages in South Africa

Providing a general overview of the legal framework regulating matrimonial property is necessary, given the different types of marriages in South Africa. Special attention is given to customary marriages as they consist of a variety of marriage regimes, mainly because they are potentially polygamous, and complexities may revolve around property.

Property is an essential aspect of any marriage, both during and after the marriage's dissolution, either by death or divorce. This is why the proprietary consequences of all marriages should be legally clear and ascertainable. Without a clear scope on how property should be regulated in marriage and between spouses and third parties, there is a higher likelihood of inequality, prejudice, or misuse of proprietary rights. Therefore, in South Africa, all recognised marriages have a defined proprietary system, which is stipulated in the respective statutes regulating the different types of marriage and regulated through the Matrimonial Property Amendment Act 3 of 1988 (MPA).

---

[17] Divorce Act 70 of 1979, s. 3, Recognition of Customary Marriages Act, s. 8; Civil Union Act, s. 13 states that civil unions have the same legal consequences as civil marriages. This implies that the same legal consequences should apply to the dissolution of such unions. This was confirmed by the court in *Steyn v Steyn* [2010] ZAWCHC 224, paras 29–30. According to the Jurisdiction of Regional Courts Amendment Act 2008, only Regional and High Courts have jurisdiction over divorce matters in South Africa.

[18] The grounds for an irretrievably broken-down marriage are no longer as tedious as in the past. Parties simply need to state that the relationship between them is no longer conducive for marriage; they can cite any other reason to that effect.

[19] Skeleton and Carnelley (2014).

4.1 Types of Matrimonial Property Systems in South African Law

According to the MPA, three types of matrimonial property systems exist. These apply to all recognised and valid marriages in South Africa (civil marriages, civil unions, and, to a certain extent, customary marriages). First, we have 'in community of property', which is the default system for all monogamous marriages in South Africa.[20] In-community of property refers to a system where spouses have a joint estate consisting of all their assets and liabilities acquired before and during the marriage.[21] This system consists of a joint or universal estate.[22] Secondly, we have the 'out of community of property,' which can either be with or without the accrual system.[23] The out-of-community property system is only achievable through an antenuptial contract.[24] An antenuptial contract is a contract that spouses must have drawn with the assistance of an attorney or notary and is approved by the court.[25] The contract will therefore stipulate how the spouse's separate estate will be regulated during the course of the marriage.

The difference between the out-of-community property regime with an accrual system and without an accrual system is quite clear. In the case of an accrual system, it applies when the spouses' estates are separate, but they share profits and losses upon dissolution of the marriage.[26] The accrual system balances estates at the termination of the marriage, whether by divorce or death, allowing the spouse with the lesser

[20] See *Gumede v President of the Republic of South Africa* [2008] ZACC 23 where the court confirmed that in community of property is a default matrimonial property system for all monogamous marriages in South Africa, including customary marriages entered into before the commencement of the Recognition Act. See also *Edelstein v Edelstein* [1952] 3 SA 1.

[21] See Matrimonial Property Act 1984, s. 14 which provides that '...a wife in a marriage in community of property has the same powers with regard to the disposal of the assets of the joint estate, the contracting of debts which lie against the joint estate, and the management of the joint estate as those which a husband in such a marriage had immediately before the commencement of this Act.' In the case of *Mazibuko v National Director of Public Prosecution* [2009] 6 SA 479, the Court held that in the event that one spouse obtained assets now belonging to the joint estate unlawfully through criminal activities, the innocent spouse's interests must be considered and protected from the forfeiture of the goods by the relevant authorities during the process of recovering the affected property or proceeds. In *Du Plessis v Pienaar* [2003] 1 671, the Court confirmed that creditors might also look into the joint estate for the recovery of debts. This means that even if the debt was incurred by one party, the creditors can join the other spouses in the recovery of the debt since their estate is joined and considered as one. See also *Persad v Persad* [1989] (4) SA 685, where the court emphasised that the joint estate begins immediately upon entering into the marriage and includes even the right to occupy leased property of one's spouse.

[22] Matrimonial Property Act 1984, s. 1 defines a joint estate as the joint estate of a husband and a wife married in community of property.

[23] See Matrimonial Property Act 1984, s. 2 which provides that an out of community of property system can only be possible with an antenuptial contract and will be of profit and loss unless such is further excluded in the contract.

[24] See Matrimonial Property Act 1984, s. 1.

[25] Matrimonial Property Act 1984, s. 1.

[26] Matrimonial Property Act 1984, s. 3.

estate to claim up to half of the difference in value from the other spouse's accrued estate.[27] The accrual value is calculated in accordance with section 4 of the MPA, starting from the date of the commencement of the marriage.[28] In the matrimonial property system of out-of-community property without an accrual system, parties keep their estates completely separate even after the dissolution of the marriage.

Consequently, for both out of community property systems, whether with or without the accrual system, an antenuptial contract is a prerequisite.[29] Without a valid antenuptial contract, the matrimonial property system will automatically be treated as a community of property, which is the default system for all marriages.[30]

While a matrimonial property system is relevant during the marriage, its significance becomes even more profound at its dissolution. This is because, at the end of the marriage, it determines how the property and liabilities acquired during the marriage should be shared between the divorcing spouses.

All the matrimonial property systems mentioned above apply to all recognised marriages in South Africa. However, customary marriages have distinct characteristics that introduce a unique matrimonial property system into the South African landscape, making them the focal point of this research. With that said, it is crucial to first provide an overview of the matrimonial systems governing the other two types of marriage before delving into the proprietary consequences of customary marriages.

4.2 Proprietary Consequences of Civil Marriages and Civil Unions

As already discussed in the preceding section, civil marriages and civil unions have the same matrimonial property systems. In other words, the proprietary consequences of civil unions correspond with those of civil marriages.[31] They are both in community of property by default, as contemplated in the Matrimonial Property Amendment Act of 1988.

4.2.1 Marriages in Community of Property

Marriages in community of property place both parties to a marriage or civil union on an equal footing when dealing with their matrimonial property. For this reason, it is

---

[27] Matrimonial Property Act 1984, s. 3.

[28] Matrimonial Property Act 1984, s. 4(1).

[29] Where the parties failed to execute or comply with certain requirements for an antenuptial contract before the commencement of the marriage, the High Court may be approached with an application to execute the intended contract as a postnuptial contract.

[30] See Matrimonial Property Act 1984, s. 2.

[31] According to the Civil Unions Act, s. 13(1), the difference between the two is that civil marriage is strictly for heterosexual couples, while civil union also include opposite-sex couples.

important to note that South African law abolished the 'marital power'.[32] This power, according to Heaton and Kruger, 'gave the husband the power to incur debts, and to buy, sell, pledge and burden joint assets as well as his wife's separate assets over which his marital power had not been excluded'.[33] Although the abolition originally applied only to certain forms of marriage, primarily prospective white, Asian, or coloured marriages contracted in 1984 or later, by 1993 it had been extended to all forms of marriage, regardless of race or the date the marriage was contracted.[34] Therefore, the new rule is one of equal administration of the community property. Section 14 of the MPA embodies this ethos by providing that both parties shall have equal rights to dispose of and manage assets in a joint estate. The Act outlines the various forms of consent required from each party when dealing with property. For instance, a spouse married in community of property requires a written consent from the other spouse or partner to alienate immovable property.[35] There are, however, other transactions that do not necessarily require written consent but only verbal consent, such as donating furniture that forms part of the joint estate.[36]

It is important to note that certain assets are excluded from the community of property and remain the separate property of a spouse, even when the marriage is in community of property.[37] Assets that do not form part of the community property include those excluded by an antenuptial contract, assets received under a will or deed of donation, property subject to a *fideicommissum* or usufruct, non-patrimonial damages, and compensation for personal injuries caused to the other spouse.[38]

4.2.2 Marriages Out of Community of Property with Accrual System

In all marriages contracted out of community of property, the accrual system applies by default, unless the antenuptial contract explicitly excludes it.[39] Parties to a marriage or union out of community of property do not share any joint estate; instead, each party maintains their separate estate. Despite this, both parties contribute to the household's necessities according to their financial means.[40] The accrual system means that upon the dissolution of a marriage or civil union, the party whose estate shows little or no growth/accrual has a right to claim half of the difference between the two estates from the estate with more value.[41] However, neither spouse has a present determinate interest in the accrued estate of the other spouse. In *Reeder v*

32 Matrimonial Property Act 1984, ss. 11 and 12.

33 Heaton and Kruger (2015, p. 70).

34 Heaton and Kruger (2015, pp. 70–71).

35 Matrimonial Property Act 1984, s. 15(2)(a).

36 Matrimonial Property Act 1984, s. 15(3).

37 *Du Plessis v Pienaar* [2002] 4 All SA 311, para. 1.

38 Heaton and Kruger (2015, pp. 64–66).

39 Matrimonial Property Act 1984, s. 2.

40 Matrimonial Property Act 1984, s. 23.

41 Matrimonial Property Act 1984, s. 3.

Softline Ltd and Another, the High Court held that 'a spouse who alleges that her estate has shown no accrual or a smaller accrual than the estate of the other spouse, and who … claims half the difference of the accrual between the two estates, has a contingent right and not a vested right'.[42] However, under section 5(1) of the Matrimonial Property Act 1984, inheritances, legacies or donations, and any other related assets do not form the accrued part of a spouse's estate.

A party to a marriage governed by the accrual system may apply to the court for an immediate division of the matrimonial property if the other spouse's conduct at the time of dissolution would seriously prejudice their rights.[43] A party who is entitled to an accrual may choose to forfeit either the whole accrual or a part thereof.[44]

4.2.3 Marriages Out of Community of Property Without the Accrual System

Each spouse retains ownership and control over their individual assets and is solely responsible for whatever liabilities they incur. In the event of a spouse's insolvency, that spouse will be subject to the applicable rules and procedures of insolvency law. Although insolvency directly affects only the insolvent spouse, it may still have an indirect impact on the solvent spouse. The solvent spouse's property may be sequestered unless they can prove that the property was: (a) acquired immediately before the marriage, (b) excluded by a marriage settlement, or (c) acquired jointly during the marriage under circumstances that render the title valid against all creditors of the insolvent spouse.[45]

The out of community system has been undercut in recent years by legal developments. For example, the Divorce Act of 1979, in tune with the introduction of the accrual system, permitted spouses previously married under the out of community system without the option of accrual to apply to a court for a redistribution order so that the court could apply the accrual system to their marriages if deemed necessary and in the interest of justice.[46] Notably, the law excluded certain categories of marriages, particularly those contracted out of community of property on or after 1984, as well as marriages contracted out of community either before or after 1984 that were subsequently dissolved by the death of one spouse.[47] The Constitutional Court has had the opportunity to comment on the different treatment given to different out of community property marriages, and in *EB v ER*,[48] the Constitutional Court found these differential treatments unconstitutional because they violated the equality rights provisions in the South African Constitution. While the court outlined

---

[42] [2001] 2 SA 844, 849.

[43] Matrimonial Property Act 1984, s. 8.

[44] Matrimonial Property Act 1984, s. 9.

[45] Insolvency Act 1936, s. 21(1–2).

[46] Divorce Act 1979, s. 7(3); see generally, Amien (2024).

[47] Amien (2024).

[48] [2023] ZACC 32.

the specific amendments needed to the statute, it suspended the immediate implementation of the judgment, allowing the legislature 24 months to pass remedial legislation.

4.2.4 Life Partnerships

In addition to the recognised marriage types, South Africa has seen recent developments of a different type of relationship where parties are in an unregistered 'life partnerships'. This is when lovers live together, replicating the relationship of married spouses. These new developments entail that parties may claim from each other's estate, should one predecease the other. This was held in the case of *Bwanya v Master of the High Court, Cape Town, and Others*.[49] According to the Court in *Bwanya*, parties in a life partnership with a reciprocated duty of support and care have the right to be considered as beneficiaries of their deceased partner's estate even if they were not married or had their partnership registered as a civil union. However, this does not mean that there is a specific or unique proprietary consequence for such relationships. In this instance, the surviving partner will only be considered a beneficiary (and not a spouse), provided they can prove that there was an undertaking of a reciprocal duty of support between them.[50]

5 An Analysis of the Matrimonial Property System in Customary Marriages

Due to the non-recognition of customary marriages in the past, it took some time for statutory and judicial developments to have an impact on these types of marriages in South Africa. Thus, parties, especially women, involved in these marriages did not enjoy significant rights or protection regarding matrimonial property, among other issues.[51] The customary law approach to proprietary rights in marriage was mostly patriarchal in nature. As the head of the family, the husband was regarded as the sole controller of the family property.[52] The wife was generally entitled to her personal belongings and allowed limited access and control over the house or

[49] [2022] 3 SA 250.

[50] See Barratt (2022).

[51] See Black Administration Act 38 of 1927, ss. 22(1) and 35. The BAA referred to customary marriages as unions and marriages at the same time. However, reading into the context of the Act, it is clear that the intention was to keep customary marriages' status inferior to that of civil marriages, hence the usage of the word 'union' instead of 'marriage'.

[52] For customary marriages this was also provided for in s. 11(3) of the Black Administrative Act 27 of 1938, which relegated a wife in a customary marriage to a perpetual minor under the guardianship of her husband. The section was later to be amended by section 11A which afforded women limited rights to acquire land property and other properties.

household property.[53] However, even such an entitlement was not applicable in most cases.[54] At the end of such marriages, which were usually through death, the wife had no tangible right or claim to the property, which she normally benefited from and contributed to during her husband's lifetime and the marriage's subsistence.[55] Most women in customary marriage were left with no significant share of the supposed family or matrimonial property.[56]

The principle of male primogeniture,[57] entrenched in section 23 of the Black Administration Act (BAA),[58] equally exacerbated this situation for women.[59] This is because women under customary law, particularly those in customary marriages, were excluded from the protection of the law when it came to matrimonial property.[60] The BAA, as the official and colonial law governing customary law matters then, regarded women as perpetual minors without any control over matrimonial property, thereby rendering them economically vulnerable, especially in the event of the dissolution of their customary marriages.[61] Furthermore, the BAA accorded husbands in customary unions, as they were called then, absolute ownership of family property, household property, and their wives' personal property and earnings.[62] In the event of the dissolution or nullification of a customary union, all matrimonial property accrued to the husband.[63]

---

[53] Also see Transkei Marriage Act 21 of 1978, ss. 14, 27 and 37, which provided for the administration of a wife's property rights under her husband's guardianship. In *Mshengu v Estate Late Mshengu* [2021] ZAKZPHC 49, the court defined house property as property which the wife and her husband (in polygamous household) jointly share and own to the exclusion of others.

[54] The practice dated even a long way back before the Transkei Marriage Act. See *Mampeyi v Rarai* [1937] NAC 148.

[55] *Bhe v Magistrate Khayelitsha* [2005] BCLR 1CC, *Gumede v President of the Republic of South Africa* [2009] 3 BCLR 243, *Nkabinde v Road Accident Fund* [2001] 3 All SA 611 and *Ramuhovhi v President of the Republic of South Africa* [2018] 2 BCLR 217. All these cases, in their entirety, deal with the issue of deprivation of women of proprietary rights and power.

[56] *Gumede v President of the Republic of South Africa* [2008] ZACC 23.

[57] This principle was based on the idea that only males had property rights in the family. It was held to be unconstitutional in the case of *Bhe v Khayelitsa Magistrate* [2005] BCLR 1CC.

[58] Black Administration Act 38 of 1927.

[59] This can also be seen in the case of *Bhe v Magistrate Khayelitsha* [2005] BCLR 1CC, where daughters were not allowed to inherit from their deceased father, and their mother from her deceased husband because of their gender.

[60] Nhlapo (1992, p. 152).

[61] Deveaux (2003).

[62] Bennett (1991). See also Recognition of Customary Marriages Act, s. 7(1)(b) which describes family property as property to which all spouses in a polygamous marriage contribute and over which they have equal ownership and control for the benefit of the entire family. Whereas house property is property belonging to or allotted to the specific unit of each wife in a polygamous marriage.

[63] *Gumede v President of the Republic of South Africa* [2008] ZACC 23; *Sithole and Another v Sithole and Another* [2021] 6 BCLR 597.

However, in the democratic dispensation under the current Constitution of South Africa of 1996,[64] a new legal order based on equality, human dignity, and freedoms emerged.[65] The South African Constitution guarantees basic human rights to all, ensuring that no one is arbitrarily deprived of their rights. This includes the right to property,[66] which is extended to women previously deprived of property rights in this context. Apart from the Constitution and other relevant legislation on the promotion and protection of women's rights, especially in marriage, South Africa has ratified many international law instruments in response to the emancipation of women, particularly in marriage.[67] As a result of this normative framework, it became necessary to reform the proprietary consequences of both monogamous and polygamous customary marriages in South Africa. This was one of the main objectives behind the enactment of the Recognition of Customary Marriages Act (RCMA).[68] This chapter briefly examines the impact of the Constitution and human rights instruments on the development of the proprietary system in customary marriages.

5.1 The Role Played by Human Rights Instruments in Developing Patrimonial Systems of Customary Marriages

The South African Constitution is considered one of the world's most progressive constitutions.[69] This is largely due to its values and inclusion of a justiciable Bill of Rights. The Constitution expressly indicates that South Africa is founded on 'human dignity, the achievement of equality and the advancement of human rights and freedoms', among other values.[70] Additionally, the Constitution was declared the country's supreme law, and any law or practice found to be inconsistent with it is deemed invalid,[71] implying that all customs relating to customary marriages and the property system had to align with the Constitution.

As already mentioned, the principle of male primogeniture largely influenced the marital property system of customary marriages. This practice, which also

[64] The Constitution of the Republic of South Africa, 1996 (herein referred to as the Constitution). The interim Constitution of 1993 was also instrumental in promoting women's rights, especially to property.

[65] See Constitution of South Africa of 1996, s. 2.

[66] Constitution of the Republic of South Africa 1996, s. 25.

[67] Convention on the Elimination of All Forms of Discrimination Against Women (ratified by South Africa in 1995) and the Protocol to the African Charter on Human and People's Rights on the Rights of Women in Africa (ratified by South Africa in December 2004).

[68] The Recognition of Customary Marriages Act 120 of 1998.

[69] Murray (2001, p. 812).

[70] Constitution of the Republic of South Africa 1996, s. 1.

[71] Constitution of the Republic of South Africa 1996, s. 2.

favoured males over females in matters relating to intestate inheritance, had a negative impact on the patrimonial system in customary marriages, as wives were not allowed to inherit their deceased husbands' estates, to which they may have significantly contributed during the subsistence of the marriage. When the principle of male primogeniture was subjected to constitutional scrutiny in the groundbreaking case of *Bhe v Magistrate Khayelitsha*,[72] it was found to be unconstitutional. Although the case did not deal with the patrimonial systems in customary marriages per se, it interrogated the constitutional validity of a principle that did not allow females to inherit from their deceased husband's estate. All customs and practices that unjustly discriminated against women had to be aligned with the Constitution. This included reforming the matrimonial property system of customary marriages to be consistent with those governing other marriages. The reform involved transitioning from a system that treated women as perpetual minors, unable to own property, to one where women are recognised as equal partners in marriage, entitled to half of the joint estate in marriages that are in community of property.

It is important to point out that the Constitution unequivocally affirms everyone's right to enjoy their culture.[73] This includes one's right to become part of a marriage regulated by one's own customs. Section 39(2), however, stipulates that, 'When interpreting any legislation, and when developing the common law or customary law, every court, tribunal or forum must promote the spirit, purport and objects of the Bill of Rights'.This means that while individuals are free to practice their culture, including entering into customary marriages, such practices must be carried out in a manner that promotes and aligns with the principles of the Bill of Rights. A customary marriage that embraces discriminatory practices like not allowing wives to own property, for instance, does not support the objects of the Bill of Rights.

In addition to section 9 of the Constitution (the equality clause),[74] which advocates for equal treatment of every person, including wives in customary marriages, the South African Constitution makes it mandatory for courts or tribunals to consider

[72] *Bhe v Magistrate Khayelitsha* [2005] BCLR 1. For a further discussion and analysis of the principle of male primogeniture and its implications see Miriki (2024).

[73] Constitution of the Republic of South Africa 1996, ss. 15, 30 and 31.

[74] Constitution of the Republic of South Africa 1996, s. 9 provides as follows:

1. Everyone is equal before the law and has the right to equal protection and benefit of the law.
2. Equality includes the full and equal enjoyment of all rights and freedoms. To promote the achievement of equality, legislative and other measures designed to protect or advance persons, or categories of persons, disadvantaged by unfair discrimination may be taken.
3. The state may not unfairly discriminate directly or indirectly against anyone on one or more grounds, including race, gender, sex, pregnancy, marital status, ethnic or social origin, colour, sexual orientation, age, disability, religion, conscience, belief, culture, language and birth.
4. No person may unfairly discriminate directly or indirectly against anyone on one or more grounds in terms of subsection (3). National legislation must be enacted to prevent or prohibit unfair discrimination.
5. Discrimination on one or more of the grounds listed in subsection (3) is unfair unless it is established that the discrimination is fair.

In a bid to prohibit unfair discrimination, the Promotion of Equality and Prevention of Unfair Discrimination Act 4 of 2000 (PEPUDA or the Equality Act) was promulgated.

international law in cases brought before them.[75] This means that when addressing a matter in a court of law, it is essential to align the decision with the principles set out in international law, including human rights instruments.

Discriminatory practices in customary marriages, most of which are perpetrated through patrimonial systems, violate several human rights conventions. For instance, the Convention on the Elimination of All Forms of Discrimination Against Women (CEDAW) condemns all discriminatory forms levied against women, including discriminatory practices in customary marriages. A practice that allows only men or husbands to own property but not wives is discriminatory and should be condemned. Article 2(f) of the CEDAW obliges member states to 'take all appropriate measures, including legislation, to modify or abolish existing laws, regulations, customs and practices which constitute discrimination against women'.[76] South Africa is a signatory to CEDAW,[77] and accordingly, its laws, including those related to the development of matrimonial property in customary marriages, have benefited from this provision.

Regional human rights instruments also play a significant role in the development of customary marriages. The Protocol to the African Charter on Human and Peoples' Rights on the Rights of Women in Africa[78] protects women's rights in all spheres, including marriage. It expressly mandates states to ensure that wives enjoy equal rights to those of husbands in marriages.[79] Although enacted and ratified after the South African Constitution, such instruments continue to shape and develop South African laws (the matrimonial property system in customary marriages, in this case). Having given a legal and human rights framework for consideration when developing matrimonial property systems, it is pertinent to now examine different matrimonial property systems for customary marriages in South Africa.

5.2 Types of Matrimonial Property Systems for Customary Marriages

The RCMA came into force on 15 November 2000 to legally recognise all customary marriages in South Africa, regardless of when they were concluded. From then onwards, customary marriages have enjoyed equal recognition and status with their

---

[75] Constitution of the Republic of South Africa 1996, s 39(1)(b) states that: 'When interpreting the Bill of Rights, a court, tribunal or forum .... b. must consider international law'.

[76] CEDAW, art 2(f).

[77] South Africa ratified CEDAW in 1995.

[78] African Union, Protocol to the African Charter on Human and Peoples' Rights on the Rights of Women in Africa (2003).

[79] Protocol to the African Charter on Human and People's Rights on the Rights of Women in Africa (African Women's Rights Protocol), art 6 provides that; 'States Parties shall ensure that women and men enjoy equal rights and are regarded as equal partners in marriage'.

common-law counterparts, namely, civil marriages. The Act provides for the recognition of customary marriages entered into before and after its commencement.[80] The Act further recognises both monogamous and polygamous customary marriages.[81]

Section 7 of the RCMA deals with the proprietary system for customary marriages.[82] The RCMA amplifies the matrimonial property systems available in South Africa by specifying how each applies to the various types of customary marriages. Four matrimonial property systems are identified in the RCMA for different types of customary marriages. The first three matrimonial property systems are the general ones already discussed in Sect. 4 above, which are in community of property with profit and loss, out of community of property with accrual system, and out of community of property without accrual system. In community of property is a default system for all monogamous customary marriages, regardless of whether they were entered into before or after the commencement of the Act, unless such is excluded by an antenuptial contract.[83] As mentioned above, an antenuptial contract applies where parties choose their own matrimonial property system. This is available for all types of customary marriages.

However, a slight extension of the three generic systems occurs when it comes to polygamous marriages. A polygamous marriage is a marriage whereby a man has more than one wife.[84] Such marriages are only recognised under customary law. The extended matrimonial property system available to polygamous marriages makes a distinction between polygamous marriages entered into before the commencement of the RCMA and those entered into after the commencement of the same.[85]

For the pre-Act or old polygamous marriages, which are polygamous customary marriages entered into before the RCMA, the matrimonial property system applicable in terms of section 7(1) of the RCMA provides that a husband jointly and equally controls and manages the property with his wives both collectively and individually.[86] In this system, the husband and all his wives collectively enjoy equal and joint

---

[80] Recognition of Customary Marriages Act 1998, s. 2.

[81] Recognition of Customary Marriages Act 1998, s. 2.

[82] Recognition of Customary Marriages Act 1998, s. 7 before the Gumede case provided that, 'the proprietary consequences of customary marriages entered into before the commencement of this Act continue to be governed by customary law'. After the case and the amendment s. 7 now states that; 'The proprietary consequences of a customary marriage in which a person is a spouse in more than one customary marriage, and which was entered into before the commencement of this Act, are that the spouses in such a marriage have joint and equal- (i)ownership and other rights; and (ii) rights of management and control, over marital property'.

[83] Recognition of Customary Marriages Act 1998, s. 7(2).

[84] Madondo (2023).

[85] Recognition of Customary Marriages Act 1998, s. 7(1) provide for the matrimonial property system for pre-Act polygamous marriages, while s. 7(6) deals with the matrimonial property system for post-Act polygamous marriages.

[86] Recognition of Customary Marriages Act 1998, s. 7(1) provides that: '(a) The proprietary consequences of a customary marriage in which a person is a spouse in more than one customary marriage, and which was entered into before the commencement of this Act, are that the spouses in such a marriage have joint and equal- (i) ownership and other rights; and (ii) rights of management and control, over marital property'.

Fig. 1 Illustration of the pre-Act matrimonial property system for polygamous marriages

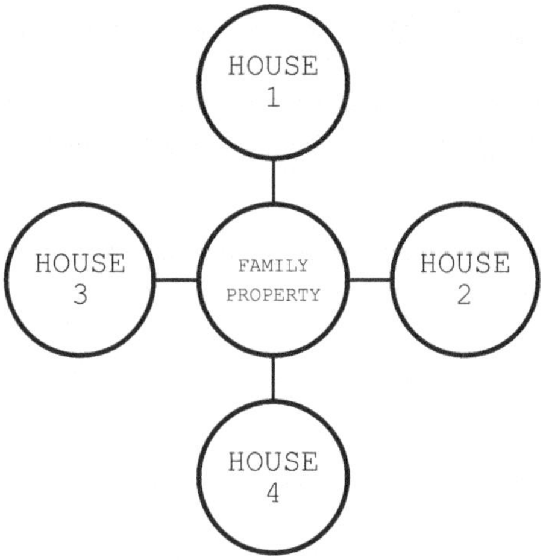

ownership and control over the family property, while the husband also enjoys a separate joint estate with each wife respectively in terms of house property.[87] This matrimonial property system may be illustrated this way (see Fig. 1):

According to the RCMA, family property is property to which all spouses in a polygamous marriage contribute and have equal ownership and control over for the benefit of the entire family.[88] House property is property belonging to or allotted to the specific unit of each wife in a polygamous marriage[89]; it is equally and jointly owned by the husband and the wife of that house.[90] This position was not so in the original customary law, where the husband, as the head of the entire family, had unilateral and full control over the family property and house property to the exclusion of the wives. The RCMA introduced significant reforms to the customary matrimonial property system by stipulating that the husband and his wives share equal control and ownership of the family property.[91]

This reform was highly significant, as polygamous marriages previously exhibited considerable inequality. The women and children in such marriages lacked patrimonial security, given that the husband had full discretion over the family's economic affairs. He could even alienate property from the different households for his own benefit or to the advantage of one household over another.[92] However, this provision was only later inserted in the RCMA 16 years after the Act came into force. Initially,

[87] Recognition of Customary Marriages Act 1998, s. 7(1)(b).

[88] Recognition of Customary Marriages Act 1998, s. 7((1)(b)(i).

[89] Recognition of Customary Marriages Act 1998, s. 7(1)(b)(ii). The concept of house property is unique to customary law and mostly refers to the real estate and household property belonging to a husband and each of the wives separately within a polygamous marriage, according to Pienaar (2021, pp. 126–129).

[90] See *Ramuhovhi v President of the Republic of South Africa* [2018] 2 BCLR.

[91] Recognition of Customary Marriages Act, s. 7(1).

[92] See discussion on polygamy before RCMA in Bennett (2004).

there was no progressive provision for the proprietary system for pre-Act polygamous marriages in the RCMA. The only provision was for marriages that occurred after the Act. However, through the decision in the case of *Ramuhovhi v President of the Republic of South Africa,* the proprietary consequences for pre-Act polygamous customary marriages were also included as section 7(1) in the RCMA to reflect this development.[93]

The last matrimonial property system for customary marriages is the matrimonial property system for post-Act polygamous marriages, where the husband applies to the court to approve a matrimonial contract between himself and his wives, stipulating which matrimonial property system will be applicable to them.[94] However, this contract depends on the court first dissolving any existing joint estate between the husband and his first wife if they were ever married in community of property.[95] This provision allows the husband and his first wife to separate their estate, making him eligible to enter a new matrimonial property system through an antenuptial contract with subsequent wives. One could argue that this provision plays a crucial role in ensuring fairness, particularly for the first wife, who is most likely to be in community of property with the husband.[96]

5.3 The Reform of the Matrimonial Property System for Customary Marriages

Let us take a brief step backwards to understand the progressive reform of the proprietary consequences of customary marriages. Initially, the proprietary consequences of customary marriages, provided for in section 7(1) of the RCMA, stipulated that all customary marriages entered into before the Act's commencement would continue to be governed by customary law. This was followed by a provision in section 7(2), which provided that all post-Act monogamous customary marriages shall be in community of property. However, this position was challenged in the case of *Gumede v President of the Republic of South Africa.*[97] As a result, these provisions were declared unconstitutional and invalid, to the extent that they discriminated between spouses from old and new customary marriages, particularly affecting women. Apart

[93] *Ramuhovhi v President of the Republic of South Africa* [2018] 2 BCLR; See Recognition on Customary Marriages Amendment Act 1 of 2021. The Recognition of Customary Marriages Amendment Act 1 of 2021 came into operation on 1 June 2021and it amended section 7 of the Recognition of Customary Marriages Act 120 of 1998 (the RCMA).

[94] Recognition of Customary Marriages Act 1998, s. 7(6). In *Ngwenyama v Mayelane and Another* [2012] ZASCA 94; the Supreme Court of Appeal held that, failure to get this contract drafted between the parties or approved by the courts will not invalidate the subsequent marriage as it is not the requirement for polygamy but a matrimonial property agreement.

[95] Recognition of Customary Marriages Act 1998, s. 7(7).

[96] Even though s. 7(6) is silent on the matter, it can be inferred that this contract must be drafted and approved every time the husband marries a new wife, and not just the second wife.

[97] *Gumede v President of the Republic of South Africa* [2008] ZACC 23.

from the fact that this would mean there would be no uniform matrimonial proprietary system for pre-Act customary marriages due to the diverse nature of customary law, the provision was problematic in many respects. Firstly, the customary law governing the proprietary system of pre-Act marriages was inherently patriarchal in nature and endorsed by the BAA.[98] Secondly, the RCMA's discrimination between pre-Act and post-Act customary marriages on proprietary consequences was illogical and discriminatory, considering that all these types of customary marriage were supposed to be recognised.[99] Lastly, this meant that women married before the RCMA would not benefit from some of the Act's key objectives, which are 'to provide for the equal status and capacity of spouses in customary marriages' and 'to regulate the proprietary consequences of customary marriages…' as stated in the Act's preamble.

Thus, in the *Gumede* decision, the Constitutional Court declared the initial section 7(1) of the RCMA unconstitutional on the grounds of unfair discrimination based on gender.[100] The Court held that just like post-Act customary marriages, the proprietary consequence of all monogamous customary marriages would be de facto in community of property, unless an antenuptial contract excluded such a consequence. However, the *Gumede* case focused solely on monogamous marriages and did not address polygamous marriages. As a result, pre-Act polygamous marriages continued to be regulated by customary law. Accordingly, the proprietary consequences of these marriages differed from those of post-Act marriages, whose proprietary consequences are clearly defined in sections 7(6)–(8) of the RCMA.[101] As expected, this meant that the proprietary rights of women in pre-Act polygamous marriages remained unchanged under the law. They would have to continue with no tangible rights over matrimonial property, and that is where the *Ramuhovhi* case took over, as already discussed above.

In the *Gumede* case, the Constitutional Court declared section 7(1) of the RCMA unconstitutional insofar as it applied to monogamous marriages on the basis that it unjustifiably and unfairly discriminated against women in terms of section 9(3) of the Constitution. As a result, the Court expunged the words 'entered into after the commencement of this Act' from section 7(2) to extend its provision to monogamous customary marriages entered into before the Act. The *Ramuhovhi* case further

[98] Black Administration Act, ss. 22 and 23.

[99] See Recognition of Customary Marriages Act 1998, s. 2 on the recognition of types of customary marriages.

[100] *Gumede v President of the Republic of South Africa* [2008] ZACC 23. In this case Mrs Gumede was challenging the subjection of her customary marriage to a matrimonial consequence that is subject to customary law instead of the same benefits as those of the post-Act customary marriages which are by default in community of property.

[101] According the Recognition of Customary Marriages Act, s 7(6–8), once a husband intends to enter into further customary marriages with other wives, he must apply for the Court to approve a marital property contract between him and his wives. Once approved, the court will dissolve the existing matrimonial property regime with his first wife and have such property equally distributed between him and her. As a result, polygamous marriage will be by default out of community of property.

declared invalid and unconstitutional the continued application of section 7(1) of the RCMA to pre-Act polygamous customary marriages.

According to the *Ramuhovhi* decision, in the unfortunate event of the husband's death, the wives in these marriages are now equally entitled to half of the family property and their husband's intestate estate.[102] This decision also implies that the same division of property would apply even in the case of divorce of one of the polygamous marriages. In the event of divorce, the wife would be entitled to half of the estate in the house property, and her equal share in the family property. The court made this decision on the basis that section 7(1) continued to discriminate against women in such marriages and deprived them of property rights. However, this declaration is only applicable to pre-Act polygamous marriages, which were still in existence and valid according to customary law at the commencement of the RCMA as provided in section 2 of the Act.[103] The *Ramuhovhi* decision also led to a significant amendment of the RCMA in 2021 to include a detailed provision on the proprietary consequences of both pre- and post-Act customary marriages.[104]

5.4 Proprietary Consequence of Customary Marriages

Before the coming into operation of the RCMA and until the Gumede and Ramuhovhi cases, the proprietary consequences of customary marriages were determined according to customary law, and in some instances, the official customary law in the BAA and other Codes, such as the KwaZulu and Natal Codes of Zulu law.[105]

As already mentioned, the generally applicable proprietary consequence of customary unions was that a husband was the sole owner of family property, excluding all family members, including his wife or wives.[106] However, the wife or wives and other family members could still benefit from its use, though they were not legally entitled to own or control it. In a polygamous household, where there were different houses and consequently different household properties, the wife had limited or no rights to the household property, depending on the customary law applicable to that particular family; this left women in a vulnerable proprietary position.[107]

---

[102] *Ramuhovhi v President of the Republic of South Africa* [2018] 2 BCLR, para 17.

[103] Recognition of Customary Marriages Act 1998, s. 2(1).

[104] Recognition of Customary Marriages Act 1 of 2021.

[105] The KwaZulu Act on the Code of Zulu Law 16 of 1985 and the Natal Code of Zulu Law (Proc R 151 in GG10966 of 9 October 1987).

[106] KwaZulu and Natal Codes, ss 20 and 22.

[107] Although contrary to the general belief in most customs that customary marriage was indissoluble, many customary marriages would still end in divorce. This would then mean that there would be no distribution of property at the end of such a marriage.

In its recommendations, the South African Law Commission,[108] in the Report on Customary Marriages,[109] stated the importance of clearly defining the proprietary consequences of customary marriages. This was true because, without a uniform, ascertainable, and official proprietary system for customary marriages, it would be nearly impossible to address the past proprietary prejudice in customary marriages. This was also necessary to fortify and give effect to the spousal equality and rights guaranteed in the Constitution[110] and the RCMA,[111] as well as to women's right to exercise their property ownership capacity.[112] Without effective statutory regulation, property matters in customary marriages would remain under the customary principles of property ownership. This would defeat the RCMA's quest to reform and develop the proprietary system of customary marriages to align with constitutional values.

Himonga and Moore,[113] in their study on the protection of the matrimonial property rights for women in customary marriages, found that there is still a long way to go in implementing a justiciable matrimonial property system in customary marriages. While the RCMA guarantees women in customary marriages the right to own and dispose of property, and to enjoy equal and joint property ownership with their husbands (especially where joint estate applies),[114] they may still be vulnerable to arbitrary customary systems. Some of which can be observed in polygamous marriages where subsequent wives do not enjoy secured matrimonial property rights compared to the first wives. This is why it is essential to establish a clear system that allows for the development of customary law.

The Recognition of Customary Marriages Amendment Act applies retrospectively, except to marriages that were already terminated when the decision was handed down.[115]

Nevertheless, the judicial development that led to the amendment of section 7 (1) of the RCMA presents yet another classic example of the interplay between customary law and human rights law, specifically in relation to customary marriages in South Africa. With the Court declaring that all 'old' polygamous marriages shall take the form of joint estates between a husband and his wives, a new and progressive reality was introduced to the complex setup of polygamous marriages. This significant intervention ensures that polygamous marriages do not continue to disadvantage the parties involved, especially the women. As it is, legal protection and promotion

---

108 This was how the South African Law Reform Commission (SALRC) was referred to back then. The South African Law Commission changed to SALRC in 2002. See Judicial Matters Amendment Act 55 of 2000, s. 5.

109 Project 90 of 1998.

110 Constitution of the Republic of South Africa, ss 9 and 25.

111 Recognition of Customary Marriages Act 1998, s. 6.

112 See note South African Law Commission Report on Customary Marriages Project 90 of 1998 note 6.3.4.8.

113 Himonga and Moore (2015).

114 Recognition of Customary Marriages Act 1998, ss 6 and 7(1).

115 This means that all customary marriage entered into before the 15 November 2000, when the Act came into force will be recognised.

of gender equality now exist in all customary marriages, regardless of the type of marriage or when it was entered into.

Nevertheless, empirical research shows that there is still ignorance and unawareness of the provisions and applicability of the RCMA as a whole, especially regarding the proprietary consequences of such marriages.[116] This suggests that although a robust and evolving legal framework for matrimonial property exists to secure proprietary rights in customary marriages, women, as parties to these marriages, are not benefiting from it, thereby allowing injustice and inequalities to persist.

6 Recent Developments in Islamic Property Rights

Islamic marriages are only recognised if the parties enter into a civil marriage subsequent to their Islamic ceremony. If the parties fail to contract a valid civil marriage, the Islamic marriage produces no legal consequences. It remains a religious affair.[117] It used to be the case that an Islamic marriage would still be subject to the rules on civil marriages on property rights.[118] However, the South African Constitutional Court has declared that the non-recognition of certain marital rights emanating from Islamic law, such as the principle of *mahr*,[119] is unconstitutional insofar as it prejudices women and children.[120] The new Divorce Amendment Act of 2024 has since made comprehensive changes to the status of Muslim spouses and their respective property rights. A court dissolving an Islamic marriage may, '...on application by one of the parties to that marriage, in the absence of any agreement between them regarding the division of their assets, order that such assets, or such part of the assets, of the other party as the court may deem just, be transferred to the first-mentioned party'.[121]

The court's exercise of discretion is dependent on the contribution of the parties. The amendment takes an expansive view of contribution. Direct and indirect financial contributions, and non-financial contributions are all covered by the scope of the law.[122] The court must also consider any contract made between the spouses of the Islamic marriage.[123]

---

[116] See Moore and Himonga (2015), De Souza (2013, p. 239) and Maphalle (2017).

[117] Bulbulia (2025).

[118] See discussion on proprietary consequences of civil marriages (Sect. 5.4).

[119] A form of dowry paid by the man to woman.

[120] *Women's Legal Centre Trust v President of the Republic of South Africa and Others* [2022] ZACC 23.

[121] Divorce Amendment Act 2024, s. 4(a), amending Divorce Act 70 of 1979, s. 7(3).

[122] Divorce Amendment Act 2024, s. 4(b), amending Divorce Act 70 of 1979, s. 7(4).

[123] Divorce Amendment Act 2024, s. 4(c)and (d), amending Divorce Act 70 of 1979, s. 7(5).

7 The Presumption of Marriage

Although South African law does not explicitly regulate or recognise a presumption of marriage, case law suggests that such a presumption exists through the court's discretion. The principle is often applied in situations where parties have cohabited in a manner resembling a marriage. For instance, in *B.S v P.M*,[124] the court considered that the parties' mutual impression of being married could justify a fair property distribution based on that perception, even if the marriage did not meet the criteria for validity. Therefore, should the presumption of marriage be accepted, property will be shared according to the Matrimonial Property Act.[125]

8 Recommendations

Having highlighted the complexities of the matrimonial property system in South Africa, it is imperative to offer recommendations. The first recommendation to improve the legal framework for matrimonial property and divorce in South Africa is to increase awareness. The persistence of inequalities in matrimonial property, especially in customary marriages, is evidence that many married persons remain unaware of their matrimonial property rights. However, a more effective intervention would be to raise awareness among unmarried persons to minimise the chances of them making uninformed choices about the matrimonial property system when they get married.

Another factor that makes divorce and matrimonial property complex, especially for laypersons, is that, as demonstrated in this chapter, South Africa uses separate pieces of legislation to regulate marriage, matrimonial property, and divorce. This not only makes matrimonial law difficult to readily understand, but may also discourage people from self-educating on the subject. A single statute that addresses all these issues simultaneously would have been very helpful in reducing the complexity of the subject for non-legal practitioners and also in making the law easily ascertainable. There is a proposed Single Marriages Bill[126] that is envisaged to do exactly this, and it would be a perfect intervention. However, the Bill is still in its formation stages and has many pitfalls, making it not even worth commenting on at this stage.

Another recommendation would be to make the existing three statutes[127] that regulate the different marriages discussed in this chapter more comprehensive, especially on the matrimonial property system. In other words, the processes, procedures, and regulations governing divorce and matrimonial property systems should not be

[124] *B.S v P.M* [2024] ZAGPJHC 508.

[125] See discussion on matrimonial property in Osman (2024). See also Sibisi (2024).

[126] Marriages Bill B43-2023.

[127] The Marriages Act of 1961, the Recognition of Customary Marriages Act of 1998, and the Civil Unions Act of 2006.

contained in separate statutes, but rather be incorporated into the three statutes dealing with each of the three recognised marriages.

9 Conclusion

In a nutshell, this chapter aimed to analyse the South African legal framework regarding matrimonial property rights and divorce. While three different types of marriages exist in South Africa, they all ascribe to the same laws regarding their dissolution. Since marriages give rise to proprietary consequences, this research analysed the legal framework regulating these, with specific reference to customary marriages, as this type of marriage used to offer a unique matrimonial property system in the past. The role of the apex law of South Africa, namely, the Constitution and the judiciary, in shaping the proprietary consequences of customary marriages is highlighted. Be that as it may, empirical research exposes a disconnect between the developments introduced by the Constitution and the practical rules or customs imposed on women in customary marriages. Such realities highlight the need for awareness campaigns on the legal framework relating to patrimonial consequences of customary marriages in South Africa.

References

Amien W (2024) South African marriage ruling is a win for divorcees and surviving spouses: It guides the sharing of their assets. The Conversation, 31 Jan 2024. https://theconversation.com/south-african-marriage-ruling-is-a-win-for-divorcees-and-surviving-spouses-it-guides-the-sharing-of-their-assets-217695. Accessed 4 Sept 2025

Bakker P (2017) Chaos in family law: A model for the recognition of intimate relationships in South Africa. Potchefstroom Electron Law J 16(3):116–150

Barratt A (2022) In which the partners undertook reciprocal duties of support—a discussion of the phrase as used in Bwanya v Master of the High Court. Cape Town. Potchefstroom Electron Law J 25(1):1–28

Bennett TW (1991) A sourcebook of African customary law for Southern Africa. Juta & Co. Ltd, Cape Town

Bennett T (2004) Customary law in South Africa. Juta, Cape Town

Bulbulia F (2025) Status of Muslim marriages: a conveyancer's perspective. De Rebus (February). https://www.derebus.org.za/status-of-muslim-marriages-a-conveyancers-perspective/. Accessed 14 Oct 2025

De Souza M (2013) When non-registration becomes non-recognition: examining the law and practice of customary marriage registration in South Africa. Acta Jurid 239–244

Deveaux M (2003) Liberal constitutions and traditional cultures: the South African customary law debate. Citizensh Stud 7(2):161–180

Heaton J (2010) South African family law, 3rd edn. Lexis Nexis, New York

Heaton J (2014) Law of divorce and dissolution of life partnerships in South Africa. Juta, Cape Town

Heaton J, Kruger H (2015) South African family law. Juta, Cape Town

Himonga C, Moore E (2015) Reform of customary marriage, divorce, and succession in South Africa. Juta, Cape Town

Madondo M (2023) Customary law in constitutional democratic South Africa. Lexis Nexis, New York

Maphalle K (2017) Succession in woman-to-woman marriages under customary law: a study of the Lobedu Kingdom. Master's thesis, University of Cape Town

Miriki T (2024) A comparative analysis of the principles of primogeniture rule and its position under international human rights law: a study of Nigeria, South Africa, and United Kingdom. https://preprints.apsanet.org/engage/apsa/article-details/6398f938b103af2abb18131d. Accessed 6 Sept 2025

Moore E, Himonga C (2015) Protection of marital property rights upon dissolution of a customary marriage in South Africa: a view from inside and outside the courts. Working Paper 350, Centre for Social Science Research, University of Cape Town. https://humanities.uct.ac.za/sites/default/files/content_migration/humanities_uct_ac_za/1380/files/WP%2520350.pdf. Accessed 4 Sept 2025

Mopai Z, Mokoena UC (2023) An analytical overview of the plurality of marital laws in South Africa. J Comp Law 18(1):267

Murray C (2001) A constitutional beginning: making South Africa's final Constitution. Univ Ark Little Rock Law Rev 23(3):809–838

Nhlapo T (1992) Marriage and divorce in Swazi Law and custom. Websters, Mbabane

Osman F (2024) The proprietary consequences of customary marriages: challenges in the new regime(s)? Potchefstroom Electron Law J 27:1–29 https://doi.org/10.17159/1727-3781/2024/v27i0a17238

Pienaar J (2021) Law of property. In: Rautenbach C (ed) Introduction to legal pluralism in South Africa, 6th edn. Lexis Nexis, New York

Rautenbach C (2022) South Africa's family laws: a potpourri of some sort? In: Yassari N, Foblets MC (eds) Normativity and diversity in family law: lessons from comparative law. Springer, Berlin

Sibisi S (2024) The legal implications of Sithole v Sithole 2021 5 SA 34 (CC) on African spouses in old civil marriages. Potchefstroom Electron Law J 27:1–22 https://doi.org/10.17159/1727-3781/2024/v27i0a17930

Skelton A, Carnelley M (2014) Family in South Africa, 5th edn. Oxford University Press, Oxford

USLegal Extrajudicial law and legal definition. https://definitions.uslegal.com/e/extrajudicial/. Accessed 4 Oct 2025

Untalimile Crystal Mokoena is a senior lecturer in the Department of Public Law, School of Law, Faculty of Management, Commerce and Law at the University of Venda (UNIVEN). She has written and co-authored various book chapters and journal articles. Her research interests mainly lie in human rights and social security law. She holds an LLD degree from the University of Pretoria.

Zamokuhle Mopai is a lecturer in the Department of Public Law in the School of Law at the University of Venda. As an academic, her area of expertise is African Customary Law. She has served on various commissions on Traditional Leadership Disputes and Claims under the Department of Traditional Affairs in South Africa. She has also written and co-authored articles and book chapters. Her research interests include Family Law, the Law of Succession, Administrative Law, and African Customary Law. She holds an LLM degree from the University of Venda.

A Double-Edged Sword: Zimbabwe's New Marriage Act and the Implications for the Matrimonial Rights of Women in Unregistered Customary Marriages

Gloria Paidamoyo Chikaonda

Abstract Zimbabwe's enactment of the Marriages Act in 2022 represents a significant attempt to harmonise the country's fragmented marriage laws and address longstanding injustices in the treatment of unregistered customary unions. These unions, while the most prevalent form of marriage in Zimbabwe, historically offered women limited property rights due to their exclusion from the protections of the Matrimonial Causes Act. This chapter adopts a comparative legal history approach to trace the evolution of marital property law in Zimbabwe, focusing on the legal position before and after the enactment of the new Act. It argues that while the new law marks a step forward by recognising unregistered customary marriages as valid for the purposes of property division, the non-retrospective application of the legislation means that many women remain unprotected under the older legal regime. The chapter explores how judicial discretion under the Matrimonial Causes Act may now extend to these unions, potentially enabling a more equitable division of marital property. However, the reform remains in its infancy, and significant uncertainty persists regarding its interpretation and impact. The chapter concludes that while the new law holds promise for enhancing women's property rights, the effectiveness of these protections will depend on the evolving jurisprudence and the judiciary's willingness to interpret the reforms in a transformative and inclusive manner.

1 Introduction

Until recently, Zimbabwe had a marriage and family law framework that was notorious for its complexity. This is because it had a multiplicity of overlapping and often contradictory sources of law governing personal relationships. Recently, a new Marriages Act was passed in response to this challenge, with the aim of harmonising the family law framework.[1] A key goal of that harmonisation was to enhance

G. P. Chikaonda (✉)
Stanford Law School, Stanford, CA, USA
e-mail: gloriach@stanford.edu

[1] Marriages Act 2022 [Chapter 5:15].

A. F. Hammond and P. Batariwah (eds.), *The Law on Marital Property in Africa*, Ius Gentium: Comparative Perspectives on Law and Justice 138,
https://doi.org/10.1007/978-3-032-19358-2_17

the property rights of spouses, particularly women and their children, in unregistered customary unions.[2] These marriages account for the majority of unions in Zimbabwe, comprising approximately 75% to 85% of all marriages.[3]

Adopted in 2022, the statute is still relatively new, and courts are only beginning to engage with its progressive provisions on the property rights of spouses. Due to the non-retrospective application of laws passed, courts still largely apply the marital property laws that existed before the new Marriages Act. Therefore, I argue that to understand the marital property regime in Zimbabwe, a legal history approach is unavoidable.

Legal history as an analytical approach has been utilised by African legal scholars to understand colonial African laws and their impact on Africa's colonial subjects, both as tools for institutionalising colonial oppression and as instruments for systemic liberation.[4] These studies explore the impact of colonial laws on the limits of state power,[5] human rights, and other social spheres,[6] including religion.[7] This paper engages with legal history scholarship that interrogates the role of law in shaping gender relations in Africa[8] to critically examine post-colonial Zimbabwean marriage laws and their implications for women's property rights. As Owolade writes, 'legislation provides a useful source for writing Africa's [colonial] legal history…the processes preceding the enactment of legislation can shed light on how [colonial] ideation informed the creation of [colonial] laws'.[9] Similarly, a critical and comparative analysis of post-independence marriage and family policies will connect the dots between Zimbabwe's colonial legal legacy and its contemporary legal framework. With the passing of a new marriage legislation that has a direct bearing on the marital property rights of Zimbabwean women as it exists in tension with gendered cultural norms, but backgrounded by a liberal international human rights order, a breakdown of the development of this legislation over the past four odd decades will most comprehensively illuminate the wins and losses of matrimonial property rights in Zimbabwe.

Thus, this chapter outlines Zimbabwean marital property along two stages: the period before 2022 and the enactment of the new Marriages Act,[10] and after the enactment of the new Marriages Act. It lays out the international and regional frameworks for gender equality, the protection of women's property rights in marriage, and the constitutional obligations relating to gender equality and property ownership, with a critical reflection on how the Zimbabwean judiciary could better apply these authorities to protect women in unregistered customary unions. It defines customary

[2] Nnoko-Mewanu (2019).
[3] ZIMSTAT (2023).
[4] Owolade (2023, p. 80).
[5] Chanock (1985).
[6] Ibhawoh (2007).
[7] Stockreiter (2015).
[8] Schmidt (1992).
[9] Owolade (2023, p. 80).
[10] Marriages Act 2022 [Chapter 5:15].

marital property and describes the division of marital property rights according to customary law. The focus here is on unregistered customary unions because of their primacy in understanding those who, until the enactment of the new Marriages Act, have been most vulnerable to property dispossession. I demonstrate that, prior to 2022 and the enactment of the new Marriages Act, those in unregistered customary unions had comparatively fewer defences to their property rights because the framework at that time did not recognise those types of unions as valid marriages for the purpose of division of marital property under the Matrimonial Causes Act.[11] Before 2022, women in unregistered customary unions had to apply discriminatory divorce principles from customary law or else rely on relatively weak common law principles of tacit universal partnership to assert their marital property rights.

The chapter continues by referencing statutory laws to describe marital property rights for registered customary marriages and civil marriages. Here, I demonstrate that during marriage, formal equality is achieved in relation to property acquisition and use due to Zimbabwe's out-of-community regime. However, substantive equality remains elusive for women in the control and use of matrimonial property during the marriage, because the law, when applied by the courts, fails to consider the gender dynamics that often characterise marital relationships in a patriarchal society such as Zimbabwe's. On the other hand, in terms of divorce, the Matrimonial Causes Act provides people in registered customary and civil marriages with more protection because of the discretionary guidance given to courts to achieve equity during the division of property.[12]

Finally, the chapter considers the impact of the enactment of the new Marriages Act 2022 on Zimbabwe's marital property rights landscape. For those in registered customary and civil marriages, not much has changed. It is arguable whether the greatest benefits are gained by women in unregistered customary unions or civil partnerships. The new Marriages Act recognised the latter for purposes of division of matrimonial property, and potentially the former as well. The Matrimonial Causes Act and its discretionary guidance to achieve equity between the spouses can potentially be applied to unregistered customary unions. However, with the amendments being so recent, considerable uncertainty remains about how the jurisprudence will develop in the interpretation of many of the reforms introduced by the new Marriages Act. The chapter then concludes with recommendations for reform.

[11] Matrimonial Causes Act 1985 [Chapter 5:13].

[12] Matrimonial Causes Act 1985 [Chapter 5:13].

2 Zimbabwe's International and Regional Commitments and Judicial Application

Zimbabwe's Constitution underscores the importance of the application of international law in the interpretation and implementation of domestic matters.[13] Section 34 of the Zimbabwe Constitution enjoins the state to incorporate international law into Zimbabwean domestic law, and section 46 places an obligation on any courts, forums, or tribunals to 'take into account international law and all treaties and conventions to which Zimbabwe is a party'.[14] Also, section 327 compels the courts to interpret legislation in a manner consistent with international conventions, treaties, or agreements.[15]

As a signatory to numerous international and regional legal instruments that guarantee, protect, and promote gender equality and the right to property for women and men, the country must uphold these guarantees and protections. Zimbabwe is a party to the Universal Declaration of Human Rights, which, under articles 2 and 17, guarantees everyone's right to non-discrimination on the basis of sex, as well as the right to own property 'alone as well as in association'.[16] Zimbabwe is a party to the Convention on the Elimination of All Forms of Discrimination Against Women (CEDAW), which, in articles 15 and 16, requires state parties to 'give women equal rights to conclude contracts and to administer property' and, in the area of marriage and family relations, requires state parties to prevent discrimination against women based on their gender. The CEDAW embodies an ethos of gender equality regarding the ownership, acquisition, management, administration, enjoyment, and disposition of property.[17] Additionally, under articles 2 and 14 of the African Charter on Human and Peoples Rights (Maputo Protocol), the property rights of women are given some attention. International and regional law, therefore, provide Zimbabwe with a robust legal framework to protect the marital property rights of women (and men).

However, a careful review of Zimbabwean law reveals that references to international law are negligible, and there is room for greater and more effective reliance on these laws to reinforce the substantive realisation of Zimbabwean women's property rights in all types of unions. One of the few recent and more comprehensive applications of international and regional standards to marital property disputes by Zimbabwean courts is seen in the case of *Katsvaira v Katsvairo and Another*.[18] It is a classic 'dual marriage problem' case where the husband married one wife according to the civil marriage system, and then, without ending the marriage, married another wife under customary law, thereby committing bigamy. The first wife then made a claim for divorce and division of the matrimonial assets, and the Court was faced with

---

[13] Constitution of Zimbabwe Amendment (No.20) Act 2013.

[14] Constitution of Zimbabwe Amendment (No.20) Act 2013, ss. 36 and 46.

[15] Constitution of Zimbabwe Amendment (No.20) Act 2013, s. 327.

[16] Universal Declaration of Human Rights, UN General Assembly (1948), arts. 2 and 17.

[17] Universal Declaration of Human Rights,UN General Assembly (1979), arts 15–16.

[18] *Katsvaira v Katsvairo and Another* [2023] ZWHHC 182.

the question of whether, and to what extent, the second wife was entitled to property from this union, as well as how to equitably and fairly distribute the assets of the marriage. The Court, quoting *Mhangani v Mhangani,*[19] underscored the importance of considering the international and regional instruments mentioned above in cases of marriage dissolution,[20] and emphasised the state's obligation to achieve 'equality and justice' for both genders 'in law and in private life'.

The difficulties presented by dual marriage cases are well-documented in the Zimbabwean marriage literature.[21] They reflect how post-colonial legal tools, mostly inherited from the colonial administration—for example, marriage registration and contract law remedies—struggle to keep up with the multiplicity of partnership arrangements and the many forms they take on the ground. In the case of *Katsvairo*, the Court decided that the second marriage was a nullity,[22] because the second 'wife' likely knew of the pre-existing civil union. In applying a combination of international and regional law standards and the discretionary considerations provided for in the Matrimonial Causes Act, the Court awarded the first wife a greater portion of the matrimonial property than the second wife. While the final order seemed just, given the specific circumstances of the case, the conclusions made by the courts about the second wife, who in effect, was in an unregistered customary union, are exemplary of the disadvantages women in these types of marriage face. The Court, in that case, felt that the evidence brought by the second wife showed that she 'went into this arrangement with her eyes wide open, well knowing that the first defendant and plaintiff were in a civil marriage' and, therefore, she 'cannot be covered on the claim of being an innocent spouse'. In their application of foreign and local laws, the courts often fail to consider the nuances of a landscape of intimate partnerships, where women have limited power in entering into, sustaining, and exiting customary marriages. This approach results in the pitting of women in civil marriages against those in unregistered customary unions, competing for limited matrimonial property, with the former often being privileged because of the colonial hierarchies that placed civil marriages over customary marriages.[23]

The Court in *Katsvairo*, however, rightly applied the principles of equality between spouses as guided by international law, and took a progressive approach to what constitutes contributions to the matrimonial assets, thus acknowledging women's historically and culturally unrecognised domestic and non-monetary labour. However, the question remains: what happens when, according to the law at the time, one is not considered a spouse for the purpose of distributing matrimonial property? The following sections will demonstrate that this was the conundrum faced by the

---

[19] *Mhangani v Mhangani* [2021] ZWHHC 523.

[20] *Mhangani v Mhangani* [2021] ZWHHC 523, para. 12.

[21] See Ncube (1989), Coldham (1994) and Chirawu (2006).

[22] Zimbabwe criminalises bigamy through s. 104 of the Criminal Law (Codification and Reform) Act [Chapter 9:23] 2004. However, in *Katsvaira v Katsvairo and Another* [2023] ZWHHC 182, the court makes clear that where a marriage is null and void—because it is a putative marriage or a bigamous marriage—it is still covered by the distribution rules under s. 7 of the Matrimonial Causes Act 1985 [Chapter 5:13]. See also *Makovah v Makovah* 1998 (2) ZLR 82 (S).

[23] Chikaonda (2020).

Zimbabwean justice system, which the new Marriage Act has attempted to resolve by recognising unregistered customary unions, with as-yet-unresolved success.

3 The Constitutional Mandate

On paper, Zimbabwe has a robust legal framework for protecting and promoting gender equality. The Zimbabwean Constitution's founding values and principles include 'a recognition of the quality of all human beings' and 'gender equality'.[24] Gender balance is also listed under the National Objectives of the Constitution Bill of Rights. Specifically, the state is mandated to 'take practical measures to ensure that women have access to resources, including land, on the basis of equality with men',[25] and it lays out that 'women and men have the right to equal treatment, including the right to equal opportunities in political, economic, cultural and social spheres'.[26] More importantly, the Constitution obliges the state to 'ensure that (c) there is equality of rights and obligations of spouses during marriage and at its dissolution'.[27] This provision giving equal rights to spouses in a marriage, along with the affordances provided for by the Legal Age of Majority Act,[28] which ended the perpetual minority of women, protects women's right to equality in marriage.

These constitutional mandates have a significant impact on marital property laws, especially when read together with section 71 of the Constitution, which guarantees each person a right to property.[29] Freedom of property ownership and the alienation of owned property are central values within the Zimbabwean property law system, with registration being the executing action that brings ownership and transfer of ownership into being.[30] As Mpofu writes:

> the right of ownership of property, is whatever nature confers the most complete and comprehensive control one can have over property. The right of an owner of land, for instance, to sell that land is almost untrammeled...whoever has his or her name endorsed on the deed conveying title is at law prima-facie recognized as the owner of the land with the most complete and comprehensive control over that land.[31]

---

[24] Constitution of Zimbabwe Amendment (No.20) Act 2013, s. 3.

[25] Constitution of Zimbabwe Amendment (No.20) Act 2013, s. 17(1)(c).

[26] Constitution of Zimbabwe Amendment (No.20) Act 2013, s. 56(2).

[27] Constitution of Zimbabwe Amendment (No.20) Act 2013, s. 56(2)(c).

[28] See General Law Amendment Act 1982 [Chapter 8:07], s. 15. This law, which has been enacted periodically by the national government, works to 'alter the general law of Zimbabwe' to make sweeping alignments of various statutes with the Constitution.

[29] Constitution of Zimbabwe Amendment (No. 20) Act 2013, s. 71(2)–(4).

[30] *Ishemunyoro (nee Mandidewa) v Ishemunyoro* (SC 14 of 2019) [2019] ZWSC 14 (17 June 2019), paras 9–10.

[31] Mpofu (2016, pp. 164–165).

4 Customary Law's Matrimonial Property Rules: With a Focus on Unregistered Customary Marriages

Zimbabwe has a dual legal system, with both indigenous African customary law and Roman-Dutch common law (often referred to as general law) being applied.[32] This means that marriages under customary law and civil law are legally recognised. In Zimbabwe today, there are four types of marriage: civil marriages, registered customary law marriages, unregistered customary law unions, and qualified civil marriages.[33]

However, prior to the recent enactment of the new Marriage Act, unregistered customary unions were not recognised as valid marriages.[34] Where an unregistered marriage was dissolved, and the question of the division of matrimonial property arose, customary law would be applied following a determination that customary law is applicable to the case in terms of section 3 of the Customary Law and Local Courts Act,[35] which provides:

Application of Customary Law

> (1) Subject to this Act and any other enactment, unless the justice of the case otherwise requires—.
>
> (a) customary law shall apply in any civil case where—.
>
> (i) the parties have expressly agreed that it should apply; or.
>
> (ii) regard being had to the nature of the case and the surrounding circumstances, it appears that the parties have agreed it should apply; or.
>
> (iii) regard being had to the nature of the case and the surrounding circumstances, it appears just and proper that it should apply;
>
> (b) the general law of Zimbabwe shall apply in all other cases.
>
> (2) For the purposes of paragraph (a) of subsection (1)—.
>
> "surrounding circumstances", in relation to a case, shall, without limiting the expression, include—.
>
> (a) the mode of life of the parties;
>
> (b) the subject matter of the case;
>
> (c) the understanding by the parties of the provisions of customary law or the general law of Zimbabwe, as the case may be, which apply to the case;
>
> (d) the relative closeness of the case and the parties to the customary law or the general law of Zimbabwe, as the case may be.[36]

---

[32] Madhuku (2010, pp. 13–35).

[33] Marriages Act 2022 [Chapter 5:15].

[34] See *Jeke v Zembe* [2018] ZWHHC 237 (5 May 2018) where the court explained that the then Customary Marriages Act [Chapter 5:07] (now repealed and replaced by the Marriages Act 2022 [Chapter 5:15]) 'gives limited recognition to an unregistered customary law marriage by recognizing it for purposes of customary law and custom relating to the status, guardianship, custody and rights of succession of children of such marriage'.

[35] Customary Law and Local Courts Act 1990 [Chapter 7:05].

[36] See *Zawaira & Others v Zawaira & Others* [2017] ZWSC 65 (12 October 2017), where this approach is applied.

The question then is: if the parties elected to apply customary law to the division of their matrimonial property, or the court deemed customary law applicable, what does customary law say about matrimonial property? Historical or official records of Shona customary law[37] stipulate that upon divorce, a woman is only entitled to *mavoko*.[38] This is described as 'property that she has acquired by dint of extra work done by her, which work is separate from that done for the family'.[39] This can be income she has earned from selling pottery or knitting.[40] She is also entitled to the *mombe yeumai*, which is the cow that she receives as part of the bridewealth (known in Shona as *roora* and in Ndebele as *lobola)* when her daughter is married (in the event that she has a daughter who gets married).[41] Apart from these, a woman is not entitled to the family property that she shared with her husband during the marriage. Even the limited belongings she is permitted to keep, usually in the form of cash, would most likely have already been spent on supporting the family.

The husband, on the other hand, is entitled to all other property. Ncube explains that:

> At the dissolution of the marriage, the husband is, under customary law, entitled to retain all the property and the wife must leave the marriage with no property except that property falling within certain recognized categories, which property is recognized as belonging to the wife exclusively.

This property includes *mombe yehumai* and *mavoko* property in the case of the Shona, and '*yohlanga* and *zezandla'* property in the case of the Ndebele ethnic community.[42]

In a case decided one year after the promulgation of the 2013 Constitution, dealing with a surviving spouse of an unregistered customary union who was disputing her husband's will, the court underscored that for women who 'opt to marry under the unregistered customary law marriage…such women would have to find some cause of action under general law if they are to benefit from the matrimonial estate outside of '*maoko* or mavoko property' at the dissolution of such a union, unless they are saved by the court's 'judicial activism'.[43] Through judicial activism, the courts recognised the property rights of women in unregistered customary unions, who were otherwise left vulnerable by the harsh rules of customary law. The courts allowed these women to find relief through alternative common law claims, such as unjustified enrichment and tacit universal partnerships. What happened is that women in unregistered marriages, who had contributed directly and financially to the family property, resorted to contract law principles to claim some of the property upon the dissolution of the marriage.[44] The contract law principle most often relied upon was

[37] The Shona ethnic group is the largest ethnic group in Zimbabwe, but even within this language group there are sub-groups with varying customary practices.

[38] Banda (2005, p. 129).

[39] *Chetty v Emile* (2005, p. 129).

[40] Chirawu (2014, p. 5).

[41] Banda (2005, p. 129).

[42] Ncube (1990). '*yohlanga* and *zezandla* property' is conterminous to *mombe yehumai* and *mavoko*.

[43] *Magedi & Anor v Samuriwo & Ors* [2014] ZWHHC 184 (7 May 2014, p. 7).

[44] Banda (2005, p. 129).

the principle of partnership. The union was treated as a sort of contractual partnership, with each party's contributions assessed and the property divided according to the proportion of their respective contributions to the partnership.[45] Alternatively, the courts also employ the concept of unjustified enrichment to ensure that neither spouse is unjustifiably enriched by the assets contributed by the other spouse.[46]

In a seminal case regarding the property rights of women in unregistered customary marriages, *Mautsa v Kuregbaseka*,[47] the Court concluded, after considering all the evidence, that the defendant (the wife) in the unregistered customary marriage, had not made any 'meaningful direct contribution to the acquisition of the immovable properties...The situation was equally the same on movables'.[48] However, Chitakunye J concluded that in the circumstances, general law should apply and not customary law, as the court is 'vested with the discretion to determine whether or not the justice of the case demands the general law or customary law should apply' and injustice would result in this case if customary law were applied.[49] He went on to comment on the rules of the customary law of marriage, which state that upon dissolution of the marriage, the wife is only entitled to *umai/mavoko*.[50]

The Court, in the end, concluded that the requirements for a tacit universal partnership were met, but did not award the half share of the assets from the partnership that was claimed by the defendant.[51] This is in line with the rules of partnership agreements, where each party is entitled to a share of the assets proportionate to their contribution to the partnership. The defendant, however, was awarded more than the plaintiff initially offered; she was awarded custody of the minor children with maintenance, as well as a considerably larger share of the movable properties and a 25 per cent share in one of the immovable properties.[52] Of significance in the judgment is the Court's call for the legislature to dedicate a more concerted effort towards legislative protection for women in unregistered customary law unions, especially where those unions are terminated.[53] The Court specifically cited recognition of such unions as a major step towards protecting such women, highlighting that 'a recognition of their marriage, albeit unregistered as a marriage for the purposes of distribution of assets acquired during the union, would go a long way in eliminating discrimination against women on the basis of the type of marriage contracted'.[54]

While the court's strategy of circumventing the lack of legislative protection for women in unregistered customary unions through common law was welcomed, I am

---

[45] Banda (2005, p. 129).

[46] Banda (2005, p. 129).

[47] *Mautsa v Kuregbaseka* [2017] ZWHHC 106.

[48] *Mautsa v Kuregbaseka* [2017] ZWHHC 106, p, 4.

[49] *Mautsa v Kuregbaseka* [2017] ZWHHC 106, p. 6.

[50] *Mautsa v Kuregbaseka* [2017] ZWHHC 106, p. 6

[51] *Mautsa v Kuregbaseka* [2017] ZWHHC 106, p. 15.

[52] *Mautsa v Kuregbaseka* [2017] ZWHHC 106, p. 15–18.

[53] *Mautsa v Kuregbaseka* [2017] ZWHHC 106, p. 8.

[54] *Mautsa v Kuregbaseka* [2017] ZWHHC 106, p. 8.

persuaded by critics who have highlighted the drawbacks of this approach. One such disadvantage was that reducing the marriage to a contract or partnership—while it achieved the desired outcome of providing the woman in an unregistered customary marriage her share of the matrimonial property upon dissolution of the marriage—had the effect of devaluing the marriage in the eyes of the woman, who understood it to be a marriage and not a 'mere' partnership/contract.[55] The Zimbabwean Constitution recognises and applies customary law with equal weight as it does general law.[56] It also recognises and upholds the right to marriage, so much so that it is listed as a fundamental human right.[57] The right to marriage has also been recognised in other jurisdictions as being central to the family unit and, therefore, to the human dignity of the members who are party to it, meaning that it must be recognised and given due respect through the law.[58] With this in mind, to equate a marriage, using general law principles as was done by the courts to assist women in unregistered customary unions simply because it was not registered, was an infringement of the cultural and equality rights of women who were parties to such unions.[59] It took away from what the marriage was understood to be. It also amounted to gender discrimination against Zimbabwean women generally, given that most Zimbabwean marriages are unregistered customary unions.[60]

A further disadvantage of the approach taken by the Court in *Kuregbaseka* is that the requirements of a partnership/contract proved to be more difficult to fulfil, and it failed to assist women in obtaining a share of the matrimonial wealth they deserved. As Chirawu highlighted: 'A partnership is a profit-making venture that is very different from a marriage. In the latter, those recognised notions of love, affection, and companionship have no place in a partnership, and yet the court asks the woman to prove what she contributed to the partnership'.[61] Moreover, as outlined by Chitakunye J in the judgment, a partnership only entitles a partner to their proportionate share of the partnership assets at the time of dissolution. Therefore, unlike women in registered customary unions or civil marriages, who are more likely to get an in-community type arrangement or an arrangement that takes into account all the specific and varying circumstances of the parties, women in unregistered customary marriages had to prove that they brought something to the partnership (or bound themselves to doing so), that the partnership was for the benefit of both parties with

---

55 Chirawu (2014, p. 6).

56 See Constitution of Zimbabwe (No. 20) Act 2013, s. 174 states that, 'customary law courts whose jurisdiction consists primarily in the application of customary law' and s. 176 which empowers the courts 'to protect and regulate their own process and to develop the common law or the customary law'.

57 Constitution of Zimbabwe (No. 20) Act 2013, ss. 26 and 78.

58 *Dawood v Minister of Home Affairs*; *Shalabi and Another v Minister of Home Affairs and Others*; *Thomas and Another v Minister of Home Affairs and Others* (CCT 35/99) [2000] ZACC 8, 2000 (3) SA 936 (CC), 2000 (8) BCLR 837, para. 37.

59 Chirawu (2014, p. 6).

60 ZIMSTAT (2023).

61 Chirawu (2014, p. 6).

the aim of profit-making, and that it was based on a legitimate agreement.[62] If, like in the case of the defendant in the *Kurebgaseka* case, the wife did not make a significant financial contribution to the marriage, other than her labour and skill in homemaking and taking care of the children, this meant she would not be entitled to much by way of the share of the matrimonial property, as she would arguably not have contributed as much financially. What this demonstrates is that the approach taken by the courts could only ever be a 'quick fix' or a temporary measure to assist women in unregistered customary marriages who had no recourse under the law when their marriage was dissolved. Therefore, the most ideal situation was ultimately one of full recognition of unregistered customary unions and allowing their matrimonial property to be equitably distributed upon the dissolution of the marriage.

Finally, scholars have observed that:

> The legal training of judges often leads them to see property as following title, so that the person in whose name the property is registered, more often than not the man is the "rightful" owner of the property and that is the end of the matter. This narrow legalism is reinforced by their socialisation, whereby they see it as women's role to look after the family home.[63]

Therefore, the use of general law principles as a substitute for legislative recognition would likely also prove ineffective. This is because, in practice, the interpretation of common law was often at the mercy of judicial officials who held gender biases and did not believe that homemaking and caregiving responsibilities undertaken by women should be or could be considered contributions to a partnership.[64]

In an interview with a High Court judge in Zimbabwe, Banda discovered that even section 7(4) of the Matrimonial Causes Act, which at the time, provided for judicial discretion in determining the distribution of matrimonial property only in *registered* customary and civil marriages, could be abused by judges who undervalued the role of a wife in rearing the children and taking care of the home.[65] The judge commented that, 'The whole system is a lottery depending on which judge you draw. We have people from a broad spectrum...It is a multi-ethnic and cross-cultural judiciary, and everybody has their own inherent prejudices'.[66]

If such judicial biases could be validated by legislation, which was intended to provide guidance on how property is to be distributed in registered marriages, whether customary or civil, this could also occur where general law principles were applied as a substitute due to the non-recognition of unregistered customary marriages. This is because a judge who had been socialised by patriarchy (which is common in Zimbabwean society) and possessed an inherent bias towards the financial contributions of the husband vis-à-vis the domestic work of the wife, would interpret the rules of partnership and contract to the latter's disadvantage. Without the legislative guidance that could come from recognising such marriages, the wife's contribution would likely always appear less significant than the husband's.

---

[62] *Mtuda v Ndudzo* 2000 (1) ZLR 710 (H), p. 716 E–G.

[63] Banda (2005, pp. 133–134).

[64] Banda (2005, p. 133).

[65] Banda (2005, p. 133).

[66] Banda (1995, pp. 71 and 76).

Over and above the customary law rules of matrimonial property, it can also be argued that there are general norms, foundational to customary law, that, when applied in Zimbabwe's socio-cultural milieu, have the potential to reinforce the patriarchal forces that disadvantage women. For example, broadly conceived, African customary law does not subscribe to the concept of private ownership. This was highlighted in a Supreme Court judgment where the division of property in an unregistered customary marriage was disputed. In that case, the couple decided to apply general law (common law) to their dispute. As an aside, the court noted that 'As the concept of private ownership of immovable property is unknown at customary law, it is virtually impossible to determine rights and obligations pertaining to privately owned immovable property in terms of any law other than general law'.[67]

In another case, the court stated:

> General law is applicable...in cases where the distribution of the estate of parties in an unregistered customary law marriage is raised and the estate includes land or rights to land, the application of general law is justified. As stated therein, this is because real rights are alien to customary law and also to avoid discrimination against women in particular who will have chosen to marry according to custom.[68]

This suggests that had the couple opted to apply customary law to their case, it would have been impossible for the court to award the woman a real right of ownership of the matrimonial home under dispute.

In sum, and to conclude our understanding of the position of Zimbabwean customary laws on matrimonial property, before 2022, women in unregistered customary marriages had limited property rights protections. This is because these marriages (which still make up the majority of marriages in Zimbabwe), were subject only to harsh customary laws or unsatisfactory common law principles. The Matrimonial Causes Act, which gave courts the discretion to divide matrimonial property equitably between spouses, did not apply to unregistered customary marriages before 2022. We move now to the Zimbabwean statutory law on matrimonial property.

5 Statutory Law Perspective

Three pieces of legislation provide a framework for understanding the property rights of those in civil marriages or registered customary marriages. I will show that this framework, while not perfect, is more far-reaching than the one under customary law, particularly for those in registered civil or customary marriages. Firstly, under Zimbabwean law, men and women have the right to acquire and own property independently, ever since the passage of the Legal Age of Majority Act,

---

[67] *Chiwenga v Mubaiwa* (Civil Appeal SC 26 of 2020; SC 86 of 2020) [2020] ZWSC 86 (25 June 2020).

[68] *Melo v Kandibero* (323 of 2023) [2023] ZWHHC 199 (24 May 2023).

which gave women the legal capacity to contract without their husband's or father's authorisation.[69]

Secondly, the Married Person's Property Act designates all civil marriages concluded between spouses domiciled in Zimbabwe as out-of-community marriages.[70] This means that property acquired before the commencement of the marriage remains the property of the spouse who acquired it, and any property acquired during the subsistence of the marriage, remains that of each spouse, unless they have concluded an antenuptial contract opting out of the out-of-community system. Third, the Customary Marriages Act (recently repealed and replaced by the new Marriages Act) recognised registered customary marriages as valid for the purposes of division of matrimonial property, provided that the customary marriage was registered.[71]

5.1 Property Rights During Marriage (Registered Customary and Civil Marriages)

Regarding the matrimonial property rights during the marriage, provides valuable insights.[72] It is a 2019 case that deals with the alienation of immovable property between co-owner spouses, through the attachment of the immovable property to debts owned by one spouse. Following the purchase of the property, which was financed entirely by the wife, the title deed of the property was registered in the names of both the husband and wife. The High Court held that, regardless of who had acquired the property, it was owned by both spouses in equal shares, by virtue of its registration to both spouses in the Deeds Registry. On appeal, the Supreme Court of Zimbabwe emphasised that notwithstanding the default application of the out-of-property regime in Zimbabwe, spouses who have registered immovable property in the Deed Registry own the property in equal and undivided shares, unless such registration took place as a result of 'a court order, fraud, undue influence, mistake, gross irregularity or other factor vitiating such registration'.[73] The Court held that the property was purchased by the wife after the couple had solemnised a civil marriage under the old Marriage Act.[74] Therefore, it was governed by the out-of-property regime under section 2 of the Married Persons Property Act, subject to the qualifications stated by the Court. The Supreme Court concluded that:

> a spouse whose name appears, for instance, in the Title Deed of any immovable property enjoys full ownership rights therein. He or she can deal with the property in any way he

[69] General Law Amendment Act 1891 [Chapter 8:07].

[70] Married Persons' Property Act 1929 [Chapter 5:12], s. 2.

[71] Customary Marriages Act 1951 [Chapter 5:07].

[72] *Ishemunyoro (nee Mandidewa) v Ishemunyoro* (SC 14 of 2019) [2019] ZWSC 14 (17 June 2019).

[73] *Ishemunyoro (nee Mandidewa) v Ishemunyoro* (SC 14 of 2019) [2019] ZWSC 14 (17 June 2019), para. 11–12.

[74] Marriage Act 1963 [Chapter 5:11].

> wishes, including alienating his rights therein or otherwise encumbering such property. Similarly, if both spouses are registered as joint owners of the property, each one enjoys full ownership rights over his or her share in the property…the appellant, having used her own resources to fully purchase the property, could have effectively safeguarded her real rights therein by having the property registered in her name only.[75]

This case illustrates the limitations on married women's property rights in Zimbabwe, which are governed by a marriage and property law framework that purports to protect the individual ownership rights of married women, yet does not meaningfully engage with the socio-cultural realities of marital relationships. These realities are characterised by gender dynamics that constrain women's choices in ways that impact their autonomy and economic freedom, realities that the court defines as existing 'outside the dictates of the law'.[76] These concerns are supported by reports of a 'crisis of dispossession which is happening to many people in marriages when their spouse decides to mortgage or sell the house without paying heed to the family's right to shelter or the contributions made to its acquisition and upkeep'.[77]

Chirawu questions whether the current family law adequately responds to a situation where a partner, whether civil or a spouse in a marriage, decides to sell or lease their property without regard to the shared use and benefits that derive from 'family property'.[78] Cases like *Ishemunyoro* deal with decisions made during the marriage that are wrapped up in and no doubt influenced by the gendered dynamics of heterosexual unions in the Zimbabwean context. In *Ishemunyoro*, the Court recognised these dynamics, restating the wife's contentions that 'her decision [to register the house in both their names] may have been motivated by societal and cultural pressures and considerations that shape and impact on gender relations within the family set up',[79] and made attempts to sympathise with the spouse whose property rights were drastically impacted, if not de jure, then at least in a de facto sense. However, it ultimately concluded that the:

> appellant was gainfully employed, freely acquired the property in question, but voluntarily chose to have it registered in her and her husband's joint names. No coercion or undue pressure on her by anyone is alleged. She therefore effectively donated one half-share of what was rightfully her property, to her husband. It is this action that lies at the root of the problems that led to her bringing the matter to court. It thus becomes difficult to comprehend how the lawful consequences of such an action can be said to have mutated into an infringement of her rights to equality in marriage, to acquire property and to shelter.[80]

---

[75] *Ishemunyoro (nee Mandidewa) v Ishemunyoro* (SC 14 of 2019) [2019] ZWSC 14 (17 June 2019), para. 13.

[76] *Ishemunyoro (nee Mandidewa) v Ishemunyoro* (SC 14 of 2019) [2019] ZWSC 14 (17 June 2019), para. 13.

[77] Chirawu (2019).

[78] Chirawu (2019).

[79] *Ishemunyoro (nee Mandidewa) v Ishemunyoro* (SC 14 of 2019) [2019] ZWSC 14 (17 June 2019), para. 13.

[80] *Ishemunyoro (nee Mandidewa) v Ishemunyoro* (SC 14 of 2019) [2019] ZWSC 14 (17 June 2019), para. 27.

Thus, despite admitting to the importance of recognising the challenging context in which women acquire and attempt to maintain control of their property, the Court shirked its powers to develop the law through judicial activism. Instead, it pointed to the failure of civil society and women's rights activists to lobby the legislature for a law that would prevent the alienation of matrimonial property without the consent of the other spouse.

5.2 Property Rights Upon Divorce for Registered Customary and Civil Marriages

Finally, for registered customary and civil marriages, the default system for dividing marital property on divorce involves each spouse retaining what they had individually acquired prior to or during the marriage. However, in practice, the courts have the discretion to apply the Matrimonial Causes Act (MCA),[81] which has provided some much-needed nuance to the out-of-community regime. The MCA introduced a recognition of the unpaid domestic work and non-monetary contributions of women, and the injustices resulting from a marital property regime which, in effect, left men, who were often the breadwinners, or controlled household finances, in a better position at the end of a marriage than their homemaker wives. The MCA provides guidance for the distribution of registered customary marriages. In determining how the property is to be distributed, section 7(4) of the Act directs the court to give regard to:

> (a) the income-earning capacity, assets and other financial resources which each spouse and child has or is likely to have in the foreseeable future;
>
> (b) the financial needs, obligations and responsibilities which each spouse and child has or is likely to have in the foreseeable future;
>
> (c) the standard of living of the family, including the manner in which any child was being educated or trained or expected to be educated or trained;
>
> (d) the age and physical and mental condition of each spouse and child;
>
> (e) the direct or indirect contribution made by each spouse to the family, including contributions made by looking after the home and caring for the family and any other domestic duties;
>
> (f) the value to either of the spouses or to any child of any benefit, including a pension or gratuity, which such spouse or child will lose as a result of the dissolution of the marriage;
>
> (g) the duration of the marriage.[82]

The jurisprudence provides guidance on what can be considered an asset subject to division, using the factors listed in section 7(4) of the MCA.

By and large, the MCA has made positive inroads into the matrimonial property rights of women in registered unions, especially those who did not have the opportunity to make significant and direct financial contributions to the matrimonial home.

---

[81] See Matrimonial Causes Act 1985 [Chapter 5:13]. s. 7(1)(a).

[82] Matrimonial Causes Act 1985 [Chapter 5:13], s. 4.

In the jurisprudence applying the MCA, the courts have emphasised equity and the principle of returning the couple to the position in which they would have been had divorce not occurred, as a guiding framework for the division of matrimonial property.[83] The courts have also clarified that assets of the spouses, in terms of the MCA provisions, mean 'all the assets owned by either spouse at the time of divorce individually and those owned jointly'.[84] They include assets acquired by either spouse before the marriage or during the period of separation, including lease agreements.[85] The case of *Gonye v Gonye* is a leading authority on this score, highlighting the 'extremely wide discrection' that courts have in both determining what counts as matrimonial assets and the proportion of the partitioning of property between the spouses. This discretion, according to Gonye, includes 'an order that *any* asset be transferred from one spouse to the other'.[86] In that case, the court was faced with property bought during and after the marriage. A more recent Supreme Court case dealt with a challenge to matrimonial property distribution of assets acquired by one spouse prior to the marriage.[87] In that case, the court quotes *Gonye* thus:

> It is important to bear in mind the concept used, because the adoption of the concept "matrimonial property" often leads to the erroneous view that assets acquired by one before marriage or when the parties are separated should be excluded from the division, apportionment or distribution exercise. The concept "the assets of the spouses" is clearly intended to have assets owned by the spouses individually (his or hers) or jointly (theirs) at the time of the dissolution of the marriage by he court considered when an order is made with regard to the division, apportionment or distribution of such assets. To hold, as the court a quo did, that as a matter of principle assets acquired by a spouse during the period of separation are to be excluded from the division, apportionment or distribution a court is required to make under s 7(1) of the Act is to introduce an unnecessary fetter to a very broad discretion, on the proper exercise of which the rights of the parties depend.[88]

Therefore, the common law position is that courts can apply the factors in section 7(4) to assets acquired by the spouses before and during the marriage and even, in some cases, during separation.

There does seem to be limited instances where section 7 cannot be applied to the property of spouses. The case of *Coumbis v Coumbis* applies this wide discretion provided for in *Gonye* but held that 'properties owned by companies in which the spouses have interests whose shareholding has not been disclosed, cannot be distributed in terms of s7(1)(a) of the MCA…'.[89]

---

[83] See *Muzongondi v Muzongondi* (Civil Appeal SC 303 of 2014; SC 66 of 2017) [2017] ZWSC 66 (20 October 2017) and *Chombo v Chombo* (Civil Appeal SC 326 of 2014; SC 41 of 2018) [2018] ZWSC 41 (6 July 2018).

[84] See *Muzongondi v Muzongondi* (Civil Appeal SC 303 of 2014; SC 66 of 2017) [2017] ZWSC 66 (20 October 2017), *Chombo v Chombo* (Civil Appeal SC 326 of 2014; SC 41 of 2018) [2018] ZWSC 41 (6 July 2018) and *Gonye v Gonye* 2009 (1) ZLR 232 (S).

[85] *Gonye v Gonye* 2009 (1) ZLR 232 (S).

[86] *Gonye v Gonye* 2009 (1) ZLR 232 (S) (emphasis added).

[87] *Lock v Lock (Nee Fischer)* [2020] ZWSC 51.

[88] *Gonye v Gonye* 2009 (1)) ZLR 232 (S).

[89] *Coumbis v Coumbis and Another* [2021] ZWSC 130.

To conclude, Zimbabwean statutory law has provided much better protection to individuals who are parties to civil marriages and registered customary marriages. This was effected through the Legal Age of Majority Act (now the General Law Amendment Act),[90] the Married Persons' Property Act,[91] and the Customary Marriages Act.[92] This statutory framework is especially significant in the context of immovable property. However, a deficiency emerges where ownership, control, and use of the property during the marriage is challenged by the female spouse. The *Ishemunyoro* case demonstrates that while Zimbabwe's statutory laws afford spouses the rights to acquire and use property within the marriage as they please,[93] these rights become superficial when the laws fail to consider how gendered power dynamics within marital relationships can be determinative factors in who is registered as owner of immovable property in the Deeds Act,[94] the primary legislation, effectuating ownership of immovable property.

On the other hand, at least on divorce, the MCA managed, to some degree, to smooth the sharp edges of the out-of-community system and bolstered property rights protections for women in registered marriages. The MCA mandated the courts to consider all relevant circumstances of the spouses and their contributions, with a view to achieving equity on divorce. Thus, this served as a response to the social realities wherein Zimbabwean women were less likely to directly contribute financially to the matrimonial household. Clearly, there is a push and pull between the law's goals on paper, and the reality in practice. It reveals the complications of statutory interpretation and application in a social context riddled with patriarchal norms and the limited autonomy of women generally, norms that are not always easily accounted for by statutory interventions.

Enter, at this stage, the newly enacted Marriages Act No. 1 of 2022. This was a significant legislative milestone, harmonising marriage regimes and addressing gaps between customary and civil unions. One of the main gaps identified by civil society, judiciary, and legal practitioners alike was the imbalance in protections of property rights between those in unregistered customary unions versus those in registered unions (civil or customary). The following section grapples with the changes introduced by the new Marriages Act and assesses whether it will adequately respond to the issue of matrimonial property rights of women in unregistered customary marriages, which constitute the majority of marriages in Zimbabwe.

[90] General Law Amendment Act 1891 [Chapter 8:07].

[91] Married Persons' Property Act 1929 [Chapter 5:12].

[92] Customary Marriages Act 1951 [Chapter 5:07].

[93] *Ishemunyoro (nee Mandidewa) v Ishemunyoro* (SC 14 of 2019) [2019] ZWSC 14 (17 June 2019).

[94] Deeds Registries Act 1960 [Chapter 20:05].

6 The New Marriages Act and What it Means for Matrimonial Property Rights

As early as 2017, several stakeholders, including civil society, legal practitioners, and legislators across the political divide, made widespread calls for a reform of Zimbabwe's marriage laws. These calls aimed to harmonise marriage laws and amend the then-applicable provisions within the Marriage Act 1963[95] and the Customary Marriages Act[96] that allowed child marriages. Locally, a landmark constitutional court judgment highlighted the necessity for the Government to outlaw child marriages.[97] Regional pressure also worked to push the issue of marriage reforms to the top of the legislative agenda, as there was a collective, regional, and international condemnation of child marriages. In addition, the Southern African Development Community (SADC) committed to legal reforms through the drafting of the SADC Model Law to Eradicate Child Marriage.[98]

Apart from the public outcry against the scourge of child marriage practices that were prevalent across the nation, the calls for legal reform within marriage and family laws were mainly centred around the non-recognition of unregistered customary marriages, which posed a threat to the property rights of women, as explained in the first half of this chapter. Comments by Chirawu-Mugomba J, a justice of the High Court of Zimbabwe, provide an example of such appeals from the judiciary:

> Given the confusion surrounding this aspect of family law, I join the clarion call that has been made in other decisions for law reform on the marriage framework in Zimbabwe. Organizations such as the Women and Law in Southern Africa (WLSA) and Zimbabwe Women Lawyers Association (ZWLA) have worked tirelessly to show the many problems caused by the non-recognition of unregistered customary law unions and have proffered suggestions on law reform. The Law Development Commission also produced an inquiry paper on the same issue...Without law reform, litigants will continue to be short-changed by legal practitioners who approach such cases as if they are registered marriages.[99]

Following a protracted cycle within the legislative process, the old marriage framework, encompassing the old Marriage Act[100] and Customary Marriages Act,[101] was repealed and replaced with a new Marriages Act,[102] which was finally passed in March 2022. Along with consolidating all the different types of marriage in Zimbabwe into one statute, the Act sets the age of marriage at 18.[103] More importantly, for the purposes of this discussion, it addresses the issue of unregistered

[95] Marriage Act 1963 [Chapter 5:11].

[96] Customary Marriages Act 1951 [Chapter 5:07].

[97] *Mudzuru & Anor v Ministry of Justice, Legal & Parliamentary Affairs N.O. & Ors* (CC 12 of 2015; Constitutional Application 79 of 2014) [2016] ZWCC 12 (20 January 2016).

[98] Southern African Development Community Parliamentary Forum (2016).

[99] *Jeke v Zembe* (HC 11663 of 2017; HH 237 of 2018) [2018] ZWHHC 237 (5 May 2018).

[100] Marriage Act 1963 [Chapter 5:11].

[101] Customary Marriages Act 1951 [Chapter 5:07].

[102] Marriages Act 2022 [Chapter 5:15].

[103] Marriages Act 2022 [Chapter 5:15], s. 3(1).

customary unions by making an explicit requirement for registration. Since Zimbabwean law does not have a common law or legislative presumption of marriage, women in unregistered customary unions may *potentially* find protection in the 'civil partnerships' clause within the new Marriage Act.[104] This provision, which drew much public controversy,[105] was touted as the most radical and progressive innovation of this new marriage legislation, as it would provide recognition to informal cohabitation relationships that did not previously benefit from the property rights of formally married couples despite being, for all intents and purposes, long-term, committed partnerships, with shared assets and often children. As previously stated, under the new Marriage Act, there are now four types of unions recognised as legal marriages for the purposes of distribution of matrimonial property under the provisions of the Matrimonial Causes Act. These are civil marriages, registered customary law marriages, unregistered customary law unions, and qualified civil marriages.

Unfortunately, because the Marriages Act was passed relatively recently, the jurisprudence has not developed sufficiently to the point where reliable claims can be made about the success of the Act in protecting unregistered customary unions and the property rights thereunder. In one 2023 judgement passed after the new Marriages Act came into effect, the court reasoned that although the couple seeking a division of their matrimonial assets before them was in an unregistered customary marriage, the previous approach of applying general law principles of universal partnership to the division of matrimonial property from such marriages still had to apply.[106] In another case that year, the court also refused to apply the new Marriages Act of 2022 retrospectively, stating that:

> In essence, this would change the essence of the already completed transactions which the parties carried on upon the faith of the then existing law. Such a position is undesirable and roundly condemned in the case law cited above. This is so because it has not been averred that the new Marriages Act of 2022 expressly provides for retrospective application… She simply has to prosecute her matter on the basis of the law which was in existence at the time of the filing of her summons. She cannot sneak in the Matrimonial Causes Act, as she had initially done before her first amendment.[107]

Therefore, the Zimbabwean courts are still grappling with the consequences of not recognising unregistered customary marriages for the purposes of dividing matrimonial property and will likely continue to do so for some time. Due to the nature of marriages and the fact that most divorce cases are brought before courts after couples have lived together for years, if not decades, we may continue to see the courts' continued application of the old framework for some time to come.

---

[104] Marriages Act 2022 [Chapter 5:15], s. 41 and Vengesai (2024, p. 223).

[105] Masiviwa (2023).

[106] See *Melo v Kandibero* (323 of 2023) [2023] ZWHHC 199 (24 May 2023), where the court stated that, 'The summons were issued on 11 February 2022. Since at the time the Matrimonial Causes Act [Chapter 5:13] applied to marriages in terms of the Marriage Act [Chapter 5:11] or the Customary Marriages Act [Chapter 5:07], both now repealed and replaced with the Marriages Act [Chapter 5:17], the plaintiff's cause of action was and is located in a tacit universal partnership with the defendant under general law'.

[107] *Almero v Sithole* (60 of 2023) [2023] ZWHHC 60 (31 January 2023).

Notwithstanding that there is yet little case law to show whether or how the Marriages Act 2022 will fare in protecting the matrimonial property of the most vulnerable in Zimbabwe, some educated guesses can be made. The new Marriages Act defines customary marriages as 'a marriage solemnised in accordance with customary law'.[108] Therefore, the definitional issues in the old Customary Marriages Act are somewhat reduced in this amended statute. What constitutes a customary marriage still remains susceptible to contestation with this definition. However, this wider definition will likely accommodate a broader range of communities and ethnic groups whose traditional marriage rites involve varying customary formalities, which may or may not include the payment of 'consideration,' i.e., *lobola*, in whole or in part. Therefore, this change, in my estimation, is by and large a welcome development in the legislative reforms related to the regulation of customary marriages.

Regarding the requirement for registration, it is significant that the new Marriages Act appears to preserve this provision from the old Act, with the important qualification that non-registration does not affect the validity of the marriage for the purpose of protecting the rights of children born from the marriage.[109] But what of the property rights of women in these unregistered customary marriages? Section 47 of the Act clarifies that for unregistered customary marriages already in existence when the Act comes into effect, there is an obligation to register the marriage 'within twelve months'.[110] It remains to be seen whether this directive will be matched with the necessary infrastructure to facilitate registration of unregistered customary unions, at scale, so that those that were already in unregistered customary marriages are in compliance with the law. Mucheto reports that one legal practitioner, Choice Damiso, has critiqued the registration requirement because:

> ...it has always been a requirement for all marriages to be registered but notwithstanding this, couples do not feel motivated to register their marriages, leading to most marriages not proceeding beyond the kubvusa pfuma/lobola stage,"... the big question this time is what the Government is going to do differently to motivate couples to register their marriages.[111]

Damiso has also pointed out that without public outreach programs to facilitate marriage registration and the redistribution of marriage offices across the country, the status quo is unlikely to change, and women in unregistered customary marriages will continue to be disadvantaged through this impotent requirement for registration.[112]

There is potential for protection for women in unregistered customary unions through a liberal reading of section 45 of the new MA, which would include unregistered customary unions. This provision reads:

> Subject to this Act, no marriage solemnised or registered or deemed to be solemnised or registered in terms of this Act shall be dissolved except by order of court of competent jurisdiction in terms of the Matrimonial Causes Act. [Chapter 5:13][113]

[108] Marriages Act 2022 [Chapter 5:15], s. 2.

[109] Marriages Act 2022 [Chapter 5:15], s. 17.

[110] Marriages Act 2022 [Chapter 5:15], s. 47.

[111] Muchetu (2022).

[112] Muchetu (2022).

[113] Marriages Act 2022 [Chapter 5:15], s. 45.

This language suggests that all marriages, whether registered or not, will be dissolved by a court, and the property divided under the Matrimonial Causes Act, which has been applied in the dissolution of registered customary and civil marriages. This is a welcome and radical change. However, if interpreted literally, the wording of that provision could also leave the possibility that a marriage that is *not* 'solemnized or registered' within the 12 months stipulated or after it, cannot be dissolved using the MCA.

Not much more can be said about what the new Marriages Act changes for the property rights of those registered customary unions and civil unions beyond what was already guaranteed by the Matrimonial Causes Act. However, related to the law and the difficulties of applying it in practice, it is worth noting that a significant portion of the analyses made by the courts turns on how lawyers are struggling to draft the appropriate pleadings to make the best case for their clients' matrimonial property claims. For example, in a 2018 case involving the division of marital property between spouses in an unregistered customary union, the Court admonished the lawyers for pleading their client's case under the wrong law. The lawyer attempted to apply the Matrimonial Causes Act to a marriage that was an unregistered customary union, but the MCA did not apply to such unions at that time.[114] Six years later, after the enactment of the new Marriages Act, the Harare High Court acknowledged the international human rights law and constitutional law mandate gender equality between spouses during and at the dissolution of the marriage. However, it concluded that it was unable to assist a woman who had made a claim for immovable property using the Matrimonial Causes Act because the immovable property was not registered in her or her spouse's name, although she alleged that she had contributed towards the acquisition of the property. The woman would have been successful had she sued for reimbursement of her contributions, but unfortunately, she sued under the wrong claim.[115] Even with the streamlining of different types of marriage in Zimbabwe through the new Marriage Act, the framework remains convoluted and tricky for legal practitioners to apply, as it was prior to the new legislation.

6.1 A Note on Islamic Marriages and Property Rights

Islamic marriages are classified as 'qualified civil marriages'. A qualified civil marriage is defined in the Marriages Act as 'a union between a man and a woman, not being a union registrable as a civil or customary law marriage under this Act'.[116] Such a marriage may be solemnised by a minister of religion who is also a marriage officer in accordance with the prescriptions of a religion. Section 11 of the Act grants the Minister the authority to designate any religious leader as 'a marriage officer for the purpose of solemnising marriages according to Christian, Jewish, *Islamic* or Hindu

[114] *Jeke v Zembe* (HC 11663 of 2017; HH 237 of 2018) [2018] ZWHHC 237 (5 May 2018, p. 237).

[115] *Chivanga v Mwakurudza* (30 of 2024) [2024] ZWHHC 30 (24 January 2024, p. 7).

[116] Marriages Act 2022 [Chapter 5:15], s. 44(1).

rites or the rites of any religion'.[117] While qualified civil marriages appear to apply uniformly across all faiths, the preference for Islamic law is clearly reflected in the wording of the Marriage Act. For instance, the definition of a minister of religion within the context of qualified civil marriages is explicitly linked to Islamic rites. A marriage officer is defined therein as 'a person designated in terms of section 11, for the purposes of solemnising marriages according to Islamic rites'.[118]

On divorce, the Matrimonial Causes Act governs the proceedings. However, for qualified civil marriages, the court must take into account any agreement between the parties that aligns with Islamic tenets, and it may accept affidavit evidence from a licensed Islamic marriage officer regarding those tenets. Section 44(12) of the Marriages Act states that:

> In proceedings for the dissolution of a qualified civil marriage under the Matrimonial Causes Act [Chapter 5:13] the court shall take into consideration any agreement between the parties as to the division of assets, custody of the children, and maintenance of the wife and children of the marriage, that is in accordance with the tenets of the faith by virtue of which the spouses contracted the qualified civil marriage, for which purpose the court may request and receive in evidence the testimony by affidavit of a licensed marriage officer who is a minister of religion competent to solemnise qualified civil marriages to the effect that the agreement is in accordance with such tenets.

Thus, Islamic couples who reach an agreement regarding their property rights in accordance with the precepts of Islamic law may have those agreements recognised by the courts and factored into property rights considerations.

7 Recommendations

In the context of the newly legislated Marriage Act, it might appear that any recommendations at this point are moot. However, there are a number of steps that the Zimbabwean governmental administration and the judiciary can take to bolster the new statute in protecting and promoting the equality rights of women in the area of matrimonial property. I discuss each in turn.

7.1 Removing Barriers to Registration

The state must implement practical measures to ensure that marriages are registered. This will reduce incidences of unregistered customary marriages and cases where women in these marriages are left vulnerable to various human rights abuses, including that of property grabbing by the other spouse. The Government should remove the practical barriers that prevent the registration of customary marriages if

[117] Emphasis added.

[118] Marriages Act 2022 [Chapter 5:15], s. 44(1).

it requires registration for their validity. In other words, the state cannot reasonably expect compliance with such a requirement if, practically, the prospective registrants are unable to do so due to structural and systematic impediments that are out of their control.

In formulating the law, it is important that we pre-empt any practical challenges that may result therefrom, and I argue that it is the responsibility of law enforcers to create an environment that is conducive to legal compliance. The provision of more registration offices and officers closer to rural areas, where community members can easily access them, is important to avoid the challenges posed by the cost and effort of travelling long distances to register a marriage, thereby preventing non-registration. Additionally, the cost of registration need not be prohibitive; it should be affordable for people belonging to these communities. The fee should be minimal to encourage registration. All the above-mentioned recommendations will no doubt require the Government to dedicate more of its resources to these efforts, if it is to insist that registration is a prerequisite for a customary marriage to fall within the MCA's ambit.

7.2 *Sustained Public Education*

In conjunction with the registration infrastructure, a nationwide campaign is needed to educate the public about their rights and duties concerning the registration of customary marriages, thereby making the recognition of customary marriages sustainable under the new Marriage Act. Education for people who are parties to unregistered customary marriages will be necessary, if the chosen approach is to retain registration as a requirement for the division of matrimonial property on divorce, because non-registration has more serious consequences in that case.

Additionally, since certain cultural beliefs and perceptions contribute to the non-registration of customary marriages,[119] state initiatives in communities where unregistered customary unions are common would be beneficial in dispelling such beliefs, myths, and misperceptions. These projects would require a collaborative effort with

[119] Chikaonda (2018) where the author explains: 'While sometimes women are aware of the advantages of registration, they often do not have much choice in the matter. With little financial independence, and due to societal pressures to be married, their ability to negotiate and bargain for registration of a customary marriage is limited. The husband in these marriages usually has the final word on whether or not registration takes place and more often than not, he is unwilling to register the marriage because registration is believed to have negative implications for him. Some of these misconceptions include the idea that the wife is not the husband's relative but rather 'the bearer of children' and therefore he should not be bound to her through a registered marriage, the fear that the husband could lose all his property if he registers his customary marriage under civil law, and the belief that it is too complicated and difficult to get a divorce when the husband wants to end the marriage. There are also superstitions held that entering a civil marriage will result in the husband being bewitched and killed by his wife so that she can inherit all his property and perceptions that that registration of the marriage, will make the wife too difficult to 'manage' and she will therefore not carry out her wifely duties, whereas the possibility that he can acquire another wife will keep her in line and performing her wifely duties as best as she can.'

community leaders, chiefs, and respected elders (male and female) who often hold significant influence over cultural norms. Providing information through workshops, media campaigns, and similar initiatives on the benefits of registering customary marriages to women and men will encourage the former to insist on registration and change the latter's negative attitudes and suspicions about the risks of losing their property if they register their marriages. The process needs to be explained in the multiple languages used by the communities, for those who may be illiterate and/or unable to understand the complex legalese in statutes or government notices. This will help reduce perceptions that registering customary marriages is too complicated to be worth undertaking. Again, leaders in these communities and registration officers are a central component of the dissemination of information effort, as they are the people who deal directly with prospective registrants. It is, therefore, imperative that they receive adequate training on the various types of marriage and the consequences of each. This will ensure that the marriage systems (civil and customary) are understood as distinct and not overlapping, and will circumvent the problem highlighted above, where husbands contract different types of marriages simultaneously or consecutively without registering them, causing confusion and leaving the wives or civil partners in these relationships economically vulnerable once the marriage dissolves and property is distributed.

7.3 Harmonisation with Family Laws

The Matrimonial Causes Act should be amended to align with the new Marriage Act to recognise and regulate unregistered customary marriages. The MCA needs to expressly recognise unregistered customary marriages in its definition of 'marriage' so that women in these unions are also protected by its section 7(4) provision, which obligates the court to consider several factors in the distribution of marital property. This amendment will provide more robust support to such women who have, for years now, only been able to seek relief through common law concepts, such as tacit universal partnership or unjustified enrichment.

As intimated by the judge in the *Kurebgaseka* case, a legislative intervention that recognises and regulates unregistered customary unions as valid marriages, eligible for the same protection as registered customary marriages, is preferable. This step will also fulfil the state's obligations to treat all marriages equally and not discriminate between them unfairly.[120] It will provide these women with the dignity they are entitled to under the Constitution, as well as international and regional laws, and will ensure that all marriages are given equal weight and significance, preventing marriages from being reduced to partnership contracts. Furthermore, women will not have to jump through all the evidentiary hoops that come with proving the existence of a partnership. While the MCA's guidelines are susceptible to judicial biases, resulting in unsatisfactory awards from the courts, the inclusion of unregistered customary

[120] Constitution of Zimbabwe Amendment (No. 20) Act 2013, ss 56(3) and 78(1).

unions in the MCA puts them in a much better position, when they are not protected by it. The amendment will also be useful for women in unregistered polygamous marriages because, in the absence of provisions within the new Marriage Act stating the rules for the proprietary consequences of polygynous unions, the courts would be able to provide guidance on how these marriages should be dissolved and the property distributed.

7.4 Judicial Application of International Law

Finally, in their analyses and rulings, the judiciary should endeavour to rely on the frameworks provided and the obligations placed by the international and regional legal instruments to which Zimbabwe is party. The guarantees of justice in the allocation and distribution of matrimonial property to achieve substantive gender equality should be clearly evident in the judgments. And the cases of women who find themselves in unregistered customary unions, especially, should be approached with a sensitivity to the patriarchal gender dynamics that lead women into these kinds of partnerships that are so common in Zimbabwean society.

8 Conclusion

I have argued that a comparative legal history approach provides a comprehensive understanding of Zimbabwe's matrimonial property regime and its practical implications for achieving gender equality. By analysing the development of Zimbabwe's marriage laws through the comparative framework of 'before' and 'after' the new Marriage Act, the critical perspective advocated by comparative legal history methodology highlights the stark contrast in the consequences for women in unregistered versus registered customary unions. Unregistered customary unions took centre stage as a subject of study in this chapter, given their prevalence in Zimbabwe and their significant impact on women's matrimonial property rights under Zimbabwe's matrimonial property laws. Through a comparative legal history approach, we can appreciate the points of tension presented by affording women in unregistered customary unions the same rights as those in registered marriages. Ultimately, it is a matter of the law coming to terms with the undeniable reality that the majority of Zimbabwean partnerships exist outside the bounds of traditional civil marriage. We have observed how the Zimbabwean plural legal system has attempted to resolve these tensions. The relevant laws have been marked by several key developments in a roughly sequential order: (1) non-recognition of unregistered customary unions and customary rules that left women using customary law with little to no rights to the matrimonial property; (2) the use of imperfect general law principles by the judiciary in an attempt to assist women in unregistered customary unions; (3) the Matrimonial Causes Act, which applied only to *registered* customary marriages and civil marriages, but did recognise the domestic and non-monetary contributions of registered wives to the matrimonial assets; (4) unequal use and control rights of property, for even those in registered marriages because of the judiciary's inability to consider the patriarchal and gendered dynamics within marriages, and finally (5) the introduction of the new Marriage Act and recognition of unregistered customary unions, whose positive impact for the property rights of women in these marriages, we are yet to see. Gender equality and marriage rights scholars in Zimbabwe must keep an eye on how the courts will apply and interpret this new legislation to determine whether it meets its lofty goal of protecting the property rights of women in the diverse forms that Zimbabwean marriages and partnerships often take in practice.

References

Banda F (1995) The provision of maintenance for women and children in Zimbabwe. Cardozo Women's Law J 1:71–76

Banda F (2005) Women, law and human rights: an African perspective. Hart Publishing, Oxford

Chanock M (1985) Law, custom and social order: the colonial experience in Malawi and Zambia. Cambridge University Press, Cambridge

Chikaonda GP (2018) Registration of customary marriages in Zimbabwe: protective shield or a source of problems. Unpublished LLM Thesis, University of Cape Town

Chikaonda GP (2020) Legal pluralism in Africa: how Zimbabwean couples navigate the path to marriage. Unpublished MSc (Law) Thesis, Stanford Law School

Chirawu S (2006) Till death do us part: marriage, HIV/AIDS and the law in Zimbabwe. Cardozo Women's Law J 13:23–44

Chirawu S (2014) Challenges faced by women in unregistered customary law unions. Women in law of southern Africa 5–6. http://www.wlsazim.co.zw/index.php/about/2-uncategorised/4-about-your-home-page. Accessed on 4 Oct 2017

Chirawu D (2019) Analysing civil partnerships in the draft Marriages Bill. https://www.herald.co.zw/analysing-civil-partnerships-in-the-draft-marriages-bill/. Accessed on 30 Oct 2025

Coldham S (1994) The government of Zimbabwe's white paper on marriage and inheritance, 1993. J Afr Law 38:67–76

Ibhawoh B (2007) Imperialism and human rights: colonial discourses of rights and liberties in African history. State University of New York Press, Albany

Madhuku L (2010) An introduction to Zimbabwean law, 1st edn. Weaver Press, Harare

Masiviwa G (2023) New law's recognition of civil partnerships stirs controversy. Glob Press J. https://globalpressjournal.com/africa/zimbabwe/new-laws-recognition-civil-partnerships-stirs-controversy/. Accessed on 29 Oct 2025

Mpofu T (2016) The property rights of women in Zimbabwe: the plight of the married woman in relation to the matrimonial home. Asian Centre for Women's studies 9th EGEP workshop, 164–165 https://www.dbpia.co.kr/journal/articleDetail?nodeId=NODE07154053. Accessed on 30 Sept 2025

Muchetu R (2022) Unpacking the Marriages Act: Don't scandalise the law. https://www.sundaynews.co.zw/unpacking-the-marriages-act-dont-scandalise-the-law/#google_vignette. Accessed on 31 Oct 2025

Ncube W (1989) Family law in Zimbabwe. Legal Resources Foundation, Harare

Ncube W (1990) Re-allocation of matrimonial property at the dissolution of marriage in Zimbabwe. J Afr Law 34(1):1–8

Nnoko-Mewanu J (2019) Zimbabwe's marriage reform should do more for women. Human Rights Watch, 21 June https://wwwhrworg/news/2019/06/21/zimbabwes-marriage-reform-should-do-more-women. Accessed on 31 Oct 2025
Owolade F (2023) Writing a colonial legal history of northern Nigeria: an analysis of methods. Hist Afr 50:73–96
Schmidt E (1992) Peasants, traders, and wives: Shona women in the history of Zimbabwe, 1870–1939. James Currey, London
Stockreiter EE (2015) Islamic law, gender, and social change in post-abolition Zanzibar town. Cambridge University Press, Cambridge
UN General Assembly (1948) Universal declaration of human rights. A/RES/217(III), 10 December
UN General Assembly (1979) Convention on the Elimination of All Forms of Discrimination Against Women. 1249 UNTS 13, adopted 18 December 1979, entered into force 3 September 1981
Vengesai P (2024) The rights of women in unregistered customary marriages in Zimbabwe: best practices from South Africa. Law, Democr Dev 28:215–223. https://doi.org/10.17159/2077-4907/2024/ldd.v28.10
ZIMSTAT (2023) Zimbabwe national statistics agency, 2022 population and housing census. Vital Stat Rep 1

Gloria Paidamoyo Chikaonda is a JSD candidate at Stanford Law School. Her research focuses on family law, marriage law, legal pluralism, and legislative reform in southern Africa. She has published internationally, including in the Journal of Comparative Law in Africa and the Stanford International Policy Review. Chikaonda is an editor for *Ornati: Journal of Emergent Socio-Legal Studies* and founder of the Young African Research Network (YARN), mentoring African scholars. She is a Stanford Knight-Hennessy Scholar and Interdisciplinary Graduate Fellow, advocating for legal reform and the empowerment of women and children. She holds an LLB and LLM (Comparative Law in Africa) from the University of Cape Town and a JSM in International Legal Studies from Stanford Law School.

Index

A. F. Hammond and P. Batariwah (eds.), *The Law on Marital Property in Africa*, Ius Gentium: Comparative Perspectives on Law and Justice 138,
https://doi.org/10.1007/978-3-032-19358-2

G

H

I

J

K